THE ETHICS OF KILLING

PROBLEMS AT THE MARGINS OF LIFE

OXFORD ETHICS SERIES
Series Editor: Derek Parfit, All Souls College, Oxford

The Limits of Morality
Shelly Kagan

Perfectionism
Thomas Hurka

Inequality
Larry S. Temkin

Morality, Mortality, Volume I
Death and Whom to Save from It
F. M. Kamm

Morality, Mortality, Volume II
Rights, Duties, and Status
F. M. Kamm

Suffering and Moral Responsibility
Jamie Mayerfeld

Moral Demands in Nonideal Theory
Liam B. Murphy

The Ethics of Killing
Problems at the Margins of Life
Jeff McMahan

THE ETHICS OF KILLING

PROBLEMS AT THE MARGINS OF LIFE

Jeff McMahan

OXFORD

UNIVERSITY PRESS

2002

OXFORD
UNIVERSITY PRESS

Oxford   New York

Athens   Auckland   Bangkok   Bogotá   Buenos Aires   Cape Town
Chennai   Dar es Salaam   Delhi   Florence   Hong Kong   Istanbul   Karachi
Kolkata   Kuala Lumpur   Madrid   Melbourne   Mexico City   Mumbai   Nairobi
Paris   São Paulo   Shanghai   Singapore   Taipei   Tokyo   Toronto   Warsaw

and associated companies in
Berlin   Ibadan

Copyright © 2002 by Jeff McMahan

Published by Oxford University Press, Inc.
198 Madison Avenue, New York, New York 10016

Oxford is a registered trademark of Oxford University Press

Library of Congress Cataloging-in-Publication Data
McMahan, Jeff.
The ethics of killing : problems at the margins of life / by Jeff McMahan.
p.   cm.—(Oxford ethics series)
Includes bibliographical references and index.
ISBN 0-19-507998-1
1. Murder—Moral and ethical aspects. 2. Abortion—Moral and ethical aspects. 3. Aged,
Killing of the—Moral and ethical aspects. 4. Insane, Killing of the—Moral and
ethical aspects. 5. Euthanasia—Moral and ethical aspects.   I. Title.   II. Series.

HV6515.M35 2001
179.7—dc21   2001021768

3 5 7 9 8 6 4 2

Printed in the United States of America
on acid-free paper

For Sally, Sophie, and William

PREFACE AND ACKNOWLEDGMENTS

We all accept that killing is in general wrong, but virtually all of us also recognize certain exceptions—that is, we concede that there can be instances in which killing is permissible. In addition to accepting the obvious permissibility of killing microbes and plants (except when this is objectionable for either instrumental or impersonal reasons), most people believe that it can be permissible in a variety of circumstances to kill animals, and also that it can be permissible to kill other human beings in self-defense and in appropriate conditions in war.

There are four distinct categories into which we may sort most or all instances of killing for which there may be a reasonable justification. Perhaps the most contentious category consists of cases in which killing would simply promote the greater good—for example, a case in which killing one person would prevent the killing, or the deaths, of a much greater number of people. Most people who believe that killing can on occasion be permissible for this sort of reason also believe that, in at least most of these instances, certain restrictions on agency have to be satisfied—for example, that the killing must be a merely foreseen side effect rather than an intended means of achieving the greater good. Although it is important, I will not be concerned with this category of possibly justifiable killings.

The second category consists of cases in which an individual has *done* something that has lowered the moral barriers to harming him, or compromised his status as inviolable, or made him liable to action that might result in his death. Cases in which killing might be thought to be justified for this sort of reason include killing in self-defense, killing in war, and killing as a mode of punishment. This range of cases will be the topic of another book, now in progress, that will be a companion volume to this one. This book, subtitled *Problems at the Margins of Life,* may thus be regarded as the first volume of a two-volume work on *The Ethics of Killing,* of which the second volume will be the projected book on self-defense, war, and capital punishment.

The third category of possibly permissible killing consists of cases in which the metaphysical or moral status of the individual killed is uncertain or controversial. Among those beings whose nature arguably entails a moral status inferior to our own are animals, human embryos and fetuses, newborn infants, anencephalic infants, congenitally severely retarded human beings, human beings who have suffered severe brain damage or dementia, and human beings who have become irreversibly comatose. These are all beings that are in one way or another "at the margins." There are pressing moral questions about the permissibility, in certain circumstances, of killing individuals of these sorts, or of allowing them to die. Among the practices (whether actual or as yet hypothetical) that raise these questions are meat eating, ani-

mal experimentation, abortion, infanticide, embryo research, the use of living anencephalic infants as organ donors, the termination of life-support for the irreversibly
comatose, perhaps in order to obtain their organs for transplantation, and the withdrawal of life-support for demented or incompetent patients in compliance with an
earlier advance directive. I will address some, though not all, of these problems in
this book, along with certain related issues, such as the morality of inflicting prenatal injury.[1]

The fourth and final category comprises cases in which death would not be a
harm to an individual but instead a benefit. In many such cases, the individual for
whom death would be a benefit also desires to die and may request to be killed or
helped to die. The practical issues that arise under this heading are suicide, assisted
suicide, and euthanasia. Although my main focus in this book will be on the marginal
cases, I will also discuss certain dimensions of the problems raised by the cases in
this fourth category.

The practical issue that I will discuss at greatest length is abortion. As this book
is going to press (October 2000), it has been announced that the "abortion pill" is
soon to be legally available in the United States. To many it may seem that this represents a decisive victory for those who favor the legal permissibility of abortion and
that the practice of abortion will become socially invisible and thus eventually cease
to be a matter of public controversy. It may therefore seem that to publish a book on
abortion at this point is rather like writing on the morality of slavery, an issue that is
now primarily of academic interest. But, although I defend the permissibility of abortion and thus welcome the introduction of the abortion pill, I do not believe the debate should end until we have the kind of intellectual and moral certainty about abortion that we have about slavery. It is important to notice that the ostensible victims of
abortion—fetuses—are not parties to the debate, while of those who *are* involved in
it, the only ones who have a significant personal interest or stake in the outcome are
those who would benefit from the practice. There is therefore a danger that abortion
could triumph in the political arena simply because it is favored by self-interest and
opposed only by ideals. We should therefore be wary of the possibility of abortion
becoming an unreflective practice, like meat eating, simply because it serves the interests of those who have the power to determine whether it is practiced. The arguments in the public debate that focus narrowly, and implausibly, on "choice" reveal a
tendency to try to convert abortion from a question of ethics into a question of interests. This book, although it offers a novel, complex, and, I hope, plausible defense of
the permissibility of abortion, nevertheless seeks to keep us focused on ethical rather
than merely political considerations.

This is a long book and may require some effort from general readers. I have tried
to go deep, which means that in places the argument can become complex. But I have
also tried to write simply and clearly and to avoid language and arguments that might
be described as technical. Thus, if there are passages in the book that some readers
may find difficult, I hope that the difficulty is in the depth of the ideas themselves and
not in their articulation. Indeed, I have in places—particularly in chapter 1—given a
certain priority to accessibility over thoroughness in argument, in that I have consciously refrained from trying to make the argument absolutely watertight by plung-
ing into arcane matters of technical philosophy. I have also avoided some of the te-

dious apparatus of academic books, such as footnotes or endnotes freighted with substantive material. The notes to this book contain only textual citations, with an occasional brief comment on one of the pieces referred to. Finally, it is perhaps worth noting that the book should get easier as it progresses, since the earlier chapters contain arguments in metaphysics and ethical theory that provide the foundations for the later, more immediately accessible material on practical issues.

I have been working on this book, albeit intermittently, since the late 1980s. Over this period, ideas or arguments that I had developed have occasionally appeared independently in the published work of others. This is especially true of the material in chapter 1 on personal identity, some of which, I confess, has begun to seem a trifle musty even to me, though it seemed fresher in the late 1980s when I first developed the position I defend here. (Even if that position now lacks the glamour of novelty, it still seems to me the most plausible view on offer.) When other writers have independently produced ideas or arguments that coincide with those that I developed during the writing of this book, I have tried to acknowledge the overlap in the endnotes. In cases in which I have knowingly borrowed from another writer, I have tried to indicate this by employing such phrases as "here I follow . . ."

I have, of course, intellectual debts other than those acknowledged in the notes. I am deeply grateful to my teachers: to the late Charles Harrison, who was profoundly influential in forming my mind when I was an undergraduate studying literature, and to my three graduate supervisors in philosophy, Jonathan Glover, Derek Parfit, and Bernard Williams. I also owe a debt of gratitude to the late Gregory Kavka for his encouragement of my work and discussion of my ideas in their embryonic stages. Many others have given me valuable comments on various parts of this book. I have been helped by discussions with N. Ann Davis, Dennis McKerlie, Paul Saka, members of the Philosophy Department of Kansas State University, and the philosophy majors of the class of 2001 at Pomona College. I have also been greatly aided by those who have given me written comments on certain chapters, or parts of these chapters. For comments on chapter 1, I am indebted to David McCarthy, Eric Olson, Ingmar Persson, and Peter Unger; on chapter 2, to David Boonin, Ruth Chang, Kai Draper, Walter Glannon, Saul Smilansky, and Alec Walen; on chapter 3 to Kasper Lippert-Rasmussen; on chapter 4 to Phillip Montague, Peter Singer, and David Wasserman; and on chapter 5 to Hugh LaFollette, Peter Singer, and Noam Zohar. Eric Rakowski very generously commented on the whole of the manuscript, as did Derek Parfit, to whose exacting standards of philosophical imaginativeness, depth, and rigor I have vainly endeavored, for more than twenty years, to conform my own work.

Finally, I gratefully acknowledge the support for my work from three sources at the University of Illinois at Urbana-Champaign: the Center for Advanced Study, the Program for the Study of Cultural Values and Ethics, and the Research Board.

CONTENTS

1. IDENTITY 3

1. Preliminaries 3
2. The Soul 7
    2.1. Hylomorphism 7
    2.2. The Cartesian Soul 14
    2.3. Divided Consciousness 19
3. Are We Human Organisms? 24
    3.1. When Does a Human Organism Begin to Exist? 24
    3.2. Organisms, Embryos, and Corpses 29
    3.3. Brain Transplantation 31
    3.4. Dicephalus 35
4. The Psychological Account 39
    4.1. Identity and Egoistic Concern 39
    4.2. Beginning to Exist and Ceasing to Exist 43
    4.3. "Pre-persons" and "Post-persons" 46
    4.4. Revisions and a Note on Method 48
    4.5. Replication and Egoistic Concern 55
    4.6. Psychological Connectedness and Continuity 59
5. The Embodied Mind Account 66
    5.1. The Embodied Mind Account of Identity 66
    5.2. The Basis of Egoistic Concern 69
    5.3. Possible Divergences Between Identity and Egoistic Concern 82
    5.4. The Individuation of Minds 86
    5.5. Mind, Brain, and Organism 88

2. DEATH 95

1. Preliminaries 95
2. The Problem of Comparison 98
    2.1. Immortality 98
    2.2. The Token Comparison 103
3. The Metaphysical Problem 107
    3.1. A Plurality of Comparisons 107
    3.2. Criteria for Determining the Appropriate Comparison 112
4. The Problem of Overdetermination 117
    4.1. When Death Would Have Occurred Soon From a Different Cause 117
    4.2. The Inheritance Strategy and the Problem of the Terminus 120
    4.3. Overall Losses in Dying 127
    4.4. The Previous Gain Account 136

4.5. *Discounting Misfortunes for Previous Gains*   *140*
5. Overall Lifelong Fortune   145
   5.1. *The Standard for Assessing Fortune*   *145*
   5.2. *A Hierarchy of Being?*   *159*
   5.3. *The Overall Fortune of Those Who Die in Infancy*   *162*
6. The Deaths of Fetuses and Infants   165
   6.1. *The Time-Relative Interest Account*   *165*
   6.2. *Narrative Unity, Retroactive Effects, Desert, and Desire*   *174*
7. A Paradox   185

3. KILLING   189

1. The Wrongness of Killing and the Badness of Death   189
   1.1. *Two Accounts*   *189*
   1.2. *The Killing of Animals*   *194*
2. Animals and Severely Cognitively Impaired Human Beings   203
   2.1. *The Options*   *203*
   2.2. *Membership in the Human Species*   *209*
   2.3. *Comembership in a Species as a Special Relation*   *217*
   2.4. *Convergent Assimilation*   *228*
3. Equality and Respect   232
   3.1. *The Time-Relative Interest Account*   *232*
   3.2. *The Requirement of Respect*   *240*
   3.3. *The Basis of the Worth of Persons*   *251*

4. BEGINNINGS   267

1. Early Abortion   267
2. Late Abortion   269
3. Prenatal Harm   280
4. Is a Later Abortion Worse?   288
5. Time-Relative Interests and Adaptation   294
6. Potential   302
   6.1. *Potential and Identity*   *302*
   6.2. *Potential as a Basis for Moral Status*   *308*
   6.3. *Potential, Cognitive Impairment, and Animals*   *316*
7. The Sanctity of Human Life   329
8. Infanticide   338
   8.1. *Abortion and Infanticide*   *338*
   8.2. *Are Infants "Replaceable?"*   *345*
9. Abortion as the Denial of Life-Support   362
   9.1. *The Argument*   *362*
   9.2. *Responsibility for the Fetus's Need for Aid*   *364*
   9.3. *Parental Responsibility*   *373*
   9.4. *Killing and Letting Die*   *378*
   9.5. *The Dependent Child Case*   *392*
10. Abortion and Self-Defense   398
   10.1. *Self-Defense Against a Nonresponsible Threat*   *398*
   10.2. *Proportionality, Third-party Intervention, and Forfeiture*   *411*
   10.3. *The Decisive Asymmetry*   *418*

5. ENDINGS   423

1. When Do We Die, or Cease to Exist?   423
    1.1. Two Concepts of Death   *423*
    1.2. Brain Death   *426*
    1.3. Persistent Vegetative State and Deep Coma   *443*
    1.4. Anencephalic Infants   *450*
2. Euthanasia and Assisted Suicide   455
    2.1. From Suicide to Euthanasia   *455*
    2.2. The Sanctity of Life, Again   *464*
    2.3. Respect for the Worth of Persons   *473*
    2.4. Nonvoluntary Euthanasia   *485*
3. The Withering Away of the Self   493
    3.1. The Metaphysics of Progressive Dementia   *493*
    3.2. The Moral Authority of Advance Directives   *496*

NOTES   505

REFERENCES   521

INDEX OF CASES   531

GENERAL INDEX   533

THE ETHICS OF KILLING

PROBLEMS AT THE MARGINS OF LIFE

1

Identity

There are many reasons why abortion remains one of the most intractably controversial of all moral issues. But the main reason is that the moral and metaphysical status of human embryos and fetuses is shrouded in darkness. In some respects these beings are similar to you and me; in others they are profoundly different. One might think, however, that at least it is certain that one *once was* an embryo and then a fetus. That, it might be thought, is an important consideration in determining the moral and metaphysical status of these beings.

There is a similar uncertainty about the status of human beings who are irreversibly comatose or who have suffered severe brain damage or dementia. But, again, one might think that we can know at least this: that one might oneself later exist in an irreversible coma or a state of advanced dementia.

One cannot, however, simply take it for granted that one once existed as an embryo or fetus, or that one could continue to exist in an irreversible coma. These ubiquitous assumptions are considerably more contentious than is commonly recognized. And it is particularly important for the purposes of this book to subject them to critical scrutiny, along with the alternative views with which they conflict. For our main concern in this book will be with the morality of killing beings of these sorts: that is, beings on the margins of life. It is therefore essential to determine whether, in killing an embryo, a fetus, or an individual in an irreversible coma, one would be killing an entity of a sort that you and I once were, or might become.

In attempting to determine when we began to exist and what the conditions of our dying or ceasing to exist are, it is important to avoid certain confusions to which it is easy to succumb. Writing about abortion, Walker Percy, who was a physician before he became a novelist, invites us to consider the common view that, "since there is no agreement about the beginning of human life, it is therefore a private religious or philosophical decision and therefore the state and the courts can do nothing about it." Percy claims:

> this is a con. I . . . submit that religion, philosophy, and private opinion have nothing
> to do with this issue. I further submit that it is a commonplace of modern biology,

3

known to every high-school student and no doubt to you the reader as well, that the life of every individual organism, human or not, begins when the chromosomes of the sperm fuse with the chromosomes of the ovum to form a new DNA complex that thenceforth directs the ontogenesis of the organism. . . . [T]he onset of individual life is not a dogma of the Church but a fact of science.[1]

It does seem true that a new human life begins to exist when a human sperm fuses with a human egg; for the resulting entity—the zygote—does not seem to be identical with either the sperm or the egg, it is indisputably alive (rather than being inanimate or dead), and it is genetically human. To this extent, Percy is right. But from the fact that something living and human begins to exist around the time of conception it does not follow that you or I began to exist at conception. To see this, note the controversial assumptions that underlie Percy's "commonplace of modern biology."

First, he assumes that the zygote is the first stage in the existence of a human organism. There are, however, serious reasons for doubting that a human organism begins to exist at conception. I will present these later; for the moment, let us simply grant this initial assumption. For even if we grant that a new human organism begins to exist at conception, it follows from this that *we* began to exist at conception only if we *are* human organisms—that is, only if each of us is numerically identical with, or one and the same thing as, the human organism that he or she animates.

As one recent writer puts it, "the answer to the question 'When did I begin to exist?' . . . seems to depend on the answer to the question 'What am I?' "[2] Thus, if I *am* a human organism, I began to exist when this organism did. But the assumption that I am numerically identical with the organism with which (to put it as neutrally as possible) I coexist is hardly uncontroversial. It is, indeed, particularly surprising that Percy, a Catholic, should implicitly assume that we are organisms. For Christian theology rejects this view and instead embraces one or another of these three views: (1) that we are souls that are distinct from our organisms, (2) that we are entities that consist of two parts—a soul and an organism—with the soul being the essential part, and (3) that we are each an essential union or fusion of soul and organism. On none of these views is it necessary that we begin to exist when our organisms do. If one is a nonphysical soul that may continue to exist after one's organism dies, or if one has a human organism as a nonessential part, or if one can exist only as an organism informed by a soul, it is possible that one began to exist only after one's organism did.

Notice another assumption that Percy makes—namely, that the answer to the question of when we begin to exist, which presupposes a view about what kind of thing we essentially are, is given by science. But the question of what kind of thing we are is not a scientific question at all. Science may tell us many things about human organisms, but it cannot tell us whether we *are* human organisms. Consider, by way of analogy, a statue that has been fashioned out of a lump of bronze. Whether the statue is one and the same thing as the lump of bronze (that is, whether it is numerically identical with the lump of bronze) is not a question that science can answer. That the statue and the lump of bronze occupy the same region of space and are composed of exactly the same constituent elements may suggest that they are identical. But the fact that the lump of bronze existed before the statue was made suggests that they cannot be identical. There are no empirical tests that could settle this issue, which is a matter of metaphysics rather than science.

Percy seems to have been misled by the way in which he posed his question. Instead of asking when *we* begin to exist, he asked, as many others do, when human life begins. As we have seen, it is possible that the correct answers to these two questions are entirely different (or, to be more precise, that there are several correct answers to the latter, depending on what kind of living human entity one has in mind, only one of which coincides with the correct answer to the former). And, if the answers are different, it is surely the answer to the question of when we begin to exist that is more important for moral purposes.

To understand when we begin to exist, as well as what is essentially involved in our ceasing to exist, we must determine what is necessarily involved in our continuing to exist over time—or, as some have put it, what our identity over time necessarily consists in. This is what is known as the problem of *personal identity,* or the problem of personal identity *over time.* It is not as simple a matter as it may seem. We are all continuously changing. One has, for example, undergone radical changes since the time one was two years old, so that one is now very different, both physically and psychologically, from the way one was then. Yet one has persisted, or continued to exist as one and the same individual, throughout all those changes. What is it that makes one now the same individual as that two-year-old child?

According to certain views, personal identity over time is not reducible to or explicable in terms of anything else. Many people, for example, believe that we are essentially nonmaterial substances, or souls. Unlike the human body, which is constituted by a vast collection of cells organized in complex ways, the soul is thought to be simple and indivisible. It is not composed of anything other than itself; it has no separable parts or constituents. Thus, while the continued existence of a human body consists in the maintenance of certain continuities and patterns of organization among its constituent elements, the continued existence of the soul cannot be analyzed in terms of anything else. Its continued existence is primitive, or irreducible.

Other views of personal identity are *reductionist.*[3] They hold that the continued existence of someone such as you or me consists in the holding of various physical or psychological continuities over time. According to these views, there is a certain relation (other than identity itself) or set of relations that must hold between a person at an earlier time and a person at a later time in order for it to be the case that these persons are one and the same person at different times. Once we know what this relation or set of relations is, we will be able to determine both when individuals like ourselves begin to exist and what is essentially involved in our ceasing to exist. To determine when we came into existence, we begin with ourselves now and track the relevant relation or relations back through the past to the time at which there first existed an entity related to us in the relevant way. It was then that we began to exist.[4] And what is, in all normal cases, involved in our ceasing to exist is that there will no longer be anyone in the future who will be related to us in the relevant way.

I should stress that, although these issues are generally discussed under the heading of "*personal* identity," we should not be misled by this phrase to suppose that this is a *de dicto* inquiry into the conditions of personhood—that is, an inquiry about what it is to be and to remain a *person.* Our interest here is in what is necessarily involved in our continuing to exist. And this may be different from what is necessarily involved in our being or remaining persons. For it may be possible for someone such as you or me to cease to be a person and yet continue to exist. Whether this is in fact possible depends, of course, both on how one understands the notion of a "person" and on what kind of thing we essentially are. Throughout this book, I will use the term "person" to refer to any entity with a mental life of a certain order of complexity and sophistication. Roughly speaking, to be a person, one must have the capacity for self-consciousness. This use of the term goes back at least as far as the philosophical writings of John Locke and is recognized by the *Oxford English Dictionary,* which gives "a self-conscious or rational being" as one definition of "person." But there are, of course, other uses that are more common in ordinary discourse.

Whether we could cease to be persons in this sense and yet continue to exist is one of the questions at issue in the debate about personal identity. The same is true in the case of other terms commonly used to designate entities of our kind. For example, it should be an open question, at this stage of the inquiry, whether one could cease to be a human being and yet continue to exist. Insofar as they are fairly sharply defined, all of the various general terms used to refer to entities of our kind—for example, "person," "human being," "human organism," "soul," "mind"—correspond to different accounts of personal identity. Thus, to avoid begging substantive questions, the inquiry must be couched, at least initially, in a neutral vocabulary. I will often, therefore, employ such locutions as "individuals like you and me" and "entities of our kind," presupposing that we can identify paradigm instances of the members of the class without necessarily being able to define the boundaries of the class. In short, exactly what kind of thing we are is something we cannot know in advance of an investigation of the problem of personal identity, but is instead something we should hope to learn from it. (I will, of course, continue to refer to us as persons, though without prejudice to the question whether we have always been or must necessarily continue to be persons.)

To clarify these matters, it will help to introduce some technical terms. *Sortal* concepts are classificatory concepts. Logicians distinguish between two different types of sortal: *phase sortals* and *substance sortals.*[5] A phase sortal designates a kind to which an individual may belong through only part of its history. "Adolescent," for example, is a phase sortal; for, although one was not an adolescent when one began to exist, one later became an adolescent and eventually ceased to be one, all the while remaining one and the same individual throughout the various transformations. A substance sortal, by contrast, designates a kind to which an individual necessarily belongs throughout its entire existence. Substance sortals indicate the sort of thing an entity *essentially* is—that is, the sort of thing it must be if it is to exist at all and thus the sort of thing it cannot cease to be without ceasing to exist. For example, although an individual that is an adolescent may exist without being an adolescent, an individual that is a plant cannot exist without being a plant. It cannot, for example, cease to be a plant and yet continue to exist. "Plant" is thus a substance sortal. Because they necessarily apply to individuals throughout their entire histories, substance sortals specify necessary conditions for the identities of those individuals. If x is a substance sortal, there are criteria for being an x that any x must satisfy as long as it exists.

It is worth stressing that the criteria given by the substance sortal appear to state only a *necessary* condition for the continued existence of an individual of the kind x. It is not always *sufficient* for the continued existence of an individual x that, beginning with that individual, one can trace the continuous presence through space and time of *an x*. Assume for the sake of argument that "dog" is a substance sortal. Suppose that, on each of ten successive days, surgeons replace one-tenth of the body parts of a male golden retriever with corresponding parts, including the brain, taken from a female German shepherd. Over the course of the ten days, there will be a living dog continuously present on the operating table. But at the beginning of the first day this will be a male golden retriever while at the end of the tenth it will be a female German shepherd. Most of us will be inclined to say that, despite the overlapping of their various parts on the operating table over the ten-day period, the golden retriever with which the surgeons began and the German shepherd with which they end up are different individual dogs. If that is right, the continuous presence through space and time of *a* dog does not guarantee the continued existence of a particular individual dog. More generally, the continuous presence of a certain kind of entity (or, more technically, spatiotemporal continuity under a substance sortal) does not guarantee the continued existence of an individual.

My earlier remark—that each of the various general terms indicating what sort of entity we are corresponds to a different account of personal identity over time—is true only on the assumption that the terms are understood as substance sortals. If, for example, "person" is a substance sortal and I am a person, then among the conditions of my continuing to exist as one and the same individual will be the conditions of personhood—that is, I must retain the capacity for self-conscious mental activity. By contrast, if "person" is a phase sortal, it will not give necessary conditions for the continued existence of anyone who is a person. For one could cease to be a person without ceasing to exist, just as a child may cease to be a child without ceasing to exist. When we ask, therefore, what kind of entity we are, with a view to determining what the conditions of our identity are, and thus when we begin to exist and cease to exist, we are inquiring after the substance sortal that indicates what we most fundamentally and essentially are.

The problem of personal identity over time may be approached in either of two ways. We may ask what is necessarily involved in our continued existence. Or we may ask what sort of thing we are essentially. In the subsequent three sections, I will canvass what I take to be the three most common views of personal identity. The first two are commonly expressed as views of what sort of thing we essentially are, while the third is typically articulated as an account of the conditions necessary for our continued existence. But, as I have suggested, this difference is superficial. A claim about what kind of thing we essentially are implies a set of conditions for our continued existence (though it may not be obvious what they are); and a claim about what is necessarily involved in our continued existence implies a certain conception of what we essentially are (though again the implication may be obscure). As Derek Parfit puts it, "the necessary features of our continued existence depend upon our nature."[6]

2. THE SOUL

2.1. *Hylomorphism*

Many people believe, with Walker Percy, that we begin to exist at conception. There are interesting arguments for this view. One argument appeals to the smooth continuity of human development. If we start with a person now and trace his biological development as far back as we can go, it is difficult to locate any event along this path until we get to conception that could plausibly be thought to mark the beginning of his existence. Surely there is no event after birth that could be identified as the beginning of the existence of an entirely new individual. Nor is it credible to suppose that birth itself is the relevant breaking point, for the changes occasioned by birth are largely extrinsic and in any case may vary from individual to individual depending on the stage of fetal development at which birth occurs. There is, moreover, no point between conception and birth when it is plausible to suppose that a new individual begins to exist, for fetal development is a process that proceeds incrementally, without abrupt changes or discontinuities. All of the points that have been proposed as the moment when a human being begins to exist—such as quickening (generally understood to refer to the time at which the pregnant woman can first feel the fetus moving) and viability (the point at which the fetus could survive outside the womb)— may be seen, on reflection, to be neither invariant in all cases nor indicative of any significant alteration in the intrinsic nature of the fetus. So, if an individual who is now a person existed at birth (if, that is, it is not merely figurative to say that he was born), and if there is no point between birth and conception that is sufficiently significant to mark the beginning of the existence of a new individual, it seems that one must conclude that this individual began to exist at conception (assuming, one should add for the sake of completeness, that he did not exist prior to conception).

This argument would be fallacious if an individual's coming into existence were a gradual process. Consider an analogous argument applied to the question of when a person becomes tall, where becoming tall *is* an imperceptibly slow process. Suppose that a person is tall now and that, as we track his biological development back through time, we can find no point at which he became tall. Should we conclude that he must have been tall from the start? Clearly not. But the argument for the view that we began to exist at conception is not like this, provided it is conjoined with the assumption that our coming into existence cannot be gradual but must occur all at once. (I will later question this assumption; but let us grant it for now.)

There are, it seems, only two views about our nature and identity that support or, at a minimum, are compatible with the belief that we begin to exist at conception. Immediately after conception, all that is empirically detectable is a single cell. If that cell is the first phase in the existence of a human organism and we are human organisms, it makes sense to suppose we begin to exist at conception. Alternatively, our presence immediately after conception might be occult, or undetectable by empirical means. If each of us is or has a soul, understood either as that which informs and animates the body or as a nonphysical substance, we might begin to exist in association with the zygote immediately after conception. These views are, in effect, exhaustive of the conceptions of what we essentially are that are compatible with the assumption that we begin to exist at conception. Because the overwhelming majority of people in contemporary western societies, including many physicians and legislators whose views profoundly affect practices involving killing and letting die, appear to accept one or the other of these views, I will examine them both at some length, beginning with the view that we are or essentially have souls. In this and the following section, I will argue that one conception of the soul that many people seem implicitly to accept is in fact empty, that another is really a form of materialism with unwelcome implications about when we begin to exist, and that a third, while more faithful to people's beliefs about the soul, is actually incompatible with what we know about the mind.

I suspect that the most common view of what we essentially are is that we are souls and that the most common view of when we begin to exist is that we begin to exist at conception. What does this combination of views imply about the nature of the soul? One possibility is that the soul is actually conscious at conception. This, however, seems at variance with the facts. Because there are no indications of consciousness in a zygote, this view suggests that the soul is "locked in"—that is, lacks access to sensory stimuli and is incapable of expressing itself—at least until some time late in pregnancy and that it suffers retroactive amnesia with regard to its conscious embryonic life. But there is no reason to believe that either of these suppositions is true. Another possibility is that the soul is from the moment of conception *capable* of consciousness but is somehow impeded in its exercise of this capacity. If, however, the soul is nonphysical, it is difficult to see what could be suppressing its exercise of its capacity for consciousness. It might be thought that the soul must await the development of the brain before it is able to be conscious; but if the soul's capacity for consciousness depends on its access to a functional brain, it seems unclear in what sense the soul itself is supposed to have the capacity for consciousness. Also on this view, even if the soul could survive the death of the body, there is no reason to suppose that it would be conscious in the afterlife. For, if the soul exists at conception but consciousness and mental activity begin only when the brain begins to function in certain ways, then, by parity of reasoning, it seems that consciousness and mental activity should cease when the brain ceases to function, even though the soul continues to exist. At least this should be the case unless or until the soul is somehow supplied with a new body and brain.

The remaining possibility, which seems most consistent with the facts, is that the soul at conception lacks the capacity for consciousness. On this conception, therefore, the soul is not the mind nor the sole basis of the mind. But most who believe that we are souls also believe that the soul is distinct from the body, and thus can exist separately from the body. Many believe, for example, that the soul continues to exist after the death of the body. This is the most common basis for the belief in an afterlife. But if the soul is distinct and separable from both the mind and the body, what exactly is it? When defined by negation, as neither body nor mind, it emerges as entirely featureless. And, even if one could give some account of what it is, what reason is there to suppose that such a thing exists? It is difficult to imagine even what would count as evidence of its existence. Finally, is not the soul, so conceived, entirely too thin and insubstantial a thing to be what we really and most deeply are?

It is significant that, apart from the deliverances of faith or dogma, there is no reason to suppose that the soul, conceived in this way, begins to exist at conception. For all one knows, one's soul may have existed for an indefinite period prior to the beginning of the existence of one's organism. Indeed, if the soul is essentially independent of both the mind and the body, almost any supposition about its history or future destiny makes about as much sense, or as little, as any other. Thus both Locke and Kant noted that the independence of the soul from both psychological and bodily continuity makes it possible that what we think of as a single person may in fact be a series of incorporeal souls, each of which inherits the mental life of its predecessor, and, correlatively, that a single soul may, for all we know, inhabit a series of bodies and have a succession of radically discontinuous mental lives over time. Locke, for example, suggested that it is "possible for Seth, Ismael, Socrates, Pilate, St. Austin, and Caesar Borgia, to be the same man. For if the identity of the *soul alone* makes the same *man;* and there be nothing in the nature of matter why the same individual spirit may not be united to different bodies, it will be possible that those men, living in different ages, . . . may have been the same man."[7] In short, if the soul is featureless— if it is nonphysical but can exist without the capacity for consciousness—anything seems possible. It may have existed in an unconscious, disembodied state prior to the origin of one's organism, it might have been wandering from body to body before or even during the period of one's conscious life, and it might continue to exist indefinitely in a discarnate, unconscious state after one's death. That it is difficult to discern any difference between this last possibility and one's simply ceasing to exist serves to highlight the vacuity of this featureless conception of the soul.

There is, however, a coherent and determinate way of conceiving of the soul as something that is neither body nor mind. This conception of the soul is one of the two conceptions that have been most influential historically. It derives from the doctrines of Aristotle and Thomas Aquinas and is now embraced primarily in Catholic circles. The other conception derives from Descartes and is even more widely accepted, both among Christians and quite generally. I will examine the first of these conceptions, according to which the soul is neither body nor mind, in the remainder of this section. I will then discuss the second, cartesian conception in the following section. When understood coherently, neither is hospitable to the idea that we begin to exist at conception. Nor does either offer a plausible account of the kind of thing we are.

The first of these two conceptions has its roots in Aristotle's metaphysics of matter and form, according to which matter can constitute a determinate individual only if it has a distinctive form. In order to constitute a human being, the matter of the body must have a certain form. That form is the human soul. This is the *hylomorphic* conception of the soul—from the Greek roots *hylē* (body) and *morphē* (form). The idea that the soul is the form of the body is often elucidated by reference to an analogy with a statue. Only when a lump of bronze (matter) is given a particular shape (form) is there a statue. According to hylomorphism, the soul is to the matter of the body as the shape is to the bronze. Just as the bronze would not be a particular statue without its particular shape, so the matter of the body would not constitute a human being without the form imparted to it by the soul.

This analogy is illuminating in another way. Just as the shape of a statue is not separable from the bronze of which the statue is made, so the soul is not separate or separable from the body. Hence, according to hylomorphism, there can be no disembodied existence, no disembodied afterlife. When a human organism dies, thereby losing the forms of organization that make it a living human being, the soul "departs" and there is no longer a human being but something different: matter that has the form of a corpse. If, on this view, we exist after death, it must be through the resurrection and reanimation of the body—indeed, according to Aquinas, the *same* body— after a period during which we have not existed at all. (This, one would think, would be rather embarrassing for proponents of hylomorphism who believe both that we begin to exist at conception and that all human beings are immortal, for it seems to commit them to a belief in the bodily resurrection of zygotes and embryos. As H. L.

Mencken once noted, if "the soul of a zygote cast out . . . an hour after fertilization . . . goes to Heaven or Hell or some vague realm between, then . . . the bishops and arch-bishops who swarm beyond the grave are forced to associate, and on terms of equal-ity, with shapes that can neither think nor speak, and resemble tadpoles far more than they resemble Christians."[8])

It is important to distinguish the hylomorphic view of what *we* are from the hy-lomorphic conception of the *soul*. For, on this view, we are not souls. We are organ-isms whose constituent matter is internally organized and "directed" (though not consciously) in such a way as to produce the capacities and powers constitutive of a human being. The soul is, to use a phrase commonly employed by proponents of this view, the "organizing principle" that imparts these capacities and powers to the matter of the body. It is thought to be a virtue of this view that it conceives of us as compound entities: each of us is an essential union of soul and body.

There is a good reason why hylomorphism does not identify us with our souls: namely, that the hylomorphic soul is not something we could *be*. We, presumably, are substances, but the hylomorphic soul is not a substance or thing at all; it is not even a part of a thing (it cannot, for example, be numbered among my parts). It is, rather, an *aspect* of the body, a property, a mode of organization or arrangement of the con-stituent matter of the body. In Bernard Williams's apt phrase, the hylomorphic soul appears "only adjectivally."[9] And for this reason, Williams contends, hylomorphism is really only "a polite form of materialism"—polite because it does not claim that we are just our bodies (since the body must be informed by a soul if one of us is to exist), but materialist all the same because it does not recognize the soul as a non-physical *substance*.[10] (Williams concedes that defenders of hylomorphism might en-able the soul "to transcend its adjectival status" by conceiving of it as a form of indi-viduated *mental* organization that could be realized in any suitably configured body. But, conceived in this way, the soul could in principle be multiply instantiated, so that each of us would have to be a *type* of thing rather than an individual entity.[11])

Proponents of hylomorphism often write as if the soul were more than just a mode of organization or the way in which the matter of the body is structured. They assume that it is in some sense a "spiritual" entity—rather more than a mere aspect of matter though less than a nonphysical substance that is wholly distinct from the body. Statements of the view in which this kind of assumption is implicit are seldom entirely clear: the soul is described, for example, as "the physico-spiritual substantial form . . . of the body"[12] or "the *living* principle (dynamic and constitutive inner source) which *actively* animates, organises and informs every aspect of one's exis-tence."[13] Typically the justification for supposing that the hylomorphic soul is spiri-tual in nature is the assumption that there must be "an irreducibly immaterial dimen-sion to self-awareness, intellection and volition."[14] Norman Ford, for example, claims that it is our "rational self-consciousness" that distinguishes us from animals and that this "cannot be explained in terms of quantified matter alone nor in space-time cate-gories. This is why a non-material life-principle or soul is required in a human being to function as an ordinary form to account for the psychosomatic unity of the one subject of all human activities."[15] There is, however, no reason to suppose that self-consciousness and rationality require a non-physical explanation if the simple con-sciousness of animals can be accounted for in wholly physical terms. Nevertheless, suppose we grant that the hylomorphic soul is some sort of nonphysical force responsible for organizing and governing the matter of the body in such as way as to produce the capacities and powers of a human being. When in the course of the developmental process initiated by conception does the soul first appear?

Some have thought that the answer to this question depends on when a human organism begins to exist. If, as many believe, this occurs at some point *subsequent* to conception, the hylomorphic soul could not be present *at* conception. For, as Joseph Donceel, S.J., observes, "the hylomorphic conception of human nature, the official Catholic doctrine, cannot admit the presence of an actual human soul in a virtual human body."[16] But, even if this is right, it states only a necessary condition for the presence of the hylomorphic soul. And it seems implausible to suppose that the presence of a living human organism is *sufficient* for the existence of a hylomorphic soul. For, on virtually any credible view of the matter, the process initiated by conception leads, if uninterrupted, to the existence of a human organism in a fairly short period—for example, two or three weeks. But if the distinctively human soul is present a few weeks after conception, before even the rudiments of the brain are formed, it seems that the essence of the soul must simply be whatever biological factor distinguishes human organisms from other animals organisms. (I will say something about what this is in section 2.2 of chapter 3.) For that seems to be the only organizational difference between the human organism and other animal organisms that is manifest at that point. But the assumption that the difference is merely biological seems incompatible with our sense that the human soul must be *importantly* different from the "organizing principle" that informs the body of an animal.

To most people it seems clear that what importantly distinguishes us from animals is our psychological nature and that this must be reflected in our conception of the human soul. If the soul is the organizing principle of the body, it seems that an essential dimension of the body's organization must be that which underlies our distinctive mental endowments. Hence the insistence that the alleged impossibility of accounting for self-consciousness and rationality in physical terms necessitates a conception of the hylomorphic soul as in some sense a spiritual entity. That the hylomorphic soul informs the body in such a way as to produce characteristically human psychological capacities is, indeed, the traditional view. It is the basis of Aquinas's commitment to the doctrine known, in Catholic theology, as *delayed hominization*—that is, the view that the product of conception *becomes* a human being some time later than the time of conception itself. Aquinas also, however, believed in *immediate animation*—that is, he recognized that a newly fertilized egg—the zygote—is biologically alive; hence it must be informed by a soul of some sort. Following Aristotle, therefore, he distinguished three phases in the organization of the matter of the human body. The zygote and embryo have a low level of organization that allows for a form of life shared by plants; they have, in other words, a *nutritive* or *vegetative* soul. This soul eventually perishes but is immediately succeeded by a *sensitive* or *animal* soul that is manifest in capacities for both nutrition and sensory experience. This type of soul, as the name suggests, is also present in sentient animals. Both the vegetative and the animal soul are products of biological development. But the third type of soul—the *rational* soul (*anima intellectiva*) that distinguishes human beings from animals—must be directly "infused" into the body by God. The event of "ensoulment" is also the moment of "hominization"—that is, the time at which the human body becomes a human being. It is at this point that one of us first begins to exist.

When does this occur? More specifically, what is the criterion for determining when the rational soul appears? Aquinas held that ensoulment occurs at forty days after conception in males and at ninety days in females. This was not sexism but simply an acceptance of the biological claims of Aristotle, who was misled by the primitive means of observation available to him to believe that the male fetus begins to move at forty days while the female does not move until ninety days have elapsed.[17] Obviously, this view is groundless. Some, reverting to the view I criticized earlier, claim that the rational soul is present from the moment that a genuine human organism is formed. But in what sense can anything that is present at that point, before the brain has formed, be said to inform the body with rational or intellectual powers? The rational soul is supposed to distinguish human beings from other animals, but the early human fetus seems, if anything, *inferior* to most animals in terms of the capacity for rationality.

A common response to this challenge is to claim that, from the moment the human organism is formed, the capacity for rationality is present, though initially it is not exercised and perhaps cannot be exercised. (This view is tantamount to "immediate hominization" if a human organism is formed at conception, but entails "delayed hominization" if a human organism begins to exist only at some later point.) If one looks at the pattern of human development and compares it with that in other animals, it becomes apparent that the capacity for rationality is the distinctive element in the design of human beings. We are the kind of thing that is internally oriented or directed toward rationality; other animals are not. Thus all things human have this capacity even if there are times when it cannot be exercised.

This is an obscure claim. Possibly it confuses the capacity for rationality with the potential to develop that capacity. For the human organism in its initial stages, before the brain has formed, can plausibly be held to have the potential for rationality. (I will later, in section 6 of chapter 4, try to elucidate the sense in which this is true, at least in the case of fetal organisms that have the gene sequences that direct the growth of a normal human brain.) But that is not the same as the capacity for rationality, which requires the actual presence of the structures causally involved in the exercise of rationality. Analogously, a newborn infant has the potential for sexual reproduction but not the capacity.

It seems, however, that the mere potential for rationality is not sufficient for the presence of a rational soul. For the hylomorphic soul is the "organizing principle" of the body: it determines how the body *is* organized, not how it might later be organized. The nature of an individual's soul is therefore manifest in that individual's present capacities or powers. The capacities that the individual has the potential to develop reveal only the kind of soul the individual might later have. The human embryo, for example, has the capacity for nutrition; therefore, according to Aquinas's hylomorphism, it has a vegetative soul. It may have the potential to develop the capacity for rationality, but only when that potential is realized will it have a rational soul. It is worth repeating that, according to traditional Aristotelian and Thomist hylomorphism, the soul is just the inherent organization of the matter of the body in a distinctive way, so that the matter constitutes an individual of a particular sort. What sort of individual it is depends on the capacities and powers it is organized to have.

We can, admittedly, discern a tendency in the Thomist tradition to reify the soul as *that which* organizes the matter of the body. This is the tendency, noted by Williams, to see the hylomorphic soul as having more than mere adjectival status. And it is, perhaps, this rather obscure conception of the soul as a spiritual entity somehow suffused through the body and directing it that underlies the claim that there can be a human being with the capacity for rationality even before the brain has been formed. For if the soul is conceived, vaguely and somewhat mysteriously, as an occult, spiritual entity, it can perhaps be thought to possess the capacity for rationality even if, prior to the formation of the brain, it is quiescent. Perhaps the capacity remains dormant until the maturation of the brain allows for its expression or exercise.

As the hylomorphic conception of the soul shifts in this way from the frankly materialist Aristotelian view to the notion of an active spiritual entity, it is in danger of collapsing into the distinctly non-hylomorphic conception I will discuss in the next section—a conception of the soul as a nonphysical substance. For unless the rational soul is a nonphysical substance, it is difficult to make sense of the claim that it is present, with the capacity for rationality, even before the apparent physical prerequisites for consciousness have been formed. The necessary assumptions of this view seem, indeed, to verge on a nonmaterialist analogue of the seventeenth century doctrine of "preformationism," which held that the human embryo actually contains a fully formed but microscopic homunculus.

Unless the hylomorphic conception of the soul shades subtly into the very different conception of the soul as a nonphysical substance, it cannot sustain the view that the rational soul is present, with the capacity for rationality, in the early stages of pregnancy when the relevant parts of the body not only have not been organized for the generation of consciousness and mental activity but have not yet even been formed. The distinctively hylomorphic conception of the rational soul entails a different and implausible account of "hominization," or the beginning of our existence. The hylomorphic soul is the form or organizing principle of the body. What *relevantly* distinguishes a human being from a living animal body, and thus indicates the presence of a different type of soul, is the capacity for rationality. This capacity is grounded in the existence and functional organization of the cerebral cortex. Indeed, the cortex must have reached quite a high level of development and organization in order to support the capacity for rationality. Because the concept of rationality is vague, it is difficult to identify the point at which the capacity for rationality first appears. But, if rationality is a level of cognition that distinguishes us from animals, the capacity is certainly not present until at least a number of months after birth. Thus the hylomorphic conception of the soul, when coherently understood, implies that we do not begin to exist until well after the birth of our organism—an implication that effectively undermines the view.

2.2. *The Cartesian Soul*

The temptation to conceive of the soul as a spiritual entity finds its clearest expression in what may be called the *cartesian* conception of the soul. According to this conception, the soul is a nonphysical substance that is distinct and separable from the body. Thus those who embrace this conception often hold, not that we *have* souls, but that we *are* souls. Yet the other view is coherent. Some who believe in the cartesian soul maintain that we are compound entities, consisting of body and soul, although the soul is our essential part. On this view, our bodies are parts of us, though we could lose them and continue to exist as disembodied souls. In what follows, I will focus on the view that we are cartesian souls. The objections to that view apply equally to the claim that we *have* cartesian souls.

The cartesian conception of the soul arises naturally as a response to the puzzlement, or indeed incomprehension, that most people have experienced in contemplating the idea that mere physical matter could be capable of thinking, feeling, and perceiving. If it seems—as it has done to most people until comparatively recently—absurd to suppose that consciousness could be a property of mere matter, it is natural to conclude that consciousness must be a property of a purely mental substance that is distinct from the body. Since we are conscious, we must be mental substances of this sort.

The cartesian conception thus effectively identifies the mind with the soul. The soul is, on this view, the subject of consciousness. It is that which thinks, feels, and perceives. It is a "thinking thing."

Those who hold this view typically assume that the soul interacts causally with the brain and body but is not dependent upon them either for its continued existence or for its ability to carry out its defining functions: consciousness and mental activity. In other words, while the soul is thought to use a particular brain and body as instruments of perception and action, it is assumed to have different identity conditions and thus to be capable of existing in an entirely disembodied state. This, of course, is gratifying, as it provides the basis for the belief in continued life after death. It is also assumed that the soul typically manifests psychological continuity over time—that is, that it has a mental life that is unified over time by overlapping series of psychological connections. But again, the soul can continue to exist in the absence of psychological continuity. Even in cases in which the particular connections between a person's mental life at different times are almost entirely expunged, as happens, for example, in the final stages of Alzheimer's disease, the existence and integrity of the soul itself are entirely unaffected.

As I noted earlier, the account of personal identity corresponding to the view that we are essentially mental substances or souls is nonreductionist in character. According to this view, the continued existence of a person over time is not reducible to any form of physical or psychological continuity. The continued existence of a person consists solely in the continued existence of the soul, which does not itself consist in the continued existence of, or functioning of, or relations between any other things. This does not mean, however, that there is no criterion for tracking the existence—or the presence—of the soul. If the soul is that which is conscious, our evidence for whether a soul exists or continues to exist in association with a particular organism is whether there is any consciousness, or capacity for consciousness, present in that organism. If the evidence indicates that there is no longer any capacity for consciousness associated with a particular human organism, we may conclude that the soul has either ceased to exist or ceased to exist in association with that organism.

In the history of speculation about the soul as the seat of consciousness, two distinct views have emerged. According to Descartes, the essence of the soul is to be conscious. Thus he claims that "the human soul . . . is always thinking . . . [It] cannot ever be without thought; it can of course be without this or that thought, but it cannot be without *some* thought."[18] By contrast, Richard Swinburne, a prominent contem-

porary representative of the cartesian tradition, holds that it is the "*capacity* for experience and action" that is the essence of the soul, without which it could not exist.[19]
To most people, Swinburne's conception is more plausible, since it allows that we
can be temporarily unconscious, even if we are essentially nonmaterial substances.

Given either of these conceptions of the soul, it seems more reasonable to believe
that the soul begins to exist in association with the organism, *not* at conception, but
when there is first evidence of the presence of consciousness in the organism. Descartes's conception implies, as we have seen, "that the human soul, wherever it be,
even in the mother's womb, is always thinking."[20] Thus Descartes is committed by his
conception of the soul to affirm "that the mind begins to think as soon as it is implanted
in the body of an infant, and that it is immediately aware of its thoughts, even though
it does not remember this afterwards because the impressions of these thoughts do not
remain in the memory."[21] Although this supposition is not incoherent, it is very difficult to believe, if we assume that the soul begins to exist at conception. We can accept that a late-term human fetus is conscious even if no one has memories of this period, because there is *evidence* of fetal consciousness at that point. But it is contrary
to all we know to suppose that a zygote or embryo is conscious and self-aware but
"locked in" and later suffers retroactive amnesia about its previous locked-in state.

According to Swinburne's conception, the soul might have existed immediately
after conception with the capacity for consciousness but without being able to exercise this capacity. Again, however, there is no reason to believe that this actually occurs. There is no reason to suppose that the soul's exercise of its essential capacity is
invariably inhibited for an extended period after the beginning of its existence. After
all, if the soul can exercise its essential capacities for consciousness and mental activity after death, when the brain has ceased to function, it seems that it should also
be able to exercise these capacities prior to the onset of functioning in the brain and
even prior to the brain's development. Either way, therefore—whether one accepts
Descartes's or Swinburne's conception of the soul—it seems reasonable to date the
beginning of the soul's existence in association with the fetal organism from the time
that there is independent evidence of the presence of consciousness.

If one accepts that the soul begins to exist in association with the human organism when consciousness first appears, one can rebut the argument cited at the beginning of this section for the claim that we began to exist at conception. For on this
view there *is* a momentous event that occurs during the otherwise smoothly continuous process of human biological development—namely, the acquisition by the fetus
of consciousness or the capacity for consciousness, which on this view marks the appearance of the soul.

While the great majority of contemporary Christian theologians appear to hold
that the soul begins to exist at conception, and thus appear to be committed to something like the featureless conception of the soul considered earlier, there is nevertheless a long tradition of Christian thought that holds that the soul begins to exist well
after conception. As we saw, this was Thomas Aquinas's view and his acceptance of
"delayed hominization" remained orthodox until well into the nineteenth century.
Thus in *The Anatomy of Melancholy,* published in 1621, several centuries after
Aquinas's death, Robert Burton states the prevailing view that "the soul . . . is infused
into the child or embryo in his mother's womb, six months after conception."[22] Views

of this sort appear to have guided the comparatively permissive stance on early abortion that prevailed in many places until about the middle of the nineteenth century. In the United States, for example, abortion during the first trimester of pregnancy was generally regarded as morally acceptable on the ground that the fetus did not come to life, or acquire a soul, until some point during the second trimester.[23] The ability of the pregnant woman to feel the fetus moving was regarded as evidence that ensoulment had occurred. We still use the term "quickening" to refer to the point in pregnancy at which fetal movement can first be detected, but many of us are unaware of the etymological significance of the term. "Quick" was once used to mean "living," as when Hamlet says, of an open grave, " 'tis for the dead, not for the quick."[24] Thus "quickening" originally meant the moment when the fetus is animated or comes to life. Although we now treat the first detectable fetal movements as *constitutive* of quickening, they were originally understood merely as *evidence* that quickening— meaning "coming to life"—had occurred. (Apparently, the distinction, presupposed by Aquinas, between "animation" and "hominization" was not always recognized.)

The idea that we are essentially mental substances may lose some of its charm, at least for some, when one realizes that it is doubtfully compatible with the belief that we begin to exist at conception. Still, this view continues to pass for common sense in many contemporary societies and it is therefore worth citing several objections to it that together seem to constitute a decisive case for rejecting it. Because most of these objections have been developed at length by other writers, I will rehearse them only cursorily here.[25]

First, it is difficult to reconcile this view of the soul with the amply documented facts about the dependence of mental events on the states of the brain. If the soul is that which is conscious and engages in mental activity, and if it is not necessarily causally tied to the brain, in the sense that it can perform its characteristic mental functions independently of any connections with a brain, how can we explain the way that mental functioning is invariably impaired by, say, the effects of alcohol on the brain, or physical damage to particular areas of the brain? While the soul must be susceptible to causal influence by the external world in order for perception through the sense organs to be possible, it is more difficult to understand how its basic capacities for cognition, imagination, emotion, and so on could be impaired or extinguished by selective damage to certain areas of the brain. I know of no plausible response to this obvious problem.

Second, most of those who believe that we are souls, so conceived, face problems of consistency with their other beliefs. If the soul is that which thinks, feels, and perceives (that is, if anything that thinks, feels, and perceives is a soul), and if many animals think, feel, and perceive, these animals must have souls, or *be* souls, as well. But for most people this suggestion would get the world unacceptably overpopulated with souls. Given the theological and moral significance that most believers in the soul attribute to the idea that that is what we are, the implications of recognizing that every cockroach is also a soul would be intolerable. The claim that we are souls is often cited, particularly in the context of the debate about abortion, as the basis for the belief in the special sanctity and inviolability of human life. If cockroaches are also souls, that may put them near enough on a par with human fetuses that the argument against abortion would have to be extended to cover the killing of cockroaches as well.

Descartes responded to this problem by simply denying that animals are conscious. Because he believed that consciousness is attributable only to mental substances and that animals clearly do not have souls, Descartes concluded that animals cannot have the capacity for consciousness. They must, therefore, be cleverly constructed automata created by God for our edification and amusement. Notoriously, this conclusion led eager cartesians to engage in ghastly forms of vivisection, marveling all the while at how convincingly the automata on which they hacked and sawed mimicked the behavior of conscious beings in agony.

This resolution of the problem is simply unavailable to us now. Skepticism about whether animals are conscious is possible, but only in the way that traditional skepticism about other minds is possible: one may treat such skepticism as a source of interesting philosophical problems, but no sane person could take either form of skepticism seriously as a basis for conduct. We have, after all, much the same evidence for consciousness in higher animals that we have for consciousness in other persons—namely, various forms of behavioral and neurophysiological evidence (though the latter may seem irrelevant to certain cartesians). All that is missing is language; but, if it were possible to treat the behavioral and neurophysiological evidence as inconclusive, it would seem that the same skepticism could be applied to the evidence supplied by language. If I may properly remain unconvinced that you experience pain when I observe your writhing, hear your howls, and contemplate the tempests in your nervous system revealed by scientific investigation, why should I then be convinced when you emit the sounds, "That hurts"? That might just be one more thing, like writhing, that you are programmed to do. If, moreover, only language can provide sufficient evidence of consciousness, it seems that we can have no more reason to suppose that infants are conscious than we have for believing that animals are. Finally, if we deny that animals are conscious while accepting that human beings are, we must either abandon the theory of evolution, accept that there was a point in the process of evolution when God began to supply souls to our ancestors, whose own ancestors were mere automata, or accept that consciousness arose along with language—though how unconscious beings could develop a language is rather a mystery.

It may be tempting to retreat to the more modest claim that, while the soul is not necessary to explain the lower forms of consciousness found in animals, it is necessary to explain the higher forms of consciousness and cognition characteristic of human beings. This proposal might explain why it is necessary to suppose that we have souls though animals do not. But it effectively abandons the conception of the soul as that which is conscious. It invites us to conceive of the soul more as a capacity than as the sort of substance that we essentially are. This response would, moreover, leave us with no reason to attribute souls to those human beings whose mental lives are no more sophisticated than those of certain animals: fetuses, infants, the gravely cognitively impaired, and so on.

A third objection that might be raised to the cartesian conception of the soul is that it is difficult to reconcile with the phenomenon of monozygotic twinning. Suppose, as many believe, that the cartesian soul begins to exist at or immediately after conception. (This assumption, as we have seen, has problematic implications, but let us ignore this for the moment.) If twinning subsequently occurs, what happens to the soul? There are several possibilities. First, although it is typically claimed that the cartesian soul is indivisible, it does not seem incoherent to suppose that a mental substance could divide. What *is* incoherent, however, is the supposition that the soul could divide but continue to exist. It is clear that the soul could not continue to exist as *both* of the twins, for that would imply that the twins were one individual, whereas they are clearly two distinct individuals. And if the original soul were to continue to exist in only one of the twins, this would not be a genuine case of division, or splitting, but a case in which the original soul would somehow generate a replica of itself. If, therefore, twinning involves a genuine division of the soul, it necessarily involves the ceasing to exist of the original soul and the coming into existence of two new souls, each conscious or possessing the capacity for consciousness. If the ceasing to exist of a human soul is tragic, the idea that twinning involves the division of the soul implies that twinning is tragic. This is hard to believe.

A second possibility is that, when the embryo divides, the soul does not divide but follows only one of the twin embryos. In that case, either a new soul is created for the other twin or the other twin is a soulless automaton.

A third possibility is that, anticipating that twinning would occur, God implanted two souls in the original zygote. But, like the second view, this claim strains credulity. There is no evidence of the presence of a conscious entity, or an entity capable of consciousness, immediately following conception. It therefore seems preposterous to suggest that, in some cases, there is not just one such entity but two.

I suggested earlier that the believer in the cartesian soul would do best to accept that the soul begins to exist with the onset of consciousness, which the evidence suggests occurs well after conception. If that is right, the soul does not join the body until after the possibility of twinning has ceased. Given this assumption, twinning poses no problem for the cartesian conception of the soul. When twinning occurs, only the physical embryo divides. Both resulting fetuses receive souls later on.

There are, however, other possibilities of splitting or dividing that pose a challenge to the cartesian that cannot be so conveniently avoided.

2.3. *Divided Consciousness*

One such possibility arises with the operation known as "hemispheric commissurotomy." In this operation, the corpus callosum—the bundle of fibers that connect the two cerebral hemispheres and enable them to communicate directly with one another—is surgically severed. This procedure has been performed on certain patients with potentially life-threatening forms of epilepsy. By preventing the spread of random discharges of electrical activity from one hemisphere to the other, it mitigates the severity of these patients' seizures.[26] In studies done on these patients following the operation, certain sensory stimuli were presented to one hemisphere only, while different stimuli were presented only to the other. What these studies revealed is that the patients have potentially separate centers of consciousness—that their consciousness can be divided.[27] This was shown by the fact that each hemisphere, communicating with the experimenters through some part of the body which it alone controlled, demonstrated awareness of having been presented with certain information of which the other hemisphere was unaware.

What can the believer in the cartesian soul say about these cases? It seems incoherent to claim that, following the operation, there is a single cartesian soul that encompasses two distinct centers of consciousness. If the soul is understood as the subject of consciousness, its boundaries are determined by what it is conscious of. All conscious events occurring simultaneously in a single soul must be co-conscious. If, for example, my soul is the substance coextensive with *this* field of consciousness, then any conscious events occurring now that are not within this field—any conscious events of which I am not now conscious—must be events within a different field of consciousness, a different soul. This is the sense in which the cartesian soul is necessarily indivisible: a single soul cannot have a divided consciousness.

The only coherent options seem to be the same as those we canvassed in the discussion of twinning. The soul might genuinely divide, resulting in the existence of two separable souls. But it is surely implausible to see this operation as causing one soul to cease to exist while simultaneously creating two new souls. Among other things, this suggests that commissurotomy is the equivalent of murder. Alternatively, one might suppose that the original soul attaches itself to one hemisphere only (presumably the dominant, verbal one). In that case, either a new soul is somehow supplied for the other hemisphere or what we take to be evidence of consciousness in the other hemisphere is really only a series of unconscious responses. Finally, it might be held that each human brain houses two souls that normally run in tandem, each unaware of the other, and that the operation somehow causes the two streams of consciousness to cease to coincide—that is, the operation somehow causes one soul to begin to have experiences, thoughts, and volitions different from those of the other.

None of these options is credible. Commissurotomy therefore poses a serious challenge to the cartesian conception of the soul as that which thinks, feels, and perceives. This challenge may be rendered more acute by means of a thought-experiment, or, rather, a series of thought-experiments. We will consider, seriatim, six different possibilities, the first five of which prepare the ground for the sixth.[28]

> *The Whole-Body Transplant.* One's entire brain is extracted and transplanted into the body of one's identical twin, who has just suffered brain death and whose brain has been removed. One's brain is appropriately connected to the nerves in one's twin's body, so that after the operation a person is revived in one's twin's body who is fully psychologically continuous with oneself as one was before the operation.

Most people believe that one would survive this operation and would continue to exist in what was formerly the body of one's identical twin. As Parfit has observed, this is just the limiting case of organ and part transplantation.[29] We accept that one could survive a heart transplant, or a kidney transplant, or an arm or leg transplant, and so on. And one could survive each of these if they occurred serially. It therefore seems that one could survive the replacement through transplantation of *all* of one's bodily parts—except the brain—even if all the replacements were to occur simultaneously.

The second case in the series is also, as yet, merely hypothetical.

> *The Brainstem Transplant.* Because one's brainstem has been damaged, it is removed and replaced by a different brainstem transplanted from the body of one's identical twin, whose cerebral hemispheres and various vital organs have been irreparably damaged.

Given what we know about the contribution of the brainstem to the mental life of a person, most people would accept that one could survive such an operation. The brainstem functions primarily to regulate both the autonomic nervous system and various other somatic processes. It is not itself the locus of consciousness or mental activity. The areas of the brain in which mental states are realized are in the cerebrum, primarily the cerebral cortex. The brainstem, by contrast, does not appear to contain any of the neurological correlates of the contents of consciousness. Thus selective damage to the brainstem does not result in the selective impairment of cognitive functioning (for example, loss of memory, perceptual disturbance, deterioration of rational capacities, and so on) in the way that selective damage to the cerebral hemispheres does.

The contribution that the brainstem makes to consciousness and mental activity is largely all-or-nothing. There is an area of the brain, located primarily in the brainstem and called the *ascending reticular activating system,* or, less cumbersomely, the *reticular formation,* that appears to function rather in the manner of an off-on switch for consciousness. If this area is damaged, coma ensues; consciousness and mental activity cease. But the functioning of the reticular formation does not appear to affect or contribute to the *contents* of consciousness. The reticular formation thus appears to be an essential support system for the parts of the brain where mentation occurs but its tissues are not tissues in which the mind or any of its elements are realized. Because of this, most of us believe, on reflection, that the continued existence and functioning of the same reticular formation is not in principle essential to a person's continued existence. One could survive the replacement of one's reticular formation through transplantation, were such an operation possible.

There is some evidence that certain areas of the brainstem do have subtle effects on the character of the contents of the mind. The brainstem may, for example, modulate the emotional hue of certain experiences and memories. But if the only contributions that the brainstem makes to the contents or character of the mind are marginal in this way, then our conclusion about the reticular formation seems to apply to the brainstem as a whole: the continued existence and functioning of the same brainstem is not in principle necessary for a person's continued existence. One could survive a brainstem transplant.

Next consider:

> *The Cerebrum Transplant.* One's cerebrum is extracted and transplanted into the body of one's identical twin, whose own cerebrum has been destroyed. One's cerebrum is detached from one's own brainstem and fully connected to the functional brainstem in one's twin's decerebrate but still living organism.

Again, most people accept that one would survive this procedure and would exist thereafter in what was previously the body of one's twin. This intuition is supported by the intuitions elicited in the two previous cases. For this case merely combines the features of those other cases. The transplantation of one's cerebrum into the decerebrate organism of one's twin is simply a whole-body transplant together with a brainstem transplant. If one could survive the transplantation of one's whole brain into a different body, and if one could also survive a brainstem transplant, then one could survive the transplantation of one's cerebrum into a different body.

Unlike the previous three cases, the fourth case is something that actually occurs from time to time.

Loss of One Hemisphere. One suffers a stroke that causes the death of an entire cerebral hemisphere.

When this actually happens, we do not doubt that the person survives, albeit in a sadly diminished state. Indeed, it seems possible, in principle, that a person could remain conscious throughout the period in which the stricken hemisphere dies from anoxia. The loss of an entire hemisphere does, of course, cause a loss of motor control of one side of the body as well as a dramatic diminution of various cognitive capacities. For while some capacities are duplicated in both hemispheres, each hemisphere normally develops certain specialized functions, beginning at an early age. Thus one hemisphere, usually the left, tends to specialize in linguistic functions. If, therefore, an adult's left hemisphere is destroyed (or surgically removed—a procedure known as "hemispherectomy"), the person's linguistic abilities may revert to the level of those of a small child, for this is the level that the right hemisphere attained before the left hemisphere took over primary responsibility for that function. If, however, a hemispherectomy is performed in childhood, before extensive hemispheric specialization occurs, the loss in cognitive functioning may be minimal. For the plasticity of the developing brain is such that the functions that were being adopted by the hemisphere that is removed are simply taken over by the remaining hemisphere. As a person grows older, however, the ability of one hemisphere to accommodate the functions of the other gradually declines.

There is speculation that, in some people, hemispheric specialization fails to occur, or occurs only minimally. In such people, if there are any, the cerebral hemispheres develop more or less symmetrically, with each carrying the full range of the person's basic psychological capacities. Moreover, these people, like other people, have memory traces of most of their experiences duplicated over both hemispheres. Imagine, in the case of the Loss of One Hemisphere, that one is such a person. Since we grant that other people in fact survive the loss of a hemisphere when their hemispheres are asymmetrically developed, it seems to follow a fortiori that one could survive the loss of a hemisphere when this would involve little or no loss either of cognitive capacity or of the contents of one's mental life.

The fifth thought-experiment combines the features of the third and fourth.

Loss Followed by Transplantation. One suffers an accident that destroys one of one's hemispheres and damages one's brainstem and body. But, because one's hemispheres were largely symmetrically developed, virtually all of one's cognitive capacities are preserved in the remaining hemisphere. Surgeons therefore extract one's undamaged hemisphere and transplant it into the cranium of one's identical twin, whose cerebrum has been destroyed but whose brainstem and body are intact.

It seems that one would survive in the body of one's twin. If one could survive the loss of a hemisphere, and if one could survive the transplantation of one's cerebrum into another body, it seems to follow that one could survive the transplantation of one's cerebrum, diminished by one hemisphere, into another body.

So far, none of these thought-experiments contains a challenge that should unduly alarm those who believe that we are essentially souls. In each case, the soul presumably follows that part of one's brain that continues to function in a way that is correlated with the continuity of one's mental life. The challenge arises in the sixth and final thought-experiment.

> *Division.* One is a member of a set of identical triplets, all of whom are involved in an accident. While one's brainstem and various vital organs are irreparably damaged, one's cerebral hemispheres are unharmed. In the case of both other triplets, however, their brainstems and bodies are undamaged but their cerebrums are destroyed. Surgeons are able to extract one's cerebrum intact but, instead of transplanting it whole, they divide it and transplant each hemisphere into the body of one of the two remaining triplets. Because one's hemispheres were symmetrically developed, the two people who are brought to consciousness after the operations are both fully psychologically continuous with oneself as one was before the operations. Both believe themselves to be oneself and both have bodies almost indistinguishable from one's own.

This thought-experiment, which, following Parfit, I have tendentiously labeled the case of Division, poses problems for all views of personal identity. But the problems are particularly acute for the belief that we are nonmaterial souls. By our original reasoning, if either of one's hemispheres had been destroyed while the other had been transplanted into the body of one of one's triplets, one would have survived as the resulting person. This conclusion seems acceptable even to those who believe that we are souls. But in the case of Division, both hemispheres are preserved and revived. What options does the believer in the soul have in understanding what happens in this case?

One suggestion is that, after the operations, the original person survives with a mind that is divided between two bodies. On certain other views of personal identity, this understanding is merely implausible; on the view that we are cartesian souls, it is incoherent, for the reason given earlier in the discussion of commissurotomy. If there are two separate centers of consciousness, each experiencing conscious states not accessible to the other, they cannot both be parts of the same soul. For the cartesian soul is individuated by reference to its synchronous unity of consciousness.

Nor is it possible to regard the people who come to consciousness after the operations as different people who are both identical with the original person prior to the operations. For this presupposes that the original soul divides but continues to exist in the form of two distinct centers of consciousness, and this, as we have seen, is incompatible with the notion of the soul as that which is conscious. If, moreover, both of the resulting people were identical with the original person, this would imply that they were identical with each other. So this understanding collapses into the previous one according to which there are not really two people but only one soul with a divided consciousness simultaneously animating two different bodies.

Some have claimed that, in Division, the original person survives as only one of the two resulting people, though neither we nor either of the resulting people can determine which of the two it is.[30] According to this view, the soul follows only one of the hemispheres, though each mind associated with each hemisphere is fully and equally psychologically continuous with the mind of the original person. The problem with this view, however, is that it leaves us with no explanation of where the other soul came from. One who believes that we are souls will be profoundly reluctant to accept that surgeons can create an nonmaterial soul de novo simply by separating a person's cerebral hemispheres.

This same problem besets another possible response to the case, which is to say that neither of the resulting people is identical with the original soul. Some philosophers have opted for this response, but it is not an attractive option for the believer in the soul, for it not only suggests that the surgeons have murdered the original person but also leaves the embarrassing problem of accounting for the presence of *two* entirely new souls.

Perhaps the believer in the soul should take an entirely different line, claiming that we are simply mistaken to assume that two persons would come to consciousness after the operations.[31] Because there is only one soul, and therefore only one consciousness, present prior to the operations, there can be only one soul, and therefore only one conscious person, after the operations. What one should expect, therefore, should such operations ever be performed, is that a person would come to consciousness in only one of the two bodies. That body would be animated by the original soul. The other body need not be lifeless and inert; after all, it would have a functional brainstem and thus might satisfy the criteria for being a living human organism. But it would have no capacity for consciousness, for it would not be host to a soul.

The problem with this response is that it seems incompatible with what we know actually happens in cases of hemispheric commissurotomy. Dividing a person's hemispheres does seem to produce two at least potentially distinct centers of consciousness. What the case of Division does is to dramatize this aspect of the actual cases by imaginatively locating the two hemispheres in different bodies rather than in the same body. If separation of the hemispheres via commissurotomy produces distinct centers of consciousness, there seems to be no reason to suppose that the consciousness associated with each hemisphere could not survive transference along with the hemisphere itself into a different body.

The mind is, it seems, potentially divisible in ways that cannot be accounted for by the view that we are cartesian souls. As I noted earlier, this view is simply incompatible with what we now know to be true about the mind and its dependence on the operations of the brain.

3. ARE WE HUMAN ORGANISMS?

3.1. *When Does a Human Organism Begin to Exist?*

Assuming that it is unreasonable to believe that we are souls, there remains only one view that seems compatible with the idea that we begin to exist at conception. This is the view that we are essentially human organisms, or, to be more precise, that each of us is numerically identical with a particular human organism or human animal. To many people, this seems obvious: it is simply scientifically educated common sense.[32]

If "human organism" applies to us as a substance sortal, indicating the kind of thing we essentially are, then "person," as I understand the term, must be a phase sortal. For it is clear that human organisms begin to exist before they acquire a mental life sufficiently complex to allow them to qualify as persons, and it is equally clear that they may lose the capacity for self-consciousness, and therefore cease to be persons, and yet not only continue to exist but also remain alive and conscious.

As we have seen, Walker Percy seems to find it uncontroversial that a human organism begins to exist at conception. It is worth considering whether this is true. The first thing to note is that conception is not a momentary event but is instead a process lasting about twenty-four hours. The process is not complete until syngamy, the point at which the genetic materials from the sperm and egg have thoroughly fused. It is arguable that no new entity exists until that point.

At syngamy, it seems clear that a new, living entity exists: the single-celled human zygote. Is the single-celled zygote the earliest stage in the existence of a single individual that will later, if all goes well, be a mature, adult human organism? Before I address that question, I should say, for the sake of clarity, how I will use certain terms. If we track the matter composing the single-celled zygote forward in time, we find the continuous presence of a collection of cells that increase in number until eventually they, or their descendents, compose an adult human organism. I will refer to this spatiotemporally continuous collection of cells as the "zygote" from syngamy to implantation, which typically occurs six days after fertilization. Following scientific practice, I will often call it the "embryo" during the early period after implantation. Technically, the collection of cells does not become a fetus until sixty days after conception, but, following ordinary language, I will often use the term "fetus" to refer to the entity during any period between implantation and birth. The fact that this collection of cells follows a continuous path through space and time does not entail that it constitutes a single individual throughout the time that it exists. Whether it is or when it becomes an individual is precisely the question at issue. (To see how a collection of individual entities might not constitute an individual, consider my computer and the books piled next to it. They form a collection of objects that together occupy a certain region of space, but it does not seem that they constitute an individual.)

Assuming that the zygote is formed at syngamy, and assuming for the sake of argument that the single-celled zygote is itself the earliest stage in the development of a human organism, it does not follow that all adult human organisms began to exist at syngamy. For something different happens when monozygotic twinning occurs. (Strictly speaking, monozygotic twinning may occur during the zygotic stage or during the embryonic stage up to about fourteen days after conception, in which case it would be monoembryonic twinning. For convenience, I will write as if twinning occurred only during the zygotic phase.) In cases in which monozygotic twinning occurs, the zygote divides to form two qualitatively identical zygotes. Because the zygotes are qualitatively identical, and because both are continuous with the original zygote in exactly the same way, there can in principle be no reason to suppose that one but not the other is identical with the original zygote. And they cannot both be identical with the original zygote for, given the transitivity of identity, that would imply that they are identical with each other, which they clearly are not. We must conclude, therefore, that, when monozygotic twinning occurs, the zygote that divides thereby ceases to exist and two new zygotes begin to exist at that point (as do two new organisms, given the assumption that the original zygote was an organism). What this means is that, even if most adult human organisms began life at conception, monozygotic twin organisms began to exist somewhat later, when a zygote that began life at conception divided.

The phenomenon of twinning raises an interesting problem. If we are human organisms and each successful conception gives rise to a new human organism, then, when a human zygote divides to form twins, one of us ceases to exist. There is a particular position for which this is rather an embarrassment. There are some who hold that abortion is wrong on the basis of two claims: first, that we begin to exist at conception and, second, that it is a terrible loss when one of us dies, even in utero. Those who hold this view seem to be committed to the conclusion that monozygotic twinning is bad, as it involves the ceasing to exist of one of us. Admittedly, the one who ceases to exist makes way for the two who come to exist; but the phenomenon should still be seen, on this view, as tragic overall. For we normally assume that, while it is bad for one of us to cease to exist, it is not in the same way good, or at least not to a comparable extent, for one (or more) of us to come into existence.

When I noted this problem in an earlier paper, I assumed that it would strike anyone as absurd to suppose that monozygotic twinning is bad or regrettable on the ground it involves a serious and uncompensated loss: the ceasing to exist of one of us, of one of our congeners.[33] Subsequently, however, David Oderberg has explicitly embraced this consequence of the pair of assumptions that lead to it. He notes that, while we do not in fact respond to instances of monozygotic twinning with a sense of loss, "our practice could change in conformity with our deeper appreciation of what *happens* when twinning occurs. . . . [It] is arguably proper for us to mourn the lost embryo in an appropriate way (which would be suitably restrained given the bareness of its relationship to anyone)."[34] For now, I simply note this view without comment. The account of personal identity that I will advance later in the chapter will, I hope, help to explain why it seems to most of us that it would be irrational to engage in mourning for the sake of an insentient cluster of cells.

It seems clear, at any rate, that not all human organisms begin to exist at conception. Monozygotic twins do not. They may or may not begin life as single-celled entities, but those entities are the direct products of fission rather than fertilization. But what about all other human organisms? If an adult human organism is not the product of monozygotic twinning (or, one might add for the sake of completeness, of zygotic or embryonic fusion, cloning, or parthenogenesis), can it be said to have begun life as a single-celled product of fertilization? In these cases, is the single-celled zygote the earliest stage in the existence of a single individual that will later be an adult human organism?

Some have held that the mere possibility that the zygote or embryo might split into twins shows that there cannot be a single human organism present until fourteen days after conception, when the possibility of twinning ceases. Helga Kuhse and Peter Singer, for example, have argued that, if there is an organism there and twinning does occur, there is no plausible explanation of what happens to the organism. It is clearly implausible to suppose that the original organism survives as only one of the twins, or as both, or that there were really two overlapping organisms present all along. Nor is it plausible, according to Kuhse and Singer, to claim that the original organism ceases to exist, for this would "put one in the difficult position . . . of having to explain how it can be that a human individual has ceased to exist when nothing has been lost or has perished—in other words, when there has been a death but there is no corpse."[35] Therefore it is best to accept that there was never an organism there at all, but merely a cell or collection of cells.

There does not, however, seem to be anything problematic about the claim that, if an organism begins to exist at conception and twinning occurs, that organism simply ceases to exist. Ceasing to exist through division is not the same kind of event as death and does not leave dead remains behind. Thus, for example, when an amoeba divides, it ceases to exist though it does not die. While living entities may cease to exist by dying, some may also cease to exist in another way, by dividing.

There are two reasonable interpretations of the processes that occur during the fourteen days following conception, before cell differentiation begins, the "primitive streak" is formed, and twinning ceases to be possible. According to one understanding, the successive cell divisions are all events in the history of a single individual. When the initial single-celled zygote divides, it becomes, or continues to exist as, a two-celled entity. The two-celled entity is simply the successor state of the initial one-celled entity. Similarly, when the cells comprising the two-celled entity divide, the same continuing individual becomes a four-celled entity. And further divisions that continue to expand the number of cells are simply further phases in the growth and development of that individual. When each cell divides, *it* ceases to exist, but the individual that is constituted by those cells continues to exist through each successive transformation of its constituent matter.

According to the alternative interpretation, when the initial single-celled zygote divides, there is nothing that continues to exist. Just as, in twinning, when the zygote divides it ceases to exist, so in the initial division the single cell ceases to exist and is supplanted by its two qualitatively identical daughter cells. Similarly, when each of the daughter cells divides, it ceases to exist and is replaced by its own two qualitatively identical daughter cells. Again, there is nothing—no individual—that persists through these transformations. Only when the cells begin to be differentiated, to take on specialized functions, and to be organized together in an integrated way do they together constitute a further individual.

If the first of these interpretations is correct, it is plausible to suppose that the zygote formed at conception is a human organism—that is, that it is the initial phase in the existence of a single individual that will eventually be recognizable as an adult human organism. If, by contrast, the second interpretation is correct, it is quite implausible to suppose that a human organism begins to exist at conception. One could, perhaps, say that the initial single-celled zygote is a human organism that ceases to exist when it divides. But then what is one to say of the two resulting daughter cells? Is each a distinct human organism? If so, and if human organisms are what we are, then Oderberg and others will have a lot of mourning to do. Is neither a human organism? This would be difficult to reconcile with the assumption that the initial single-celled zygote *is* a human organism, for there is little that distinguishes the parent cell from the daughters. One seems forced to conclude that the second interpretation makes it unreasonable to believe that what exists at or shortly after conception is a human organism.

Which interpretation is correct?[36] The fundamental difference is that the first interpretation holds that the clustered, proliferating cells together constitute a further

individual that is distinct though not separable from them, while the second interpretation denies this. The case for the first interpretation depends on the observation that the
cells are bundled together within a single membrane (the *zona pellucida*) and eventually their descendants begin to take on specialized tasks in the constitution of the organism and its prenatal environment. Unlike a series of amoebas, where division produces daughter cells that may wander off to lead quite independent lives, the zygotic
cells and their progeny form a discrete unit. That unit, it is claimed, is the organism.

The case for the second interpretation is that, during the first two weeks after conception, the cells are only loosely grouped within the zona pellucida. They are independent and uncoordinated and, at least until the eight-cell stage, each is *totipotent*—
that is, capable, if separated from the others, of developing into, or giving rise to, a
complete adult organism. It is this lack of integration among the cells that suggests
that they do not together constitute a distinct entity, an individual.

Consider, as an analogy, an island on which there are people. Suppose these
people are entirely unrelated: each came to the island independently of the others,
each lives a solitary life with no communication or cooperation with the others, and
each is even unaware of the existence of most of the others. In that case it seems clear
that these individuals do not together constitute an individual of any substantial sort.
If, by contrast, various relations obtained among them—if, for example, they were
related genealogically, spoke the same language, accepted the same moral and religious beliefs, followed the same customs, cooperated together in complex ways, and
so on—then it would be plausible to suppose that they would together constitute a
distinct individual: a nation, for example.

If the zygotic cells are relevantly like the inhabitants of the island in the scenario
in which the latter are unrelated, it seems that the cells do not constitute an individual and, a fortiori, are not an organism. If instead they are relevantly like the com-
plexly related inhabitants, it is considerably more plausible to regard them as together constituting an organism.

The analogy with the people on the island may be revealing in another way. Most
of us are reductionists about human collectivities such as nations.[37] A nation is an individual, but it consists simply of a collection of people related to one another in certain ways. The nation has no existence independent of the existence of the people and
their relations with one another. Our concept of a nation, moreover, admits of vagueness. If certain people share some of the commonalities typically constitutive of na-
tionhood but not others, there may be no yes-or-no answer to the question whether
they constitute a nation. There is no further information that could resolve this question; the matter is simply indeterminate. When we know the facts about the people,
their histories, and their relations with one another, we know all the facts, other than
those concerning our use of the word "nation," that are relevant to determining
whether the people constitute a nation.

I suspect that similar claims are true of the cluster of zygotic cells within the
zona pellucida during the fortnight following conception. There is no deep, recondite
truth to be discovered about whether these cells together constitute an organism or
whether instead the organism begins to exist only later, when the proliferating cells
lose their totipotency, become differentiated, and begin to be tightly allied both orga-
nizationally and functionally. Neither of these views is definitely true—or definitely

false. This is because there is really nothing more to a human organism than a collection of cells functioning together in complex ways. Whether the cells within the zona pellucida are sufficiently integrated to constitute an organism is simply underdetermined by our concept of an organism. The claim that the zygote is the earliest stage of the organism is something that we are neither rationally compelled to accept nor rationally compelled to deny.

3.2. *Organisms, Embryos, and Corpses*

The view that each of us is numerically identical with a particular human organism entails that one's history is the history of an organism. The beginning of one's existence necessarily coincides with the coming into existence of an organism and one will cease to exist when that organism does. It would seem, however, that neither of these implications is, on reflection, easy to accept.

Assume for the sake of argument that a human organism begins to exist roughly two weeks after conception, when the proliferating cells have begun to specialize and to function together in an integrated way. Could *I* really have once been such a humble little entity? One obstacle to thinking critically about the idea that one once existed as an insentient, microscopic cluster of cells is that the retrospective viewpoint one adopts in considering this suggestion effectively excludes the engagement of one's emotions, in particular those, such as hope and fear, concerned with self-interest. To get these engaged, it is helpful to consider, not whether one *was* a tiny cluster of cells, but whether one could ever *become* such an entity. Imagine, for example, that in some of us the process of biological development were somehow reversed. Those to whom this happened would begin to grow younger, in biological terms. Eventually they would revert to being babies and thereafter would have to be placed in artificial wombs in order to survive. As their brains reverted to the infantile and fetal stages of their development, their mental lives would become increasingly rudimentary and would eventually disappear altogether when their brains ceased to be capable of supporting consciousness. Suppose now that one were to face this prospect. It is instructive to ask oneself when in this process of biological regression one would cease to exist. For my part, I find it impossible to believe that I would still be around when what we may neutrally designate as my organism had been reduced to a microscopic network of cells from which any possibility of consciousness had vanished.

If one is an organism, one will cease to exist when that organism ceases to exist. This suggests that most of us do indeed survive death—not in an afterlife but as corpses. Again, however, this is not what most of us believe. Unless one is an immortal soul or one's brain has been transplanted into a different body, the death of one's organism is a sufficient condition of one's ceasing to exist—even if the organism itself continues to exist as a corpse until it reaches a state of decomposition sufficiently advanced that there is no longer a physical object there at all. But, if one may cease to exist while one's organism continues to exist, one cannot be numerically identical with that organism.

One way that those who believe that we are organisms may attempt to salvage their view without accepting that we can exist as corpses is to deny that the human organism continues to exist after it dies. This denial may be implied by Locke's con-

ception of an organism as an entity "which has . . . an organization of parts in one coherent body, partaking of one common life";[38] for the suggestion is that if there is no
common life in which the parts partake, there is no organism. In any case, the view
that an organism ceases to exist when it dies is explicitly embraced by Eric Olson, a
more recent advocate of the view that we are organisms, who writes that "an animal
necessarily ceases to exist when it dies. In that case there is no such thing as a dead
animal, strictly so called. We may call something lying by the side of the road a dead
animal, but strictly speaking what is lying there are only the lifeless remains of an animal that no longer exists."[39]

If, however, an organism ceases to exist when it dies, what exactly is the corpse
and where does it come from? Merely labeling it the "remains" of the organism is un-
illuminating. There seem to be four possibilities. One is that the corpse is an entirely
new entity, one that springs into existence in the area of space that the organism previously occupied immediately upon the organism's death. This option has little allure.
When an organism dies, the physical object that remains does not seem to be a new
creation; it seems to have been there all along. The second option is to concede that
the entity that becomes the corpse has been there all along but to hold that it was never
identical with the organism. But it is surely implausible to suppose that, while the organism was alive, there were two distinct physical entities coexisting in the space it
occupied, only one of which would continue to exist as the corpse after the death of
the other. The third option is to hold that a human organism is a phase in the history
of an ontologically more fundamental entity (for example, a physical body) that, at
the moment of death, ceases to be an organism and becomes a corpse. This, however,
is clearly unsatisfactory for those who maintain that we are organisms, for on this
view "organism" is a phase sortal and hence is not the kind of thing that we could essentially be, assuming that we are substantial individuals. Fourth, and finally, one
might deny that there is any such thing as the corpse. One might claim that, when an
organism dies, all that is left behind is a collection of cells or even more basic elements that were once constitutive of an organism but now do not constitute any object at all. Although this option has its defenders, it is very hard to believe.[40]

It seems that none of these four options is as credible as the simple commonsense
view that, when an organism dies, it undergoes a catastrophic change—the change
from being a living organism to being a dead one—but that, unless its death also involves its obliteration, it continues to exist for a limited period in the form of a
corpse. If that is so and we are organisms, it follows that most of us—those whose
deaths will not involve physical obliteration—will become corpses at some point.
And this, as I have said, counts against the view that we are organisms, for it seems
clear that, unless one is a soul that bides awhile before fluttering away to its celestial
abode, one will no longer be present when one's organism becomes a corpse.

These apparent implications of the view that we are organisms—that one once
existed as an insentient, microscopic cluster of cells and that one is likely to exist at
some point as a corpse—are disturbing but not literally unacceptable. Most of us believe that we could not exist in these states—that *I,* for example, could never be a tiny
cluster of cells or a dead body. But it might be objected: "You are confusing your
being there with your being able to imagine what it was or would be like to be there.
You were there as an embryo but, because your conscious life had not yet begun,

there was nothing that it was like for you to be there then. Similarly, you will be there if you become a corpse; but, because you will no longer be alive, there is nothing that it will be like to exist in that state." This sort of reply has some force. In these counter-examples, the view that we are essentially human organisms implies that one would exist as a certain entity when we believe that one would not exist at all. It would be more damaging if there were a counterexample in which the view implied that one would exist as a certain entity when we not only believe that one would not exist as that entity but also strongly believe that one would exist as an entirely different entity. The familiar example of the brain transplant is just such a counterexample.

3.3. *Brain Transplantation*

In the first of the series of thought-experiments I presented in section 2.2, one's entire brain is extracted and transplanted into the body of one's identical twin. Most people, on considering this possibility, believe that one would continue to exist in what was formerly the body of one's twin. And the usual interpretation of what would happen in this case is that one would come to animate a different organism. The organism with which one began life would continue to exist separately from oneself. There are various fates that we can imagine befalling it once the brain has been removed. It might be left to die; it might receive a brainstem transplant, thereby remaining alive though incapable of supporting consciousness; most of the functions that were previously directed by the original brainstem might instead be sustained indefinitely with the aid of various artificial life-support systems; or it might have the whole of someone else's brain transplanted into it, thereby not only remaining alive but also becoming host to an entirely different person. Whichever course of events we imagine happening, one's original organism would continue to exist (as a corpse, in a persistent vegetative state, etc.) on one bed in the operating theater while one would oneself regain consciousness in a different organism on another bed. One would now be an individual separate and distinct from one's organism. But, if one would not be identical with that organism now, then one never was identical with it; for an individual cannot cease to be itself and yet continue to exist.

What are the options for those who believe that we are essentially organisms? One response is to hold that the theory is sufficiently well grounded to warrant our embracing the counterintuitive implication that one's fate in this case would be the fate of the brainless body.[41] We might just accept that if, for example, the brainless body is left to die, one would become a corpse, while one's twin would survive, albeit with a mental life remarkably similar to one's own. This, however, seems tantamount to surrender. It saves the theory only if there are considerations favoring the theory that are sufficiently rationally compelling to overpower the conviction that most of us have that one would survive in the body of one's twin. I know of nothing that has been advanced in favor of the theory that has that degree of rational force.

It is, moreover, one thing to *say* that one accepts a certain implication, another actually to accept it. Those proponents of the view that we are organisms, who profess to accept that one's fate in the brain transplant case would be the fate of the body from which the brain had been removed, might instructively consider what they would really prefer if given the following choice. Suppose that you have an identical twin whose brain has been destroyed but whose body has until now been kept in a healthy state through intensive artificial support. Serendipitously, you discover today that you have an invariably fatal condition. If your entire brain were transplanted into your twin's body, it is estimated that that body could support life for another thirty years. But this option must be seized immediately; for, unless the artificial life support is replaced by the fuller ministrations of a human brain, the organs in your twin's body will in a matter of days begin a precipitous process of deterioration. Alternatively, you can continue for about a year in an unimpaired state, whereupon you will die painlessly from rapidly developing complications of the fatal condition. I think that one could be said to accept the implications of the view that we are organisms *only* if one would *really* prefer death within a year to having one's brain sustained alive in a different organism for thirty years.

A more plausible response to the case of the brain transplant is to claim that one would continue to exist and would follow one's brain into what was formerly the body of one's twin precisely because, in the circumstances, one would *be* one's brain. For one is, according to the view under consideration, an organism, and the living brain extracted from one's skull would *be* an organism pared down virtually to its minimal physical components. This is the position taken by Peter van Inwagen, who argues that the core or nucleus of an organism is the "control center," that which regulates and coordinates the multifarious activities of its various parts.[42] Because the brain has this role, it is possible to cut away all of an organism's extraneous or inessential matter until it is shaved down to a bare brain, provided that the brain receives the external support it requires to remain alive.

This response raises awkward questions. If, for example, the organism survives in the form of a brain, what is the thing from which the brain has been extracted? The typical response is to assume that it *is* the organism—an organism from which a vital organ has been removed. But if the brain is the organism, its former casing must be something else. It cannot, of course, be the "remains" of an organism, for the organism is alive and well, although drastically reduced in size. Perhaps it is best regarded as a collection of severed parts. Van Inwagen, who denies that an organism has parts larger than a cell, would say that what is left behind when the brain departs is not an object or thing at all—not even a collection of parts in the usual sense, but a mere collection of cells. The point is that, if one believes that the living brain is the organism, one must deny that what the brain leaves behind is an organism. But this is very difficult to deny if what is left behind can, with the provision of minimal external "life support" (for example, a respirator, intravenous nutrition and hydration, and a daily hormone injection), continue to perform in an integrated and coordinated manner all of the characteristic functions of an organism, such as circulation, metabolism, growth, immune response, and even reproduction. (For evidence that this is possible, see chapter 5, section 1.2.)

(One option that does not imply that what is left behind when the brain is removed is not an organism is to treat the surgical extraction of the brain as an instance of fission in which one organism splits into two distinct organisms: a living brain and a brainless organism. But this understanding of the case fails to capture the intuition that we want to preserve—namely, that one would continue to exist after the operation in the body of one's twin. For in fission, as it is normally understood, the parent entity ceases to exist when it divides to form new descendent entities. So, even if the brain and the body from which it had been extracted would both be organisms, neither would be identical with the organism that existed prior to the surgical extraction of the brain.)

There is a corresponding puzzle about the entity that contains one's brain after the transplant has been performed. Again, the natural view is that this is the human organism that once housed one's twin but is now occupied and animated by oneself. According to this commonsense view, one has come to have or to inhabit a new organism. But we are assuming that one's brain is itself an organism when it is transplanted into the emptied skull that once housed the brain of one's twin. Is there now an organism within an organism? Or have two distinct organisms fused to form a single composite organism? Both suggestions are problematic in various ways. Following the reasoning in the previous paragraph, it seems best to say that, when one's twin's brain is removed, what remains is merely a collection of severed parts. What we are inclined to call the transplantation of one's brain into the body of one's twin is really the grafting onto one's brain of the matter that remained after one's twin's brain was separated from it. According to this understanding, the organism of which one's brain is a part after the transplant surgery is identical to the organism of which one's brain was a part prior to the surgery. It is one and the same organism that survives the cutting away of most of its tissues, exists for a brief period as an artificially sustained brain, and then has a mass of new tissue grafted onto it.[43]

This, too, is hard to accept. Suppose that one's twin was not an identical twin but a fraternal twin of the other sex. If one is oneself female, what we tend to describe as the transplantation of one's brain into the body of one's twin would, on this view, involve the transformation of a female organism into a male organism. Or imagine that one's brain were transplanted into the body of an ape. The resulting entity would, on this view, be a human organism (albeit one with a preponderance of hitherto simian parts). Similarly, if the brain of my dog Rufus were transplanted into the body of a pig, the resulting animal would, on this view, be a dog, a canine organism to which some porcine bits had been surgically added.

It is more natural to describe these as cases in which a woman comes to inhabit the body of a man, a person becomes lodged in the body of an ape, and Rufus, a dog, comes to have the body of a pig—with the implication that in each case an individual moves from one organism to another. These cases are, however, sufficiently bizarre that it is difficult to know how best to understand them. Hence it would be unwise to rest the case against van Inwagen's position on them alone.

Recall that van Inwagen's claim that the organism can be pared down to the living brain, but not to any other organ, is based on the idea that the brain is the control center of the organism. He asks us to imagine, first, that a human head is severed from the rest of the body and that both the head and the entity consisting of the trunk and limbs are provided with external life support. (Because of his understanding of the metaphysics of parthood, he expresses all of this a bit differently.) The organism, he contends, has now been reduced to a severed head. He argues for this claim by reference to a political analogy. Imagine an empire controlled entirely by an administration that resides in the Imperial Palace. If the palace becomes isolated, so that no information or matériel can flow into or out of it and the citizenry outside the palace descends into chaos, the empire will have shrunk to the palace and its staff. For the boundaries of the empire are determined by the extent of the political control exercised by the government. Similarly, an organism is individuated by reference to its controlling entelechy, which is the brain: "Give the severed head the proper environment and it will maintain itself, but the headless body will need a constant supply of 'instructions' in the form of electrically transmitted information."[44] It is for this reason that "the living severed head, the analogue of the isolated Imperial Palace, is the organism."[45] And, since it is really the brain that matters and not the entire head, van Inwagen concludes that "if a man may become a severed head, then he may become a naked brain."[46]

This political analogy can be disputed. In the political case, the isolated administration cannot claim to be the empire on the ground that it is the center of political control. For it no longer exercises political control. It may control its domestic arrangements, but this is not the same as exercising political control over an empire. The reasonable thing to say in this case is that the empire continues to exist within the full extent of its former boundaries as long as a certain degree of unity and coordination is maintained among the citizens, even if the administration no longer exercises control; but as political and social disintegration increases, the empire ceases to exist. In the same way, while the brain may exercise control over the organism while they are united, it ceases to exercise significant control functions once it is separated from the rest of the organism. Thus van Inwagen's claim that the severed head "will maintain itself" is overstated. A severed head or an isolated brain manifests no greater degree of internal self-regulation, and requires no less external life support, than the rest of the body from which it has been detached. (Again, I will return to this in section 1.2 of chapter 5.) The fact that the brain was the center of control in the organism when it was a part of the organism does not entail that the organism survives as the brain when the brain is separated from the other parts of the organism. To suppose that it does is comparable to supposing that, if the control panel is removed from the cockpit of an airplane, the airplane continues to exist as the control panel while the remainder, consisting of the fuselage, wings, and so on, becomes just an assembly of spare parts.

These rejoinders to van Inwagen's argument will not persuade everyone. Some will continue to believe that, if the brain of a human organism is extracted from the cranium and kept alive, either by being transplanted into another body or simply by being oxygenated in a tank of fluid, the original organism will survive, albeit in a reduced state, in the form of that living brain. But the argument for the claim that we are not identical with our organisms can appeal to a different case, one not involving the removal of the entire brain. Recall the third of the six cases described in section 2.3: the case of the cerebrum transplant. As I argued earlier, if it is plausible to suppose that one would follow one's brain if it were transplanted in its entirety into a new body, it is also plausible to suppose that one would follow one's cerebrum if it alone were transplanted into a new body. But van Inwagen's view distinguishes sharply between these cases. For the regulatory functions of the brain are localized not in the cerebrum but in the brainstem. Hence, on van Inwagen's view, an organism cannot be pared down to a functional cerebrum. If one's cerebrum were surgically severed from one's brainstem and transplanted into a different body while one's brainstem remained intact and functional, one's original organism would survive as the collection of organs and tissues governed by the operations of the brainstem. If one *is* that organism, one would survive the procedure as a decerebrate organism, an organism in a persistent vegetative state, even if one's mental life would in some sense be continued in the organism into which one's cerebrum had been transplanted. This is what van Inwagen's view implies, but it is not what we believe.[47]

3.4. *Dicephalus*

So far, then, the challenge to the view that we are human organisms that is posed by the possibility of brain transplantation still stands, though van Inwagen's claim that a human organism could be pared down to a living brain may show that the challenge must come from a case involving a cerebrum transplant only rather than the transplantation of the entire brain. Various writers have, however, contended that our intuitive responses to examples such as these that are and are likely to remain merely hypothetical are not reliable guides to the metaphysics of personal identity.[48] Let us assume that this charge has at least enough force to make the appeal to brain or cerebrum transplantation inconclusive. There is another challenge to the view that we are organisms that need not appeal to examples drawn from science fiction but instead focuses on an actual, though extremely rare, condition known as *dicephalus*. Dicephalus (from Greek roots, meaning "two-headedness") occurs when a human zygote divides incompletely, resulting in twins conjoined below the neck.[49] In dicephalic twinning, as in other forms of twinning, it is clear that there are two people. In a case featured in a recent issue of *Life* magazine, Abigail and Brittany Hensel present a spectacle of two heads sprouting from a single torso; yet no one doubts that they are separate and distinct little girls.[50] Each has her own private mental life and her own character, each feels sensations only on her own side of the body, and each has exclusive control over the limbs on her side (though, interestingly, each brain gets enough information about the other that the girls are able to coordinate their movements in running, swimming, riding a bicycle, and so on). But, although Abigail and Brittany are two different persons, there seems to be only one organism between them. If so, then neither girl is identical with that organism. For they cannot both be identical with the organism, as that would imply that they were identical with each other, which they are not. Nor is it plausible to suppose that one of them is identical with the organism while the other is some sort of parasite hosted by the organism. (Even if this understanding were plausible, it would involve a concession that there is at least one person who is not an organism.) So it seems that we should accept that neither is identical with the organism they share. But if dicephalic twins are not human organisms, this strongly suggests that none of us is an organism. For, despite their anomalous physical condition, there is no reason to suppose that dicephalic twins are fundamentally different types of being from the rest of us.

Those who hold that we are essentially human organisms would seem to have only three options. One is to claim that, because dicephalic twins constitute a single human organism, that organism can be at most one person—a person with a divided mind.[51] In Mark Twain's farcical novella, *Those Extraordinary Twins,* inspired by an actual case of dicephalus (the Tocci brothers, born in Sardinia in 1877), the townspeople initially treat a pair of dicephalic twins as one person. One character says, "Ma, you ought n't to begin by getting up a prejudice against him. I'm sure he is good-hearted and means well. Both of his faces show it." As the story progresses, however, the perception changes and the twins come to be regarded as distinct persons—so much so that the townspeople end up ignoring the fact that they share a single body. At the end of the story, when a mob proposes to hang one of the twins, some protest that the other twin is innocent. "Who said anything about hanging him?" is the reply. "We are only going to hang the other one."[52] This reply is taken to be entirely satisfactory.

The idea that dicephalic twins constitute a single person obviously denies the reality of one or both of the Hensel twins. It implies that neither is in herself any more an independently existing thing than the separate centers of consciousness in a commissurotomy patient. It implies that, if one of the twins' brains were to die, this would be no more destructive of a person than if a commissurotomy patient were to suffer a stroke that would kill a cerebral hemisphere. This seems clearly unacceptable.

The second option is equally unacceptable, for the same reason. This is to claim that dicephalic twins constitute a single organism with two distinct minds. But here again the implication is that the Hensel girls cannot be separate and independently existing things—at least not things of the sort that we are. For, if we are human organisms and there is only one organism present where the Hensel twins are, then there is only one entity of our sort present there. Thus if one of their brains were to die, leaving the other to regulate the various somatic functions of the organism, the organism would merely have lost one of its centers of mental life; no entity of our sort would have ceased to exist, for no organism would have died. Again this is unacceptable.

The third and most promising option is to claim that dicephalic twins are actually two distinct though overlapping organisms. Van Inwagen may hold this view, for at one point he writes, parenthetically, of "a fusion of two or more multicellular organisms, after the manner of Siamese twins."[53] This understanding is, of course, entirely compelling in the case of conjoined twins who are only superficially melded (and therefore potentially separable) and who each have a full complement of organs and parts. It is also plausible in cases in which there is a limited sharing of certain organs or parts but extensive duplication of others. It is substantially less plausible, however, when, as in the case of the Hensel sisters, there is only very limited duplication of organs and all the organs function together as a unit. Although the Hensel twins have two hearts and two stomachs, they share three lungs, have a single liver, a single small intestine, a single large intestine, a single urinary system, and a single reproductive system (thus any child they might conceive would be the child of both, a child with three parents: a father and two mothers). The organs are packaged together within a single rib cage and function together in a harmoniously coordinated manner. The limited duplication of organs—the two hearts and two stomachs—would appear to be fortuitous. Recorded cases of dicephalus show varying degrees of duplication and it seems possible that there could be an even purer case than that of the Hensel twins in which there would be virtually no duplication of organs below the neck.

If the Hensel twins were two distinct but partially fused organisms, there should in principle be a conceptual distinction between the death of the one and the death of the other. Even if their deaths would be inevitably linked, in the sense that the death of one would infallibly and immediately cause the death of the other, we should nevertheless be able to say what would count, in principle, as the death of only one. But if the death of a biological organism is understood in the usual way as the irreversible cessation of integrated functioning among the organism's constituent organs and parts, then in the case of the Hensel twins there can be only one death of an organism. For, despite the presence of two hearts and two stomachs, there is basically only one set of organs. When those organs have irreversibly ceased to function together in an integrated manner, an organism will die. But there will then be no other organs whose continued functioning could count as the continued life of another organism. In the case of the Hensel twins, there are two personal lives but only one biological life.

(It is highly probable, though not certain, that the Hensel twins could continue to live even if the supernumerary heart and stomach on one side were to die or be removed. For blood pumped by each heart circulates through the body as a whole and food digested by each stomach nourishes the entire body. So, while the loss of one each of the duplicated organs would undoubtedly impose a strain on the remaining organs, it would not necessarily involve the death of anything other than the organs themselves.)

At this point we might recall van Inwagen's claim that the core of a human organism—that to which it may in principle be reduced by stripping away its inessential parts—is its control center, the brain. One who held this view could argue that the Hensel twins are two distinct organisms because there are two distinct and independent brains. The two organisms share a great many organs in common. But each brain exercises various regulative functions with respect to a certain system of organs and parts, even if the system that each regulates has many members in common with the other. This understanding of the idea that the Hensel twins are two overlapping human organisms makes sense of the possibility of one organism could die while the other would remain alive. If one of the twins were to suffer brain death, that would constitute the death of one of the organisms and would in principle be compatible with the other remaining alive.

Some may find this response satisfying. I do not. It is rather (though not exactly) like the claim that a plane with duplicate control mechanisms for a pilot and a copilot is really two distinct but overlapping planes. Dicephalic twins such as the Hensel girls constitute a single integrally functioning set of organs wrapped in a single skin, sustained by a single coordinated system of metabolism, served by a single bloodstream, protected by a single immune system (which, significantly, recognizes every cell that either twin could claim to be a part of her body as "self"), and so on. These systems and the processes they sustain together constitute a single biological life, despite the fact that various aspects of this life are somehow jointly governed by two brains. There are, of course, two personal or biographical lives; thus if one of the twins were to suffer brain death, a person would die or cease to exist. But that, as I will try to show later, does not entail that an organism would likewise die or cease to exist. In cases of dicephalus, a single biological life supports the existence and thus the lives of two distinct persons.

Earlier, in introducing the case of dicephalus as a challenge to the view that we are human organisms, I claimed that the challenge did not require examples drawn from the realms of science fiction; for dicephalus, though rare, is real enough. But in order to respond to the claim that dicephalic twins are actually two organisms because each head contains a separate control center, it will be helpful to invoke a hypothetical example. Imagine an extreme case of dicephalus, a case in which the division is even less complete than it is in the cases on record. In this case, instead of two necks emerging from a single torso, there are two heads diverging from a common neck. But even the separation of the heads is incomplete. They are, we may imagine, fused at the base, though only in the back. There are two faces—two pairs of eyes, two mouths that function independently, and so on—and, more important, two cerebrums, each controlling its own face and the limbs on its side of the body. But the cerebrums diverge from a single brainstem. Assuming that neuroscientists are right that the cerebrum is the locus of consciousness, it seems as reasonable to believe that there are two persons present in this case as it is to believe this about the recorded instances of dicephalus, such as the Hensel twins. There are two separate centers of consciousness, each with its own private sensory pathways and each capable of independent thought, emotion, expression, and movement. But, because there is only one brainstem regulating a single autonomic nervous system for a single set of organs with no duplication below the level of the brainstem itself, it seems clear that there is only one organism, even if organisms are individuated with reference to their control centers. For it is the brainstem—not the cerebrum—that regulates and coordinates the functioning of the various organs and somatic systems. (It is true that the hypothalamus at the base of the cerebrum has certain regulatory functions, such as maintenance of body temperature and control of the balance of water within the body. If necessary, one can imagine the cerebrums diverging above the hypothalamus.)

This case is intermediate between the case of the commissurotomy patient, in which there may be at least intermittently divided consciousness even though there is only one brainstem, and the cases of dicephalus with which we are familiar. So, even though the case is hypothetical, it is sufficiently similar to known anatomical phenomena to be readily imaginable. Most of us believe that the body of the commissurotomy patient houses only one person, even though each hemisphere may experience thoughts and perceptions that are not directly accessible to the other. In the known cases of dicephalus, by contrast, we believe that there are two persons present. Why do we distinguish so sharply between these two cases? Clearly it is not because the commissurotomy patient has only one brainstem while dicephalic twins have two. It has to do, rather, with our sense that there is somehow sufficient unity of consciousness in the commissurotomy patient to make it unreasonable to believe that there are actually two persons present, whereas in known cases of dicephalus there are clearly two separate and independent mental lives in progress. (We can, however, imagine commissurotomy cases in which it would be reasonable to believe that there were two persons sharing a single organism. Suppose, for example, that a commissurotomy was performed at birth and that each hemisphere was then for many years presented with different stimuli.[54] This could lead to the existence of two different minds, each with a different set of experiences, dispositions, beliefs, memories, and so on. This is, perhaps, a more realistic illustration than my hypothetical dicephalus case of a single organism with a single brainstem that supports the existence of two distinct persons.)

Because the hypothetical case of dicephalus, like the actual cases, clearly involves the existence of two separate and distinct mental lives, we readily assume that there are two persons present, one per cerebrum. It makes no more sense in this case than in the known cases to suppose that there is only a single person with a divided mind or two distinct minds. This seems a clear case in which there are two persons who coexist with and are supported by a single organism. Because it is implausible to suppose either that only one of them is identical with the organism or that both are, we should conclude that neither is. And because there is no reason to suppose that dicephalic twins are a different kind of entity from ourselves, or that a different account of personal identity applies to them, we should further conclude that we are not organisms either.

4. THE PSYCHOLOGICAL ACCOUNT

4.1. *Identity and Egoistic Concern*

Having reviewed and rejected the two views of what we essentially are that are most commonly held among the general population, I turn now to the view that, at least in recent years, has been dominant within philosophical discussions of personal identity. According to this view, we are essentially psychological beings. Because this view holds that psychological continuity is the criterion of personal identity, I will refer to it as the *Psychological Account*.

The notion of psychological continuity as it figures in this theory requires elucidation. But first we must define certain notions that figure in the definition of psychological continuity. The following relations are instances of *direct psychological connections:* the relation between an experience and a memory of it, the relation between the formation of a desire and the experience of the satisfaction or frustration of that desire, and the relation between an earlier and a later manifestation of a belief, value, intention, or character trait. When there are direct psychological connections between a person P_1 at time t_1 and a person P_2 at t_2, P_1 and P_2 are *psychologically connected* with one another. Because the number of such connections may be many or few, psychological connectedness over time is a matter of degree. It may be strong or weak. Derek Parfit stipulates that there is *strong psychological connectedness* if, "over any day, [there are] *at least half* the number of direct connections that hold, over every day, in the lives of nearly every actual person."[55]

Psychological connectedness is not only a matter of degree; it is also an intransitive relation. Thus, if P_1 is psychologically connected to P_2 and P_2 is psychologically connected to P_3, it does *not* follow that P_1 is psychologically connected to P_3. Because psychological connectedness is intransitive, it cannot be the criterion of personal identity over time. For the criterion of identity must have the same logical form as the relation of identity itself, and identity is both transitive and all-or-nothing (that is, there cannot be degrees of identity).

There is, however, a different relation compounded out of psychological connectedness that is transitive and may be construed as all-or-nothing. This is psychological continuity. It consists, in Parfit's words, of "the holding of overlapping chains of *strong* connectedness."[56] Suppose, for example, that P_1 at t_1 and P_2 at t_2 are strongly psychologically connected and that the same is true of P_2 and P_3, P_3 and P_4, and so on through time to P_n at t_n. Between P_1 and P_n there is a series of overlapping relations of strong psychological connectedness. (There is overlap if, for example, P_1 is psychologically connected to P_3 as well as to P_2). P_1 and P_n are therefore *psychologically continuous* with one another. This is true even if there are *no* direct psychological connections between them—that is, even if they are not psychologically *connected* at all.

Psychological continuity is clearly transitive. And it can, as I also noted, be construed as all-or-nothing: either there is strong psychological connectedness from day to day or there is not. Even when defined in this way, however, psychological continuity *could* be interpreted as a matter of degree. One might, for example, stipulate that there is weak psychological continuity if there are only a little more than half the normal number of psychological connections from day to day, but that there is strong psychological continuity if there are more than the normal number. I will later suggest an alternative understanding of psychological continuity that makes it explicitly a matter of degree. Even interpreted as a matter of degree, psychological continuity could be the criterion of identity. For it could be stipulated that there is identity whenever psychological continuity holds to *any* degree. But Parfit and others have not understood psychological continuity in this way. The Psychological Account treats psychological continuity as an all-or-nothing relation.

According to the Psychological Account, psychological continuity is the criterion of personal identity. Thus a person P_1 at time t_1 and a person P_2 at time t_2 are one and the same person only if P_2 is psychologically continuous with P_1. But, although psychological continuity is a necessary condition of personal identity, it is not a sufficient condition. The reason that it is not sufficient is that psychological continuity can take a *branching* form—that is, it is possible for one person to be psychologically continuous with two or more people. Reconsider the case of Division, the case in which a person, P_1, has his brain divided, with each hemisphere being transplanted into a different body. After the operation, two people, P_2 and P_3, are both psychologically continuous with P_1. Initially P_2 and P_3 are qualitatively identical, but they are numerically distinct—that is, they are not one and the same person. Since P_2 and P_3 are not identical with one another, they cannot both be identical with P_1, for identity is a transitive relation.

Psychological continuity is not sufficient for personal identity in cases in which it takes a branching form. But it is, according to the Psychological Account, both a necessary and a sufficient condition of personal identity in cases in which it holds in a nonbranching or one-to-one form.

According to the Psychological Account, then, personal identity consists in nonbranching psychological continuity. What does the theory imply about the case of Division, in which P_1 is psychologically continuous with two distinct people, P_2 and P_3? As we saw in section 2 of this chapter, the view that we are souls seems incapable of yielding a plausible response to this case. But as I also remarked earlier, other theories tend to run aground on this case as well, for none of the obvious options seems acceptable. This ground has been endlessly tilled in the literature, so I will be brief. As we have seen, P_1 cannot be identical with both P_2 and P_3, for that would imply that P_2 and P_3 are themselves identical, which they are not. Nor is it plausible to suppose that P_1 is one but not the other, for there is no difference between the two that could ground the claim that P_1 is that one rather than the other. (This is true also of the interesting suggestion that P_1 is either P_2 or P_3 but it is indeterminate which of the two he is.)[57] Finally, it also seems unacceptable to say that P_1 is neither P_2 nor P_3—that P_1 has either ceased to exist or else continues to exist as the unconscious body from which the cerebral hemispheres have been removed. For intuitively it seems that P_1 should look forward to living *both* lives—that of P_2 and that of P_3. We concede that, if P_3 had not existed, P_1 would have been identical with P_2 and would thus have been justified in being egoistically concerned about P_2. But surely the additional existence of P_3 cannot nullify P_1's reasons for concern about P_2.[58] For there is nothing significant that is missing from P_1's relation to P_2. The only problem is that this relation is duplicated in P_1's relation to P_3. The same reasoning applies to P_1's relation to P_3. Nothing is missing there either. So it seems that P_1 is warranted in being egoistically concerned about both P_2 and P_3. But how can this be, if P_1 will *be* neither P_2 nor P_3?

It seems that there is no intuitively satisfying answer to the question of what happens to P_1 in the case of Division *if* the question whether P_1 continues to exist is invested with all the significance, for P_1 himself and for those who care about him, that it is normally supposed to have. Derek Parfit has, however, proposed an alternative way of thinking about this case. His remarkable insight is that this case forces us to reject the hitherto unquestioned assumption that it is personal identity that provides the grounds for egoistic concern about the future.

Each of us has a special sort of concern for his or her own future. We anticipate our own future experiences, fearing future pains and looking forward to future pleasures, in a way that is different from our attitude to the future experiences of others. As Marya Schechtman notes, "we all know the difference between fearing for our own pain and fearing for the pain of someone else. The difference here consists not in *degree*—I may care more about the pain of my beloved than about my own—but in kind."[59] Let us call this special kind of concern about the future *egoistic concern.*

It may seem to be a necessary truth that it is rational to feel egoistic concern about what may or will happen to some person only if that person will be oneself. That is, it seems that egoistic concern is rationally justified only if there is personal identity. While it may be debatable whether identity is a sufficient condition of the rationality of egoistic concern, it may seem to be a necessary truth that identity is a necessary condition of justified egoistic concern. In order for me now to be rationally egoistically concerned about some future person, it may seem at least *necessary* that this person should be *me*. It is in this sense that identity is normally thought to provide the grounds for rational egoistic concern.

Parfit's claim is that the case of Division shows this to be false. In this case, it seems that P_1 is rationally justified in being egoistically concerned about both P_2 and P_3. Although he cannot *be* both P_2 and P_3, he can rationally anticipate, in an egoistic way, living both their lives. The reason why branching egoistic concern is justified in this case is that the relation that is constitutive of personal identity in the normal case is present *both* in P_1's relation to P_2 *and* in his relation to P_3. Everything important that is normally present in a person's relation to himself in the future is present in P_1's relations to both P_2 and P_3 except identity itself. From this, together with our strong sense that it is rational for P_1 to be egoistically concerned about both P_2 and P_3, Parfit concludes that identity is not what provides the basis for egoistic concern—or, as he himself puts it, that identity is not what matters.

If this is right, it can in principle be rational and appropriate to be egoistically concerned about a person in the future even if that person will not be oneself. This presupposes, of course, that the concept of egoistic concern does not imply that concern about the future is egoistic only if it is concern about oneself. Thus the concept of egoistic concern, as I will understand it, is the concept of a form of concern that is phenomenologically indistinguishable from concern for oneself, but conceptually need not be focused on oneself. Egoistic concern is conceptually possible and may in principle be rational in the absence of personal identity. (To avoid misunderstanding, it might be preferable to use the phrase "special, egoistic-like concern" instead of "egoistic concern." But that would be cumbersome. I will instead simply stipulate that "egoistic concern," as I will use it, is shorthand for "special, egoistic-like concern.")

Let us call the relations that ground rational egoistic concern about the future the *prudential unity relations.* According to the traditional view, there is only one such relation: identity. According to Parfit, the prudential unity relations are psychological connectedness and psychological continuity. The idea that identity is the sole prudential unity relation is a natural mistake, for in all actual cases there cannot be psychological continuity and connectedness without identity, and whenever there is identity there is also psychological continuity. That is, in practice, identity and what matters in fact coincide. But in the case of Division, psychological continuity and connectedness diverge from identity. Our intuitions about this case reveal that, in this and other cases, it is not identity, but the relations that underlie identity, that ultimately matter.

Parfit contends that the best description of what happens in Division is that P_1 ceases to exist. But ceasing to exist in this way is radically different from ceasing to exist in the ordinary way. For, as we have seen, while neither P_1's relation to P_2 nor his relation to P_3 is a relation of identity, each contains all (or nearly all) that matters to us in ordinary cases of survival.[60] Thus, addressing his remarks to a person about to undergo Division, Parfit writes: "You will lose your identity. But there are different ways of doing this. Dying is one, dividing is another. To regard these as the same is to confuse two with zero. Double survival is not the same as ordinary survival. But this does not make it death. It is even less like death."[61] (In these remarks, Parfit is appealing to a sense of the term "survive" that he had introduced in his earlier work, according to which there can be survival without identity.[62] Given this way of speaking, we could say that although P_1 will *be* neither P_2 nor P_3, he will *survive* as both. In the subsequent discussion, I will not follow this usage, but will assume that survival presupposes identity.)

The Psychological Account, as understood here, itself divides into two distinct theories—an account of personal identity and an account of the basis for egoistic concern about the future. I will refer to these as the *Psychological Account of Identity* and the *Psychological Account of Egoistic Concern,* respectively. For convenience, I will often use the simple label "Psychological Account" to refer to the account of personal identity and will use the cumbersome full label only for the Psychological Account of Egoistic Concern. While the Psychological Account holds that nonbranching psychological continuity is the criterion of identity, the corresponding account of egoistic concern holds that psychological continuity and connectedness—irrespective of whether they take a one-one or a one-many form—are what rationally justify egoistic concern. Even though in actual cases there are never relations of psychological continuity and connectedness without identity, the separation of the theory of identity and the theory of egoistic concern is of great practical significance. For while it seems that identity is all-or-nothing and does not admit of degrees, psychological connectedness is a matter of degree. And if part of what grounds the rationality of egoistic concern is a matter of degree, then rational egoistic concern may itself be a matter of degree. Parfit writes: "My concern for my future may correspond to the degree of connectedness between me now and myself in the future. Connectedness is one of the two relations that give me reasons to be specially concerned about my own future. It can be rational to care less, when one of the grounds for caring will hold to a lesser degree."[63]

I believe that Parfit is right that Division shows that identity is not what matters— that is, that it is not what rationally grounds egoistic concern about the future. My view differs from Parfit's, however, both about the nature of the relations are that are constitutive of personal identity and about the prudential unity relations. I will pursue the objections to his accounts in the remainder of this section and then argue for a pair of alternative views in section 5.

4.2. *Beginning to Exist and Ceasing to Exist*

What does the Psychological Account imply about the critical questions of when we begin to exist and what the conditions of our ceasing to exist are? The exposition will be clearer if we take the second problem first. According to the Psychological Account of Identity, the criterion of personal identity is nonbranching psychological continuity. To determine when a person ceases to exist, we track his life forward in time by following the relation of psychological continuity until it ceases to hold. When it ceases to hold, the person ceases to exist. That is, a person ceases to exist when it ceases to be the case that there will be someone existing in the future with whom he will be psychologically continuous.

In many cases it is obvious when psychological continuity ceases to hold—for example, when a person suffers brain death, or lapses into a persistent vegetative state as a result of the destruction of the cerebral hemispheres. There are other cases, however, in which the matter is not so simple. For example, in cases of progressive dementia, such as occurs in Alzheimer's disease, the degree of psychological connectedness from day to day diminishes gradually and there seems to be no determinate point at which psychological continuity ceases to hold. Recall that psychological continuity (as understood by the Psychological Account) consists of overlapping chains of strong psychological connectedness and that there is strong connectedness when the number of direct psychological connections from day to day is at least half the number that hold over each day in the life of a normal person. Because we do not know how to count psychological connections, there is considerable vagueness about when the degree of connectedness within a mental life counts as strong. In cases involving gradual mental deterioration, it may be impossible to determine when the number of connections from day to day drops below the threshold, so that strong connectedness, and therefore psychological continuity, comes to an end.

What, then, does the Psychological Account imply about the fate of a person with Alzheimer's disease? We know what will happen as the disease progresses: assuming that the person's body remains alive, his mental capacities, including memory, will gradually deteriorate until his brain will cease to be capable of even the most rudimentary forms of thought or perception. By that point, the person will clearly have ceased to exist, according to the Psychological Account, for the patient with advanced Alzheimer's will clearly not be psychologically continuous with the person in the early stages of the disease. But since the progress of the disease is a smooth, continuous process without abrupt discontinuities, there is no precise point at which psychological continuity is lost.

The theory's vagueness about when psychological connectedness ceases to hold should be regarded as a virtue rather than a failing. It would be incredible if there were a sharp threshold to strong connectedness, so that there would be some determinate point at which the loss of a single further psychological connection would constitute the death of the patient with Alzheimer's disease. The Psychological Account instead holds that it is *indeterminate* when the patient with Alzheimer's disease ceases to exist. While it is clear and determinate that there is psychological continuity within the patient's life during the early stages of the disease, and while it is also clear that psychological continuity is absent in the later stages, there is also an intermediate period in which, owing to the vagueness in the notion of strong psychological connectedness, it is simply indeterminate whether the mental life in progress is psychologically continuous with that of the patient in the earlier stages. During this period (which itself does not have sharp boundaries), it is neither true nor false that the person continues to exist—that is, it is not the case either that the person continues to exist or that he has ceased to exist.[64]

The coming into existence of a person is, according to the Psychological Account, in many ways a mirror image of the process whereby the patient with Alzheimer's disease ceases to exist. For the process by which a mental life develops in richness and complexity in association with the development of an immature human organism closely parallels, though in reverse, the process of gradual mental deterioration characteristic of dementia in Alzheimer's disease.

To determine when a person began to exist, on this view, we track the relation of psychological continuity back through time to the point of its origin. In the life of a normal person, there are overlapping chains of strong psychological connectedness that stretch back at least to early childhood. Thus each of us has existed at least since then. But earlier in infancy the degree of psychological connectedness from day to day is not clearly strong, and in very early infancy and during fetal gestation, what connectedness there is is clearly not strong—that is, there are far fewer psychological connections from day to day than half the number that hold over a day in the life of a normal adult.

It follows that, according to the Psychological Account, we began to exist sometime in early childhood. Prior to that, during infancy, our existence was indeterminate—that is, it was neither true nor false that we existed during that period. But the period of indeterminacy probably does not extend back into early infancy. If that is right, it is determinately true, according to the Psychological Account, that we never existed as newborn infants or fetuses. Parfit himself would have to accept this. He writes that it "is not true . . . that I am now strongly connected to myself twenty years ago . . . Between me now and myself twenty years ago there are many fewer than the number of direct psychological connections that hold over any day in the lives of nearly all adults."[65] It seems clear, however, that there are normally many more direct psychological connections between a person at forty and himself at twenty than there are between a two-day-old infant and the same infant the day before. For between the forty-year-old and the twenty-year-old there are various connections of memory, desire, intention, belief, and character; whereas a newborn infant's mental life is so sparse that there cannot be more than a few direct psychological connections from day to day. It follows that the two-day-old infant cannot be strongly psychologically connected with itself the day before, that there is therefore no psychological continuity in early infancy, that none of us now is psychologically continuous with a newborn infant, and thus that none of us is now numerically the same individual as a newborn infant.

There is, perhaps, an alternative way of expressing the implications of the Psychological Account. Recall that, as I use the term, a "person" is a being with a rich and complex mental life, a mental life of a high order of sophistication. Parfit has a similar understanding: he stipulates that "to be a person, a being must be self-conscious, aware of its identity and its continued existence over time."[66] It seems that a being that lacked self-consciousness could not have a mental life that was strongly psychologically connected from day to day. For self-consciousness is necessary for most of our memories, our desires and intentions for the future, our beliefs about the world, and so on. Without self-consciousness there would not be the ingredients for strong psychological connectedness. From this it follows that psychological continuity cannot obtain within the life of a nonperson. If, therefore, one's mental life contracted and one ceased to be a person, psychological continuity would come to an end; and if psychological continuity came to an end, one would cease to exist according to the Psychological Account. If this is right, the Psychological Account implies that we are essentially persons. For a person, on this view, is just an entity with a mental life that is sufficiently rich for there to be strong psychological connectedness from day to day.

Understood in this way, "person" becomes a substance sortal within the Psychological Account of Identity. If one of us ceases to be a person in this sense, he or she ceases to exist. Again, because the notion of personhood admits of vagueness, there may be cases, such as those involving progressive dementia, in which it is indeterminate whether there is still a person present. In the case of a patient with Alzheimer's disease, for example, a point may be reached in which there is no correct yes-or-no answer to the question, "Is he still a person?"

Because human psychological development is gradual, there is also indeterminacy about when we begin to exist. If, as the Psychological Account seems to imply, we are essentially persons, one did not begin to exist until there was a person present in association with one's physical organism. A person is an entity with a mental life that is strongly psychologically connected from day to day, which is possible only when self-consciousness is achieved. But there is no precisely determinate moment when self-consciousness appears in the development of a human organism. In early infancy, there is clearly no self-conscious entity present.[67] At some point in early childhood, there clearly is a self-conscious entity present. During at least some of the intervening period, it is indeterminate whether one of us—a person—exists or not. In my own case, for example, the Psychological Account implies that I did not exist when the organism I now animate was born, that there may be no yes-or-no answer to the question whether I existed when that organism was six months old, but that I undoubtedly did exist by the time that it was a year or two old.

4.3. *"Pre-persons" and "Post-persons"*

According to the Psychological Account, one did not begin to exist until after the birth of one's physical organism. But during the later stages of pregnancy and immediately following the birth of one's organism, there was a more or less continuous mental life associated with one's organism. There was, at a minimum, continuity of consciousness (though not, of course, continuous consciousness), in the sense that there was a series of conscious events all generated in the same areas of the same brain. And this mental life was unified over time by at least a weak form of psychological connectedness—exemplified, for instance, in the fact that an infant will react differently to music to which it was exposed in utero, thereby indicating that the experience of the music was registered in memory and is later, at some level, recalled. There was, in short, a conscious being present both immediately before and after the birth of one's organism—a being whose mental life was in some ways continuous with one's own and whom one's parents and others took to be oneself. But the assumption that this being was actually oneself is, of course, mistaken if the Psychological Account is right. For, according to that account, one did not exist then. Who, or what, was this conscious being? And what happened to it when one began to exist?

Perhaps the defender of the Psychological Account should simply deny that, prior to the existence of the person, there is any conscious being present that is distinct from the human organism. Before the person appears, there is merely a series of mental events generated by the functioning of the organism. Only with the appearance of the person is there an individual distinct from the organism. The problem with this response, however, is that if it is the organism that is conscious, thinks, feels, perceives, and so on, it seems that, as the organism's mental life becomes progressively richer and more complex, it must be the organism itself that becomes a person. For it will be the organism that will then have a mental life that is sufficiently sophisticated for it to count as a person. But if the organism can literally *become* a person, then the person must simply be a phase in the history of the organism. "Person" must be a phase sortal rather than a substance sortal. "Person" is simply a label that applies to the organism during a certain period. But this is incompatible with the Psychological Account, which implies that "person" is a substance sortal. The view that holds that the person is merely a phase in the history of an organism is the view that we are essentially human organisms. Hence the idea that it is simply the organism that is conscious prior to the appearance of the person is not available to the defender of the Psychological Account.

What the Psychological Account seems to imply is that the conscious subject that exists in association with the human organism prior to the coming into existence of the person is some sort of *pre-person,* a subpersonal subject of consciousness that begins to exist when the organism becomes capable of supporting consciousness and mental activity and ceases to exist when the person comes into existence. This, of course, is an extravagant supposition, one that offends against the principle of parsimony, which holds that a theory is less plausible the more new entities it is required to postulate.

A similar problem arises in cases in which psychological continuity within a person's mental life ceases but the flow of consciousness generated by the person's brain continues. This may happen abruptly, as a result of a stroke or an injury to the brain, or it may occur gradually, as it does in progressive dementia such as that caused by Alzheimer's disease. When psychological continuity comes to an end, the person ceases to exist, according to the Psychological Account of Identity. So the question arises who or what the conscious entity is that exists thereafter in association with the person's organism. Again the best answer seems to be that this is a sort of *post-person* that begins to exist immediately upon the ceasing to exist of the person and continues to exist in association with the organism until the organism ceases to be capable of supporting consciousness and mental activity.

The necessity of recognizing a post-person in these cases is perhaps even more embarrassing for the Psychological Account than the necessity of postulating the existence of a pre-person. For the prospective viewpoint one adopts in considering the possibility of suffering brain damage or being afflicted with Alzheimer's disease readily engages one's self-interested intuitions. If, for example, one were to imagine oneself in the early stages of Alzheimer's disease, one would be very unlikely to accept that the conscious life associated with one's body in the later stages of the disease would belong to someone other than oneself. One recognizes that, if one were to fall prey to Alzheimer's disease, one would fear any suffering attendant upon the final stages of the condition in a self-interested or egoistic way.

Many who accept the Psychological Account might be untroubled to recognize the existence of pre- and post-persons. They might, as Parfit once did, accept a rather strong form of reductionism about personal identity according to which persons are just logical constructions compounded out of ontologically more fundamental items—mental states—and the relations among them. Thus Parfit once made the claim, which he has subsequently retracted, that one "could give a *complete* description of reality *without* claiming that persons exist."[68] One who accepts such a radically reductionist conception of persons could see the distinction between persons and pre- and post-persons as just one way of grouping or categorizing mental events. One might see a parallel here with our understanding of clubs. Suppose that two people get together regularly to play tennis and have drinks afterwards. Others gradually join in and eventually there is a group of twenty people who meet regularly for two hours a week at the tennis courts and then adjourn to a nearby bar for drinks and socializing. The group of twenty recognize themselves as constituting a club. When did the club begin to exist? There may be a certain arbitrariness to our answer. But it may be plausible to say that two people are too few to constitute a club. So, although there is a sense in which the club can trace its existence back to the regular meetings of the two original players, we might say that the club proper did not yet exist at that point and that the two people meeting regularly constituted only a sort of pre-club. In saying this, however, we would simply be reporting how we use the term "club." And it would not much matter if we decided to use it differently—if, for example, we decided not to impose any restrictions concerning size on what could count as a club. Because we are reductionists about the nature of clubs and thus do not regard clubs as elements of our basic ontology, the question whether the two original players constituted the club in its earliest stages or only a pre-club is not a question of ontology but simply a question about language. The radical reductionist about personal identity may take an analogous view about whether a newborn infant is a person or merely a pre-person.

It is, however, difficult to accept this radical reductionism as applied to ourselves. Even if we think that there may be circumstances in which our existence would be indeterminate, it is hard to believe that we ourselves are no more ontologically basic than clubs. The question whether one would continue to exist during the later phases of Alzheimer's disease seems to be much more than just a question about the way in which we use the word "person."

The radical reductionist might respond that this is to confuse identity with what matters—that is, with that which provides the grounds for egoistic concern. If we wish to know whether one should now care in an egoistic way about what might happen to one's body in the later stages of Alzheimer's disease, one should, it might be argued, consult the Psychological Account of Egoistic Concern. And that theory, perhaps surprisingly, implies that one might well have reason in the early stages of Alzheimer's disease to care in an egoistic way about what might happen to one's body in the later stages, even if, according the Psychological Account of Identity, one would no longer exist at that later time. For recall that the Psychological Account of Egoistic Concern holds that psychological continuity and connectedness are what matter. As we have seen, the person in the early stages of Alzheimer's disease would not be psychologically continuous with the post-person who would exist in the later stages. For in the later stages the number of psychological connections that would hold from day to day would be far fewer than half the number that hold over each day in the life of a normal adult. But, at least until the very final stages of the disease, there would likely be a certain number of direct psychological connections between the person in the early stages and the post-person in the later stages—for example, the latter might have a certain number of memories (or what, as I will explain in section 4.6, are called "quasi-memories") of events experienced by the former. If there would be direct psychological connections between the person and the post-person, there would be a basis for egoistic concern, albeit only an attenuated degree of concern, according to the Psychological Account of Egoistic Concern.

The Psychological Account of Egoistic Concern thus yields the right result in this case, though the result coheres rather awkwardly with the implication of the Psychological Account of Identity that the individual for whom one has reason to be egoistically concerned would not be oneself. It is, however, open to the defender of the Psychological Account to reply that this anomaly must be tolerated, just as it must in the case of Division. If there can be egoistic concern in the absence of identity in cases involving branching, why cannot there be a basis for egoistic concern when there is nonbranching connectedness but not identity?

4.4. *Revisions and a Note on Method*

Perhaps this is an adequate response in cases in which there are direct psychological connections between the person in the early stages of Alzheimer's disease and the post-person in the later stages. But a problem remains. Suppose that there would be no direct psychological connections between the person in the early stages and the post-person in the very late stages. In that case the Psychological Account of Egoistic Concern implies that the person has no reason to be egoistically concerned about what might happen to the post-person at that point. But intuitively we believe that, if the person knew that the post-person was likely to experience excruciating physical suffering, it would be reasonable for the person to care about that prospect in an egoistic way—to fear it, for example.

Most people think that it would be reasonable for the person to fear the suffering that the post-person would experience because they believe, contrary to what the Psychological Account implies, that the person and the post-person would be the same individual. But even if we assume that the person and the post-person would be different individuals, there is still reason, of a sort congenial to the Psychological Account, to suppose that the person should have some egoistic concern for what might happen to the post-person. For although the person and the post-person would not be directly psychologically connected and would not be psychologically continuous (that is, would not be related by overlapping chains of *strong* psychological connectedness), they still might, and presumably would, be bound together by overlapping chains of *weak* psychological connectedness. And it is easy to see how this could give the person a reason to be egoistically concerned about the post-person. Let "P_1" be the person at the onset of the disease; let "P_2" be the person a month later, "P_3" the same person after another month, and so on until we reach "P_{50}," the post-person in the final, fiftieth month of the disease. Suppose that P_1 is psychologically continuous with P_2 but that the number of direct psychological connections from day to day steadily diminishes, so that P_{29} is *not* psychological continuous with P_{30}. Nevertheless, P_{29} is (we may plausibly suppose) directly psychologically connected to P_{30}. Even if P_1 is neither psychologically continuous with nor directly psychologically connected to P_{30}, he is continuous with P_{29}, who is connected with P_{30}. Since P_{29} has reason to care egoistically about P_{30} and P_1 has reason to care about P_{29}, it is reasonable to suppose that P_1 has reason to care about P_{30}, for if P_1 has reason to care egoistically about P_{29}, he would seem to have some reason (however slight) to care egoistically about what P_{29} has reason to care egoistically about, which includes what will happen to P_{30}.

Suppose that, by reiterating this logic, we reach the conclusion that P_1 has reason to care egoistically about P_{49}. But suppose that, between P_{49} and P_{50}, there are no direct psychological connections. According to the Psychological Account of Egoistic Concern, P_{49} has no reason to be egoistically concerned about P_{50}, and third parties who care about P_{49} for his own sake have no reason deriving from their concern for P_{49} to care about what will happen to P_{50}. Yet P_{49} and P_{50} are (let us assume) related by overlapping chains of weak psychological connectedness *from day to day*. That is, let us assume that, over the month that separates P_{49} and P_{50}, $P_{49.1}$ (i.e., the post-person on the first day of the month) is directly but weakly psychologically connected to $P_{49.2}$ (the post-person a day later), $P_{49.2}$ to $P_{49.3}$, and so on down to P_{50}, although by the time we get to P_{50} there may be very few psychological connections from day to day. Thus, according to the Psychological Account of Egoistic Concern, on each day during this month, the post-person has reason to be egoistically concerned about himself on the following day. (This assumes, of course, that we have some criterion for the identity of the post-person, although it obviously cannot be psychological continuity. I leave this issue aside.) It seems, moreover, that there should be a certain transitivity to egoistic caring. If $P_{49.1}$ has reason to care about $P_{49.2}$, and $P_{49.2}$ has reason to care about $P_{49.3}$, and so on down to P_{50}, it seems that $P_{49.1}$ has some reason, however slight, to care egoistically about P_{50}. And if P_1 has reason to care egoistically about $P_{49.1}$, who has reason to care about P_{50}, then P_1 too should have reason to care about P_{50}. This reasoning seems congenial to the spirit of the Psychological Account of Egoistic Concern, even though P_1 and P_{50} are neither psychologically continuous (and hence are not the same individual, according to the Psychological Account of Identity) nor directly psychologically connected.

For it seems arbitrary to claim, as the Psychological Account of Egoistic Concern does, that overlapping chains of strong psychological connectedness provide grounds for egoistic concern, and yet deny that overlapping chains of weaker psychological connectedness could also provide grounds, albeit weaker ones, for the same kind of concern. Most of us, in any case, readily accept that overlapping chains of weak connectedness provide grounds for egoistic concern—or, rather, the third-person analogue of egoistic concern—in the case of beings that are not persons. The degree of psychological connectedness from day to day within the life of a higher nonhuman animal may be quite weak, yet overlapping chains of weak connectedness seem sufficient for what matters. Over any given day in the life of my dog, for example, there are fewer than half the number of psychological connections that hold over a day in the life of a normal adult human being; but even this relatively weak degree of psychological unity in my dog's life seems a sufficient basis for me to care, *for the dog's own sake now,* about what will happen to it in the future. But if overlapping chains of weak psychological connectedness are a sufficient basis for egoistic concern (or its third-person analogue) within the life of an animal, the same should also be true in the case of beings of our sort.

The Psychological Account of Egoistic Concern would be considerably more plausible if it were revised to accommodate these intuitions. The necessary revision is simple and obvious. It is to redefine the notion of psychological continuity so that it admits of degrees. Let us say that there is *broad psychological continuity* whenever there are overlapping chains of psychological connectedness of *any* degree of strength. Broad psychological continuity may be strong or weak. When the chains are of *strong* psychological connectedness from day to day, there is what I will call *strong psychological continuity.* (Strong psychological continuity is not the same as what Parfit calls "psychological continuity," for even strong psychological continuity comes in varying degrees of strength—it may, for example, be moderately strong or extremely strong—whereas Parfit stipulates that psychological continuity is all-or-nothing.) When the chains are of weak psychological connectedness (that is, fewer than half the number of psychological connections that hold over each day in the life of a normal adult), there is *weak psychological continuity.* I suggest that the Psychological Account of Egoistic Concern be revised to hold that what matters are psychological connectedness and *broad* psychological continuity. When revised in this way, the Psychological Account of Egoistic Concern acknowledges that a person in the early stages of Alzheimer's disease has reason to care in an egoistic way about what may befall the post-person in the later stages of the disease, for the two will be broadly psychologically continuous. The overlapping chains of psychological connectedness will admittedly be increasingly weak as the disease progresses. But the revised theory can concede that the basis for egoistic concern is weaker when broad psychological continuity is weaker rather than stronger—just as both the original and revised versions of the theory hold that the grounds for egoistic concern are weaker the fewer direct psychological connections there are. (Again, recall Parfit's claim that "it can be rational to care less, when one of the grounds for caring will hold to a lesser degree.")[69]

Although this proposed revision enhances the plausibility of the Psychological Account of Egoistic Concern, it also widens the divergence between that theory and the corresponding Psychological Account of Identity. But again proponents of the Psychological Account may be undismayed. They may cite two claims that I have already endorsed in support of the view that it does not count against an account of personal identity if it diverges, even fairly extensively, from our beliefs about what matters. First, I have followed Parfit in accepting that identity is not what matters— that is, it is not in itself the basis of egoistic concern. If that is right, then in principle it is possible that there could be identity but no basis for egoistic concern; or there could be grounds for egoistic concern in the absence of identity (as in the case of Division). Once our account of egoistic concern is in principle distinguished from our account of personal identity, it is possible that nothing of substance hinges on the account of personal identity. For if personal identity is not what matters, disagreements about whether a person would continue to exist do not necessarily have any implications for what that person has reason to care about in an egoistic way. Considerations of egoistic concern would necessarily constrain our account of personal identity only if personal identity were itself the basis of egoistic concern. If that were true, a divergence between the implications of our account of personal identity and our sense of what matters would clearly count against the account of personal identity. But divergence is not otherwise a threat.

Second, if we are reductionists about personal identity, we should concede that disagreements about personal identity are for the most part disagreements about how our existence is constituted out of the various facts about physical and psychological continuity. Identity, as Parfit puts it, is not a fact that is independent of the facts about these continuities. When we disagree about what constitutes the best account of personal identity, we are simply disagreeing about the best understanding or interpretation of the known facts about physical and psychological continuity, not about some fact that obtains separately from these other facts. There is, in other words, no deep fact about identity that rationally compels us to accept one account rather than another and, a fortiori, no fact that compels us to accept an account that minimizes the divergence between identity and egoistic concern.

I nevertheless believe that it is best to seek an account of personal identity that is as closely aligned as possible with our understanding of the basis of egoistic concern. I therefore think that the revision I have proposed of the Psychological Account of Egoistic Concern exerts pressure to make a corresponding revision of the Psychological Account of Identity.

It is not an accident that we have hitherto assumed that personal identity is what matters and thus that the scope of rational egoistic concern coincides with personal identity. Consider the vast range of cases in which we are utterly confident in our judgments about personal identity: all the ordinary actual cases involving reidentification of ourselves and others. Any minimally plausible account of personal identity must endorse these judgments. Whatever relations are constitutive of personal identity, they are surely present in these cases. In all of these cases, we intuitively find a basis for egoistic concern. This strongly suggests that the relations that are constitutive of personal identity are at least part of what we believe to be the basis of egoistic concern. It is of course possible that this is merely a coincidence—that the relations constitutive of personal identity and those that ground egoistic concern are entirely different but just happen to be present across this range of cases. But it is surely more plausible to suppose that they coincide because the relations that are constitutive of personal identity are among those that matter.

From this it seems reasonable to conclude that personal identity is always a sufficient basis for egoistic concern. That basis may be very weak, however, for either or both of two reasons. First, recall that personal identity is commonly assumed to be all-or-nothing, even though the relations that are constitutive of it may vary in degree. If the relations are present only to a weak degree, the basis for egoistic concern may be correspondingly weak even though there is identity. Second, the relations that are constitutive of personal identity may be only part of what matters. There may be other relations that matter, either in conjunction with the relations that underlie identity or even in the absence of identity. If that is the case, the basis for egoistic concern may be weak even when there is identity because those other relations are entirely absent. And, of course, both these conditions may obtain simultaneously: the relations that are constitutive of personal identity may be present to only a very weak degree while none of the other relations that matter are present at all. In such a case, even though there would be identity, the basis for egoistic concern would be very weak.

Perhaps this is too bold. Perhaps there might be cases—for example, the lives of immortals—in which there is personal identity but no basis for egoistic concern over very long stretches of time. If there are any such cases—cases in which the relations constitutive of personal identity are present but do not provide a basis for egoistic concern—they are likely to be hypothetical and sure to be controversial. Still, it may be unwise to rule them out ex cathedra. So perhaps we should retreat to the claim that there is a strong *presumption* that personal identity is a sufficient basis for egoistic concern. That alone would support the requirement that, in developing an account of personal identity, we should seek to achieve maximum congruence between personal identity and the reach of egoistic concern.

It has also been a presupposition of our thought about personal identity that when there are grounds for egoistic concern, there is also identity. This assumption is evident in many of the cases in the literature on personal identity, from Bernard Williams's early cases in which the distinctive features of a person's psychology are erased to Peter Unger's repeated use of what he calls the "avoidance of future great pain test."[70] I believe, of course, that the case of Division shows that the presence of rational egoistic concern is not sufficient for personal identity, and thus that personal identity is not a necessary condition of rational egoistic concern. Even in the case of Division, however, there are grounds for egoistic concern only where the relations that are constitutive of personal identity in the normal case are also present.

I have conceded that it is in principle possible that there are relations that provide a sufficient basis for egoistic concern that are different from and may occur independently of the relations that are constitutive of personal identity. If that is the case, the presence of rational egoistic concern would not be sufficient for personal identity even in cases that did not involve branching of the relations constitutive of personal identity. For my part, I doubt that there are any such relations. If there are no such relations, we should expect personal identity and what matters to coincide in all cases except those involving the branching of the relations that are constitutive of personal identity. For if the relations that are constitutive of personal identity are part of what matters, then there is at least a strong presumption that personal identity is sufficient for the rationality of some degree of egoistic concern. And if there are no other relations that are by themselves sufficient for egoistic concern, the presence of justified egoistic concern is sufficient for personal identity in all cases except those involving branching.

These, it seems, are good reasons for expecting that the scope of egoistic concern should coincide with personal identity. There is therefore a presumption that an account of personal identity should imply that where there is personal identity, there is a basis, however weak, for egoistic concern, and that where egoistic concern is rational, there is, except in cases involving branching, personal identity. It is, in short, a test of an account of personal identity, albeit a defeasible one, that its implications should be congruent with our understanding of what matters.

Some of the objections I have urged against the accounts of personal identity that I have rejected have taken this form. I noted, for example, that the view that we are human organisms seems to imply that at some point most of us will exist, for a while, as corpses. But, because it seems irrational to be egoistically concerned about what may happen to one's corpse, it is hard to believe that one will *be* that corpse. (One may, of course, be concerned in a self-interested way about what will happen to one's corpse in much the way that one may be concerned about one's reputation. But this is an indirect form of egoistic concern: one can no more anticipate what will happen to one's corpse "from the inside" than one can anticipate what will happen to one's reputation from the inside.) This, I suggested, counts against the view that we are organisms.

There are, of course, other criteria for the adequacy of an account of personal identity. Thus my most elaborately developed objection to the view that we are organisms—based on the case of dicephalus—makes no appeal to considerations of egoistic concern. This objection is purely metaphysical: in dicephalus, there are incontestably two persons—two beings of our sort—but apparently only one organism, a circumstance that is incoherent according to the view that we are organisms. This account of our identity therefore fails to satisfy a requirement of compatibility with our criteria for the individuation of entities of particular kinds. And any account must satisfy this and various other requirements that are purely metaphysical in character. This suggests a potential problem. For the account of personal identity that is best aligned with our intuitions about what matters may satisfy the various metaphysical criteria less well than some rival account. For example, all accounts of our identity other than that which claims that we are human organisms may have difficulty explaining what the relation is that we bear to our organisms if it is not identity. At some point, in attempting to determine what the best account of personal identity is, it may become necessary to choose whether to give priority to metaphysical considerations or to congruence with our sense of what matters.

For the time being, however, I will assume that there is a presumption that our account of personal identity should coincide as closely as possible with our sense of what matters. If our account of personal identity follows our sense of what matters where it is logically possible for it to do so, there will be a strong presumption that there is a basis for egoistic concern whenever there is identity and that there is identity where there is a basis for egoistic concern. And this will facilitate the clear and forceful articulation of certain evaluative claims. It is, for example, more immediately compelling to say, "That future individual will be *you;* hence you have reason to be egoistically concerned about what will happen to him," than it is to say, "That future individual will not be you; nevertheless certain relations that ground egoistic concern will hold between you and him; therefore you have reason to care egoistically about what will happen to him." Admittedly, this exploits and no doubt reinforces our mistaken belief that it is identity itself that matters; but it is the way of describing certain situations that involves the least cognitive dissonance, the least upheaval in our system of concepts and beliefs.

Return now to the case of the person in the early stages of Alzheimer's disease. I have suggested that we revise the Psychological Account of Egoistic Concern so that it implies that this person has reason to be egoistically concerned about the conscious subject who will exist in association with his body during the later stages of the disease. But because this conscious subject will not be psychologically continuous with the person in the early stages, the two must be different individuals, according to the Psychological Account of Identity. I claimed earlier that this failure of congruence between the revised account of egoistic concern and the unrevised account of identity exerts pressure to make a corresponding revision to the latter, for reasons that I have tried to explain. The necessary revision is quite simple. Instead of holding that nonbranching psychological continuity (in Parfit's sense) is the criterion of identity, the revised Psychological Account would hold that the criterion of identity for a person or other conscious subject is nonbranching *broad* psychological continuity (that is, overlapping chains of psychological connectedness, of any degree of strength). On this view, the person in the early stages of Alzheimer's disease would continue to exist until there was no longer anyone to whom he would be even weakly psychologically connected in the immediate future. When psychological connectedness terminates, the individual ceases to exist.

The revised version of the Psychological Account accepts that the existence of the person with Alzheimer's disease extends as far into the future as it is rational for his egoistic concern to extend, according to the revised version of the Psychological Account of Egoistic Concern. It also better matches our intuitions about our own survival and persistence than the unrevised version. Virtually everyone believes that persons who develop Alzheimer's disease continue to exist at least until the final phases of the disease, in which the mind disintegrates entirely. The revision also greatly mitigates the problem of the post-person—though it does not dispose of it entirely. The revised account of identity implies that the individual with Alzheimer's disease continues to exist as long as there are psychological connections from day to day. When this ceases to be the case, he ceases to exist. But it is possible that the cessation of psychological connectedness from day to day may leave, for a short while, a conscious entity—a subject capable, for example, of experiencing pain. Even on the revised Psychological Account, this conscious subject would not be the same individual as the person who existed in the early stages of the disease. He—or it—is therefore a post-person, albeit an extremely transient or ephemeral one, who succeeds the original person in his own body. Let us refer to this merely conscious entity as the "isolated subject." (Each of us is presumably also preceded by a correspondingly isolated pre-person: a conscious subject that exists in utero prior to the point at which psychological connections begin to be formed. It is unnecessary to discuss this parallel problem here.)

This residual commitment to the existence of a post-person seems a minor embarrassment for the revised version of the Psychological Account. The critical issue here, however, concerns what matters. Does the person in the early stages of Alzheimer's disease have reason to be concerned in a egoistic way about the isolated subject to whom he will not be related even by the weakest strands of psychological connectedness? I suspect that most people would believe that he does. But this belief, though probably common, is hard to assess. It may not be a spontaneous deliverance of one's sense of what matters but may instead be an inference drawn, perhaps unconsciously, from the conjunction of the view that we are living organisms and the belief that identity is what matters.

There is room for reasonable disagreement here. If we think that the person who develops Alzheimer's disease has no ground for egoistic concern about what may befall the isolated subject, the revised versions of the Psychological Accounts of Identity and Egoistic Concern will seem satisfactory despite the necessity of recognizing the existence of a conscious successor to the person. If, by contrast, we think that the person could rationally be egoistically concerned about the fate of the isolated subject, the Psychological Account of Egoistic Concern will require further revision. And it would then be desirable to make a corresponding revision to the Psychological Account of Identity in order that it would imply that the isolated subject is the same individual as the person who initially developed Alzheimer's disease.

If those who are attracted to the Psychological Account are willing to accept the revisions I have proposed, they will have to abandon the idea that "person" is a substance sortal. If, as I suggested earlier, strong psychological continuity is necessary for personhood and yet we can continue to exist with only a very weak degree of psychological connectedness from day to day, we are not essentially persons. We could cease to be persons and yet continue to exist. This does not, however, mean that the revised Psychological Account of Identity cannot count as a theory of *personal* identity. As I noted in section 1 of this chapter, the debate about personal identity concerns the conditions for the existence or continued existence of entities of our sort—whatever sort of thing we may be.

4.5. *Replication and Egoistic Concern*

I have proposed that we revise both the Psychological Account of Egoistic Concern and the Psychological Account of Identity in such a way that they will better accommodate our beliefs about what matters us and about our own survival and persistence in cases in which the mental life of a person drops below the threshold for psychological continuity but in which the person's brain continues to support a flow of consciousness and mental activity whose constituent mental events are less tightly unified. My proposed revision is that we recognize that *broad* psychological continuity (a relation that admits of degrees and is compounded of overlapping relations of psychological connectedness, of any degree of strength) is a sufficient basis for egoistic concern and a necessary but not sufficient condition of personal identity. Broad psychological continuity is not sufficient for personal identity because of the possibility that it could take a branching form. In the subsequent discussion of the Psychological Account, I will assume that we have accepted these revisions.

The case of Division is important for a number of reasons. It challenges both the view that we are cartesian souls and the view that we are identical with our physical organisms. And it appears to show that identity is not what grounds egoistic concern about the future. Does it also show that psychological connectedness and broad psychological continuity are the bases of egoistic concern, as the Psychological Account of Egoistic Concern holds? I believe that it does not. To understand why, consider another example introduced by Parfit. It involves an imaginary device, familiar to readers of science fiction, by which people travel instantaneously over great distances.

> *Teletransportation.* One enters a "scanning booth" and presses a button. The Scanner records information about the exact states and structural relations of all of the cells in one's body. This process causes the instantaneous disintegration of one's body. The information thus obtained is then transmitted by the speed of light to a "replicating booth" at some distant location where the Replicator instantly creates, out of new matter, an exact, cell-for-cell duplicate of one's original body. The person who emerges from the replication booth is exactly similar, both physically and psychologically, to oneself as one was when one pressed the button in the scanning booth.

Let us call the person who emerges from the replicating booth the "replica." Is the replica the same individual as the person who pressed the button in the scanning booth? In his book *Reasons and Persons,* Parfit distinguishes two versions of the Psychological Account of Identity. According to the *wide* version, the criterion of personal identity is nonbranching psychological continuity (which we now understand as *broad* psychological continuity) *with any cause.* This version implies that the original person and the replica are one and the same individual. Teletransportation is just a very fast mode of transportation. According to the *narrow* version, however, the criterion of personal identity is nonbranching psychological continuity *with its normal cause*—namely, the functional continuity of the relevant areas of the same brain. On this version, the replica is a different individual from the original person because he does not have that person's brain. Parfit remains agnostic about the choice between the two versions but is inclined to believe that the narrow version better captures our intuitions about personal identity.[71]

For Parfit, however, the choice is unimportant. It is just a choice between different ways of using the words "same person." What is important is the issue about what matters, or about egoistic concern. Does the person who enters the scanning booth have reason to be concerned in an egoistic way about what will happen to the replica?

Parfit believes that the answer to this question is unequivocal: everything (or virtually everything) that matters is present in the relation that the original person bears to the replica. The original person has as much reason to care egoistically about the replica as an ordinary person has to care about herself on the following day.

Many people share Parfit's intuition.[72] But many others, myself included, do not. Cases involving replication can be elaborated in ways that bring out or enhance the intuitive reluctance of many people to accept that what matters is present in the relation between a person and his replica. Imagine, for example, that an advanced-model Replicator has been produced that has a scanning mechanism that leaves the original person entirely undamaged. (When this machine creates a replica, there are then two qualitatively identical people. If we accept the wide version of the Psychological Account of Identity, we should accept that neither of these people is the original person; for on the wide version, this would be a case of Division. If, however, we accept the narrow version, the person who leaves the scanning booth—and not the replica—is the original person. For convenience of exposition, I will assume that we accept the narrow version.) Now consider:

> *The Suicide Mission.* In a time of war, one has been chosen to carry out a military mission that will involve certain death. Although the operation of the Replicator is very expensive and has therefore been strictly rationed, one's superiors have granted one the privilege of having a replica of oneself made prior to the mission. They will also allow one to choose, prior to the process of replication, whether one will go on the mission oneself or whether the replica will be sent. (Because one is a dutiful soldier, one's replica will be dutiful as well. One knows that if ordered, he will go on the mission.)

If we were to choose entirely on the basis of what matters to us in an egoistic way, most of us would choose without hesitation that our replica should be sent on the mission. Yet, according to the Psychological Account of Egoistic Concern, all that matters in the relation that the original person bears to himself in the future is also present in the relation that he will bear to his replica. On this view, it should make no difference to the person, prior to replication, whether it is he himself or his replica who will be sent on the mission.

Next imagine a further improved Replicator—one that does not even require a scanning booth but can scan a person's body for the information necessary for replication from a considerable distance. This further detail makes the following case possible.

> *Multiple Replication.* Extortionists, having acquired control of a Replicator, have obtained one's cellular blueprint via long-distance scanning. They threaten that, unless one transfers all of one's wealth to them, they will create multiple replicas of oneself whom they will then torture and kill.

One would probably be willing to pay rather more to prevent the torture of replicas of oneself than one would to prevent a comparable fate for an equivalent number of unknown dissidents in a police state. But one would hesitate to pay as much as one would to prevent this fate from befalling *oneself.*

It must be conceded, however, that most of us feel some uncertainty about what matters in these cases. Our ambivalence emerges in response to the following example.

The Nuclear Attack. One is an employee at the Pentagon, which has a Replicator capable of transmitting one's cellular blueprint to a replicating booth in Alaska. One receives confirmation that a nuclear missile, targeted on the Pentagon, has penetrated the country's defenses and will obliterate the entire area within a minute. That is just enough time to have oneself scanned and for the data to be transmitted to Alaska.

Most of us believe that it would be better to have a replica created in Alaska than to be obliterated without leaving a replica. But this response is curiously inharmonious with the reactions that many of us have to the Suicide Mission and the case of Multiple Replication. It does not seem that our view is that replication would offer part but not all of what matters, or a partial basis for egoistic concern. And it would be a mistake to suppose that we have some antecedent sense of what matters but cannot tell whether replication would provide it. That is, it would be a mistake to regard replication as a risk or gamble, in the sense that we could not know until after the fact whether replication had preserved what matters. For there is no uncertainty about what would happen. In the Nuclear Attack, for example, one knows exactly what would happen. There is nothing that one's replica could know or discover that would be hidden from one prior to replication. Our uncertainty, revealed in our differing responses to the cases of the Suicide Mission and the Nuclear Attack, is simply an uncertainty about what matters to us. We can know all of the nonevaluative facts without being certain whether there is a basis for egoistic concern.

Suppose that one is inclined, as I am, to believe that what matters is missing in replication, so that, for example, one's concern for one's replica in the Suicide Mission would be like one's concern for someone closely related to oneself rather than like concern for oneself. Because one would be both directly and strongly psychologically connected and psychologically continuous with one's replica, these relations cannot be all that matters. There must be more. What is it?

Parfit's argument for the claim that psychological connectedness and continuity are what matter begins with the case of Division. The story he tells in order to illustrate the phenomenon of division is the one cited earlier in which a person's cerebral hemispheres are surgically separated from each other, detached from the person's brainstem, and each separately transplanted into a different decerebrate organism. Most of us respond to this case in the desired way—that is, we feel that it is natural and appropriate for the person who faces the prospect of division in this way to care in an egoistic way about both resulting persons. We feel that he is justified in fearing each's suffering, looking forward to each's pleasures, planning for each's future, and so on. Parfit might, however, have illustrated the phenomenon of division in a different way. He might have appealed to:

Double Replication. A person steps into one of the earlier-model Replicators and presses a button, whereupon his body is simultaneously scanned and destroyed, while two exact replicas are created in adjacent replicating booths.

As in the original case of Division, involving the bisection and double transplantation of a person's cerebrum, neither of the replicas would be identical with the person who entered the replicating booth. Yet, according to the Psychological Account of Egoistic Concern, everything that matters is present in the relation that the original person bears to both replicas. There is, on this view, no relevant difference between division via double replication and division via hemispheric separation and double transplantation. Yet, had Parfit presented the phenomenon of division with the example involving replication, he would have been unable to persuade many of his readers to accept his conclusion; for when division occurs by replication, many of us doubt that the original person has reason to be egoistically concerned about his replicas. Had Parfit used double replication to illustrate the phenomenon of division, we would have retained our original conviction that it is identity that matters.

To repeat: most of us agree that what matters is present in the relation between the original person and *both* of his successors in the case of Division; but many of us do not find a basis for egoistic concern in the relation between the original person and his replicas in the case of Double Replication. The difference between the cases is that, in the case of Division, psychological connectedness and continuity are grounded in the physical and functional continuity of the parts of the brain in which consciousness and mental activity are realized; whereas, in Double Replication, psychological connectedness and continuity have a different cause—namely, the replication of the relevant areas of the brain. This difference appears to matter: it seems to make a difference whether psychological connectedness and continuity are grounded in the continued existence and functioning of the relevant areas of the same brain.

4.6. *Psychological Connectedness and Continuity*

The problem revealed by the comparison between the cases of Division and Double Replication is traceable to the concepts of psychological connectedness and continuity as they are used in the literature. Let us examine these concepts more closely.

In the literature in which the Psychological Account is developed, the notion of a psychological connection is defined ostensively—by citing instances—as I did earlier. Typical examples are an experience and the memory of it, the "connection . . . which holds between an intention and the later act in which this intention is carried out," and the "connections . . . which hold when a belief, or a desire, or any other psychological feature, continues to be had."[73] As has frequently been observed, however, an ostensible memory-experience must, to count as a genuine memory, be causally dependent on the experience of which it is a memory in the normal way. Because of this, it has often been claimed that memory connections presuppose personal identity, so that one can remember only *one's own* experiences.

To avoid circularity in the statement of the Psychological Account, proponents of that view have introduced the notion of a *quasi-memory*. A person is said to have a quasi-memory of some past experience if (1) the person seems to remember having the experience, (2) someone did have the experience, and (3) the person's apparent memory is causally dependent, in the right sort of way, on that past experience.[74] For many adherents of the theory, the right sort of cause can be *any* cause. For example, suppose that a person has a certain experience but later loses the memory of it through damage to her brain. Later still, under hypnosis, she has the experience described to her in detail from the point of view of one having the experience, with the suggestion that she has had this experience. Or suppose, alternatively, that a neuro-scientist is able to remove the damaged tissues from her brain and graft a close replica of the tissues prior to their being damaged into the same area of her brain. After either process she will have what she believes to be a memory of the experi-ence, and indeed the apparent memory she will have may be subjectively indistin-guishable from her original genuine memory. She may therefore have a reasonably accurate quasi-memory of the experience.

According to the Psychological Account, the relation between an experience and a quasi-memory of it counts as a psychological connection. This is important, for it enables the theorist to treat the relation between a person's experience and his replica's quasi-memory of it as a psychological connection.

A parallel assumption has to be made about a person's belief and the correspon-ding belief that is later held by his replica. The Psychological Account assumes that these two beliefs establish a psychological connection, despite the fact that this is not a case in which the same belief "continues to be had"—for the replica's belief is a different belief, despite its being qualitatively identical to the earlier belief of the original person. Similar assumptions, of course, have to be made with respect to de-sires, dispositions, and other psychological states.

The concept of a psychological connection that accommodates these assump-tions is usually held to set two criteria that a later mental state must satisfy in order to form a psychological connection with an earlier mental state. One is that the later state must be causally dependent on the earlier one. The other is that the later state must have the phenomenological character and behavioral consequences appropriate for a normal successor state. The characterization of what is appropriate may differ from one type of psychological state to another. For example, a memory must in some way be a representation of the original experience, while a desire must have the same motivational force when conjoined with certain relevant beliefs, and so on. The precise characterization in each case is a difficult issue in the philosophy of mind that I will not go into here. I will use the general term "qualitative similarity" to express this second requirement. Thus the usual view is that, for example, a later belief forms a psychological connection with an earlier one if the later one is qualitatively similar to and causally dependent on the earlier one.

It seems, however, that the requirement of causal dependency is otiose. Does it really matter that the hypnotist should know about the woman's experience and try to induce in her a state resembling that which she would have had if not for the brain damage? Suppose instead that the hypnotist induces the same state in her without try-ing to duplicate her lost memory and without even knowing of her former experience. His duplication of her memory-experience is quite fortuitous. Or suppose that the same extraordinary coincidence occurs with the brain graft: the tissue that the sur-geon grafts onto her brain duplicates the original state of the damaged tissue quite by accident. In either case, the woman's later apparent memory would not be causally dependent on her earlier experience. Should we nonetheless say that she quasi-remembers her earlier experience?

I believe that those who defend the Psychological Account of Egoistic Concern should recognize relations between earlier and later psychological states that are qualitatively identical as constituting psychological connections even in the absence of any causal relations between the states. For if the *nature* of the causal relation between an earlier state and a later state does not matter, it is hard to see why it should matter whether there is a causal relation at all. To make this claim intuitively clearer, compare the earlier case of Teletransportation with the following case.

> *Unintended Replication.* A person dies. Immediately thereafter, the operators of a Replicator program the machine to create a person that they believe would not be a replica of any actual person. But, by an improbable coincidence, the brain and body of the person created in the replicating booth are exact cell-for-cell duplicates of the brain and body of the person who has just died.

According to Parfit and other proponents of the Psychological Account of Egoistic Concern, what matters is present in the relation between the person and his replica in Teletransportation. And it is very hard to believe that, while what matters is present in that case, it is absent in Unintended Replication. For the only difference is that, because the replication is intended in Teletransportation, the existence of the replica is causally dependent on the existence of the original person, whereas the existence of the replica is not causally dependent on the existence of the original person in Unintended Replication. But if what matters is present in the relation between the original person and his replica in Unintended Replication, proponents of the Psychological Account of Egoistic Concern seem committed to accepting that the original person's psychological states form psychological connections with those of the replica even though the latter are not causally dependent on the former. If that is right, causation is not a necessary feature of a psychological connection.

This leaves the requirement of qualitative similarity between an earlier and a later psychological state as all that is necessary in order for the two to form a psychological connection. This, however, may lead to an implausible proliferation of psychological connections. Suppose, for example, that you and I witness the same event from almost the exact same point of view. Years later I remember this event. If my memory-experience is sufficiently qualitatively similar to yours, it would seem to establish a psychological connection not only with my experience of the event but with yours as well.

This suggests a further a problem. How close does the resemblance between an earlier and a later mental state have to be in order for the two of them to constitute a psychological connection? Ordinarily we grant that the divergence between two states can be fairly great. A memory may be an extremely blurry or inexact representation of the original experience and still count as a memory. Indeed, a memory may become increasingly blurry over time and still remain the same memory. If we grant a comparable latitude in establishing quasi-memories, while at the same time dispensing with the requirement of causal dependency, it seems that psychological connections across different lives will be abundant.

This phenomenon would be particularly pronounced in the case of dicephalic twins. Dicephalic twins necessarily go to the same places and for the most part see and hear the same things from virtually the same point of view. Suppose that they read the same books together and so on. Each twin will therefore be quite closely psychologically connected with the other as she was in the recent past. According to the Psychological Account of Egoistic Concern, what matters in the life of each twin will therefore be present to a substantial degree in each's relation to the other. If one were going to die (that is, if one twin's brainstem and cerebrum were going to be destroyed and the functions of that brainstem were going to be taken over by the other's), she could console herself with the thought that much of what matters is present in the relation she bears to her twin in the future.

This is an extreme example of a phenomenon that, if we accept that qualitative similarity is all that is necessary for mental states at different times to form a psychological connection, will be quite pervasive in ordinary life: namely, psychological connections across different lives. Given these assumptions, moreover, the Psychological Account of Egoistic Concern (even the original, unrevised version) will imply that there are numerous actual cases (of which dicephalic twins would be only one clear and obvious instance) in which it is appropriate for one person to be concerned in an egoistic way about what happens to another. Most of us believe, however, that this conclusion would involve an excessive blurring of the boundaries between lives.

This problem arises from the liberality of the Psychological Account of Egoistic Concern in what it is willing to recognize as a psychological connection. The problem is not, however, with the general notion of quasi-memory, or any other quasi-states. If we grant for the sake of argument that it is indeed a conceptual truth that one can remember only one's own experiences, the notion of a quasi-memory is a useful one. Suppose that one of the memory traces from my brain is grafted onto your brain in such a way that it becomes accessible to your consciousness. This seems to be a case in which one and the same psychological state is experienced first by me and then by you. The two experiences are different manifestations of the same psychological state. If it is a conceptual truth that this state cannot be a genuine memory in its new home, we can call it a quasi-memory. There is clearly a real, albeit deviant, psychological connection between my earlier experience and your quasi-memory. So we may grant that some quasi-psychological states can be elements in genuine psychological connections. There can, in short, be a genuine psychological connection between an earlier mental state and a later one even when the person who has the later state is not same individual as the person who had the earlier one.

But many quasi-memories and other psychological states that are qualitatively similar to earlier states that may have been had by a different person are not like this. In cases involving replication, for example, one's replica has quasi-memories of one's experiences. But the replica's psychological states are not one's own states at a later time. They are merely duplicates of one's earlier states. (We should note that the wide version of the Psychological Account may deny this. It implies that, if the original person is destroyed and only one replica is then produced, the replica's psychological states *are* the person's states at a later time. For on this view, the replica *is* that person, so that his states must be that person's own states.)

Does the replica's belief that $2 + 2 = 4$ form a psychological connection with one's own earlier belief that $2 + 2 = 4$, despite the fact that the two beliefs are not earlier and later manifestations of the same (i.e., numerically identical) belief? It does, according to the notion of a psychological connection employed by those who accept the Psychological Account of Egoistic Concern. For if psychological connectedness and continuity are what matters, and what matters is present in one's relation to one's replica, there must be psychological connections between oneself and one's replica.

But to many of us, this is the point at which the Psychological Account of Egoistic Concern seems to go wrong. For one psychological state to establish a psychological connection with another, more is required than that the later one should be qualitatively similar to and causally dependent on the earlier one. Your later belief that 2 + 2 = 4 may be qualitatively identical to mine and may have been caused by it (if I taught you arithmetic), but that seems insufficient to make your belief a continuation of mine. There is no genuine psychological connection here at all. As we have seen, moreover, this conception's requirement of causal dependency seems incompatible with the intuitions that underlie the Psychological Account of Egoistic Concern. But its abandonment seems to lead to a proliferation of psychological connections across lives in the actual world, so that the account then has the implausible implication that what matters in an egoistic way is present to varying degrees in our relations with others even now.

We may concede that there would be psychological connections between you and me if parts of my brain containing memories and other elements of my mental life were excised and grafted onto your brain. And we might concede, further, that if enough such matter were going to be transplanted from my brain to yours, I would have grounds, although relatively weak ones, for being concerned in an egoistic way about what would later happen to you. But many of us doubt that the mere replication of a mental state establishes a psychological connection or that pseudo-connections established via replication would constitute a basis for egoistic concern. If we are to accept that psychological connectedness is part of what matters, we might therefore insist on a concept of a psychological connection according to which an earlier and a later psychological state form a psychological connection only if the two are qualitatively similar and the later state is causally dependent on the earlier one in the right way. And, we might further insist, there is the right sort of causal dependency only if there is continuity between the physical realization of the earlier state and the physical realization of the later state—that is, only if the states are constituted or generated by the same region of the same brain.

To distinguish this narrower conception of a psychological connection from the more familiar conception, I will use the tendentious label, *real psychological connection*. With this notion as the basic element, one can go on to formulate corresponding conceptions of real psychological connectedness, broad real psychological continuity, and so on.

I noted earlier that Parfit distinguishes between a narrow and a wide version of the Psychological Account of Identity. The narrow version insists that psychological continuity should have its normal cause: the continued existence and functioning of enough of the same brain. Because it denies that one could survive as a replica of oneself, the narrow version seems to many of us to match our beliefs about personal identity better than the wide version. If, as I suggested earlier, there is a presumption that our account of identity and our account of the reach of egoistic concern should coincide to the greatest degree possible, we should expect that a correspondingly narrow version of the Psychological Account of Egoistic Concern would better capture our beliefs about what matters than the standard version. The notion of a real psychological connection enables us to formulate this narrow version. According to this version, psychological connectedness or broad psychological continuity provides a basis for egoistic concern if the psychological connections that are constitutive of these relations are *real* psychological connections—that is, if connectedness and continuity are sustained by the continued existence and functioning of the brain tissues in which the original states were realized.

This narrow version of the Psychological Account of Egoistic Concern is doubly revised. It is more restrictive than the original version in that it insists that only those relations compounded out of real psychological connections provide a basis for egoistic concern. But it is in another respect less restrictive, in that it accepts that not only psychological continuity in Parfit's sense but broad psychological continuity of any degree of strength provides some basis for egoistic concern.

For many of us, the implications of this doubly revised version match our intuitions about what matters more closely than those of the original. This version implies, for example, that a person facing a prospect of progressive dementia has reason to be egoistically concerned about what will happen to him (or to his body, if our account of personal identity diverges here from our account of egoistic concern) until his mind reaches the stage of deterioration at which it will not be psychologically connected to any mental states in the near future. It also distinguishes sharply between the cases of Division and Double Replication. Because there is real psychological connectedness and continuity in the case of Division, one has reason to be strongly egoistically concerned about both of one's successors; but there is no basis for egoistic concern in Double Replication because one's relations with one's replicas will be compounded entirely out of pseudo-psychological connections.

It has to be recognized, however, that different people's intuitions conflict about what matters in these cases. Some people may continue to believe that we are essentially persons. They may think it a mistake to suppose that a person in the early stages of Alzheimer's disease could have reason to be egoistically concerned about what would happen to his body in the later phases of the disease. I suspect, however, that this intuition is comparatively rare. Most people would find my initial revision to the Psychological Account of Egoistic Concern persuasive. But there are many people, including Parfit and a number of other philosophers, who find it plausible, or even compelling, to suppose that psychological connectedness and continuity provide a basis for egoistic concern even in the absence of their normal cause—that is, even in the absence of the continued existence or functioning of the relevant areas of the same brain. I am uncertain about how one would even argue about this conflict of intuitions and I am therefore reluctant to claim that it is a mistake to suppose that one can have grounds for egoistic concern about the future in the absence of the continued existence of one's brain. Either version—wide or narrow—seems acceptable.

Given that our principal concerns in this book are ethical, these are reasonably agreeable conclusions. The first revision to the Psychological Account of Egoistic Concern that I have proposed has extensive and important prudential and moral implications. It is, for example, a significant matter whether a person in the early stages of Alzheimer's disease has grounds for egoistic concern about what will happen to his body in the later stages. But my revision of this aspect of the account is widely compelling. This revision has considerable practical significance, but it is also intuitively secure.

The second proposed revision—the suggested move from the original to the narrow version—is intuitively less secure; but it is also less significant. It might seem, indeed, that the difference between the narrow and the wide versions of the Psychological Account of Egoistic Concern shows up only in hypothetical examples involving replication, and hence is altogether irrelevant to prudential rationality and ethics. That will be true, however, only if we define a psychological connection in such a way that the later state must be causally dependent on the earlier one. If our concept of a psychological connection contains this causal requirement, there will in practice be no psychological connections across different lives and the wide and narrow versions of the Psychological Account of Egoistic Concern will coincide in all actual cases. The problem is that those whose intuitions are best captured by the wide version will want to claim that what matters is present in the case of Unintended Replication; but they cannot do so if the causal requirement is retained as part of the concept of a psychological connection. They therefore appear to face a dilemma: if they insist that the causal requirement is an essential element in the concept of a psychological connection, they will be unable to defend their intuition about the case of Unintended Replication; but if they jettison the causal requirement, they will apparently be committed to recognizing the existence of direct psychological connections, and therefore grounds for egoistic concern, between different lives in the actual world.

This may not be a serious problem. Even if the wide version is based on a concept of a psychological connection that does not include a requirement of causal dependency, the divergence between that version's implications for the actual world and those of the narrow version may be negligible. Even if we dispense with the requirement of causal dependency, the psychological connections between a person at one time and a different person at a later time would seldom if ever be very extensive; therefore the grounds that one person might have for egoistic concern about the future life of another would never be sufficiently significant to be of practical relevance. If that is right, it should not matter, where ethics is concerned, whether we accept the narrow or the wide version of the Psychological Account of Egoistic Concern.

There is, however, one further worry that applies to both versions. Recall that, as Alzheimer's disease progresses, it gradually destroys the neurological basis of a person's mental life until the psychological states generated by the person's brain cease to form psychological connections from day to day. All versions of the Psychological Account of Egoistic Concern imply that the person in the early stages of the disease has no grounds for egoistic concern about what happens after that point (and the corresponding versions of the Psychological Account of Identity imply that the person will have ceased to exist by that time). But the person's brain may continue to generate conscious states even after that point. Earlier I suggested that we refer to the conscious entity that remains after the flow of consciousness ceases to be psychologically connected over time as the "isolated subject." Many people believe that it would be rational for the person in the early stages of Alzheimer's disease to be egoistically concerned about what might later happen to the isolated subject. If, for example, it were a feature of Alzheimer's disease that there were often episodes of great pain in the very final stages, this would strike most of us as an additional reason for dreading the disease.

The problem of the isolated subject is an instance drawn from real life of a problem noticed in the earlier literature on personal identity. In a seminal paper, Bernard Williams presented the following case:

> *Deprogramming.* A mad scientist has developed a device that can erase all of the features of one's mental life that are elements in psychological connections—for example, memories, beliefs, desires, intentions, and so on. The device can also reprogram one's brain with an entirely new set of psychological characteristics. The process of deprogramming and reprogramming does not, moreover, require any interruption of the flow of consciousness. The scientist announces that he intends to deprogram one's brain and then to torture one's body.

Williams expects that most of us, if faced with the scientist's threat, would fear not only the deprogramming itself but also the torture that would follow it. But because there would be no direct psychological connections and no degree of broad psychological continuity between oneself prior to deprogramming and the conscious entity who would exist in association with one's body afterward, all the versions of the Psychological Account of Egoistic Concern agree that, prior to the deprogramming, one could have no basis for egoistic concern about the subsequent torture of one's body.

Our intuition that what matters would survive the process of deprogramming is perhaps stronger than the belief that the person in the early stages of Alzheimer's disease has reason to care egoistically about the isolated subject. This is because the discontinuity caused by Alzheimer's disease is more radical than that caused by deprogramming, even though it is less abrupt. In Alzheimer's disease, not only is there an eventual end of psychological connectedness even over short periods, but there is also an extensive loss of basic psychological capacities. Still, the intuition that what matters is present throughout the progress of Alzheimer's disease, at least until the victim loses the capacity for consciousness, is fairly robust. And because Alzheimer's disease and other conditions that involve progressive dementia are relatively common, it really matters what matters in these cases. If even the doubly revised version of the Psychological Account of Egoistic Concern cannot accommodate our intuitions about what matters in these cases, perhaps we should explore alternative accounts.

5. THE EMBODIED MIND ACCOUNT

5.1. *The Embodied Mind Account of Identity*

What is the basis of egoistic concern about the future? Cases involving replication suggest, at least to many of us, that neither psychological connectedness nor even broad psychological continuity provides a foundation for egoistic concern unless it is compounded from *real* psychological connections—that is, psychological connections grounded in continuity of the physical bases of the constituent psychological states. Only if psychological connectedness and continuity are "real" do they provide a basis for egoistic concern. (And even real psychological connectedness may not, by itself, be a sufficient basis for egoistic concern, as I will suggest in section 5.3 of this chapter.) But cases involving deprogramming or progressive dementia suggest that neither real psychological connectedness nor real psychological continuity is *neces-*

sary for egoistic concern. A person in the early stages of Alzheimer's disease has reason to be egoistically concerned about what may happen to his body even in the final phases in which the mental life associated with his body will no longer be even weakly psychologically connected from day to day.

Consideration of these various cases suggests that what matters, or what provides the basis for egoistic concern about the future, is continuity or sameness of consciousness—continuity, in my case for example, of *this* consciousness. Of course, what is required is not *continuous* consciousness—one does not have to remain perpetually awake—but continuity of the *capacity* for consciousness, so that the renewed appearance of conscious states following a period of unconsciousness is always the reappearance of the same consciousness, or the same mind.

How are we to understand the intuitive notion of sameness of consciousness? Some have contended that this notion presupposes personal identity: a particular field of consciousness at one time is the same consciousness as a certain field of consciousness at another time if and only if all the various conscious states are states of one and the same person. But because we are seeking an account of personal identity as well as an understanding of what matters, and also because we are assuming that identity is not what matters, it is clearly undesirable to rest our account of what matters on an unanalyzed conception of personal identity.

The notion of the "same consciousness" is equivalent to the notion of the same mind. And one can, it seems, give an account of this latter notion that does not presuppose personal identity. A mind, it seems, is individuated by reference to its physical embodiment, just as an individual mental state is. Just as a particular memory (for example) continues to exist only if the tissues of the brain in which it is realized continue to exist in a potentially functional state, so a particular mind continues to exist only if enough of the brain in which it is realized continues to exist in a functional or potentially functional state. The continued existence and functioning of the same brain is, however, only a necessary condition of the continued existence of the same mind. For it seems possible, at least in principle, for a single brain to support the existence of two different minds, either serially or even simultaneously. I will return to these possibilities in section 5.4 of this chapter. What I think can be asserted with some confidence is that, if a single mind has hitherto been realized in certain regions of a single brain, the undivided survival and continued, self-sufficient, functional integrity of those specific regions is both a necessary and sufficient condition of the continued existence of the same mind.

(What is important is the continuation of the same consciousness. But not all parts of the brain are involved in the generation of consciousness. The areas of the brain whose survival and functional integrity are important are those areas, whichever they may be, in which consciousness is directly realized. Henceforth when I refer to "the brain" while discussing the basis for egoistic concern and the criterion of personal identity, this should in general be understood to be shorthand for "those regions of the brain in which consciousness is realized.")

I suggest that the basis for an individual's egoistic concern about the future—that which is both necessary and sufficient for rational egoistic concern—is the physical and functional continuity of enough of those areas of the individual's brain in which consciousness is realized to preserve the capacity to support consciousness or mental activity. Usually the functional continuity of these areas of the brain involves broad psychological continuity, but in the very earliest phases of an individual's life and in some instances near the end, the same mind or consciousness persists in the absence of any degree of psychological connectedness from day to day. And as we have seen, what matters may be present in these cases, at least to some minimal degree.

Earlier I proposed that we should seek the closest congruence possible between our understanding of the basis of egoistic concern and our account of personal identity. We should therefore seek to determine what account of personal identity best coincides with the understanding of egoistic concern that has emerged from our review of the various cases. As a first approximation (which I will subsequently qualify and refine), I suggest that the corresponding criterion of personal identity is the continued existence and functioning, in nonbranching form, of enough of the same brain to be capable of generating consciousness or mental activity. This criterion stresses the survival of one's basic psychological *capacities,* in particular the capacity for consciousness. It does not require continuity of any of the particular *contents* of one's mental life. This allows that one may survive the deprogramming of one's brain and that one continues to exist throughout the progress of Alzheimer's disease, until the disease destroys one's capacity for consciousness.

As I noted at the beginning of this chapter, different criteria of personal identity over time correspond to different conceptions of what kind of entity we essentially are. The criterion that I have sketched corresponds to the view that we are essentially embodied *minds.* Let us therefore call this account of personal identity the *Embodied Mind Account.*[75] It parallels what we may call, more cumbersomely, the *Embodied Mind Account of Egoistic Concern.*

In order to clarify the nature of the Embodied Mind Account and to differentiate it from other accounts, it will help to distinguish three forms of continuity of the brain. *Physical continuity* of an organ such as the brain requires either the continued existence of the same constituent matter or the gradual, incremental replacement of the constituent matter over time. The cells in the skin, for example, undergo a continuous process of replacement that is compatible with physical continuity. By contrast, the cells in most areas of the brain are not subject to replacement. But they might have been. Our concept of physical continuity is in principle hospitable to the possibility that the same brain could continue to exist throughout a gradual process of cellular turnover comparable to that which takes place in other organs (a possibility to which I will shortly return). *Functional continuity* involves the retention of the brain's basic psychological *capacities.* And, finally, *organizational* or *structural continuity* involves the preservation of those configurations of tissue that underlie the connections and continuities among the *contents* of an individual's mental life over time.

Do these concepts allow for the possibility of functional or organizational continuity in the absence of physical continuity? I suspect that, as these terms are used in ordinary language, functional and organizational continuity presuppose physical continuity. But I will use these terms in a different way. I will assume that, as long as certain functions or patterns of organization are preserved, there will be functional or organizational continuity even if the relevant functions or patterns or organization are not preserved in the same matter. So, for example, one may say that there is functional and organizational continuity of the brain when a person is replicated (as in Teletransportation), even though there is no physical continuity at all—that is, even though the relevant functions and patterns of organization are not preserved in the same brain.

According to the Embodied Mind Account, the criterion of personal identity is physical and minimal functional continuity of the brain. This distinguishes it from other accounts that include organizational continuity in the criterion of personal identity. Michael Lockwood, for example, argues that the mistake of the Psychological Account is to "*define* personal identity . . . in terms of . . . discernible continuities" among mental states. "For our ordinary concept of identity through time of a human being is not of something that is *constituted* by these discernible continuities, but as something that *underlies* these continuities and accounts for them—something of which these discernible continuities are merely a manifestation. . . . [W]hat underlies the discernible continuities of memory and personality is a continuity of physical organization within some part or parts of a living human brain persisting through time."[76] On this view, one could not survive deprogramming. Thus Lockwood notes that deprogramming followed by reprogramming "would effect too radical a *dis*continuity of organisation in the parts of [the brain] that subserved mental functioning."[77] This also appears to be the view of Michael B. Green and Daniel Wikler, who write that personal identity requires "continuity of certain brain *processes,* carried out through microstructural and microfunctional registrations in the brain tissue," and that the relevant processes are those that "normally underlie . . . psychological continuity and connectedness."[78] Accounts such as these, which insist on the preservation of some form of psychological continuity, are instances of the narrow Psychological Account of Identity.

In order to match the intuitions that many of us have about the necessary and sufficient conditions for the rationality of egoistic concern, our account of personal identity must focus, as these authors insist, not on the superficial continuities of mental life but on that which underlies and sustains them. I differ from these authors primarily in thinking that identity requires less structural or organizational continuity in the brain than they believe is necessary. While they believe that identity requires sufficient structural continuity to preserve certain continuities in the content of an individual's mental life, I believe that there need be only enough physical and functional continuity to preserve certain basic psychological capacities, particularly the capacity for consciousness. This, I believe, is a sufficient basis for egoistic concern; it should, therefore, be a sufficient basis for identity, other things being equal.

5.2. *The Basis for Egoistic Concern*

Return now to the problem of egoistic concern. The Embodied Mind Account insists that physical but not organizational continuity of the brain is necessary in order for egoistic concern to be rational. The Psychological Account of Egoistic Concern, by contrast, insists that organizational but not physical continuity is necessary—that is, it insists on the preservation of certain patterns of organization in the bases of mental life but denies that these patterns require continuous realization in the same physical matter. Thus, as I noted in section 4.5 of this chapter, the Psychological Account of Egoistic Concern holds that what matters is preserved in cases of replication. But most people intuitively doubt that this is so. Most of us believe that physical continuity of the brain is necessary.

It will be helpful at this point to reconsider the importance of physical continuity. Parfit has developed a challenge to the significance of physical continuity that takes the argument deeper than the appeal to superficial intuitions about replication. Consideration of this challenge will then lead naturally to a fuller consideration of the relevance of organizational continuity to the rationality of egoistic concern.

Parfit's challenge seeks to undermine the importance of physical continuity by showing how slight a difference there is, in certain cases, between there being and there not being physical continuity of the brain. He invites us to consider a pair of cases, both involving the replacement of the various parts of a brain with exact duplicates. "Suppose," Parfit writes, "that I need surgery. All of my brain cells have a defect which, in time, would be fatal. But a surgeon can replace all these cells. He can insert new cells that are exact replicas of the existing cells except that they have no defect. We can distinguish two cases."

> In *Case One,* the surgeon performs a hundred operations. In each of these, he removes a hundredth part of my brain, and inserts a replica of this part.
>
> In *Case Two,* the surgeon follows a different procedure. He first removes all of the parts of my brain, and then inserts all of their replicas.[79]

Parfit concedes that his brain would survive in Case One but not in Case Two. But he argues that the difference between the two cases can be seen, upon reflection, to be trivial. "The difference between the cases," he writes, "is merely . . . a difference in the ordering of removals and insertions. In Case One, the surgeon alternates between removing and inserting. In Case Two he does all the removing before all the inserting. Can *this,*" he asks, "be the difference between life and death? . . . Can it be so important, for my survival, whether the new parts are, for a time, joined to the old parts?"[80]

Parfit's own intuitive response to this case is firm: "I cannot believe that what would matter for my survival is whether, over some period, the replicas of parts of my brain would be inserted in one of these two ways."[81] Because in both cases psychological continuity (in his sense, which does not require what I have called "real" psychological connections) would be preserved, he believes that what matters would be present in both cases. Again, however, I suspect that most people's intuitions are different. For most people, just as there would be no basis for egoistic concern about a replica of oneself, so there would be no basis for egoistic concern about a person who would have a replica of one's entire brain, even if that person would have the rest of one's body. By contrast, one's grounds for egoistic concern about oneself tomorrow would not be seriously compromised by the loss of one one-hundredth of one's brain today—provided, of course, that the remaining ninety-nine one-hundredths would retain the capacity to support consciousness and mental activity. And this is, if anything, even more obviously true if the one-hundredth part that would be lost would be replaced by an exact duplicate. Furthermore, if one's grounds for egoistic concern about the future would not be substantially affected if this process were to happen once, it seems that they would also not be undermined if the process were repeated at infrequent intervals.

In short, to many of us, myself included, it does not seem arbitrary to suppose that the difference between Case One and Case Two is crucial to whether there is a basis for egoistic concern. Yet, as Parfit shows, that difference can be described in a way that makes it odd to suppose that it could be important. And Parfit himself, reflecting on the difference in this light, finds it trivial. What are we to make of this intuitive disagreement? Is Parfit mistaken? Are those whose intuitions differ from his mistaken? Or are both understandings of what matters tenable, so that it could be reasonable for Parfit to believe that the all-at-once replacement of his brain would be as good as ordinary survival though it would also be reasonable for me to believe that it would be as bad as ordinary death? It would, I think, be a mistake to embrace the relativist view that whatever a person believes to be the basis for egoistic concern is in fact a necessary and sufficient basis for egoistic concern *for that person*. But perhaps there is a limited range of defensible views, none of which can be shown to be more reasonable than the others. If so, I suggest that both Parfit's Psychological Account of Egoistic Concern (provided that it is based on the *broad* concept of psychological continuity) and the Embodied Mind Account of Egoistic Concern are within that range.

There is, however, more that can be said about Cases One and Two. For those who accept the Embodied Mind Account of Egoistic Concern, it matters how long the intervals are between the replacements in Case One. If, for example, fifty replacements were carried out each day, at intervals of fifteen minutes, over a period of two days, it seems highly doubtful, even on the Embodied Mind Account of Egoistic Concern, that what matters would be preserved. The turnover would be too rapid for there to be physical continuity of the relevant areas of the brain. If, however, the series of replacements were very gradual—for example, one replacement every six months over a period of fifty years—it seems compelling both that there would be continuity of the relevant areas of Parfit's brain and that Parfit's grounds for egoistic concern about the future would, at each point, be preserved. There would be physical continuity, despite the replacements, because our understanding of the continued existence of a physical object normally tolerates a replacement of the object's constituent elements or parts, provided that no one of the parts is essential to the existence of the whole and that the turnover is sufficiently gradual that each new tissue would coexist for a significant period of time with substantially greater amounts of older matter.

There is a spectrum of possible cases between Case One and Case Two. (The parallel with Parfit's well-known Physical Spectrum will be obvious, the main difference being that, in the spectrum between Cases One and Two, the variable is not the amount of the brain that is ultimately replaced by duplicate matter but the length of the interval between the replacements.)[82] Consideration of this spectrum may help to elucidate the Embodied Mind Account of Egoistic Concern. At one end of the spectrum—Case Two—the replacement of the matter of Parfit's brain occurs all at once. At the other end of the spectrum—Case One—the replacement is carried out in a hundred operations spread out at equal intervals over a period of fifty years. In most cases along the spectrum, it seems plausible to suppose that what matters is preserved. But as we approach Case Two, it becomes less clear that Parfit would have egoistic reason at the beginning of the process to care about the person who would exist at the end. Suppose, for example, that Parfit's surgeon were to replace one one-hundredth part of his brain twice a day for fifty days. Is there physical continuity of the brain in this case? I suspect that there is no right answer to this question. It is simply indeterminate whether, at the end of the fifty-day period, there is the same brain that there was at the beginning. Those whose intuitions are best captured by the Embodied Mind Account of Egoistic Concern may therefore find that it is also indeterminate whether Parfit has reason at the beginning of the process of replacement to be egoistically concerned about the person who will exist at the end. In the region of the spectrum between the area of indeterminacy and Case Two, the rate of turnover is too great to be compatible with physical continuity.

(There are other spectra that might be invoked to illustrate the same point. Instead of a spectrum with a fixed proportion of the brain being replaced with a duplicate at varying intervals, there might be a spectrum with a fixed interval between replacements but varying amounts of the brain replaced at each operation. Or there might be a spectrum in which both the amount of the brain replaced and the interval between replacements would vary. In this spectrum, the greater the proportion of the matter that is replaced at each operation and the shorter the intervals between operations, the less likely it is that what matters will be preserved—if physical continuity of the brain is part of what matters.)

The cases in this spectrum raise an important question. Between Case One and the region of indeterminacy, there is a range of cases in which there is decreasing physical continuity but always enough to make it rational for one at the beginning of the process to be at least minimally egoistically concerned about oneself at the end. The question is whether the degree of one's egoistic concern may rationally vary with the degree of physical continuity or whether the grounds for egoistic concern are equal in strength in the range of cases between Case One and the region of indeterminacy. What makes this range of the spectrum a useful test for the importance of physical continuity is that, while the cases involve differing degrees of physical continuity, there is nevertheless full functional and organizational continuity in each case within the range.

As we saw earlier, Parfit argues that "it can be rational to care less, when one of the grounds for caring will hold to a lesser degree."[83] I have suggested that physical continuity of those areas of the brain in which consciousness is realized is part of the basis for egoistic concern (in that a certain degree of physical continuity is a necessary condition of rational egoistic concern). In the spectrum of cases we are considering, physical continuity of the brain is a matter of degree: there is greater physical continuity in the cases nearer to Case One, in which the intervals between replacements are longest. In the cases in this spectrum, therefore, the degree to which one is egoistically concerned at the beginning of the process of replacement about oneself at the end may rationally vary with the degree of physical continuity between one's brain at the beginning and the end of the process.

This conclusion depends on two claims: the claim that physical continuity is part of what matters and Parfit's claim that egoistic concern may rationally vary with the strength of the prudential unity relations. Some people, considering this spectrum of cases, will find it intuitively plausible to suppose that one has equal reason in each case to be egoistically concerned about oneself in the future. If that is one's reaction, one may decide to reject one or both of the claims just cited.

The cases in this spectrum have no analogues in the world as it is. Areas of the brain cannot in fact be replaced by duplicates; hence there are no actual cases in which there is full functional and organizational continuity in the brain but in which there are also varying degrees of physical continuity. The cases in the spectrum are, in a sense, irrelevant in practical terms. But there are, of course, actual cases involving diminished physical continuity of the brain. In the most obvious of these types of case, diminished physical continuity is not the result of the replacement of cerebral tissue but of the *loss* of cerebral tissue. In Alzheimer's disease, for example, cerebral tissues atrophy and die; the brain shrinks. (There is also physical discontinuity between the earlier and later phases of brain *growth*. I will consider this other form of discontinuity in section 6.1 of chapter 2.)

We can imagine a spectrum of cases involving decreasing physical continuity in the brain as a result of the loss of cerebral tissues. At one end would be a case involving the loss of a single neuron; at the other, a case in which both hemispheres are utterly destroyed. Somewhere in the middle there would be a range of losses—losses of different areas—that would be just beyond the maximum loss compatible with the retention of the capacity for consciousness. Between the case in which a single neuron is lost and this range of cases at which the capacity for consciousness is lost altogether, there is a subspectrum of cases in which enough of the brain survives to be capable of supporting consciousness. But along this subspectrum, there is decreasing physical continuity. And because this physical discontinuity is the result of the loss or death of living tissues, it causes or entails an increasing diminution of functional and organizational continuity as well. As we move along the subspectrum in the direction of increasing physical discontinuity, there is increasing loss of psychological capacity as well as decreased psychological connectedness and continuity.

The cases along this subspectrum involving decreasing physical, functional, and organizational continuity of the brain are all distressingly familiar in actual life. Most points along the spectrum presumably correspond to some actual form of brain damage. And persons suffering from progressive dementia may exemplify one case after another as they descend grimly along the path to oblivion.

It is instructive to compare the cases in this subspectrum with the corresponding cases in the previous spectrum. In that spectrum of hypothetical cases, there is decreasing physical continuity from case to case (because the intervals between replacements by duplicate tissues are increasingly frequent), but functional and organizational continuity remain constant. In the subspectrum, by contrast, decreasing physical continuity is accompanied by decreasing functional and organizational continuity. One important question is whether our intuitive sense is that the basis of egoistic concern is more sharply eroded in the subspectrum. If it is, that suggests that functional and organizational continuity matter in addition to mere physical continuity. (In the subsequent discussion, I will assume that functional and organizational continuity are based on or sustained by physical continuity. I will ignore hypothetical cases in which there might be functional and organizational continuity in the absence of physical continuity.)

I have contended that minimal functional continuity of the relevant areas of the brain is a necessary condition both of egoistic concern and of identity. In order for a person to survive and to have a basis for egoistic concern about his future, his brain must retain its capacity for consciousness. So functional continuity is part of what matters, and there is a presumption that the degree of egoistic concern that a person is rationally warranted in having about his own future varies with the degree of functional continuity between himself now and himself in the future.

Organizational continuity is different. There seems to be a minimal basis for egoistic concern about the future even when the structural organization of the brain that underlies psychological connectedness and continuity will be destroyed—as often happens over the course of progressive dementia. If this is right, organizational continuity is not a necessary condition of rational egoistic concern. Nor is it, according to the Embodied Mind Account, among the relations constitutive of personal identity. I will argue, however, that it is among the prudential unity relations, in this sense: although organizational continuity is not necessary for minimal egoistic concern, the degree of egoistic concern that is rationally warranted nevertheless varies with the degree of organizational continuity.

The arguments for this claim appeal to intuitions about egoistic concern. These intuitions emerge more clearly if we focus our attention on the psychological manifestations of organizational continuity, which itself (in all actual cases) presupposes substantial physical and functional continuity of the brain. If we can see that the various unities and continuities of psychology over time are among the bases of egoistic concern, that will be tantamount to recognizing that the continuities of neural organization and function that underlie them also matter.

What I will argue is that the rational degree of egoistic concern about one's own future varies with the degree of *psychological unity* between oneself now and oneself in the future. Psychological unity is a complex notion, encompassing both psychological connectedness and continuity. To understand more clearly the various elements or dimensions of psychological unity within a life, let us distinguish between two types of psychological connection. Some psychological connections are constituted simply by an earlier and a later manifestation of the same mental state—for example, a belief or disposition of character that exists at time t_1 and continues to exist later at time t_2. Other psychological connections are constituted by mental states that occur at different times but contain some internal reference to one another—for example, an experience and a later memory of that experience, or the formation of a desire or intention and the later experience of the fulfillment of that desire or intention.

One form of psychological connectedness consists of connections of the first sort. This form of connectedness consists simply in the carrying forward through time of the elements of an individual's psychological makeup. It may, however, be a comparatively insignificant form of psychological connectedness. It obtains, for example, in the life of a dog to the extent that the dog retains its various beliefs, dispositions of character, memories, and so on. But at least two important dimensions of psychological unity are only minimally present in this case. First, because the dog's mental life is sparse, the sheer number of psychological connections is comparatively small. The magnitude or density of the mental life carried forward is comparatively slight. Second, there is little internal reference among the earlier and later mental states: few memories of particular experiences, few acts that fulfill desires or intentions formed significantly earlier, and so on. The concept of psychological unity takes all these factors into account. The degree of psychological unity within a life between times t_1 and t_2 is a function of the proportion of the mental life that is sustained over that period, the richness or density of that mental life, and the degree of internal reference among the various earlier and later mental states. These three factors are normally buried within the notion of the degree of psychological connectedness between an individual at the two different times. But they need to be explicitly distinguished. If the period between t_1 and t_2 is quite long, so that there are comparatively few direct psychological connections spanning the entire period, the degree of psychological unity within the life can still be expressed using a notion of psychological continuity that admits of degrees. If the relations of psychological connectedness over shorter periods are strong in terms of the three factors just noted, we can say that there is strong psychological continuity between t_1 and t_2 and therefore that there is substantial psychological unity over the whole of that period.

It is obvious, but worth stating, that substantial psychological unity within a life presupposes parallel conditions for psychological capacities. The degree of psychological unity over a certain period will be higher the greater the variety of capacities the individual possesses, the higher the proportion of the capacities carried forward, and the more highly developed the capacities are. Richness and continuity of psychological capacities are essential to psychological unity if only because they are necessary conditions of strong psychological connectedness and continuity. Overall, one might say that the degree of psychological unity within a life is a function of the richness, complexity, and coherence of the psychological architecture that is carried forward through time.

Earlier I mentioned the case of a dog in whose mental life over time there may be a certain continuity, in that most of the elements of the mental life are carried forward, though the level of overall psychological unity is comparatively low. Consider now a hypothetical creature in whose life there is markedly less psychological unity than there is in the life of a dog. Imagine a sentient creature whose mental life consists of a stream of consciousness without any psychological connections. It lives entirely in the present, so that the poet Robert Burns might address to it the words he utters to the mouse: "The present only toucheth thee." But let us imagine that our sentient creature's mental horizons are even more temporally circumscribed than those of Burns's mouse. Our creature lives entirely in what is known as the "specious present." While it has sufficient short-term memory to enable it to see the motion of the second hand on a clock as a continuous motion, that is all the memory it has. It cannot remember what happened to it a few seconds ago. It is not self-conscious and has no conception of the future. Not only does it have no memory or foresight, it also has no psychological architecture to carry forward: no structure of beliefs, desires, attitudes, dispositions, or traits of character. All it has, we may suppose, are experiences. But most of these experiences are extremely pleasant. Perhaps we can imagine this creature as having a well-formed pleasure center in the brain but little else in the way of neurological development.

Would there be reason to care, for this creature's own sake now, whether it would continue to live? The mere continuity of consciousness within its life that is a corollary of the physical and functional continuity of its brain seems to provide a basis for the claim that there is some reason to be concerned about the creature's future for its own sake. But our intuitive sense is that the reason to care *for its sake* is absolutely minimal. And we can see intuitively that it is the lack of psychological relations between the creature now and itself in the future that diminishes our grounds for concern about the creature for its own sake. Its future, were it to continue to live, might contain a considerable sum of good in the form of unalloyed physical pleasure. But the creature is not related to itself in the future in anything like the way that you and I are related to our future selves. Each experience in the creature's life is discrete, isolated, unconnected with any of the experiences that precede or follow it. Later psychological states are neither caused by nor have any internal reference to earlier ones. Thus, while we may think that the experiences have value individually, it is less plausible to attribute independent value to them as a collection or aggregate. Lacking any *unity* apart from their common grounding in the same brain, they fail to form a *unit* in any but the most minimal sense. Thus we can see, by contrast, that the psychological unity within the lives of persons such as ourselves gives our lives as wholes a moral and prudential significance that the mere sum of our experiences lacks—or, to put it differently, that makes our lives as wholes significant *units* for moral and prudential evaluation.

Because the experiences of the merely sentient creature fail to form a significant unit, it may seem that what matters is mainly that experiences of this sort should continue to occur (and even this may not matter much, given the disconnected character of the experiences). It does not much matter whether the experiences occur within this same life. As Parfit has argued, when the unity within individual lives is less deep, the distinctions between the lives are correspondingly less significant. And when the boundaries between lives are less significant, "it becomes more plausible, when thinking morally, to focus less upon the person, the subject of experiences, and instead to focus more upon the experiences themselves."[84] Thus it would not much matter if the merely sentient creature were to die while another creature of the same sort were to begin to exist and to have experiences of the same sort. That which is of most significance—the individual experiences themselves—would continue to occur. Little or nothing of significance would be lost simply because the experiences would be occurring in a different series—that is, within a different life. For the experiences themselves, and not the lives as wholes or units, would be the focus of our concern. The creature itself would be, in Peter Singer's phrase, "replaceable."[85]

There are cases of adult human beings who are relevantly similar to the sentient creature in being marooned wholly in the present. These cases of course involve severe pathological states. One such individual, a middle-aged patient with Korsakov's syndrome, has no memories of his life after the age of nineteen. His episodic memory is ephemeral: "whatever was said or shown to him was apt to be forgotten in a few seconds' time."[86] Oliver Sacks describes him as "isolated in a single moment of being, with a moat or lacuna of forgetting all round him . . . He is [a] man without a past (or future), stuck in a constantly changing, meaningless moment."[87] An even more radical case is that of the musician and musicologist, Clive Wearing, who in 1985 suffered an episode of herpes simplex encephalitis that left him with retrograde amnesia so severe that he can remember almost nothing of his life prior to the illness. It also virtually destroyed his capacity for episodic memory, so that, like Sacks's Korsakov patient, he can remember nothing that happens to him for more than a minute or so. According to his wife, his "world now consists of a *moment* with no past to anchor it and no future to look ahead to. . . . Clive is unaware there have been other days prior to the one in which he finds himself. He only ever has knowledge of being conscious for a couple of minutes."[88] For years he has lived with the persistent, ever-present sense of having just emerged into consciousness. He has kept numerous diaries in which he writes, repeatedly throughout each day, that he is now awake for the first time.[89]

I believe that, as in the case of the sentient creature, the basis for egoistic concern about the future is radically diminished in each of these people. It is not just that there is no prospect of significant good in either life—though that is true as well, for, without the ability to remember one's thoughts and experiences for more than a few moments, one cannot have a structured life, cannot have plans or projects, significant personal relations, or any of the constituents of a rewarding life other than the most evanescent and superficial pleasures. There are, however, ordinary people whose lives similarly consist largely in a succession of disconnected passive experiences and pleasures—television and then more television. These people's futures may promise little other than more of the same, and yet there is sufficient psychological unity in their lives to ground a robust degree of egoistic concern. The problem in these cases is in the content rather than the structure of the life. But in the case of the individuals who are forever lost in the present, the basis for caring about the future is drastically eroded. The successive moments in each life are so utterly unconnected subjectively that they scarcely constitute a life at all in any but the purely biological sense. (Thus, musing on his patient with Korsakov's syndrome, Sacks questions "whether, indeed, one could speak of an 'existence,' given so absolute a privation of memory or continuity.")[90]

These claims may become intuitively clearer if we consider a hypothetical case in which radical psychological discontinuity would be followed by an abundance of future good.

> *The Cure.* Imagine that you are twenty years old and are diagnosed with a disease that, if untreated, invariably causes death (though not pain or disability) within five years. There is a treatment that reliably cures the disease but also, as a side effect, causes total retrograde amnesia and radical personality change. Long-term studies of others who have had the treatment show that they almost always go on to have long and happy lives, though these lives are informed by desires and values that differ profoundly from those that the person had prior to treatment. You can therefore reasonably expect that, if you take the treatment, you will live for roughly sixty more years, though the life you will have will be utterly discontinuous with your life as it has been. You will remember nothing of your past and your character and values will be radically altered. Suppose, however, that this can be reliably predicted: that the future you would have between the ages of twenty and eighty if you were to take the treatment would, by itself, be better, as a whole, than your entire life will be if you do not take the treatment.

Would it be egoistically rational for you to take the treatment? Most of us would at least be skeptical of the wisdom of taking the treatment and many would be deeply opposed to it. How can this be explained, given the stipulation that you could reasonably expect not only that the treatment would give you a better future (roughly sixty years rather than five) but also that your future with the treatment would be better, as a whole, than your entire life will be without it? I suggest that the best explanation is that psychological unity is among the prudential unity relations. The future you would have with the treatment would contain vastly more good than you will have if you refuse the treatment, but the future offered by the treatment is too much like someone else's future. In that future, you would be a complete stranger to yourself as you are now. The psychological distance between you now and yourself as you would be after the treatment is too great for you to think of the goods in that future as fully *yours*. Of course, if the Embodied Mind Account is the correct account of personal identity, these goods would lie in your future, but you now would not be sufficiently related to yourself in the future in the ways that matter to make it rational for you to care about them in the normal way. It may seem rational instead to opt for the lesser good (five more years only), which would more clearly be *your* good, or to which you would be more strongly related in the ways that matter.

Consideration of the Cure is, I think, a helpful test of our intuitions. If, in the circumstances, you would strongly desire to have the treatment, that suggests that you may doubt that psychological unity is among the prudential unity relations. If, by contrast, you would be reluctant to take the treatment, that suggests that you believe not only that identity is not the basis of egoistic concern, but also that psychological unity is among the prudential unity relations.

It is worth mentioning here one other kind of case—one that is actually ubiquitous—in which there is little or no psychological unity between an individual now and himself in the future but in which there is now a prospect of abundant future good. These are cases involving human fetuses and infants. Consider, for example, a late-term human fetus. Assume that the amount of good that lies in prospect for it is very great: the amount of good in the whole of a normal human life. How much does it matter, for the fetus's own sake now, that it should live to have that good? If the extent to which it matters is commensurate with the magnitude of the good in prospect, it seems that it would be terribly bad if the fetus were to die instead. But most of us believe that the death of a human fetus is not a terrible tragedy, at least not for the fetus itself. In the next chapter I will argue that we can convincingly defend this otherwise puzzling belief (puzzling because the magnitude of the loss is so great) by appealing to the claim that psychological unity is among the prudential unity relations. Anticipating that later discussion, I suggest that the ability of this claim to explain and justify our beliefs about fetal and infant death is one of the strongest reasons for accepting it.

This suggestion invites a charge of circularity. For I here appeal to our intuitions about fetal and infant death to defend the claim that psychological unity is among the bases of egoistic concern, yet in the next chapter I will invoke this claim in order to defend these same intuitions. Although there is a certain circularity here, I do not believe that it vitiates either the defense of the claim or the defense of the intuitions. In epistemology, it is widely accepted that coherence among beliefs sometimes strengthens the case for thinking that each belief is justified. In the present instance, in which both the general claim and the intuition about fetuses and infants enjoy a certain initial credibility, it seems plausible to suppose that the credibility of each is enhanced or reinforced by their mutual support.

Let me now summarize these reflections about the basis for egoistic concern. The relation that is constitutive of identity—sufficient physical and functional continuity of the areas of the brain in which consciousness is realized in order for those areas to retain the capacity to support consciousness—is both a necessary and a sufficient condition of a minimal degree of rational egoistic concern. Beyond that, the degree of egoistic concern that it is rational to have about the future may vary with the degree of physical, functional, or organizational continuity in the brain (or, to be more exact, those areas of the brain in which consciousness is realized). All three forms of continuity matter; and variations in the strength of any of the three are manifest, in practice, in variations in the degree of psychological unity within the life. Because all three forms of continuity matter, progressive dementia can attack the basis for egoistic concern in a more radical way even than deprogramming would—for the latter destroys only organizational continuity, while the former erodes all three forms of continuity in the brain.

I have argued that psychological unity is among the prudential unity relations, even though it is not among the relations that are constitutive of personal identity. Yet earlier I suggested that the two sets of relations should coincide as closely as possible. Is this an objection to the inclusion of psychological unity among the prudential unity relations? I think not. There is in fact a close coincidence between the two sets of relations. I have conceded that psychological unity is not necessary for personal identity. But I also concede that it is not necessary for rational egoistic concern, as in the case of someone at the onset of progressive dementia, who can rationally care in an egoistic way about the pain he will suffer in the late stages of the disease, when the psychological separation from his present self will be total. My claim is only that the degree of egoistic concern that is warranted can vary with the degree of psychological unity. No parallel claim about personal identity can be made because personal identity is not a matter of degree. Moreover, provided we assume that, other things being equal, there is greater physical and functional continuity of the relevant areas of the brain the more highly developed those areas are to begin with, it turns out that, in all actual cases, the degree of psychological unity varies with the degree of physical and functional continuity. It is only in hypothetical cases such as Deprogramming that there can be a high degree of physical and functional continuity but only weak psychological unity. And this is what we should expect: that in the cases that have shaped our beliefs about what matters, variations in the strength of the relations that matter are paralleled by variations in relations that are constitutive of personal identity. (Note that the two Psychological Continuity Accounts also hold that one of the prudential unity relations—namely, psychological connectedness—is not a necessary condition of identity. It is, however, a constituent of the relation—psychological continuity—that is the criterion of identity.)

Having indicated what I think the prudential unity relations are, let me now say more precisely how they affect what it is egoistically rational for an individual to care about. Consider some event within one's own future life. The extent to which one ought now to be egoistically concerned about that event is a function of two factors: first, the value, positive or negative, that the event would have for one at the time when it would occur, and second, the extent to which the prudential unity relations would hold between oneself now and oneself at the later time when the event would occur. The prudential unity relations in effect function as a multiplier with respect to the value of the event. If, for example, the prudential unity relations would be of maximum strength, we calculate the importance of the event from one's present point of view by multiplying the value the event will have when it occurs by 1; thus the extent to which one ought rationally to be egoistically concerned about the event is proportional to the value the event will contribute to one's life. If, however, the prudential unity relations would be weaker, the extent to which the event matters from one's present point of view declines. We should multiply the value that the event will have when it occurs by some fraction representing the strength of the prudential unity relations. There is, in short, a discount rate for weakened prudential unity.

This discounting operation—the value that future events would have within one's life at the time they would occur multiplied by a number (either 1 or a positive fraction) representing the strength of the prudential unity relations between oneself now and oneself at those times when the events would occur—determines the strength of what I will call one's present *time-relative interests* in the possibilities of one's own future life. It will help, in elucidating this notion, to draw a preliminary distinction between two senses of the notion of an interest. This is the distinction between *being interested in* something and *having an interest in* something. To be interested in something is to be curious or concerned about it, whereas to have an interest in something is to have a stake in it. If, for example, I am intellectually fascinated by the behavior of the stock market but have no investments in it, one could say that I am interested in it without *having* an interest in it. If, on the contrary, I have investments but am incurious or unconcerned about the way my stocks are performing, one could say that I am uninterested in the stock market even though I have an interest in it. In the subsequent discussion of interests, I will be concerned primarily with interests in the second of these two senses: the sense in which to have an interest in something is for one's well-being to be engaged with it.

One's present time-relative interests are what one has egoistic reason to care about *now* (or, in the case of a non-self-conscious being incapable of being egoistically concerned about the future, its present time-relative interests are what a third party would have reason to care about for the being's own sake now). One's time-relative interests are always, as the label is intended to suggest, relativized to one's state at a time. They are different from one's *interests* (as traditionally understood) in that they are affected by the strength of the prospective prudential unity relations whereas one's interests are not. One's interests are concerned with what would be better or worse for oneself as a temporally extended being; they reflect what would be better or worse for one's life as a whole. If identity were the basis of rational egoistic concern, there could be no divergence between one's interests and one's time-relative interests. For the prudential unity relation—identity—would not be a matter of degree and would always be present whenever there was any basis for egoistic concern. In short, if identity were the basis of egoistic concern, the concept of a time-relative interest would be otiose. But if identity is not the basis of egoistic concern and the prudential unity relations can hold to varying degrees, we need a concept that is temporally relativized—one that expresses the idea that the degree of rationally warranted egoistic concern over some possible event may vary over time depending on the strength of the prudential unity relations.

I will conclude this section by returning to the claim that psychological unity is among the prudential unity relations. There is an important objection to this claim, which is that it seems to imply that personal growth and improvement are, in prospect at least, undesirable insofar as they would involve a weakening of psychological unity between oneself before they would occur and oneself afterwards. For growth and improvement necessarily involve changes of belief, desire, and character—that is, severings of various kinds of psychological connection. Thus, to the extent that growth and improvement involve a weakening of psychological unity over time, they diminish the strength of one's time-relative interests in the goods of one's future.

Two points may be made in reply. First, personal improvement is typically the product of a person's own efforts; it results from a person's conscious striving after a certain ideal of character or action. When this is the case, although the evolution of character may involve the severing of certain psychological connections that would otherwise have held (for example, connections of belief, desire, or disposition), it also involves the establishment of other connections, often at a higher level (for example, between the formation and the satisfaction of a second-order desire to overcome an obsessive or obstructive first-order desire). The establishment of psychological connections through the intentional molding of character may actually strengthen overall psychological integration over time. A life in which there is substantial change and diversity may, if the diverse elements of the psychology are held together by strands of desire and intention, be unified in a deeper and richer way than a life in which one's character remains largely static. (This suggests that, of the two types of psychological connection distinguished earlier—those that involve the mere persistence of some psychological property and those that involve mental states that somehow refer to one another—the latter are more deeply psychologically unifying than the former.)

In some cases, however, personal growth or improvement just *happens* to a person, without conscious effort and perhaps without the person even being aware that it is occurring. In this kind of case, there may actually be a net loss of psychological integration. It is well to remember, however, that we are discussing growth and improvement rather than pathological conditions involving significant erosions of psychological connectedness. Even in the more dramatic instances of unintended change—for example, moral or religious conversion—the effect on overall psychological unity over time is relatively insignificant. Thus even when there is some attenuation of psychological connectedness, growth or improvement may still be desirable, for the enhancement of virtue or rationality may increase the good in one's life, or make one a higher or better being, in such a way as to outweigh the comparatively trivial weakening of psychological unity over time. (It is worth noting, however, that there is a limit to the extent to which the good derived from the enhancement of one's mind or character can offset the weakening of psychological unity—at least in principle, if not in practice. If it were possible—for example, through some exotic form of genetic therapy—for a person to become suddenly like a god, altogether different and unimaginably higher in character, it is not obvious that it would be in that person's time-relative interest to do so. I will return to this point in section 6.3 of chapter 4.)

I have suggested that certain kinds of psychological connection between mental states that refer to one another—particularly "higher-order" connections such as that between the formation and the satisfaction of a desire to live a certain kind of life or to be a certain kind of person—are more deeply unifying psychologically than connections that consist in the mere persistence of a psychological state. This seems to imply the desirability of maintaining one's links with one's past through the exercise of memory and of trying to anticipate and prepare for the future. Yet this seems contrary to the folk wisdom that urges immersion in the present or, in the Buddhist idiom, mindfulness of what is occurring at the moment. I suggest, however, that, at least if the folk wisdom is generously interpreted, there need be no conflict. The common exhortation to focus on the present may mean only to avoid becoming so preoccupied with the future that the goods of the present pass by unnoticed; or it may mean to adjust one's concern about the future to take account of uncertainty, for there is no point in sacrificing the present to evils that may never occur. It is also worse than pointless to contaminate the present with brooding about future evils when nothing can be done to avert them. Thus, in times of affliction the advice of the Reverend Sydney Smith, recently quoted with approval by John Bayley in his account of Iris Murdoch's descent into dementia, may make good sense: "Take short views of human life—never further than dinner or tea."[91]

Beyond conditions of adversity, however, it is primarily our ability, through memory and imagination, to transcend the temporally and spatially local that raises us above the level of animals. As Samuel Johnson once noted, "Whatever withdraws us from the power of our senses; whatever makes the past, the distant, or the future predominate over the present, advances us in the dignity of thinking beings."[92] Consider, by contrast, Aldous Huxley's description of a woman whose "life was spent in enjoying the successive instants of present contentment of which it was composed; and if ever circumstances forced her out of this mindless eternity into the world of time, it was a narrow little universe in which she found herself, a world whose farthest boundaries were never more than a week or two away."[93] If a person who lives this way does so deliberately—on principle, as it were—that very shaping of the life around an ideal of atemporality may give it a certain overall psychological integrity. If, however, the immersion in a mindless eternity is unreflective, it reduces the life uncomfortably near to the level of a non-self-conscious animal. One cannot get much more deeply immersed in the present, while remaining a human being, than Clive Wearing.

5.3. *Possible Divergences between Identity and Egoistic Concern*

In what ways might the Embodied Mind Account and the Embodied Mind Account of Egoistic Concern diverge? Might there be identity but no basis for egoistic concern? Or, alternatively, might there be a basis for egoistic concern in the absence of identity? Because the Embodied Mind Account of Egoistic Concern holds that the relations that are constitutive of identity are part of what matters, it seems that identity guarantees that there will be some basis for egoistic concern, however minimal. As I noted in section 4.4, there might be some doubt about this in hypothetical cases in which the same embodied mind continues to exist for an extremely long period of time but with little psychological connectedness from day to day. But in all actual cases, within the space of an actual human life span, when enough of the brain will persist to carry forward the conscious life of the original subject, there seems to be some basis for egoistic concern about the future even if (as in later phases of Alz-heimer's disease) there will be no connectedness from day to day.

There are two familiar types of case, both hypothetical, in which there might be a basis for egoistic concern in the absence of identity. One of these is when a person undergoes fission, as in the case of Division. The other is when two or more people undergo fusion.[94] Consider:

> *Fusion.* You and I are friends. Each of us has lost one cerebral hemisphere as a re-sult of a stroke. Each of us also has a condition that will soon result in the death of his brainstem. Another friend of ours has suffered the death of his entire cerebrum, though his brainstem and body remain intact and functional. Before he lapsed into the persistent vegetative state, this friend agreed to donate his body so that either my or your surviving hemisphere could be transplanted into it. Unable to choose that one of us should survive while the other dies, we decide that both our hemispheres should be transplanted into that body where, in order to function in a coordinated way, their severed corpora callosa will be joined.

There are various ways of understanding what happens in this case. One is that, when our hemispheres are harnessed together in the body of our friend, there is only one person there. This will seem reasonable if our hemispheres function together in roughly the way that paired hemispheres normally do, generating substantial unity of consciousness despite the high levels of cognitive dissonance resulting from the fu-sion of the elements of our disparate mental lives. Suppose that this is right: there is only one person there. Who is it? Most of us will reject the claim that it is the friend whose body this was before he lapsed into a persistent vegetative state. There may be some reason to suppose that the person is me; but there is presumably equal reason to suppose that he is you. This is more obviously the case if each of our surviving hemispheres was the dominant hemisphere prior to the operation. If there is only one person, he cannot be both of us, as this would imply that you and I were all along the same person. We may therefore conclude that this is an entirely new person—someone who is not identical with anyone who existed prior to the double transplant operation.

This person has, however, enough of my brain to generate consciousness and mental activity. He also has enough of yours. In this case, therefore, the relations that are constitutive of personal identity branch, but backwards rather than forwards in time. If the relations that are constitutive of identity are part of what matters, this per-son will be related to you and to me in a way that makes it rational for both of us, prior to the operation, to be egoistically concerned about him, even though he will *be* neither of us. This, then, seems to be another case in which identity and what matters fail to coincide according to the Embodied Mind Account. (There are, it should be noted, several respects in which the basis for egoistic concern may be weaker in this case. First, even the relations that are normally constitutive of identity may be weaker in both my case and yours as a result of the strokes we suffered earlier. Second, as Parfit notes, some of what matters to me may be lost if elements of my psychology clash with yours. If the new person is not to be forever at war with himself, some of my beliefs, tastes, desires, intentions, and so on may have to be abandoned or, alter-natively, may simply be crowded out by the conflicting elements of your mental life.

And even those elements that survive may be diluted by the pervasive presence of an alien psychology.)

There is a third possible way in which identity and egoistic concern might diverge. Suppose, as seems to be true, that certain elements of a person's mental life are located in precisely delimited tissues of the brain. This seems to be true, for example, of memories. Next, consider again the possibility I mentioned earlier that a particular memory trace might be surgically extracted from my brain and grafted onto yours in such a way that it becomes accessible to your consciousness. If this were to be done, it seems that there would be no branching of the relations that are constitutive of identity. I would continue to exist here in the body that I had always inhabited. For a single memory trace does not seem to constitute enough of my brain to be capable of generating consciousness or mental activity. This would not be a case in which my mind would divide, forming two new minds; rather, a tiny portion of my mind would become a part of your mind. Because you and I would thus remain distinct, this would also not be a case involving fusion. But there is a question here about what matters. The brain graft would establish a real psychological connection between me now and you at later time. Would this transfer of a real element of my mental life to your mind give me a reason for egoistic concern about what might happen to you in the future?

Imagine that the transfer is not of a single memory but of ten, or a hundred. With each increase in number, there is greater blending of my mind with yours. But even the grafting of a thousand distinct memory traces from my brain to yours would not constitute an instance of fission followed by fusion. Even a thousand bits of tissue from my brain, each consisting of a single memory, would not constitute enough of my brain to support consciousness and mental activity. But the grafting of a thousand memory traces from my brain into yours would establish a significant degree of psychological connectedness between us. With the numbers thus increased, it may seem more reasonable for me, prior to the grafting of the tissues, to feel some degree of egoistic concern about what might happen to you after the grafts had been completed.

I suspect that there may be irresoluble disagreement, and perhaps genuine indeterminacy, about what matters in these cases involving the grafting of limited portions of one brain into another. Even those whose intuitions support the Embodied Mind Account of Egoistic Concern may be unable to agree about whether grafting provides a basis for egoistic concern. One might think that if some small portions of one's brain bearing elements of one's psychology were about to be grafted into the brain of another, the prospect would merely be that one would lose some aspects of one's mental life while someone else's mind would be gaining access to them. That, one might hold, would be an insufficient basis for any degree of egoistic concern, no matter how minimal. Alternatively, one might reflect that the grafts would mean that portions of one's own mind would be blended with but preserved within the mental life of another; there would be a partial fusion of one's own mind with that of the other person, even though the other person's mind would remain the dominant presence. When understood in this way, it may seem more reasonable to be egoistically concerned, if only minimally, about the person into whom some elements of one's own mind would be transferred.

How are we to understand the Embodied Mind Account of Egoistic Concern, given this uncertainty about grafting? One may distinguish two competing conceptions of what matters, either of which might be paired with or be held to correspond to the Embodied Mind Account of Identity. According to one view, the relations that are constitutive of personal identity are a necessary and sufficient condition for egoistic concern. For one to have reason to be egoistically concerned about some future individual, that individual must have enough of one's brain to be able to support consciousness. This is the minimal condition both for identity and for egoistic concern. The more the individual will have of the relevant functional areas of one's brain, and thus the more of one's mind that will be preserved or carried forward, the stronger one's basis will be for egoistic concern about that individual.

According to the second view, the relations that are constitutive of identity are sufficient for egoistic concern but not necessary. Any degree of real psychological connectedness, even in the absence of identity, is a sufficient basis for some, perhaps minimal, degree of egoistic concern. On this view, grafting would be a basis for egoistic concern.

I have suggested that we may reasonably remain agnostic between these two views. Neither is rationally compelling; neither is obviously wrong. So we may leave it undecided whether grafting constitutes a third type of case in which identity and what matters might diverge according to the Embodied Mind Account.

These apparently alternative conceptions of what matters might be coextensive, given a certain understanding of what would count as "enough" of the same brain. For it might be said that, if some tissue from one's brain in which only a single mental state (for example, a single memory) was realized were grafted into another person's brain, that grafted tissue would constitute enough of one's brain to support consciousness. For, in its new setting, that memory could be a conscious mental state. A part of one's brain would, in a sense, be supporting consciousness.

This, clearly, is not the sense of "enough of the brain to support consciousness" that one needs for the Embodied Mind Account. It seems absurd to regard a single graft as constituting an instance of asymmetrical fission in which one of the descendent minds undergoes fusion with another. The question is how we can exclude this understanding of "enough of the same brain to support consciousness." Perhaps we can stipulate that it means "enough of the same brain to be capable of supporting consciousness without assistance from tissues drawn from any other brain." When we consider the case of the brain graft, we understand why this stipulation is not ad hoc: continuity of mind involves more than just the preservation of some element or elements of one's mental life. The capacity for consciousness must be preserved in the same tissues of the same brain; it cannot be imported from a different brain, for that would not be the same consciousness.

The problem with this response is that the regions of the brain in which the conscious mind is realized are incapable of generating conscious mental activity on their own. As I noted in section 2 of this chapter, the reticular formation, which is located primarily in the brainstem and apparently contributes nothing to the contents of consciousness, must nevertheless be functional in order for consciousness to be generated by and in the relevant areas of the higher brain. But continuity of one and the same reticular formation does not appear to be a condition of personal identity. As I noted earlier, because the reticular formation appears to function as an on-off switch for consciousness without any of the actual stuff of consciousness being realized in its tissues, sameness of consciousness does not seem to require sameness of reticular formation. One could survive the replacement of one's reticular formation with a transplanted substitute in just the same way that one could survive a heart transplant. *That* part of the brain could be imported from another without compromising one's identity, despite the fact that it is clearly involved in the production of consciousness.

Our criterion of personal identity, therefore, should not require "enough of the same brain to be capable of supporting consciousness." It must instead require "enough of those regions of the same brain in which consciousness occurs to be able, with relevant support systems, to continue to support consciousness." And it must be understood that the support systems necessary for the generation of consciousness cannot include tissues from another brain in which consciousness or conscious states are realized, though they can include other tissues from a different brain, such as the reticular formation. The support systems are necessary for the mind to work, though they may not be necessary for one's survival. Thus one might survive in a coma if one's reticular formation were damaged and incapable of functioning. (I will return to this in section 1.3 of chapter 5.) Loss of other support systems, such as a blood supply to the brain, normally leads not only to loss of functionality in the areas in which consciousness occurs but also rather rapidly to their destruction.

In what areas of the brain is consciousness actually realized? At present this is not known with any accuracy, although it does seem that the relevant areas are in the cerebral hemispheres rather than in the brainstem. Some scientists have speculated that there is a specific localized area of the brain in which consciousness is realized, while many of the objects of conscious awareness, such as memories, are physically stored elsewhere in the brain and episodically brought within the scope of consciousness by being somehow accessed by the mechanisms in the consciousness-generating area.[95] If this is right, it is the functional continuity of this area of the brain that is the criterion of personal identity and perhaps the basis of (that is, the necessary and sufficient condition of) egoistic concern as well. (The fact that a person can retain the capacity for consciousness following the loss of either hemisphere, together with evidence of divided consciousness in the commissurotomy cases, indicates that, if there is such an area, it must somehow span both hemispheres and be potentially divisible.)

Alternatively, consciousness might be a global function of the combined, simultaneous operations of many areas of the brain. Rather than arising from any single site, it might be a property of various areas functioning in unison. If this is right, it may be more difficult to distinguish between those areas of the brain in which consciousness is realized and those that are essentially just support systems.

5.4. The Individuation of Minds

Let us turn from the issue of grafting (which at present is of merely theoretical interest) to a range or further questions raised by the Embodied Mind Account. There are, first, questions about the unity of the mind. The most fundamental such question is whether the same brain could support the existence of more than one mind. This question divides into two more specific questions. First, might the same brain support more than one mind at a single time? And, second, might the same brain support more than one mind at different times?

There are phenomena that challenge our assumptions about the synchronic unity of mind: in particular, cases of commissurotomy and cases of multiple personality disorder. I will not comment on the latter; there is as yet insufficient understanding of what actually goes on in these cases, and in particular little understanding of the neurological bases of the disorder.[96] In the case of the commissurotomy patients, most observers, including the patients themselves, believe that each brain with divided hemispheres supports the existence of only one mind. Even in these cases, there is substantial subjective unity. Following the operations, the patients typically notice no difference and those close to them report very few behavioral anomalies. Although each hemisphere no longer has "direct access" to conscious events in the other via the corpus callosum, they find other ways to communicate. Nevertheless, it seems well documented through experimentation that the brains of these patients support two separate and distinct centers of consciousness. This has led some to claim that there must have been two centers of consciousness prior to the commissurotomy operation and thus that each of us actually has two centers of consciousness. All the commissurotomy operation does is to make this more apparent by disrupting the smooth and instantaneous exchange of information between them.

There is nothing, I think, that compels us to accept the inference that there must have been two centers of consciousness prior to the operation. It is compatible with what we know about these cases that prior to the operation, all conscious events in the brain were accessible within the same field of consciousness. The severing of the corpus callosum might have the effect of dividing what was a single field of consciousness into two distinct fields. The challenge that these cases pose is not necessarily to the unity of consciousness prior to the operation, but to our intuitive identification of "same mind" with "same consciousness." Whatever is the case about the unity of consciousness in an undivided brain, it seems clear that in the divided brains there are two centers of consciousness; yet most observers do not conclude that there must therefore be two minds present. These cases pry us away from our intuitive understanding of the mind as having or being a single center or field of consciousness. They confront us with a dilemma: either we must accept that the post-operative patients have two minds (and therefore are perhaps two distinct people) or we must accept that it is possible for a single mind to have separate centers of consciousness. But if a single mind can have more than one center of consciousness, we seem to be left with no clear criterion for the individuation of minds. What makes two or more centers of consciousness a single mind rather than a collection of different minds?

It is not just that the separate centers of consciousness in the commissurotomy cases are generated by the same brain. We can imagine that the results of the operation might have been different. Suppose that following the operation, the patients had begun to behave in increasingly anomalous ways. Suppose that as time passed, their left hands began to write out messages expressing desires, feelings, and beliefs contrary to those they articulated verbally, that (as in Stanley Kubrick's film *Dr. Strangelove*) one of their hands would often interfere with what the other was doing, and that their bodies would often move haltingly in one direction and then another, eventually becoming immobilized, even though they would say that they wanted to go somewhere. (When the dicephalic Hensel twins cannot agree about where to go, they become incapable of moving anywhere. Each controls half of their shared body; neither can drag the other half of the body against her twin's will.)[97] If events of this sort had begun to occur consistently, on a daily basis, we would, I think, have accepted that there were two minds present, both supported by the operations of a single brain. If the results of commissurotomy had been like this, it would have been plausible to regard the procedure as a form of Division. It seems, therefore, that whether a range of mental phenomena constitute one mind or two depends not only on whether the phenomena are generated by one brain or two, but also on the degree of integration among the various mental events. The actual cases of commissurotomy show that our concept of a mind is tolerant of a limited degree of mental fragmentation, even to the extent of accepting that a single mind can encompass more than one center of consciousness. But as the degree of separation between centers of consciousness increases, with each developing a distinctive mental life of its own, it becomes increasingly plausible to recognize the existence of more than one mind.

Might the same brain support different minds serially? There seem to be at least two possibilities. (Multiple personality is possibly a third.) First, suppose that certain regions of a particular brain necessary for the generation of consciousness were removed and replaced by corresponding tissues from a different brain. If the areas replaced constituted only a tiny proportion of the original brain (for example, if only certain portions of the cerebral cortex were replaced), it would be reasonable to suppose that the same brain existed both before and after the replacement. But the mind generated by the new consciousness-supporting tissues would arguably be different. Second, recall the possibility I noted earlier: that consciousness might be a function of the operation of some specific region of the brain. Suppose that that is correct and that the relevant region (whatever it might be) of a particular brain is destroyed. If somehow a different region of the same brain were then reconfigured so that it acquired the capacity to support consciousness, the mind generated in this different area would arguably be a different mind—even if the reconfigured area functioned in part by casting the spotlight of consciousness on memories, desires, and so on preserved in other areas of the brain in which they were originally registered.[98]

5.5. Mind, Brain, and Organism

It might be thought that one who claims that we are essentially embodied minds must be prepared to say what the relation between the mind and the brain is. I believe, however, that the defender of the Embodied Mind Account may remain agnostic about this. For all of the plausible understandings of the relation between mind and brain agree that the mind is *either* causally generated by *or* identical with certain parts of the brain when they are in certain states, and hence that the mind cannot be tracked or traced independently of the brain. The continued existence of the same mind thus requires the continued existence and functioning of certain regions of the same brain irrespective of whether mental states are brain states, functional states, or causal products of brain states. In short, the Embodied Mind Account is compatible with virtually all of the leading theories about the relation between the mind and the brain: identity theories, functionalist theories, property dualism, dual aspect theory, and so on. The one obvious exception is of course cartesian dualism, but I have presented arguments for rejecting that view earlier in section 2.

A considerably more problematic question for the Embodied Mind Account is what the relation is between the mind and the human organism—or alternatively, on the assumption that one *is* a mind, between oneself and one's physical organism. Following the arguments I presented in section 3 of this chapter, the Embodied Mind Account denies that the relation is identity. But an account that denies that we are organisms owes us an alternative account of what the relation is between ourselves and our organisms.

The Psychological Account also implicitly denies that we are organisms. Some proponents of that view have contended that our organisms stand to us in the relation of *constitution*. Sidney Shoemaker describes the relation in this way:

> One can allow that there is a sense of "is" in which a person is an animal. But this will not be the "is" of predication or of identity; it will be, perhaps, the sort of "is" we have in "The statue is a hunk of bronze"—it will mean something like "is composed of the very same stuff as." Arguably, the statue and the hunk of bronze are not one and the same thing, since if the hunk of bronze were hammered into another statue, the statue we had originally would no longer exist, but the hunk of bronze would still be there. So two things, the statue and the hunk of bronze, can occupy the same place and share the same matter and the same non-historical properties. . . . The suggestion is that a person "is" an animal, not in the sense of being identical to one, but in the sense of sharing its matter with one.[99]

Let us call the view articulated here the "constitution view." According to this view, one is composed of the same matter as one's organism and shares its nonhistorical properties. One's organism also shares one's own nonhistorical properties. This, however, leads to a serious problem, first noticed, I believe, by W. R. Carter. I am now conscious; therefore my organism must also be conscious. "Are we then to say," Carter asks, "that *two* conscious beings presently are located in the chair in which I am sitting? Doesn't 'my' organism feel a toothache when I feel a toothache? How many toothaches are in question in such a case? Those of us who believe that there is only one toothache. . . , and who also believe that different beings do not (ordinarily at least) feel the same toothache, will say that we *are* our organisms."[100]

There is some scope for misunderstanding here. The idea that I am constituted by my organism does not imply that there are two toothaches or two consciousnesses. But it does imply something that Carter finds odd: namely, that I and my organism feel the same toothache. The oddness of this implication may be mitigated somewhat by consideration of the analogy with the relation between the statue and the hunk of bronze. The statue and the hunk of bronze share the same shape. But that does not mean that there are two qualitatively identical shapes present. There is only one shape. The two entities share numerically one and the same shape, which is not surprising if they share the same matter. Still, the appeal to the analogy does not eliminate the oddness of the constitution view entirely. For this view does imply that there are now two conscious entities present in my chair (even if there is only one consciousness that they share), and that clearly seems to be one too many.

The constitution view faces another objection. To articulate this objection, we need a word or phrase that indicates what we essentially are. To refer to ourselves as minds may be literally correct; but it is unfamiliar. So, in order to articulate this second objection to the constitution view, it will be convenient to use the term "person" to refer in a generic way to what we essentially are. In stating the following argument, therefore, I drop the assumption that I have hitherto made that to be a person one must have the capacity for self-consciousness and, perhaps, a mental life with a high degree of unity.

1. One is a person by virtue of one's possession of certain nonhistorical properties—for example, the capacity for consciousness.
2. The possession of these properties is necessary and sufficient for being a person.
3. If one is constituted by one's organism, one's organism shares all of one's nonhistorical properties.
4. One's organism must therefore have the properties that are necessary and sufficient for being a person.
5. One's organism must therefore *be* a person rather than merely constituting one.
6. If one is a person and one's organism is a person, and if one is not identical with one's organism, there must be two persons present where one is now: oneself and one's organism.

The conclusion—claim 6—violates the assumption that there can be no more than one entity of a particular kind at a given place at a given time.

A parallel argument can be formulated in support of the conclusion that we are organisms.

1. An entity is an organism by virtue of possessing certain nonhistorical properties.
2. The possession of these properties is necessary and sufficient for being an organism.
3. If one is constituted by one's organism, one shares all of its nonhistorical properties.
4. One must therefore have the properties that are necessary and sufficient for being an organism.
5. One must therefore *be* an organism rather than merely sharing one's matter with one.

The final claim—5—contradicts the motivating assumption of the constitution view that one is not identical with one's organism (or, of course, any other organism).

These objections challenge the coherence of the notion of constitution, suggesting that it collapses into the relation of identity.[101] It would, however, be surprising if philosophical logicians had all along been mistaken in supposing that there is a coherent notion of constitution. (Notice that parallel arguments could be formulated to show that the statue is—the "is" of identity—a hunk of bronze and that the hunk of bronze is a statue.) Perhaps the defender of the constitution view can respond by denying the second premise in each of these arguments. Perhaps the mere possession of the defining properties of a certain type of entity is not sufficient for actually being an entity of that type. Suppose, for example, that the capacity for consciousness is a defining property of persons (where "person" is understood to be a substance sortal). Nevertheless, possession of the capacity for consciousness (together with any other defining properties of persons) might not be sufficient for actually being a person. Instead, it might be necessary for being a person that one possess the defining properties of personhood as *essential* properties. That is, to be a person, not only must one have the defining properties of personhood, but it must also be impossible for one to exist without them. So, for example, because one has the capacity for consciousness and could not exist without it, one satisfies the conditions for being a person. But although one's organism has the capacity for consciousness (according to the constitution view), it does not have this property essentially. For it could lose the capacity for consciousness and yet continue to exist. (No one supposes that the capacity for consciousness is an essential property of organisms—not even of human organisms.) Thus, on the view I am suggesting, the organism would not be a person even though it possessed the defining properties of a person.[102]

Even if the coherence of the constitution view can be defended in this way (or perhaps in some other way), this view still leaves us with the unsettling implication that there are two conscious entities occupying my chair at the moment. Perhaps we should explore alternatives to the constitution view that either avoid this implication or at least elucidate it in a way that makes it less bizarre.

One option is to abandon the assumption of the constitution view that I and my organism share all of each other's nonhistorical properties. If I am not identical with my organism, and if I am now conscious and there is only one conscious entity in my chair, it follows that my organism is not conscious. Perhaps, indeed, *no* psychological properties are in a literal way ascribable to the organism. If we say, for example, that this organism is hungry, that is just an oblique or elliptical way of saying that I am. Similarly, it may be that not all of my organism's physical properties are literally ascribable to me. As Parfit points out, to say that I weigh 150 pounds when it is literally this organism that does might be analogous to saying that I got splashed with mud when it was literally only my coat that got mud on it.[103] While there are two distinct substances occupying my chair as I write (an implication that seems unavoidable if we assume that I am not identical with my organism and that each of us is a substance rather than, for example, a mere phase in the history of something else), these two substances divide between them at least some of the properties that the constitution view holds that they share. Let us call this view *radical dualism.*[104]

Radical dualism conceives of the human organism as what Warren Quinn has called a "subentity." The following remarks of Quinn's apply to the human body but, insofar as the body is distinguishable from the organism, they could equally well apply to the organism. Understood as a subentity, the human body,

> while logically incapable of intentional actions (that is, unable to read, converse, perceive), is the *primary agent* of a human being's metabolic and purely reflexive activities. So conceived, it is our body that digests, that converts nourishment to protoplasm, that sweats, that jerks when struck in certain ways, and *we* (human beings) are seen to metabolize, jerk, sweat, or even to occupy physical space only because our bodies do. According to this conception, we supervene upon, contain, or bear some other exotic relation to a distinguishable source of activities which then become attributable to us by a kind of logical courtesy.[105]

This is quite difficult to accept. W. R. Carter objects that "there is reason to think that 'higher forms' of animal life can and do feel pain (hunger, fear, etc.) and so reason to think that a variety of physical organisms are in some sense *conscious* beings. Surely there is no plausibility to the thesis that non-human organisms are conscious beings and human organisms are not."[106] What this shows, I think, is not that psychological predicates must be applicable to human organisms but that radical dualism, to be consistent, must deny that psychological predicates apply to *any* organisms. Carter's argument appeals to our sense that it is a truism that animals simply *are* organisms. But the same arguments that purport to show that we are not identical with our organisms are also applicable to sentient animals. If, for example, my dog Rufus's cerebrum were transplanted into the body of a different dog, the dog with Rufus's cerebrum would be Rufus, while the organism that Rufus once animated, and which would still exist and might indeed continue to live, would be a different individual. Thus radical dualism must hold that any conscious subject, any being with a mind, is distinct from the organism it animates and in which it is embodied. And it must hold that, whenever an organism supports the existence of a mind or conscious subject, psychological properties are directly and literally ascribable only to the latter and are ascribable to the organism only by extension or "logical courtesy."

In denying that organisms have psychological properties, radical dualism seems coherent; but it is offensive to common sense. It seems perverse, for example, to deny that, when a developing organism's brain acquires the capacity to support consciousness, the organism itself becomes conscious. Moreover, even though radical dualism enables us to avoid the implication that there are two conscious beings in my chair at the moment, it does not itself offer an account of the nature of the relation between the person and the organism. We should see whether there is an alternative understanding that illuminates the nature of the relation and is more respectful of common sense.

One possibility is that the relation between ourselves and our organisms is the relation of part to whole. This suggestion will seem most cogent if we assume that the mind is entirely reducible to certain regions of the brain. If, for example, the mind just *is* those regions of the brain in certain functional states, and if I am this mind, then I am, in effect, this functional brain, which is itself a part of this organism; therefore I am a part of my organism. But even if the mind is not entirely reducible to the brain, it is still something that is generated by the operations of the brain and is a critical component of the systems controlling the functions of the organism. Hence it may be regarded as a part of the organism even if it is not so obviously a part as is an organ such as the brain.

It makes sense to think of an organism as having a mind among its many and various parts. Accordingly, it makes sense to think of the organism as having at least some of the psychological properties of the mind by virtue of having the mind as a part.[107] Thus the organism may be said to be conscious by virtue of having a mind that is conscious. Does this imply that there are two conscious entities where I am now? Perhaps it does, but we can now explain this fact in a way that seems benign rather than bizarre. Suppose, for the sake of comparison, that over a certain period of time the only part of a tree that grows is a particular limb. When this limb grows, the tree grows. The tree grows by virtue of having a part that grows. A property of the part— growth—is in this instance necessarily a property of the whole. There are thus two things that are growing: the limb and the tree of which it is a part. Similarly, when I blow the horn in my car, the horn makes a noise but so does the car. There are two things that have the property of emitting a noise: the horn and the car of which it is a part. In the same sense in which the tree grows because its limb does, and in which the car honks because its horn does, my organism may be said to think, feel, and perceive because I do. This is just another case in which a whole (the organism) has certain properties by virtue of having a part (the mind or person) that has those properties.

These analogies help elucidate the sense in which there are two conscious entities present where I am. My organism is conscious only in a derivative sense, only by virtue of having a conscious part. Similarly, when I blow the horn of my car, the car makes a noise only in the sense that one of its parts makes a noise. There is only one noise; and there is a clear sense in which there is only one noisemaker: the horn. But we attribute the making of the noise not just to the horn but also, in a derivative way, to the larger whole that contains it. It is clear, however, that the car is not some additional occult presence that mysteriously joins the horn in producing the honking noise. Nor is the organism as a whole involved in the experience of consciousness except by containing that which is conscious.

This view preserves the claim that we are not identical with our organisms. It seems, indeed, a conceptual truth that a part is not identical with the whole of which it is a part. According to this view, I am not identical with an organism, nor am I constituted by one; but I am a part of one. I am, however, a separable part, one capable of existing and retaining its identity and integrity apart from the whole. If I were to be separated from my organism, as would happen if my cerebrum were transplanted into a different organism, my own essential nature would not be diminished. Thus, even though I am now a part of this organism, I am a distinct and independent substance. I am, indeed, a whole, with parts of my own. This is not uncommon: it is often the case that a thing may itself be a whole, comprised of many parts, while at the same time being a part not just of a single larger whole but of numerous different wholes.

Recall that, according to the constitution view, I and my organism share all of the same nonhistorical properties. This, I noted, makes it at least prima facie puzzling why I am not an organism (in the sense of being identical with one) and my organism is not a person. If, however, I am a part of my organism, there is no reason to suppose that I must share all of my organism's properties or that it must have all of mine. A part may share some of the properties of the whole to which it belongs but not others. My car's horn, for example, has the property of traveling at sixty miles per hour when the car has that property, but does not share with the car the property of weighing a ton. And as we have seen, my car has the property of emitting a honking noise when its horn does, but it does not share with the horn the property of weighing exactly three pounds. If, similarly, I do not have all of my organism's properties and it does not have all of mine, the challenge of explaining why I am not an organism and it is not a person does not arise.

Our actual practice in ascribing properties to ourselves and our organisms is not particularly revealing. Typically, one tends to ascribe all of the properties of one's organism to oneself. Yet one may be reluctant to ascribe all of one's psychological properties to the organism. For example, one may acknowledge that one is in a bad mood and yet resist the claim that one's organism is. Perhaps, however, this is to conflate the organism with the body. Many writers distinguish between the two. Perhaps it is just the body that fails to share one's psychological properties; perhaps the organism, which is, after all, an animal, shares them. (For example, although it seems absurd to say that one's body is in a bad mood, it may make sense to say that one's organism is.) If our practice were not only to ascribe the physical properties of our organisms to ourselves but also to ascribe our psychological properties to our organisms, that would tend to support the constitution view. Yet a case can be made that in practice we do not discriminate sharply between the body and the organism. Thus one tends to ascribe all of the properties of one's body to oneself. If, for example, my body has a freckle, *I* have a freckle. And we often apply psychological predicates to bodies or parts of bodies—for example, when we say that a person has a pain in her toe. It is not obvious that there is anything substantive to be gleaned from our actual practices in ascribing properties to persons, organisms, and bodies.

It is curious, nonetheless, that one tends to ascribe all of the properties of one's organism to oneself. For typically a part does not have all of the properties of the whole to which it belongs. If I am just a part of this organism, how could I have *all* of its properties? Perhaps the explanation is that I am the master or controlling part: from my point of view, the rest of the organism functions to sustain my existence, serves as a vehicle for my agency, and provides me with sensory access to the external world. In short, although I am only a part of this organism, I am the conscious and controlling part and therefore tend to regard its other parts as extensions of myself. This may also help to explain the common view—of which the view I have espoused is an inversion—that this organism is a part of me. Because I control these hands, I regard them as parts of me. But this common view, if taken literally, seems implausible. On this view, my organism would be one of my parts (thus my hands would be parts of one of my parts). What other part or parts am I supposed to have that, together with the organism, constitute the whole that is me? If there is no soul, the only other part I might have is my mind. But unlike the soul, the mind is itself generated by the operations of one part of the organism: the brain. Therefore it does not seem to be independent from the organism in the way that is necessary in order for the mind and the organism to be distinct parts that together compose individuals such as you and me.

Another worry about the idea that one is a part of one's organism is that it may seem that mere parts are not fully real entities, or at least that status as a part is rather lowly, and certainly ontologically subordinate or inferior to status as a whole. One response to this concern is to note that some philosophers have held an opposing view according to which only the more basic constituents of the world (for example, atoms, or latterly, fundamental particles) are fully real, and that all else (including all the wholes of which these basic elements are the parts) are mere logical constructions. Alternatively, it might be argued that there is in fact no ontological hierarchy in which parts are generally ranked lower than wholes, or wholes higher than parts. As I noted earlier, many things are simultaneously both parts and wholes. Thus one may be a whole mind, with parts consisting of mental states, even if one is also a part of an organism, or a whole person at the same time that one is a part of a family or a nation. Hence, to be recognized as a part is not tantamount to demotion from full to merely partial reality.

2

Death

Our ultimate aim is to understand the morality of killing. In those instances in which killing is wrong, it seems that it must be a critical component of the explanation of why it is wrong that it causes something dreadful to happen to the victim: it causes him to die. It is, indeed, natural to suppose that it is because it is normally such a terrible misfortune to die that murder is, in general, the most grievously immoral of crimes. Murder is the most egregious crime because what it inflicts is, in general, the gravest harm: death.

If this is right, we must, to understand the morality of killing, understand why and to what extent death is bad for those who die and, in particular, whether some deaths may be worse than others. The question here is not whether one death can be worse than another in the manner of its occurrence, for of course it can: one death may, for example, be more painful or less dignified than another. Nor is the question whether one person's death can be worse than another's for people other than the victims. The answer to that is also obvious: the death of a person who is widely loved and on whom many others depend will be worse for the survivors than the death of a person who was simply a nuisance. Our question is instead whether, holding the manner of death constant, one person may suffer a greater harm in simply ceasing to exist than another. If the answer to this question is "Yes," this raises the further question whether, if other things are equal, it would be more seriously wrong to kill the one person than to kill the other.

There are many who believe that the degree to which an act of killing is wrong varies, if other things are equal, with the extent to which it harms its victim and therefore with the extent to which death is bad for the victim. I will examine this and a closely related view in detail in chapter 3. If either of these views is correct, then in order to determine how seriously wrong an act of killing is, it is essential be able to determine, so far as is possible, how bad death is for the victim. Thus, it is if this way of understanding the wrongness of killing is correct that the subject of this chapter is most relevant to the morality of killing. It would, however, be unduly coy to conceal at this point my conviction that this type of view is mistaken. Nevertheless, a view of this sort will have a crucial role in my larger argument. While such a view seems un-

95

acceptable as a *general* account of the wrongness of killing, it is, I believe, substantially correct as an account of the morality of *some* acts of killing with which this book will be particularly concerned.

The evaluation of death is, moreover, of interest in its own right. The subject is of intense personal interest to many people, particularly those who are oppressed by an obsessive or morbid fear of death. In attempting to reconcile themselves to mortality, or to achieve a modus vivendi with the prospect of death, these people often seek wisdom in the writings of great thinkers from the past. But what they are more likely to find there is a dreary record of evasion and sophistry.

Just as ordinary people tend to do, many otherwise sagacious people have succumbed to one or another strategy of denial. Often they avert their thoughts altogether, dismissing death from their minds with the aid of shibboleths such as "We all have to go sometime," without bothering to consider whether it is worse to go earlier rather than later. More commonly they anesthetize themselves with visions of a beatific afterlife. Even Socrates, for example, serenely drank his hemlock while prating about his "hope to obtain the greatest good in the other world" and the opportunities he hoped to have to "converse with Orpheus, Musaeus and Hesiod and Homer."[1] Epicurus and his followers had very different and more interesting arguments for denying that death can be bad for those who die. I have, however, criticized these arguments at length elsewhere and will not repeat those criticisms here.[2]

The practice of wringing a meager drop of consolation from the rags of bad argument reaches its apogee in the work of Schopenhauer, who otherwise confronted reality so unflinchingly that he arrived at a vastly grimmer conception of it than is warranted. He is notorious for having maintained that life is never worth living, that it would have been better had none of us ever existed. This should, of course, have dictated his view of death, assuming that to die is to cease to exist. He should have concluded that death is always to be welcomed as a release from a life of intolerable misery. But although he gestured at this inference in passing, he never really embraced it and certainly did not act on it. Instead he devised arguments for the conclusion that death does not really involve our annihilation, the central one being that "the imperishability of matter" ensures "the indestructibility of our true being-in-itself."[3] When we die, we nevertheless continue to exist because the matter that composed our bodies continues to exist: "the living being does not suffer any absolute annihilation through death, but continues to exist in and with the whole of nature."[4]

To the obvious objection that the stuff into which the matter of one's body will eventually be resolved will not be oneself, Schopenhauer has two replies. Here is the first:

> But it will be asked, 'How is the permanence of mere dust, of crude matter, to be regarded as a continuance of our true inner nature?' Oh! Do you know this dust then? Do you know what it is and what it can do? Learn to know it before you despise it. This matter, now lying there as dust and ashes, will soon form into crystals when dissolved in water; it will shine as metal; it will then emit electric sparks. . . . It will, indeed, of its own accord, form itself into plant and animal; and from its mysterious womb it will develop that life, about the loss of which you in your narrowness of mind are so nervous and anxious.[5]

In short, even inorganic matter is pretty impressive stuff; so one must not imagine that one is too exalted to be transmuted into it. The second reply appeals to an analogy: "the insect that dies in autumn [is] in itself and according to its true essence just as identical with the insect hatched in spring as the person who lies down to sleep is with the one who gets up."[6]

Perhaps dimly sensing that these replies are less than wholly compelling, Schopenhauer concedes that death involves some loss of individuality. Although at various points he confidently asserts that death "does not in the least disturb [our] true and real inner being," he elsewhere accepts the more muted claim that our survival of death in the form of inanimate matter is "only as in an image and simile, or rather only as in a shadowy outline."[7] In order that his reader not take this as capitulation, he hastens to add that "*nature,* which never lies," holds "that the life or death of the individual is of absolutely no consequence. She expresses this by abandoning the life of every animal, and even of man, to the most insignificant accidents without coming to the rescue."[8] The lesson we should draw from this is that our deaths "should be, in a certain sense, a matter of indifference to us; for in fact, we ourselves are nature. If only we saw deeply enough, we should certainly agree with nature, and regard life or death as indifferently as does she."[9] Fortunately, Schopenhauer's restless mind does not linger to work out the implications of this view for the ethics of killing and saving but rushes past this argument to yet another. Reverting to the analogy with the insect and the recurring cycle of birth and death, he contends that "it is the species that always lives, and the individuals cheerfully exist in the consciousness of the imperishability of the species and their identity with it."[10]

And so the chapter goes. It makes painful reading, and contrasts jarringly with the lucid and penetrating nature of much of the rest of Schopenhauer's work.

The collapse of Schopenhauer's intellect in the confrontation with death is paralleled by an equally conspicuous evasion in Tolstoy's *Death of Ivan Ilych,* one of the few acknowledged classics on the subject of death. It is in many ways a masterpiece; it searingly articulates a number of striking insights, most notably that death is particularly poignant when its prospect brings a realization that the life has been badly lived. The protagonist, Ivan Ilych, achieves this insight near the end. Yet he is immediately rescued from it by the deus ex machina: for, just as Ivan Ilych is on the verge of death, Tolstoy grants him an unelucidated epiphany.

> "And death? Where is it?"
> He searched for his accustomed fear of death and could not find it. Where was death? What death? There was no fear of death because there was no death.
> Instead of death there was light.
> "So that's it!" he exclaimed. "What bliss!" . . .
> "Death is over," he said to himself. "There is no more death."[11]

And then he dies. The revelation is, it is true, immediately preceded by an awakening of sympathy and compassion for his family; but that alone is insufficient to explain the ecstatic surrender to death, or the bizarre denial of death, or delusion of immortality, or whatever it is that occurs. We are simply left to guess what the reassuring illumination is. One of Tolstoy's biographers comments that "it is merely the acceptance of mortality itself which brings him peace"; but not only is there no textual support for this conjecture, but insofar as Ivan Ilych accepts mortality, this is not an explanation of his finding peace but is itself precisely what requires explanation.[12] Tolstoy in fact offers nothing to explain Ivan Ilych's sudden shift from howling terror to quiet serenity at the moment of his death. Death has not been robbed of its sting; rather, we, and perhaps Tolstoy himself, have simply been soothed with a bit of literary legerdemain.

One could go on multiplying examples of this sort of thing, but those I have given suffice to indicate how specious much of the classical literature is in the consolations it offers. It is more profitable to turn to our own exploration. First, it is important to note that, in what follows, I will assume that when we die we cease to exist. Unless there is reason to suppose that our brains will be resurrected, the Embodied Mind Account of Identity seems to rule out the hope of an afterlife. But I should stress that I do not *define* a person's death as his ceasing to exist. If that were one's definition of death, then to say that we all die would be to imply that there is no afterlife; and, conversely, to say that there is an afterlife would be to imply that no one really dies. While there is some support in ordinary language for the idea that an afterlife would somehow negate the reality of death, it seems best to leave conceptual space for the idea that, although we die, we nevertheless continue to exist in another form, or mode, or world. I will say more about the concept of death in section 1.1 of chapter 5.

2. THE PROBLEM OF COMPARISON

2.1. *Immortality*

If it is right that when we die we cease to exist, it seems to follow that death cannot be bad because of its intrinsic features in the way that, for example, suffering is. For nonexistence has no intrinsic properties, positive or negative. Since the badness of death cannot be intrinsic, it must instead be comparative. Death must be bad by comparison with what it excludes. Thus the central problem in the evaluation of death is understanding what exactly is excluded by death in any particular case. Obviously the alternative to death must be continued life, but what sort of life and of what duration?

There is a temptation to suppose that the badness of death must be directly proportional to the value of the life that it excludes. I will later explain why this assumption is mistaken. Death is not bad *in exact proportion* to the net amount of good that the life it excludes would have contained. Nevertheless the degree to which death is bad is a *function* of the value of that life. So to evaluate the badness of a particular death we must have some sense of the value of the life that is lost. A complete account of the badness of death must therefore incorporate an account of the good life: an account of what it is for a life to go well or badly, what makes some lives better or more worth living than others, and so on. I will, however, have little to say of a substantive nature about the good life; rather, the account of the badness of death will be based on a more formal or schematic account of the value of life, one that focuses more on the *structure* of a good life (for example, how length of life and psychological unity are relevant to the overall value of a life) than on what the *contents* of a good life might be.

It may seem that the obvious answer to the question, "What is the alternative to death?" must be continuing to live forever, infinite life, immortality. It seems, indeed, a necessary truth that, in the absence of death, one would live forever. This would not be immortality in the form of an afterlife—that is, an altered existence that *follows* death—but an immortality that would consist in an infinite continuation of *this* life. It is sometimes assumed that if such an immortal life would be good, it follows that death must be bad; whereas if an immortal life would not be good, then death is not necessarily bad, and if an immortal life would be bad, then death—at least at some point—must be good.

Whether an immortal life would be good or bad depends on what it would be like. There are indefinitely many possible conceptions of an immortal life. How do we decide which one is appropriate for comparison with death in order to arrive at an evaluation of death?

In the technical literature, there are various proposals for determining whether a statement of the form "If it were the case that p, then it would be the case that q" is true. It might be thought that we could appeal to such a proposal in order to arrive at an appropriate conception of an immortal life. According to the best known of these proposals, in order to determine what would happen if a person were never to die, we should imagine that everything would be as much as possible as it actually is except that the person would never die.[13] We should, it seems, imagine that the person would continue to age (presumably up to the point at which the aging process could continue no further without resulting in death), that he would remain vulnerable to nonlethal injuries and diseases, and so on—because these conditions would be closer to the way things actually are than if the person were to cease to age at some earlier point or to become invulnerable to nonlethal injury or disease. But if a person were to continue to live forever in these conditions, he would soon become incapacitated by the effects of aging, and it is statistically certain that he would be injured in various permanently disabling ways and afflicted with chronic and painful though nonlethal diseases. He would, in short, spend an infinite amount of time paralyzed, or blind, or demented, or depressed, or in chronic pain, or in some combination of these states.

This vision of an immortal life blighted by decrepitude and perpetual disease has been a persistent theme in mythology and literature. It appears in the myth of Tithonus, later explored in the verse of Tennyson, and receives a stark fictional depiction in the chapter in Swift's *Gulliver's Travels* that describes the struldbrugs, who, like Tithonus, live forever but without "a perpetuity of youth, health, and vigour."[14] The struldbrugs have

> no distinction of taste but eat and drink whatever they can get, without relish or appetite. The diseases they were subject to continue, without increasing or diminishing. In talking they forget the common appellation of things, and the names of persons, even those who are their nearest friends and relations. For the same reason they can never amuse themselves with reading because their memory will not serve to carry them from the beginning of a sentence to the end; and by this defect they are deprived of the only entertainment whereof they might otherwise be capable.[15]

On learning of them, Gulliver wishes he "could send a couple of struldbrugs to my own country, to arm our people against the fear of death."[16] And indeed death would surely be preferable to an infinite life of disease, dementia, isolation, and misery.

There is, however, no reason to suppose that this is the only coherent or appropriate conception of an immortal life. No theory of the logic or semantics of counterfactuals can rule out a conception of an immortal life in which the conditions of our lives would continue indefinitely to be much the same as they are now. There is, however, a body of literature that has sought to show that, even with favorable assumptions about the character of an immortal life, immortality would be undesirable; hence it cannot be bad that we must die at some point. One representative argument of this sort has been advanced by Richard Wollheim, who writes that, if we were immortal,

> many of the reasons we currently have for choosing this rather than that would be removed . . . Questions whether we should do this rather than that would rewrite themselves as questions whether we should do this before or after that, and answers to those new questions would be found by considering not the intensity of our wants or the ends to which they are directed, but the favourable opportunities that the present provides.[17]

Thus immortality would be bad, according to Wollheim, because it would drastically diminish our opportunities for choice; and choice, and all that surrounds it, is part of what gives life its meaning and interest.

This argument is unconvincing, for three reasons. First, it exaggerates the limitations on choice that immortality would entail. Immortality would not necessarily entail that we could have everything that we want, so that the only problem would be to arrange the goods of life in an agreeable temporal order. Immortality alone carries no guarantees about the quality of life and thus even in an endless life there would presumably have to be continual trade-offs between, say, leisurely pursuits and the efforts required to sustain a certain quality of life, between idle pleasures and the satisfactions derived from achievement, and so on.

But we can concede that immortality would reduce the occasions for choice, or at least their relative frequency, and still reject Wollheim's conclusion. For he also exaggerates the value of choice. Insofar as immortality would narrow the scope for choice, it would be mainly by eliminating the necessity of choosing among good things. And while it would be bad if one were to lose the opportunity to choose between two good things because one of them becomes unobtainable, or because both become unobtainable, it is seldom a misfortune to lose the opportunity to choose between two goods because one can have both. (Of course, there is cause for concern if, as C. P. Snow puts it, "the range of choices becomes so wide that choice becomes impossible."[18] But this is just a contingent psychological phenomenon—being overwhelmed and bewildered by an incalculable array of options—and an immortal would have ample time to adjust to his or her circumstances and overcome any temporary paralysis of the will.)

Finally, even if we concede that immortality would deprive us of certain opportunities for the exercise of choice, and that this would be a real loss, it does not follow that immortality would be bad on balance, or all things considered; for clearly the benefits of immortality could outweigh the loss of certain opportunities for choice.

A stronger argument for the undesirability of immortality has been advanced by Bernard Williams. Suppose we were to become immortal. There would then be two possibilities. Either our characters could remain constant or they could vary, evolving over time. Suppose that they were to remain constant. In that case, if our future lives were to involve an endless repetition of the same types of event that we had experienced previously, immortality would become intolerably boring. If, alternatively, our experience were to be endlessly varied, it would seem that, if our characters were to remain fixed and invariant, we would have to be essentially unaffected by our experience. We would, according to Williams, have to be "detached and withdrawn."[19] In either case an immortal life would not be worth living.

There is, however, the other possibility: that our characters could evolve over time. This is in fact the more realistic assumption, since it is common in actual life for people's characters to change through adaptation to shifting circumstances. If our characters and our interests were susceptible to indefinite alteration and growth in response to new experiences and challenges, we might forever stay one step ahead of boredom and satiety.

Williams canvasses this possibility, stating two conditions that would have to be met for an immortal life of this sort to be desirable. First, "it should clearly be *me* who lives forever." And, second, "the state in which I survive should be one which to me looking forward, will be adequately related, in the life it presents, to those aims which I now have in wanting to survive at all."[20] Williams expresses doubts about whether these conditions could be satisfied in the case of an individual whose character is in continuous flux over infinite time. It is not obvious, however, that either is a reasonable condition of the desirability of immortality. Nor is it obvious that either condition could not be met.

The first condition is that an individual at an earlier time and an individual at a later time must be the same individual in order for the earlier individual to be egoistically concerned about the life of the later individual. Williams suggests that the radical psychological discontinuity over vast temporal distances in an immortal life would be incompatible with personal identity (a suggestion that, incidentally, is in tension with the account of personal identity that he develops elsewhere, according to which mere bodily continuity is sufficient for personal identity).[21] (Tennyson's Tithonus laments, "with what another heart / In days far-off, and with what other eyes / I used to watch—if I be he that watched . . .")[22] Thus, if the conditions of personal identity make it impossible for a person to continue to exist over an infinite expanse of time, then it is also impossible for anyone to have an interest in an immortal life.

Both of Williams's assumptions seem false. First, as we saw in chapter 1, personal identity is not a necessary condition of rational egoistic concern for the future. In order for it to be rational for an individual now to be egoistically concerned about an individual in the future, it is not necessary that they be one and the same individual; it is sufficient that they be linked by the prudential unity relations. In the case of an immortal life, however, there is no reason to suppose that the prudential unity relations would diverge from the relation of personal identity itself. But could personal identity be sustained forever? According to the Embodied Mind Account, the criterion of personal identity is the physical and functional continuity of certain cerebral structures. And it is of course physically impossible that a human brain could remain alive and functional forever. While this may seem to clinch Williams's case, it is in fact irrelevant to his argument. *Any* conception of immortality requires deviations from the laws of nature as we know them; but since he assumes that we can coherently discuss and evaluate an immortal life, he must be setting that problem aside. His concern is instead that there may be a *necessary* incompatibility between personal survival and the continuous mutation of individual character over infinite time. But if the account of personal identity that I have developed is acceptable, personal survival is compatible with radical psychological discontinuity.

Whether Williams's second condition is reasonable depends on how generously the phrase "adequately related" is interpreted. If the idea is that all parts of one's infinite future would have to cohere harmoniously with one's present values, desires, and ambitions, then clearly an immortal future in which one's character would be continuously evolving would fail to satisfy the condition. But interpreted in this way, the condition is wholly implausible. Because one's character would always be gradually changing in ways that would permit a sustained interest in life, many of one's distant future activities and pleasures would be utterly alien to one's present values and interests. But this alone is insufficient to show that immortality would be *bad*. Admittedly, it might be the case that one would now have little or no present time-relative interest in living to experience those potential parts of one's future life. This, however, is only partly explicable by reference to the alien character of the values and interests one would acquire in the further future. If one had to choose between dying now and undergoing surgery that would have as a side-effect the alteration of one's present values and interests, it would not be irrational to think that the surgery would be in one's best time-relative interest now. So even the prospect of a sudden, sharp discontinuity in one's values and interests is insufficient to nullify one's time-relative interest in continuing to live, other things being equal. That being the case, there must be more to the explanation of why one might now have little or no time-relative interest in the more distant parts of an immortal life. It is not just that one's later values and interests would be different; it is also, assuming that the minds of immortals would work in roughly the same ways that ours do, that only the weakest possible form of psychological continuity would hold between oneself in the present and oneself in the more distant parts of one's immortal future. There would be no direct psychological connections at all, and continuity would obtain, if at all, only by virtue of the transitive nature of the relation. Because of the immense psychological gulf that would always separate an immortal from himself in the distant future, the strength of his present time-relative interest in his own life in the remote future would be marginal *even* if that future life would be fully harmonious with his present character and values. For his time-relative interest in his own distant future would be discounted virtually to zero for the virtual absence of psychological relations between himself in the present and himself in the far distant future.

Again, however, it is worth stressing that this does not imply that immortality would be bad. At most, an immortal life would, from one's present point of view, be no better than a life that would extend as far into the future as the last element of one's present psychology. It seems, however, that it would be better than that. One need only imagine oneself approaching that later time at which one's *present* interest in continued life would supposedly run out. One would *then* have a strong time-relative interest in continuing to live beyond that point. And one has some interest now in assuring the satisfaction of the interests one would have then. Perhaps an indefinite iteration of this concern for one's future concerns is sufficient to ensure that almost any future life of one's own would be "adequately related" to one's present aims to justify some degree of egoistic concern. But the more important point is that an immortal with a gradually evolving character would always, at any given moment, have a strong time-relative interest in continuing to live for a further considerable time (assuming, or course, that his life would be worth living). Hence death at any time would always be against the time-relative interests he would have for a considerable period prior to that time. Thus even if an immortal would always, at any given time, have little or no time-relative interest in living into the very distant future, there would still be no time at which death would not be bad for him.

I see no reason, therefore, why an immortal life would have to be undesirable. And the corollary is that there is no reason to suppose that, at some point, death would necessarily cease to be a misfortune and instead become a desirable release.

Notice, moreover, that even if Williams were right about immortality, this would not necessarily show that any actual death was not bad. For even if it would be bad to live forever, the conditions that would supposedly make an immortal life intolerable might never arise until well beyond the present maximum life span. Thus the alleged undesirability of immortality is compatible with the claim that every actual death is bad for the person who dies, relative to continuing to live for a certain further period and then dying. In short, even if there were necessarily some point at which death would cease to be bad, it is possible that no one ever reaches that point within the short space of life as we know it.

2.2. *The Token Comparison*

There is a distinction implicit in the preceding paragraph that is considerably more important than the point the paragraph explicitly makes. This is the distinction between a particular death and the fact that we have to die at some point. When a person has died, we may reflect what a pity it is that he had to die at some point, that he could not have lived forever; but we are more likely to lament that he died when and how he did, that he was unable to live somewhat longer—long enough, for example, to bring his life's work to completion, to see his children grow to maturity, or to gain recognition for his accomplishments. If we wish to assess how great his misfortune was in dying, we do not compare his actual death with a hypothetical course of events in which he would have lived forever; rather, we compare it with a hypothetical course of events in which he would not have died that particular death but in which he would eventually have died some other way. We imagine, that is, a course of events in which the particular cause of his actual death would not have occurred, not one in which *no* cause of death would *ever* have operated.

In other words, when a person dies and we seek to determine how serious a misfortune it was for him to have died, our concern is with how bad it is that he died *this* death rather than some later hypothetical death, not that he died rather than never dying at all. If this is right, reflections about the desirability or undesirability of immortality are largely irrelevant to our effort to understand the badness of death—at least when our concern with death takes its usual form. It is of course entirely sensible to ask whether it is bad that we must die rather than continue to live forever; but this is a different question from the one that weighs so heavily on us when we contemplate death in some particular instance. When we reflect on certain particular deaths—Keats's death at twenty-six, Shaw's at ninety-four, Swift's at seventy-eight after years of slow disintegration into a dreaded dementia—we recognize that some are tragic, others are relatively benign, and some are belated rescues from a bitterly detested fate. It is hard to make sense of this spectrum of judgments if we suppose that the implicit comparison is with immortal life. These judgments instead reflect our preoccupation with how bad (or good) the particular death is in comparison with death at some later time.

My concern in this chapter is with the evaluation of particular deaths: how bad it is for a person to die *this* death now rather than a later death from a different cause. Our intuitive judgments about the comparative badness of death for different people are responses to this question. And, in exploring this question, I will be respectful of those intuitions. Just as in moral theory I take intuitions that are deeply and pervasively held to be presumptively reliable, so in thinking about the badness of death I will take strongly held intuitions (e.g., that it is generally worse to die in early adulthood than in one's dotage) to be starting points for inquiry that are not to be lightly abandoned. My aim is in part to discover the deep values and assumptions that underlie our intuitive discriminations among different deaths; but if I am able to identify a unified foundation for our intuitions, I will also try to determine the extent to which it is rationally defensible and how it might be made more rigorous and coherent.

We have acknowledged that the badness of death must be comparative. If we ask "How bad is death?" we must therefore answer the further question, "What is the alternative to death?" We have seen that to pose the question this way is to invite a comparison between death and the complete absence of death—that is, immortality. But this is the wrong comparison; it is not what we are most interested in. Borrowing from linguistics the distinction between type and token, one might say that we are less interested in what would happen if the *type* of event—death itself—were not to occur than in what would happen if a particular *token* instance of the type—that is, *this* particular death—were not to occur. So our question should be "How bad is (or was) *this* death?" And to answer it we must answer the further question, "What would have happened if this particular death—death at this time and of this cause—had not occurred?" We then compare the actual death with the life the victim would have had if he had not died when and how he did, and this comparison gives us the measure of the badness of his death. Since our concern is with what would have happened had the particular token instance of death not occurred, we can call this the *Token Comparison.*

The Token Comparison seems to support a variety of common and compelling intuitions about death. It explains, for example, why it is in general worse to die earlier rather than later. For, as a rule, a person who dies in early adulthood would, had she not died then, have enjoyed more of the goods of life before meeting with death from some other cause than a person who dies in old age. This approach also explains how death can be good, or a benefit. If the life a person would have if she were not to die now would be "worth not living," or worse than no life at all, it would be better for her to die now rather than later. This recognition allows us to see how either suicide or euthanasia could be in a person's interest.

The Token Comparison does, however, raise several difficult questions. We are supposed to compare a particular death with the life the person would have if he were not to die this particular death. Some have interpreted this in the following way. We should compare the life he has if this particular death occurs with the life he would have if the death were not to occur. The difference between these two possible lives is the difference that this particular death would make. If the longer life would be a better life for the person than the shorter life, the death would be bad for him. This is the interpretation favored by Fred Feldman, who contends that "we must ask about the value for him of the life he leads if he dies when he in fact dies; and we must compare that value to the value for him of the life he would have led if he had not died then. If the life terminated by that death is worse for [him] than the life not terminated by that death, then his death . . . was extrinsically bad for him; otherwise not."[23] Feldman notes that this approach has various merits: for example, it does not involve any dubious comparison between continued life and nonexistence, but instead simply compares two possible lives.

This approach may tell us not only *whether* a particular death is bad but also *how* bad it is. The extent to which a particular death would be bad is just the extent to which the shorter life that ends with that death would be worse than the longer life that the person would have if the death were not to occur. According to the simplest version, the extent to which the shorter possible life would be worse is exactly proportional to the net amount of good in the additional period of time that would occur only in the longer possible life. Feldman's view is of this simple sort, though it is not crudely additive, for he insists that the value that an additional segment of time would add to a life is a complex function of the amount of intrinsic good the segment would contain and the amount of good the person deserves. The extent to which the addition of a certain good would contribute to the value of the life depends on whether and to what extent the good is deserved.[24]

The important point to notice is that the badness of a death is measured in terms of its effect on the overall value of the life as a whole. The extent to which death is worse (or better) than continuing to exist is proportional to the difference between the total value the life as a whole would have if the death were to occur and the total value the life would have if the death were not to occur. Call this the *Life Comparative Account* of the badness of death.

The Life Comparative Account appears to presuppose that identity is what matters. If identity is not what matters, there may be cases in which the loss of future goods through death may matter less from the point of view of the victim at the time of death because the relations that do matter—the prudential unity relations—would have held to a weaker degree between himself at that time and himself as he would later have been had he lived. In these cases, the individual's interest in continuing to live, which reflects the extent to which death would be worse for his life as a whole, is stronger than his *time-relative interest in continuing to live*. The strength of an individual's time-relative interest in continuing to live is, in effect, the extent to which it matters, for his sake now or from his present point of view, that he should continue to live. It takes into account how strong the prudential unity relations would be between himself now and himself in his subsequent life, assuming he were to live.

The notion of a time-relative interest is the basis of a rival approach to the badness of death. The *Time-Relative Interest Account* of the badness of death evaluates death in terms of the effect that it has on the victim's time-relative interests rather than on the value of his life as a whole. It holds that the badness of death is proportional to the strength of the victim's time-relative interest in continuing to live. The strength of his time-relative interest in continuing to live is a function of both the net amount of good his life would contain if he were not to die, and the extent to which he would be bound to himself in the future, if he were not to die, by the prudential unity relations.

The Life Comparative Account and the Time-Relative Interest Account coincide in cases in which the prudential unity relations would be strong. But they diverge when those relations would be weak. In these cases, the implications of the Time-Relative Interest Account are more congruent with our intuitions. Consider, for example, the death of a developed fetus through spontaneous abortion. According to the Life Comparative Account, this should be an especially bad death, for the difference in value between a full human life and a life that ends in utero is enormous. It seems, indeed, that the Life Comparative Account implies that the worse possible death is one that occurs immediately after an individual begins to exist. This, however, is hard to believe. The Time-Relative Interest Account, by contrast, implies that the death of a developed fetus is substantially less bad, since the badness of its loss of the vast amount of good that lay in prospect for it has to be discounted for the weakness of the prudential unity relations that would have connected it to itself in the future.

I will defend this claim in greater detail in section 6.1 of this chapter. (I will also consider and reject an argument of Feldman's that attempts to show that the Life Comparative Account can recognize that the death of a developed fetus is a less bad death than the death of an older child or adult.) For now, it is enough to note that my claim is *not* that it is illegitimate to evaluate a death in the way required by the Life Comparative Account. On the contrary, the Life Comparative Account requires us to notice the difference that a particular death makes to the amount of value that a life, and therefore the world, contains, and that may be an important consideration. My claim is only that it is not the basis of our intuitive comparative evaluations of different deaths.

For the moment, let us put aside the contrast between the Life Comparative Account and the Time-Relative Interest Account and focus our attention instead on cases in which they coincide: cases in which the prudential unity relations would be strong. Even in these cases, the Token Comparison raises further problems. Consider:

The Young Cancer Patient. A man dies of cancer at the age of twenty.

To determine how bad death is for the Young Cancer Patient, one must compare his death with what would have happened to him if he had not died when he did. But how can one possibly know what would have happened to him had he not died of cancer? How long would he have lived? What goods would his life have contained? Just as it is difficult to predict the future with any accuracy, so it is at least equally difficult to know what would have happened in a future that is entirely hypothetical. This *Epistemological Problem* is formidable even if the future is fully determined; the difficulties are magnified if people are assumed to have libertarian free will that leaves the future undetermined to the extent that it depends on human choice.

One response to this problem is to abandon the ambition of evaluating death in terms of the value of the life it excludes and instead focus just on the *opportunities* that it denies us. We can concede, for example, that we have no idea whether the

Young Cancer Patient would have become a parent if he had not died when he did; for he might have freely decided not to have children or have been unable to have them for some reason quite independent of the cancer. Hence we may not be able to claim that his death denied him the good of being a parent. But we can at least claim that it denied him the opportunity to become one. In general, we can retreat from claims about the loss of specific goods occasioned by death and instead evaluate the badness of death in terms of the opportunities for having various goods that it denies us. The loss of a certain opportunity can be a misfortune even if one would not have seized that opportunity had it arisen.

While shifting the focus from goods to opportunities would mitigate the Epistemological Problem somewhat, it would not eliminate it altogether; for just as we cannot be certain what goods a person would have had if he had not died, so we cannot be certain exactly what opportunities he would have had either. And if he would not have had a certain opportunity even if he had lived, we cannot say that his death denied him that opportunity.

The Epistemological Problem is real and unavoidable. It forces us to acknowledge that our ability to evaluate a particular death is limited. It would be a mistake, however, to conclude that evaluation is impossible. Evaluations of death must have a probabilistic or statistical basis. Based on our knowledge of the way in which a certain kind of life tends to go, we can hazard a reasonable conjecture, though only at a fairly high level of generality, about what a given person's future life would have held if he had not died when he did. We know, for example, that people who are intelligent, attractive, good-natured, and highly educated and who come from families that are loving and supportive tend, in general, to enjoy a relatively high level of well-being and to have lower than average mortality rates. Hence, if the Young Cancer Patient was such a person, it may be reasonable to assume that, if he had not died of cancer, he would have had a lengthy and satisfying future. While projections of this sort are difficult, untestable, and highly fallible, they cannot be dismissed as utterly unreliable and they do in fact underlie many of the judgments about death that we make with considerable confidence.

Because our projections of what a person's life would have been like are of necessity founded on probabilistic reasoning, they should be discounted for uncertainty. So, for example, even if the evidence suggests that the Young Cancer Patient would have had a glorious future had he not died when he did, we should nevertheless moderate our assessment of the badness of his death to take account of the possibility that the future life that he lost would have been less good than we suppose.

3. THE METAPHYSICAL PROBLEM

3.1. *A Plurality of Comparisons*

There is a deeper, more obscure problem we face in making the Token Comparison. The Token Comparison requires that we ask what would have happened to a person if he had not died when he did. The problem is that there are indefinitely many ways in which the person might have avoided that particular death and the different ways in which he might not have died would have led to his having very different futures.

In order for the person not to have died, the cause of his death must not have operated. But there were many different causal conditions that were necessary for the occurrence of that particular death and, for each of these many causal conditions, there were many ways in which it might have been suppressed or might not have operated to produce that death.

These claims can be illustrated by reference to the following elaboration of the preceding case.

> *The Young Cancer Patient.* During a holiday at the beach, a child was exposed to radiation from a leak in a nearby nuclear power plant. The radiation damaged a strand of DNA, causing a mutation in a cell. Later, when the child had grown to young adulthood, a certain catalyst precipitated the uncontrolled replication of the damaged cell, resulting in the person's developing acute leukemia. When this person was twenty, he suffered a severe hemorrhage that deprived his brain of its blood supply, thereby causing the death of his cerebral tissues, the cessation of brain function, and systemic organ failure.

Which factor in this sequence of events was the cause of his death? One can of course say simply that the cancer was the cause of his death. But one could also say that the cancer was caused by the radiation, so that, ultimately, exposure to radiation was the cause of his death. Lawyers suing the power plant on behalf of his relatives could plausibly claim that the leakage from the plant, or the carelessness of the plant managers, was the cause of his death. Or one could say, with equal propriety, that the cause of his death was the event that precipitated the replication of the cell containing the damaged DNA. Or if the Young Cancer Patient's physician were asked by another physician who knew that the patient had leukemia what the cause of his death was, the appropriate response would be that he had died of a hemorrhage. So any of these things—the cancer, the leakage, the exposure to radiation, the catalyst, the hemorrhage—might plausibly be identified as the cause of the Young Cancer Patient's death. In any case, each was a necessary condition of his dying when and how he did: if any one of these things had not occurred, he would not have died that particular death.

But what would have happened if the Young Cancer Patient had never got cancer is very different from what would have happened if the hemorrhage had not occurred. Let us suppose that, had he not got cancer, he would have had a long and prosperous future. But if he had not died when he did simply because the hemorrhage did not occur, he would, we may suppose, have lived only for a few more days in a torpid, semi-conscious state with a certain amount of pain before dying from another complication of the cancer. With which of these alternative courses of events should his actual death be compared for the purpose of evaluation? Compared to a long and prosperous future, his death was tragic; compared to living a few more days in a groggy and painful condition, it might have been a welcome release.

The problem is actually more complicated than this suggests. Not only are there numerous necessary causal conditions of a particular death, but there are also many ways in which each particular cause or causal condition might not have resulted in the death. If, for example, we identify the cancer as the cause of the Young Cancer Patient's death, then we can recognize various ways in which this cause might not have resulted in the particular death: for instance, the cancer might never have occurred, it might have been cured, it might have gone into remission only to recur later, and so on. Again, each way in which the cause might not have operated to produce the particular death would have resulted in a different future for the Young Cancer Patient.

Let us call this problem—the problem of determining which of the many different ways in which a person might not have died when he did is the appropriate one for the purpose of comparison—the *Metaphysical Problem*. To appreciate how this problem might be relevant to the morality of killing, note that it is often held that the wrongness of killing is explained at least in part in terms of the harm that an act of killing inflicts on its victim, which in turn is measured in terms of the loss the victim suffers by dying. For example, the fundamental premise of one of the most influential arguments about the morality of abortion is that "the prima facie wrong-making feature of a killing is the loss to the victim of the value of its future."[25] But as we have seen, many different futures were possible for a person who is killed, each one corresponding to a different way in which he might not have died. And these different futures are often widely varying in value. Without an adequate response to the Metaphysical Problem, we will be unable to determine on which of these futures to focus in estimating the victim's loss in being killed.

It might be thought that certain reasonably plausible ways of understanding the badness of death manage to avoid the Metaphysical Problem altogether. It might be suggested, for example, that, to determine how bad a person's death is for him, one should simply survey the desires that the person has at the time of death and treat the badness of his death as proportional to the badness for him of those desires being unsatisfied.[26] Because most of the person's desires about how his own life should go are necessarily left unsatisfied when he dies (the possible exceptions being desires about what should *not* happen to him, and the desire to die), it may seem that there is no need to speculate about what would have happened if he had not died in order to determine how bad his death was.

I have argued elsewhere that views that analyze the badness of death solely in terms of the effect on the victim's desires are inadequate.[27] (I will briefly rehearse the objections in section 6.2 of this chapter.) The relevant point here is that, even if such a view were otherwise plausible, it would not evade the Metaphysical Problem. For in order to explain the badness of a person's death in terms of the failure of his desires to be satisfied, it must be the case that the desires go unsatisfied *because* of the death. The fact that the desires fail to be satisfied can be attributed to the person's death only if the desires would have been satisfied (or, perhaps, would have had a reasonable probability of being satisfied) if the person had not died when and how he did. It seems a mistake to suppose that the desires go unsatisfied because of the death when they would not have been satisfied even if the death had not occurred. If, for example, a man dies who desperately wanted to become president of the United States, it would be a mistake to say that his death frustrated his desire if there was no possibility that he would have become president if he had lived. And in fact we know that in all people's lives many desires fade away, are renounced or overcome, or otherwise fail to persist, while many others are either frustrated or remain forever unsatisfied because opportunities for their satisfaction fail to arise. In order, therefore, to know which of a person's desires his death prevents from being satisfied, one must at least have reasonable beliefs about which of his desires would have been likely to be satisfied if he had not died. One must, that is, ask what would have happened if he had not died when and how he did—in short, one must confront the Metaphysical Problem.

Suppose that, on the day before the Young Cancer Patient's hemorrhage occurred, his physician had been wondering how grave a misfortune the patient's death would be for him. His reason for wondering about this was that he believed it relevant to his deliberations about whether to take action to avert a possible hemorrhage. His reasoning was simple: if the Young Cancer Patient's death in the immediate future would be a serious misfortune, the physician would implement costly measures to avert a possible hemorrhage; whereas if the patient's death would not be a serious misfortune, no action would be taken. Suppose the physician concluded that, if the patient were not to die in the immediate future, he would linger on for a short while in a dull haze through which only pain could penetrate; and, compared to that, an immediate death would not be bad. On the basis of this comparison, the physician decided not to try to avert a hemorrhage, which duly occurred the following day.

Did the physician make a mistake? Did he base his evaluation of the Young Cancer Patient's death on the wrong comparison? Clearly not: this was the right comparison to make in deciding whether to attempt to avert a possible hemorrhage. If the circumstances had been different, a different comparison would have been appropriate. If, for example, a therapy had unexpectedly become available that promised the possibility of a remission lasting several years, the appropriate comparison would have been between an immediate death and the patient's living for several years free from cancer and then perhaps dying of a recurrence. In determining whether it would be worthwhile to administer the new therapy to the Young Cancer Patient, it would be absurd to evaluate the possibility of an immediate death using the same comparison that is appropriate for determining whether to try to avert a hemorrhage. Different comparisons, and therefore different evaluations of the death, are appropriate for different purposes. The Young Cancer Patient's immediate death from a hemorrhage is not bad compared with living on for a few days in a painful and stuporous condition, as he would if the hemorrhage were averted. But his death now from a hemorrhage would be quite bad compared with living several more years free from cancer, which would be the alternative to the immediate death if the new therapy were to become available.

The fact that a death may appropriately be compared to more than one alternative helps to explain our profound ambivalence about certain deaths. It seems appropriate, for example, for the friends and family of the Young Cancer Patient to be both relieved and deeply distressed by his death. They will naturally regard the death as both a beneficial release from suffering and a terrible tragedy, involving great loss, not only to themselves but to the Young Cancer Patient as well. Although these responses may initially seem incompatible and thus confused, they make sense if we see each as implicitly based on a different comparison. It makes sense, for example, to regard the death as good in comparison to the Young Cancer Patient's living for only a few more days in great pain, but bad in comparison with the possibility of his being cured and going on to live a normal life.

These reflections suggest a simple response to the Metaphysical Problem: perhaps we should abandon the aim of identifying a single alternative to which a death can be compared in order to arrive at a single evaluation of the death. Perhaps instead we should accept that all the ways in which the person might not have died are relevant to the evaluation of his actual death. In the case of the Young Cancer Patient, his death was good compared to living a few more days in pain, bad compared to experiencing a temporary remission from cancer, and even worse compared to being cured of cancer altogether. All of these alternatives were possible, as of course were many others, and the comparison between the actual death and each of the possible alternatives yields a valid evaluation of the death. So we are left with a variety of evaluations of the death, all of which are valid, though one may be appropriate in a certain context or for a certain choice, while another is appropriate for a different context or choice. But no one of them is the uniquely correct evaluation; none has a stronger claim to be considered definitive than any other.

A view of this sort has been advanced by John Broome. Broome holds that in no case does a death have an absolute or nonrelative value, bad or good. Inquiring about the badness of death at age eighty-two, he contends that "all the significant facts have been fully stated once we have said what dying at 82 is better than and what it is worse than. There is no further significant question whether or not dying at 82 is an absolutely bad thing."[28] He holds this view because he believes that *nothing* is good or bad in itself or in a noncomparative way—a belief that is succinctly captured in the title of the essay in which it is defended: "Goodness Is Reducible to Betterness."

I believe we should reject Broome's general claim about value, for reasons that are irrelevant here. But death is a special case: its goodness or badness is, as I noted earlier, essentially comparative. If there is no one comparison that is more apt or revealing or significant than the other comparisons that are possible, we may have to accept that there are indefinitely many answers—each different but all equally correct—to the question whether and to what extent a particular death is bad or good. The various different evaluations of the death could be equally correct because each would implicitly appeal to a different comparison between death and some alternative possible course of events in which the token death would not have occurred.

It would, however, be puzzling if this were true. Although in a small number of cases, such as that of the Young Cancer Patient, we acknowledge that divergent and seemingly conflicting evaluations of the same death make equal sense, in most cases we find that a single evaluation is adequate and comprehensive, even if we concede that there were indefinitely many ways in which the death might not have occurred. Consider, for example:

> *The Pedestrian.* A person is absorbed in his own thoughts and steps absentmindedly off the curb into the path of a bus. He is killed instantly by the impact.

It seems obvious that the relevant alternative to the Pedestrian's death was for him simply to be more alert and not step into the path of the bus. Thus we naturally evaluate the death by comparing it to the life he would have had if everything had been the same except that he had not stepped in front of the bus. It is equally possible, of course, that he might not have died if, for example, he had taken a shorter step, so that the bus would have struck him a glancing blow rather than hitting him head-on. Suppose that, if that had happened, he would have survived but with permanent brain damage and painful physical disabilities. Compared with that way in which he might not have died, his actual death may not seem so bad. But even though this was a possible alternative, we do not consider it. Even if we know that this was possible, that knowledge does not cause us to have ambivalent feelings about the death. Our sense that it was tragic that the Pedestrian died rather than staying out of the path of the bus is in no way tempered by a sense that the death is not so bad compared to the alternative of living on with severe mental and physical disabilities.

It is, of course, possible that our single evaluation in cases of this sort is actually an intuitive distillation from a variety of unconsciously processed comparisons between the death and some of the ways in which it might not have occurred. But this seems unlikely. Again, it seems clear that, in thinking about the Pedestrian, we simply consider the life he would have had if he had looked before stepping into the street. If that life would have been long and happy, we judge the death to have been tragic. Other possibilities seem irrelevant.

If this is right, it seems that in most cases we unconsciously follow certain loose and unarticulated criteria in determining what the relevant alternative to a particular death is for the purpose of evaluation. In the following subsection, I will try to identify some of those criteria. But I should stress the limited nature of my ambitions. My main aim is descriptive: to indicate how we in fact select the terms of comparison when evaluating a particular death. I will not attempt to defend the rationality of the ways of thinking that I will identify, though later parts of the argument in this chapter will presuppose ways of thinking of just these sorts. I would of course prefer to have firmer foundations for those parts of the argument, but I have been unable to discover a solution to the Metaphysical Problem that seems rationally required. As others do, I simply follow our practice. Finally, although I will try to indicate how in many cases, for the purpose of evaluating a person's death, we come to focus on one way in which he might not have died, I do not mean to imply that there is always, or ever, a single, uniquely correct evaluation of any particular death. Often different and seemingly conflicting evaluations of a death can be justified, each based on a different comparison between the death and some way in which it might not have occurred, and each can be a rational guide to action in the appropriate context.

3.2 *Criteria for Determining the Appropriate Comparison*

It is normally the case that, prior to a person's death, innumerable futures were possible for him. Indeed, unless all that occurs is rigidly determined, each of the many ways in which a person might not have died leaves open an indefinite number of ways in which his life might have unfolded. Death closes off all these possible futures. In one sense, therefore, the person loses all of the futures that were possible for him. But these losses are not additive. While indefinitely many futures were possible, at most one could ever have been actual. The lost futures are thus related disjunctively rather than conjunctively: he lost this future, or that one, or that. In general, we tend to see the greatest loss as subsuming all the lesser ones. We tend to think that, if other things are equal, the person's loss of the *best* of the futures that were possible for him reveals the full extent of his misfortune in dying.

Our usual practice, in other words, is to compare the death with the way in which the person might not have died that would have given him the best future that was possible for him. One way in which we do this is to focus on the way in which he might not have died that would have involved the most complete possible absence of the condition or event that we identify as the cause of his death. So, for example, in the case of the Pedestrian we compare the death with an alternative course of events in which he would not have been hit by the bus at all rather than with one in which the bus would have struck him a glancing blow, thereby merely injuring rather than killing him.

There are, however, at least two significant restrictions on our practice of comparing a death with a salient possible alternative in which the condition that caused the death is fully absent and in which the future is thus maximally untainted by other possible deleterious effects of that condition. One such restriction is that the sequence of events with which we compare the death must preserve as much of the person's actual past as would have been compatible with his not dying. We tend not, in other words, to compare a person's death with an alternative possible course of events in which his earlier life would have been substantially different from the way it actually was.

In cases in which the cause of death appears suddenly and abruptly (as in an accident) or is of recent onset (as in a rapidly fatal illness), it is easy to imagine a course of events in which the cause of death would have been completely absent but in which the person's past would have been substantially the same as it actually was. But in other cases in which the cause of death is a long-standing condition with ill effects beyond its tendency to result in death, there is no alternative course of events in which the person's past would have been much the same but in which the cause of death would have been completely absent. In these cases, holding the past constant generally takes priority over imagining the cause of death to be wholly absent. Suppose, for example, that we want to determine how bad it is for someone to die from a slowly progressive disease that has caused gradual disablement and disfigurement over a period of decades. We do not compare the death with an alternative in which the victim never contracted the disease in the first place. For in supposing that he might not have died, we do not imagine his earlier life to have been different from the way it actually was. Rather, we compare the death with the possibility of his living on in a disabled and disfigured condition.

Or consider a variant of the case of the Pedestrian. Suppose that the Pedestrian is struck by the bus but survives for several years before dying from complications arising from his injuries. We may still see the accident as the ultimate cause of his death but, in evaluating that death, our tendency is not to compare it to an alternative possible course of events in which he was never hit by the bus at all. That supposition involves too radical an alteration of the past. Rather, we compare the death to an alternative in which the injuries he sustained would not have proved fatal.

In this insistence on holding the past constant until very near the time of death, there is more than an echo of David Lewis's well-known account of counterfactuals.[29] According to Lewis, in order to determine whether a proposition of the form "If x had not occurred, y would have occurred" is true, we consider the hypothetical course of events (or possible world) in which everything is as much as possible as it actually was except that x did not occur. If it is reasonable to believe that, in those conditions, and given the laws of nature, y would have occurred, it is also reasonable to believe that the counterfactual proposition is true. (This, of course, is a crude paraphrase of Lewis's more precise but also more technical analysis.) It is perhaps worth noting that an appeal to Lewis's account does not, by itself, seem to solve the Metaphysical Problem. For the account can be applied independently to all the various interpretations of "If he had not died"—for example, "If the hemorrhage had not occurred," "If he had been cured," "If he had never contracted cancer," and so on. Moreover, insofar as Lewis's analysis discriminates among these interpretations, it seems to favor the one in which there is least deviation from the way things actually were prior to the person's death. In the case of the Young Cancer Patient, this seems to be the alternative in which he gets cancer and is not cured but in which the hemorrhage does not occur. It is clear, however, that if we compare the death with only that alternative, our evaluation will be incomplete and even distorted.

Although we tend to hold the past constant in our reflections on what would have happened if a person had not died, the case of the Young Cancer Patient shows that our practice is not inflexible. We accept that in this case more than one evaluation is appropriate and that an evaluation of the death as tragic may appropriately appeal to a comparison with an alternative in which the victim's earlier life would have been rather different. In most other cases, however, the comparison between death and an alternative in which the victim's earlier life would have been different normally yields something different from just an evaluation of the death. Consider again the person who dies from a long-standing, progressive disease. A comparison between the actual course of events and an alternative course of events in which the person would never have contracted the disease in the first place seems to ground an evaluation not of the death alone but of his *having the disease,* with all its attendant effects, including disability, disfigurement, and death.

There is at least one further consideration that is worth mentioning. This is that, in asking what would have happened if a person had not died, we consider only realistic alternatives to the death, alternatives that were in some sense possible. In the case of the Pedestrian, for example, we do not consider the scenario in which he is "beamed up" by benevolent aliens just prior to impact with the bus. But it is difficult to say exactly what the terms of this insistence on realism are, beyond merely ruling out obviously fanciful alternatives to death involving alien intervention and the like.

One suggestion might be that we should (or that we unconsciously *do*) focus on the alternative to death (or the way in which a person might not have died) that was *most probable.* There are various problems with this, one of which is that in many cases it does not significantly narrow the field, because there are no discriminable differences in probability among the various alternatives. It seems, for example, equally realistic to suppose that the Pedestrian might have been struck a glancing, nonlethal blow by the bus as it is to suppose that he might not have been hit at all. And in other cases in which this suggestion does seem to pick out a single alternative to death as more probable than any other, its selection may be implausible as a basis for evaluation. Suppose, for example, that in the case of the Young Cancer Patient, we do not compare the death with alternatives in which he never got cancer at all, as they all involve his having a very different past. This leaves such possibilities as being cured, going into remission, avoiding the hemorrhage, and so on. Suppose that it would have been easy to avert the hemorrhage but that the probability of a cure or remission was very low. In that case the most probable alternative to the actual death seems to have been the course of events in which the hemorrhage would have been averted and the Young Cancer Patient would have continued to live for a few more days in pain. But, as we have seen, there is no necessity to suppose that the Young Cancer Patient's death can be appropriately evaluated only in comparison with that alternative.

So, even in those cases (which may be relatively few) in which we can identify the likeliest way in which a person might not have died, we are not constrained to evaluate the death only in relation to that alternative. In what sense, then, must our understanding of the alternative to death be realistic? The constraint might be understood simply as a minimal requirement of possibility: that is, the alternative to the death must have been realistically possible. As Thomas Nagel contends in his seminal discussion of the badness of death, "we . . . have to set some limits on *how* possible a possibility must be for its nonrealization to be a misfortune."[30] If the avoidance of a death was simply *not possible,* perhaps we should conclude that the death cannot have been a misfortune.

That even this is open to doubt is suggested by the following case.

> *The Incurable Patient.* A person dies at age twenty from a congenital, genetically based condition. This condition is invariably fatal and no one who has had it has ever lived beyond the age of twenty. There is no cure and none on the horizon, no treatment to extend the victims' lives, and no recorded instance of regression, remission, or spontaneous recovery. Although the condition causes premature death, it does not cause significant pain or disability during the victim's life.

This seems to be a tragic death. But if it is bad, that must be by comparison with a possible alternative. What is the alternative? There is a clear sense in which it is impossible, if one has the condition, to survive beyond the age of twenty. Perhaps, then, we are suppressing our scruples about comparing the death with an alternative in which the victim's earlier life would have been different. Perhaps we are implicitly comparing the death with the possibility that the person might never have had the condition at all.

Suppose that it was also not possible for the Incurable Patient to have existed without the condition. It might be true that the condition was essential to his identity in the sense that, if the zygote from which he in fact developed had had normal genes rather than the abnormal ones responsible for the condition, that zygote would have developed into a different person. In short, without the genes that cause the condition, the Incurable Patient would never have existed. (Whether a gene or set of genes of this sort can be essential to a person's identity in this sense is controversial. I have discussed this issue briefly elsewhere.[31] For the moment, assume for the sake of argument that the Incurable Patient could not have existed without having this invariably fatal genetic defect. It is worth stressing, however, that this assumption does *not* imply that a cure for the condition is necessarily impossible. The claim that the Incurable Patient could not have existed without the genetic defect is a claim about whether a person who actually exists could ever have existed had certain conditions been different at or prior to the point at which he came into existence. It is, in other words, a claim about the conditions of an individual's coming into existence, or *ever existing.* It is different in kind from a claim about the conditions of an individual's *continuing to exist.* It is possible that a person could not have come into existence without certain genes but that, once he exists, he could survive the alteration, replacement, or suppression of the action of those genes.)

We are assuming, then, both that it was not possible for the Incurable Patient to be cured and that it was impossible for him not to have contracted the condition (since it was congenital and the genes responsible for it were essential to his identity). It may therefore seem that it was simply impossible for him to have avoided the particular death he suffered, except, of course, by dying even earlier. But if there is no realistic way that he could have lived longer than he did, should our commitment to realism lead us to conclude that his death cannot have been a misfortune, since it did not exclude any realistic alternative that would have been better for him?

Suppose that the Pedestrian was also twenty when he was killed by the bus. Is it plausible to suppose that, because his death was easily avoidable, it was tragic, while the Incurable Patient's death, being unavoidable, was not bad at all? Most of us intuitively find that the two deaths were equally bad, assuming that other things were equal. This suggests that our commitment to realism in the evaluation of death is flexible. What exactly are we thinking when we judge the Incurable Patient's death to have been tragic?

I suggest that we are implicitly comparing the death to an alternative in which the Incurable Patient would have lived out a normal life span with a normal quality of life (given that the condition had not, at the time of death, caused any significant disability). This, of course, presupposes the possibility of some sort of cure, which we have stipulated was in fact impossible. But the impossibility was of a contingent sort. It was not that a cure was in principle or necessarily impossible—for example, that the suppression of the effects of the condition was incompatible with the Incurable Patient's continued existence. Rather, a cure was in principle possible; it was simply beyond the resources of science to bring it about at the time. This would be demonstrated if a cure were eventually discovered. Friends and relatives of the Incurable Patient might then lament that the cure was not discovered earlier, in time to save him.

It might be objected that it was also possible, in this same sense, that aliens might have intervened to save the Incurable Patient with some exotic extraterrestrial technology. But this is the kind of stipulation that is supposed to be ruled out as unrealistic. This suggests that it matters to us that the forms of possibility that we invoke should be familiar. Even if alien intervention is only contingently impossible, it is not something that ever happens. But it does sometimes happen that a cure is found for a previously incurable illness. It is therefore reasonable to lament that this did not happen in the case of the Incurable Patient, even if it is not appropriate to lament the absence of alien intervention.

In summary, when we seek to evaluate a person's death, we must concede that there are indefinitely many ways in which he might not have died and that, in some cases, comparisons with more than one of these alternatives to death may be appropriate and may yield two or more different yet equally justified evaluations of the death. In other cases, however, we focus on one alternative and ignore the others. Among the criteria that seem unconsciously to guide our selection of the relevant alternative are that, to the greatest extent possible, it should completely exclude the cause of death and its effects, it should give the person the best future that was open to him, it should preserve his earlier life as it actually was, and it should have been, in a suitably weak sense, a realistic possibility, though not necessarily a practical possibility in the circumstances. These various criteria—and there may be others that I have missed—may conflict with one another so that trade-offs have to be made. How we negotiate these conflicts seems to be more a matter of psychology than of rationality.

4. THE PROBLEM OF OVERDETERMINATION

4.1. *When Death Would Have Occurred Soon from a Different Cause*

It may seem that, once we get past the Metaphysical Problem, the only real problems with the Token Comparison are epistemological. But this is not so. One further problem is illustrated by the following case.

> *The Geriatric Patient.* A woman reaches the maximum human life span, the biological limits of human life. Every organ is on the verge of failing when she dies suddenly of a massive hemorrhagic stroke.

This woman's death in the immediate future was overdetermined in the sense that any realistic way in which she might not have died of the stroke would have left her vulnerable to the virtually immediate action of a different cause of death. (The same would be true again if we asked what would have happened if the alternative cause of death had not operated either.) Thus the Token Comparison, applied to the case of the Geriatric Patient, implies that her actual death was hardly a misfortune at all, since it deprived her of at most only a moment of life.

While it seems clear that the death of the Geriatric Patient is a lesser misfortune than the deaths of most younger people, it seems wrong to suppose that it is not a misfortune at all. Thomas Nagel captures our sense of the Geriatric Patient's misfortune when he observes that "existence defines for [a person] an essentially open-ended possible future, containing the usual mixture of goods and evils that he has found so tolerable in the past. . . . Viewed in this way, death, no matter how inevitable, is an abrupt cancellation of indefinitely extensive possible goods. . . . If there is no limit to the amount of life that it would be good to have, then it may be that a bad end is in store for us all."[32]

If the case of the Geriatric Patient arouses suspicions about the Token Comparison, our skepticism is likely to be further inflamed if we consider a variant of the earlier case of the Pedestrian.

> *The Young Pedestrian.* A young man, aged twenty, absentmindedly steps off the curb into the path of a bus and is instantly and painlessly killed. During the autopsy, it is discovered that he had a hitherto silent cerebral aneurysm that would inevitably have burst within a week if he had not been hit by the bus. And the bursting of the aneurysm would certainly have been fatal.

In this case, the autopsy reveals that the Young Pedestrian would have died within a week even if he had not been hit by the bus. The Token Comparison therefore implies that his actual death was hardly bad at all, for it deprived him of at most a week's worth of life.

This evaluation of the case of the Young Pedestrian seems extremely implausible. Imagine rushing to the Young Pedestrian's grieving mother and saying, "Cheer up! They've discovered good news at the autopsy. He would have died within a week anyway, so his actual death was hardly a misfortune at all." There is clearly no ground for consolation in the discovery of the aneurysm.

The Young Pedestrian's death is overdetermined in a way similar to that of the Geriatric Patient. By this I do not, of course, mean that the token death was causally overdetermined in the sense that there were two or more causes, each sufficient on its own to bring about the actual death, that operated simultaneously. Rather, a type of event—death—was overdetermined in the near future in that, if the cause of the actual token death had not operated, a different death would have resulted soon from the operation of a different cause. In cases in which death is overdetermined in this latter sense, the Token Comparison has implications that seem implausible. The implausibility may be slight in the case of the Geriatric Patient, but it is glaring in the case of the Young Pedestrian. Let us call the challenge that cases involving overdetermination pose to the Token Comparison the *Problem of Overdetermination.*

There are some cases in which the causal overdetermination of a person's death in the near future does not seem to challenge the Token Comparison. Here is one example:

> *The Cavalry Officer.* A gallant young cavalry officer is shot and killed during the charge of the Light Brigade by a Russian soldier named Ivan. If he had not been killed by Ivan, however, he would have been killed only seconds later by a bullet fired by another soldier, Boris, who also had him in his sights.[33]

It may seem that, if we ask what would have happened if the Cavalry Officer had not died when and how he did—that is, if he had not been killed by Ivan's bullet—the answer must be that he would have died moments later. According to the Token Comparison, his actual death was hardly a misfortune at all, as it deprived him of only a second or two of further life. That seems absurd; but it is not necessarily implied by the Token Comparison. As we have seen in discussing the Metaphysical Problem, there are many ways in which the officer might not have died. If everything had been the same up to the moment before his death except that Ivan's hand trembled, altering the trajectory of his bullet, then the officer would indeed have been killed a moment later by Boris. But that is not the way we suppose that he might not have died for the purpose of reaching an overall evaluation of his death. Instead, we naturally see the threats from both Russian soldiers as parts of the same causal sequence. When we imagine the officer not being killed by Ivan, we imagine him not being killed by Boris either. We imagine—for example—his riding onto a different area of the battlefield where he would not have been in range of either soldier's gun. That was certainly a possible alternative.

The fact that the causal overdetermination of death seems innocuous in the case of the officer provides some reason for skepticism about the problem in the case of the Young Pedestrian. If we are so easily able to avoid the implication that the officer's death is only a trivial misfortune, it seems that we should be able to avoid the comparable implication in the case of the Young Pedestrian. But the solution in the case of the Cavalry Officer is not available in the case of the Young Pedestrian. The bus and the aneurysm are not parts of the same causal sequence. While it may be true that some of the ways in which the threat of the aneurysm might have been averted (for example, if it had been detected earlier and surgically corrected) would have altered his life in ways that would also have prevented the bus accident, these are not ways in which we naturally suppose that he might not have died. All of the ways in which we naturally imagine the bus accident not occurring would leave the threat from the aneurysm in place. So there is no realistic interpretation of the clause "if he had not died" that would enable us to compare the Young Pedestrian's actual death with an alternative in which he would have had a long and prosperous future. Yet surely the mere fact that the threats from both soldiers seem to be part of a single causal sequence is insufficiently significant to explain how the officer's death could be tragic while the Young Pedestrian's death is only marginally worse than that of the Geriatric Patient.

Fred Feldman has offered a response to the case of the Cavalry Officer that might be thought to solve the Problem of Overdetermination in the case of the Young Pedestrian as well. Feldman, as we have seen, advances an account of the badness of death that combines the Token Comparison and the Life Comparative Account. Basing his account on what he calls "the standard account of the meaning of subjunctive conditionals" (that is, Lewis's theory), and invoking its associated apparatus of possible worlds, he offers the following general account:

> Suppose we are wondering whether it would be bad for a certain person, s, to die at a certain time t. Then we must ask about the value for s of the [nearest] possible world that would exist if s were to die at t; and we must compare that value to the value for s of the [nearest] possible world that would exist if s were not to die at t. If the death-world is worse for s than the non-death-world, then s's death at t would be bad for s; otherwise not.[34]

Feldman acknowledges that this account is challenged by the case of the Cavalry Officer. His response is, first, to distinguish among a variety of distinct states of affairs—for example, that the officer "dies exactly at t," that the officer "dies as a result of being shot by Ivan," and that the officer "dies in his youth." The first two of these, he contends, "are not very bad for" the officer; neither deprived him "of much happiness, since if he hadn't been killed at t by Ivan, he would have been killed seconds later by Boris. . . . The real tragedy here is not that he died exactly at t, or that he died as a result of being shot by Ivan; the real tragedy is that he died so young."[35] According to Feldman, the appropriate comparison is with "the nearest possible world in which" the officer does not die young—that is, with the alternative in which the officer "does not die in his youth, but is otherwise as much as possible like he is here in the actual world."[36] If we ask what would have happened if the officer had not died young, the answer is presumably that he would have lived "a long and happy life."[37]

Perhaps a similar solution can be applied to the case of the Young Pedestrian. Feldman's approach invites us to find the state of affairs associated with a person's death that seems to capture our sense of why the death was bad and then to compare the death with the alternative that is most like the actual course of events except that

that state of affairs does not occur. In the case of the Young Pedestrian, the very same maneuver may seem to work: we identify his misfortune as "dying young" and then compare the death with the nearest alternative in which he does not die young.

There are, however, objections to this approach. First, Feldman's response to the case of the Cavalry Officer effectively shifts from the evaluation of the actual death—the token event—to the evaluation of a *type* of event: death in the near future. The comparison is no longer with the nearest possible world in which the victim's actual, particular death does not occur but with the nearest possible world in which he does not die *any* death until he is no longer young. What this comparison reveals is not how bad the particular death was but how bad a certain type of event—death while young—would be in his case. Feldman has, in effect, changed the subject. It should be no surprise that, once the subject has been changed in this way, the Problem of Overdetermination disappears. The Problem of Overdetermination arises when various potential causes of death are lined up seriatim in the relatively near future. When Feldman stipulates that the officer's misfortune is to die young and compares his death with his not dying young, he is comparing the death with an alternative in which none of the potential causes of death that might have operated while the officer was young are present. There is no longer a Problem of Overdetermination because the death is compared with a hypothetical alternative in which none of the potential overdetermining causes of death operates.

Second, there is a disturbing arbitrariness about identifying the misfortune of either the Young Pedestrian or the Cavalry Officer as "dying young." We are, according to Feldman, to imagine the absence of successive causes of death up to the end of the victim's youth. But why stop there? There seems to be no principled reason why the death should be compared with the closest alternative in which the victim does not die young rather than, for example, with the closest alternative in which he does not die prematurely, or in which he does not die before reaching old age, or in which he does not die before attaining the maximum human life span, or in which he does not die at all.

Feldman's response to the Problem of Overdetermination is ad hoc. But it seems to be inspired by a line of thought that has a certain plausibility. I will sketch that line of thought in the following section. We need an explanation and defense of our sense that the Young Pedestrian suffers a tragic misfortune—a misfortune that is significantly greater than that of the Geriatric Patient. The problem is that, because for both of them death is overdetermined in the near future, the Token Comparison implies that neither's death constitutes a significant misfortune. I will return later to the question whether the Geriatric Patient suffers a misfortune. For the moment, I will focus on the case of the Young Pedestrian.

4.2. *The Inheritance Strategy and the Problem of the Terminus*

I have suggested that one who cared about the Young Pedestrian would derive no consolation from learning that, if he had not been killed by the bus, he would have died soon anyway. Let us consider why that is. Suppose that the Young Pedestrian had not been killed by the bus but had then died a week later from the bursting of the aneurysm. How ought that hypothetical death to be evaluated? Presumably it would have been a tragic death. Assume that there would have been no overdetermination of death in the near future in that case: for example, if the Young Pedestrian had not died from the aneurysm, he would have lived another forty years before dying of a heart attack at age sixty. According to the Token Comparison, the death from the aneurysm would have deprived the Young Pedestrian of forty years of life. But if death from the aneurysm would have been tragic, how could the death in the bus accident a week *earlier* fail to be even worse? Let t_1 be the time of the bus accident and t_2 be the time of the bursting of the aneurysm. It seems that, if the death at t_2 from the aneurysm would have deprived the Young Pedestrian of a great deal of good beyond t_2, the death at t_1 must have deprived him of all of that good *as well as* the good between t_1 and t_2. For it simply makes no sense to suppose that the earlier death at t_1 could be less bad, indeed substantially less bad, than the death at t_2—though this is what the Token Comparison, applied discretely to each death, seems to imply.

This argument can be iterated. Let t_3 be the time that the Young Pedestrian would have had the heart attack at age sixty if he had not died either in the bus accident or from the aneurysm. Death from the heart attack at t_3 could also have been bad, and the Token Comparison explains why. Suppose that if he had not died from the heart attack at t_3, he would have lived another twenty years until he died from a stroke at time t_4. But if death at t_2 from the aneurysm would have been worse than death at t_3 from the heart attack, and death at t_3 would have been worse than death at t_4, then it follows that death at t_2 would be worse than death at t_4. And surely that is plausible: it *would* be worse for the Young Pedestrian to die at age twenty from an aneurysm than to die at age eighty from a stroke (assuming, of course, that the intervening life would be worth living). But notice that the same reasoning applies to death at t_1 in the bus accident. If death at t_2 is worse than death at t_3, surely death at t_1 is worse than both. If death at t_2 would have been bad because it would have deprived the Young Pedestrian of the good his life would have contained between t_2 and t_3, then death at t_1 must be worse than death at t_2 for the same reason. Death at t_1, therefore, must deprive the Young Pedestrian not only of the good his life would have contained between t_1 and t_2 but also the good it would have contained between t_2 and t_3; otherwise it is difficult to see how the death at t_1 could be worse than the death at t_2. The death at t_1 *inherits* the badness of the hypothetical death at t_2. But the logic of the argument transfers along the entire series of potential deaths. If death at t_1 is bad relative to death at t_2, and death at t_2 is bad relative to t_3, and death at t_3 is bad relative to death at t_4, and so on up to death at t_n, then death at t_1 is bad relative to death at t_n. The actual death at t_1 must inherit the badness of each potential death relative to the next hypothetical death in the queue all the way to death at t_n.

| actual death: | burst | | | |
| bus accident | aneurysm | | heart attack | stroke |

t_1 t_2 t_3 t_4 t_n

age 20   age 60   age 80

Let us call this approach to the Problem of Overdetermination the *Inheritance Strategy*. It suggests that the Token Comparison cannot be right. According to the Inheritance Strategy, we do not in fact evaluate a death by comparison with the future life that the victim would have had if only the actual death had not occurred. Rather, we evaluate it by comparison with the future the victim would have had if the actual death had not occurred *and* if all subsequent potential deaths up to some point would not have occurred either. In imagining this alternative to the victim's death, we imagine that the cause of the actual death did not operate; and we imagine that the next cause of death that would have operated if the actual death had not occurred also would not operate; and so on. But we do not imagine that other evils that would have been independent of the various causes of death would not occur. These we hold constant in an effort to evaluate the quality of the life that the victim would have had in the absence of death up to a certain point.

The Inheritance Strategy is intended to capture the idea that the death in the bus accident already deprives the Young Pedestrian of all that the death from the aneurysm would have deprived him of had he lived. But there is an alternative way of arriving at this conclusion. We assume that the Young Pedestrian loses, or is deprived of, an adult life. Even though the aneurysm would have deprived him of that life if the rendezvous with the bus had not, it was the bus that *in fact* brought about the loss. Thus we attribute the loss of his adult life to its actual cause—the actual death in the bus accident—rather than to any further hypothetical causes. This view is supported by a comparison with our reasoning about the attribution of responsibility for a loss in cases involving killing. An example of this reasoning is given by Matthew Hanser. He sketches an example in which X maliciously kills Y knowing that, if he were not to do so, a group of Mafia hit men would certainly kill him (i.e., Y) only moments later. Hanser comments that "there is a sense in which Y's death . . . deprives him of no more than a few moments of life . . . Taking the broader view, however, Y suffers the same loss he would have suffered had the hit men not been in the picture: the loss of being cut down in the prime of his life. If Y's actual death (brought about by X) does not produce this loss, what does? Not anything the hit men cause to happen, for they have no influence on how events actually unfold."[38] A similar point might be made with respect to saving a life. If X snatches a child out of the path of an oncoming truck, we credit X with having saved the child's life even if Z was standing by ready to save the child if X had not.[39]

There is, however, a problem with these claims—a problem that I believe ultimately undermines the Inheritance Strategy as well. Hanser assumes that, in the case he presents, X's killing Y causes a loss of life beyond that which Y would have had up to the point of being killed by the hit men. But what reason is there to suppose that X's act causes the loss of life that Y would not in fact have had even if X not done the act? It seems false to say that X's act prevents Y from having a life that he would not in fact have had even if X had not acted. I suspect that our readiness to accept that X's act deprives Y of a lengthy future derives from a confusion. We implicitly make two assumptions about this example: that Y is deprived of a lengthy future and that X's killing Y is seriously morally wrong. And given the normal connection between killing and deprivation, the two beliefs are naturally associated in our minds: we assume that X's wrongful act causes Y's loss and that this explains the egregious wrongness of X's act. But this association can be broken. As I will argue in chapter 3, most of us believe, on reflection, that killing is wrong for reasons other than that it inflicts a loss on the victim. Thus most of us believe that it would be wrong for X maliciously to kill Y even if he knew for certain that Y would otherwise die within minutes of a cerebral hemorrhage. In this case, however, we would be less inclined to claim that X's act caused Y to lose a lengthy future. Perhaps this is because we regard the occurrence of a hemorrhage as outside the scope of human volition and thus certain to occur in a way that what we assume to be the free action of the hit men could never be.

This is just speculation. The important point is that Hanser assumes that Y suffers a great loss. And he claims that the only plausible candidate for the cause of that great loss is X's act of killing. But he can assume that Y's loss is great only if it is a loss of life that Y would have had if he had not been killed by X *and* if he would not have been killed by the hit men. Here we see the similarity between Hanser's view and the Inheritance Strategy. Both presuppose that a person may lose more in dying than merely what he would have had if his actual death had not occurred. Both presuppose that, in assessing a person's losses in dying, we are entitled to compare the person's actual death with what would have happened not only if that death had not occurred but also if other, later, hypothetical deaths would not have occurred either.

Again, Hanser must be assuming that, if Y had not been killed by X, his life *might* not have been ended by the hit men either (even though in fact it *would* have been) and that this is essential to measuring Y's *loss*. Similarly, the Inheritance Strategy assumes that the Young Pedestrian loses life beyond both the actual bus accident and the various further hypothetical causes of death. The crucial question is this: What is the full extent of each's loss? What is the limit to the losses we are entitled to attribute to each? The answer, of course, depends on what we take to be the outermost boundary of the life that each could (not would) have had in the absence of the actual death. In the case of Hanser's Y, if he lost more than just the few moments between his actual killing by X and the death he would have met at the hands of the hit men, at what point should we imagine the lengthy life he lost as ending? In the case of the Young Pedestrian, the Inheritance Strategy measures the loss he suffers from the actual death at t_1 by comparing the life that ends then with a hypothetical life that terminates at time t_n; but what is t_n? In each case, at what point does it become inappropriate to imagine the hypothetical life being further extended by asking what would have happened if yet another hypothetical death would not have occurred? These various questions pose what I will call the *Problem of the Terminus*.

Earlier I suggested that there are inchoate intimations of the Inheritance Strategy in Feldman's response to the Problem of Overdetermination. There is also a response to the Problem of the Terminus. Recall that, in the case of the Cavalry Officer, Feldman claims that "the real tragedy is that he died so young." The suggestion is that the officer's actual death should be compared with an alternative possible course of events in which he does not die young. And there is a similar suggestion in Hanser's claim that X "suffers the . . . loss of being cut down in the prime of his life." We are, it seems, to evaluate X's death by comparison with a life in which he dies beyond his prime.

These suggestions are ad hoc and rather arbitrary. But perhaps they can be refined. What they have in common is the sense that, because death is at some point inevitable, what is bad is a *premature* or, as it is often said, "untimely" death. On this view, we should compare a person's death with a life that he could otherwise have had in which he would not have died prematurely. We would continue to ask what would have happened if each successive hypothetical death had not occurred, but only up to the point at which death would not longer have been premature. At what point does death cease to be premature? One answer is that a death is not premature if it occurs after a person has lived a normal life span.

There are, of course, many problems in determining what constitutes a normal life span. The *average* life span at a given time varies enormously over human history and even now varies considerably from one society to another. Should we take the normal human life span to be something like the average over all of human history? (If so, when do we suppose human history to have started?) Should we take it to be the present average for our own society? There is, I think, an ineliminable element of arbitrariness to the selection of a measure of the norm. There is no single objective standard for a normal human life span. What counts as normal depends on whom we are concerned to compare ourselves with. Our actual tendency seems to be to compare ourselves with the members of the population with whom we most strongly identify ourselves. If one is an American of the early twenty-first century and the average life span for members of that population is around the mid-seventies, then one may feel cheated if one expects to die significantly prior to reaching that age, even if one's life will be significantly longer than the average life span for sub-Saharan Africa during the same period of time. Similarly, if one is a sub-Saharan African who lives well beyond the average for one's own society, one may feel fortunate even if one expects one's life to be considerably shorter than the average American life span.

There is also, however, a tendency to compare oneself with the members of the most fortunate population among one's contemporaries. Thus sub-Saharan Africans who are aware of the difference between their average life span and that of contemporary Americans are likely to conclude that they themselves are dying prematurely. But when Americans who live into their seventies are confronted with the same information about differences in mortality rates, they are unlikely to think of themselves as having lived well beyond a normal human life span. Roughly speaking, one tends to think of a death as premature if it occurs prior to the average time of death for the most advantaged populations among one's contemporaries or near contemporaries.

Whatever we take the normal human life span to be, it is absurd to suppose that it sets the limit to the degree of misfortune that a person can suffer by dying. If we were entitled to compare a person's death with the life he could otherwise have had but only up to the end of a normal life span, then no one who dies after having lived beyond the normal life span could be said to have suffered a misfortune. Yet even if we assume that the normal life span is quite long, an energetic person brimming with plans and ambitions surely suffers a misfortune in being run over by a bus irrespective of whether he has already lived beyond the normal life span.

The normal human life span cannot, therefore, be the end point of the hypothetical life—the life a person could have had—with which we compare his actual life in order to evaluate his losses in dying. But we have not exhausted the possible understandings of what counts as a premature death. An alternative understanding is that any death is premature that occurs prior to the maximum human life span. According to this notion of the terminus for comparisons, we should continue to ask what would have happened if successive possible causes of death had not occurred until we reach the point at which the hypothetical life could not have continued without exceeding the maximum possible life span. In evaluating a person's death, we ought, in effect, to compare the life that ended with that death to the life the person could have had if no cause of death had operated until he reached the maximum life span.

Schopenhauer held that any death that occurs before the body reaches its own internally determined limit is a premature death. In *Parerga and Paralipomena,* he wrote:

> in the *Upanishad* of the *Veda . . . the natural duration of human life* is stated to be a hundred years. I think this is correct because I have noticed that only those who have passed their ninetieth year attain to *euthanasia,* that is to say, die without illness, apoplexy, convulsions, or rattles in the throat; sometimes they die without turning pale, often when seated and after a meal; or rather they do not exactly die, but simply cease to live. At any earlier age one dies merely of disease and hence prematurely.[40]

Schopenhauer does not explicitly say that it cannot be bad to die when the body reaches its own natural limit; but the implication may be there.

It is now commonly assumed that the natural limit to human life, or the maximum human life span, is not a hundred years but just a little over 120 years. The longest-lived person about whose birth and death dates we have reliable data was a French woman who died in 1997 at the age of 122.[41] So we might interpret the current proposal to mean that we should evaluate a person's overall loss in dying by comparing the actual death to an alternative in which the person would have lived to be about 122.

This, however, presupposes a particular sense of the notion of the maximum human life span—namely, the maximum life span that any human being is known to have attained. An alternative understanding of the maximum is the longest that it is biologically possible for human beings to live as they are now constituted. Many gerontologists believe that it is possible for human beings as they are now constituted to live longer than anyone has lived hitherto by restricting the number of calories they consume daily while at the same time satisfying various nutritional requirements. No one knows what the maximum human life span is in this sense.

One argument for making the maximum life span the terminus for comparisons might be that it keeps the comparisons within the bounds of physical possibility. But there is surely some variation in what is physically possible for different individuals. Thus if part of the concern is with realism, we must accept that the maximum, and thus the terminus for comparisons, is variable. Otherwise we might have to compare an individual's death with a life that was longer than what was physically possible for him. But if the terminus is variable in this way, one implication might be that an individual who dies at a substantially earlier age than another would nevertheless suffer a lesser misfortune because his maximum was correspondingly lower. This seems implausible.

There are other objections. The Inheritance Strategy requires that we compare a person's death with the life he would have had if successive causes of death had been absent but in which other conditions had evolved naturally. Because we assume that other conditions would be unaltered, taking the terminus for comparisons to be the maximum life span will yield evaluations of death as less bad than it seems intuitively. To see this, consider the case of someone who dies at age 60 when the presumed maximum life span (whether this is his individual maximum or the maximum for human beings as they are presently constituted) is 140 years. Suppose that when he died he was beginning to suffer from certain progressive degenerative conditions. While he could have lived comfortably with these conditions for another 20 or 30 years, they would after that have begun to cause increasing pain that could not have been fully relieved. Suppose that they would have made the final 40 of his projected 140 years unbearable. If the agony of those final 40 years would have outweighed the good of the projected years from 60 to 100, the Inheritance Strategy implies that his actual death was good for him. Given that he would not in fact have lived to be 140, this seems absurd.

Finally, taking the terminus to be the maximum life span for human beings as they are currently constituted implies that it cannot be a misfortune to die at that maximum. But we must consider the possibility that the maximum life span could be extended by altering the present biological constitution of human beings, perhaps through genetic engineering. Suppose that a scientist discovers how to modify our genetic constitution in a way that would extend the present maximum human life span. But just as he is about to reveal how we could extend our lives beyond the present maximum, he is struck by lightning and his secret dies with him. If that would be a misfortune for us, the maximum life span for human beings as they are currently constituted cannot be the terminus for comparisons.

I have argued that neither the normal human life span nor the maximum life span is the appropriate terminus for comparisons in evaluating the losses involved in death. It seems, in fact, that we can always continue to ask: "What would have happened if the person had not died *then?*" That is, for each successive death a person might have died, we can always ask what would have happened if that death would not have occurred—even if the continuation of life would, in the circumstances, have in fact been impossible. (It makes perfect sense to ask what would have happened if something that is in fact impossible were to occur—for example, if the law of universal gravitation were an inverse cube law rather than an inverse square law.) If this is true, there is no terminus, no point at which, if a person's actual death had not occurred, the life he could have had *must* be assumed to end, or could not be supposed to have gone on.

But if we continue to pose the question indefinitely—what would have happened if that cause of death would not have operated, or the next one, or the next . . . — we can know in advance the pattern that the answers will take. If we assume that the other conditions of life, such as aging, would evolve as they normally do, we know that there must be some point, which no doubt varies from person to person, at which a person's life would cease to be worth living. In short, if we imagine a person continuing to live indefinitely while remaining vulnerable to such evils as disease, injury, and aging, we are in effect imagining a struldbruggian immortality. If we compare each actual death with such a hypothetical life, we will conclude that every death is good because the evils of the struldbruggian life would outweigh any goods the person could have had before his life ceased to be worth living. This is clearly absurd. Of course, we would not be limited to comparing a death just with a hypothetical life with no terminus. We could compare an actual death with any of the hypothetical deaths that might have occurred later, and we could compare different hypothetical deaths with one another. But again the pattern of evaluations is obvious.

Just as we know that any actual death is better than living forever in a struldbruggian state (which is the moral of Swift's tale), so we also know that an actual death is worse than dying later but prior to the point at which one's life would have ceased to be worth living. And an actual death might be worse or might be better than a hypothetical death somewhat beyond the point at which the life would have ceased to be worth living, depending on whether the remaining good life would have outweighed the period that would not have been worth living. Finally, any actual death would be better than any hypothetical death well beyond the point at which the life would have ceased to be worth living. We are left, in short, with a plurality of evaluations, all of which are obvious and none of which seems genuinely informative. We might learn something of interest if we could determine by how much an actual death preceded the point at which the life would have ceased to be worth living. But that point, too, is wholly arbitrary as a terminus for comparisons: sometimes life does continue after it has ceased to be worth living.

This entire line of thought is in any case idle, for after a point the necessary comparisons simply cannot be made. The Inheritance Strategy requires that we compare a person's actual death with the life he could have had if the actual death had not occurred *and* if successive possible deaths would not have occurred either. But we must assume that other conditions of the person's life would have evolved normally (or as normally as possible in the absence of death); for otherwise we will not be asking only what would have happened in the absence of successive causes of death. We will instead be asking what would have happened in the absence of death and certain other conditions as well. And that question yields an evaluation of more than death alone. But in fact it is incoherent to suppose that life could continue indefinitely while conditions such as disease, injury, and aging would evolve normally. Conditions such as these often evolve toward death. Indeed, the process of aging and the progression of certain diseases are such that the disintegration and death of the organism are the necessary ultimate outcome of their indefinite continuation. It is therefore a necessary impossibility for a life to contain these evils in the forms in which we know them without terminating in death. The struldbruggian immortality is incoherent.

4.3. *Overall Losses in Dying*

If there is no terminus, and if we cannot coherently continue to ask what would have happened if death had continued not to occur but other conditions had evolved normally, we must abandon the Inheritance Strategy. We should, I believe, return to the Token Comparison. But this leaves us where we began with the Problem of Overdetermination. In the case of the Young Pedestrian, for example, the Token Comparison implies that his death is only a minor misfortune, since it deprives him of only a week's worth of life. Is it possible to accept the Token Comparison and yet preserve our sense that the Young Pedestrian suffers a grave misfortune?

I believe it is. The Young Pedestrian's misfortune, we may suppose, is to lose a long and happy future—at a minimum, the forty years of life he could have had up to the fatal heart attack he would have suffered at age sixty. This is a serious misfortune. But the loss of that future is not attributable just to the Young Pedestrian's death. For it is not true that he would have had a long and happy future if only his actual death had not occurred. This is, in fact, a central objection to the Inheritance Strategy: it sees the Young Pedestrian's death as responsible for his losing goods that he would not have had even if the death had not occurred. The truth is that the Young Pedestrian would have had a long and happy future *only* if *two* circumstances had been different: namely, if he had not been killed by the bus *and* if, had he not been killed by the bus, he would not have died of a burst aneurysm. His misfortune in being deprived of a long and happy future is therefore attributable not just to his actual death but also to the fact that, if he had not died in the bus accident, he would have died a week later from a burst aneurysm. His loss is attributable to these two misfortunes, one actual and one hypothetical. (Even though the second *misfortune* was hypothetical, the *threat*—the aneurysm—was actual.)

The temptation to blame the Young Pedestrian's death for his loss of a long and happy future may arise from the fact that the loss *is* attributable to death, understood as a *type* of event rather than a particular token event. His loss is properly attributed to a disjunction: his actual death or, if not that, then a different death soon thereafter. If we blur the actual and the counterfactual death together, we may simply assign the loss to death without noticing that it is not solely the actual death that is responsible for the full loss.

To avoid this kind of confusion, we should distinguish the loss that is attributable entirely to a person's death from his *overall loss,* which is his loss of whatever good was in prospect for him but of which he was deprived by a variety of factors, including his death. The notion of a person's overall loss is illustrated by the following case:

> *The Accident Victim.* A young man of twenty suffers an accident that causes extensive brain damage, leaving him severely cognitively impaired in a way that blights his previous hopes for the future. A week later he is killed in the middle of the night by an earthquake that completely destroys the house in which he lives.

Suppose that if neither the accident nor the earthquake had occurred, the Accident Victim would have had a long and happy future. It is obvious in this case (as it is not in the case of the Young Pedestrian) that his loss of that future is not attributable to the death alone, for the accident had, in a sense, *already* deprived him of much of the good of which, had the accident *not* occurred, he *would* have been deprived by death. (In this respect his situation is similar to that of the Young Cancer Patient, whose disease has altered his prospects for the future in a way that affects the value of his death.) The loss of a long and happy future is the Accident Victim's overall loss and is attributable to the combined misfortunes of the accident and the death.

The Young Pedestrian, too, loses a long and happy future (at least forty years of life up to the point at which he would have died of a heart attack), though, as in the case of the Accident Victim, the whole of this loss is not attributable to his death. The loss of a lengthy future is his overall loss and is, as I noted earlier, attributable to the conjunction of his actual death and the fact that, if that death had not occurred, he would have died soon of the aneurysm. Note that his overall loss is the same as his loss from death would have been if he had been run over by the bus but had not had an aneurysm at all.

There is an understandable tendency in the literature on death to conflate the loss that a person suffers from death alone with the overall losses he suffers in dying. Nagel, for example, writes that "countless possibilities for [an individual's] continued existence are imaginable, and we can clearly conceive of what it would be for him to go on existing indefinitely. However inevitable it is that this will not come about, its possibility is still that of the continuation of a good for him, if life is the good we take it to be."[42] Thus, as I noted earlier, he concludes that "death, no matter how inevitable, is an abrupt cancellation of indefinitely extensive possible goods."[43] Given that his claim takes this general form, Nagel cannot be referring to what would happen in the absence of only the actual death, or even (as the Inheritance Strategy invites us to imagine) to what would happen if death were indefinitely postponed but the other conditions of life were to evolve normally. He must instead be referring to what would happen if not only death were indefinitely postponed but also various other causes of misfortune and deprivation were not to occur either—for example, if aging were slowed or arrested. In other words, if every person loses an indefinitely extensive set of possible goods when he dies, this must be his overall loss, not his loss from death alone. This loss is attributable to the death in conjunction with a variety of other possible causes of deprivation that would have operated had the death not occurred.

A similar implicit focus on overall losses seems to underlie this otherwise paradoxical claim by Richard Wollheim: "That there are circumstances in which we would prefer to die rather than to live is . . . compatible with death being a misfortune because there are circumstances in which life has become a yet greater misfortune."[44] This is paradoxical if, as I have claimed, death can be good or bad only by comparison with what it excludes. For in the circumstances Wollheim describes, the life that the person would in fact have in the absence of death would be bad; therefore it seems that the death must be good. Wollheim's claim that the death is a misfortune must therefore be based on a comparison with a life other than the one the person would in fact have had in the absence of the death. His claim must be that death is bad in comparison with what would have happened if the death had not occurred *and* if certain *other* sources of deprivation or misfortune had been absent as well. *This* loss is not attributable to the death alone; it is the person's overall loss.

In the case of the Young Pedestrian, the discovery of the aneurysm should prompt us to revise our evaluation of his death, though what we took to be his loss from death we should now see as his overall loss. When we learn of the aneurysm, we should not conclude that his loss is less than we thought; rather, we should simply reassign responsibility for that loss. This is why there is no comfort for the grieving mother in the discovery that his loss *from death* is less than we had supposed. In other cases, events that occur after a person has died may retroactively affect how bad his death was for him without, however, affecting his overall losses. This can be illustrated by citing and responding to a general objection to the idea that death is bad to the extent that it deprives the victim of goods that he would have had if he had not died. Suppose that shortly after the death of someone whom we may call *Victim,* it becomes possible to raise the general quality of life. It might be argued that it is a reason not to raise the quality of life that this would make Victim's death worse; for it would mean that the quality of the life that he lost would have been higher. But surely this is wrong. And it is not just that the benefits to the living of increasing the quality of life would outweigh the increase in the badness of Victim's death. It seems instead that the effect on the badness of Victim's death constitutes *no* objection to raising the quality of life.

There are various ways of responding to this problem. One is to argue that events that occur after a person has died cannot affect either that person's life or his death. I reject that response. Let us grant, at least for the sake of argument, that raising the quality of life would make Victim's death worse by increasing the losses attributable to the death. We should then ask whether refraining from raising the quality of life would actually limit Victim's losses. Clearly it would not; it would simply relocate those losses. His overall loss would remain the same.[45] What was possible for him, and therefore what he lost, was life at the higher level of quality. That is his overall loss: it is what he would have had if he had not died *and if* we raise the quality of life. If we do raise the quality of life, his loss of life at the higher level of quality will be attributable to the death alone. But if we do not raise the quality of life and would not have done so even if he had lived, then his death is responsible only for the loss of life at a lower level of quality. The remainder of his overall loss is attributable to our failure to raise the quality of life. Thus his death *and* our subsequent failure to raise the quality of life would together deprive him of a future life at the higher level. (Notice that, if we do not raise the quality of life *precisely because* he died, so that his death is what indirectly prevents the quality of life from being raised, we may credit his death itself with his loss of life at the higher level. In that case, the loss attributable to death will be the same as it would have been if we *had* raised the quality of life. In short, to refrain from raising the quality of life in order to reduce his loss from death would be self-defeating.)

Although the notion of a person's overall loss in dying seems essential if we are to explain our sense that the Young Pedestrian (and others whose death within a short period is overdetermined) suffers a terrible misfortune, it is also highly problematic. One problem concerns the apportioning of responsibility for overall losses among the various sources of deprivation, both actual and hypothetical. In the case of the Young Pedestrian, for example, should we say that the actual death deprived him of only one week of life, while his loss of forty years beyond that week is attributable to the fact that he would have died of the aneurysm? Because the problem of apportioning responsibility for losses between an actual and a hypothetical event raises the difficult question of how an actual loss may be attributable to a merely hypothetical event, I will illustrate the general problem with a simpler case: that of the Accident Victim.

It seems that we should accept that the Accident Victim's death is a comparatively minor misfortune, since the accident had already deprived him of the prospect of a future that would have been well worth living. The death causes him to lose only a future that would scarcely have been worth living. Here we evaluate the later event (the death) against the background of what has already occurred (the accident). But notice that this conflicts with what we are inclined to say about Young Pedestrian, which is that the initial event (the actual death) should be evaluated in the light of what would have happened if it had not occurred (which is that he would have died in a week from the aneurysm). And this alternative approach makes just as much sense in the case of the Accident Victim. It seems plausible to say that the accident was only a comparatively minor misfortune given that the death was going to occur in a week anyway. Viewed in this way, it seems that the only difference the accident made was to make the Accident Victim's last week of life less good than it would otherwise have been.

Each of these ways of viewing the Accident Victim's losses seems plausible. It seems reasonable to say that the accident was not responsible for a great loss because the death was going to occur soon anyway. It seems equally reasonable to say that the death did not cause a great loss because his prospects at the time of death were already grim as a result of the accident. But these claims, taken together, cannot both be right. It cannot be true that the loss caused by the accident was only that the Accident Victim had a week with severe cognitive disabilities rather than a week with normal cognitive capacities *and* that the loss caused by the death was only the loss of a future of severe cognitive disability. For these two losses do not add up to the Accident Victim's overall loss, which is the loss of the life he would have had if neither the accident nor the death had occurred. What this shows is that we cannot assess both losses by taking each against the backdrop of the other.

In some cases involving this kind of overdetermination, it may be important to apportion losses to their proper causes. We may need to know how much harm a person has caused in order to determine how much blame or punishment he deserves. This might be true, for example, if one were to cause a person an injury similar to that suffered by the Accident Victim when it was known for certain that the person was going to die in a week anyway, or if one were to cause the death of a person who one week previously had suffered irreversible brain damage of the sort suffered by the Accident Victim. I am uncertain about what we should say in these cases.

In some instances, which event we take as given for purposes of evaluation depends on what we know. If someone suffers brain damage and seems as if he will live on for years, we assume that the brain damage is responsible for his loss of many years of happy life. Suppose he then dies of independent causes—causes that would have operated even if the brain damage had not occurred. Since we have already taken the brain damage to have eliminated his prospects for good, we take the death not to be a serious misfortune. But we might have seen the damage differently had we known for certain that the death was going to occur. Thus, if it is known that someone is going to die at a specific time (for example, because he is scheduled to be executed and there is no possibility of a pardon or even a reprieve), we may think that an accident that causes brain damage a week prior to that time is not a serious misfortune, for we take the death as given. Notice, however, that there is no real difference between these cases; in both, a person suffers an accident that causes brain damage and then dies of independent causes a week later. What is different, in the second case, is our knowledge at the time the accident occurs that the death is impending.

I will not pursue this problem further. It will be sufficient for our purposes if we can determine what a person's overall losses are in cases involving the forms of overdetermination found in such cases as the Young Pedestrian and the Accident Victim. We may not need to know how to assign each distinct misfortune, actual or hypothetical, its share of the overall loss. But even the determination of overall losses is highly problematic. I will briefly note three related problems.

Recall that the Inheritance Strategy invites us to measure a person's losses from death by asking what would have happened if his actual death had not occurred and if successive possible deaths he might have suffered would not have occurred either. In calculating a person's overall losses, we need to know what would have happened not only if he had not died but also if certain other causes of deprivation would not have occurred either. Imagine, for example, a variant of the case of the Young Pedestrian in which, if he had not been killed by the bus, his aneurysm would have burst a week later but would have caused brain damage rather than death. In determining his overall losses in dying, we ask what would have happened if neither cause of loss had occurred, even though the bursting of the aneurysm would not have caused him to die. But if we take a person's overall losses to include whatever he could have had if *no* causes of loss—death, aging, disease, injury, and so on—would have occurred, his losses may seem virtually infinite. But surely there is some limit to a person's overall losses. The problem of determining what this limit is is a new version of the Problem of the Terminus.

Even if each person's overall losses were, to use Nagel's term, indefinitely extensive, it would not follow that all people's overall losses are equal. For unless we include among a person's overall losses what his life could have been like in the future if both his past and his future were devoid of misfortune, we will calculate his overall losses by asking what he could have had if only very recent and future causes of loss had not occurred or would not have occurred. (I include very recent causes of loss in order to accommodate such losses as those that the Accident Victim suffers from the accident a week before his death.) This means that what a person would have in prospect in the absence of recent and future causes of deprivation depends on what his recent or present state is. And this raises a second problem. If we take a person's overall loss to consist of the life he would have had if his recent or present life had evolved indefinitely in the absence of further causes of loss, we will be greatly magnifying the differences between people's recent or present states by projecting them into an indefinite future. We will be doing little more than multiplying a person's recent or present state by time, and it seems doubtful that that yields a genuine measure of loss.

Notice, finally, that in speculating about a person's overall losses, we are asking what would have happened if causes of loss had not occurred or would not have occurred; but we assume that sources of benefit or gain would remain the same, to the extent that this would be compatible with the absence of causes of loss. This kind of reflection (though with perhaps a more moderate assumption about the absence of causes of loss) seems to be what underlies Nagel's claim, quoted earlier, that "countless possibilities for [an individual's] continued existence are imaginable," so that "for him to go on existing indefinitely" would be "the continuation of a good for him." This is why he concludes that, "if there is no limit to the amount of life that it would be good to have, then it may be that a bad end is in store for us all."[46] But we could, with equal propriety, reverse the pattern of assumptions on which these reflections depend. We could instead ask what a person's life would have been like if he had not died and if causes of benefit would not have occurred, while causes of loss and misfortune would have occurred as they normally do insofar as this would be compatible with the absence of sources of benefit. A possible future of this sort is equally imaginable and yields a measure, perhaps, of how much the person has been spared by dying. We are thus left with a plurality of possible comparisons and corresponding evaluations—of what the person has lost and what he has been spared. If we focus solely on the losses, we may conclude, with Nagel, that a bad end is in store for us all. If, however, we focus on the possible evils a person may avoid by dying, we may conclude instead that a beneficent end awaits us all. Is there any way to integrate these various evaluations? Is it possible that a person's overall losses in dying and his avoidance of possible evils simply cancel each other out?

These speculations seem unpromising. Intuitively, what is needed at this point is the imposition of some constraint on what can be considered to be realistically in prospect for a person shortly before or at the time of his death. Nagel himself gestures in this direction when he notes that "we . . . have to set some limits on *how* possible a possibility must be for its nonrealization to be a misfortune (or good fortune, should the possibility be a bad one)."[47] The mere nonoccurrence of a good is not, after all, a *loss* (nor is the mere nonoccurrence of an evil a benefit). For there to be a loss, a good must have been genuinely in prospect but then have been prevented by some intervening condition. Let us call this stipulation the *Realism Condition.*

To insist on the Realism Condition in our accounting of a person's overall losses is an obvious response to the new Problem of the Terminus. It also prevents us, in reckoning a person's losses, from simply extrapolating his present state into the indefinite future. Finally, it constrains our sense of what a person is spared by death as well. To illustrate the intuitive force of the Realism Condition, recall our earlier contrast between the cases of the Young Pedestrian and the Geriatric Patient. For both of these people, death is overdetermined in the near future. Nevertheless, we sense that an abundance of good is genuinely in prospect for the Young Pedestrian, whereas this is not true of the Geriatric Patient. It is difficult to say, in a general way, what the precise form of the difference is. There are, perhaps, two major differences. First, there are fewer obstacles to significant good in the case of the Young Pedestrian than in the case of the Geriatric Patient. If only two circumstances had been (or would have been) different, the Young Pedestrian would have had at least forty more years of life. But the obstacles to further good in the Geriatric Patient's life are legion. Second, there is a sense in which it was within the realm of practical possibility that the causes of the Young Pedestrian's overall loss might not have occurred. It was entirely possible for him to be more alert so that he would not have stepped in front of the bus; and often cerebral aneurysms do not burst, or they can be discovered and repaired before they burst. But there is a sense in which it would be deeply impossible for the Geriatric Patient to enjoy significantly more good. The progression of certain conditions, such as aging and disease, would not only have to be arrested, it would also have to be reversed. She would have to be restored to a physical state to which, to the best of our knowledge, it would be physically impossible to restore her. This is particularly obvious if she is already profoundly demented as well as physically incapacitated.

Something like the Realism Condition is necessary if we are to try to assess people's overall losses in dying. But the condition is extremely vague. Moreover, there may be cases in which we feel that a person who dies suffers a grave misfortune but in which the Realism Condition implies that there is no loss. Here is a case of this sort.

There is a very rare condition known as progeria that involves accelerated aging beginning around the age of four. The condition is visibly manifested in striking ways: children afflicted by it come to have thin, white hair, sagging, withered skin, and an overall wizened, birdlike appearance. Victims typically die in adolescence from advanced atherosclerosis. Curiously, although it has been found that the victim's cells divide fewer than the normal number of times, the condition does not involve all aspects of aging; so the processes involved are not identical to those involved in normal aging. But let us assume, for the sake of argument, that the mechanisms behind progeria are exactly the same as those in normal aging, except that they have a much earlier onset and progress more rapidly. Given this assumption, progeria is no more curable than ordinary aging. Any treatment that would extend the life of a child with progeria by fifty years could also do the same for the Geriatric Patient if it were administered at a comparable stage in the latter's process of aging.

With these assumptions, consider the following case:

> *The Progeria Patient.* A child of twelve dies from progeria in a state of advanced decrepitude.

Since the Progeria Patient had reached the far end of the process of aging, it was no more possible for him to continue living than it is for the Geriatric Patient. If the Realism Condition implies that there is no genuine prospect of further good life for the Geriatric Patient, it must have the same implication in the case of the Progeria Patient. Neither suffers a loss in dying.

We have, however, a strong, recalcitrant sense that the Progeria Patient suffers a very grave misfortune. How can that be if there was nothing that was realistically in prospect for him—that is, if there was nothing good for him to lose? I believe that we should regard that fact itself as his misfortune: that he had arrived at a point at which the possibilities for good in his life were exhausted. His misfortune, in short, was that no more good was possible for him.

We may crudely divide misfortunes into positive evils, such as suffering, and those that consist in the absence of good. Among the latter are losses: misfortunes that involve the failure to get a certain good that was in prospect. But it can also be a misfortune for a person if a certain good is simply not in prospect at all. (It may, of course, be worse to have a good in prospect and then lose it than it is not to have it in prospect at all. A loss, in short, may be worse than a mere absence. Most of us, I think, are inclined to believe this in a general way, though it is not clear whether losses are really worse or whether they are just harder to bear.)

I claim that the Progeria Patient's misfortune is to have run out of possibilities for good. But there is a puzzle. Why is this misfortune not counterbalanced or canceled out by the corresponding good fortune of being out of reach of further evil? Various poets and philosophers have claimed this as a virtue of death: that it frees one at last from the tyranny of suffering. And since, in ethics at least, we normally tend to think that it is more important to avoid suffering than to increase the good, one might expect that, if anything, we would think that the general good fortune of having no further suffering in prospect would more than cancel out the general misfortune of having no further good in prospect. But in fact we do not tend to think of the Progeria Patient in this way. We do not see his release from the threat of evil (or at least the threat of *experienced* evil) as outweighing or even beginning to compensate for his having reached a point at which no more good (or experienced good) is possible for him. Perhaps it is just that we make the assumption, rejected perhaps by certain poets and philosophers but affirmed by our own experience, that life is in general good; and this supports the presumption that to come to the end of life's possibilities is a misfortune, even if it does not involve a loss. If life as we know it were in general not worth living, so that suicide would characteristically be prudentially rational, our view might be different.

(I can think of one reason why someone might be tempted to see the closing of life's possibilities as a release rather than a misfortune. As we have seen, conditions in life can become so bad as to exclude any further prospect of significant good. But while the conditions of life can put further good out of reach, they cannot put us out of reach of further evil or suffering. The one possible exception to this claim is continued life in an irreversible coma. I will argue in section 1.3 of chapter 5, however, that in most cases of irreversible coma, the individual does not in fact continue to exist. The only kind of irreversible coma through which a person may continue to exist is quite rare, and it is reasonable to believe that continued existence in this state may be a misfortune, even though it cannot involve suffering. So it seems that there is an asymmetry: the conditions of life can make further good impossible but rarely if ever can they guarantee us immunity to further misfortune.)

There is another problem. The Progeria Patient has arrived at a point at which he has no realistic prospect of further good. This case was deliberately modeled to parallel the case of the Geriatric Patient. In each case, the avoidance or even postponement of death is not a realistic possibility. But even if the life could continue—with, perhaps, the person's physical state arrested just before the point of dissolution—the conditions of the life exclude any prospect of significant good. In each case, there is no good in prospect, not so much because death is physically inevitable, but because the life could not continue *and be worth living* unless some of the effects of aging were reversed or eliminated. And it is precisely this kind of supposition that is ruled out by the Realism Condition. In both cases there is an absence of any prospect of further good, and for the same reason. If this is a grave misfortune for the Progeria Patient, it seems that it should also be a grave misfortune for the Geriatric Patient. But most of us would distinguish sharply between these two cases. We tend, I think, to believe that that Geriatric Patient suffers a misfortune, though not a tragic misfortune. The Progeria Patient, however, is a victim of tragedy.

What, then, is the difference between these cases? In each case, death causes no loss, for the reasons given. Thus the death is not the misfortune. The misfortune lies in the circumstances of the life: namely, that it no longer offers a prospect of good. Our question now is why this is a greater misfortune in the case of the Progeria Patient than in the case of the Geriatric Patient. Again, the answer lies in another fact about the life rather than about the death. The reason that it seems a greater misfortune for the Progeria Patient to have arrived at a point at which no further good is possible is that he has gained so little—and so much less—from life. The Geriatric Patient has already had a full life; the Progeria Patient has not.

4.4. *The Previous Gain Account*

Before elaborating on these last claims, I will briefly summarize the argument so far. My approach to the badness of death has been forward-looking, focusing on the victim's losses. I began with the Token Comparison but found that it is challenged by the Problem of Overdetermination. While considering certain cases that involve overdetermination, I explored the Inheritance Strategy but found that it is undermined by the Problem of the Terminus. I then returned to the Token Comparison, suggesting that we might capture our sense of the misfortune that people suffer in cases in which death is overdetermined by appealing to the notion of a person's overall loss in dying. But the Problem of the Terminus arose again in connection with overall losses and, together with certain related problems, made the evaluation of losses again problematic. I next suggested that a Realism Condition plausibly enables us to impose a vague limitation on overall losses. But there are cases—the Geriatric Patient and the Progeria Patient—in which our sense of a person's misfortune in dying altogether eludes articulation in terms of the notion of loss. These people seem to suffer a misfortune—though the misfortune of one is much greater than that of the other—even though the Realism Condition implies that neither suffers a loss.

The cases of the Geriatric Patient and the Progeria Patient force us to look back at the life rather than forward to some hypothetical future in order to understand the peculiar misfortune of each. This suggests a radically different approach to understanding the badness of death. Rather than attempting to measure a person's losses in dying, perhaps we should evaluate how bad it is that the life is over by looking back to see what it has contained. The fuller and more complete it has been, the less bad it is that it has ended. One might even claim, more precisely, that the badness of a death is inversely proportional to the extent to which the life it ends was good overall. Call this the *Previous Gain Account* of the badness of death. It offers a plausible explanation and defense of our sense that it is a greater misfortune for the Progeria Patient than for the Geriatric Patient to reach a point at which no further good would be in prospect even if life were to continue. At the point at which the Progeria Patient's life runs out of possibilities for good and ends, it is a tragically unfulfilled and incomplete life.

There are two bases for measuring the badness of a life's coming to an end in terms of what the life has already contained rather than in terms of what it would or might have contained had it continued. One basis is comparative, the other noncomparative. The comparative idea is that we should determine how bad it is that a person's life comes to an end by seeing how the life compares with those of others. If the person has gained less from life than others typically do, the death is particularly bad; if he has gained more than most people do, the death is less bad. One might say that, in the latter case, the person has had his fair share. If the person has gained as much from life as anyone ever does, his death may not seem a misfortune at all.

For example, we might say that the death of the Geriatric Patient is hardly a misfortune at all, for she has had more than her fair share. But of what? How do we measure gains from life? A crude measure would be the number of years lived. This may make some sense in the case of the Geriatric Patient. Her life has been as long as a life of our sort can be. In that respect—in avoiding death or holding it at bay—she has been as successful as it is possible to be. Compared with others, she has had her fair share of life; she has no ground for complaint.

But suppose that the Geriatric Patient has lived long but has had very few opportunities for good in her life. It hardly seems right to say that her death is a lesser misfortune just because she has been around a long time, independently of what has actually happened in her life. Perhaps we should instead take *opportunities* for good as the measure of what a person gains from life. If a person has had a long life with ample opportunities for good, that may be the most that a person may reasonably ask from life. On this view, death is less bad to the extent that life has already afforded at least the normal amount of opportunity for good. What of a person who has had abundant opportunities for good—more than most have—but has failed to exploit them and consequently has gained little actual good from life? One response is to accept that the death is indeed less bad. Responsibility for the lack of good is, after all, attributable to the person rather than to his death. As Walter Kaufmann astutely observes, "we like to blame death rather than those who died, if we loved them; hence we deceive ourselves as they might have deceived themselves. We do not say, 'How many months did they waste!' but, 'If only they had had a few more weeks!' Not, 'How sad that they did not do more!' but, 'How unfair that they died so soon!' "[48] But an alternative response seems at least equally plausible. This is that, when a person dies, there is no consolation in knowing that her life offered abundant opportunities for good. On the contrary, looking back on a life of missed or squandered opportunities may make death all the more bitter. It should be consoling, however, to reflect that one's life was at least as good as most other people's. The comparative version of the Previous Gain Account should, it seems, focus on the good that a life has contained, not merely on the number of years or amount of opportunity it has afforded.

The same seems true of the noncomparative version. The general idea behind the noncomparative version is that the more of a good one has already had, the less important it is that one should have even more. This is true, of course, of specific types of good, often because of the effects of satiety, or because increasing quantities of a particular good may crowd out goods of other types. But it may be true of the good quite generally, and not necessarily because of satiety. It may be true of a particular type of good—achievement—in a way that is particularly relevant to the badness of death.

The idea that a certain kind of achievement can reconcile a person to his death is expressed in Hölderlin's poem, "To the Fates":

> A single summer grant me, great powers, and
> A single autumn for fully ripened song
> That, sated with the sweetness of my
> Playing, my heart may more willingly die.
>
> The soul that, living, did not attain its divine
> Right cannot repose in the netherworld.
> But once what I am bent on, what is
> Holy, my poetry, is accomplished,
>
> Be welcome then, stillness of the shadows' world!
> I shall be satisfied though my lyre will not
> Accompany me down there. Once I
> Lived like the gods, and more is not needed.[49]

Walter Kaufmann's reflection on the poem is worth quoting as well.

> Not only in childhood but long after one may retain the feeling that one is . . . at the mercy of death. "But once what I am bent on, what is holy, my poetry, is accomplished," once I have succeeded in achieving—in the face of death, in a race with death—a project that is truly mine, . . . then the picture changes: I have won the race and in a sense have triumphed over death. Death and madness come too late.[50]

Many have found that, once they accomplished at least some significant part of what they regarded as their mission in life, no matter how early in life that might have been, death lost some of its terror. Raymond Carver, who died at the age of fifty when at the height of his powers as a writer, wrote that "in the end, the satisfaction of having done our best, and the proof of that labor, is the one thing we can take into the grave."[51] After his death, his first wife commented, "I think Ray did his job in this life."[52] Nearing his own end, Einstein pronounced a strikingly similar judgment on his own life. C. P. Snow reports that, in his final years, Einstein "stayed cheerful, serene, detached from his own illness and the approach of death. He worked on. The end of his life was neither miserable nor pathetic. 'Here on earth I have done my job,' he said, without self-pity."[53] This understanding of how the badness of death may be mitigated of course implies an injunction about how best to live. One should live in such a way that, if one is ambushed by death in medias res, one can make one's defiant surrender without excessive regret because one has seized the opportunities so far offered and made the best of one's life in the time allotted.

Kaufmann is almost obsessive in his insistence that it is one's work and achievement that have the power to reconcile oneself to one's death. This reflects a certain understanding of what gives meaning and value to life. If it is achievement that gives life its point, then, having made one's mark, one may resign oneself to death without undue anguish or agitation. But this is an impoverished conception of the good life. A life wholly devoted to achievement and thus devoid of close personal relations may, in retrospect, seem hollow, even desolate, to one confronting an imminent death. Indeed, some who throw themselves into the unremitting pursuit of achievement do so primarily, whether consciously or unconsciously, as a desperate means of inspiring affection and respect.

Pluralism with respect to the good is a commonplace in contemporary philosophical circles; but in this case the conventional wisdom seems true. There are many different dimensions to the good life, some of which may be incommensurable and many of which are uncombinable within a single life. They include pleasure, personal relations, achievement, knowledge, virtue, aesthetic experience, and so on. For most goods of these sorts, it is better to have more rather than less. This is true even of achievement: Mozart's life would have been even better if he had written ten more symphonies, all at least as good as the 40th. But as we have seen, there is a point at which the value of further achievement begins to decline. A 42nd symphony would have added more to the value of Mozart's life than an equally good 101st. And the same seems true of other goods. Thus we should expand Kaufmann's claim that a certain level of achievement makes death less threatening. It is not just having achieved some important aim, but, more broadly, having lived well and fully in the time that one has had, that may enable a person to accept death with a measure of equanimity. While more good would no doubt always be better, there may also be a point at which one has had enough to be satisfied.

Having endorsed a pluralistic account of the good life, I nevertheless concede that Kaufmann is right that past achievement may assume an unusual degree of importance as death approaches. Knowing that one has accomplished something with one's life may be a source of profound solace in a way that knowing that one has had a good time may not. As Thackeray remarked, "recollections of the best-ordained banquets will scarcely cheer sick epicures."[54]

In a passage written when he was very near to death from AIDS, Harold Brodkey declared, "I like what I've written, the stories and two novels. If I had to give up what I've written in order to be clear of this disease, I wouldn't do it."[55] Some may quarrel with the estimation of the work, finding it inflated. Perhaps also Brodkey's view would have been different if, having produced the same work, he had been dying at the age of forty-five rather than in his early sixties. (He elsewhere concedes, "I am not being cut down before I have had a chance to live. . . . I feel cut off from old age, it's true, but that's not like someone young feeling cut off from most of his or her possible life.")[56] Nevertheless, his words are testimony to his conviction that his life had been well lived, that his achievements mattered, and that these facts are more important than the absence of any prospect of future good.

This may indeed be a useful test to apply to any life. How many of us, facing Brodkey's limited future, could say the same about our lives? Of course, for those who die young without having had Brodkey's opportunities for achievement, the view he took may not be a possibility. That is one of the main reasons that these deaths are particularly tragic: they preclude the possibility of achievement as well as the consolation that previous achievement may provide. For those who are older, an inability to refuse a devil's bargain of the kind Brodkey imagines may be a symptom of a misspent life—which, according to the noncomparative version of the Previous Gain Account, necessarily ensures that one's death will be worse than it would be if one had lived better.

There are deeper issues here that, if I were to take them up, might yield challenges to these observations. One such issue is the adjudication of conflicts between a person's preferences at different times. Nearing death, one may wish that one had devoted less of one's life to the pursuit of pleasure and more to the achievement of significant goals. But earlier in life, even anticipating that one's preference will change, one might prefer the sacrifice of significant achievement for the sake of present pleasures. Sometimes this is the result of a failure of will or imagination—as when a smoker says that he would rather have a shorter life that contains the pleasures of smoking than a longer life without those pleasures. In other instances it may be difficult to adjudicate rationally between conflicting preferences at different times.

There is, moreover, a general objection to the claim that significant achievement blunts the fangs of death. (A similar objection applies to the parallel pluralist claim that death is less bad to the extent that life has already been well lived. But for simplicity of exposition, I will focus on the narrower claim about achievement.) The claim is that, once one has accomplished one's mission, one has triumphed over death, which then arrives too late, after one has become immune to its most fearful effect, which is to prevent one's life from amounting to anything. But in one sense this seems a pyrrhic victory: for death is less bad only because one now has less to live for, less in prospect of which one might be deprived by death. Imagine, for example, someone who triumphs in this way early in life. He resolves very early to devote his life to the achievement of some important goal—for example, writing an epic novel. In a sustained fever of creativity, he completes what he anticipated would be the work of a lifetime with unexpected rapidity. The novel is a masterpiece; he has won his race with death, which cannot rob him of this achievement. But now what? If his life is to retain a comparable level of quality, he will have to set new goals—for example, to write a sequel. Then he will again become vulnerable to loss; death will have reacquired a power over him.

The general lesson here is that, whenever the future promises to be worth living, and perhaps especially when continuing to live is necessary for the achievement of some important goal, death poses a threat of loss that cannot be fully nullified by any degree of previous achievement or, more generally, previous gain from life. For an example that supports this claim, we can do no better than to return to the case of Mozart. Mozart died at the age of thirty-five having achieved more than most of us could achieve in an eternity. So good was his life along this one important dimension of well-being that it is no exaggeration to say that he had one of the most fulfilling lives possible for a human being. Because he achieved so much, it may seem almost indecent to lament that he was prevented by death from achieving even more. Thus, according to the Previous Gain Account, his death was a lesser misfortune than that of anyone who dies having lived less well. Yet at the time of his death, Mozart's genius was steadily maturing. If he had had another thirty years in which to continue composing, his subsequent achievements might have been unrivaled in the history of music. In *this* respect—in the magnitude of his loss—his death was incomparably more tragic than most. This demonstrates the inadequacy of the Previous Gain Account. A death cannot be evaluated simply by evaluating the life it ends. How bad—or good—it is that a life is over depends primarily on what it would have contained if it had continued. It depends on what the death deprives the person of, or on what it spares him from having to endure.

The comparative version of the Previous Gain Account is unacceptable for the same reason that the noncomparative version is. Imagine two elderly men who die at the same time, having gained equally from life—for example, their accomplishments are comparable. If one of them had much more in prospect had he not died, his death was worse. It is possible, of course, that the other was equally unfortunate precisely because he had less to lose—but that misfortune is not properly ascribable to his death.

4.5. *Discounting Misfortunes for Previous Gains*

Although the Previous Gain Account is mistaken, it attempts to articulate, however crudely, an important insight. Recall the case of the young novelist. If he dies, his having accomplished something of great and enduring significance does seem to make his death less bad than it would otherwise have been. How can this be explained?

Recall the three types of misfortune we have distinguished that a person may suffer in dying. There are the loss from death itself, overall losses, and the misfortune of arriving at a point at which there is no more good in prospect. Mozart, for example, suffered a tragic loss from death itself. By contrast, the Young Pedestrian and the Accident Victim may each suffer only a comparatively minor loss from death itself, but both suffer significant overall losses. The Progeria Patient and the Geriatric Patient have virtually no losses at all, but this is because the conditions of their lives preclude the possibility of further good, and this itself may be a misfortune. I suggest that all three types of misfortune can plausibly be *discounted* for the magnitude of the victim's previous gains from life.

Consider, for example, the difference between the Progeria Patient and the Geriatric Patient. Both suffer the misfortune of having no further good in prospect, yet the Progeria Patient's misfortune seems vastly greater than that of the Geriatric Patient. I suggest that it matters less that the Geriatric Patient has run out of good because she has had so much more already. There are both comparative and noncomparative dimensions to this explanation. Unlike the Progeria Patient, the Geriatric Patient has had her fair share of the good. Compared to the rest of us, she has done well: she has gotten more from life than most. This puts her misfortune into perspective. But there is also this: she has had a full, reasonably complete life. Quite independently of comparisons with others, the relative completeness of her life mitigates the severity of her misfortune in having it come to an end. All this is in striking contrast to the case of the Progeria Patient, who arrives at the end having got very much less from life than most people do and without having been able to make something significant of his life. His life is a fragment rather than a whole; and he is denied the consolation that comes from knowing that one leaves the world substantially better for one's having existed in it.

The same points apply in cases involving loss. Mozart's loss in dying was surpassingly great: he was very young, at the height of his powers, with unparalleled promise for future achievement. Yet the opportunities his life had offered for the exercise of musical genius had already placed him among the most favored and fortunate of human beings, and his prior accomplishments gave his life a grandeur and a proximity to perfection that may make the additional life that was possible for him seem almost superfluous.

It might be thought that there is an alternative comparative basis for discounting the badness of certain losses that a person may suffer in dying. Consider someone who dies at the age of eighty whose prospects, had he not died, would have been rather better than those of most people of that age. Irrespective of how much this person has already gained from life, it may seem that the badness of his losses should be discounted for the fact that they are widely shared—for the fact, that is, that he loses only what most other people lose, or fail to have, as well. His losses are, one might say, of goods beyond the norm for human life.

To illustrate this suggestion further, imagine that a person dies in a freak accident at the age of fifty but that, if he had not died, he would have lived a full and rewarding life to the age of ninety. Suppose that the quality of this person's life between the ages of eighty-five and ninety would have been much the same as it would have been between the ages of fifty and fifty-five. Even so, it may seem that the loss of the years between eighty-five and ninety is a lesser part of his overall misfortune than the loss of the years between fifty and fifty-five. If so, this may be because the losses between eighty-five and ninety are more widely shared. Most people live to fifty-five; far

fewer live beyond eighty-five. In general, we may progressively discount the misfortune involved in the loss of a certain period of life for the extent to which the loss is
shared by others.

The intuitive idea here is difficult to formulate with precision. What does it mean
to say that a person's losses in dying are widely shared, or that the goods that the person loses are ones that most others fail to get as well? It does seem that whether and
to what extent it is a misfortune for a person not to have certain specific goods can be
affected by whether they are goods that other people also fail to have. It would, for
example, be a very great good for me to be able to fly, or to explore the moons of
Jupiter in a protected craft. I would like to be able to do both. But my inability to do
either hardly counts as a misfortune, or at least not a misfortune that it is appropriate
to lament. And it seems that a significant part of the explanation for this is that, in
failing to have these goods, I am no worse off than anyone else, for these are goods
that no one gets.

It might be argued that the absence of these goods is ruled out as a misfortune by
the Realism Condition. But this would be a mistake. What the Realism Condition implies is that, because these goods have never been realistically in prospect for me, my
failure to have them cannot count as a *loss*. But their *absence* in my life could, in
principle, be a misfortune. And it does seem that at least part of the reason why the
absence of these goods is not a misfortune for me, or at least not a significant misfortune, is that we do not count the mere absence of a good as a misfortune when the
lack of that good is universally shared, or even just very widely shared. (Another part
of the explanation may have to do with the distinction between goods that are normal
and central to human life and goods that are highly specific to a particular way of life
or set of ideals; but I will not pursue this here.)

This explanation of why the mere absence of certain goods is not a misfortune is,
however, irrelevant to the evaluation of death. When death is responsible for the absence of a good in a person's life, it is because death causes the *loss* of that good. The
mere absence of a good that was never in prospect, and would never have been, cannot be attributable to death.

What about the loss through death of a specific good that would have been very
rare—a good that few if any other people ever have? Does the fact that most other
people's lives lack this good make its loss through death a lesser misfortune than it
would otherwise be? I believe that it does not, or at least that it does not mitigate
the severity of the misfortune by much. Suppose that a person dies the day before he
would have been awarded the Nobel Prize. This is a case in which death causes the
loss of a great but exceedingly rare or uncommon good, for the prize cannot be
awarded posthumously. Intuitively, the loss of this good is a grave misfortune even
though the absence of this good in the person's life is something that he shares with
all but a few of the people who have ever lived. Similarly, a person who is forced by
an approaching storm to descend from Everest just as he was about the reach the
summit also suffers a significant misfortune, despite the fact that reaching the summit of Everest is a good that very few ever enjoy. There is, it seems, no reason to discount the badness of these losses for the rarity of the goods lost.

In any case, comparatively few of the goods of which people are deprived by
death tend to be rare in the way that goods such as winning the Nobel Prize or reach-

ing the summit of Everest are rare. Thus, even if we were to discount the loss of goods of these sorts for their rarity, this would hardly affect our evaluations of the most people's deaths at all.

We began with the vague idea that the losses that someone suffers in dying at eighty matter less because they are widely shared—that is, because the good that the person loses is missing in most other people's lives as well. It is not, as we have seen, that this good is rare in the way that winning the Nobel Prize is rare. In what sense, then, is it rare? One suggestion is that some goods are specific to old age and are therefore comparatively rare because most people do not live well into old age. Among these age-specific goods might be retiring from work, having grandchildren, having the satisfaction of looking back over a long life well spent, and so on. But again, discounting a person's loss of these goods for the commonness of the loss would not substantially affect the evaluation of the death, for most of the goods that an eighty-year-old loses in dying—for example, friendship, aesthetic pleasure, recognition of achievement, and so on—are not limited to old age and so are not rare in the relevant sense. An alternative and even simpler suggestion is that we should progressively discount the loss of goods for their occurrence later in life. We might, for example, say that the loss of *goods beyond eighty* is a common loss, and therefore a lesser misfortune, because most people do not live beyond the age of eighty. But it seems that this is equivalent to discounting a person's losses in dying for the number of years (or the amount of time) he has already lived. If so, this is just a version of the idea that we should discount a person's losses in dying for the magnitude of his previous gains from life, taking years lived as a crude measure of gains.

I doubt that there is any relevant sense in which the good that people lose by dying in old age is a rare good or a good that few people have. But suppose for the sake of argument that there is. Does the loss of this good matter less because the absence of the good in people's lives is widely shared? Imagine a Longevity Pill that would enable one who took it to live, in stable health, to be five hundred years old. It is not, as things are, a misfortune for some eighty-year-old woman that she cannot take such a pill. In part this is because there is no such pill; therefore, in not having it, she is no worse off than anyone else. But suppose her lack of the pill were not the mere absence of a good but were instead a loss. Suppose, for example, that she happened fortuitously to gain possession of the only Longevity Pill in existence and that the pill could not be duplicated. Just as she was about to take it, she dropped it down the sink. Soon thereafter, she died. Her loss of the Longevity Pill deprived her of 420 years of further life. Let us assume that there is some clear sense in which virtually all of the good she lost is also absent from the lives of others. It seems, nevertheless, that her loss is a serious misfortune. (That it would be a serious misfortune for her to lose the pill even though it is not a significant misfortune for us that there is no such pill suggests that, in some instances at least, the loss of a good is worse than its mere absence. On the other hand, if there were a large but limited supply of these pills and they were distributed by lottery, losing a pill that one had been allocated would not be a significantly greater misfortune than simply not being allocated one.)

Would this woman's loss be a more serious misfortune if most other people were to have the good she lost? Suppose everyone has been given a Longevity Pill. There are no replacements and the woman drops hers down the sink. In this case, she loses what everyone else gets, and that does indeed seem to be a greater misfortune. But notice that this is in fact equivalent to a claim about her gains from life. In these circumstances, her gains from life would be vastly inferior to those of her contemporaries. Her loss matters more, or is a greater misfortune, the less she gets from life compared to others. Her misfortune in the circumstances described would be comparable to that of a person who dies quite young in the world as it actually is.

There is, in general, no need to invoke such notions as the commonness of a loss or the rarity of the good lost. Our intuitions in the relevant range of cases can be explained by reference to people's gains from life. Consider, for example, the case mentioned earlier of the person who dies in an accident at fifty but would otherwise have lived to be ninety. I suggested that his loss of the years between fifty and fifty-five seems a greater part of his misfortune than the loss of the years between eighty-five and ninety, and that this is so even if we suppose that his quality of life during the two periods would have been comparable. The need to account for this intuition led me to speculate that, other things being equal, his misfortune in losing certain goods is less the later in his life those goods would have occurred. The reason for this, I provisionally suggested, is that the loss of a good matters less, the more common it is for people's lives to lack that good—an explanation that has turned out to make little sense. But there is an alternative and better explanation of our intuition in this case. This is that the loss of later goods matters progressively less, other things being equal, because the older the person would have been at the time the good would have occurred, the more he would already have gained from life. In short, we discount the badness of the later losses by more for the greater gains that *would* have preceded them.

To confirm that this is the better explanation, consider a variant of this case in which, if the person had not died at fifty, his life would have been barely worth living for the next thirty years (perhaps, for example, because he was condemned to imprisonment with hard labor), but that in the final ten years of his life, from eighty to ninety, he would have experienced peace and contentment. I am assuming that there is some relevant sense in which this person's losses beyond the age of eighty are widely shared, or common. Nevertheless, it does not seem that, in this case, his misfortune in losing the goods of those years should be discounted. Because his gains from life up to the age of eighty would have been modest, his losses beyond that point count fully despite the supposition that they are widely shared.

I believe, therefore, that we should not discount the misfortune involved in suffering a loss for the commonness of the loss; rather, we should discount the misfortune a person suffers in dying (whether the misfortune is the loss caused by death, the overall loss, or simply the arrival at a point at which no further good is possible) for the magnitude of the person's previous gains from life. But this, of course, raises a question I have yet to address—namely, how a person's gains from life are to be measured. As I suggested earlier, we cannot plausibly measure how much a person has gained from life just in terms of the number of years he has lived or in terms of the amount of opportunity his life has afforded. Nor, perhaps surprisingly, can we measure an individual's gains from life just in terms of the amount of good his life has contained. For we do not want our account of the badness of death to be arbitrarily limited to members of the human species. But if our account is to apply across species, and if we discount the misfortune involved in death for the amount of good that an individual's life has contained, we will be committed to accepting that the loss of a certain good by a person matters less than the loss of the same good by a dog, to the extent that the person's life has contained a greater amount of good. This is wholly implausible.

This implication can be avoided if what we discount for is not the total amount of good an individual's life has contained, but instead the extent to which the individual has been fortunate in life or, as I will say, the extent of the individual's overall life-long fortune. What counts as a good or fortunate life for a dog is different from a fortunate life for a person and contains a substantially lower total of good. Because of this, it would be a mistake to discount a person's losses from death for the extent to which his life has been better than that of a dog. Rather, we should, as a general matter, assess an individual's losses from death by reference to whether the individual has had a fortunate life for an individual with his nature. What dimensions of an individual's nature are particularly relevant to this kind of evaluation will be the subject of the following section.

5. OVERALL LIFELONG FORTUNE

5.1. *The Standard for Assessing Fortune*

A good life for a dog and a good life for a person contain very different totals of well-being. Having a good or fortunate life is therefore not just a matter of the amount of good or well-being one's life contains. Whether an individual is well or badly off, flourishing or faring badly, or fortunate or unfortunate—in short, how well an individual's life is going or has gone—appears to express a relation between that individual's level or total of well-being and a standard against which well-being is assessed. It would be useful to have an abstract noun for this notion, a noun that denotes the range of conditions or states of being from extreme misfortune to extreme prosperity or flourishing. The closest that English offers appears to be "fortune." This is not quite right, both because it is suggestive of extrinsic conditions and because the corresponding nouns referring to the conditions at the ends of the spectrum—"misfortune" and "good fortune"—more naturally refer to events than to states of the individual. Still, the adjectival forms—"fortunate" and "unfortunate"—do suggest states of being of significant duration. For want of a better term, therefore, I will use "fortune" as a technical term to refer to how well or badly an individual's life is going or has gone.

Fortune may be synchronic or diachronic—that is, an individual may be fortunate or unfortunate at a particular time or over a period of time. Our concern here is with how fortunate or unfortunate an entire life has been. I will refer to how good or bad an individual's entire life has been as that individual's "overall lifelong fortune." My claim is that the proper measure of an individual's gains from life is his overall lifelong fortune. If we discount a person's misfortune in dying (whether that misfortune takes the form of a loss or whether it is just the misfortune of having no realistic prospect of further good) for the magnitude of his gains from life, we are discounting for the degree of his overall lifelong fortune, not for the quantity of good or well-being his life has contained. (Of course, the notion of a person's overall lifelong fortune may be of interest independently of any concern about death.)

To assess an individual's overall lifelong fortune, what is the standard against which his life's well-being should be compared? We have seen that a dog may be considered to have been fortunate, or to have had a good life, even if the amount of well-being in its life would be woefully insufficient for a fortunate life for a person. Consider next a congenitally severely retarded human being. Suppose that this human being, having cognitive capacities comparable to those of a dog and having also a shortened life span, has a life with an overall total of well-being that would be sufficient for a good life for a dog. Is this a fortunate or an unfortunate life? The commonsense view is of course that this human being has a terribly unfortunate life—even, perhaps, if the life is characterized by a steady dull contentment, without significant suffering or unhappiness. While the dog has a good life *for a dog,* the severely retarded human being's life is a bad life *for a human being.* According to this commonsense view, the standard against which an individual's well-being must be assessed is a norm for well-being that is specific to the individual's biological species.

Our judgments reflect an implicit appeal to the idea that each species is defined in part by the range of psychological capacities characteristic of its members, and that this range of capacities sets limits to the goods accessible to the members. Each species, therefore, has a specific range of states of well-being open to its members. Dogs, for example, are capable of experiencing a greater range of types and magnitudes of good than caterpillars are. According to this view, then, an individual's biological nature, the contours of which are determined by its species, sets limits to the forms and amounts of good or well-being its life can contain. In particular, the highest psychological capacities that are possible for any member of a given species set an upper limit to the amount of good, and thus the best sort of life, that is accessible to a member of that species. To determine whether a member of that species has had a fortunate or unfortunate life, we try to ascertain where its life lies along the spectrum of lives, from worst to best, that are possible for the members of that species, given their characteristic range of psychological capacities. If, for example, the life is near the high end of the spectrum of lives that are possible for beings with psychological capacities within the range for the species, the individual may be considered to have had a fortunate life. There is, however, slightly more to it than this. Our estimation of an individual's overall lifelong fortune is sensitive not just to where his life lies along the spectrum of *possible* lives but also to the relative proportion of *actual* lives at that level. Suppose, again, that an individual's life is near the peak for members of its species. If 90 percent of the members of the species have lives at that level, we will consider the individual to be less fortunate than it would be if only 1 percent of the members of the species had lives near the peak. In short, our sense of an individual's overall lifelong fortune reflects not only a comparison of the individual's life with the range of lives that are possible for a member of its species but also a comparison of the individual's life with the range of actual lives of the other members of the species. (In most species, there is not a lot of variation in the amount of good in the lives of the members. Most lives tend to cluster around the median level of fortune. The species with the greatest range of variation is, of course, the human species.)

Call this account of the nature of fortune the *Species Norm Account.*[57] If it were correct, we would calculate a person's gains from life, or determine how fortunate or unfortunate his life has been overall, by comparing his life with the range of lives possible for human beings in the world as it is, taking into account how the lives of actual human beings are distributed across this range. But the Species Norm Account is undermined by counterexamples. If how fortunate a being is overall were determined by how its life compares with the range of lives possible for members of its species, an anencephalic infant, born without cerebral hemispheres, would be near the far end of the scale of misfortune. For it is certainly a member of the human species and it falls even farther short of any plausible specification of the human good than any human being with a capacity for consciousness whose life is minimally worth living. It is an utterly failed human being. Yet it seems that an anencephalic infant is not the sort of being that can be either fortunate or unfortunate, well or badly off. Lacking even the capacity for consciousness, it has no capacity for well-being at all. It makes no more sense to claim that an anencephalic is unfortunate, or badly off, than it does to make this claim about a plant.

Anencephalic infants may seem to be a decisive counterexample to any account that assesses whether an individual is fortunate or unfortunate (or neither) by comparing its life with those of other members of its species. But it might be argued that, since the Species Norm Account is an account of fortune—of whether or to what extent an individual is fortunate or unfortunate—it applies only to those beings with a capacity for well-being, since the latter is a necessary condition for being fortunate or unfortunate, or well or badly off. When restricted in this way, the account no longer applies to anencephalics. There are, however, other counterexamples.

> *The Superchimp.* A newborn chimpanzee is administered a form of gene therapy that causes its brain to continue to develop in ways that parallel the development of the human brain. As a consequence, this chimpanzee, as an adult, comes to have cognitive and emotional capacities comparable to those of a ten-year-old human child. After some years of exercising these capacities, however, this Superchimp suffers brain damage that reduces him to the psychological level of a normal chimpanzee, after which he lives a contented life among other chimpanzees, with a mental life indistinguishable from that of a normal chimpanzee.

The Species Norm Account recognizes that, during the period when he exercised his enhanced psychological capacities, the Superchimp was a uniquely fortunate chimpanzee. (There are, to be accurate, two distinct species of chimpanzee—*Pan troglodytes* and *Pan paniscus*. It does not matter which of these we assume the Superchimp belongs to.) It also recognizes that, when he lost his superior capacities, he suffered a misfortune. But it implies that this was not a misfortune that left the Superchimp in a deprived or unfortunate state. According to the Species Norm Account, the Superchimp in his brain-damaged state is no more unfortunate than an ordinary chimpanzee. The Superchimp's loss of his enhanced capacities and the consequent sharp decline in his level of well-being are treated by the Species Norm Account in much the way we think of a multimillionaire's loss of a million dollars: the loss constitutes a serious misfortune, but one that leaves the victim in quite a good state overall.

This, however, is the wrong way to think about this case. The brain damage that the Superchimp suffers causes his psychological capacities to drop from a level characteristic of a ten-year-old human being to a level characteristic of a normal chimpanzee. When a comparable decline occurs in the case of a ten-year-old human being, we regard it as a tragic misfortune that leaves the victim in a pitifully unfortunate condition (one of moderately severe mental retardation). But the Species Norm Account implies that, when this same decline occurs in the case of the Superchimp, the victim is not unfortunate at all, though he has suffered a misfortune. It seems arbitrary, however, to suppose that the mere difference in species should make the human being's state an unfortunate one while the same state in the Superchimp is not. If the human being and the Superchimp have both fallen from the same height to the same lower state, it seems that either both are unfortunate or neither is. (This is consistent with supposing that the ten-year-old human being is even more unfortunate than the Superchimp, which, for reasons I will give later, I believe to be true.)

The Superchimp challenges the Species Norm Account in another way. The expansion of the Superchimp's psychological capacities greatly extends the range of well-being found within its species. The existence of the Superchimp therefore resets the standard against which a chimpanzee's lifelong well-being is to be assessed in order to determine whether the chimpanzee has a fortunate or unfortunate life. The Superchimp's existence has the effect of making all other chimpanzees less fortunate than they previously were—not, of course, by affecting their levels of well-being but by placing their levels of well-being relatively lower on the scale of possible well-being for a chimpanzee.

This effect need not, however, be a significant one. For the Species Norm Account takes account of the distribution of actual lives along the spectrum of lives that are possible within the limits set by the range of psychological capacities within the species. Thus if all but one member of the species have lives that are well below the best life possible for a member of the species, any individual whose life is above the norm may count as fortunate even if its life is well below the peak.

This objection becomes more worrying, however, if we imagine that the distribution of lives is different. Suppose that the type of genetic alteration responsible for the Superchimp's enhanced intelligence affects the germ cells and thus is heritable. Imagine that a number of cognitively enhanced chimpanzees are created at a time when chimpanzees have become an endangered species and that the new, intelligent chimpanzees begin interbreeding and eventually become more numerous than ordinary chimpanzees. At that point, the median for the range of well-being possible for chimpanzees in normal external conditions will have shifted to a substantially higher point on the scale that measures well-being. The hitherto normal chimpanzees will have become abnormal, or retarded, and their levels of well-being will have dropped below the median level for the species. According to the Species Norm Account, therefore, they will have become unfortunate. But this seems absurd. If they have lives that are good relative to the best life they can have given their congenital capacities and potentials, it seems unreasonable to suppose that they have become unfortunate just because an expanded range of well-being has become possible for a majority of the members of their species. (It is worth noting that this objection applies even if we take the Species Norm Account to state a sufficient condition of an individual's being unfortunate rather than a necessary and sufficient condition.[58] Understood in this way, the account concedes that there may be other grounds for declaring an individual to be unfortunate than that the individual's life is in the lower part of the range for its species. One advantage of interpreting the account in this way is that it then allows for the possibility that the brain-damaged Superchimp is unfortunate even if his level of well-being is moderately high for the species as a whole. But in this extension of the Superchimp example, the hitherto normal chimpanzees are below the median level; hence the account implies that they are unfortunate even if it concedes that falling below that level is not a necessary condition of their being unfortunate.)

The implication that the previously normal chimpanzees become unfortunate as the cognitively enhanced chimpanzees become more numerous cannot be evaded by claiming that the Superchimps would constitute a new species, with its own distinctive set of capacities and range of well-being. For this suggestion is contrary to the canons of biological taxonomy. The first generation (at least) of Superchimps would be descended from chimpanzee parents and would, we may suppose, be capable of interbreeding with other chimpanzees. They would, of course, be genetically different in a significant way. But if genetically based cognitive deviation in the direction of improvement could give rise to a new species, so should equally extreme deviation in the other direction, in which case those human beings whose severe cognitive impairment is genetically based (and perhaps heritable) should also constitute a different, nonhuman species—which, of course, they do not.

It seems, therefore, that we must abandon the idea that whether a being is fortunate or unfortunate depends on a comparison between its life and the lives of the other members of its species.[59] For like the Superchimp, an individual may be a highly deviant member of its species; significant aspects of its nature may be very different from the corresponding characteristics of most or all of the other members of its species. It therefore seems arbitrary to assess how fortunate such an individual is by reference to what is possible for beings whose nature it may not share. The case of the Superchimp suggests that whether an individual's life is fortunate or unfortunate depends, in the first instance at least, on how its life compares with what is possible given *its own individual nature or constitution*. In what follows, I will attempt to develop and refine this suggestion.

The brain of every individual, whatever that individual's species may be, appears to be limited in its psychological capacities: its neural hardware sets limits to its cognitive and emotional capacities and potentials. These limits in turn define or delimit the individual's capacity for well-being. Just as a dog's cognitive and emotional capacities set limits to the varieties and heights of good it may attain, so a person's psychological capacities impose limits on the forms and amounts of good his life may contain. There is nothing surprising about this. However long I set my dog in front of my print of Goya's *Devota Profesión,* he will never derive the least spark of aesthetic gratification from it. As far as I can tell, my dog is incapable of any sort of aesthetic response, at least to visual phenomena. This is a dimension of the good from which my dog seems to be constitutionally excluded. This is a limitation of his nature; but it does not seem to be a misfortune. There may, indeed, be a general limitation here on what we are willing to count as a misfortune. If it is an individual's nature to lack the psychological capacity to have a certain good in its life, the absence of that good from its life is not a misfortune.

I have tried to choose my words with care. There are various ways in which the absence of a good in an individual's life can be a misfortune even if the individual presently lacks the capacity to have that good. The absence of a good from an individual's life can be a misfortune if it is the result of a *physical* incapacity, even a congenital physical incapacity. It can also be a misfortune if the absence is a result of a *transient* psychological incapacity, a *loss* of psychological capacity, or even a loss of *potential* for the relevant psychological capacity. But if the incapacity to have or experience a certain good is psychological in origin and is part of an individual's congenital or native psychological constitution, the absence of that good in the individual's life is not so much a misfortune as simply a fact about that individual's essential nature.

If it is not a misfortune to lack a good that one is by nature psychologically incapable of having, an individual's overall lifelong fortune cannot be assessed by comparison with a life that may contain goods that the individual is by nature psychologically incapable of having. For example, a dog's overall lifelong fortune should not be assessed by comparison with the life of a person with a highly developed capacity for well-being. If the dog's life were assessed relative to that standard, the dog would have to be regarded as terribly unfortunate, even if it had as good a life as it could possibly have given the limitations imposed by its cognitive and emotional capacities.

A dog's life should, it seems, be assessed by reference to what is possible given its own psychological nature. Generalizing, perhaps we can say that, to determine an individual's overall lifelong fortune, we should compare its life with the range of lives that are possible in the world as we know it, given the limitations on that individual's capacity for well-being imposed by its own psychological capacities. This requires some elucidation. We are to compare the actual life with the range of hypothetical lives, from worst to best, that would be possible for someone with this individual's psychological capacities. There is, however, a realism constraint. The range of possible lives includes only lives that are possible in realistic conditions, which are not limited to the actual circumstances of the individual's own life but nevertheless exclude what would be possible only if the world itself were fundamentally different.

There is also the fact that a person's psychological capacities vary over time. Our psychological capacities develop gradually and are also vulnerable to decline and loss. If we are to compare a person's life to the range of lives that are possible given his psychological capacities, how are we to identify what his capacities are, given that they evolve and change over time?

Our account of fortune should accommodate several compelling beliefs. First, it should not imply that infancy and childhood are unfortunate states. It therefore must not assess an individual's present state by reference to what would be possible given his *future* psychological capacities. Second, the account should imply that states of cognitive decline—for example, dementia—are unfortunate states. Thus we should evaluate the condition of someone who has suffered cognitive decline by reference to what would be possible given his *former,* higher capacities. Third, the account should imply that, at least within certain limits, someone who undergoes cognitive enhancement is fortunate, other things being equal. Thus we should evaluate the condition of someone who has received cognitive enhancement (for example, through genetic therapy) by reference to what is possible given his *present* rather than his former capacities.

One way to accommodate all three beliefs is to insist that a person's present state be evaluated by reference to the range of states that would be accessible given the *highest* psychological capacities that he has so far achieved. This allows that an infant may be flourishing if its state is high relative to the range of states accessible to it given its present capacities, even if its well-being is comparable to that of a contented dog. It implies that a person who has suffered brain damage is in an unfortunate state if his well-being is low relative to what was possible given his former capacities. And it implies that a person who has undergone cognitive enhancement is in a fortunate condition, provided that his well-being rises accordingly. If, however, his level of well-being remains the same as it was prior to the enhancement, his present state is worse, or less fortunate, than it was before, for he is now worse off relative to the best that is possible for him. Notice, however, that although we evaluate his present state relative to his present capacities, this is not because they are his *present* capacities but because they are his *peak* capacities.

Call this the *Peak Capacity Account* of the nature of fortune. In order to extend the account so that it yields an evaluation of a person's overall lifelong fortune, we must see a life as a series of stages, assess each stage relative to what was possible given the highest capacities that the person had achieved at that point, then somehow combine the various assessments of the stages into a single comprehensive assessment of the life as a whole.

The Peak Capacity Account is, however, challenged by a counterexample—one involving neither cognitive enhancement nor cognitive decline, but rather the absence of normal cognitive development.

> *The Brain-Damaged Individual.* An infant suffers brain damage that arrests its psychological capacities at their present level. As this individual grows and matures physically, his psychological capacities remain comparable to those of an infant.

Most of us believe that this individual has suffered a misfortune and that, as he gets older, his condition will be a pitiable one. If, however, we assess misfortune relative to the range of well-being made possible by the peak capacities that an individual has so far had, this individual may not be unfortunate at all. Both now and in the future he may fare as well as possible relative to the highest capacity for well-being he ever possesses. (The Peak Capacity Account may, indeed, be unable to explain why it is objectionable, because of the effect on the infant itself, to *cause* it to suffer brain damage that arrests its psychological capacities at their present level.)

What seems unfortunate about the Brain-Damaged Individual is that, soon after the brain damage occurs, he begins to fare poorly relative to the range of well-being he once had the *potential* to achieve. This suggests a way of revising the Peak Capacity Account. To determine whether a person's state is fortunate or unfortunate, we should compare it to the range of states possible given the highest psychological capacities that the person has so far achieved, or the highest psychological capacities he has had the potential to achieve at his present stage of development. Notice that this takes into account only those psychological capacities that the person has already achieved or that he has had the potential to have *by now*. It does not evaluate his present state by reference to what would be possible given capacities he now has the potential to have only in the future. Thus the account does not evaluate the state of a child by comparing it to what would be possible if he had the psychological capacities he has the potential to have as an adult. In short, the account treats only the *fail-*

ure to realize one's psychological potential as a misfortune. The possession of unrealized potential for higher psychological capacities is a misfortune only if the potential could by now have been realized.

Again, in order to assess a person's overall lifelong fortune, one must see his life as a series of stages and assess each stage relative to the psychological capacities he has had, or has had the potential to have, up to that point. The assessments of the various stages must then be somehow combined into a single assessment of the life as a whole.

But even this is still not quite right. Consider again the Superchimp. There must be a sense in which, prior to receiving the genetic therapy, the Superchimp (then just an ordinary chimpanzee) had the potential to have cognitive capacities characteristic of a person. Because the Superchimp did actually come to have such capacities, it must be true that, even before receiving the therapy, it had the potential to have them. But if the mere possibility of receiving the therapy was sufficient to give the Superchimp the potential to become a person, it seems that every chimpanzee in a world in which such a therapy exists must also have the potential to have the psychological capacities of a person. In that case, the view I stated in the previous paragraph would imply that all chimpanzees in such a world would be terribly unfortunate, for their actual lives would be very inferior to the best kind of life they could have if their potential to become persons were realized.

This is implausible. Although there is a sense in which all chimpanzees would have the potential to become persons if a genetic therapy existed that could transform them into persons, they would not be unfortunate if they did not receive the therapy. It is not a misfortune for a chimpanzee to retain its psychological nature as a chimpanzee. So the potential to have higher psychological capacities that the Superchimp had *prior* to receiving the therapy does not seem to be the kind of potential that is relevant to the evaluation of fortune.

What is needed, it seems, is a distinction between types of potential. In order for the Superchimp to have the psychological capacities of a person, it was necessary that the physical basis for those capacities be supplied from the outside—in this case via genetic therapy. This potential for having higher psychological capacities is *extrinsic:* it involves only a susceptibility or receptivity to having the relevant capacities externally provided in a way that is compatible with the beneficiary's retaining its identity (that is, continuing to exist). It contrasts with *intrinsic* potential, which requires that the physical basis for the development of the capacities be present in the individual. This distinction is difficult to draw with precision, for all potential for the development of psychological capacities requires external provision of some sort or other (for example, nutrients) for its realization. I will later, in section 6.2 of chapter 4, try to indicate how very problematic the distinction is. For the moment, however, it seems necessary to assume that a coherent distinction of this sort can be drawn. Consider again the Superchimp. Prior to receiving the genetic therapy, the Superchimp was just like any other chimpanzee. It had the extrinsic potential (given the existence of the therapy) to have the psychological capacities of a person, but it would not have been unfortunate to have remained an ordinary chimpanzee. The therapy, however, changes its nature. After it receives the therapy, it becomes relevantly like a human infant: it then has the intrinsic potential to develop the psychological capacities of a person (that is, the physical basis for the development of the capacities is now in place). At any point subsequent to its acquisition of that intrinsic potential, its state must be evaluated relative to the range of well-being made possible by the highest psychological capacities it has had the intrinsic potential to develop at that point. If, for example, it had suffered brain damage shortly after receiving the therapy, its subsequent life would have been unfortunate in much the way the Brain-Damaged Individual's is, except that the latter is even more unfortunate since he had the intrinsic potential for an even higher range of psychological capacities that would have made a higher range of well-being accessible to him.

Our account of fortune must therefore be revised so that it focuses only on intrinsic potential. To determine whether a person is fortunate or unfortunate, we should compare his condition to the range of conditions that would be realistically possible for him given the highest psychological capacities he has so far achieved or that he has had the intrinsic potential to achieve thus far. Call this the *Intrinsic Potential Account* of fortune. (It takes this disjunctive form in order to allow for the possibility—at present merely hypothetical—of a being's acquiring higher psychological capacities via external augmentation, without ever having had the intrinsic potential to develop them.)

The Intrinsic Potential Account is not immune to objections. I will here mention just one. The account seems to imply that a congenitally severely retarded human being, which lacks the intrinsic potential to have psychological capacities higher than those of certain animals, is not unfortunate. As I have noted, common sense rebels at this suggestion. Suppose, moreover, that there were a genetic therapy that would cause new areas to grow in a congenitally severely retarded infant's brain, thereby enhancing its cognitive capacities. The Intrinsic Potential Account seems to imply that there is little more reason to administer this therapy to a human infant than there would be to administer it to an animal, assuming that it would have a comparable effect in the latter case as well. The account can of course recognize that it might be very important for the parents of such an infant to have its capacities raised in this way. It can also recognize that life in human society might be very awkward for a Superchimp. Because of considerations of these sorts, the account can accept that in practice there would be stronger reasons to administer such a therapy to retarded human infants than to animals. But these contingent reasons are the only reasons that the account will recognize.

Suppose that one is able to accept the implication that a severely retarded human being is not unfortunate to have the psychological nature he natively has, just as a dog is not unfortunate to have the psychological nature it is endowed with. There is still a further charge that the Intrinsic Potential Account draws arbitrary distinctions. While it implies that a congenitally severely retarded infant is not unfortunate, it accepts that a previously normal infant that suffers brain damage *is* unfortunate, even if its actual state is indistinguishable from that of the congenitally retarded infant. Yet if one were to see the two infants in adjacent cots in the hospital, each unable ever to progress beyond its present psychological capacities, it would seem arbitrary to suppose that one was terribly unfortunate while the other was not.

This may not, however, be as implausible as it initially seems. After all, someone who was a person but suffered brain damage may now and in the future have cognitive capacities and a level of well-being indistinguishable from those of a contented dog but will nevertheless be unfortunate in a way that the dog is not. This shows that much depends on an individual's history, or on what his (or its) nature has been. In the case of the two infants, one began life as a being with high potential but suffered the misfortune of losing that potential, whereas it is simply the nature of the congenitally impaired infant to have the capacities it has. This difference may emerge intuitively if we imagine that it is possible to do one or the other of two things, but not both. Suppose we can either augment the brain of the congenitally retarded infant, providing it with neural hardware that it presently lacks that would enable it eventually to become a person, or we can repair the damaged areas of the other infant's brain, restoring the potential it has lost. To many of us, it seems more important to repair the brain-damaged infant's loss than it is to transform the other's congenital nature.

The charge of arbitrariness might, however, be refocused on a different comparison. Suppose that a congenitally retarded infant is administered a genetic therapy that gives it the intrinsic potential to develop the psychological capacities of a person. Suppose that very soon thereafter it suffers brain damage that undoes the work of the therapy, returning it to exactly the condition it was in prior to the therapy. The Intrinsic Potential Account seems to imply that this infant is unfortunate in a way that a congenitally retarded infant that has never received the therapy is not. Can the one's brief possession of the intrinsic potential for higher cognitive capacities really make that much difference—or indeed any difference at all?

There is something to be said in response to this challenge, but it is best reserved until the end of section 5.3 of this chapter, after I have developed the idea on which it depends. For the moment, let me sketch another way in which the Intrinsic Potential Account requires modification.

The Intrinsic Potential Account, as I have stated it, assesses whether an individual's life has been fortunate or unfortunate by comparing it to the range of lives, from worst to best, that are possible in realistic conditions given that individual's psychological capacities or the psychological capacities he has had the intrinsic potential to achieve. But insofar as the Intrinsic Potential Account aims to explain and defend our actual evaluations of fortune, it must go beyond comparisons with lives that are merely possible to comparisons with the actual lives of others. For our evaluations of fortune seem implicitly comparative. We judge a person's life in relation to the lives of others. Thus the points along the spectrum of lives that are possible given an individual's psychological capacities have to be weighted for the distribution of actual lives along the spectrum. If, for example, most actual people's lives fell along the lower half of the spectrum of possible lives, a person whose life was right at the midpoint of the range might be considered unusually fortunate, even though his life would be as far from the peak of the range as it would be from the nadir. But if, by contrast, most people's lives were above the midpoint, a life at that point might be considered rather unfortunate.

This modification of the account raises a difficult question. What is the relevant comparison class? The Intrinsic Potential Account, of course, has a general answer to this. For any given individual, human or nonhuman, the group with whose lives its life must be compared is not its species but the group of individuals with comparable psychological capacities or potential. Yet psychological capacity and potential are not precisely measurable. And even if they were, and we could divide people into a large range of groups, each defined by subtle differences of psychological capacity or potential that would differentiate its members from those in other groups, it would seem absurd to make comparisons only within such groups. Even if your psychological capacities are slightly higher than mine, it is not irrelevant to how fortunate my life is to determine how it compares with yours. On the other hand, how fortunate or unfortunate a congenitally severely retarded human being is should not be determined by comparing his life with the lives of persons with normal psychological capacities, or vice versa. This, as we have seen, is contrary to common sense but is clearly implied by the Intrinsic Potential Account. So the Intrinsic Potential Account requires that the human species be divided into at least two groups—those with normal cognitive capacities and those with subnormal cognitive capacities—and holds that how well or badly off the members of one group are is irrelevant to assessing whether a member of the other is fortunate or unfortunate. The critical question, then, is whether there should be further subdivisions within the category of those with normal cognitive capacities.

Let us, without worrying too much about the actual facts about his nature, take Albert Einstein to have been a person with exceptionally high cognitive and emotional capacities. Let us suppose that the range of states accessible to him—from the peaks of well-being to the depths of misery that his exceptional sensitivities made possible—was at least as broad as that of any other human being who has ever lived. Our question, then, is whether the range of states accessible to a person with normal but below-average psychological capacities is sufficiently close to the range accessible to Einstein to make comparisons between their lives relevant to evaluating the overall lifelong fortune of each.

Suppose, for the sake of argument, that the range of possible states of well-being (and therefore the range of possible lives) open to a person with Einstein's capacities is significantly broader than the range open to a person with below-average capacities—so much broader, in fact, that the gap between the two persons makes comparisons between them inappropriate for determining either's level of fortune, in much the same way that the gap between the below-average person and a dog makes it inappropriate to assess how well off the person is by comparing his life with that of the dog. Such a view—that two persons within the normal range for cognitive capacity could belong in different comparison classes—is bound to have inegalitarian implications. It has been suggested that inegalitarian consequences could arise in the following way.[60] Einstein might have a higher level of well-being than the below-average person and yet be significantly further below his own maximum level of well-being than the below-average person is below his. Einstein would therefore be less well off, or less fortunate, than the below-average person. If principles of justice or equality give priority to the well-being of the less fortunate, they will imply that Einstein has priority over the below-average person in the distribution of resources, despite the fact that Einstein's level of well-being is actually higher. This is clearly repugnant. But the Intrinsic Potential Account does not obviously have this implication. For, if Einstein and the below-average person belong to different comparison classes, the Intrinsic Potential Account, as I have developed it so far, has no implications about whether one is more fortunate than the other. The account as stated is silent about comparisons across categories. It can identify a fortunate person with psychological capacities within a certain range and it can pick out a fortunate dog, but it does not imply that one is more fortunate than the other or that they are equally fortunate.

I will defer discussion of how the Intrinsic Potential Account should deal with comparisons across categories until the next subsection. For the moment, it is important to recognize that we do assess how fortunate or unfortunate a person is or has been by comparing his life with the lives of others whose range of well-being may be wider or narrower than his. There are, of course, limits to the degree of divergence that is tolerable. We do not regard a person as fortunate because his level of well-being, either at a time or over the whole of his life, greatly exceeds that of a dog. And some of us, at least, do not regard a congenitally severely retarded human being as extremely unfortunate just because his level of well-being is significantly lower than the heights of well-being accessible to a person. But we do accept that it is relevant to determining how fortunate or unfortunate a person is or has been, to see how his life compares with the lives of other *persons,* or other human beings with psychological capacities within the normal range. If, therefore, the Intrinsic Potential Account is to reflect certain core aspects of our actual practice, it must accept that Einstein and the below-average person belong to the same comparison class. If it accepts that, it allows that there is a clear sense in which Einstein is more fortunate than the below-average person if his level of well-being, either at a time or over a lifetime, is higher.

There is, however, an obvious problem. The Intrinsic Potential Account has both a comparative and a noncomparative dimension. The noncomparative evaluation of a person's overall lifelong fortune depends on where his life lies along the spectrum of lives that are possible given his psychological capacities and potential. The comparative evaluation assesses his life in relation to the lives of others in his comparison class—that is, those with psychological capacities or potential comparable to his own. Earlier I suggested that the comparative evaluation is just a matter of weighting the points along the spectrum of possible lives for the distribution of actual lives. But this cannot be right if Einstein and the below-average person are in the same comparison class. For their ranges of possible well-being, and therefore of possible lives, are different. Einstein's present state, or even his life as a whole, might be off the below-average person's scale—that is, it might be higher than is possible for the below-average person given the limitations imposed by his psychological nature. This can lead to discrepancies between the two evaluations. For example, Einstein might be less fortunate noncomparatively than the below-average person (if he is proportionately farther below his personal maximum) but comparatively more fortunate (if he has a higher level of well-being).

One response to this problem is just to divide the Intrinsic Potential Account into its two components—the comparative account and the noncomparative account—and accept that they are different and can diverge. We could accept that the comparative and the noncomparative evaluations may not be combinable into a single overall evaluation. That, I suspect, is the best solution, for as I will presently indicate, we tend to make a variety of potentially conflicting comparative evaluations both of people's present states and of their lives as wholes, and this suggests that our comparative evaluations do not aspire to the kind of objectivity offered by the Intrinsic Potential Account's noncomparative component.

An alternative response is to define each comparison class as the group of all individuals whose psychological capacities are within a certain range and then noncomparatively evaluate each life in the class by reference to the range of lives, from worst to best, made possible by the highest psychological capacities within the class. (Only by taking the limits to the range to be set by what is possible given the *highest* capacities can we ensure that every life in the comparison class can find a place on the spectrum.) For example, *persons* might constitute a single comparison class, so that the life of each person would be comparatively evaluated by reference to the lives of all other persons. And each person's life would be noncomparatively evaluated by seeing where it lies along the spectrum of possible lives accessible to someone with the highest psychological capacities found among persons. (I call this "noncomparative" because it does not involve a comparison with other people's actual lives, though it does involve a comparison between the person's actual life and a range of merely hypothetical lives.)

According to this proposal, it is relevant to the evaluation of the overall lifelong fortune of the below-average person that his level of well-being is lower than Einstein's. That is one datum that the comparative evaluation has to take into account. And now the noncomparative evaluation cannot conflict with this, for we are to evaluate the below-average person's life relative to the range of lives accessible to someone with Einstein's psychological capacities (his being the highest in the class of persons). If the below-average person has a lower level of well-being than Einstein, he is necessarily farther from the relevant maximum than Einstein is. But of course this is now a very different form of noncomparative evaluation. We are now evaluating the life of the below-average person relative to a range of possible lives not all of which are even in principle accessible to him. On this view, even if the below-average person achieves the best kind of life possible for one with his psychological capacities and potential, he is still not ideally fortunate. For he still falls short of the best kind of life accessible to some members of his comparison class. His misfortune, perhaps, is that his psychological capacities and potential fall short of the maximum for individuals of his kind—that is, persons.

There are at least two objections to this. One is that this proposal moves away from the core idea of the Intrinsic Potential Account—namely, that an individual's overall lifelong fortune should be evaluated relative to what is possible given his *own* psychological nature (capacities and potential)—to the idea that his overall lifelong fortune should be evaluated relative to the range of lives possible *for individuals of his kind.* This latter idea is what underlies the Species Norm Account, which I have rejected. What distinguishes the Species Norm Account is that it holds that an individual's species defines what *kind* of being it is for the purpose of this sort of evaluation. Species, in short, are the relevant comparison classes. The proposal I have outlined, which takes "person" as the relevant kind to which both Einstein and the below-average person belong, seems an advance over the Species Norm Account if only because the range of psychological capacities within the category of persons is narrower than that within the biological category of human beings. But there is still no deep difference between the Species Norm Account and the Intrinsic Potential Account, if the latter is understood in the way I have outlined. If the range of psychological capacities within the class of persons were as wide as it is among chimpanzees in the case of the Superchimp, the Intrinsic Potential Account, understood in this way, would have implications as implausible as those of the Species Norm Account.

The second objection arises from the fact that the Intrinsic Potential Account now treats the below-average person as less than fully fortunate, even if he has the best life that is possible for someone with his psychological capacities, because his capacities are lower than the highest capacities found among persons. If the account allows that in general an individual can be unfortunate because its psychological capacities are lower than those of certain other individuals, we have to confront the question why it seems that, for example, dogs are not unfortunate for having only the limited psychological capacities characteristic of dogs. Of course, even on this new understanding of the Intrinsic Potential Account, a dog would be unfortunate only to the extent that its capacities fell short of the highest capacities found among members of its kind—so that even on this view, a dog would not be unfortunate not to be a person. But if kinds are individuated by level of psychological capacity rather than by species, it may well be that dogs and chimpanzees should be in the same comparison class—for, after all, the difference between a dog's psychological capacities and those of a chimpanzee may be less than the difference between those of the below-average person and those of Einstein. But if dogs and chimpanzees were in the same comparison class, dogs would be unfortunate to the extent that their capacities, and hence their levels of well-being, were below those of chimpanzees. And that does not seem plausible.

For these reasons, I suspect that it is best to see the Intrinsic Potential Account as encompassing two distinct accounts—one involving comparative evaluation, the other involving noncomparative evaluation—whose judgments need not coincide. Indeed, the comparative dimension to our evaluation of overall lifelong fortune may itself be pluralistic, involving comparisons not only with all other persons but also with certain subgroups among persons. Thus, for example, a person who is among the poorest 10 percent of the people in the United States today may be regarded as unfortunate, both by herself and by her peers, even if she is better off than 95 percent of the world's current population and 99.9 percent of the world's population over the past three millennia. It seems that, in general, the tendency is to compare a person's life with the lives of those with whom the person is closely identified, particularly those with whom the person identifies herself—for example, the members of her nation, social class, or peer group. An American who is relatively unfortunate by American standards but extraordinarily fortunate by Haitian standards will naturally regard herself as unfortunate because she tends to identify herself with other Americans rather than with Haitians.

Is this tendency defensible? I believe that comparisons between an individual's life and the lives of those in some comparison class narrower than the group of all persons have to be accepted as legitimate. An American who is worse off than most other Americans but considerably better off than most Haitians is unfortunate *for an American.* There is certainly nothing *mistaken* about a person's assessing how well or badly off she is by comparison with others with whom she identifies herself. But this kind of comparison has to be recognized for what it is: a limited assessment of the individual's fortune, made by reference to a narrow comparison class. It has to be acknowledged that there is more to the person's fortune than this.

I think we should recognize the legitimacy and importance of several different types of comparison. Ultimately, the comparison between a person's life and the range of lives possible given that person's own psychological capacities and potential yields the most objective measure of how well or badly off that person is. But one's sense of how fortunate or unfortunate one is is also affected by the comparison between one's own life and the lives of others with capacities comparable to one's own, which most of us take to include most other human beings. By that standard, most of those who will read this book are fortunate indeed. Beyond this, one is free to compare one's life with the lives of those with whom one most closely identifies oneself. If one is worse off than most of these people, there is a limited sense in which one is unfortunate. But this must not be allowed to obscure the larger sense in which one may be quite fortunate. A person who aspires to the highest sort of life and identifies himself with those who have attained such a life may feel unfortunate if he never quite succeeds in attaining it himself; but if he thinks of himself as simply unfortunate—unfortunate in some absolute way—and thinks that comparisons between his own life and the lives of the mass of humankind are simply irrelevant to understanding how fortunate or unfortunate he is, then he is suffering from a failure of imagination.

5.2. *A Hierarchy of Being?*

If a dog has a life that is about as good as is possible given the limitations imposed by its cognitive and emotional capacities, we consider the dog to be fortunate, or to have a good life. If a person has a life that is about as good as is possible for him, he too is very fortunate. Surely, however, we do not want to say that the dog and the person are equally fortunate. For, obviously, the person has a vastly better life than the dog. How, then, are we to compare the levels of overall fortune of individuals with widely divergent psychological capacities (who will therefore be in different comparison classes)?

We must distinguish several distinct dimensions of evaluation. There is, first, the evaluation of an individual's level of well-being, of how good its present state is. We can also, of course, evaluate well-being over time: how good an individual's life is during a certain period or how good, or well worth living, the life is as a whole. If we compare the life of a person with the life of an animal, the person's life will typically have a vastly higher level of well-being, or contain vastly more good, or be vastly more worth living than the life of the animal. (This is not always true, of course. Just as the peaks of well-being accessible to a person are higher than those accessible to an animal, the depths are also deeper. A human life can be tragic, containing depths of suffering, misery, grief, and degradation, in a way that no animal's life can. I will return to this in section 1.2 of chapter 3.)

The second dimension of evaluation is the evaluation of what I have called "fortune." This is the evaluation of whether an individual flourishes or fares poorly, is fortunate or unfortunate, or well or badly off, either at a particular time or over a period of time, including an entire lifetime. Fortune, as I understand it, adds a comparative dimension to the evaluation of well-being. Fortune is a matter of how an individual's level of well-being compares with a certain standard. The various competing accounts of fortune differ in their specification of the relevant standard.

What is singular about the evaluation of fortune is that, whatever the relevant standard may be against which an individual's level of well-being is to be assessed, comparisons between the levels of fortune of different individuals must be internal to the categories defined by the standard. Comparative evaluations of individuals in different categories seem to go beyond our notion of fortune. The Species Norm Account, for example, may judge that one dog is more fortunate than another, but it is silent about whether a supremely fortunate dog is more or less fortunate than a moderately fortunate human being.

So how ought the Species Norm Account to handle comparisons across species? It seems that there must be a third dimension of evaluation—beyond the evaluation of well-being and the evaluation of fortune—that is concerned explicitly with the *ranking* of the categories defined by the relevant standard. The Species Norm Account, for example, must conceive of species as at least potentially ordered in a hierarchy—a Great Chain of Being, in A. O. Lovejoy's familiar phrase. Dogs, for instance, constitute a species that is higher than any insect species but lower than the human species.

What about the Intrinsic Potential Account? It holds that the standard against which an individual's well-being should be assessed in order to arrive at a noncomparative evaluation of that individual's level of fortune is the range of well-being accessible to that individual given his own psychological capacities and potential. It might be suggested that individuals should be ranked hierarchically according to their level of psychological capacity or potential. On this view, all individuals with equivalent capacities or potential would count as higher forms of being than individuals with lower capacities and potential. This offers a way of articulating our sense that it is better to be a person than to be a dog. Persons are higher forms of being: their capacities are higher, the range of good accessible to them is higher, and in general their lives are better, or more valuable, or more worth living, than those of dogs. But we do not articulate these claims by saying that persons are more fortunate than dogs. We do not regard a dog as unfortunate simply for being a dog. It is not a misfortune to be a dog. In particular, it is not a misfortune to be a dog rather than a person, even though it is better to be a person. Nor are we unfortunate to be persons rather than gods—though gods, if there were any, would be higher forms of being than we are.

The objection to this view is, of course, that it is deeply and perniciously inegalitarian, as it ranks people even within the normal range for cognitive capacity as higher and lower. One response to this objection parallels the understanding of comparative evaluation I suggested earlier. We do not comparatively evaluate how fortunate an individual is by comparing his well-being (or his life) with that of every subject of well-being, from the lowest conscious animal on up; nor do we compare his well-being only with the well-being of those with exactly the same level of psychological capacity. Rather, we restrict comparisons to a class of individuals defined by a certain broad range of psychological capacity—for example, the class of all persons. If we comparatively evaluate how fortunate or unfortunate an individual is by comparing his level of well-being, or his life, with that of all others in his comparison class, it seems that comparisons between individuals from different comparison classes do not yield judgments of fortune, but judgments of a different sort. They are, presumably, judgments of whether one individual is higher or lower than another. Thus all dogs, whatever the boundaries of their comparison class may be, are lower forms of being than persons. On this understanding of the Intrinsic Potential Account, it is comparison classes, each comprising all the individuals with psychological capacities within a particular range, that are ranked as higher or lower.

Human beings, it seems, have to be divided into at least two different comparison classes—those with psychological capacities within the normal range and those with capacities below that range. If it is irrelevant, in determining how well off a person is, to compare his life to that of a dog, it is difficult to avoid the conclusion that it is equally irrelevant to compare that person's life to that of a human being whose psychological capacities are comparable to those of a dog. If we think that a person is a higher form of being than a dog, it is difficult to avoid the conclusion that a person is a higher form of being than a human being with psychological capacities and potential comparable to those of a dog. We can avoid these conclusions only if we take species membership to set the standard for the evaluation of fortune and if we rank individuals by species rather than by psychological capacities and potential—in short, we can avoid these conclusions only if we accept the Species Norm Account, which I have argued is unacceptable. These conclusions will, however, undoubtedly be offensive to many people. I will return to the question of the moral status of congenitally severely retarded human beings in section 2.4 of chapter 3.

(It is worth noting that it is plausible to suppose that principles of equality are restricted in their application to the members of particular categories or comparison classes defined by our standard for assessing fortune. In the case of the Intrinsic Potential Account, for example, principles of equality will apply only within the comparison classes defined by level of psychological capacity. While it matters that persons should be equal in relevant ways if other things are equal, there is no reason to think that there should be equality between persons and dogs—though it may matter that individuals within the comparison class that includes most dogs should be as equal as possible in relevant respects *to one another*.)

While it seems inevitable that the Intrinsic Potential Account should assign congenitally severely retarded human beings to a different comparison class from human beings with normal cognitive capacities, it seems clear that we ought not to recognize any other divisions within the human species. We clearly accept that Einstein's life and that of the below-average person are appropriately compared with one another in determining whether either person is fortunate or unfortunate. And we clearly do not accept that Einstein is a higher form of being than the below-average person. Our egalitarian intuitions thus demand that each comparison class encompass a broad range of psychological capacity.

It should be acknowledged, of course, that psychological capacities and potential are distributed roughly along species lines, so that the comparison classes specified and ranked by the Intrinsic Potential Account coincide roughly with those of the Species Norm Account. But the hierarchies of the two accounts may diverge in their classification of individuals whose psychological capacities are profoundly deviant within their species. Thus, according to the Intrinsic Potential Account, a dog congenitally endowed with cognitive and emotional capacities no higher than those of a turtle counts as a lower being than other dogs.

5.3. *The Overall Fortune of Those Who Die in Infancy*

Normally, when a human being's life as a whole has contained very little good, this means that he was a deeply unfortunate individual whose life was tragic, for one or more of several reasons—for example, because the life contained a great deal of misery, because opportunities for good were scarce, or because the life ended very prematurely. But there seem to be exceptions: cases in which an individual's life has contained comparatively little good but does not seem to be a conspicuously unfortunate life. I will note two such types of case, one of which is particularly significant for our purposes.

First, we decline to regard a person's life as unfortunate to the extent that the absence of good is the person's own responsibility—particularly when it is the direct result of defects of moral character, such as wickedness or laziness. In these cases, we are inclined to say simply that the person deserved no better than he got.

There is an assumption here that, though intuitively plausible, may nevertheless be challenged. The assumption is that it is not a misfortune to be endowed with a certain type of moral nature, even if such a nature tends to diminish the amount of good in the life of one who has it. Possibly there is a deeper assumption in back of this one—namely, the assumption that one is responsible for one's own moral nature and therefore that it is inadmissible to treat one's moral nature or its expression in action simply as a piece of bad luck, an external imposition. Yet this assumption is challenged both by determinists and by liberal egalitarians, who regard the dispensations of the "natural lottery" as no less morally arbitrary than those of the social lottery, which distributes advantages and disadvantages according to the contingencies of a person's birth. And it does in fact seem obvious that it is impossible for a person to be wholly responsible for his own moral nature. Even if a substantial degree of self-creation is possible, it must have its source in an initial nature that is unchosen. But suppose, as most people believe, that one has enough control over one's moral nature to be to some degree responsible for it, at least in compatibilist terms. Even that may be insufficient to show that a bad moral nature cannot be a misfortune. For there are other dimensions of character that we recognize as misfortunes even though they are no less plastic than the specifically moral dispositions. A disposition to pessimism or depression, for example, tends to diminish the amount of good in a person's life. Although such a disposition seems both constitutive of the person's nature as well as potentially alterable through an effort of the will, we nevertheless regard its presence and operation as an affliction or misfortune. We regard the disposition as sufficiently extrinsic to count among the factors that affect the person's overall lifelong fortune. But if we allow that the effects of depression may diminish a person's overall fortune, how can we consistently deny that the effects of an evil character may do the same?

I will not pursue this further, as it is not directly relevant to our concerns in this book. Let us turn instead to the second type of case in which an individual does not seem terribly unfortunate for having a life with a very low overall level of well-being. Consider, for example, the life of a human being who dies shortly after birth. This brief life contained very little good at all. Yet it does not seem to have been a tragic life; nor does the infant seem to have been a deeply unfortunate individual. Why not?

One suggestion is that the infant is relevantly like a nonhuman animal. We have noted that animals too have low levels of lifelong well-being but are not considered unfortunate for that. I argued that, in the case of an animal, the explanation is that its overall fortune must be assessed relative to the best sort of life that would be possible given that animal's psychological capacities and potential. Because the best life of which an animal is capable is one with a level of well-being that is vastly lower than that of a normal human life, an animal may be considered to have been fortunate, or to have had a good life, even if the amount of good its life contained was very low compared to that of the average person. This explanation is unavailable in the case of a human infant who dies shortly after birth. If we compare the life that the infant actually had with the best life it could have had given its intrinsic potential, we of course find that it has fallen disastrously short of its potential.

Yet, again, the infant who dies shortly after birth does not seem to be the victim of a terrible tragedy or the have had a terribly unfortunate life. This seems to be an intermediate case. The life of a human being who dies in early infancy seems unfortunate in a way that the life of an animal—even an animal that dies in early infancy—is not; yet, intuitively, it is not nearly so unfortunate as a human life that is difficult and deprived, though worth living, that ends after only thirty years. Our problem, however, is to make sense of this last comparative judgment, which is puzzling because the life of the infant who dies may contain a considerably lower net amount of good than the life of a person who dies at the age of thirty.

It is difficult at this point to make clear what I believe the solution to this problem to be. That solution will come into focus gradually over the course of the book, as we address various issues about the nature and status of human infants—and human fetuses, in whose case the present problem also arises. At this point a few telegraphic remarks will have to suffice—though they will be at least partially elucidated in the following section.

When an individual's actual life contains considerably less good than it might have, we judge that individual to be unfortunate for basically two reasons. There is the sense that the individual has suffered an enormous loss as well as the sense that it is unfair for that individual to get so little from life when others get so much more. The individual seems to us a *victim*—a victim both of deprivation and of natural injustice. In the case of a newborn infant who dies, even though the disparity between its abbreviated life and the life it might have had may be very great indeed, it is nevertheless difficult to conceive of the infant itself as a victim, or at least as a victim of a tragic misfortune. For a newborn infant, like an animal, is simply not a substantial enough individual psychologically to be susceptible to tragedy or injustice. While the infant's objective loss is great, the infant itself is too shallow a vessel to contain that loss; the badness of the loss is as much impersonal as it is something suffered by the infant. Thus even though the total amount of good in the infant's brief life was pathetically meager, we do not judge the infant itself to have been greatly unfortunate or to have been the victim of a tragic misfortune.

In assessing the infant's overall lifelong fortune, we are not merely measuring the amount of good its life has contained against the amount it had the potential to have. We are also evaluating how bad it is for the infant to have had a life that is so deficient in good. What explains why we do not think the life of the infant is very bad is that the notion of badness we are invoking is relational: badness *for the infant*. Our intuition is that it is not terribly bad for the infant to have had that life. For even though the life contained about as little good as it is possible for a human life to contain without dropping into the negative dimension on balance, it is not very bad for the victim because the victim is insufficiently developed to be the subject of great misfortune—or at least of great misfortunes of certain sorts.

An infant can, of course, suffer great pain, and that can be a great misfortune. But most forms of great misfortune—for example, blighted hopes, failed efforts at significant achievement, the loss of something that one cares about deeply—presuppose a psychologically substantial subject. It seems that all misfortunes that consist of the loss or the absence of good require a psychologically well developed subject in order to be *grave* misfortunes.

If this is right, it offers a defense of the Intrinsic Potential Account against the objections mentioned earlier. I noted, for example, that the Intrinsic Potential Account implies that a congenitally severely retarded human being is not unfortunate as long as he fares well relative to what is possible given the limitations of his psychological nature. I then noted that the account implies that the Brain-Damaged Individual is unfortunate in a way that a congenitally severely retarded human being is not, even if they both have the same psychological capacities and the same level of well-being. The reason is that the Brain-Damaged Individual falls well short of the best life possible given the psychological capacities that he once had the intrinsic potential to have. Indeed, given the disparity between the Brain-Damaged Individual's actual life and the best life he once had the potential to have, it may seem that he is terribly or tragically unfortunate. But to suppose that he is terribly unfortunate while a congenitally severely retarded human being is not unfortunate at all is to distinguish between them in a way that will strike most people as arbitrary.

If, however, the Intrinsic Potential Account is restricted by the recognition that the loss or absence of good can be a *grave* misfortune only for individuals who at some point have substantial or well-developed psychological capacities, the charge of arbitrariness loses much of its force. For with this recognition, the distinctions that the Intrinsic Potential Account draws between the cases have less significance. While the account continues to distinguish between a congenitally severely retarded human being and the Brain-Damaged Individual, it does not imply that the difference between them is great. A congenitally severely retarded human being may not be unfortunate at all if there is not too great a gap between its actual well-being and the highest levels of well-being of which it is capable given its psychological capacities and the psychological capacities it has had the intrinsic potential to develop. The Brain-Damaged Individual, by contrast, is unfortunate, for there is a great shortfall between the highest state he had the intrinsic potential to achieve and his actual state. But because he remains a psychologically insubstantial subject, a shallow or incomplete self, the Brain-Damaged Individual cannot be terribly unfortunate; therefore the difference between him and a congenitally severely retarded human being cannot be very great. Finally, an infant who dies shortly after birth may be even more unfortunate than the Brain-Damaged Individual, since the infant gets even less good from life and thus has an even lower lifelong level of well-being. But again the difference is limited by the nature of the victims.

This is not to return to the Peak Capacity Account. The Intrinsic Potential Account recognizes that it can be a misfortune to have psychological capacities lower than those one has had the potential to have. But it does seem that psychological potential matters less to the evaluation of fortune than psychological capacity. It is, for example, a greater misfortune to fall short of heights of well-being that one is, or has been, psychologically capable of achieving than it is to fall equally short of heights of well-being that would have been possible only if one had had psychological capacities that one had the potential to develop but did not in fact develop. And loss of certain psychological capacities is a greater misfortune, other things being equal, than the loss of the potential to have those capacities.

In this section, I have discussed a couple of exceptions to the rule that the life of a human being is unfortunate if it contains very little good. A person may not be unfortunate if the relative lack of good in his life is his own fault; and an infant or fetus that dies is insufficiently substantial as an individual to be the victim of a tragic loss. It is interesting to note that, while these types of individual are not gravely unfortunate, neither are they fortunate. They are neither fortunate nor profoundly unfortunate.

6. THE DEATHS OF FETUSES AND INFANTS

6.1. *The Time-Relative Interest Account*

It may be easier to understand why we do not regard the life of a human being who dies shortly after birth to be among the most unfortunate possible lives if we consider a parallel problem: the badness of death for an infant or fetus.[61] The account of the badness of death as I have developed it thus far focuses on the magnitude of the loss suffered by the one who dies. Thus it implies that it is worse for a person to die earlier rather than later: for example, it is worse to die at thirty than at eighty, provided the intervening fifty years of life would be worth living. It also implies that, if other things are equal, it is worse for one person to die at thirty than it is for another to die at eighty: the one suffers a greater loss or misfortune than the other. By this same logic, however, it seems that it should be worse to die one day after birth, or even before birth (assuming that we begin to exist before birth), than it is to die at thirty. And it should be worse for one individual to die a day after birth than it is for another to die at thirty, other things being equal. This is what we should believe if we assume that the badness of death is a function *entirely* of the magnitude of the loss suffered by the victim. This assumption defines what I earlier referred to as the Life Comparative Account of the badness of death. Yet it is contrary to what most of us believe to suppose that a very early death—death in utero or in earliest infancy—is worse than a later death.

It is worth pausing to cite evidence for the claim that most people believe that the death of a fetus or infant is less bad than the death of an older child or adult. Consider first that most people believe that we begin to exist at conception. They therefore believe that the death even of an embryo prior to implantation is the death of one of us. Yet on a conservative estimate, two of every three products of human conception die of natural causes prior to birth.[62] If we thought that the death of a fetus or infant was as serious a misfortune as the death of an older child or adult, we would have to think of the vast number of spontaneous abortions that occur as a continuing tragedy of major proportions. We would surely mobilize ourselves, as a society, to lower the prenatal death rate. Yet the level of social spending on the prevention of spontaneous abortion remains exceedingly low—lower by far than the social investment in the search for a cure for diseases, such as AIDS, that result in far fewer deaths. The explanation for this is that we simply do not regard the death of an embryo of fetus as a serious misfortune, even though most of us believe that the victim is one of us. In general, people seem more concerned about the effect of spontaneous abortion on the potential parents than about the effect on the fetus.

It can, of course, be argued that there are alternative explanations of our apparent complacency about spontaneous abortion. One is that the possible causes of spontaneous abortion are so varied or heterogeneous that no single research agenda for discovering a means of prevention is possible. This is true, but if our level of concern about these deaths were high, we would at least seek to isolate and suppress the most common causes. But this is not a goal of any visible, publicly supported research effort. Another possible explanation is that we recognize that many spontaneous abortions occur because the embryo or fetus is defective in some way; thus our resigned acceptance of spontaneous abortion as nature's way of correcting mistakes is compatible with the belief that these deaths are nonetheless tragic. This, however, would be convincing only if we were equally unconcerned to prevent the deaths of older children with congenital genetic or other defects.

Assuming, then, that most people really do believe that death is a less serious misfortune for a fetus or infant than it is for an older child or adult, we need to consider whether and how this common view can be justified, given that it clashes with the obvious fact that the fetus or infant suffers a greater loss of future good. One possibility is that the view can be explained, though the explanation fails to constitute a justification. Some have noticed that evolutionary biology offers a quite powerful explanation of our tendency to regard the deaths of fetuses and infants as less bad. One writer, Robert Wright, offers a clear exposition of this view, suggesting at the end that the search for rational grounds for thinking these deaths are less bad is chimerical. His account is worth quoting at length.

> A fifty-year-old of either sex has, on average, many fewer potential offspring in his or her future than he or she did at thirty—at which point, in turn, the potential was less than it had been at fifteen. On the other hand, the average fifteen-year-old has more future offspring than the average one-year-old, since the one-year-old may yet die before adolescence—a fairly common thing during much of human evolution.
>
> . . . Since reproductive potential is embedded in both the cost and benefit sides of the altruism equation, the age of both the giver and the recipient help to determine whether the altruism will tend to raise inclusive fitness, and thus be favored by natural selection. In other words, how warm and generous we feel toward kin depends, theoretically, both on our age and on the kin's age. There should, for example, be continuous change, throughout a child's life, in how dear that life seems to parents.
>
> Specifically, parental devotion should grow until around early adolescence, when reproductive potential peaks, and then begin to drop. Just as a horse breeder is more disappointed by the death of a thoroughbred the day before its first race than the day after its birth, a parent should be more heartbroken by the death of an adolescent than by the death of an infant. Both the adolescent and the mature racehorse are assets on the brink of bringing rewards, and in both cases it will take much time and effort, starting from scratch, to get another asset to that point. . . .
>
> As predicted, parents do grieve more over the death of an adolescent than of a three-month-old—or, also in keeping with theory, of a forty-year-old. It is tempting to dismiss such results: *of course* we regret a young man's death more than an older

man's; it's obviously tragic to die with so much life unlived. To which Darwinians reply: Yes, but remember—the very "obviousness" of the pattern may be a product of the same genes that, we propose, created it. . . .

In this case, we should ask: If an adolescent boy's vast unlived life is what makes his death seem so sad, why doesn't the death of an infant seem even sadder? One answer is that we've had more time to get to know the adolescent and can thus see the unlived life more clearly. But what a coincidence that the countervailing changes in these two quantities—the growing intimacy with a person over time and the shrinking size of that person's unlived life—happen to reach some sort of maximum combined grief value right around adolescence, when that person's reproductive potential is highest. Why doesn't the peak come, say, at age twenty-five, when the contours of the unlived life are *really* clear? Or at age five, when there's so *much* unlived life?[63]

According to this view, our intuitions about the comparative badness of death at different ages are biologically determined; explanations that seek to portray our attitudes as rational are mere rationalizations.

The details of this explanation, as presented, are slightly off target. If parents will evaluate the death of a child in terms of its effect on the child's reproductive potential, they should be equally distressed by the death of a day-old infant and the death of a fifteen-year-old. For both deaths are equally decisive in preventing the child from reproducing. (It makes no sense to regret the day-old infant's death less simply because there was a higher probability that it might have suffered a different death before being able to reproduce.) The real explanation is in the third paragraph quoted. It has to do with the greater investment that is lost when an older child dies, and with the greater difficulty of reestablishing a comparable probability of reproductive payoff.

Even this plausible explanation, however, does not exclude complementary and potentially justifying explanations. The claim that the Darwinian explanation excludes other explanations is challenged by the fact that we accept the view that the death of an infant is less bad than the death of an adolescent whether or not the children are our own. The Darwinian explanation seems to apply only to *parental* attitudes. While there may be a biological advantage in thinking that it would be worse for one's own child to die in adolescence than in infancy, there is no obvious biological advantage in having the same attitude to the deaths of children who are not one's own. The Darwinian might reply, of course, that natural selection need not produce attitudes that discriminate between one's own children and those of others. It could endow one with attitudes to the deaths of children that fail to make that discrimination as long as they provided appropriate motivation with respect to one's own children. Yet there are reasons why evolutionary biology should predict that one would have a rather different view of the deaths of other children. It might be advantageous, for example, to be less concerned about the deaths of other children when they are the same age and sex as one's own children; for those other children would otherwise become potential competitors with one's own children for the more desirable mates of the other sex. But, so far as I know, this is not a common attitude to have. It seems, on the contrary, that the judgments we make about the comparative badness of death at different ages for other people's children are similar to those we would make about the badness of death at different ages for our own children. If the Darwinian view fails to explain this, or even predicts that we would have attitudes quite different from this, this suggests that there is an independent basis for our beliefs about the comparative badness of death at different ages.

In general, evolutionary explanations are compatible with other forms of explanation. There is, for example, an extremely powerful and plausible Darwinian explanation of our sense that parents have special responsibilities to their own children that they do not have to the children of others. But this hardly excludes the possibility that parental duties may also have a rational basis in morality. The two forms of explanation may run happily in tandem. The explanations I will suggest of the view that the deaths of fetuses and infants are less bad than the deaths of older children and adults are similarly compatible with the Darwinian explanation cited above.

Before developing the elements of the explanation that I believe is most plausible, I should briefly discuss a different explanation that I believe is inadequate. Fred Feldman has argued that the death of a human fetus shortly after conception does not involve a serious loss of value because value is a matter of individuals getting the amount and kinds of good they deserve and the fetus deserves very few, if any, of the goods that its subsequent life would have contained. He believes that a late-term fetus—and thus, by extension, a newborn infant—deserves more than a newly conceived fetus simply by virtue of the greater "investment" it has made in its own future, albeit without consciously aiming to prepare for that future. But while an infant deserves more than an early-term fetus, its level of desert is normally much lower than that of an adult. Thus Feldman concludes that, while the death of an infant would be bad because the infant would be failing to get the good it would deserve, its death would be substantially less bad than the death of an adult would normally be. And this would be because the amount of good that it would deserve would be only a tiny fraction of the total good its subsequent life would have contained. Its loss would be adjusted for desert: only the loss of the amount of good that the infant deserved would count as bad.

This argument is intended to defend the Life Comparative Account by showing that it is compatible with that account to recognize that the death of a fetus or infant is less bad than the death of an older child or adult. I believe that this defense fails. There are grounds for skepticism about the account of desert on which the argument depends (according to which a fetus or infant's desert increases with its biological investment in its life), but these need not detain us. For the principal objection is that, when the role of desert is understood properly, the Life Comparative Account cannot avoid implying that the death of a fetus or infant is worse than the death of an older child or adult, if other things are equal.

Let us focus on the death of a newborn infant. In order to conclude that the death of the infant is substantially less bad than the death of a young adult, the advocate of the Life Comparative Account must show that the difference in value between the infant's short life and the life it would have had if it had not died is substantially less than the difference in value between the actual life of the young adult and the longer life he would have had if he had not died. To show this, one must show that the lengthy segment of life that the infant loses by dying (that is, the whole of a normal human life from just after birth to old age) contains less value than the shorter future life that the young adult loses. How could this be? Feldman's answer is that the life the infant loses is less valuable because most of the good it would contain would be beyond what the infant now deserves, whereas much or most of the good that the young adult would lose would presumably be deserved.

This, however, is to evaluate each future life relative to each individual's desert at the present time. If this is to be compatible with the Life Comparative Account, the claim about the value of the longer life that the infant might have had must not be a claim about the value that the life has for the infant *at that time;* rather, it must be a claim about the value that the life would have had atemporally. It must be true that, if the infant had not died but had instead lived the longer life, the value of that life as a whole would have been greatly diminished because the goods it would have contained would not have been deserved when the person was an infant. But that is absurd. Consider any completed life that we recognize as having been exceptionally good or valuable, supremely worth living for its possessor. On any criterion of desert that Feldman would be willing to accept, virtually none of the good that this life contained was deserved by the person whose life it was when he was an infant. This shows that what the person deserved when he was an infant is irrelevant to the assessment of the value of his life as a completed whole. This must be true in the case of our infant's hypothetical life as well.

If the Life Comparative Account is to adjust the value that a good would add to a life by reference to the person's desert, it must do so by considering whether and to what extent the good would be deserved *at the time that it would occur.* If, for example, a good would be undeserved at the time that it would occur, the value that it would contribute to the life might be discounted; or the good might not contribute to the value of the life at all. The precise details need not concern us here. The crucial points can be made by reference to a pair of examples. Suppose there are two infants, both of whom are in danger of dying. If both infants were to survive, the life of each would contain roughly as much good as the other's. But in one case, most of the goods in the life would be deserved when they occurred; in the other, few would be deserved. It may well be plausible to suppose that the first of these lives would be significantly more valuable than the second and that, consequently, death would be worse for the first infant. It might even be true, depending on how steeply we discount the value of a good for the absence of desert, that the second life would not be very valuable at all, despite the fact that it would contain a great deal of good. In practice, however, this is irrelevant to the evaluation of the deaths of infants. For in the case of infants (or fetuses), we cannot predict whether the goods their lives would contain would be deserved when they would occur. We must instead estimate the amount of good an infant's life would be likely to contain and assume that the infant's subsequent deserts would fall within the normal range. There can be no basis for predicting, of any particular infant, that it would later have an abnormally low level of desert, and hence there is no basis for discounting the value of its prospective life for diminished desert. Therefore, even if we accept that how much a certain good contributes to the value of a life depends on whether it is deserved, this provides no reason for thinking that the deaths of infants or fetuses are in general less bad than the deaths of older children or adults.

In order to defend our intuitive sense that the deaths of fetuses and infants matter less, or are less serious misfortunes, we must abandon the Life Comparative Account of the badness of death. We must instead appeal to a view that relativizes the evaluation of the death to the state of the victim at the time of death. The evaluation must be based on the effect that the death has on the victim as he is at the time of death rather than on the effect it has on his life as a whole. This is what the Time-Relative Interest Account of the badness of death does. It discounts the importance of the death to the victim at the time for any weakness there would have been in the prudential unity relations that would have bound him to himself in the future.

Consider again the death of a newborn infant. Intuitively, it is the vast psychological distance that there would have been between the infant and itself later as a person that explains our sense that the death is a less serious misfortune than the death of an older child or adult—despite the greater magnitude of the good it loses. An infant is unaware of itself, unaware that it has a future; it therefore has no future-directed mental states: no desires or intentions for its future. Because its mental life is so limited, there would be very few continuities of character or belief between itself now and itself as a person. And if it had lived to become a person, it would then remember nothing of its life as an infant. It is, in short, almost completely severed psychologically from itself as it would have been in the future. This is the principal reason why its time-relative interest in continuing to live is so weak. It is almost as if the future it loses might just as well have belonged to someone else.

To appreciate this last claim, it may help to consider how the badness of death for an infant is intermediate between the badness of death for a person and the badness of a person's failing to come into existence at all. Let us refer to the situation in which a person might come into existence, but does not, as "nonconception." In the case of nonconception, there is a loss of an enormous amount of possible future good but there is no victim of the loss, no existing individual whose good it would have been. For the good is lost precisely because the individual whose good it would have been never comes to exist. The loss is therefore entirely impersonal. Because of this, most people think that the loss matters much less. Most people, indeed, think that it does not matter at all—that is, they think that it is morally irrelevant that there might have been a great deal of good in the future if there never is anyone whose good it might have been. If the loss cannot be attributed to someone who exists at some point, it is morally insignificant.

Nonconception contrasts markedly with the death of a person. When a person dies, the amount of future good that is lost may be less than that which is lost through nonconception, but there is, in this case, a *victim* of the loss, an existing individual in whose life the good would have occurred. This latter consideration may seem to make all the difference. It may seem to be what distinguishes the death of a person so sharply from nonconception. But that is true only if identity is the basis of egoistic concern about the future. For what *really* distinguishes the death of a person from nonconception is that, when a person dies, there is a loss of future good *and* there is someone who would have been related, *in the ways that matter,* to the recipient of that good. If identity is what matters (that is, what grounds rational egoistic concern about the future), we have a complete explanation of the difference between the death of a person and nonconception when we point out that when a person dies there is a loss of great good and the person who would have been the subject of that good would have been the same person as the person who dies. But I argued earlier, following Parfit, that identity is not what matters. If that is right, then, to explain the difference between nonconception and the death of a person, we need to note both that the death of a person involves the loss of a great deal of good *and* that the person who dies would have been strongly related, in the ways that matter, to the person who would have been the subject of the good. This shows the *relevant* sense in which the death of a person involves a victim while nonconception does not. When a person dies, there is someone who would have been related *in the right way* to the good that is lost.

We can now see how the death of an infant is relevantly intermediate between nonconception and the death of a person. In the case of nonconception, there is a loss of a great deal of good, but there is no victim who would have been related to that good in the ways that matter. When a person dies, there is a loss of a great deal of good, and there is a victim who would have been strongly related to that good in the ways that matter. When an infant dies, there is a loss of a great deal of good, and there is a victim of that loss, in the sense that there is someone who would have been identical with the person who would have been the subject of the good. If identity were what matters, the loss suffered by the infant would matter at least as much as, and perhaps more than, the loss a person suffers in dying, for the loss would be greater and the basis for caring about that loss would be the same. The difference is that, unlike a person who dies, the infant would have been only weakly related, *in the ways that matter*, to the subject of the good that is lost. The infant is not a victim in the same way as a person who dies; but neither is the loss occasioned by its death a wholly impersonal or victimless loss in the same way as the loss involved in nonconception.

If identity were what matters, the worst death, involving the most significant loss, would be the death of an individual immediately after the beginning of his existence. But the loss that would have occurred if that individual had simply been prevented from beginning to exist would not have been significant at all. This is hard to believe. It suggests that it is profoundly important to prevent the existence of an individual who would die within seconds of beginning to exist. This might make sense if we came into existence fully formed psychologically, as Athena emerged from the head of Zeus. But given the way we in fact develop, this view is very hard to accept.

I have stressed that, intuitively, it is the fact that an infant is almost entirely cut off psychologically from its own future self that accounts for our sense that its death is a lesser misfortune than the death of an older child or adult. One objection to this claim is that there are other cases involving a comparable degree of psychological discontinuity in which there is nevertheless a moderately strong basis for egoistic concern about the future. Suppose, for example, that one's brain were going to be deprogrammed in the manner described in section 4.6 of chapter 1. Provided that one would retain one's psychological capacities and that there would be continuity of consciousness, the breach in psychological connectedness would weaken but not altogether subvert one's basis for egoistic concern about the future. To die shortly before the process of deprogramming would be a serious misfortune, despite the tenuousness of one's expected psychological connections to oneself in the future. But if the death of a person facing a prospect of immediate deprogramming would be a serious misfortune, the same should be true of the death of an infant—indeed, the death of the infant should, if anything, be a greater misfortune, given the greater magnitude of its loss.[64]

There are, however, two respects in which the prudential unity relations would be stronger in the case of deprogramming than in the case of an infant. First, recall that I argued in section 5.2 of chapter 1 that the degree of psychological unity within a life depends on the richness, complexity, and coherence of the overall psychological architecture that is carried forward through time. Because a person facing deprogramming would retain his psychological capacities, he would carry forward a significantly more extensive set of psychological structures than an infant, which has comparatively few psychological capacities to begin with. Second, although deprogramming involves radical organizational discontinuity in the brain, it causes no physical or functional discontinuity (hence the victim's retention of his psychological capacities). But in the relation that the infant would bear to its future self, there would be significant physical and functional discontinuity as well as an absence of significant psychological unity.

This may seem a surprising claim, for it may seem that there would be, if anything, heightened forms of physical and functional continuity of the brain between the infant and itself later as a person; for its brain is in the process of growing, expanding, and developing its capacities. But this is a mistake. Growth and development of the brain involve physical and functional additions, just as the deterioration of the brain in dementia involves physical and functional losses. In neither case is there just preservation or continuity. The radical changes involved in growth and development are therefore forms of discontinuity. (One can appreciate this point intuitively by imagining a form of gene therapy that would greatly alter the physical structure of a person's brain, expanding his cognitive capacities until they were almost those of a god. As I suggested in section 5.2 of chapter 1, this could weaken rather than enhance the basis for egoistic concern about the future. A person could rationally regard this kind of transformation as a threat rather than a benefit on the ground that the being he might become would be too alien to be an appropriate object of egoistic concern.)

In short, in the relation between an infant and itself as an adult there would not only be a weaker degree of psychological connectedness but also weaker forms of physical and functional continuity of the brain than there would be between a person before and after deprogramming. Therefore the recognition that a person facing a prospect of deprogramming would nevertheless have a substantial basis for egoistic concern about the future is compatible with acceptance of the claim that an infant's time-relative interest in continuing to live is extremely weak.

I have argued that the Time-Relative Interest Account of the badness of death plausibly explains our sense that the death of a fetus or infant is a lesser misfortune by noting that the prudential unity relations between the fetus or infant and its future self would be conspicuously weak. When the prudential unity relations that would bind an individual to himself in the future would be weak, death matters less *for that individual at the time*. Notice, however, that it seems reasonable to want one's own death to be less bad—to be a lesser rather than a greater misfortune. If weaker prudential unity relations make death less bad, might one make one's own death, or the death of someone one cares about, less bad by ensuring, prior to the death, that the prudential unity relations would have been weaker? Consider:

The Benefactor. One's dearest friend is certain to die within a few hours. Because he is still young and, in a sense, full of promise, it will be a tragic death. Suddenly one has an inspiration. One has access to a deprogramming device. Believing that psychological unity is among the prudential unity relations, one deprograms one's friend's brain, thereby dramatically weakening the extent to which he would have been related, in some of the ways that matter, to himself in the future had he lived.

Does the would-be benefactor in this case actually reduce the severity of the misfortune his friend suffers in dying? If so, does he thereby benefit his friend? If the Time-Relative Interest Account implies that he does, that counts against the plausibility of the account. For surely there would be no benefit in having one's brain deprogrammed just prior to death.[65]

The Time-Relative Interest Account must be able to recognize that deprogramming the friend's brain would not benefit him or promote or protect his time-relative interests. One reason for believing that there is no benefit is that deprogramming affects not just the strength of the prudential unity relations but also the amount of good there would be in the person's future. For as I noted earlier, psychological unity is a condition of many goods, such as friendship and achievement, that require a continuing access to one's past through memory. So the deprogramming, even if it was done only moments before the death occurred, preemptively precluded a great many of the goods that would otherwise have been made impossible by the death. The case of the Benefactor is therefore a case involving overdetermination. We can therefore acknowledge that there is a sense in which the deprogramming does indeed make the death a less serious misfortune, but only by ensuring that the life the person would have had if he had lived would have been less good. The loss attributable to the death is less, but only because much of the deprivation that would have been attributable to the death has been preemptively caused by the deprogramming itself. The overall loss is the same.[66] (As in the earlier case of the Accident Victim, it may be unclear how responsibility for the overall loss is to be apportioned between the overdetermining causes: the deprogramming and the death. One can claim that the deprogramming caused virtually no loss given that the death was going to occur independently; and one can claim that the death caused a significantly lesser loss given that the deprogramming had already occurred. But the overall loss is clearly greater than the sum of these two losses as described.)

This reply, while plausible, is really beside the point. For if, in the case of the Benefactor, the weakening of the prudential unity relations also makes various goods impossible, the example then fails as a test of the plausibility of the Time-Relative Interest Account. What we want to know is whether the Time-Relative Interest Account implies that the weakening of the prudential unity relations *by itself* makes death less bad in a way that could make the weakening of those relations beneficial or desirable. To test for this, we must alter the case in such a way that deprogramming would not affect the amount of good that would lie in prospect for the friend if he were not to die. Let us simply stipulate that this is so (perhaps we can imagine that the deprogramming would alter the friend's character in a way that would make him more receptive to friendship, more attractive to others, and more responsive to the good things in life). Understood in this way, the Benefactor becomes a case in which the amount of good that the friend's future would contain were he not to die remains constant before and after the deprogramming, but in which his time-relative interest in continuing to live becomes significantly weaker as a result of the deprogramming. The weakening of the prudential unity relations therefore makes the death less bad or matter less, even though the loss from death remains as great. Does the Time-Relative Interest Account treat that as beneficial?

It does not. For it is perfectly plausible, and compatible with the Time-Relative Interest Account, to regard the weakening of the prudential unity relations as itself a misfortune. We can see this intuitively by reflecting back on the case of the Cure, presented in section 5.2 of chapter 1. The treatment described in that case would greatly increase the amount of good in prospect for a person but would also significantly weaken the prudential unity relations that would bind him to himself in the future. I suggested that, intuitively, it could be egoistically rational to decline the treatment. If that is right, it must be because the weakening of the prudential unity relations would be a misfortune sufficiently grave to offset the increase in future good. It would, of course, be a peculiar sort of misfortune. The misfortune would be to become psychologically isolated from one's own future self, to be islanded in the present, to have less reason to anticipate or look forward to the goods of one's own future in an egoistic way. (The weakening of the prudential unity relations between oneself now and oneself in the future might be compared to the involuntary elimination of certain of one's desires for the future—indeed, if the Embodied Mind Account is correct, the latter is an instance of the former. In general, the involuntary elimination of a desire is as much a misfortune as the frustration of that desire. Thus there would be no benefit in erasing a person's desires for the future just prior to his death. Similarly, it might be argued that one has a second-order time-relative interest in preserving and maintaining the strength of most of one's present time-relative interests.)

Even this revised version of the Benefactor thus turns out to be a case involving overdetermination. Again the deprogramming may make the death less bad, but only by transferring some of the overall misfortune to another cause. In the revised case, there are now two misfortunes, which occur serially: the victim is first deprived of much of his basis for caring about his own future, and then he is deprived of the future itself. The second misfortune may matter less when it occurs, but only because the first has already severed many of the connections that would make the goods he loses matter to him. So, again, the death itself may be a lesser misfortune, or matter less, when it occurs, but the overall misfortune is the same.

One important lesson to be drawn from this defense of the Time-Relative Interest Account is that there are various ways in which one's death might be less bad, only some of which are desirable. There is no consolation in one's death being a lesser misfortune if the reason is only that one's future would have been less good, or that the relations that would have bound one to oneself in the future have been weakened.

6.2. *Narrative Unity, Retroactive Effects, Desert, and Desire*

In addition to psychological unity, there is another form of diachronic unity or integration within a life that may affect the extent to which death is bad for a person. This form of unity, which Alasdair MacIntyre refers to as "narrative unity,"[67] exists when the elements in a life fit together to form a meaningful whole, a series of events that have an intelligible purpose, direction, and overall structure—specifically, as Aristotle demanded of dramatic art, a beginning, middle, and end. When a life has narrative unity, the meaning or significance of each segment is derived in part from its relations both to what has gone before and to what comes after—for example, when a later segment fulfills the promise of an earlier one.

The future life that a person loses through death might have affected the narrative unity of his life as a whole in various ways. If the future that a person loses could reasonably have been expected to round out his life or bring it to completion, the death is tragic for a particular reason: it leaves the life in suspension, without resolution or closure. If, by contrast, the future life that death excludes would have been unlikely to provide a fitting conclusion to the person's life story, the death will lack this particular tragic dimension. Indeed, if the death prevents what would have been a jarring, inappropriate, or inharmonious conclusion to the life, it may not be bad at all, or might even be good for the person, even if the life the person would otherwise have had would have been perfectly pleasant and therefore, in one sense at least, worth living.

Suppose that two people each suffer a stroke.[68] Each can be expected to live for about another year in a state of bovine contentment. One implication of the concern with narrative unity is that whether and to what extent that further year of life would be good for each depends on its relation to the person's previous life. Thus even if the additional year of each person's life would be much the same in terms of its intrinsic features, it might be good in one life but bad in the other. Suppose that one of the two people had devoted his earlier life to the experience of passive pleasures. For this person, the additional year of contented dementia seems in harmony with the values that informed his previous life and thus may be an acceptable, though sadly diminished, extension of that life. Suppose that the other person, by contrast, has previously led a life of the mind, devoted to intellectual and spiritual concerns. Set in the context of this person's previous life, the additional year may seem a travesty of life that is worth living. For this person, the additional year may be a dreadful misfortune, despite his remaining content throughout it. Within *this* life, the additional year has negative value. It is bad for the person while he lives through it and diminishes the value of his life as a whole. (I will discuss this claim in greater detail in section 3.2 of chapter 5.)

To many it will seem implausible to hold that the additional year is not worth living for the second of these two people if the person himself finds it tolerable, as he does by hypothesis. But the fact that the person remains content throughout the period of dementia means only that that segment of his life is good along one dimension of well-being. The additional year would of course be even worse if the person were miserable as well as demented. The point is that, given the character of his previous life, his condition during the additional year is bad along another dimension of well-being, and the badness of the year in this respect may outweigh the fact that it is subjectively experienced as good. There is, of course, a serious question about how the two dimensions of well-being can be combined on a single scale. I will not pursue this matter here, though it has been admirably discussed elsewhere.[69]

The importance of narrative unity helps to explain why the deaths of human fetuses and infants are less bad. It is only as a life progresses that its story lines become more focused and determinate. And as the story of one's life becomes more defined, the narrative significance of succeeding events becomes increasingly important. When the story is well advanced, its narrative structure may demand completion in one of a limited number of ways. As David Velleman aptly puts it, "by middle age, one finds oneself composing the climax to a particular story—a story that is now determinate enough to be spoiled."[70] The life of a fetus or infant, by contrast, has barely begun: there is no focused narrative in progress, the story is inchoate, and thus no particular conclusion is required by the elements already in place. Death does not spoil a good story for the simple reason that the story has hardly begun. If all we have are the words, "Once upon a time . . . ," we do not have a story that ends badly; we do not have a story at all.

It might be objected that this insistence on the importance of narrative unity is in tension with the rejection of the Life Comparative Account of the badness of death in favor of the Time-Relative Interest Account. For narrative unity is a feature of a life as a whole; therefore a concern with narrative unity is a concern for the value of a life as a whole. This is not, however, a problem for the Time-Relative Interest Account, properly understood. During that period within a life when the prudential unity relations are strong (and in most cases this period stretches from childhood through old age), what an individual has most egoistic reason to want, at any given time, will be what would be best for his life as a whole, and this will be importantly affected by considerations of narrative unity. As I noted earlier, when the prudential unity relations are strong, a person's time-relative interests coincide with his interests. A person's time-relative interests at a given time need not be—and typically are not—concerned only with his good at that time.

I should perhaps stress that I take narrative unity to be only one of a number of considerations that combine to determine the value for a person of a particular future. Certain writers, by contrast, seem to treat it as the sole criterion of what would be good for a person. MacIntyre, for example, contends that the unity of a life "is the unity of a narrative embodied in a single life. To ask 'What is the good for me?' is to ask how best I might live out that unity and bring it to completion."[71] If, however, considerations of narrative unity were all that determined how important it was for a person that his life should continue, the death of a very elderly person, who needed perhaps one more year to round out and complete his life in a fully satisfying way, would be far worse than the death of a ten-year-old whose life still lacked a definite trajectory or narrative structure. As this implication is plainly implausible, we must concede that considerations of narrative unity provide only a partial explanation of the badness of death.

Thus far my contention has been that the way the parts of a life fit together may affect the value for a person of the future that she would have if death were not to intervene. But just as the character of a person's past may affect the value that a certain future would have for her, so what happens or fails to happen in the future may also affect the value of her life in the past.[72] Particularly important for our purposes is the fact that death may prevent a person from fulfilling projects or ambitions in which she has invested considerable time and effort. The loss of the future in which those ambitions would have been achieved retroactively condemns to futility much of the activity that had been dedicated to them. Suppose, for example, that a brilliant but desperately impoverished student aspires to become a surgeon. She is accepted for study at a prestigious medical school but, in order to help her family, has to hold a part-time job throughout the years of her training. These are therefore years of unremitting toil and hardship, in which she is chronically deprived of sleep and has virtually no opportunities for personal indulgence or pleasure. At the end, however, she graduates at the head of her class and is thus on track for a glorious career in medicine. Suppose that, shortly after she completes her residency, she is killed in an accident. Her death seems retroactively to affect the value for her life of the years in medical school. Had the trials of those years fulfilled their intended purpose of enabling her to become a celebrated surgeon whose skills saved the lives of many, they would have been redeemed by their contribution to her later achievements. But the death has instead made those years a period of needless misery and wasted opportunities for activities whose value would not have been so drastically diminished by an early death.

The medical student's death does not, of course, affect the dimension of her well-being concerned with the character of her subjective states during the years in medical school. Suppose, moreover, that her successful striving in the face of adversity added to the value of her life during those years—that this was a feature of her life that contributed to her own overall good. If so, that aspect of the value of those years is also unaffected by her death. What *is* affected are certain dimensions of the *meaning* of her activities during those years. If she had lived and become a eminent surgeon, her efforts in medical school would have had a point, a crucial role in a story of success, that they lack when they have in fact led to nothing. Michael Lockwood expresses this well: "Set against an ideal of human life as a meaningful whole, we can see that premature death can, as it were, make nonsense of much of what has gone before. Earlier actions, preparations, planning, whose entire purpose and rationale lay in their being directed towards some future goal, become, in the face of an untimely death, retrospectively pointless—bridges, so to speak, that terminate in midair, roads that lead nowhere."[73] In the case of the medical student, the years that might have been the foundation of a brilliant medical career have been transformed by death into something else entirely: a tragic waste of time.

In general, death is worse to the extent that it frustrates the efforts that a person has invested in preparing for the future that the death prevents.[74] This is not just because the future that is lost would have been better by virtue of its narrative relations with the past but also because the value of the past may be decreased if the meaning with which it would have been imbued by subsequent events is lost. This, too, helps to explain why the deaths of fetuses and infants are less bad. For fetuses and infants are obviously incapable of making the sorts of investment in their own futures that may be rendered futile by a premature death. There is therefore no possibility of their past lives being retroactively devalued by death. This is a dimension to the badness of death that we find in the case of most adults that is necessarily absent in the case of fetuses and infants.

It is worth stressing that my claim—that death is worse, other things being equal, to the extent that it frustrates previous investments in the victim's future—applies only to efforts consciously intended by the person to achieve certain goals. Other writers, motivated by a concern to explain why late abortion and infanticide seem morally more serious than early abortion, have claimed that other forms of investment are relevant. Fred Feldman, for example, writes:

> an eight-month-old fetus probably has made a much greater investment [than a day-old fetus]. She has endured the boredom of a long, claustrophobic, underwater captivity. She has [devoted] energy and other resources to the tasks involved in growth and development. Though she has made a substantial investment, she has not yet had an opportunity to enjoy the benefits of her prenatal labors. In light of the fact that she has made a significant commitment to her future life, it is reasonable to maintain that she is fully deserving of the opportunity to enjoy that life. . . . In general . . . a fetus's investment in its life steadily increases from conception to birth.[75]

It is hard to see how the investments involved in mere biological growth and development could affect the extent to which death would be bad for the fetus. These investments do not contribute to a narrative process that would be disrupted by death. The processes of growth and development are things that *happen to* the fetus rather than things it *does.* Because they are not purposeful activities, and because the fetus is not even aware of it when they are occurring, these processes are no part of the biography, which has, indeed, yet to begin. They would have been no part of the meaning that the life might have had. And because these processes lack any meaning in the nascent story of the individual's life, there is no meaning in the life thus far that death might retroactively alter.

Ronald Dworkin also argues that the badness of a fetus's or infant's death is increased by the "investments" that nature, or God, or other people have made in the life. And he is quite explicit that "even unconscious natural processes of creation should be treated as investments worthy of respect."[76] Thus, he contends, "fetal development is a continuing creative process, a process that has barely begun at the instant of conception. . . . [A]s fetal growth continues, the natural investment that would be wasted in an abortion grows steadily larger and more significant."[77] He also notes that, as the life of a fetus continues, there is an increasing "waste of personal emotional investments made in that life by others" if the fetus dies.[78]

Dworkin's view is actually quite different from Feldman's. Feldman sees the fetus's growth and development as investments the fetus itself makes in its own future life, so that if these investments are frustrated by death, this is bad for the fetus, who should be regarded as a victim of natural injustice for failing to receive benefits that it has come to deserve through its "labors." According to Dworkin, however, investments made in the life of a fetus by nature or by other people do not affect the strength of any interest the fetus might have in continuing to live or the extent to which it would be bad *for the fetus* if it were to die. Rather, these investments help to determine the degree to which the fetus's life is "sacred" or "inviolable"—terms he uses to indicate the *intrinsic, impersonal* value of the life. Intrinsic value, on Dworkin's understanding, "is independent of what people happen to enjoy or want or need or what is good for them."[79] It is a kind of value that may be possessed not only by fetuses and persons but also by biological species, works of art, and other entities that altogether lack interests or a personal good. Thus even if Dworkin is right that the investment by nature in a fetus's growth and development increases the fetus's intrinsic value, it does not follow that the investment affects the fetus's life in a way that would make its death worse *for it*—though the investment does (according to Dworkin) make the death worse from an impersonal point of view, since it means that the death involves a greater loss of intrinsic value. Because our concern is with the badness of death *for those to whom it happens,* Dworkin's claims about the effects of previous investments by nature or by other people on the impersonal badness of an individual's death are essentially irrelevant for our purposes here.

Dworkin himself does, however, invoke these claims in order to explain "our common view that it is worse when a late-stage fetus . . . miscarries than an early-stage one, and worse when a ten-year-old child dies than an infant."[80] It seems to me, however, that most of the intuitions he cites—that the death of an infant is worse than the death of a late-term fetus, that the death of a three-year-old is worse than the death of an infant, and that the death of an adolescent is worse than the death of a three-year-old—are not essentially intuitions about the impersonal badness of death, or intuitions about the intrinsic value of the life of the individual who ceases to exist, but are instead intuitions about how bad death is *for the individual* at the time the death occurs. If this is right, Dworkin's claims are off target and we do better, in explaining these intuitions, to appeal to the considerations I have cited: psychological unity, narrative unity, retroactive effects, and so on. But even if Dworkin's claims are irrelevant to understanding the badness of death for those who die, they may be relevant to the morality of killing, and we will thus have occasion to return to them in section 7 of chapter 4 and again in section 2.2 of chapter 5.

The idea that the value of a person's past may be retroactively affected by what happens later will strike many of us as implausible. David Velleman, for example, contends that "the daily well-being of your former self is a feature of the past, beyond alteration. . . . [Thus] when subsequent developments alter the meaning of an event they can alter its contribution to the value of one's life, but they cannot retroactively change the impact that it had on one's well-being at the time."[81] Velleman develops several arguments for this claim. One is that, at the intuitive level, we do not in fact believe that a person's past well-being can be retroactively affected. We do not say "of a person raised in adversity, that his youth wasn't so bad, after all, simply because his youthful hopes were eventually fulfilled later in life. We might say that such a person's adulthood compensated for an unfortunate youth, but we wouldn't say that it made his youth any better."[82] This, however, is not a very telling example. For in order for future events to make a person's past life better, they must make it more meaningful in some way; but in this case nothing in the person's future imbues the past adversity with meaning that it lacked at the time. If instead the future had involved triumphs that would not have been possible in the absence of the earlier adversity, it might be more reasonable to claim that the future had altered the meaning and therefore the value of the past.

There is also the idea, in the quotation cited above, that the past is fixed and unalterable. Yet Velleman immediately notes that later events may alter the *meaning* of an event in the past. Surely this is right, for meaning may be in part relational, and the relational aspects of the past are certainly alterable. Thus the meaning for a person of an event that occurs now may depend on what has happened previously. Velleman himself cites illuminating examples, such as that "a particular success can be either a windfall or a well-earned reward, depending on the amount of effort that preceded it."[83] But it seems that some types of value are relational in the same way that meaning may be, so that, in Velleman's example, how good the present success is for the person depends in the same way on whether it is a mere windfall or is instead deserved. And if value is relational in the way meaning is, and if the meaning of past events can be altered by subsequent ones, it seems that the value of past events can be altered in the same way.

Velleman denies this. "How well off someone is judged to be at one moment," he writes, "does not reflect potential interactions between the value of what obtains and happens then and the value of earlier or later events."[84] According to Velleman, the value of an event in a person's life, or the way that the event effects the person's well-being at the time, is not relational. The problem with this, however, is that it divorces the value that an event has for a person at the time it occurs from the meaning that the event has within the person's life. Whether a success is a reward or a mere windfall must, therefore, be irrelevant to how it affects the person's well-being at the time. But this seems implausible. A success is better than a windfall, even if the tangible aspects of the event are the same in either case.

Many people may be inclined to reject the idea that a person's past well-being can be affected by subsequent events, because they accept an unduly narrow conception of well-being. If, for example, one believes that well-being is entirely a matter of the subjective character of a person's mental states at any given time, then it is clear that a person's previous well-being must be unalterable. For on this view, a person's well-being at a particular time is not relational but is instead entirely a matter of the person's intrinsic properties at that time. There are, I believe, *dimensions* of well-being that are like this—that is, that are fully determined by certain nonrelational properties. I think, for example, that it would be a mistake to deny that the subjective character of a person's mental state is an important dimension of his overall well-being at a given time. But I think that we must also recognize that well-being is multidimensional and that some of its dimensions are relational—in particular those concerned with the meaning that a state or event has within a person's life.

One final point. As we have seen, Velleman concedes that "when subsequent developments alter the meaning of an event they can alter its contribution to the value of one's life." If, however, subsequent developments alter an event's contribution to the value of the life, it seems to follow that they thereby alter the value of the life. If we can interpret this as an alteration of the value of the life up to that point, it seems that Velleman is conceding that there can be retroactive effects on well-being. For he distinguishes between two dimensions of well-being: synchronic well-being, or well-being at a time, and diachronic well-being, or well-being over time.[85] His view seems to be that, while a later event can retroactively affect the value of a person's life as a whole, and therefore his diachronic well-being, it cannot affect the value of any previous moment, or his previous momentary well-being. This seems arbitrary. There is no fundamental ontological difference between a moment and a longer period. Indeed, unless we understand a moment as an indivisible temporal atom, moments are nothing but rather short periods. If the value of a lengthy period of time, such as a life as a whole up to the present, can be affected by subsequent events, then surely the value of a very short period of time can be similarly affected.

There are several other matters that ought to be briefly noted before this section is concluded. For the most part, these matters are just elaborations or extensions of ideas already articulated. First, one should acknowledge the possible relevance of personal desert to the badness of death. Earlier I stressed the significance of prior investment in the future. If a person has invested time and effort in preparing for his future, the badness of the loss of that future through death may be magnified by virtue of the role the future might have had in rounding out and completing the life in conformity with its narrative structure. (I also argued that the loss of that future may retroactively affect the meaning and therefore the value of the earlier future-directed activities.) But as Feldman points out, one may also understand the frustration of the investment as a failure on the part of the victim to receive what he deserves. On this view, the person's efforts establish a presumption that he deserves the goods for which he has striven; therefore, if death intervenes, it frustrates his deserts as well as his time-relative interests.

This idea can be expanded. Although effort is a prominent criterion of desert, there may be others. Many people believe, for example, that what a person deserves depends in part on what he has achieved or what he has contributed to the common good. Others believe that a person is more deserving the more virtuous he is or the better he is morally. If either of these views is right, death may be worse, other things being equal, for those who have been unusually productive or virtuous. The point here is not, I should stress, that the deaths of those who are conspicuously productive or virtuous are worse for others or for society generally, though that may be true as well. The point is, rather, that the badness of the loss that an industrious, productive, or morally worthy person suffers through death is exacerbated *for him* by virtue of his deserving, at the time of death, the goods of which he is deprived. If two people, one who is deserving and one who is not, both suffer the loss of the same amount of good through death, the deserving one arguably has a stronger time-relative interest in continuing to live, if other things are equal.

If this is right—and I do not wish to insist too strongly that it is—it adds a further dimension to the explanation of why death is less bad for fetuses and infants. For, setting aside notions of fetal labor or the perfect moral purity of infants (who enter the world "trailing clouds of glory"), it is clear that fetuses and infants have done nothing to deserve the goods of which they are deprived by death; hence the strength of their time-relative interest in continuing to live cannot be magnified by considerations of desert, as it may be in the case of older children or adults.

In addition to desert, there is the further matter of desire. Some philosophers have argued that the badness of death can be explained in terms of death's frustration of the victim's desires. Bernard Williams, for example, writes:

> if I desire something, then, other things being equal, I prefer a state of affairs in which I get it from one in which I do not get it. . . . But one future, for sure, in which I would not get it would be one in which I was dead. To want something . . . is to that extent to have reason for resisting what excludes having that thing: and death certainly does that, for a very large range of things that one wants. If that is right, then for any of those things, wanting something itself gives one a reason for avoiding death.[86]

Williams is careful to note both that there are some desires that are not frustrated by death and that there are other desires whose frustration by death does not contribute to the badness of death. Desires that may not be frustrated by a person's death include those that are not concerned with the person's own life or activities. And desires whose frustration by death does not contribute to making the death bad are those that are not "categorical"—categorical desires being those that give one a reason to continue to live in order to ensure their satisfaction. The desire to scratch an itch is not categorical; hence its frustration by death would not be among the reasons why the death was bad.

The idea that the badness of death can be fully explained by reference to the frustration of categorical desires is, I think, decisively undermined by two considerations that I will note here only in passing (since I have stated them more fully elsewhere).[87] One is that this idea cannot recognize that death can be bad for fetuses, infants, and animals. The other is that it seems clear that the loss of future goods that are undesired at the time of death can contribute to the badness of death. There are various reasons why an individual may, at the time he dies, fail to desire certain goods that his future life would have contained if he had lived. He might be incapable of desiring them (for example, if he is an infant and is therefore incapable of conceiving of them); he might fail to consider or envisage them; or he might consider them but remain indifferent to them. Older children and teenagers, for example, very often fail to contemplate the goods of middle and old age or, if they do, they typically remain indifferent to them, as these goods have little attraction for persons of their age (just as the goods of childhood fail to excite the desires of the elderly). But surely the loss of these goods is a considerable part of the tragedy when a child or teenager dies.

Although one cannot fully explain the badness of death by reference to the frustration or elimination of desires, desires do figure in several ways in the full explanation. First, the persistence of a desire from one time to another constitutes an important form of psychological connection, as does the formation or possession of a desire and its later satisfaction. A life that contains an abundance of categorical desires that persist until they are satisfied—especially desires that underlie long-range ambitions, plans, goals, and projects—is therefore necessarily a life that is richly unified and integrated psychologically. There is thus a positive correlation between the badness of death and the frustration or elimination by death of categorical desires. The more categorical desires death causes to go unsatisfied, the more future goods are lost, other things being equal, and the worse the loss of those goods is, since the desires themselves would have bound the life together psychologically over time.

Furthermore, categorical desires—especially insofar as they are expressions of an individual's personal values—are central constituents of narrative unity within a life. The story of a life is a story informed by certain values; its triumphs and tragedies concern the fate of those values. When death entails the loss of a future in which a person would have satisfied desires reflecting his core values, ideals, or aspirations, the loss is particularly grave because of its effect on the meaning of the life as a whole.

Just below the surface of the point about narrative unity is an assumption that should be made explicit. This is that some of a person's desires are partly determinative of his personal good, or what would count as a good life *for him*. It seems obvious that there is no single kind of life that is good for everyone. Although there seem to be a number of general goods that contribute more or less uniformly and invariably to the value of any life (though they may take different forms in different people's lives), there are, in addition, other things that are good only for certain people and not others. There is a dimension of the good for each person that depends on, and thus varies with, his own distinctive character, abilities, and, above all, desires and values. In short, many of a person's most important interests depend directly on his desires. It should therefore be unsurprising that the strength of a person's time-relative interest in continuing to live depends in part on the extent to which his present desires (or at least a subset of his present desires that satisfy certain epistemic conditions) would be likely to be satisfied if he were to remain alive. Thus, while the loss of any future good seems to contribute to the badness of death, it also seems that we should discount the badness for a person of the loss of goods for which he has no desire at the time at which he dies. Even though the person might later come to have a stronger time-relative interest in a later good by virtue of coming to care about it, the absence of desire at present weakens his present time-relative interest and therefore makes the loss of the good through death a lesser misfortune than it would be if the good were one he presently cared about.

Because a person's desires help to determine the character of at least some of his present time-relative interests, desire has a role in explaining the badness of death that is independent of considerations of psychological continuity and narrative unity. This further element in our overall account of the badness of death also helps to explain why the deaths of fetuses and infants are less bad. Because fetuses and infants are incapable of a robust form of self-consciousness, they cannot conceive of their own futures and thus have no categorical desires for future goods. Thus, although a fetus or infant may lose an enormous amount of good if it dies, its time-relative interest in those goods is weakened by its own lack of desire for them. We must therefore discount the badness of the loss it suffers in dying for the absence of any desire for the goods it loses.

The account of the badness of death that I have developed in this lengthy chapter is quite complex. It may be helpful at this point to offer a brief summary of its main elements. We cannot, I have argued, assess how bad it is for a person to die simply by ascertaining how much better his life as a whole would have been if he had not died when and how he did. Nor can we determine how strong the person's time-relative interest in continuing to live was simply by ascertaining how much good his subsequent life would have contained if he had not died. There are many other factors that are relevant to determining the strength of that interest. In addition to asking how much good a person's future life would have contained, we must also ask the following questions:

1. How close would the prudential unity relations have been between the individual as he was at the time of his death and himself as he would have been at those later times when the goods of his future life would have occurred?
2. Are the individual's previous gains from life below or beyond the norm for people with psychological capacities comparable to his own?
3. Did the individual's life have a narrative structure that would have been rounded out or completed by the future life of which death deprived him?
4. Had the individual made significant investments in his own future that were retroactively rendered futile or pointless by his death?
5. Were the individual's previous actions or character such as to make him deserving of the goods he lost?
6. Would the goods of which the individual was deprived have been ones that he desired at the time of his death?

On the basis of these considerations, we may conclude that a death is worse or more tragic to the extent that the following characterizations are applicable to it: (1) The amount of good that is lost is great. (2) The prudential unity relations would have been strong between the victim at the time of death and himself in the future if he had lived. (3) The victim had so far gained relatively little from life. (4) The victim's future life could reasonably have been expected to bring the story of his life to a satisfying state of completion. (5) The victim had invested considerable efforts in preparing for the future that he lost. (6) The victim was notably deserving of the goods that his future life would have contained. (7) The goods that the victim's future life would have contained were largely ones that he desired or valued at the time of death.

A death is correspondingly less bad to the extent that it is not characterized by these seven features. Accordingly, death is probably least bad when it occurs at a very great age, when there is little prospect of further good, but following a life of great achievement, a life in which the person's efforts were rewarded with success, his desires and ambitions fulfilled, and his deserts satisfied—in short, a life well lived: one that is richly integrated, satisfying, and successful and that culminates in a serene old age, so complete at that point as to leave little else to be desired. The death of a fetus or infant is not quite so benign; for the loss is great and the victim has so far gained little or nothing from life. But the misfortune is greatly diminished by the virtual absence of potential psychological connections to the life that is lost, the absence of narrative structure in the life, the absence of investment in the future, the absence of desert, and the absence of categorical desires for future goods. The badness of the loss must be discounted for the absence of each of these factors.

The badness of death thus varies with a great many factors. But the various factors are strongly correlated with age. When an individual first begins to exist, the amount of good in prospect is at its maximum; but the prudential unity relations binding that individual to his own future are about as weak as is compatible with identity. The weakness of these relations greatly diminishes the strength of his time-relative interest in continuing to live. As the individual develops psychologically, he becomes increasingly closely related to himself in the future in the ways that matter. Because the quality of life in utero and in the initial months of postnatal existence is arguably quite low, the amount of good in prospect remains more or less constant during this period. But this is a period in which the prudential unity relations gain in strength with great rapidity. Throughout this period and well into childhood, it seems that the effect of this strengthening of the prudential unity relations on the strength of the individual's time-relative interest in continuing to live greatly exceeds the effect of the diminution of the amount of good in prospect. Hence the individual's time-relative interest in continuing to live gains steadily in strength, and the badness of death increases dramatically, throughout infancy and early childhood. As childhood passes into adolescence, the amount of good remaining in the life steadily declines, though this continues to be more than offset by increases in psychological integration, narrative unity, the number and intensity of the individual's desires and ambitions, and the investments he makes in order to fulfill them. Exactly where the peak is, and whether the peak is actually a plateau, are questions that it is difficult to answer with confidence. There is surely some variation from individual to individual. And there is certainly a case to be made for the view that the peak comes even before adolescence. But it is clear that, after late adolescence or early adulthood, when an individual's psychological capacities are fully developed and the prudential unity relations reach their full strength, the badness of death slowly but steadily declines with age, as the amount of good remaining in the life decreases. If old age brings a decline in an individual's psychological capacities, and a consequent weakening of the prudential unity relations, the pace at which the badness of death diminishes with age will accelerate. Eventually a point will be reached at which death will scarcely be a misfortune at all—though, as I noted earlier, that in itself may be a misfortune of sorts.

7. A PARADOX

In this chapter, I have developed a complex account of why death is generally worse the earlier it occurs, the main exception being during the early period of a life, when death becomes worse the *later* it occurs. According to this account, death is worse at thirty-five than at seventy, though death at one day after birth is not worse than death at thirty-five; indeed it is substantially less bad. There is, however, a surprising problem with this view, which emerges when we consider certain choices between different possible deaths for the same individual.[88] Suppose that a thirty-five-year-old man will die unless the doctor saves him, in which case he will live to be seventy. Provided that the life that the man would have between the ages of thirty-five and seventy would be worth living, it would clearly be better for the doctor to save him, which of course is consistent with our judgment that it is worse to die at thirty-five than at seventy. But now consider a parallel case in which the protagonist is thirty-five years younger:

> *The Choice between Deaths.* A day-old infant will die unless the doctor saves him. Although the infant can be saved, the condition that threatens his life cannot be cured and will certainly cause his death later around the age of thirty-five.

Surely, despite the inevitability that he will suffer a premature death, it would be better for this individual for the doctor to save him; for it is better to have thirty-five years of life that are worth living than to have only a day under the sun. But, if the doctor saves the infant, this ensures that the individual will die at thirty-five rather than a day after his birth. This case therefore challenges the view I have developed. It seems clear that the doctor ought to save the infant. And it seems that this is because it would be better for the infant to live thirty-five more years—that is, that it would be *worse* for the infant to die now than at age thirty-five. But what I have argued is precisely that death in early infancy is *less bad* than death at thirty-five.

It will help to clarify the problem if we compare this case with another involving a choice between the deaths of different individuals. Because this is a choice of whom to save, I call it the Choice between Lives.

> *The Choice between Lives.* A thirty-five-year-old woman is due to give birth the next day but there are complications with the pregnancy. If nothing is done, the fetus will die and the woman can reasonably expect to live another thirty-five years. The doctor can, however, administer a treatment that will save the fetus. But if the fetus lives, the continuation of the pregnancy will be unavoidably fatal to the woman. Moreover, because of an incurable congenital condition, the fetus will later die around the age of thirty-five.

If the doctor does nothing, the fetus will die. If he saves the fetus, the woman will die. Either way, someone will lose thirty-five years of life that would have been worth living. Most of us believe that the doctor ought not to save the fetus. And the basis for this belief is our sense that the death of the fetus would be less bad—that it would be the less serious of the two possible misfortunes.

These two cases give rise to a paradox. In the Choice between Lives, the view for which I have argued seems vindicated: death at thirty-five would be worse than death a day before birth. But the Choice between Deaths supports a different conclusion: death a day after birth would be worse than death at thirty-five. Assuming that that there is no significant difference between death a day before birth and a day after, these two conclusions are in conflict. Let us refer to this conflict as *The Paradox.*

One way to resolve the Paradox refers back the distinction drawn earlier between two different approaches to the evaluation of death: the Time-Relative Interest Account and the Life Comparative Account. In my argument thus far, I have been presupposing the Time-Relative Interest Account—that is, I have been concerned to evaluate the badness of death in terms of the impact that death has on the victim's time-relative interests at the time of his death. But both approaches are possible. There is certainly nothing *mistaken* about evaluating a death in terms of the effect that it would have on the value of a life as a whole. One way of resolving the Paradox, therefore, is to see our responses to the two cases as deriving from the two different approaches.

The common intuitive response to the Choice between Lives clearly relies on the Time-Relative Interest Account of the badness of death. We believe that the death of the thirty-five-year-old woman would be worse than the death of the fetus because we understand that she would be closely bound to herself in the future by the prudential unity relations, while the fetus is psychologically cut off from its own future life: it lacks self-consciousness and therefore has no desires or ambitions for the future. The woman's life is now in full flow; the fetus's biography has yet to begin. Thus, if we evaluate each death in terms of the impact it would have on the victim at the time rather than in terms of the effect it would have on the value of the life as a whole, we will naturally judge the death of the woman to be worse.

Our intuitive response to the Choice between Deaths may, by contrast, be seen as deriving from or appealing to the Life Comparative Account. When we judge that the doctor ought to save the infant rather than allow it to die, we seem to be guided by the thought that it is better for the infant to live for thirty-five years than to live for only a day. It is better to have a longer rather than a shorter life. This is why, in this case, we judge death in infancy to be worse than death at thirty-five.

This is sufficient to resolve the Paradox. If we adopt the Time-Relative Interest Account of the evaluation of death, we find that death at thirty-five is worse than death in early infancy. If we adopt the Life Comparative Account, we find that death in early infancy (or late in pregnancy) is worse than death at thirty-five. These two evaluations are not contradictory. They are based on different comparisons and are concerned with different dimensions of the badness of death. Even the appearance of conflict vanishes when the perspectival presuppositions are made explicit. Death at thirty-five is worse than death in early infancy in terms of the effect on the victim's time-relative interests at the time of death; but death in early infancy is worse than death at thirty-five in terms of the effect on the value of the victim's life as a whole.

This way of resolving the Paradox raises a further problem. It suggests that, in determining which life the doctor ought to save in the Choice between Lives, we should be guided by the Time-Relative Interest Account of the badness of death, whereas in deciding what the doctor ought to do in the Choice between Deaths, we should be guided by the Life Comparative Account. If both accounts are valid but are appropriately applied to different kinds of case, or different choices, how can we know when to follow the Time-Relative Interest Account and when to appeal to the Life Comparative Account? Is our understanding of the badness of death and its application to practical choices really so schizophrenic?

I believe that it is possible to avoid having to appeal to one account in some cases and to the other account in others. We can, for example, reach the correct practical conclusion in the Choice between Deaths by appealing to time-relative interests only—that is, without appealing to the effect of death on the value of a life as a whole. In that case, it is true that the infant's time-relative interest in continuing to live is weak and that the time-relative interest in continuing to live that it will later have if it lives to be thirty-five will be strong. Nevertheless, its present time-relative interest, however weak, favors life and opposes death. If the doctor saves the infant, he will have done what is in its best time-relative interest now. And the infant will never have a later time-relative interest that would have been better served by allowing it to die. If, however, he allows the infant to die now, he will have frustrated the only time-relative interests it will ever have (since its death will preclude its having any further time-relative interests). It seems clear, therefore, that if he is guided by a concern for its time-relative interests, he should save the infant, which of course is what we intuitively believe he ought to do.

It remains true, however, that if we continue to adhere exclusively to the Time-Relative Interest Account, we will have to accept that death will be worse for the individual at thirty-five than it would have been in early infancy. We must therefore accept that, when the doctor saves the infant, he ensures that it will have the worse of two possible deaths. His concern for the infant's time-relative interests thus leads him to choose for it the worse of two possible deaths, the death that will frustrate a stronger time-relative interest. And that in itself seems paradoxical.

There is much that can be said about this. Among other things, as I have remarked before, it is not always desirable to have a less bad death—though the reasons why this is true vary from case to case. In the present case, the explanation has to do with the peculiar nature of the misfortune involved in death. To see this, consider an objection that might be urged against the Time-Relative Interest Account. It might be objected that, because the time-relative interest in continuing to live that the individual would have at thirty-five would be far stronger than that which he has as an infant, the Time-Relative Interest Account implies that the reason to prevent the frustration of that later time-relative interest is stronger than the reason to prevent the frustration of the earlier, weaker one.

There is a sense in which this is true. Preventing the frustration of that later possible time-relative interest is important, though only certain means of prevention are acceptable. Others are self-defeating. If we could prevent the death at thirty-five (and thus of course the frustration of the time-relative interest) by *saving* the individual at that time (which, by hypothesis, we could not), our reason to do so would indeed be stronger than the reason the doctor has to save the infant now—for a stronger time-relative interest would be at stake. But it is not a reasonable way of preventing the later time-relative interest from being frustrated to ensure that the individual will not then exist. In this respect, the time-relative interest in continuing to live—or the time-relative interest in avoiding death—is quite unlike the time-relative interest in avoiding suffering. It is sometimes rational to prevent an individual's future suffering by preventing him from existing—for example, when the suffering cannot be prevented in any other way and it would outweigh any goods that the individual could expect to have both during and after it. But it is never rational to prevent the frustration of a later time-relative interest in avoiding death by preventing the individual from existing—that is, by ensuring an earlier death. This may seem obvious. For those who are skeptical, I will offer a more detailed explanation in section 4 and again in section 9.2 of chapter 4.

3

Killing

1. THE WRONGNESS OF KILLING AND THE BADNESS OF DEATH

1.1. *Two Accounts*

There is no moral belief that is more universal, stable, and unquestioned, both across different societies and throughout history, than the belief that killing people is normally wrong. Yet no one, to my knowledge, has ever offered an account of why killing is wrong that even begins to do justice to the full range of commonsense beliefs about the morality of killing. Perhaps the overwhelming obviousness of the general belief— its luminous self-evidence—discourages inquiry into its foundations. Yet it does not appear to be a basic or ultimate moral belief—that is, one that cannot be derived from or justified by reference to some more fundamental moral principle or principles. Rather, the belief that killing is normally wrong seems susceptible of defense or justification: reasons can be given that purport to explain why killing is wrong.

It might be thought that an understanding of why killing is wrong is merely of academic interest. From a practical point of view, the important piece of knowledge— that in general killing *is* wrong—is already known with sufficient certainty that it would be idle to offer clever proofs that trace the belief to its source in more fundamental beliefs or principles. What could be gained from an exercise in demonstrating the obvious?

There is in fact an answer to this, which is that an understanding of why killing is normally wrong should help us to identify the conditions in which killing may *not* be wrong. For, in cases of killing in which the reasons that make killing normally wrong do not apply, there may be no objection to killing: it may be permissible or, if there are moral reasons that favor it, even morally required. And there may be other cases involving killing in which the reasons that normally militate against killing are present but only to a weaker degree, or in which some reasons apply while others do not. In either case, the presumption against killing may be correspondingly weaker, or more readily overridden by countervailing considerations.

Understanding the basis of the wrongness of killing is therefore of considerable practical significance. How might we seek to deepen our understanding of the morality of killing? One approach is to compare the killing of persons with the killing of

s. (Recall that by "persons" I mean individuals who are self-conscious, irre-
ive of species. By "animals" I mean nonhuman animals. In general, I will use
u. word "people" as the plural of "person" rather than as the plural of "human
being." Thus "people" could conceivably include some nonhuman individuals. But in
general I will treat "people" and "animals" as categories that do not overlap. Thus, in
most of what follows, one should assume that "animals" refers to animals that are not
only nonhuman but also not persons. For simplicity, I will put aside, for the time
being, the questions that are raised by the possibility that there are nonhuman animals that—or who—are persons.)

It is uncontroversial that the killing of an animal is normally less seriously wrong
than the killing of a person. If we could determine *why* this is so, this could illuminate the reasons why killing is in general wrong. Either some of the reasons why
killing a person is wrong do not apply in the case of animals, or the reasons that apply
in the case of persons apply less strongly in the case of animals. Or both could be
true. If we could identify what is missing in the case of animals, this would reveal
why killing people is normally *more* wrong. And that would provide a substantial
part of the explanation of why killing people is wrong at all.

The idea that wrongness is a matter of degree may seem puzzling. This is the result of an ambiguity in the notion of wrongness. In the most familiar sense of the
term, to say that an act is wrong is to say that it ought not to be done, all things considered. In this sense, wrongness is not a matter of degree, for it either is or is not the
case that an act ought not to be done. There is, however, another sense of the term,
according to which the wrongness of an act is just its moral objectionableness. An act
may have various morally objectionable or, as some have said, "wrong-making" features. These features may, in certain contexts, be outweighed by other considerations,
so that the act, though morally objectionable in some respects, may be permissible,
or not wrong (in the sense that it ought not to be done), all things considered. But if
the reasons why it is morally objectionable are not outweighed (or nullified or otherwise overcome), it will be wrong, in the sense that it ought not to be done. Still, the
degree to which it is morally objectionable is variable. If the moral objections to it,
or the reasons why it ought not to be done, are very strong and are not substantially
opposed by countervailing considerations, we say that the act would be seriously
wrong. If, by contrast, the objections to it are weak, or are almost counterbalanced by
countervailing moral considerations, it may be only slightly wrong.

Return now to the claim that killing people is generally more wrong than killing
animals. One strikingly obvious difference between killing a person and killing an
animal is that a person who is killed normally thereby suffers a significantly greater
harm than an animal does if it is killed. And it seems obvious that there is a close connection between the wrongness of killing and the fact that killing normally involves
the infliction of a grievous harm on the victim. Indeed, many people think that it is
precisely because killing harms its victim that it is morally wrong. James Rachels, for
example, contends that, "[i]f we should not kill, it is because in killing we are harming someone. That is the reason killing is wrong. The rule against killing has as its
point the protection of the victims."[1] And in a well-known article on abortion, Don
Marquis echoes Rachels's claim: "What primarily makes killing wrong is . . . its effect on the victim. The loss of one's life is one of the greatest losses one can suffer.

The loss of one's life deprives one of all the experiences, activities, projects, and enjoyments that would otherwise have constituted one's future. Therefore, killing someone is wrong, primarily because the killing inflicts (one of) the greatest possible losses on the victim."[2] With one further assumption, this view of the morality of killing offers a tidy and plausible explanation of why killing people is normally more wrong than killing animals. What Rachels, Marquis, and others claim is that killing is wrong because it harms the individual who is killed. But of the great many acts that are harmful, few if any are as seriously wrong as killing. Why is killing more gravely wrong than most other acts that also cause harm? For someone sympathetic to the account offered by Rachels and Marquis, the answer is obvious. As Marquis notes in the passage just quoted, the harm inflicted by killing is normally very great. If we assume that the degree to which a harmful act is wrong varies with the degree of harm it causes, this would explain why killing is normally more seriously wrong than other harmful acts. It would also explain why some acts of killing are more wrong than others—in particular, it would explain why killing a person is normally more wrong than killing an animal.

The assumption that is needed to generate these explanations may take a weaker or a stronger form. According to the weaker version, if an act of killing is wrong, or morally objectionable, at least in part because it harms its victim, then another act that is the same in all relevant respects except that it harms its victim to an even greater extent will be wrong, or morally objectionable, to a greater degree. Call this *the assumption of correlative variation*. The stronger version is that, if an act of killing is wrong, or morally objectionable, at least in part because it harms its victim, then another act that is the same in all relevant respects except that it harms its victim to an even greater extent will be more wrong, or more morally objectionable, *in proportion to* the extent to which the amount of harm it causes is greater. Call this *the assumption of proportional variation*. Because the assumption of correlative variation is weaker and is entailed by the assumption of proportional variation, it has a better chance of being true. Hence in the subsequent discussion I will focus primarily on it.

In order to explain why killing people is in general more seriously wrong than killing animals, we can combine the view articulated by Rachels and Marquis with the assumption of correlative variation. The resulting view, which we may call the *Harm-Based Account* of the wrongness of killing, holds that acts of killing are normally wrong principally because of the harm they inflict on the victims, and that the degree to which an act of killing is wrong varies with the degree of harm it causes to the victim, other things being equal. (This account has to be refined in order to account for the wrongness of attempted, unsuccessful killing, presumably by focusing on expected or intended rather than actual harm. Though important, this refinement need not detain us here.) According to this account, killing people is usually gravely wrong, for death is typically among the worst harms a person can suffer. By contrast, the harm an animal suffers in dying is considerably less; hence killing the animal is less seriously wrong.

The Harm-Based Account of the morality of killing is naturally associated with the denial of moral significance to the distinction between killing and letting die. If it is the harm that the victim suffers that explains why killing is wrong, then letting someone die should also be wrong, if other things are equal, for the same reason. For the harm that results when one lets someone die—namely, death—is the same as the harm caused by killing.[3] The idea that letting a person die is, other things being equal, as objectionable as killing is not, however, *entailed* by the Harm-Based Account. That view does not claim that the only factor relevant to assessing the morality of killing is the amount of harm suffered by the victim. It claims only that the *fundamental* explanation of the wrongness of killing appeals to the wrongness of inflicting harm. It is compatible with that claim to suppose that the way in which an agent is instrumental in the occurrence of harm could make a moral difference.

The Harm-Based Account has certain virtues. For example, it offers a credible explanation not only of why the killing of persons is in general more seriously wrong than the killing of animals but also of why the killing of animals of certain types is generally more objectionable than the killing of animals of other types. Because animals vary considerably in their capacities for well-being, some may be harmed to a greater extent by death than others. For example, because a dog's life is normally richer (in pleasure, social relations, and so on) than a frog's, dogs generally suffer a greater harm in dying. Therefore the Harm-Based Account implies that it is normally more wrong to kill a dog than it is to kill a frog. These claims—that the killing of persons is normally more seriously wrong than the killing of animals and that the killing of higher animals is generally more seriously wrong than the killing of lower animals—are ones that our account of the wrongness of killing should be able to explain and defend.

Despite these virtues, however, the Harm-Based Account faces certain objections. There is only one we need to consider, since it alone is sufficient to undermine the account. This is that the Harm-Based Account presupposes that identity is what matters. For the harm involved in death is equivalent to the extent to which the death is worse for the individual who dies—that is, the extent to which the death makes the life as a whole worse than it would otherwise have been. In short, the Harm-Based Account presupposes a Life Comparative Account of the badness of death. Its implications for certain cases are consequently profoundly counterintuitive. For example, it implies that, if other things are equal, the killing of a fetus or infant is more seriously wrong than the killing of an older child or adult, because the death of the fetus or infant involves a greater harm—that is, the effect of the death on the value of the life as a whole is worse.

Some advocates of the Harm-Based Account have embraced the conclusion that abortion is wrong for the same reason that the killing of adults is normally wrong.[4] Others have sought to evade this conclusion by various stratagems—for example, by asserting a conceptual link between harm and desire and arguing that a fetus cannot be harmed by death because it cannot desire to continue to live.[5] But another option is to abandon the assumption that identity is the rational basis of egoistic concern. If we recognize that identity is not what really matters, our moral concern ought not to follow identity but ought instead to follow what really matters. If morality requires us to be concerned for an individual for his own sake, it should direct our concern to what he has most egoistic reason to care about—that is, to his time-relative interests. These, as I have noted, may diverge from his interests, which are what would be best for his life as a whole. The divergence is, of course, most striking in hypothetical cases involving division. These cases can raise moral questions that may assist us to see the appropriateness of focusing our concern on an individual's time-relative interests rather than on his interests.

Spontaneous Division. Suppose that people sometimes spontaneously divide. (Readers may imagine their own details, which will have to be rather bizarre. The sole constraint is that the process of division must preserve the prudential unity relations: between the original person and each of his successors, there must be sufficient physical, functional, and organizational continuity of the brain to support a degree of psychological unity over time comparable to that within the life of an ordinary person over the same period of time.) The process of spontaneous division is preceded by the person's lapsing into a coma. In the early phases, while the person is comatose, the process can be reversed and division prevented. Suppose a person suddenly enters this process without having indicated whether she would prefer to be prevented from dividing. Suppose, too, that we know that, if she does not divide, she will die in about a year but that, if she divides, her successors will both be able to live for many years.

Ought we to prevent this person from dividing or ought we to allow it to happen? We cannot consult her preferences, for she is comatose. It would be against her interests to divide, for she would cease to exist now rather than in a year. What does she have most egoistic reason to want? She might, of course, have contingent egoistic reasons to want not to divide—for example, she might greatly value the relation she has with her husband, a relation that could not be sustained by both of her successors. But suppose there are no such reasons. Suppose, on the contrary, that she has been vacillating between becoming a concert pianist and becoming a historian and has been frustrated by her inability to do both, given the amount of time that each would require. If she were to divide, one of her successors could become a pianist while the other could engage in historical research. In these circumstances, she has strong egoistic reason to want to divide. For if she divides, she will be related in the ways that matter to *two* future lives, in each of which her successor would be able to achieve one of her ambitions. And each of her successors would live much longer than she would if she were not to divide. If the prudential unity relations, and not identity, are what matter, it would be perverse to prevent her from dividing.

The only actual cases in which an individual's time-relative interests may diverge from his interests are cases in which the prudential unity relations would be conspicuously weak. In these cases, the divergence is considerably less pronounced than in cases involving division. And in most of these cases this weaker divergence is of little or no practical significance. This is because morality requires us to show the same respect for an individual's future time-relative interests as we must show for his present ones. So, for example, even if an individual's present time-relative interest in some future event is weak, it may be that our treatment of him should be the same as it would be if we were guided by a concern for his interests; for we can now anticipate that his *later* time-relative interest in that event will be strong. (I will return to this in section 3 of chapter 4.)

Among the actual cases in which there may be significant divergence between an individual's interests and his time-relative interests, the only ones that are common are those involving a choice that will affect whether an individual will continue to exist and in which the prudential unity relations linking that individual to himself in the future would be weak. In these cases, the individual's present time-relative interest in continuing to live may be weak even if his interest in continuing to live is strong. And the present time-relative interest is the only one that would be frustrated by the individual's ceasing to exist, for his ceasing to exist would prevent his having any future time-relative interests. In these cases, it can make an enormous difference whether we are guided by a concern for the individual's interests or his time-relative interests. I claim that, if identity is not what matters, it would be a mistake to be guided by a concern for his interests, just as it would be in the case of Spontaneous Division. It would therefore be a mistake to be guided by the Harm-Based Account.

It is, however, obviously possible to formulate an alternative account of the wrongness of killing that captures the spirit of the Harm-Based Account but rejects the assumption that identity is what matters. Like the Harm-Based Account, this alternative account would explain what is fundamentally wrong about killing in terms of the effect on the victim. But it would insist that it is the prudential unity relations, which may hold to varying degrees, that matter. Therefore it will explain the wrongness of killing in terms of the effect on the victim's time-relative interests. According to this account, what is fundamentally wrong about killing, when it is wrong, is that it frustrates the victim's time-relative interest in continuing to live. It should incorporate its own assumption of correlative variation, which holds that the degree to which an act of killing is wrong varies, other things being equal, with the strength of the victim's time-relative interest in continuing to live. (Substituting for this an assumption of proportional variation would yield a more determinate, slightly more controversial account.) Call this the *Time-Relative Interest Account* of the wrongness of killing. (The label is, of course, the same as that of the parallel account of the badness of death. I will normally rely on the context to indicate to which account I will be referring.)

As was true of the Harm-Based Account, the Time-Relative Interest Account does not claim that the factor that it identifies as fundamental is the only factor relevant to the morality of an act of killing. It is compatible with this account to accept that a variety of other factors can affect the moral status of an act of killing and that these factors can interact in complex ways. Relevant factors divide into several distinct types, among which are the agent's motives, intentions, and mode of agency, side effects, whether the victim is responsible in a way that makes him liable to be killed as a matter of justice, whether the victim consents to be killed, whether the agent is specially related to the victim, and so on. I will return to these factors in section 3 of this chapter.

1.2. *The Killing of Animals*

As one might expect, the Time-Relative Interest Account of the wrongness of killing has much the same set of virtues as the Harm-Based Account. It implies, for example, that the killing of an animal is normally substantially less seriously wrong than the killing of a person and that the killing of a lower animal is normally less objectionable than the killing of a higher animal. Indeed, one way in which the account differs in its implications from the Harm-Based Account is that it implies that the difference in the degree of wrongness between killing a person and killing an animal is even greater. For like the Harm-Based Account, the Time-Relative Interest Account accepts that it is directly relevant to the evaluation of killing that the amount of good an animal loses by dying is typically much less than the good a person loses. But the

Time-Relative Interest Account recognizes a further consideration as relevant that the Harm-Based Account ignores: namely, the strength of the prudential unity relations that would have bound an individual to himself (or itself) in the future. Because these relations are typically weaker in the case of an animal, the Time-Relative Interest Account implies that there is a further reason for discounting the degree to which the killing of an animal is objectionable.

Let us pause to consider in greater detail why it is that an animal's time-relative interest in continuing to live is typically much weaker than that of a person. To assess the strength of an animal's time-relative interest in continuing to live, one must first consider how much good its life would have contained if it had not died. It is unnecessary, however, to become embroiled here in the various aspects of the Problem of Comparison, such as the Metaphysical Problem. If, in comparing the death of an animal with what would have happened if the animal had not died, we hold the animal's nature constant, it is clear that the maximum good its life might have contained, *given any of the ways in which it might not have died,* is substantially less than the amount of good that a typical person's future holds in prospect. There are two obvious reasons for this. First, the goods characteristic of an animal's life are of a lower quality than the goods characteristic of the lives of persons. Because of their limited cognitive and emotional capacities, most animals lack the capacity for many of the forms of experience and action that give the lives of persons their special richness and meaning, and without which our lives would be greatly impoverished. Animals are incapable of deep personal relations based on mutual understanding; they lack both imagination and an aesthetic sense and hence are unable to experience works of art, literature, or music or to appreciate the aesthetic dimensions of the natural world; they are incapable of engaging in complex and skilled activities or achieving difficult goals or ambitions—for example, through artistic creation or scientific discovery; and so on.

There have, of course, been those who have dissented from the view that the more developed cognitive powers of persons facilitate higher levels of well-being. Here, for example, is a passage by H. L. Mencken, which I reproduce without comment. Of "the Dawn Man," he writes:

> For many generations, perhaps for many thousands of years, he had been finding life increasingly unpleasant, for the cells of his cortex had been gradually proliferating, and the more they proliferated the more he was afflicted with a new curse: the power to think. Having escaped his enemies and eaten his fill, he could no longer take his brutal ease under a kindly tree. The dog-like beasts who were his playmates and the apes who were his sardonic cousins were far happier. Their minds were empty; they could not generalize experience; they were innocent. But man suffered under the stealthy, insidious assaults of his awakening brain, now bulging and busy like a bulb in Spring. It not only caused him to remember the tree that came near falling upon him last week; it also enabled him to picture the tree that might actually fetch him tomorrow.[6]

There are, I confess, moments when one doubts the superiority of the goods of human life, at least in comparison to those of certain types of animal life. If, for example, one has ever had a dog, one must surely at some point have suspected that a dog's life contains more pure, unalloyed joy than one's own. But even if it is true that, as a sober and responsible adult, one seldom seems to attain quite the peaks of ecstasy that a dog experiences at the prospect of going for a walk, most of us can remember having, as a child, a capacity for almost boundless delight in various equally simple and trivial activities. Thus one may console oneself with the reflection that one's life *as a whole* contains much the same goods that a dog's contains, and much more besides. This reflection, however, has little bearing on the comparative evaluation of human and animal *death,* since the simple ecstasies of childhood are, for most of us, in the past. Still, it seems that even adult human life tends to contain its share of exuberant joys that rival in intensity those experienced by dogs. They are simply not so conspicuous as they are within the lives of dogs, where they dramatically punctuate days otherwise given over to torpor and sleep. Human well-being, by contrast, is more continuous, dense, and varied, so that the ecstatic moments, which may be more diffusely spread over longer periods, are less salient. And what fills the intervals between these moments is normally altogether better than the dull vacancy of a dog at rest.

The goods that an animal loses in dying are not only of a lower quality; they are lesser in quantity as well. Most animal species are condemned by their biology to live lives with a maximum length that is considerably shorter than the maximum, or even the average, human life span. Because we must hold an animal's nature constant when we speculate about what its life would have been like if it had not died, we must assume that it would have died from some other cause before reaching the maximum life span for its species. In general, therefore, the quantity of life that an animal loses in dying is less than that which a person loses.

In the previous chapter, I suggested that we should not evaluate a death by comparing it to the life that the victim would have had if that individual had lived to the maximum life span for the members of the species to which he (or she, or it) belongs. I am not retracting that suggestion here. I am simply assuming that *all* of the possible ways in which an animal might not have died its actual death would have resulted in its dying in some other way prior to reaching the biologically determined maximum life span for its species, and that its actual death must be evaluated by comparison with one (or some, or all) of these alternative possible futures. Of course, as I conceded in the previous chapter, it is possible to evaluate the fact that an individual must die at all, and one can imagine alternatives to an individual's dying even at the outer limits of that individual's biologically determined life span. But speculations about what it would be like for an individual (either a person or an animal) to live beyond the maximum life span for that individual's species seem irrelevant to our present concern, which is to understand the harm that is inflicted by an act of killing. For killing an animal cannot deprive it of what it would never in fact have had even if it had not been killed. Finally, even if we were to evaluate an animal's death by comparing it with a possible future in which the animal would have lived beyond the maximum life span for its species, we would, in order to maintain parity, have to evaluate the badness of death for persons in the same way. Hence, assuming that a typical person's future would be of a significantly higher quality than that of a typical animal (of whatever species), the conclusion remains the same: persons typically lose considerably more good by dying than animals do.

There are other reasons why animals normally lose considerably less good by dying than persons do. It may be, for example, that a good contributes more to the value of a life to the extent that it has been and continues to be desired when it occurs. If so, we should discount the value of most of the goods in an animal's life, which tend to arrive unbidden and indeed unanticipated, for the absence of prior desire. And a similar claim may be true with respect to desert. It may be that a good contributes more to the value of a life to the extent that it is deserved when it occurs. But since, in general, desert presupposes responsibility and animals are not responsible agents, their deserts, if any, are sparse and attenuated. Therefore we should also discount the value of most of the goods in an animal's life for the absence of desert.

One way in which the value that a good contributes to a life may be enhanced is through its relations to earlier and later events within the life. In the previous chapter, I endorsed the commonly noted claim that the lives of persons typically have a narrative structure that may demand completion in a certain way. People autonomously establish purposes for their lives, form patterns of structured relations with others, and thereby create expectations and dependencies that require fulfillment. The importance of later events in a typical human life may thus be greatly magnified by their relation to ambitions formed and activities engaged in earlier. The goods of a person's expected future life may assume a special significance within the life as a whole if they would bring longstanding projects to fruition, extend previous achievements, resolve conflicts, harmonize hitherto dissonant ambitions, redeem past mistakes, or in general round out or complete the narrative structures established earlier. In these and other ways, future goods may enhance the meaning and significance of patterns of experience and activity throughout the life. And the values of the goods themselves may be enhanced by their relations to what has gone before. In the lives of animals, however, this potential for complex narrative unity is entirely absent. There are no projects that require completion, mistakes that demand rectification, or personal relations that promise to ripen or mature. Rather, as Aldous Huxley once put it, "the dumb creation lives a life made up of discreet and mutually irrelevant episodes."[7] Each day is merely more of the same. As an animal continues to live, goods may continue to accumulate in sequence, but the effect is merely additive. There is no scope for tragedy—for hopes passing unrealized, projects unwillingly aborted, mistakes or misunderstandings left uncorrected, or apologies left unmade. Because the amount of good that an animal can lose through death is limited in this way while that which a person may lose is not, the absence of narrative unity within the lives of animals is another reason why death is typically far worse for persons than it is for animals. (It might be argued that the possibility of tragedy in the lives of persons makes their deaths *less bad,* since death may preclude the occurrence of tragedy in the life of a person but not in the life of an animal. But this would be true only if the possibility of tragedy made the future lives of persons in general less worth living than the future lives of animals, an assumption that I take to be false, in spite of what Mencken says.)

Also in the previous chapter, I noted a further dimension to the badness of death, which is that death not only precludes the addition of further goods to a life but may also retroactively affect the meaning and therefore the value of certain aspects of the victim's previous life. Many of the events or activities in our lives may have no value, or even negative value, considered only in themselves, but may acquire meaning and therefore positive value in the context of a larger pattern of experience or activity. This is related to the previous claims about desire and narrative unity. Because people have long-range desires, they invest time and other resources in preparing for the future. The eventual fulfillment of their desires may endow their earlier efforts, which may have been painful or tedious in themselves, with meaning and value that they would have lacked had the desires remained unfulfilled. Thus when death prevents the fulfillment of projects or ambitions around which a life has been autonomously structured, it not only denies the addition of further good to the life but may also prevent elements of the past from having a deeper meaning or value. Again, however, this dimension of the badness of death is absent in the case of animals. Because they lack self-consciousness, animals generally lack long-range desires; hence they do not consciously plan or make sacrifices for the sake of the future. Death cannot rob their previous activities of a meaning or value that was contingent upon future fulfillment.

There is, of course, a sense in which a squirrel's efforts in gathering nuts for the winter are rendered futile if it is run over by a car. But the squirrel's action was merely instinctive, not deliberate; there was no goal that the squirrel was consciously seeking to achieve. And even if the squirrel had been consciously pursuing a goal, that goal would merely have been survival itself. It would not have been a goal that gave the squirrel a *reason* for surviving or for wanting to survive. Finally, the squirrel's action involved no sacrifice for the sake of the future: for the squirrel did not gather nuts at the expense of some alternative course of action that it might more profitably have pursued instead. One cannot look back on the time that the squirrel spent gathering nuts as a tragic waste of opportunities. In short, there is no reason to suppose that the squirrel's death retroactively deprives its prior action in gathering nuts of a special meaning or value that it would have had if the squirrel had survived and the action had realized its instrumental function.

There are, finally, comparative dimensions to the badness of death in the case of persons, reasons why a death may be worse that essentially involve comparisons between the life of the person who dies and the lives of others who are, for one reason or another, appropriate subjects for comparison. A death may be worse, for example, if many of the goods the victim loses are ones that are found in most other people's lives, or if the victim's previous gains from life are below the norm for persons generally, or even if they are below the norm for members of some more specific comparison class with whom the victim is closely identified. Again, however, these comparative dimensions to the evaluation of death seem inapplicable or irrelevant in the case of animals. The death of an animal does not, in general, seem worse simply because some of the goods it loses are ones that are common in the lives of most of the other members of its species.

These are various ways in which the amount of good that an animal loses through death is typically much less than that which a person loses. Thus even if the prudential unity relations that would bind the animal to itself in the future would be strong, its time-relative interest in continuing to live would still be comparatively weak. But in fact the prudential unity relations are also quite weak. This is most obvious if we focus on the psychological manifestations of physical, functional, and organizational continuity of the brain. There is, in the life of an animal, very little psychological architecture to be carried forward, and earlier and later mental states seldom refer to one another. There is, in short, very little psychological unity within the lives of most animals. Thus an animal's time-relative interest in continuing to live is doubly weak:

the goods in prospect for it are comparatively meager, and the prudential unity relations that would bind it to itself in the future would be weak. Because of this, the Time-Relative Interest Account of the wrongness of killing implies that the killing of an animal is normally significantly less seriously wrong than the killing of a person.

Earlier, in section 6.1 of chapter 2, I tried to show how the badness of death for a fetus or infant is intermediate between the impersonal badness of nonconception and the badness of death for a person. It is perhaps worth noting where the death of an animal fits in relation to these other cases. At one end of the spectrum is the death of a person. In that case, there is great good in prospect that is lost, there is identity between the one who dies and the one who would have been the subject of the good, and the one who dies would have been strongly related in the ways that matter to the subject of the good. At the other end of the spectrum is nonconception. In that case, great good is lost, but there is no one who would have been identical with the subject of the good and no one who would have been related to the subject of the good in any of the ways that matter. When an infant (or a late-term human fetus) dies, great good is lost and the one who dies would have been identical with the subject of the good, but the one who dies would have been only weakly related to the subject of the good in the ways that matter. Finally, when an animal dies, there is relatively little good in prospect and, although the animal that dies would have been identical with the subject of the good that is lost, that animal would have been only weakly related in the ways that matter to itself in the future. Thus, even if an animal would be slightly more closely related in the ways that matter to itself in the future than an infant would be, the amount of good that an infant or fetus loses by dying is vastly greater. Because the infant's time-relative interest in continuing to live is therefore stronger, the Time-Relative Interest Account of the wrongness of killing can endorse and explain the common conviction that infanticide (and late-term abortion, as well) is morally a more serious matter than the killing of an adult animal, if other things are equal.

Before concluding this section on the killing of animals, it is worth pausing to consider a common view about the comparative badness of suffering and death for animals—a view that seems to influence people's thinking about killing and causing suffering to animals. Many people, perhaps particularly among those who are unusually concerned about animals and their well-being, accept that death is not a terribly tragic misfortune for an animal and yet also accept that the suffering of an animal matters in much the same way that the suffering of a person does. Let us call this combination of beliefs the view that *suffering matters more.* What is interesting about this view is that it is in sharp contrast with the corresponding view that people typically have about other persons. Consider, for example, common beliefs about human and animal euthanasia. Many people are reluctant to accept that euthanasia can be legitimate in the case of persons. One reason for this reluctance is that they believe that the life of a person has such great value that it should generally be preserved even if continued life will involve the endurance of great suffering. By contrast, most people readily approve of euthanasia in the case of animals. For example, even among those who are willing to devote their time and energy to caring for animals, most approve of the painless killing of stray animals for whom homes cannot be found. The apparent assumption is that death is preferable, for the animal's own sake, to even the quite limited amount of suffering it might experience as a stray. And those who make that assumption presumably do so because they believe that the value of an animal's life is insufficiently great to justify allowing the animal to suffer.

This same view seems to underlie the position that many people take of common practices that involve the killing of animals. These people believe that the killing of animals can be morally justified, often for apparently quite trivial reasons, provided that the animals are not caused to suffer. It is, for example, easier to obtain approval from committees that oversee animal experimentation for experiments that involve the painless killing of animals than for ones that involve the infliction of suffering. The burden of justification is greater for experiments of the latter sort. And many people who worry about the morality of eating meat are more disturbed by the suffering that is typically inflicted during the rearing and slaughtering of food animals than by the killing itself. In a story by J. M. Coetzee, the view that suffering matters more is articulated by a fictional academic philosopher: "It is licit to kill animals, I would say, because their lives are not as important to them as our lives are to us. . . . Gratuitous cruelty, on the other hand, I would regard as illicit. Therefore it is quite appropriate that we should agitate for the humane treatment of animals, even and particularly in slaughterhouses."[8] An even stronger asymmetry is advanced by Judith Jarvis Thomson, who contends

> that animals do not have claims to not be killed and, in particular, that it is not an infringement of any claim of a chicken's to kill it for dinner. . . . Causing an animal pain, however, is surely a different matter. It seems to me, in fact, that other things being equal it is worse to cause an animal pain than to cause an adult human being pain. An adult human being can, as it were, think his or her way around the pain to what lies beyond it in the future; an animal—like a human baby—cannot do this, so that there is nothing for the animal but the pain.[9]

The view that suffering matters more is strikingly manifest in the work of Temple Grandin, a designer of facilities for the slaughter of animals that are intended to cause minimal fear, distress, and pain to the animals. Grandin, who is autistic, believes— apparently with ample justification—that although she has difficulty understanding the states of mind of other people, she has an acute sensitivity to and special sympathy for the feelings of animals, and that these have enabled her to devise mechanisms for the killing of animals that are exquisitely attuned to the animals' sensibilities. Oliver Sacks, who visited with Grandin in an effort to understand how she has been able to achieve so much despite—or perhaps because of—her autism, reports:

> her deepest feelings are for cattle; she feels a tenderness, a compassion for them that is akin to love. She spoke of this at length. . .—how she sought gentleness, holding cattle in the chute, how she sought to transmit calmness to the animals, to bring peace in the last moments of their lives. This, for her, is half-physical, half-sacred, this cradling of an animal in the last moments of its life, and it is something she endlessly tries to teach the people who operate the chutes in the slaughter plants.[10]

Her "whole effort," Sacks observes, is "to remove anything that could frighten or stress the animals so that they could go peacefully, gently, unknowingly, to their death."[11]

Grandin is passionate in her insistence that animals not be caused to suffer in the process of being killed. But she seems to find nothing objectionable in the killing per se. She tells Sacks that "I want to reform the meat industry. The activists want to shut it down. . . . I have a radical dislike of radicals."[12] Sacks, however, still feels "queasy about the whole thing," and expresses, on leaving the slaughterhouse, "an enormous relief, morally, to get away from the idea of killing." He questions her about this. " 'Nobody should kill animals all the time,' she said, and she told me she had written much on the importance of rotating personnel, so that they would not be constantly employed in killing, bleeding, or driving."[13] One gets the impression that, in Grandin's view, the killing itself is morally significant only insofar as it affects the sensibilities of the people who do it—a rather surprising attitude in one who is able to enter so deeply into the emotional lives of animals. As I have suggested, however, her view is far from anomalous. It is only a slightly extreme variant of the common view that, in a general way, it is more important to prevent the significant suffering of animals than it is to prevent, or not to cause, their deaths.

In its more extreme variants, the view that suffering matters more threatens to have implications that seem absurd. Let us confine our attention to animals whose suffering or death would not be indirectly harmful to human beings. If the suffering of these animals matters in much the way that human suffering does but there is no serious moral reason not to kill them, it seems that it would usually be best, other things being equal, to kill any such animal painlessly. For that would be a means of preventing the animal from suffering that would be both unobjectionable and certainly more reliable than any alternative means. Thus, according to the stronger versions of the view that suffering matters more, almost any painless killing of an animal would count as euthanasia.

This is not necessarily a matter of entailment. The quotation from Thomson, for example, does not say that killing an animal is morally unobjectionable, only that it does not violate any claim that the animal might have not to be killed. Let us assume, however, that she means to imply that the moral reason, if any, not to kill an animal is sufficiently weak to make it permissible to kill it for dinner. That claim, together with the view that the reason to prevent an animal from suffering is much the same as the reason to prevent a human being from experiencing a comparable degree of suffering, seems to have the implausible implication I cited. For if it is permissible to kill an animal for dinner, it must surely be permissible to kill that same animal to prevent human suffering. But if animal suffering matters in the way that human suffering does, it should also be permissible to kill that animal in order to prevent an animal from suffering. And there is no reason to alter this conclusion if the animal that is killed is also the animal whose suffering is thereby to be prevented.

For this reason, I believe that the variants of the view that suffering matters more that hold that the killing of animals is hardly objectionable at all (except insofar as it is bad for human beings) are unacceptable. Nevertheless, the elements of the weaker versions of this view seem defensible. I have argued that death is normally substantially less bad for an animal, in the sense that the animal's time-relative interest in continuing to live is substantially weaker than a person's normally is. This supports the view that the killing of animals is less seriously objectionable—indeed, it entails this view if the Time-Relative Interest Account is the correct account of the wrongness of killing. It is also plausible to suppose that the significant suffering of an animal matters in much the way that the comparable suffering of a person matters. I will say more about that in section 2.4 of this chapter. For now, the question is whether these plausible claims imply that death is often preferable for an animal—even a quite young animal—to having to endure significant suffering. In particular, is killing often an acceptable means of preventing an animal from suffering? And, if so, why is it different in the case of a person? I will discuss these questions only briefly here, but will revisit them in section 2.4 of chapter 5, after some further groundwork has been laid in chapter 4.

There is a limited range of cases in which the view that suffering matters more appears to be supported by the focus on time-relative interests. I have argued that death is a lesser misfortune for an animal because the weakness of the prudential unity relations within its life diminishes the strength of its present time-relative interest in having the goods of its later future life. If, however, the prospect of suffering is immediate, the animal's time-relative interest in avoiding it will be stronger than its time-relative interest in having remoter goods, since the prudential unity relations diminish in strength with time and are therefore stronger over shorter periods. (Even from moment to moment, however, the prudential unity relations are weaker in the life of an animal than in the life of a person, since the entire psychological architecture carried forward is thinner.) Thus in this sort of case—in which the significant suffering would be immediate but the goods of further life would be more remote—it may be in an animal's present time-relative interest to die rather than to continue to live, even if the amount of good in prospect exceeds, perhaps to a significant degree, the expected amount of suffering.

This, however, is only one kind of case, and the common view is not restricted to cases of this sort. As I noted, many people believe that it is preferable even for a quite young stray dog to be painlessly killed than to be allowed to live with a prospect of significant future suffering. But if both the goods of further life and the expected suffering would be evenly spread over the future, or particularly if the suffering would come later, the animal's present time-relative interest in avoiding future suffering would be weak for the same reason that its time-relative interest in the goods of its future would be weak: namely, that the prudential unity relations would be weak. Whether it would be in the animal's time-relative interest to continue to live would, it seems, be determined simply by the balance of expected good and evil. But if that is right, there is no fundamental difference between animals and people in cases of this sort. If death would be preferable for an animal in these circumstances, it should also be preferable for a person in relevantly similar circumstances (that is, circumstances in which the expected suffering would exceed or outweigh the expected good). (There might, of course, be additional constraints on *killing* that would apply in the case of persons but not in the case of animals—for example, constraints imposed by respect for autonomy. I will return to this in section 3 of this chapter.) Thus the focus on time-relative interests offers no reason to suppose that, *in general,* death would be a lesser misfortune for an animal than the experience of significant suffering. Even if it is true that death is a lesser misfortune for an animal than for a person, and even if the suffering of an animal matters in much the same way as the suffering of a person, it does not follow that death is more likely to be preferable to significant suffering in the case of an animal than it is in the case of a person.

To the extent that the common view that suffering matters more can be defended at all, I think the defense must appeal to an asymmetry between an animal's capacity for happiness and its capacity for suffering. As I noted earlier in this section, animals are incapable of many of the higher dimensions of well-being accessible to persons: for example, deep personal relations, aesthetic experience, achievement through the exercise of complex skills, and so on. In short, the peaks of experience and activity for animals fall far short of the peaks potentially attainable by persons. And, although their capacity for misfortune and suffering is limited in a similar way—in that there is little or no scope for genuine tragedy—the limitation is much less significant. Because physical pain is the source of some of the worst forms of suffering, animals can get considerably closer to the lowest depths of human misery than they can to the heights of human well-being. This, I think, is what best explains the common view that death is more often preferable to a prospect of significant suffering in the case of animals than in the case of persons. When an animal, such as a stray dog, faces a prospect of suffering, the potential for terrible suffering may be significant, while the probability that there will be compensating goods may be low. This is because the animal may simply be incapable, within its expected life span, of experiencing sufficient good to outweigh the suffering of which it is capable and which it stands a serious chance of experiencing. In the case of a person, by contrast, the possibilities for good are normally not so decisively limited by the person's nature.

Although this asymmetry in an animal's capacities for happiness and suffering supports the view that euthanasia is more often an option in the case of animals, it does not support the view, which Grandin and many others hold, that the killing of animals is generally unobjectionable if it is done without causing suffering. While there may be other dimensions to the wrongness of killing, the Time-Relative Interest Account seems correct in asserting that it is generally an objection to the killing of an animal that it would frustrate the animal's time-relative interest in continuing to live. For in most cases, in the absence of human intervention, animals do not face a prospect of significant suffering that clearly outweighs the possibilities for future good. Thus if one is to be justified in killing an animal, one must, *at a minimum,* have a purpose that is sufficiently serious to outweigh the animal's time-relative interest in continuing to live. While I accept that there are certain purposes that can meet this burden of justification—for example, certain medical experiments—there are other widespread human practices, such as the social practice of eating meat, that I believe cannot.[14]

2. ANIMALS AND SEVERELY COGNITIVELY IMPAIRED HUMAN BEINGS

2.1. *The Options*

The claim of the Time-Relative Interest Account that the wrongness of killing is primarily a function of the effect that killing has on the time-relative interests of the victim raises two profound problems of equality. I will discuss the first of these in this section and then devote section 2.2 to the second. I will contend that, although the first problem shows that the Time-Relative Interest Account has implications that are disagreeable, this is not fatal to the account; for the problem is one that no theory can solve without either embracing certain counterintuitive conclusions, or accepting as morally relevant certain distinctions that are quite clearly morally irrelevant. This is,

in short, a problem to which there is no solution that will salvage all of our moral intuitions. Some rather deep intuitions will have to be repudiated if we are to achieve
consistency without arbitrariness. The only real question, as we will see, is which intuitions should be abandoned. I will also contend, however, that the second problem
of equality *is* fatal to the Time-Relative Interest Account of the morality of killing.
While the Time-Relative Interest Account may give the right results in a broad range
of cases, it is not a fully plausible general account of the morality of killing.

The Time-Relative Interest Account offers an explanation of why the killing of
animals is less seriously objectionable than the killing of persons. Because the psychological capacities of animals are significantly less well developed than those of
persons, the range of goods accessible to them is narrower and the degree of psychological unity within their lives is less. They therefore have a weaker time-relative interest in continuing to live than a person normally does. For not only do they lose less
good in dying, but the relations that ground their time-relative interest in the goods
they might have had are weaker; thus the loss of those goods matters less in an egoistic way than the loss of a comparable amount of good would matter in the life of a
person. If the strength of the moral objection to killing varies with the strength of the
victim's time-relative interest in continuing to live, it follows that the killing of animals is in general significantly less seriously wrong than the killing of persons.

This explanation fits comfortably with common intuitions. When challenged to
defend our treatment of animals, we typically respond by citing various differences
between the psychological capacities of persons and those of animals: for example,
that we—but not they—are capable of self-consciousness, rationality, and autonomy, of planning for the future, using language, distinguishing right from wrong, and
so on. Our possession of these capacities, we say, is what relevantly distinguishes us
from animals and makes killing us more seriously wrong. The connection with the
Time-Relative Interest Account is that it is precisely our possession of these various
psychological capacities that enables us to have a time-relative interest in continuing
to live that is so much stronger than that of any other animal. The Time-Relative Interest Account, in short, offers a plausible explanation of the moral significance of the
differences between ourselves and animals that we typically cite when challenged to
justify our belief that killing animals is morally much less serious than killing persons.

There is, however, a serious problem here, which is that, whatever we take to be
the range of psychological capacities that differentiate us morally from animals,
there are some human beings whose psychological capacities are no more advanced
than those of certain animals. We can distinguish three groups of which this is true:
(1) those whose psychological capacities have yet to mature (for example, fetuses
and infants), (2) those with *acquired* cognitive deficits—that is, those who once had
highly developed capacities but have lost them (for example, those who have suffered
brain damage or dementia), and (3) congenitally severely cognitively impaired
human beings. Because of their rudimentary cognitive and emotional capacities,
human beings of all three types have a comparatively weak time-relative interest in
continuing to live. In the case of fetuses and infants, the amount of good their futures
might contain is very great, but the prudential unity relations would hold only weakly
between them now and themselves later, when the goods of their future lives would
occur. Because the amount of good in their futures would be so great, it is arguable

that fetuses and infants have a considerably stronger time-relative interest in continuing to live than animals with comparable capacities. Yet the difference in the amount of future good may be partially offset by the fact that a fetus's or a newborn infant's psychological ties to itself in the future may be weaker than those that bind an animal to itself in the future, if the animal's present psychological capacities are higher than those of the fetus or infant. Thus, while the Time-Relative Interest Account arguably implies that the killing of a human fetus or infant is normally more seriously objectionable than the killing of an animal with comparable psychological capacities, it cannot claim that the difference is substantial. Some people, of course, may find this a welcome conclusion—at least in the case of fetuses—for it provides the basis for an argument for the permissibility of abortion.

Members of the other two groups of human beings—those with acquired dementia and the congenitally severely retarded—would not only be weakly related in the ways that matter with themselves in the future, but also would have comparatively little good that they could in principle anticipate in an egoistic way. Thus it seems that Time-Relative Interest Account implies that it would be no more seriously wrong, other things being equal, to kill a human being of one of these two types than it would be to kill an animal with comparable psychological capacities. Very few people will find this a welcome conclusion.

Most fetuses and infants, of course, have the potential to develop sophisticated cognitive and emotional capacities. Many people believe that this distinguishes them in a morally important way from animals to which they are at present comparable. The Time-Relative Interest Account recognizes this difference as significant only insofar as it makes it the case that fetuses and infants have a stronger time-relative interest in continuing to live. But even if the Time-Relative Interest Account fails to recognize the full significance of the potential of fetuses and infants, it could be modified or supplemented in such a way that it would. (If it were revised or supplemented in this way, of course, it might cease to provide the basis for an argument for the permissibility of abortion.) Similarly, human beings who have suffered brain damage or dementia are distinguishable from animals on the basis of their having once had high cognitive and emotional capacities. This seems to most of us to be a morally significant difference. Again, the Time-Relative Interest Account fails to recognize this difference as relevant; but it could be revised or supplemented so that it would.

The most problematic case is that of congenitally severely cognitively impaired human beings, or, as I will refer to them, the severely retarded. These human beings have cognitive and emotional capacities no higher than those of certain animals. As a consequence, their time-relative interest in continuing to live is no stronger than that of their nonhuman counterparts. According to the Time-Relative Interest Account, therefore, it is no more wrong, other things being equal, to kill a severely retarded human being than it is to kill an animal with comparable psychological capacities. And this, it hardly needs pointing out, is strongly at variance with what most people believe. This is, however, more than just a counterexample for proponents of the Time-Relative Interest Account to wrestle with. It is a more general problem. For not only are the psychological capacities of the severely retarded comparable to those of certain animals (so that their interests—and their time-relative interests—are no stronger), but they also have no more potential than those animals. They are not, therefore, distinguishable from animals in the way that fetuses and infants are. Nor do they have a former status that differentiates them from animals in the same way as the demented. In short, it is difficult to identify *any* intrinsic difference between the severely retarded and animals with comparable psychological capacities that is relevant to the morality of killing them. But, as I noted, commonsense intuition, embodied in the law, strongly affirms that the killing of a severely retarded human being is a far more serious matter than the killing of an animal—even an animal with *higher* cognitive and emotional capacities. Thus the challenge of reconciling this commonsense belief with the absence of any apparent intrinsic difference between the severely retarded and animals with comparable capacities is one that confronts not just the proponent of the Time-Relative Interest Account, but the rest of us as well.

We can distinguish four broad strategies for resolving the tension between our moral intuitions about severely mentally impaired human beings and our intuitions about animals.[15] (1) The first strategy is to follow common sense in asserting that neither animals nor cognitively impaired human beings can be morally assimilated to the other, because there are factors in addition to an individual's psychological capacities and potential that are major determinants of that individual's moral status and how it may be treated, and animals and the severely retarded differ with respect to some of these factors. (2) Alternatively, we might preserve common intuitions about the proper treatment of animals and accept that it is permissible, other things being equal, to treat human beings with comparable psychological capacities and potentials in the same ways we have hitherto treated animals. (3) Or we might hold constant traditional intuitions about the moral status of cognitively impaired human beings, and accept that animals with comparable cognitive and emotional capacities and potentials must be accorded a comparable status. (4) Finally, we might accept that animals and the severely retarded share roughly the same moral status, though the moral status of neither is quite what it has traditionally and popularly been supposed to be.

These different options might be labeled and represented as follows, with the arrows indicating the direction of assimilation.

1. Anthropomorphism: severely retarded human beings $\longleftrightarrow$ animals
2. Consistent Elitism: severely retarded human beings $\longrightarrow$ animals
3. Radical Egalitarianism: severely retarded human beings $\longleftarrow$ animals
4. Convergent Assimilation: severely retarded human beings $\rightarrow\leftarrow$ animals

I will explore the possible defenses of the commonsense view—*Anthropocentrism*—in detail. First, however, I will briefly consider the middle two options. In the end my conclusion will be that the fourth option is the only reasonable strategy to adopt.

The second option, *Consistent Elitism,* finds no morally significant differences between animals and human beings with equivalent psychological capacities and potentials, yet refuses to abandon or modify common beliefs about the morality of killing and harming animals. Consistent Elitism, in short, regards congenitally severely mentally impaired human beings as morally comparable to animals, accepting the radical implication that it is permissible, other things being equal, to treat these human beings in the same ways in which we have hitherto found it acceptable to treat animals with comparable psychological capacities—for example, using them for experimental purposes, killing them for food, and so on. Of course, the ceteris paribus clause in this last claim is crucial. Consideration of side effects may rule out the use of severely retarded human beings in ways in which we have traditionally used animals with comparable capacities and potentials—for example, in medical experimentation. Even the most severely cognitively impaired human being is someone's child or sibling, and the relatives have reasons that others may not to ensure that the retarded individual is protected from the harms that medical experimentation typically inflicts. These reasons that derive from the relatives' special relation to the retarded individual are ones that the rest of us must respect. For to harm a severely retarded individual is thereby gravely to harm those persons who are specially related to that individual. Thus even Consistent Elitism may have to acknowledge that it is unacceptable to experiment on retarded human beings rather than on animals with comparable capacities, even when the experimental results would be considerably more reliable if the experiments were performed on human beings. Still—and this is the important point—our moral reason for refusing to experiment on a severely retarded human being rather than an animal with comparable capacities would not, according to Consistent Elitism, derive from a respect for the retarded individual himself. It would not be a response to that individual's intrinsic properties. It would instead be analogous to our reason to experiment on a stray animal rather than on someone's pet, with this difference: that the relation that a person bears to a severely retarded child or sibling is deeper and more significant than the relation that a pet owner bears to a comparably endowed pet animal.

I will assume that Consistent Elitism is so deeply repugnant that it need not be explored in depth. It is not really an option. The third of the four possible views, *Radical Egalitarianism,* reverses the direction of assimilation. It claims that animals must be regarded as the moral equals of human beings with equivalent capacities, while it holds constant a range of traditional beliefs about the sanctity or inviolability of the lives of severely mentally retarded human beings. This view accepts the common assumption that, if conditions are such that it would be wrong intentionally to kill or inflict suffering on a normal adult human being, it would be equally wrong intentionally to kill or inflict equal suffering on a severely mentally retarded human being in those same conditions. And if it would be wrong to harm a severely retarded human being in these ways, it must be equally wrong to inflict the same harm on an animal with equivalent capacities, other things being equal. In short, animals with capacities equivalent to those of severely mentally impaired human beings must be our moral equals in those respects in which the impaired human beings are our moral equals.

The general strategy embodied in Radical Egalitarianism underlies the commitment that many people have to the idea that animals have rights—in particular, the right to life.[16] These people claim that the commonly recognized rights of severely mentally retarded human beings must be based on or grounded in certain relevant properties and capacities that these individuals share with us. Rights must, they insist, supervene upon certain relevant natural properties or capacities that are intrinsic to the individuals who are the possessors of the rights. But since the properties that ground the rights of severely mentally impaired human beings are in fact possessed by many animals as well, these animals must be recognized as possessing the same rights.

Radical Egalitarianism so described tends to self-destruct at the lower ends of the scales of human and animal life. According to the traditional understanding of the sanctity of human life, even the most profoundly mentally impaired human beings have a right to life equal to that of normal adult human beings. Thus it remains illegal, and is widely considered immoral, to kill an anencephalic infant in order to use its organs for transplantation, despite the fact that there is virtually unanimous agreement among neuroscientists that anencephalic infants have neither the capacity nor the potential for even the faintest glimmer of consciousness. If, as we are assuming, Radical Egalitarianism holds that the moral status of severely retarded human beings is grounded primarily in certain intrinsic properties other than mere membership in the human species, and if it retains the traditional belief that killing an anencephalic infant is just as wrong, or at least nearly as wrong, as killing a normal adult human being, then it follows that the relevant intrinsic properties cannot be psychological. For anencephalics have no psychological properties. But if the properties that ground the anencephalic's rather exalted moral status are neither psychological nor specific to the human species, it seems inevitable that they must be possessed by even the most rudimentary forms of animal life, and perhaps by plants as well.

It must be conceded, however, that commonsense beliefs about the moral status of anencephalic infants are evolving. Anencephalic infants normally die within a few days of birth. But by the time they are diagnosed as brain dead, reduced blood flow to their organs has usually caused these organs to deteriorate to a point at which they are no longer suitable for transplantation. Perhaps sensing the tragic absurdity of allowing the healthy organs of a moribund and necessarily nonconscious human organism to deteriorate while, possibly in the same hospital building, a child dies for want of an organ transplant, the American Medical Association in 1995 endorsed the moral permissibility (with parental permission, of course) of extracting the organs from anencephalic infants prior to brain death for the purpose of transplantation. This position provoked protests from certain quarters, and was soon retracted by the AMA. Still, if one can construe this episode as evidence that commonsense morality no longer unambiguously regards the killing of an anencephalic infant as morally comparable to the killing of a normal adult human being, Radical Egalitarianism might then be understood as the view that we should preserve the belief that the killing of any human being possessing either the capacity or the potential for some form of conscious life is seriously wrong, and also accept that the killing of an animal with comparable psychological capacities or potential is equally wrong. This would exclude from the scope of the view both plants and any forms of animal life that lacked consciousness (or perhaps had a form of consciousness dimmer than that of even the most retarded human being). But even when interpreted in this way, Radical Egalitarianism implies that the killing of, say, a fish is as seriously wrong, other things being equal, as the killing of a human being whose psychological capacities and potential are no greater than those of a fish. And, assuming that the commonsense view is that the killing of such a human being is (again, if other things are equal) just as wrong, or nearly as wrong, as the killing of a normal adult human being, Radical Egalitarianism must imply that, if other things are equal, the killing of a fish is as seriously wrong as the killing of a person—which is absurd.

To avoid implications of this sort, proponents of animals' rights often specify a threshold along the scale that measures the complexity and sophistication of a being's psychological life such that individuals with psychological capacities above the threshold are said to have the right to life, while those whose capacities are below it do not. The threshold is typically set low enough to ensure that mature mammalian animals and most mentally impaired human beings are located above it.[17] And while it is conceded that those animals and profoundly mentally impaired human beings that fall below the threshold do not have the right to life, it is normally held that this fact alone does not automatically make it permissible to kill them or, of course, to harm them in other ways. There are, it is insisted, moral constraints governing the treatment of animals and human beings that lack the right to life, though these constraints are less stringent than those imposed by the right to life.

Views of this sort—ones that do not discriminate between human beings and animals on the basis of species membership alone, but do draw a line between those animals and human beings that enjoy certain moral protections and those that do not—are not really variants of Radical Egalitarianism. For Radical Egalitarianism is distinguished by the fact that it preserves traditional beliefs about the special sanctity of the lives of even the most profoundly psychologically impaired human beings. But views that set a species-neutral threshold for the possession of certain fundamental moral rights or immunities require the abandonment or revision of certain of these traditional beliefs; for these views inevitably locate some mentally impaired human beings below the threshold. As will soon become apparent, views that posit a species-neutral threshold are instead variants of the view I have identified as *Convergent Assimilation,* to which I will return. First, however, it is necessary to consider the view I have labeled Anthropocentrism.

2.2. *Membership in the Human Species*

Anthropocentrism insists on retaining traditional beliefs both about the appropriate treatment of severely retarded human beings and about the permissibility of various widely accepted practices involving the use and, in particular, the killing of animals. It therefore combines the elements of both Consistent Elitism and Radical Egalitarianism that are incompatible with the Time-Relative Interest Account. It permits us to treat animals less well than a proper concern for their time-relative interests requires, while also insisting that we treat the severely retarded with greater solicitude than is required by a concern merely for their time-relative interests. Anthropocentrism is defined so that it necessarily coincides with commonsense beliefs. Whether it is defensible depends on whether there are morally significant differences between animals and human beings with comparable psychological capacities and potentials. And not only must such differences exist, but they must also be sufficiently significant to justify the wide divergence between the norms that in practice govern our treatment of the profoundly retarded and those that sanction our practices involving the use of animals. The challenge for Anthropocentrism is to identify and defend the significance of some such difference or differences.

The usual strategy is to seek to identify some difference in *intrinsic* or nonrelational properties. It is often claimed, for example, that all human beings have souls, while no nonhuman animals do. This is a fundamentally theological claim. But it is not thereby altogether extracted from the realm of the empirical or rendered immune to rational examination. And, as I argued in chapter 1, the idea that all human beings have souls, or are souls, seems indefensible, particularly if the soul is understood in a metaphysically robust way, rather than figuratively as, for example, a reification of individual spirituality. For either this idea is incompatible with what we know about the dependence of the mind on the functioning of the brain, or else the conception of the soul as the seat of consciousness has to be abandoned, in which case our notion of the soul becomes too insubstantial or lacking in content to support the view that those who have souls are exalted well above those who lack them.

Moreover, even if the theological claim that all human beings have immortal souls while animals do not were true, it is not obvious that this would support common-sense intuitions about the moral disparity between killing human beings and killing animals. For, if the soul is immortal, killing an individual with a soul does not terminate that individual's existence. It merely causes that individual to undergo an involuntary transition from one realm or mode of existence to another. If, therefore, all human beings have immortal souls while animals do not, it may actually be worse to kill an animal than it is to kill a human being, all things considered; for, given this assumption, killing an animal deprives it of any further good it might otherwise have, while killing a human being does not. (One response to this problem has been to reinterpret the wrongness of killing as an offense against God rather than the victim of the killing. This idea may, in fact, be necessary in order to make sense of the common belief that God can forgive a person for the commission of murder. For unless God is the party to whom the wrong has been done, it is unclear how it is possible for God to grant forgiveness. Normally it is incoherent to suppose that one can forgive wrongs done not to oneself but to others.)

It is often assumed that the mere fact that human beings are *human* gives them a special status that other animals lack. In an important recent book on abortion and euthanasia, for example, Ronald Dworkin argues that both conservative and liberal views of abortion are best understood as based on some version of the idea that every individual human life is "sacred" and "inviolable." According to this view, which Dworkin claims is virtually universally accepted in one form or another, "the life of a human organism has intrinsic value in *any* form it takes, even in the extremely undeveloped form of a very early, just-implanted embryo. . . . *Any* form of human life [is therefore] something we should respect and honor and protect as marvelous in itself."[18] But notice that the sacredness of a just-implanted human embryo is not cashed out or explicated in terms of its possession of any properties other than its bare humanness, its membership in the human species. Thus, assuming that just-implanted *animal* embryos are *not* sacred and inviolable, Dworkin's claim implies that a defective human embryo that lacks the potential to develop into anything other than an anencephalic infant is nevertheless sacred and inviolable in a way that no animal embryo, and perhaps no mature animal, is.

Is that credible? Again, the special value of the defective human embryo cannot be attributable to its psychological capacities, for it has none. Nor can its special status derive from its psychological potential, for again it has none. The ground of its superior status must therefore be physical. But a newly implanted embryo is just a tiny cluster of cells that are only beginning to become differentiated. Its physical intricacy and functional complexity are less marvelous than those of an ant. Hence its physical or functional complexity cannot be the source of its sacredness or special status. This seems to leave its mere humanness—whatever it is that makes it a member of the human species rather than some other species—as the basis of its special value or status. Or, to be more precise, it is not its mere humanness alone; for a skin cell may be human without being sacred. Rather, what Dworkin seems to be assuming is that the embryo is sacred because it is a distinct individual *organism* belonging to the human species. (I will henceforth make the natural assumption that the phrase "member of the human species" refers only to individual human organisms or human beings rather than to all living entities, including single cells and organs, that are human rather than nonhuman.)

The assumption here need not be that membership in the human species is a necessary condition of sacredness or inviolability. Suppose that there were a form of gene therapy that allowed us to alter the expression of genes responsible for the development of the cerebral cortex and thus to endow an individual with cognitive capacities greatly superior to those he would have had in the absence of the therapy. If this were possible in the case of a human being, it would presumably be possible also in the case of a chimpanzee. Recall, for example, the case from chapter 2 of the Superchimp, a chimpanzee that through genetic therapy has developed psychological capacities comparable to those of a ten-year-old human child. Surely the Superchimp would be entitled to whatever forms of respect are due to normal ten-year-old human beings. So we would not want our understanding of the significance of membership in the human species to commit us to the view that it would be permissible to treat the Superchimp in exactly the same ways in which ordinary chimpanzees are treated in our society.

We can avoid this by assuming that membership in the human species is only a *sufficient* condition of sacredness and inviolability and not a necessary condition. While membership in the human species would alone be sufficient for the status of inviolability, so would possession of certain psychological capacities—for example, capacities for self-consciousness, rationality, and autonomy. According to this view, both the anencephalic infant and the Superchimp would be sacred and inviolable. The various bases of inviolability would not, however, be additive. For, while the Superchimp would satisfy only one sufficient condition for status as sacred (the possession of certain psychological capacities), a normal ten-year-old human being would satisfy two (the possession of those capacities and membership in the human species). But the status of the human being would not necessarily be any higher. The Superchimp would arguably be the moral equal of the child. If so, the different bases of sacredness could not be added together to yield higher moral status, a higher form of sacredness.

This leaves the central question unresolved: what reason is there to suppose that membership in the human species is sufficient for high moral status while membership in a different species is not? To address this question, we must first understand what a species is and how different species are distinguished from one another. This is not an uncontroversial matter—though one aspect of the matter is universally accepted: namely, that the concept of a species is a component in a scheme of biological classification, a taxonomy for the classification of biological organisms. And this alone is one reason for doubting whether our membership in a particular species could have the kind of moral significance that Dworkin and others suppose it has. For if I am right in my earlier contention that we are not identical with our physical organisms, it follows that membership in the human species is, strictly speaking, a property of our organisms and therefore is predicated of *us* by extension, by virtue of the intimate relation that we bear to our organisms. This is not to deny that it can be correctly said of us that we are members of the species *Homo sapiens.* But it is to question whether properties that we have only because they are properties of our organisms can have the same sort of moral significance as properties—such as psychological properties—that are directly attributable to *us.*

I will return to this point later in this section. For the moment, let us return to the question of what it is for an organism to belong to a particular species. Some people have thought that the members of a single species are united by their common possession of a certain *essence,* an essence that defines their particular species. This essence cannot, however, be a matter of phenotype. There are some recognized species—called "polytypic species"—whose members have widely divergent phenotypes but nevertheless can interbreed. In other cases, we find animals that are virtually indistinguishable phenotypically but cannot interbreed, and thus are classified as members of different species. These different species whose members share a common gross morphology are known as "sibling species." The recognition of polytypic and sibling species is incompatible with the idea that species are differentiated in terms of phenotypic essences.[19]

If there are species essences, they must be essences of genotype rather than phenotype. Yet it is unclear how *this* difference—the bare difference between the types of genes that individuals carry in their cells—could have any moral significance at all. One can understand how differences in the phenotypic manifestations of genetic differences could be morally significant, but we have just seen that species are not differentiated in terms of common phenotypes. Moreover, the magnitude of the difference—again at the level of genotype—between the human species and certain other species is comparatively trivial: approximately 98.4 percent of a human being's genes will be shared by any given chimpanzee.

In any case, whatever the degree of overlap there may be between certain human and animal genomes, the genetic differences between human beings and animals of other species are not immutable. Genes from members of different species can be combined in a single animal. It is possible, for example, to take a sheep zygote, insert into it various genes taken from the cells of a goat, and implant the genetically altered zygote into a sheep's womb. The result will be the birth a chimera, a creature with mixed sheep and goat genetic material. In the chimera, genes of both contributing species may be expressed phenotypically: for example, the animal may have patches of short, straight hair like that of a goat interspersed with tufts of sheep's wool.

No one is, of course, making fully-fledged human-animal chimeras, though the thin edge of the wedge has already been inserted. There are at present laboratories engaged in breeding "transgenic" animals—animals with a tiny amount of human genetic material. The aim is to breed pigs with livers suitable for transplantation into human beings. In pursuit of this aim, scientists have inserted a single human gene into each of a number of newly fertilized porcine eggs and then implanted the altered zygotes in the womb of a sow. The human gene is intended to give the animal's organ characteristics that would moderate the immune response to it if it were transplanted into a human being. The human gene usually does not "take," but a small proportion—about one in a hundred—of the genetically altered zygotes do develop into piglets that carry a human gene in every cell in their bodies.

If it is possible to insert a single human gene into an animal zygote, it should be possible to insert two or more. We can imagine a spectrum of possibilities. At one end of the spectrum, there is a transgenic animal—say, a chimpanzee—with a single human gene. (A human gene does not come marked "human." As I noted, most human and chimpanzee genes are the same. What I mean here by a "human gene" is any gene found in and taken from a human being.) Next in the spectrum there is a transgenic chimpanzee with two human genes. And so on, with each animal farther along in the spectrum having one more human gene than the animal before it. Since the overlap between the human and the chimpanzee genomes is high, it may be well beyond the middle range of the imagined spectrum before one reaches individuals that are phenotypically chimerical: individuals that seem half-human, half-chimpanzee, with bizarre blends of human and chimpanzee characteristics. At the far end of the spectrum is an individual grown from a chimpanzee zygote from which all the chimpanzee genes but one have been removed and replaced by human genes. This would, presumably, be a human being with a single chimpanzee gene.

Is there a point along this spectrum at which the individuals cease to be chimpanzees and become human beings? Is there, in other words, a point at which there is an individual with just enough human genetic material to count as a member of our species? And, if so, is it only at that point that there begin to be individuals with special moral status—for example, individuals whose lives are sacred and inviolable? (We might also ask, as a challenge to the view that only human beings have souls, at what point along the spectrum the individuals would begin to have souls.)

I suspect that the chimeras near the middle of the spectrum would be neither human beings nor chimpanzees. On either side of these would be individuals whose species membership would be genuinely indeterminate. But these issues, though interesting, need not detain us here. The important point is that it would be absurd to suppose that the moral status of any individual in the spectrum would be determined by how many, or what proportion, of its genes were human or were taken from a human being. Rather, it seems that the moral status of each individual would be determined by its individual phenotypic characteristics, particularly its psychological capacities. Compare, for example, two possible chimeras. In one, more than 99 percent of its genes are of human origin, though the genes responsible for the growth and development of its brain are from the original chimpanzee zygote. If species membership is determined by the genome, this chimera is presumably a human being, though its mental capacities are those of a chimpanzee. In a second chimera, more than 99 percent of its genes are of chimpanzee origin, but the genes responsible for the development of its brain have a human source. This is presumably a chimpanzee with human intelligence. If membership in the human species is sufficient for a certain high moral status, the chimera with the intelligence of a chimpanzee should have a moral status at least equal to that of the one with human intelligence. This, I believe, is implausible.

Some who believe that membership in the human species is itself morally significant may respond to these arguments by denying that the criterion of species membership is genetic. What, then, is the criterion? The orthodox method of sorting organisms into species is to determine whether they can or do interbreed. If they do
interbreed (or, perhaps, if they could, even if in fact they do not), they are regarded as
belonging to the same species; if they do not (or, perhaps, cannot), they are regarded
as belonging to different species. There are, however, numerous well-known problems with this method, most notable of which is that it can lead to contradictions. In
the case of "ring species," for example, a collection of animals, A, can interbreed with
the members of an adjacent population, B; the members of B can interbreed with the
members of a different population, C, whose members can interbreed with the members of population D. If interbreeding is the criterion of species membership, the
members of population B must be of the same species as those of A, those of C the
same species as B, and those of D the same as C. If the relation "member of the same
species as" is a transitive relation, as it seems to be, the members of population D
must be of the same species as the members of A. But in some instances, in which
populations A and D are geographically isolated, they are also reproductively isolated—that is, they cannot interbreed.[20] Hence the interbreeding criterion of species
membership seems to imply that the members of populations A and D both are and
are not members of the same species. There are exactly analogous intransitivities that
occur over time in the evolution of species. We, for example, would certainly be incapable of interbreeding with our remote evolutionary ancestors; but the members of
each generation in the long chain of our ancestry were necessarily capable of interbreeding with the members of the generations that came immediately before and
after them.

In any case, if potential for interbreeding were the criterion of species membership, that would make it unlikely that membership in the human species could by itself be a morally significant property. It seems ridiculous to suppose that an anencephalic infant is sacred simply because it is potentially capable of interbreeding
with people like you and me.

Whatever the exact criterion for membership in the human species is, it will be a
purely biological criterion. As such, it is difficult to see how it could have any intrinsic moral significance—particularly if we are not actually biological organisms, as I
have claimed. Just as racial and sexual differences are purely biological and thus in
themselves morally insignificant, so a mere difference of species, by itself, is also
morally insignificant. Hence discrimination among individuals on the basis of species membership alone has earned the epithet "speciesism," which stresses the parallel with racism and sexism and other forms of arbitrary discrimination on the basis of
an individual's belonging in a category that is itself devoid of moral significance.
While the line between the human species and other species is of course strongly *correlated* with differences that are of clear moral significance—such as differences of
psychological capacity or potential—these correlations are not invariant. And they
break down in precisely the cases with which we are concerned: namely, those involving human beings with severe congenital cognitive impairments.

Some have thought that the significance of species membership is slightly different. They hold that the appropriate treatment of individuals is determined, not by ref-

erence to individuals' own psychological capacities or potential, but by reference to the psychological capacities that are characteristic of normal individuals of their *kind*.[21] John Finnis, for example, claims that "to be a person is to belong to a kind of being characterized by rational (self-conscious, intelligent) nature."[22] Thus he claims that all human beings, including the severely retarded, are persons and must be treated in ways that are appropriate for rational beings. Thomas Scanlon has advanced a similar view. He claims that there is a part of morality concerned with duties that we owe to each other, and that the class of those to whom we can owe these duties includes "those beings to whom we have good reason to want our actions to be justifiable."[23] These are the beings who can be *wronged* in addition to being merely harmed or mistreated. What Scanlon claims is that "the class of beings whom it is possible to wrong will include at least all those beings who are of a kind that is normally capable of judgment-sensitive attitudes."[24] Thus he concludes that "our treatment of [severely retarded human beings] should be governed by principles that they could not reasonably reject, even though they themselves do not and will not have the capacity to understand or weigh justifications."[25] By contrast, our treatment of animals with comparable psychological capacities should be governed by such principles only if it makes sense to think of them as potentially represented by trustees to whom we might in principle present our justifications. Although he is inclined to reject this latter idea, he does not rule it out. The important point for our purposes, however, is that, unlike animals, the severely retarded do not require trustees: they come within the scope of the part of morality concerned with duties we owe to others by virtue of being members of our kind.

For Scanlon and most others who invoke this notion, the relevant kind or class is the species. Severely retarded human beings, but not animals with comparable psychological capacities, are owed treatment appropriate for beings with high psychological capacities *by virtue of* their membership in a species whose normal members have high psychological capacities. This view has obvious affinities with the view that, in section 5.1 of chapter 2, I called the Species Norm Account. That, of course, was a view about the nature of fortune and misfortune, whereas the view we are now considering is a view about the appropriate treatment of individuals. But the two views may be connected. For the view that how an individual should be treated is determined by its species membership may derive from a rather obscure sense that defective members of a species are unfortunate in having capacities and potentials that are diminished relative to the norm for the species, even though individuals of other species for which those same capacities and potentials are the norm are not similarly unfortunate. Most people feel, for example, that it is a terrible misfortune for a congenitally severely mentally retarded human being to have psychological capacities comparable to those of an animal, though they also feel that it is not a misfortune for an animal to have only those capacities. If this is true, it suggests that an individual's good is not measured by reference to forms and levels of well-being that its own native capacities or potential make possible, but must instead be assessed relative to the norm for members of its species. And, if what counts as good for an individual is determined at least in part by what is good for normal members of its species, this may support the claim that the moral principles that govern the treatment of normal members of a species must also govern the treatment of abnormal or defective members of that species. For the appropriateness of certain modes of treatment of an individual must be gauged relative to an assessment of what constitutes the good for that individual.

The deeper assumptions here seem to be that an individual's moral status is determined by its essential nature, that its essential nature is given or defined by the *kind* of thing it most fundamentally is, and that the relevant kind for each living being is its species. As I noted earlier, if we are not in fact human organisms, it makes less sense to suppose that the kind of thing we fundamentally are is given by our species membership. But let us put that aside. Suppose, for the sake of argument, that each living individual is essentially a member of its own species, and that in that sense an individual's species membership indicates its essential nature. Even if that is true, there is no reason to suppose that its species membership determines its moral status. For the properties—whatever they may be—that are necessary and sufficient for membership in the species, and are thus the properties that define the individual's essential nature, are *not* the properties that are deemed to be *morally* significant. For Finnis, for example, what is ultimately morally significant is the possession of a rational nature, whereas for Scanlon it is the capacity for judgment-sensitive attitudes. In both cases, there seems to be no reason why the moral status that comes from having the morally significant properties should also be awarded in some honorary sense to those who do not and never will possess those properties simply on the ground that they possess the *different* properties that make them members of a certain species.

The problems with views of this sort emerge more clearly when we consider such cases as the Superchimp. Even though the Superchimp has a rational nature, he remains a chimpanzee, and thus does not belong to a kind that is characterized by having a rational nature. By Finnis's definition, therefore, the Superchimp is not a person, and presumably also lacks the moral status that persons have by virtue of belonging to a kind characterized by the possession of a rational nature. This seems absurd. Scanlon's view seems more plausible because it is stated in such a way that kind-membership is only a sufficient condition of a certain moral status, not a necessary condition. Because the Superchimp is himself capable of judgment-sensitive attitudes, Scanlon can recognize him as a being who can be wronged even though he is not of a kind normally capable of these attitudes.

But even Scanlon's view is vulnerable to a related objection based on a case I also introduced in criticizing the Species Norm Account. Suppose that, as a result of reduced numbers and selective breeding, Superchimps come to outnumber what were previously considered normal chimpanzees. In that case, the norm for the species would have changed: its normal members would now be capable of judgment-sensitive attitudes in the same way that ten-year-old human children are. According to Scanlon's view, our treatment of the less intelligent animals would have to be governed by "principles that they could not reasonably reject," in the same way that our treatment of severely retarded human beings is supposed to be. This seems implausible.

Thus far we have noted two possible defenses of Anthropocentrism, both of which claim that there are intrinsic, morally significant differences between animals and human beings with comparable psychological capacities and potentials. One of these alleged differences—that all human beings have souls, while no animals do— might be a morally significant difference if it were a real difference; but in fact there is no such difference. No one has a soul of the sort that would relevantly distinguish all members of the human species from all other animals. There is simply no such thing. The other difference—the biological difference between the human species and other species—is real, or at least as real as any line drawn between species. But, at least considered as an intrinsic difference, it is morally irrelevant. The mere fact that an individual is a member of one biological species rather than another does not constitute an agent-neutral reason (that is, a reason that applies to any moral agent) to treat that individual differently from the way one ought to treat the members of another species. (There is, of course, one form of treatment that is an exception: biological classification itself.)

2.3. *Comembership in a Species as a Special Relation*

An alternative defense of Anthropocentrism is to abandon the search for intrinsic differences between animals and human beings with comparable psychological capacities and to claim instead that the relevant difference is extrinsic, or relational. We might have reason to be specially solicitous of severely retarded human beings because we are related to them in certain significant ways—ways in which we are not related to animals. Interestingly, the reason that Scanlon gives for distinguishing morally between severely retarded human beings and animals with comparable psychological capacities makes just such an appeal to the relation that we bear to the former. "The mere fact that a being is 'of human born,'" he writes, "provides a strong reason for according it the same status as other humans." Thus "our relation to [the severely retarded] gives us reason to accept the requirement that our actions should be justifiable to them"; for they "are ones who are born to us or to others to whom we are bound by the requirements of justifiability. This tie of birth gives us good reason to want to treat them 'as human' despite their limited capacities."[26]

Scanlon's appeal to the relation that we bear to the severely retarded is important in at least two respects. First, it provides a basis for denying that his view has the implications that I claimed it does in the case involving the Superchimps. If the basis of the special status enjoyed by the severely retarded is that they are related to us by "the tie of birth," there is no reason to suppose that the less intelligent chimpanzees in a population containing a majority of Superchimps should have the same status; for they, certainly, would not be related to us in this special way. This helps to reveal the second important point, which is that Scanlon's fundamental claim—that the severely retarded have the status he attributes to them by virtue of their relation to us—is different from and does not support the view that he explicitly states: namely, the view that "the beings whom it is possible to wrong will include at least all those beings who are of a kind that is normally capable of judgment-sensitive attitudes." According to this latter view, intelligent and morally sensitive Martians would be required to treat severely retarded human beings in the same way they would be required to treat us. For severely retarded human beings are beings "of a kind that is normally capable of judgment-sensitive attitudes." But, if the reason we have to accord the severely retarded the same moral status as other human beings is that we are related to them through "the tie of birth," then Martians would not have this reason.

Let us consider in more detail the view that Scanlon appears to take as fundamental: namely, that the severely retarded are among those to whom we owe special duties because of the way in which they are related to us. A view of this sort was suggested earlier, though without much elaboration, by Scanlon's colleague at Harvard, Robert Nozick. In a review of a book about animal rights, Nozick speculated that "perhaps it will turn out that the bare species characteristic of simply being human, as the most severely retarded people are, will command special respect only from other humans—this is an instance of the general principle that the members of any species may legitimately give their fellows more weight than they give members of other species (or at least more weight than a neutral view would grant them)."[27]

The background to this view is a conception of morality according to which there are at least two distinguishable sources of moral reasons.[28] Many—perhaps most—of the moral reasons we have to act or not to act in certain ways derive from a consideration of the intrinsic properties of other beings who might be affected by our action. There are certain ways in which we ought or ought not to act toward an individual that are required simply by virtue of the nature of that individual. Thus the mere fact that a being is capable of suffering is the source of a moral reason not to do what would cause it to suffer. One has reason not to cause that being to suffer that is independent of any relation that one might have to it. Similarly, the fact that a being has an interest, or time-relative interest, in continuing to live is the source of a moral reason not to kill it. And again this reason is independent of the ways in which one might be related to that being. But reasons of this first sort may be supplemented, strengthened, or reinforced by reasons deriving from one's relations to others. Thus, while one has a reason to save an imperiled child just because the child is the kind of being who would be greatly harmed by dying, one has an additional reason (or, perhaps, the same reason but considerably strengthened) to save that child if the child is one's own. One has more reason, or a stronger reason, to save the child if one is related to it in this important way than if one is not specially related to it. In short, special relations, such as the relation between a parent and child, are an independent and autonomous source of moral reasons.

Nozick's suggestion, then, is that, if we confine ourselves to a consideration of their intrinsic properties only, there may be nothing that morally distinguishes the severely retarded from animals with comparable psychological capacities; nevertheless, the fact that we are related to the severely retarded in a way that we are not related to animals—namely, through our membership in the same species—gives us reason to care for the severely retarded in ways that go beyond the respect that we are required to show them because of their intrinsic properties.

The idea that comembership in the human species is a special relation that either permits or requires us to show greater concern for severely retarded members of our own species than we are required to show for comparably endowed animals should not be confused with the related but different idea that some moral reasons are generated within the personal point of view. According to this latter idea, morality must reflect our nature as persons; it must therefore acknowledge that each of us views the world from a unique point of view that naturally generates a pattern of concern and valuation that is inherently perspectival rather than impartial. Morality must somehow accommodate our various individual values and ideals; it must permit people to give some weight to the things that matter to them, even if those things do not matter, or matter much less, from an impartial point of view. The personal point of view is thus held to be an autonomous and authoritative source of moral reasons for action, though most theorists concede that it is not the only such source. According to one prominent theory, our most basic moral reasons derive from impartial considerations; yet morality acknowledges the authority of the personal point of view by permitting each person to give somewhat greater weight to those things that specially matter from his or her own point of view than they would be assigned from the impartial point of view.[29] Call this the *Personal Priority View.*

The Personal Priority View does not offer an adequate account of the moral significance of special relations. It is not really a view about special relations at all. Instead it stresses, to borrow the title of a recent book, the importance of what we care about. But it is possible that one might not care specially about those to whom one is in fact specially related. It is possible, for example, that a parent might care no more about his own child than about another child to whom he is not specially related—for example, a famous child actor whom he admires. But this fact about the parent's psychology is irrelevant to his responsibility as a parent. His responsibility to be specially solicitous of his own child's well-being is independent of his sentiments or affections. It is, however, compatible with the Personal Priority View to suppose that the parent is permitted to give priority to the interests of the child actor over the interests of his own child. The Personal Priority View, therefore, cannot account for the moral significance of the special parent-child relation.

It is also possible that those one cares most about may not be people to whom one is specially related. For example, one might care specially about people to whom one is related in a way that in fact lacks objective moral significance. Most people believe that membership in the same race is not a special relation; thus, that two people are members of the same race does not by itself give them a reason to favor each other over members of other races. Yet according to the Personal Priority View, if one of these two people cares more about members of his own race, he is permitted to give the other's interests a certain limited priority over the interests of members of other races. The objective insignificance of the relation between them is irrelevant.

The application of these points to the comparison between the severely retarded and animals with comparable capacities should be obvious. There may be people who do not care more about severely retarded human beings than they do about animals with comparable capacities. It is compatible with the Personal Priority View to suppose that these people have no reason to give priority to the interests of the severely retarded. Indeed, even if one *does* care more about the severely retarded than about comparably endowed animals, it is compatible with the Personal Priority View not to give the interests of the severely retarded any priority. For according to the Personal Priority View, partiality is optional rather than required. If one cares more about treating oneself to a fine meal than about donating one's money to the relief of poverty, the Personal Priority View may imply that it is permissible to indulge oneself in the meal; but it does not imply that one *must* have the meal. Similarly, even if one cares more about the retarded, the Personal Priority View does not imply that one must give them priority. But commonsense morality—and thus Anthropocentrism— holds that we are *required* to give priority to the interests of the severely retarded over the comparable interests of animals.

For those who care more about severely retarded human beings than about animals with comparable psychological capacities, the Personal Priority View implies that it is permissible to give greater weight to the interests of the retarded than to the equal interests of animals. But because it imposes no restrictions on what people may care about, the Personal Priority View also allows this priority to be inverted. It permits the reversal of the pattern of concern endorsed by commonsense morality. If, for example, a person cares more about his pet dog than about a congenitally retarded human being with comparable psychological capacities, the Personal Priority View implies that it is permissible, other things being equal, for that person to give greater weight to the interests of his dog than to the equal interests of the human being. It seems clear, therefore, that the Personal Priority View cannot be invoked in defense of Anthropocentrism.

It is a corollary of our rejection of the Personal Priority View as an account of the morality of special relations that the mere fact that a relation tends to *elicit* partiality does nothing to show that the presence of the relation *justifies* partiality. This should be obvious in any case. Psychologists have found that virtually any group affiliation is sufficient to elicit a tendency to favor other members of one's group. In one experiment, an experimenter told some of the subjects that they tended consistently to overestimate the number of dots that they saw flashed on a screen. Other subjects were told that they tended to underestimate the number of dots. The result was that those who thought that they tended to estimate the number of dots in a certain way (even if in fact they did not) were then disposed to be partial to others whom they believed to share this trait and to be less kindly disposed to those they believed to estimate the number of dots in a different way.[30] Yet nothing could be more obvious than that sharing with someone else a disposition to over- or underestimate the number of dots flashed on a screen is a relation utterly devoid of moral significance.

Or perhaps this is not obvious at all. What *is* obvious is that the relation lacks intrinsic significance. But if the presence of a relation tends to elicit feelings of sympathy, affection, fraternity, or solidarity, this is certainly morally significant. In such a case, however, it is not the relation itself that has moral significance, but the effects of the relation (or of the recognition of the relation among those so related). We must distinguish, therefore, between relations that have *intrinsic* moral significance and those that are only *instrumentally* significant. A relation has intrinsic moral significance if it generates moral reasons for action that are independent of or irreducible to the contribution that the relation might make to any other good. Intrinsically significant relations—of which relations between parents and children or relations between friends or lovers are paradigm and relatively uncontroversial examples—are thus a fundamental or nonderivative source of moral reasons for action. A parent, for example, has a special moral reason to give certain forms of priority to the well-being of his or her child, a reason that is not derived from any considerations other than that she is the parent of this child. A relation is instrumentally significant if its presence has good effects, either for those involved in the relation or for others.

Most relations that are intrinsically significant are also instrumentally valuable. The relation a parent bears to his or her child, for example, is significant in itself but is also a profound source of meaning and happiness in the life of the parent. In other cases, the presence of a relation may have good effects even if the relation itself lacks any intrinsic significance. If, for example, a number of hitherto lonely individuals were prompted to care specially about one another, thereby enriching one another's lives, by believing that they all shared a rare tendency to overestimate the number of dots flashed on a screen, that intrinsically trivial relation would have acquired a certain instrumental significance.

The question whether comembership in the human species is a special relation thus divides into two questions: "Is it intrinsically morally significant?" and "Is it instrumentally significant?" Let us consider the second question first.

Most people believe that our belonging to the same species as the severely retarded constitutes a significant bond between us and them. This belief that membership in the human species is special might have beneficial effects for us, for them, or for both. In many cases, a person's belief that his membership in a certain group is significant can have beneficial effects within his own life. Membership in a nation, for example, is for many people an important source of psychological stability: it provides them a sense of security and belonging and, by merging their individual identities into the larger national identity, enables them to expand the boundaries of the self, thereby enhancing their self-esteem. There is, however, no parallel to this in the case of membership in the human species. Unlike membership in a nation, membership in the human species is not a focus of collective identity. Being human does not significantly differentiate us from anything else; it therefore fails to engage our pride or enhance our sense of identity. Just as no one's sense of self is enlarged by the recognition that one is an animal rather than a plant, so no one's sense of identity is importantly shaped by an awareness of being human rather than being, for example, a rabbit.

There is, however, an alternative possibility, which is that our belief in the significance of membership in the human species is instrumentally valuable for the severely retarded. Perhaps we are motivated by our sense of kinship with the severely retarded to minister to their well-being in ways that exceed what we would be required to do for them by impartial considerations (that is, exceed what would be required by a proper respect for their intrinsic natures). If so, the relation would have a positive instrumental significance. It is arguable, however, that a further effect of our partiality for members of our own species is a tendency to decreased sensitivity to the lives and well-being of those sentient beings that are not members of our species.

One can discern an analogous phenomenon in the case of nationalism. It frequently happens that the sense of solidarity among the members of a nation motivates them to do for one another all that—and perhaps even more than—they are required to do by impartial considerations. But the powerful sense of collective identity within a nation is often achieved by contrasting an idealized conception of the national character with caricatures of other nations, whose members are regarded as less important or worthy or, in many cases, are dehumanized and despised as inferior or even odious. When nationalist solidarity is maintained in this way—as it has been in recent years in such places as Yugoslavia and its former provinces—the result is often brutality and atrocity on an enormous scale. Thus, while nationalist sentiment may have beneficial effects within the nation, these are greatly outweighed from an impartial point of view by the dreadful effects that it has on relations between nations.

I believe that our treatment of the severely retarded and our treatment of animals follow a similar pattern. While our sense of kinship with the severely retarded moves us to treat them with great solicitude, our perception of animals as radically "other" numbs our sensitivity to them, allowing us to abuse them in various ways with an untroubled conscience. We are not, of course, aggressively hostile to them the way nationalists often are to the members of rival nations; we are simply indifferent. But indifference to their lives and well-being is sufficient, when conjoined with motives of self-interest, for the flourishing of various practices that involve both killing and the infliction of suffering on a truly massive scale and that go virtually unchallenged in all contemporary human societies: factory farming, slaughtering animals for food or to take their furs, using them for the testing of cosmetic products, killing them for sport, and so on. When one compares the relatively small number of severely retarded human beings who benefit from our solicitude with the vast number of animals who suffer at our hands, it is impossible to avoid the conclusion that the good effects of our species-based partiality are greatly outweighed by the bad.

One might protest that this claim begs the question: for I have not shown that these various practices involving the use of animals are in fact unjustified. If they are not unjustified, it may not be appropriate to count them as undesirable consequences of our partiality for members of our own species. I believe, however, that the argument so far has indeed established at least a presumption that many of these practices are unjustifiable. That there is such a presumption follows from two assumptions: first, that there are no morally significant intrinsic differences between certain animals and severely retarded human beings with comparable psychological capacities, and second, that we would not be justified in treating severely retarded human beings the way we treat these animals *even if we were not specially related to them*. I have argued for the first of these assumptions, and I believe that most people will find the second intuitively compelling. It is, however, worth pausing to offer an explicit defense of the second assumption.

The second assumption is, in effect, that the difference between our treatment of animals and our treatment of congenitally retarded human beings with comparable psychological capacities cannot be fully justified by reference to our special relation to the latter. For if the only factor that relevantly differentiated the severely retarded from animals with comparable capacities was that the severely retarded are specially related to us, it would follow that it would be permissible, other things being equal, for those who are *not* specially related to them to treat them in the ways in which we treat animals (assuming, of course, we provisionally grant Anthropocentrism's premise that traditional practices involving the use of animals are justified). This means that, if intelligent and morally sensitive Martians were to arrive on Earth, they would be justified, other things being equal, in treating severely retarded human beings in the ways in which we treat animals with comparable capacities. They would, of course, be required to exercise forbearance out of respect for us, for we are (or at least some of us are) specially related to the severely retarded; thus any harms the Martians might inflict on the severely retarded would constitute indirect offenses against us. But this would, it seems, be the *only* reason Martians might have not to subject the severely retarded to forms of treatment that we reserve for animals: for example, eating them, hunting them, experimenting on them, and so on. It is doubtful that this conclusion would be congenial to commonsense intuition. If that is right, an appeal to the special relation we bear to the severely retarded cannot provide a full justification for our treating animals considerably less well than we believe we are required to treat the severely retarded.

To assume otherwise—that is, to assume that our comembership in the human species is the source of the various requirements to treat the severely retarded better than we are permitted to treat comparably endowed animals—seems to have implications that are wholly implausible.[31] To show this, it is necessary to make several assumptions explicit. First, let us assume that there are no morally significant intrinsic differences between animals and severely retarded human beings with comparable psychological capacities and potential. Second, let us grant that comembership in the human species is a special relation. Finally, let us assume that a special relation with another individual strengthens or extends one's moral reasons to benefit or not to harm that individual in a way that is commensurate with or proportional to the moral significance of the relation.

This third assumption—which I will call the *assumption of proportional significance*—requires some elucidation. Suppose that A and B are individuals who have the same intrinsic nature and moral status, but that one is specially related to A in a certain way but not to B. Suppose that all else is equal—in particular, one either bears no other special relation to either or one is specially related to both in other ways but the relations are the same in each case. It seems clear that, insofar as one's moral reasons to benefit or not to harm A are stronger or more extensive than one's reasons to benefit or not to harm B, the degree to which this is the case is proportional to the moral significance of the special relation one bears to A but not to B.

A similar claim holds for the comparative significance of different special relations. Suppose, for example, that one has both a child and a nephew and that, apart from the parental and avuncular relations and their normal entailments, one's relations to both are the same. According to commonsense morality, one owes more to one's child than to one's nephew. And it seems clear that the extent to which one's responsibilities to one's child are greater is proportional to the extent to which the parental relation is more significant morally than the avuncular relation. This is true even though one is equally related to one's child and to one's nephew by comembership in the human species. The moral effects of both the parental relation and the avuncular relation appear to be additive with respect to the effect of the species relation.

Next consider two comparisons between what we are commonly thought to owe to individuals of certain kinds. First, compare what one is thought to owe to a stranger and what one is thought to owe to one's own child. One owes to both, of course, whatever is owed by virtue of their intrinsic natures. Assume that this is the same in both cases. One is related to both by the species relation and to one's child by the parental relation. Assume that one is not specially related to either in any other way. According to the assumption of proportional significance, the divergence between what one owes to a stranger and what one owes to one's child provides a measure of the moral significance of the parental relation.

How great is the divergence? This is of course controversial, even within the boundaries of commonsense morality. Part of the problem is that it is unclear what one owes to strangers. According to commonsense intuition, we have virtually no positive duties (for example, duties to provide aid) to distant strangers, though we do have moral reasons of a modest sort to aid strangers whose plight is immediately present to us. This suggests, perhaps, that mere immediacy is a special relation of sorts, or at least that commonsense morality treats it as such. Let us therefore focus on the distant stranger.

As I noted, commonsense morality holds that there are virtually no requirements to protect or promote the interests or well-being of distant strangers. Yet one's negative duties to distant strangers are much the same as one's negative duties to anyone else. It would be seriously wrong, for example, to cause the death of a remote stranger in order to secure his organs for transplantation—even if this were the only means of saving one's own life. One's negative duties to one's own child are, arguably, somewhat stronger—at least in this sense: that to harm one's own child without justification would be even more seriously wrong than to inflict the same unjustified harm on a stranger. But the main difference between what one owes to one's own child and what one owes to a distant stranger is that one's positive duties to one's child are vastly stronger and more extensive. The main effect of the parental relation is to strengthen and expand the moral reasons one has to protect and promote one's child's well-being.

Consider now a second comparison: that between what, according to common sense, one owes to an animal and what one owes to a severely retarded human being with comparable psychological capacities. For the sake of parallelism, assume that the severely retarded human being is a distant stranger. And assume further that one bears no special relation to the animal. It is, for example, no one's pet. Finally, assume that there are no relevant intrinsic differences between them. It may be that commonsense morality holds that one owes somewhat less to a distant stranger who is severely retarded than to one who is cognitively normal. Commonsense morality may assign the latter a somewhat higher status because of his higher intrinsic nature. But, because common sense holds that one's positive duties to a distant stranger are already minimal, there is no possibility that one's positive duties to a severely retarded stranger could be significantly weaker. And one's negative duties seem, for the most part, equally strong. For example, commonsense morality seems to judge that whether a distant stranger is cognitively impaired makes little or no difference to the wrongness of causing his death in order to obtain his organs for transplantation.

What one is thought to owe to an animal is, by contrast, negligible. Any aid to an animal that is not someone's pet (and not specially valued by human beings for some other reason) is generally regarded as entirely supererogatory. And one's negative duties to animals are effectively limited to a requirement not to cause them harm that is wholly gratuitous. The commonsense view, revealed in our everyday practices, is that it is permissible to harm or kill animals for the sake of almost any end, however trivial. One is permitted, for example, to rear them in misery and kill them for the sake of gratifying one's palate or decorating one's body, to hunt them for sport, to experiment on them to test new cosmetics, and so on. Assuming that there is no relevant intrinsic difference between an animal and a comparably endowed severely retarded human being, the source of one's vastly stronger negative duties to the latter must be the species relation. If we take commonsense intuitions as given, the principal effect of the species relation seems to be an enormous magnification of the scope and strength of one's moral reasons not to cause harm.

In summary, while the parental relation seems primarily to expand and strengthen the moral reasons one has to protect and promote an individual's well-being, the species relation seems to strengthen the reasons one has not to cause harm. It is tempting to conclude that the divergence between what one owes to an animal and what one owes to a severely retarded stranger is greater than the divergence between what one owes to a distant stranger and what one owes to one's own child. To treat a severely retarded stranger in the ways in which we treat animals (for example, to cause him to suffer and die, to eat his flesh, and to wear his skin for decoration) would, it seems, be regarded by common sense as even more heinous than to treat one's own child the way we believe it is permissible to treat distant strangers (for example, to ignore his well-being altogether, to fail to make even minimal sacrifices to save his life). But it has to be conceded that the strengths of the different requirements, as they appear in commonsense judgments about cases, are difficult to measure and compare. Thus I suggest a weaker conclusion: that the divergence between what one owes to an animal and what one owes to a severely retarded stranger is *as great, or nearly as great,* as the divergence between what one owes to a distant stranger and what one owes to one's own child.

Given the assumption of proportional significance, this conclusion implies that the species relation is as significant morally, or nearly as significant, as the parental relation. That, however, is clearly false. Thus, unless we can find a significant intrinsic difference between animals and severely retarded human beings with corresponding capacities, we must conclude that commonsense views require revision. The appeal to the species relation cannot justify the full difference between the forms of treatment common sense approves for animals and those it requires for the severely retarded. We could conclude that common sense greatly underestimates what parents owe to their children. Or we could conclude that it overestimates the scope and strength of our negative duties to distant strangers. It seems more plausible, however, to conclude that it underestimates the scope and strength of our negative duties (and perhaps our positive duties) to animals.

In developing the foregoing argument, I have been assuming that the species relation is morally significant. The question posed was: "Assuming the relation is significant, is it sufficiently significant to justify the difference between our treatment of animals and our treatment of the severely retarded?" But it may be more plausible to deny that the species relation is a special relation at all. There is, after all, no morally significant essence that all the members of the human species have in common. Comembership in the human species is, like membership in the same race, a purely biological relation: it is a matter of genealogy, similarity of genome, or potential for interbreeding. It seems hardly credible that *these* commonalities could be morally significant, any more than membership in the same race could be.

Indeed, as I suggested earlier, our species membership may seem more obviously insignificant if we accept that we are not essentially biological organisms. To see this, consider the relations in which one stands to an anencephalic human infant and to a chimpanzee. An anencephalic infant is a mindless biological organism belonging to the human species. A chimpanzee is a conscious being whose organism belongs to a different species. If one is not an organism but is essentially an embodied mind, one's relation to the chimpanzee may be closer and more significant than one's relation to the anencephalic infant. For one's relation to the infant is only that one *has* an organism that is, like the anencephalic organism, biologically human. But one's relation to the chimpanzee is that one *is,* like the chimpanzee, an embodied mind. The chimpanzee, in short, is of the same kind that one essentially is, whereas the anencephalic infant is only of the same kind that one's organism is.

It might be argued, however, that the mere fact that membership in the same species is a purely biological relation does not prevent it from being morally significant. After all, even the paradigm of a morally significant special relation—the relation between parent and child—has a purely biological component. In the normal case, of course, there is much more to the relation that a parent bears to her child than the mere biological connection: she is at least partiality responsible for its existence and its need for aid, she has voluntarily assumed responsibility for it, she has bonded with it and it with her, and so on. But even in cases in which these factors are absent, the biological connection alone may be morally significant. Consider, for example, the following case:

> *The Sperm Donor.* A man donates sperm at a sperm bank, having signed an agreement that both guarantees him anonymity and absolves him of all responsibility for any child who might be conceived using his sperm. Later, however, a woman who has been artificially inseminated using the man's sperm gives birth to a child with a serious medical condition. Only a bone marrow transplant can save its life. Desperate to find a suitable donor, the woman illegally obtains access to the records at the bank, discovers the identity of the sperm donor, and approaches him with a plea to donate bone marrow in order to save her child's life.

The relation that the sperm donor bears to the child is purely biological in character. It is, like species membership, a genealogical relation, involving a substantial sharing of DNA; but that is all there is to it. In the abstract, it hardly seems that such a relation could be intrinsically morally significant. Yet many people believe, intuitively, that this biological relation gives the sperm donor a special reason to provide bone marrow for the child. To say that the sperm donor has a special reason is not to say that he is obligated to provide the bone marrow. It is only to say that he has a moral reason to provide it that someone completely unrelated to the child does not have. It is entirely possible that that reason is outweighed by countervailing considerations.

If the relation of parent to child, stripped down to its purely biological component, is morally significant, perhaps the relation of membership in the same species is as well. This possibility cannot, I think, be wholly excluded. But if membership in the same species is an intrinsically significant special relation, it is surely one with only minimal moral significance. It can hardly have more significance, for example, than membership in the same race, which is a similar kind of biological relation. And it almost certainly has less significance even than the relation of a pet owner to his or her pet, which is at least a personal relation, involving a history of shared experience and companionship.

The parallel with racial partiality is particularly instructive, for it reminds us that, in general, the moral effect of a special relation is to demand that one do more for those to whom one is specially related than one is required to do for others. (When one is specially related to someone who is specially related to oneself in the same way, one is required to do more for that individual but, in some cases, one may demand more of him or her as well.) The effect of a special relation is *not* to *lower* the moral barriers with respect to those to whom one is not specially related. So, for example, even if membership in the same race is a special relation, the effect may be to require that one do marginally more for members of one's own race than one would be required to do by a proper respect for their intrinsic properties alone; it is not to permit one to do less well by members of other races than is demanded by a proper respect for their intrinsic natures. The baseline for respect for persons—the set of minimal requirements for treating others decently—remains the same. Thus, even if membership in the human species is a special relation, the upshot is only that we may be required to do marginally more for severely retarded members of our own species than we are required to do for comparably endowed animals. The baseline for our treatment of animals is unaffected by the recognition of our special relation to the severely retarded. And one way to determine what that baseline is—to determine what we owe to animals based on a regard for their intrinsic natures—is to ask what we would owe to the severely retarded in the absence of the special relation we bear to them. Thus a rough guide to what we owe to animals is this: we owe to them whatever kind of treatment we believe the severely retarded would be owed in virtue of their intrinsic natures by morally sensitive Martians. We should, in short, treat animals no worse than we believe severely retarded human beings with comparable capacities should be treated by moral agents who are not specially related to them.

Before concluding this section, I should note one further possible defense of Anthropocentrism. There is obviously a great difference between ourselves and animals. Between us and them, there is a deep and significant moral boundary. Suppose we do not know exactly where that boundary lies. In particular, we may be uncertain whether the severely retarded lie on our side of it. But there are pragmatic reasons for drawing a highly visible or conspicuous line. One reason is self-interested: we want to ensure that we are ourselves always on the right—that is, the protected—side of the line. A line that divides our species from others gets all of us permanently on the protected side, whereas a line based on psychological capacity does not. Even though no reader of this book could ever become a congenitally severely retarded human being, each of us could be reduced—by brain damage, stroke, or dementia—to the cognitive level of such a human being. And, if a congenitally severely retarded human being is on the other side of the line, it may in practice be difficult to resist the conclusion that a person who has been reduced to the same cognitive level must be on the other side of the line as well. Thus any line that has the severely retarded on the other side from us leaves us more vulnerable than we would be with a line that has all of the members of our species on the protected side.

There are various things that might be said in response to this argument, but it is sufficient to note only one, which is that the argument implicitly concedes that in reality there is no morally relevant intrinsic difference between the severely retarded and animals with comparable psychological capacities. It urges us to act as if there were such a difference for the sake of self-protection. It is clear, however, that this is an insufficient basis for the commonsense intuitions that Anthropocentrism insists on preserving. Common sense holds that the severely retarded really are significantly different morally from animals with comparable capacities, not just that it is in our interests to pretend that they are.

2.4. *Convergent Assimilation*

I have argued that there are no morally significant intrinsic differences between severely retarded human beings and animals with comparable psychological capacities. And, if we are specially related to the severely retarded but not to animals, the moral significance of the relation is minimal. Thus our options in thinking about the comparative status of the severely retarded and animals with comparable psychological capacities seem to have narrowed to one: that, apart from possibly being permitted a slight degree of partiality for the severely retarded on the basis of their membership in our species, we are required to accord the same degree of concern and respect to severely retarded human beings and animals with comparable capacities. Since we have rejected Consistent Elitism (which holds that we are permitted to treat the severely retarded in the same ways in which we have hitherto treated animals with comparable capacities) and Radical Egalitarianism (which holds that we should treat animals in the same ways in which we have hitherto treated severely retarded human beings at the same cognitive and emotional levels), it seems that we must revise our understanding of the moral status of *both* animals and the severely retarded. According to this view, which we may call *Convergent Assimilation,* we must accept that animals have a higher moral status than we have previously supposed, while also accepting that that moral status of severely retarded human beings is lower than we have assumed. The constraints on our treatment of animals are more stringent than we have supposed, while those on our treatment of the severely retarded are more relaxed.

There are numberless variants of this view. For there are various possible points of convergence between our view of animals and our view of the severely retarded. We might, for example, drastically revise our view of the moral status of animals while revising our view of the severely retarded only a little; or we might alter our view of animals only a little while greatly revising our understanding of the severely retarded. These two possibilities might be represented as follows. (The starting points for the arrows represent the traditional views. The length of an arrow represents the extent to which the traditional view changes.)

severely retarded human beings   →←————————   animals
severely retarded human beings   ————————→←   animals

There are, of course, indefinitely many possible views between these two extremes.

The representations are, however, oversimplifications. It is implausible to suppose that we must seek convergence by equally revising all of our views about animals so that they all more closely resemble our previous views about the severely retarded while also shifting all of our views about the severely retarded in the other direction. It is more reasonable to expect that we should instead alter some of our views about animals quite radically, alter others only a little, and retain yet others unchanged. If we do the same with our traditional beliefs about the severely retarded, we can achieve overall convergence even though some of our original beliefs will remain unmodified.

Consider, for example, traditional beliefs about the permissibility of causing pain (focusing, for purposes of this discussion, on the typical kind of case in which pain is found disagreeable by those who experience it). The commonsense view is that it is as objectionable to cause a certain degree of pain to a severely retarded human being as it is to cause the same amount of pain to a person with normal cognitive capacities. There is, I think, no reason why this view should be substantially modified. The badness of pain is primarily intrinsic; it is not bad only by comparison with what it excludes or only because of its further effects: it is bad in itself. Pains of equal intensity are therefore equally bad, or very nearly equally bad, wherever they occur. (Pain that is equally intense may be equally bad even in the absence of self-consciousness. It is not necessary to have the thought "I am in pain" in order for pain to be bad. As people who have experienced the more intense forms of pain are aware, pain can blot out self-consciousness altogether. Intense pain can dominate consciousness completely, filling it and crowding out all self-conscious thoughts.)

One may, of course, care more about one's own pain, or about that of someone to whom one is specially related; and this pattern of concern may be both rational and moral. But the permissibility of showing greater concern for one's own pain or for the pain of someone to whom one is specially related derives from the significance of the relevant relations (including identity), not from the greater intrinsic importance of the pain. It is thus similar to the permissibility of saving the life of one's own child in preference to the life of a stranger. The reason this is permissible has to do with the importance of the relation; there is no suggestion that the life of one's child is worth more, or is more valuable.

If we are to hold constant the traditional view that the pain of the severely retarded matters as much as the equivalent pain of persons with normal cognitive capacities, the strategy of Convergent Assimilation implies that we must radically revise the traditional view of the moral significance of causing pain to animals. According to this view, animal pain matters much less than human pain. But unless we are willing to accept that the pain of severely retarded human beings matters much less, we should conclude that the pain of animals matters about as much as the equivalent pain of human beings.

It should be conceded, I think, that there are reasons for thinking that the pain of animals matters slightly less. One derives from the fact that the badness of pain is not entirely intrinsic. Pain is also bad because of what economists would call its "opportunity costs"—that is, because it excludes or prevents people from doing or experiencing things that would have had positive value. When one is in intense pain, one cannot, for example, savor the taste of food, concentrate on one's writing, or focus on a conversation with a friend. Because the activities and experiences of persons are generally more valuable than those of an animal, the opportunity costs of pain are in general greater for persons than for animals.

Pain may also have effects that ramify throughout the whole of a life. The infliction of pain on a human infant, for example, may have damaging effects that last for the whole of its subsequent life. Of course, pain or cruelty can have similar effects in the life of an animal. Mistreatment of a puppy can produce a timorous and withdrawn adult dog. But because the life of an animal is shorter, simpler, and contains less of value that can be spoiled by psychic scarring than the life of a person does, these effects are less significant.

There are two other types of effect that pain can have within the life of a person that it generally does not have in the life of an animal. One is that persons can suffer from the anticipation of pain. The other is that persons can suffer from anxiety about the medical significance of pain. Both anticipatory anxiety and anxiety about the meaning of pain can on occasion be worse than the pain itself. (The fact that people can be anxious about the meaning of pain is to some extent offset by the fact that they can also be reassured, in some cases, that pain is temporary and insignificant. Thus the panic and terror that sometimes accompany pain can be mitigated in the case of a person in a way that they cannot in the case of an animal. And, as Thomson has noted in the passage quoted earlier, persons can distract themselves from pain by thinking beyond it.)

These reasons for thinking that the pain of an animal matters slightly less than the equally intense pain of a person are also reasons for thinking that the pain of a severely retarded human being may matter less. For the lives of the severely retarded also contain less of value that is disrupted by pain, and the severely retarded are, like animals, incapable of anticipating future pain or of fretting that pain may be the harbinger of a debilitating or life-threatening illness. If we conclude that the pain of animals in general matters slightly less than the pain of persons, we must draw the same conclusion about the pain of the severely retarded, if other things are equal. (There may, of course, be reasons having to do with side effects for being somewhat more scrupulous about avoiding causing pain to the severely retarded—for example, because the pain of a severely retarded human being is more likely to excite sympathetic distress in other human beings.)

While it seems reasonable to modify traditional beliefs about the wrongness of causing pain to the severely retarded only very slightly (if at all), it is doubtful that we can retain our traditional beliefs about the importance of preserving the lives of the severely retarded with so little alteration. As I noted earlier, the traditional view is that it is seriously wrong to kill an anencephalic infant—perhaps just as wrong as it is to kill an innocent adult human being with normal cognitive capacities. But if Convergent Assimilation is correct, the preservation of this traditional view will commit us to the conclusion that it would be seriously wrong to kill an animal that altogether lacks the capacity for consciousness. And this is unacceptable. Hence it seems that our traditional beliefs about the special sanctity of the lives of severely retarded human beings will have to yield. How much they must yield depends on how drastically we are willing to revise traditional beliefs about the permissibility of killing animals with psychological capacities comparable to those of cognitively impaired human beings. I believe that reaching the optimal point of convergence with respect to killing and letting die requires that traditional beliefs about animals be more extensively revised than traditional beliefs about the severely retarded. Killing animals, and allowing them to die, are morally far more serious matters than we have supposed. But allowing severely retarded human beings to die, and perhaps even killing them, are correspondingly somewhat less serious matters than we have believed. To return again to the most extreme case, I believe that, given a request from the parents (so that there is no objection based on the morality of special relations), it is permissible to kill an anencephalic infant in order to use its organs to save the life of a child with the potential for a life that is worth living. And it is possible that the killing of other infants with extremely severe cognitive impairments may on occasion be justified as well. My reasons for asserting this—both positive reasons and responses to possible objections—will emerge more fully as my argument continues to develop through this and the following two chapters.

Does the acceptance of Convergent Assimilation commit us to the shocking conclusion that severely retarded human beings and animals with comparable psychological capacities should receive the same forms of treatment? I believe that it does not, though the concessions that can be made to commonsense intuitions are not as significant as most people will wish. First, it is unlikely that there is a requirement that we treat the severely retarded no better than we treat animals. It is our prerogative, it seems, to treat the severely retarded as well as we wish. There is no restriction on supererogation, unless a commitment to equality would forbid our making the severely retarded significantly better off than their animal counterparts. And I doubt that a plausible commitment to equality would have this implication. If not, we are morally permitted to lavish resources on the care and comfort of the severely retarded, even if we decline to do the same for animals with comparable capacities.

Of course, if the benefits we bestow on the severely retarded beyond what we owe to comparably endowed animals are supererogatory, we could just as well bestow them on animals instead, if we wished. This is in fact the practice of some people, who dote excessively on their pets. This phenomenon suggests a further restriction on supererogation, which is that the bestowal of a benefit can be supererogatory only if there are no moral demands that the bestowal of the benefit would prevent one from fulfilling. A person who, for example, leaves a fortune in his will with the instruction that it be devoted to the provision of luxuries for his pet cat is arguably neglecting his duties. In a world in which people are dying for want of basic necessities, it is obscene to spend large sums of money on frivolous indulgences for a pet, most of which the pet is incapable of appreciating or benefiting from at all. Prodigality of this sort is wrong, though it may not be the kind of wrong that ought to be legally regulated. Similarly, in a society in which many people experience preventable suffering and premature death, there may be moral limits (though perhaps not ones that are legally enforceable) to the social resources that may be devoted to the care of the severely retarded. Also, as I noted earlier, we need to ensure that our partiality for the severely retarded does not have the effect of dulling our sensitivity to the status of animals. But within these limits, it is certainly permissible to do more for the severely retarded than we are required to do for animals with comparable capacities.

A second possible reason for denying that Convergent Assimilation commits us to treating the severely retarded and comparably endowed animals the same is that we may be specially related to the severely retarded by virtue of our membership in the same species. As I argued earlier, however, this relation cannot have more than minimal moral significance. It may permit us in some circumstances to give priority to the interests of the severely retarded over the similar interests of comparably endowed animals, but the extent of the priority will be extremely limited.

There is, however, a third and much more important reason why it may be not only permissible but morally required to treat severely retarded human beings differently from comparably endowed animals. This reason, too, appeals to the significance of special relations, but the relations in this case are much closer and more important than mere membership in the same biological species. As I noted earlier, each severely retarded human being is someone's child. In most cases, that individual is also someone's sibling, niece, nephew, or cousin. The people who are closely personally related to severely retarded human beings have special reasons to protect and care for them and are typically strongly and appropriately motivated by love and compassion to do so. And the rest of us are morally bound to respect these people's feelings and commitments. We therefore have indirect or oblique moral reasons to be specially solicitous about the well-being of the severely retarded that we do not have in the case of comparably endowed animals.

Our reasons, it should be stressed, do not derive from *our* special relations. It is not because we are specially related to certain people that we must respect their commitments to their children or siblings. Our reason to respect the commitments that other people have because of *their* special relations is independent of any relation we might bear to them. Thus the reason to respect a person's commitment to a severely retarded relative applies to anyone—including Martians, if there were any.

There are, of course, rare cases in which a severely retarded human infant is an orphan, with no one who is specially related to it. It might still be appropriate not to treat it in ways in which it would be permissible to treat a comparably endowed animal, if to do so would be distressing to other people who feel an affinity for the human child that they do not feel for an animal. This is an appeal to a contingent side effect, but it cannot be dismissed as utterly irrelevant.

Many people will find it offensive to suppose that our main reason to treat the severely retarded better than we treat comparably endowed animals is to respect their special relations with others. For this seems to make the status of a severely retarded human being vis-à-vis most of us relevantly like the status of someone else's pet. Just as it is only respect for other people that forbids us to treat a person's pet in ways that it would be permissible to treat a wild animal, so it is mainly this same consideration that forbids us to treat a severely retarded human being in ways in which it would be permissible to treat a comparably endowed animal. But people who are specially related to severely retarded human beings would surely be right to be offended by the suggestion that the individual to whom they are specially related has the status of a pet.

This, however, is to misunderstand the claim that I have made. I have not suggested that the severely retarded are like pets. I have claimed only that they have an enhanced moral standing—or merit a wider array of protections—by virtue of their being specially related to certain people. In this respect, there is a parallel between the situation of the severely retarded and that of pets.

3. EQUALITY AND RESPECT

3.1. *The Time-Relative Interest Account*

Let us pause to take stock. I argued earlier that the Harm-Based Account of the morality of killing is unacceptable, in part because it has the implausible implication that the killing of a fetus is, other things being equal, more seriously objectionable than the killing of child or an adult. Ultimately, the reason it has this implication is that it presupposes that identity is the basis of rational egoistic concern about the future. It evaluates killing in terms of the harm caused to the victim, and it measures the harm by comparing the life as a whole that the victim would have if he were to die with the longer life he would have if he were not to die. The difference in value between these two possible lives is the measure of how much worse it is for the victim to be killed, or of the extent to which the victim is harmed by being killed. The problem with this is that, if identity is not the basis of egoistic concern, what is better or worse for an individual—that is, better or worse where his life as a whole is concerned—may not be what that individual, at a given time, has most reason to care about from a purely egoistic point of view. In such cases, in which there is a divergence between what is better for an individual and what it is rational from an egoistic point of view for that individual to prefer, morality seems to direct us to be guided by the latter. Because of this, the Time-Relative Interest Account, which evaluates an act of killing on the basis of its effect on the victim's time-relative interest in continuing to live, is a superior account of the morality of killing. It preserves the spirit of the Harm-Based Account while rejecting its assumption that identity is the basis of egoistic concern.

In the previous section, we considered an objection to the Time-Relative Interest Account, which is that the account seems to imply that the killing of some innocent human beings—in particular, congenitally severely retarded human beings—is no worse, other things being equal, than the killing of certain animals. While this seemed a powerful objection because the implication is radically at variance with common sense, I have argued that the account can withstand the objection because the objection itself is misguided. For the implication is in fact correct. In this conflict between common sense and the Time-Relative Interest Account, it is common sense that must yield. Certain commonsense beliefs, both about animals and about the severely retarded, have to be revised. Our vague, intuitive commitment to a fundamental moral equality among all human beings—all members of the species *Homo sapiens*—has to be abandoned.

There is, however, another belief about equality that is also threatened by the Time-Relative Interest Account and that we may be even more reluctant to reject. Recall that the Time-Relative Interest Account asserts that the degree to which killing is wrong varies, other things being equal, with the strength of the victim's time-relative interest in continuing to live. The strength of an individual's time-relative interest in continuing to live, in turn, varies primarily with either or both of two things: first, the net amount of good that the individual's future would contain if he were to continue to live and second, the extent to which the prudential unity relations would hold between the individual now and himself later when the goods of his future life would occur. With respect to the second of these two variables, there is relatively little difference among mature, cognitively normal human beings. Significant divergences arise only in the case of human beings with substantially diminished psychological capacities: fetuses, infants, the congenitally severely cognitively impaired, and human beings suffering from brain damage, dementia, and so on. However, with respect to the first variable—that is, the amount of good that an individual's future can reasonably be expected to contain—there is substantial divergence even among mature, cognitively normal human beings.

The amount of good that an individual's future can be expected to contain varies with numerous different factors: for example, the degree of development of the individual's cognitive and emotional capacities, the nature of the individual's temperament and dispositions, the character of the individual's circumstances, the individual's life expectancy, of which the principal determinant is age, and so on. Consequently, people differ widely in the strength of their time-relative interest in continuing to live. In many people—those whose futures promise a great deal of good—the time-relative interest is strong; in others, it is comparatively weak. According to the Time-Relative Interest Account, therefore, killing people of the latter sort is substantially less objectionable morally than killing people of the former sort, if other things are equal. And this implication profoundly offends our sense of the moral equality of persons.

It will help to have some cases for purposes of illustration. The background and circumstances of each case are the same. Raskolnikov is a young man who has read a number of works of contemporary moral philosophy and has become convinced of the overriding importance of saving the lives of innocent people around the world threatened by starvation, dehydration, preventable disease, and so on. He has also been persuaded that there is no morally significant difference, if other things are equal, between killing people and allowing them to die. In each of the following eight cases, therefore, Raskolnikov has painlessly killed one innocent person because, for one reason or another, that person's death would put at his disposal a large sum of money that he could then give to Oxfam for the purpose of saving lives in impoverished areas of the world. Each case can be stated simply by describing the person killed, each of whom is given a name that indicates his salient characteristic. Raskolnikov was aware of each victim's salient characteristic at the time of the killing.

> *Bright* was a person with exceptionally high cognitive and emotional capacities that made possible for him an unusually high level of well-being.

> *Dull* was the same age as Bright but was constitutionally dim-witted and stolid. There was thus a range of goods—including engagement in rich, complexly and subtly layered personal relations, the experience of intense, refined aesthetic states, and so on—that were accessible to Bright but from which Dull was by nature excluded.

> *Cheerful* was, as economists say, an efficient converter of resources into well-being. Whatever happened, he managed to find the bright side.

> *Melancholy* was perpetually lugubrious and depressive. Whatever happened, he derived little satisfaction from it.

> *Fortunate's* circumstances were highly favorable. He was good-looking, wealthy, socially powerful, and physically robust and healthy.

> *Unfortunate* was plagued by bad luck in all the corresponding areas of his life.

> *Young* was twenty years old.

> *Old* was ninety.

These cases come in pairs in which there is a marked contrast between the two victims. Bright contrasts with Dull, Cheerful with Melancholy, and so on. What should be conspicuous is that one victim in each pair has a significantly stronger time-relative interest in continuing to live than the other. Consider, for example, Bright and Dull. I noted earlier that what seems to distinguish us morally from animals is our possession of various higher cognitive capacities: self-consciousness, rationality, autonomy, and so on. But for each capacity that we have and animals lack, or that we have to a significantly higher degree than animals, some of us possess that capacity to a higher degree than others. That is, in each relevant respect in which we differ from animals, we also differ from one another, albeit less markedly. If these differences are so important in distinguishing us morally from animals, how could they fail to distinguish us morally from one another? If, for example, it is because of our higher cognitive and emotional capacities that it is more seriously objectionable to kill one of us than it is to kill an animal, it may seem that, by parity of reasoning, Bright's possession of higher cognitive and emotional capacities must make his killing by Raskolnikov more seriously objectionable than the killing of Dull.

This is, of course, exactly what is implied by the Time-Relative Interest Account of the wrongness of killing. The difference in degree of objectionableness, according to the Time-Relative Interest Account, is perhaps most pronounced in the comparison between the killing of Young and the killing of Old. For the amount of good that Young's life would have contained had he not been killed is, we may assume, many times greater than that which the remaining few years of Old's life would have contained.

Whether the Time-Relative Interest Account implies that Raskolnikov's acts of killing are wrong depends on, among other things, whether it recognizes a moral difference between killing and letting die. Most of us, however, strongly believe that Raskolnikov's acts of killing are wrong. We may well accept that his moral beliefs have a certain plausibility. And we should recognize that he is motivated by a desire to achieve goals that are obviously good. But while we may not think of Raskolnikov as an evil person, we nevertheless believe that he acted wrongly each time he killed an innocent person in order to save a greater number of others. Indeed, the common intuition, which is given expression in the law, is that each act of killing was equally wrong, despite the variable strengths of the victims' time-relative interests in continuing to live. That Bright had a better future in prospect than Dull seems to make no difference to the extent to which the two killings were wrong.

The common view, in short, is that the wrongness of killing persons does not vary with such factors as the degree of harm caused to the victim, the age, intelligence, temperament, or social circumstances of the victim, whether the victim is well liked or generally despised, and so on. Call this the *Equal Wrongness Thesis*. It insists that our understanding of the wrongness of killing should reflect our commitment to the fundamental moral equality of persons. But despite my choice of label, the Equal Wrongness Thesis does not imply that the wrongness of killing persons never varies. It is compatible with that thesis to recognize that the wrongness of killing can vary in ways that are consistent with the fundamental moral equality of persons. It is worth pausing to enumerate the principal factors of this sort, some of which were briefly noted earlier, in order to be clear about the implications of the Equal Wrongness Thesis. (Each consideration I will mention is of course contentious; for each consideration, there are some who deny its relevance to the morality of killing. While I believe that all the factors I will mention may affect the morality of killing, I will not try to defend that belief here—though I will later say a little in defense of the significance of one or two of these factors. For the moment, one may interpret the following paragraphs as an enumeration of some, though not necessarily all, of the variables that are held by commonsense morality to affect the degree to which an act of killing is wrong.)

One type of consideration that may affect the extent to which an act of killing is wrong has to do with the killer's *mode of agency*. Killing itself is an instance of doing rather than allowing and, as such, may be more seriously objectionable, in cases in which death is bad for the person who dies, than a corresponding act that is the same in all respects except that it involves letting a person die. Within the class of killings, an act that involves the creation of a new lethal threat to the victim may be more objectionable than an otherwise similar act that involves the redirection of, or the removal of a barrier to, a preexisting threat.[32] Or, again within the class of killings, an act that kills by intentionally affecting the victim in a certain way may be worse, or more objectionable, than a corresponding act that foreseeably kills the victim but without intending to affect him in any way.[33] Finally, the character of the agent's motive for killing may affect the degree to which his act is wrong—though this (like all the other claims about the significance of a killer's mode of agency) is disputed, with some claiming that the nature of the agent's motive should affect only our evaluation of the moral character of the agent and not our assessment of the morality of his act.

In some cases, the killing of a person is not only not as wrong as other killings of persons, but is not wrong at all. In these cases, some factor or set of factors functions to nullify or override the considerations that normally make killing wrong. I refer to factors of this sort as *defeaters*. There may be various types of defeater; I will mention only the two most obvious. One is a person's moral responsibility—in many but not all cases involving guilt or culpability—for the actual or impending occurrence of a bad outcome, such as a harm or an injustice. A defeater of this sort must be invoked, I believe, in order to explain the permissibility of killing in self-defense or war and, if it *is* permissible, killing as a mode of punishment. (One point of controversy in debates about killing in self-defense and war is whether mere causal responsibility for an unjustified threat, in the absence of fault or even moral responsibility, constitutes a defeater. This is what is at issue in the debate about the permissibility of killing an innocent threat in self-defense.)[34] The second type of defeater is a person's freely requesting or consenting to be killed. An appeal to this defeater must, I believe, be a component of any satisfactory argument for the permissibility of suicide, physician-assisted suicide, or euthanasia.

A third factor that may make one act of killing more seriously wrong than another is the *number* of people killed. In general, and if other things are equal, an act of killing is more seriously wrong the more people it has among its victims.

A fourth factor is the presence of a *special relation* between the killer and the victim. Because a special relation can increase the strength of one's responsibility to another person, it can also exacerbate the wrongness of failing to fulfill one's responsibilities to that person. It is in part the failure to appreciate this fact that is the source of the nearly universal but nevertheless mistaken belief that, if a baby dies because its parents fail to feed it, the parents have killed or murdered the baby. It is obvious, on reflection, that the parents have merely let the baby die; for the failure to provide food to an individual who will otherwise starve is simply a failure to save that individual, and whether the individual is a stranger or one's own child does not affect the nature of the agency involved. But because of the parents' special relation to the child, their failure to feed it is an unusually egregious instance of letting someone die; it is more seriously wrong than standard instances of letting someone die and, indeed, is at least as seriously wrong as standard instances of killing. Thus, because letting one's own child die is as bad as a typical instance of killing, people tend to think that it must *be* an instance of killing. They neglect to take into account that the parent-child relation exacerbates or magnifies the wrongness of allowing the child to die. The important point here, however, is that the presence of this relation has the same effect in the case of killing—hence the deep, visceral abhorrence people felt toward Susan Smith, the woman from South Carolina who a few years ago drowned her two little boys in order to free herself for romance with a man who was averse to being involved with a woman encumbered with children.

There are doubtless other factors that may make one act of killing a person more seriously wrong than another. The foregoing catalogue is meant to be merely suggestive, not exhaustive.

It is important to note that there are cases in which differences of the sorts that distinguish Raskolnikov's various victims are morally relevant. If, for example, one could save Young's life or Old's life, but not both, it seems that it would be better, if other things were equal, to save Young. The fact that he would lose more by dying seems relevant to this choice. There are, in fact, cases involving *killing* in which these differences seem relevant. These are, by hypothesis, cases in which the Equal Wrongness Thesis does not hold. This is not surprising, because these are cases in which killing is not wrong. There are, it seems, rare cases in which it is morally permissible, and perhaps even morally required, to kill an innocent person. Here is an example, a variant of the familiar cases involving runaway trolleys.

> *The Three-Option Trolley Case.* A runaway trolley is careering down the mainline track. If it continues along this track, it will crash into the station, killing hundreds of people, both passengers and people in the station. Although it cannot be stopped or slowed down, it can be diverted onto one or the other of two branchline tracks. Suppose that you are a bystander who happens to have access to the switch that can divert the trolley. You see that there is an innocent bystander on each of the branchline tracks: Young is on the track to the left and Old is on the track to the right. Because the banks are steep, neither will be able to get out of the way of the trolley if you divert it.

Most people believe that, in these circumstances, it would be permissible for you to divert the trolley, thereby killing an innocent person. Some, indeed, believe that you would be morally required to do so. Assuming that it is permissible to kill one or the other, the choice of whom to kill becomes morally like a choice of whom to save. Considerations such as the ages of the potential victims, their respective capacities for well-being, and so on—in short, considerations relevant to determining which has a stronger time-relative interest in continuing to live—become relevant to the choice of whom to kill.

In spite of this, it remains true that, in the various cases in which Raskolnikov kills an innocent person, most of us believe that the killings are not only wrong but equally wrong. The Time-Relative Interest Account, however, has different implications. For it holds that the moral objection to each act of killing varies with the strength of the victim's time-relative interest in continuing to live. Thus, if it were to imply that the killings were all permissible, it would also imply that the justification was stronger in some cases than in others. And if it were to imply that all the killings were wrong, it would also imply that some were less seriously wrong than others—for example, that the killing of Old was less seriously wrong than the killing of Young, since the objection to killing Old was significantly weaker. These implications clash with most people's intuitions.

There are two broad types of response to this conflict. One is to reject the common intuitions as errors of moral phenomenology. The other is to accept the intuitions and seek to determine what it is in these cases that is apparently nullifying the normal role that the degree of harm caused by an act has in determining the extent to which the act is morally wrong.

The proponent of the Time-Relative Interest Account must defend the first of these responses. There are two options. One is to claim that moral intuitions, as such, lack any epistemological authority. I believe that this is unacceptable, though the issue is too involved for me to try to defend my view here.[35] I am going to assume, in this book, that, unless they can be explained away as obvious products of collective self-interest, exploded metaphysics, factual errors, or some other discrediting source, common moral intuitions should be treated as presumptively reliable, or as having some presumptive authority. The other option for the proponent of the Time-Relative Interest Account is to provide a convincing explanation of how we can have been misled in our intuitive responses to the specific cases I have cited in which the various acts of killing seem equally wrong. I will develop and respond to a few suggestions about how our intuitions might be misguided in these cases. I will then turn to the alternative response to these cases, which is to accept that our intuitions are reliable and therefore indicate something important about the morality of killing.

One deflationary explanation of our intuitions in these cases is that they derive from a failure to distinguish between the evaluation of *acts* of killing and the evaluation of *agents*. It may be that our intuition is really only that in each case Raskolnikov reveals himself to be equally fanatical and insensitive, so that we think no worse of him in one case than in another; but we then illegitimately and perhaps unconsciously extrapolate this judgment, mutatis mutandis, to the comparative evaluation of the various acts themselves.

It is true that our judgments about agents and our judgments of their acts are distinguishable. Most of us, however, will continue to judge Raskolnikov's acts of killing to be equally wrong even after we have cautioned ourselves about the danger of conflating the evaluation of agents and the evaluation of their acts. One way to test for this is to alter one of the cases. Suppose that it was not Raskolnikov who killed Young but another philosophy student acting for the same reason: to save a greater number of lives. This other student, however, particularly disliked Young and thus took a certain measure of personal satisfaction in killing him. We should, I think, evaluate this person more harshly than we do Raskolnikov, whom we may imagine to have killed with reluctance and aversion. Thus, *whether or not we retain our tendency to conflate act-evaluation with agent-evaluation,* we should now, *if* we accept the Time-Relative Interest Account, evaluate Raskolnikov's killing of Old as less seriously wrong than the other student's killing of Young. For Raskolnikov's act violated a weaker time-relative interest *and* he, as agent, was less reprehensible. But most of us continue to find the two killings equally wrong.

A second explanation of how our intuition might be an illusion appeals to our sense that all of Raskolnikov's acts of killing were *terribly* wrong. Our sense that they were *equally* wrong might be a result of the fact that the difference between the relative degree of wrongness of any two of these acts may seem insignificant *in comparison with* the absolute magnitude of the wrongness of each. The difference in degree of wrongness tends to be obscured by the enormity of the two crimes.

As a defense of the Time-Relative Interest Account, this is inadequate, for two reasons. Compare the killings of Young and Old. This explanation presupposes that the killing of Old is an egregious wrong. But if the wrongness of killing is a function of the strength of the victim's time-relative interest in continuing to live, and if Old really would have had only a short time to live in any case, so that his time-relative interest in living out his remaining days was comparatively weak, then killing him cannot have been a great crime and may not have been wrong at all. The explanation, in short, presupposes a claim that the Time-Relative Interest Account is committed to denying. Moreover, according to the Time-Relative Interest Account, the difference in strength between the objection to killing Young and the objection to killing Old must *in fact* be enormous, other things being equal, and therefore not easily obscured in the way that this explanation suggests. For the harm that Young suffers is the loss of many decades of life worth living, while that which Old suffers is the loss of only a few months or years. If the degree of objectionableness were a function of the strengths of the victims' time-relative interests in continuing to live, then, even if we assume that the Time-Relative Interest Account judges both acts to have been wrong, the difference in the degree of wrongness would exceed and overshadow the absolute degree of wrongness of killing Old—exactly the reverse of what this explanation suggests.

A third and final critique of the common intuition counters it with another intuition. Let us focus again on the comparison between the killing of Young and the killing of Old. Suppose that one could have prevented one or the other of the two killings but not both. It seems reasonable to suppose that one ought, other things being equal, to have prevented the killing of Young, since he had so much more to lose than Old. And this suggests that the act of killing Young was more seriously wrong, since one ought to have prevented the more serious of the two wrongs.

It is, however, a mistake to assume that which of two acts one should prevent is determined by which would be more wrong. For the importance of preventing others from doing wrong lies primarily in the prevention of the *consequences* of wrongful action. Insofar as we should be concerned to prevent wrongdoing independently of the prevention of its consequences, that concern should be primarily agent-relative: that is, we should be concerned to avoid *doing* wrong. There is little or no reason to minimize the incidence of wrongdoing by others apart from the reason one has to minimize the bad consequences of wrongdoing.

To see this, suppose that one could either prevent a terrorist from detonating a bomb that would kill fifty innocent people or prevent the accidental explosion of a gas main that would kill fifty other innocent people *and* cause minor injuries and trauma to a few others. If one could not prevent both, and assuming that there would be no further relevant differences in consequences (for example, the terrorist will subsequently be captured and prevented from causing further harm whatever one chooses to do), it is not unreasonable to suppose that one ought to prevent the explosion of the gas main. If so, then while the prevention of wrongdoing may be of some significance independently of the prevention of its consequences, it cannot matter much. Thus, even if one ought to have prevented the killing of Young rather than the killing of Old, this is not because the killing of Young was more seriously wrong, but only because it had worse consequences.

There may be other ways of attempting to undermine the common intuition in these cases, but I can think of none that is more persuasive than those I have reviewed. It therefore seems warranted to determine whether a convincing case can be mounted in defense of the common intuition that Raskolnikov's killings in the various cases are equally wrong.

3.2 The Requirement of Respect for Persons

Let us assume that the Equal Wrongness Thesis is correct: all acts of killing persons are equally wrong, if other things—such as agency, defeaters, numbers, and so on—are equal. I have suggested that, if this view is correct, it is fatal to the Time-Relative Interest Account. Is that necessarily true? It is true if people differ in the strength of their time-relative interest in continuing to live. But if each person's time-relative interest in continuing to live is of the same strength, then the Time-Relative Interest Account will be compatible with the Equal Wrongness Thesis. It may, of course, seem absurd to suppose that all people's time-relative interests in continuing to live are of equivalent strength. But a case might be made for this claim, as follows. Recall that the strength of an individual's time-relative interest in continuing to live is a function of two variables: first, the extent to which the prudential unity relations would hold between the individual now and himself in the future and second, the value of the life the individual would have if he were to live. I have already suggested that, in the case of *persons,* there is very little variation in the first of these variables. It is only in cases in which the complexity of an individual's mental life falls, or is about to fall, below the level that defines personhood that psychological unity is sufficiently diminished to have a significant effect on the strength of the individual's time-relative interest in continuing to live. And where the second variable is concerned, it is commonly claimed that the lives of all persons have equal value. This is, indeed, a fundamental tenet of liberal egalitarianism: that no person's life matters more or has greater value than the life of any other person. Putting these claims together, one might draw the conclusion that all people (where "people," recall, is the plural of "person") have an equal time-relative interest in continuing to live.

While this conclusion is wholly incompatible with the argument of chapter 2, it is not unknown in the literature. It seems, for example, that the assumption that all human lives (and therefore the lives of all human persons) are of equal value is what lies behind the claim of Paul Ramsey that "all our days and years are of equal worth whatever the consequence; death is not more a tragedy at one time than another," nor worse for one person than another.[36]

The idea that all people have an equal time-relative interest in continuing to live because all people's lives are of equal value involves an equivocation. There are two concepts of the value of a life that are being conflated here.

1. In one sense, the value of a life is determined by the character of the contents of the life. The value of a life in this sense is the value that the life has for the person who lives it; it is equivalent to the extent to which the life is worth living.
2. In another sense, the value of a life is the value or worth of the individual or person whose life it is. This value is largely or completely unaffected by what happens within the life—by the character of its contents. It is instead determined by the nature of the subject of the life—by the particular properties and capacities that make that individual the kind of thing that he or she is.

Let us reserve the phrase *the value of a life* for the first of these two notions and refer to the second as *the worth of the individual* or person whose life it is.[37]

It is obvious that not all people's lives have equal value in the first sense. Some people are more fortunate: their lives go better than those of most others. This is compatible with the idea that all lives—or, more precisely, all people—have equal value in the second sense. It is clearly not necessary, in order for two people to matter equally or to have equal value or worth, that they should have lives that are equally good or worth living.

Let us return to the question whether all people have an equal time-relative interest in continuing to live. We are assuming that all killings of *persons* are equally wrong, if other things are equal. Because we are concerned only with persons, we can assume that there are no substantial variations in the strength of the prudential unity relations. If, therefore, people's time-relative interests in continuing to live are all equal, it must be because the values of their future lives are all equal. And that will be true only if we interpret the value of a life in the second of the two senses distinguished above. But is the strength of a person's time-relative interest in continuing to live a function of his worth as a person? Is the badness of death proportional to the worth of the victim?

If the badness of death were proportional to the worth of the person, and if all persons have positive worth, death would always be bad (and, of course, equally bad, if all persons have equal worth). This is implausible; in some cases, when a person's future life would be past the point at which life ceases to be worth living, it can be good for that person to die, irrespective of his or her inherent worth as a person. It is obvious, in other words, that the badness of death is a function of the value of life in the first rather than the second of our two senses. The badness of death is, other things being equal, proportional to the expected value of the *contents* of a person's projected future life. But the value of life in this sense varies from person to person. Thus all deaths are not equally bad; therefore, because the strength of a person's time-relative interest in continuing to live varies with the degree to which death would be bad for him, people's time-relative interests in continuing to live are not all equal in strength. Therefore the Time-Relative Interest Account of the wrongness of killing is incompatible with the commonsense view that all killings of persons are equally wrong.

The Time-Relative Interest Account cannot be rescued by implausibly altering our understanding of the badness of death. We must, therefore, seek a different understanding of the wrongness of killing. The foregoing discussion prompts an obvious suggestion. If the killing of persons is always equally wrong, and if all persons are of equal worth, the wrongness of killing may be a function of the worth of the person (rather than of the value of the person's subsequent life). According to this view, while the *badness of death* is correlative with the value of the victim's possible future life, the *wrongness of killing* is correlative with the value or worth of the victim himself.

The intuitive idea behind this view is that a person, a being of incalculable worth, demands the highest respect. To kill a person, in contravention of that person's own will, is an egregious failure of respect for the person and his worth. It is to annihilate that which is irreplaceable, to show contempt for that which demands reverence, to assert a spurious authority over one who alone has proper authority over his own life, and to assume a superior position vis-à-vis one who is in reality one's moral equal. Killing is, in short, an offence against what might be called a *requirement of respect* for persons and their worth. Indeed, because killing inflicts the ultimate loss—the obliteration of the person himself—and is both irreversible and uncompensable, it is no exaggeration to say that it constitutes the ultimate violation of the requirement of respect.

If all persons have equal worth, their worth cannot be based on their achievements, which vary. Thus, unlike the familiar form of respect that is a proper response to achievement, the respect that one is due as a person is not earned; it is one's due simply by virtue of one's intrinsic nature as a person. What are the properties of persons that are the basis of their worth? It is clear that they must be those properties, or some subset of those properties, that relevantly differentiate persons from animals. I have claimed that these properties are psychological capacities, though I have not attempted to defend the special significance of any particular capacity or set of capacities.

If this is right—that the basis of one's worth as a person is some set of psychological capacities—then one cannot lose one's worth except, perhaps, by losing the relevant capacities. (Because the capacities are, by hypothesis, possessed by all persons, and because personhood is essentially a matter of psychological capacity, it is reasonable to assume that the relevant capacities are both necessary and sufficient for personhood. If so, the loss of these capacities would entail the loss of personhood. One could not lose the capacities that are the basis of one's worth without ceasing to be a person.) Just as the respect one is owed as a person is not earned by deeds, so it cannot be forfeited by deeds. People who, for example, do evil, or indeed *are* evil, do not thereby lose their worth as persons or forfeit their claim to respect. They are not reduced to the status of dangerous wild animals. While it may be right to restrain or punish or perhaps even kill them, the justification cannot be that they have lost their entitlement to respect. The demands of respect for persons must somehow be compatible with the infliction of such harms—perhaps because, in these cases, they are overridden by countervailing demands, such as the demand that harms be distributed in accordance with justice, where justice is sensitive to considerations of innocence and responsibility.

There is another possible misunderstanding of the notion of respect for persons that must be guarded against. I have suggested (following a familiar pattern of reasoning) that persons deserve respect because of their worth, and that their worth derives from their intrinsic nature as persons—in particular, from their possession of certain higher psychological capacities that distinguish them from animals. But although these psychological capacities are ultimately the *basis* for respect, or that which makes persons worthy of respect, they are not themselves the *objects* of respect. Respect is for persons, not for their capacities alone.

It is important to stress this aspect of the view I am advancing, for there are related views that have importantly different implications. Some people, for example, believe that human life has a certain intrinsic value or sanctity, and that respect for the sanctity of human life is different from and may even conflict with respect for the person whose life it is. Thus, in a concurring judgment in a case concerning the right to die, Supreme Court Justice Antonin Scalia asserted that it can be imperative to protect the sanctity of human life by refusing to allow a person to die, even if continued life would be both contrary to that person's interests and opposed by his or her autonomous will.[38] (I will return to this view in section 7 of chapter 4 and in section 2.2 of chapter 5.) The view that I have sketched might be interpreted in a similar way. It might be thought that, if certain psychological capacities are the basis of respect, killing must be equally wrong whenever those capacities are present. If that were the case, then even if a person's life had passed beyond the point at which it ceased to be worth living, and even if the person autonomously wished to die, it would nevertheless be a violation of the requirement of respect to kill him or even, perhaps, to assist him in committing suicide. For killing the person would still constitute the destruction of a being with incalculable worth.

One must not be misled by the possible connotations of the notion of worth to suppose that killing is wrong simply because, by eliminating a person who has worth, it reduces the total amount of worth in the world, or the total of that which has worth. Properly understood, the view I wish to defend does not recognize a concept of respect for a person's worth that is independent of respect for the person himself. A person may have special worth by virtue of having certain capacities, but he is not merely a container for those capacities. I will defend this understanding of respect for the worth of persons at considerable length in section 2.2 of chapter 5.

The foregoing remarks are intended to elucidate a general, alternative account of the wrongness of killing. According to this view, killing is wrong because it involves a failure of respect for the worth of the victim, where the worth of the victim is entirely independent of the value—be it personal value (that is, the value to him), instrumental value (the value to others), or impersonal value—of the contents of his possible life in the future. The wrongness of killing, therefore, does not vary with the strength of the victim's time-relative interest in continuing to live or with the degree of harm the victim suffers in being killed; it varies instead with the worth of the victim. Assuming, as liberal egalitarianism does, that all persons have equal worth, this account, which I will call the *Intrinsic Worth Account,* implies that all killings of persons are equally wrong, if other things are equal.

The Intrinsic Worth Account appears to have the same virtues that I earlier ascribed to both the Harm-Based Account and the Time-Relative Interest Account; that is, it, too, offers plausible explanations of why killing persons is more seriously wrong than killing animals and why killing animals of some types is more wrong than killing animals of other types. Because the worth of persons is based on their possession of psychological capacities that animals either lack altogether or possess only in more rudimentary forms, animals must have significantly lesser worth than persons. This, according to the Intrinsic Worth Account, is why killing them is significantly less morally objectionable. Moreover, because some animals possess much higher psychological capacities than others, their worth is greater and therefore killing them is more seriously wrong, if other things are equal, than killing animals with lower capacities.

According to the Intrinsic Worth Account, the degree to which an act of killing is wrong is not directly affected by the degree of harm caused to the victim. But there remains a contingent correlation between the two. For those whom it is most wrong to kill are, on this view, those with the highest worth, and those with the highest worth are those with the highest cognitive and emotional capacities. But higher cognitive and emotional capacities also make it possible for an individual to experience higher levels of well-being—levels that are not accessible to beings with lower capacities. Hence those individuals with the highest worth will also tend to have lives with the greatest value—that is, lives that are most worth living. They are therefore likely to be harmed to a greater degree by death, and thus by being killed, than those of lesser worth. When this is so, the implications of the Intrinsic Worth Account coincide with those of the Time-Relative Interest Account. But the correlation here is only rough; for even those with the highest capacities are not immune to misfortune. In cases in which a person's future life would be short or of a low level of quality despite her high capacities (or perhaps even *because* of them, since unusual sensitivity can also make one vulnerable to depths of misfortune that are not possible for those with lesser cognitive endowments), the Intrinsic Worth Account and the Time-Relative Interest Account could diverge quite considerably in their assessments of how wrong it would be to kill that person.

Another virtue of the Intrinsic Worth Account is that it seems to offer an explanation of the common view that, while neither the quality of life nor the life expectancy of the victim affects the degree to which an act of killing is wrong, the *number* of victims that the act has *does*. For while neither the quality of a person's life nor the expected quantity of his future life affects his worth as a person or, therefore, the wrongness of killing him, it is at least arguable that killing a greater number of people constitutes a greater offense against the worth of persons than killing a lesser number. Thus, for example, an act that kills two persons constitutes two offenses against the worth of persons, while an act that kills one person involves only one such offense.

As it stands, however, the Intrinsic Worth Account is also vulnerable to serious objections. I will mention two. First, it makes the wrongness of killing vary with the worth of the victim all the way down to the lowliest animal, ignoring the degree of harm caused to the victim. Below the level of persons, however, this seems a mistake. In contrast to the common judgment about the cases involving the killings of Young and Old, it seems less objectionable to kill a dog of advanced years than to kill a dog in the flush of youth, even if both have comparable psychological capacities and therefore, presumably, equal worth. In the case of animals, the wrongness of killing does seem to vary with the degree of harm caused to the victim.

The idea that the wrongness of killing varies with the worth of the victim all the way down the scale of animal life also presupposes that the notions of worth and respect for worth retain their applicability all the way down; but this assumption becomes increasingly doubtful the farther down the scale one goes. In Kant's moral theory, which is the source of our notion of the worth of persons, "worth" denotes a form of value beyond the possibility of price, beyond estimation. It is absolute, does not admit of degrees, and is possessed only by rational, autonomous beings—that is, by persons. Thus, for Kant, all worth is equal worth. I am not committed to that concept of worth (though neither am I convinced that it is wrong). As I understand it, the claim that persons have intrinsic worth is intended only to articulate the idea that persons have a form of moral standing that demands respect but is entirely independent of the value their lives have, or of the goods their lives might contain. But it is not obvious that even this is true in the case of animals, or at least the lower animals. It is not obvious, in particular, that our reason not to kill an animal extends beyond our reason to preserve for it, or at least not to deny it, whatever goods its future might contain. In the case of persons, by contrast, our central reason seems, as the case of Old suggests, to stem at least in part from a demand that we respect their autonomous wills in a matter of supreme concern to them. Animals, or at least most animals, do not have autonomous wills; nor can their wills be set against their being killed. They may react instinctively to threats, including lethal threats, but that is another matter. To set one's will in opposition to death, and thus to being killed, one must be able to conceive of the contrasting possibilities of one's own life continuing or, alternatively, ceasing. And this is something that very few, if any, animals are able to do.

This first objection to the Intrinsic Worth Account may be addressed by stipulating that there is a threshold along the scale that measures the psychological capacities that relevantly distinguish persons from animals. The wrongness of killing beings above this threshold is to be explained primarily in terms of the requirement of respect for the worth of persons. In the case of beings above the threshold, the wrongness of killing does not vary with the strength of the victim's time-relative interest in continuing to live or with the degree of harm the victim suffers in being killed. But the wrongness of killing beings that lie below the threshold is explained primarily in terms of the frustration of their time-relative interest in continuing to live. Below the threshold, the morality of killing is governed entirely by the Time-Relative Interest Account.

This response to the first objection to the Intrinsic Worth Account in effect proposes two distinct accounts of the morality of killing, each of which applies to a different range of cases. The Intrinsic Worth Account governs the morality of killing individuals above the threshold—for example, persons—while the Time-Relative Interest Account governs the morality of killing individuals below the threshold—for example, animals. Let us call this hybrid account of the morality of killing the *Two-Tiered Account*.

The idea that the morality of killing is divided in this way echoes the familiar idea that morality itself is divided into different spheres—for example, one concerned with beneficence and another concerned with rights or justice. The version of this general idea that best corresponds to the Two-Tiered Account is Warren Quinn's division of morality into what he calls the "morality of humanity" (which I will rechristen the *morality of interests*) and the *morality of respect*. The morality of interests is concerned with the effects our action has on the well-being, the interests, or the time-relative interests of others. By contrast, the morality of respect is, as Quinn puts it, "made up of constraints on our behavior toward others that spring from our recognition of others as mature agents on an equal moral footing with ourselves. The fundamental attitude underlying virtuous action of this type seems to be respect for what can be thought of as the moral authority of others."[39] (Scanlon's view, to which I alluded earlier, involves a similar partitioning of morality. His claim that our treatment of certain others must be governed by principles that they could not reasonably reject may be interpreted as one way of understanding what is required by respect.) The two spheres, it should be stressed, are not necessarily exhaustive. There is, I believe, a further sphere concerned with *impersonal* considerations. There may be others as well.

Although Quinn represents himself as following a Kantian tradition,[40] his view differs radically from that of Kant, who, on one plausible interpretation, held that the morality of respect is in fact coextensive with the *whole* of morality. Thus he denied that there could be duties with respect to animals other than those that are owed to people but of which animals are the accidental beneficiaries (for example, a duty to avoid cruelty to animals lest it coarsen one's nature, making it likelier that one will be cruel to people). Like Quinn, I believe that this is a serious mistake. Our treatment of animals lies securely within the scope of morality; but it lies entirely within the sphere of the morality of interests. Our relations with other persons, by contrast, come within both spheres: we are required to show proper regard for the interests and well-being of other persons, but we are also constrained by a further set of protections that apply to persons but not to animals.[41] The threshold along the scale that measures psychological capacity marks the point at which individuals not only merit consideration of their interests but also have sufficient worth to command respect. Let us therefore call this threshold the *threshold of respect.*

If we are to recognize an area of morality in which the principal requirement is one of respect, we will obviously want to know what is required of us in order to show proper respect for those to whom it is due. According to some accounts of the morality of respect, one may proceed inferentially from the concept of respect together with a set of claims about the grounds or bases of respect to conclusions about what sorts of act are or are not compatible with respect for persons.[42] For various reasons, some of which will emerge later, I do not believe that this is a plausible or fruitful strategy. I believe, in fact, that we must proceed in exactly the opposite way, despite the misgivings we may have about the seemingly unsystematic nature of this method of inquiry. I believe that we must instead begin with a range of intuitions that arise from sustained reflection about particular problems and cases and then seek to organize, make sense of, and in some cases revise these beliefs within a coherent framework of principles and concepts. In the present case, we begin with a set of sharply contrasting intuitions about the killing of persons and the killing of animals. We believe, for example, that the killing of an animal may be more or less morally objectionable depending on how strong a time-relative interest that animal has in continuing to live. In the case of persons, however, the wrongness of killing does not vary in this way; killing is always equally wrong, if other things are equal. Similarly, we believe that it can be permissible to sacrifice an animal for the greater benefit of other animals or persons. (Thus Judith Jarvis Thomson speaks for common sense when she writes that it would "be permissible to kill one chicken to save five chickens."[43]) In the case of persons, however, we believe that it is wrong to kill one person as a means of preventing the killing of a greater number of others. (Many people, myself included, believe that if the number of others becomes sufficiently high, killing the one may become permissible. In extreme cases, the demands of respect may simply be overwhelmed by countervailing pressures from the morality of interests.) My suggestion is that the idea that there is a requirement of respect for the worth of persons helps to illuminate and support these common intuitions. What else is involved in or required by respect for persons is something that we have to discover, not by deduction, but by further exploration of how and why some of our most compelling intuitions are resistant to explanation or accommodation within the morality of interests.

If this is right, then to fill out the details of what is required by the morality of respect we must explore the intuitive terrain both carefully and extensively. And there are certainly many pressing questions to be addressed. Here I will briefly note several important challenges to the idea that the morality of killing persons is governed by a requirement of respect that implies or supports the Equal Wrongness Thesis.

There are, first, questions about how considerations of interests and considerations of respect combine or interact to determine the morality of various acts involving the infliction of harm. It *seems* that, in most cases involving the killing of persons, the two types of consideration do not combine at all. Certainly they are not additive. If they were, Raskolnikov's killing of Young would be more seriously wrong than his killing of Old, for the killing of Young would involve an *equal* violation of respect and yet inflict a *greater* harm. It would, that is, be opposed by a stronger array of considerations and would, therefore, be more seriously objectionable, or wrong. Yet these two killings see equally wrong. In cases of these sorts, the morality of interests seems altogether supplanted by the morality of respect—except that, as I noted earlier, it also seems that, in certain extreme cases, considerations of interests can override considerations of respect, which shows that considerations of interests seem always to be at least *potentially* relevant.

There is also the question why the Equal Wrongness Thesis holds for acts of killing, while there is, apparently, no parallel in the case of acts of nonlethal harming. It seems that the requirement of respect for persons condemns not just killing but various forms of nonlethal harming as well. Surely, for example, it is incompatible with respect for a person, if other things are equal, to cause him extreme agony for an hour. It also seems a failure of respect, again if other things are equal, to cause him moderately severe pain for ten minutes. But, though both of these acts are violations of respect, the infliction of extreme agony for an hour seems a more serious violation, and is more seriously wrong. But if the gravity of the violation varies with the extent of the harm in nonlethal instances, why should it not do so in cases of killing as well? Indeed, is it not a good explanation of why killing is generally more seriously wrong than acts of nonlethal harming that it inflicts a greater harm and therefore constitutes a more egregious violation of respect?

There are also cases that challenge the plausibility of the Equal Wrongness Thesis. Here are two examples.[44] Consider, first, an act of killing a person exactly one week before he would otherwise certainly have died from an entirely different cause. The Equal Wrongness Thesis implies that this act is as seriously wrong as an otherwise comparable act of killing that deprives its victim of many years of life. Now consider an act that causes a person to be unconscious during the last week of his life. Suppose that, for this person, this is no worse than it would have been to have been made unconscious for a week during an earlier part of his life. It seems that killing this person a week before he would have died is no worse for him than making him unconscious for that week. But surely, in general, killing a person is a more serious violation of respect than making him unconscious for a week. Should we, therefore, conclude that killing this person a week before he would have died is more seriously wrong than making him unconscious for that week, even though the two acts are equally bad for him? That is hard to believe. Perhaps we should say that making him unconscious for that week is as wrong as killing him a week before he would have died. But, given the Equal Wrongness Thesis, this implies that making him unconscious during his last week of life is as wrong as an act of killing that deprives its victim of many years of life. And that is implausible. Perhaps the most plausible option is to reject the Equal Wrongness Thesis and accept that killing a person a week before he would otherwise have died is not so seriously wrong as killing someone who would otherwise have lived many years.

Second, compare two acts of killing, both by poisoning. One of the killings is accomplished with a fast-acting poison that kills within minutes, while the other is done with a slow-acting poison that causes death only after ten years. The Equal Wrongness Thesis holds that the two acts are equally wrong. But it may be tempting to think of the use of the slow-acting poison as less seriously wrong.

There may well be entirely convincing replies to these and other questions and challenges. I will not attempt to formulate them here. For my concern in this book is not with the morality of killing persons—that is, with the morality of killings that are wrong because they involve a violation of the requirement of respect. My concern is instead with the morality of killing in marginal cases, where the presumption is that the individual killed is below the threshold of respect. In cases in which that presumption stands, the details of what is required by the morality of respect are irrelevant. If, on the other hand, there are cases in which an apparently marginal individual is in fact above the threshold (which could conceivably be true of an individual who is not now a person but once was, or who has the potential to become one), then we already know something of quite fundamental importance: that there is at least a presumption that killing that individual would be as wrong as killing any other person normally is (that is, gravely wrong), if other things are equal. There are, of course, controversial questions about when other things are not equal—questions concerning different modes of agency, defeaters, special relations, and so on. I will address some of these questions later as they arise in particular contexts—contexts in which special circumstances may seem to make it permissible, or objectionable to a lesser degree than normal, to kill an individual even if we assume that that individual is above the threshold of respect. But I will not attempt to develop a general account of the morality of respect, even as it applies to the morality of killing.[45]

Let us now turn to a second objection to the Intrinsic Worth Account. Recall that we have restricted the scope of that account so that, as a component of the more comprehensive Two-Tiered Account, it applies only to the killing of individuals above the threshold of respect. Assuming that personhood is a sufficient condition for being above that threshold, the account continues to apply to all cases involving the killing of persons. Even given this restriction of its scope, the Intrinsic Worth Account remains vulnerable to a second objection provided we assume, as I think we must, that the basis for the sort of worth that demands respect is some set of psychological capacities. For even among persons, the relevant psychological capacities are possessed to a higher degree by some than by others. We have been assuming that all persons have equal worth; but, if one's worth is determined by one's psychological capacities and these are variable among persons, it may seem that we should conclude that some persons have a higher degree of worth than others. But, if we were to draw that conclusion, we would lose our basis for the Equal Wrongness Thesis. The Intrinsic Worth Account would imply that it is more seriously wrong, other things being equal, to kill people with higher capacities than it is to kill those with lower capacities. Although it would, for example, imply that the killings of Young and Old were equally wrong, it would imply that the killing of Dull was less seriously objectionable than the killing of Bright. It would, in short, have some of the inegalitarian implications that subverted the Time-Relative Interest Account.

There is an obvious response to this objection that parallels the suggested response to the first objection. This is to claim that, somewhere along the scale that measures psychological capacity, there is a point at which individual worth ceases to fluctuate with variations in psychological capacity. There is a certain level of psychological capacity such that the corresponding level of worth cannot be exceeded. All individuals above that level of capacity have equal worth. Call this point on the scale the *threshold of equal worth.*

It seems plausible to suppose that the threshold of equal worth and the threshold of respect coincide—that is, that the point at which individuals have sufficient worth to command respect is also the point at which worth ceases to vary in degree. If this is so, then for most purposes we can refer to the two thresholds together as "the threshold." We can also stipulate—though this seems independently plausible—that a "person" is simply an individual with psychological capacities sufficiently high to be above the threshold. Given these assumptions, the Two-Tiered Account implies that the killing of persons is wrong (in those cases in which it is wrong) because it violates a requirement of respect, and that all such acts of killing are equally wrong, if other things are equal, irrespective of the degree of harm that the victim suffers in being killed.

This is all neat and tidy, but does it have any plausibility? If certain psychological capacities are the basis of a person's worth, it seems that the possession of those capacities to a markedly higher degree ought to give a person a higher degree of worth. The idea that there is a threshold beyond which worth ceases to vary with the capacities that are its basis may seem an arbitrary, ad hoc stipulation motivated entirely by a desire to salvage our egalitarian intuitions.

There are certainly cases in which claims to equality can be founded on people's possession of a property which itself has a basis that varies from person to person. The property that grounds the claim to equality must be what John Rawls calls a "range property." "The property," Rawls notes by way of illustration, "of being in the interior of the unit circle is a range property of points in the plane. All points inside this circle have this property although their coordinates vary within a certain range. And they equally have this property, since no point interior to a circle is more or less interior to it than any other interior point."[46] One example of a range property commonly invoked in ethical debates is competence. Most human beings have, we believe, an equal right to make certain sorts of decision affecting their own lives. Some human beings, however—small children and individuals with certain types of cognitive deficiency—lack this right. They lack it because they lack the cognitive capacities that would enable them to understand what is at issue, deliberate intelligently about the matter, and reach a rational decision. The cognitive capacities that make rational deliberation possible are, however, a matter of degree. Some people possess them to a higher degree than others. Yet we do not believe that those who possess them to a preeminent degree have a stronger right to autonomy or self-determination than those who possess them only minimally. We believe, instead, that the right to self-determination is possessed equally among all those whose cognitive capacities exceed a certain threshold—that is, all those who are *competent*. The justification for this is, as Daniel Wikler has argued, that "a given challenge may be wholly and fully met by the use of a certain amount of intelligence, if the challenge is not too great. Although some persons may have more intelligence than others, they will be no more competent at performing certain tasks; their added power is simply unused surplus."[47] Competence here is understood as a range property that does not admit of degrees, though it is based on an individual's possession of various cognitive capacities that do vary in degree. One response to the charge that it is arbitrary to postulate a threshold of equal worth is to claim that worth is a range property based on psychological capacities that vary, in just the way that competence is a range property based on cognitive capacities that vary.

There are, however, objections to the analogy with competence. First, our tendency to treat competence as a range property—a property that is all-or-nothing rather than a matter of degree—is morally motivated. There is a clear sense in which competence may be regarded as a matter of degree. One person is more competent than another with respect to making decisions of a certain sort if his cognitive capacities are more highly developed in ways that make it more likely that his deliberations will yield decisions that are rational. The fact that in most matters of social policy we decline to understand competence in this way appears to be a result rather than the basis of our commitment to recognizing an *equal* right to self-determination among most human beings. There is, in other words, a problem of justifying our treatment of competence as a range property that closely parallels the challenge of justifying our understanding of worth as a range property.

Wikler's remarks suggest a response. There are surely some sorts of decision that demand a certain minimum degree of intelligence but that are likely to be made equally rationally by all those who have the necessary minimum intelligence. In these instances, further intelligence above the minimum is, as Wikler says, "surplus" with respect to the relevant decision-making capacity. It would be pointless to suppose that those with intelligence beyond the minimum would have a stronger right to self-determination with respect to decisions of the relevant sort. In these cases, there is a compelling reason for treating competence as a range property.

The problem is that there is no obvious parallel between the notion of competence in these cases and our notion of worth. The moral significance of competence in these cases is instrumental: competence is necessary for the achievement of a certain goal—namely, reaching a rational decision. If additional increments in the basis of competence are not useful in achieving that goal, there is no reason to treat competence as a matter of degree. But the moral significance of the worth that demands respect is not instrumental. There is nothing that worth is good or useful *for.* Hence there is no reason, parallel to that in the case in which competence is an instrumental value, to suppose that the worth of individuals ceases to vary with the capacities that are its basis.

I will not pursue this problem further. If we wish to preserve the common intuition that, if other things are equal, all killings of persons are equally wrong, we may well have to mount a defense of the idea that, beyond a certain threshold, all worth is equal worth—that is, that worth is, beyond that point, a range property. I myself share the common intuition and believe that intuitions that are as strong and as widely accepted as this ought not to be lightly abandoned. Every effort ought to be made to determine what can be said in their support before we accept that they must be revised or rejected. Nevertheless, if the argument in subsequent parts of the book is correct, it is not important for my purposes here to defend the idea that all killings of individuals above the threshold are equally wrong, other things being equal. My main purposes are, as I noted earlier, to defend the permissibility of certain killings of beings below the threshold, and to show that some killings of persons are not wrong at all because they are compatible with what is required by respect. What would be most helpful for my argument, therefore, is a criterion for determining whether an individual belongs above or below the threshold.

3.3. *The Basis of the Worth of Persons*

This book is concerned with the moral status of various beings that are "marginal" in the sense of being very different in seemingly important ways from morally innocent, cognitively normal adult human beings, our dealings with whom constitute the core of the subject matter of moral philosophy. Among these marginal beings are animals, human fetuses and infants, anencephalic infants, severely retarded human beings, and human beings with acquired cognitive deficiencies of varying degrees of severity. If the Two-Tiered Account of the wrongness of killing is correct, we must determine whether beings of each of these types lie above or below the threshold in order to understand the conditions in which killing them might be permissible. If a being lies below the threshold, the conditions that would justify killing it will be different from and less stringent (that is, easier to satisfy) than those that would have to be satisfied in order to justify the killing of a being above the threshold.

To determine whether different beings belong above or below the threshold, we obviously must know where the threshold lies, and this depends, of course, on what the basis is of the worth that demands respect. It is the nature of the basis of worth that determines the scope of the requirement of respect.

There is a history of speculation about the basis of the worth that demands respect. Some of this speculation occurs outside the context of discussions explicitly concerned with the notions of worth and respect. For example, on the assumption that the basis of our worth is also what makes us one another's moral equals, certain discussions of the foundations of equality can be instructively read as discussions of the basis of our equal worth. In these discussions of equality and elsewhere in the history of liberal thought, there is a persistent assumption that at some deep level we are all the same in some fundamental respect. Here is the way William James expressed it, in his characteristically colorful way.

> In God's eyes the differences of social position, of intellect, of culture, of cleanliness, of dress, which different men exhibit, and all the other rarities and exceptions on which they so fantastically pin their pride, must be so small as practically quite to vanish; and all that should remain is the common fact that here we are, a countless multitude of vessels of life, each of us pent in to peculiar difficulties, with which we must severally struggle by using whatever fortitude and goodness we can summon up. The exercise of courage, patience, and kindness must be the significant portion of the whole business; and the distinctions of position can only be a manner of diversifying the phenomenal surface upon which these underground virtues may manifest their effects. At this rate, the deepest human life is everywhere, is eternal. And, if any human attributes exist only in particular individuals, they must belong to the mere trapping and decoration of the surface-show.[48]

The problem, of course, has been to identify the eternal, underground essence that we all share.

The earliest source of our contemporary notions of worth and respect is Kant. Kant argued that our capacities to reason and to act autonomously, which enable us to legislate rules for ourselves and to be guided by them in our action, give us an intrinsic worth or "dignity" that is "exalted above all price and so admits of no equivalent."[49] Kant, of course, was aware that some human beings are better able to think rationally and to act autonomously than others; nor was he blind to the fact that some human beings—for example, infants and the severely retarded—seem to lack these abilities altogether. His response was not, however, to treat worth as a range property beyond a certain threshold and to regard as irrelevant any variations in rationality and autonomy beyond that point. For Kant, it was inconceivable that moral worth could depend on any contingencies of natural endowment. His solution, then, was to distinguish between the "sensible world," or the empirical world governed by natural causality, and the "intelligible world," a "noumenal" realm outside of time and governed by reason rather than causation.[50] The rationality and autonomy that are the bases of our worth are transcendental properties of our noumenal selves, our selves as inhabitants of the intelligible world. These transcendental capacities may be variously and only incompletely manifested, or even not manifested at all, by our empirical selves in the sensible world.

One may wonder which among the beings one finds in the sensible world have corresponding noumenal selves that are ideally and equally rational and autonomous and thus have an intrinsic worth that is equal to one's own. Apart from ruling out animals, Kant apparently never explicitly addressed or even considered this query about the scope of his view. It would seem that both Kant and most subsequent theorists who have embraced some variant of his doctrines of worth and respect have simply assumed that the realm of noumenal selves coincides with the population of human beings.

Most contemporary readers, I think, will find it impossible to accept or even to make clear sense of Kant's notion of the noumenal self existing outside the world of causation and contingency. Those of us who can find only empirical selves must either abandon Kant's suggested basis of worth—the capacities for rationality and autonomy—or else accept that the requirement of respect is restricted in its application only to beings that are detectably rational and autonomous—that is, persons.

A view quite similar to Kant's, except that it draws no distinction between sensible and intelligible worlds, has been advanced by John Rawls in his influential *Theory of Justice*. Rawls agrees with Kant that the capacities that are the foundation of equality are our moral capacities—that is, the capacities that make us moral agents. According to Rawls, the basis of equality is the "capacity for moral personality," which he claims has two components: the capacity to have a conception of the good and the capacity to have a sense of justice.[51] Rawls stipulates, of course, that moral personality is to be understood as a range property; thus, "provided the minimum for moral personality is satisfied, a person is owed all the guarantees of justice."[52] Unlike Kant, who regards rationality and autonomy as necessary conditions for the possession of intrinsic worth, Rawls claims only that the capacity for moral personality is a sufficient condition for full equality. He leaves it an open question whether it is also a necessary condition. He is also quite explicit that the moral theory he advances is a two-tiered theory with a threshold separating two distinct areas of morality. Above the threshold are "moral persons"—that is, those with the capacity for moral personality—all of whom are owed equal justice, while below it are animals, who are not owed duties of justice. But, again unlike Kant, Rawls denies that animals are altogether outside the scope of morality. "The capacity for feelings of pleasure and pain," he writes, "and for the forms of life of which animals are capable clearly impose duties of compassion and humanity in their case."[53] Our treatment of animals, in other words, comes within the scope of the morality of interests. Rawls's overall moral theory (of which his theory of justice is only one component—albeit the only component he develops in detail) thus has the same structure as the Two-Tiered Account.

Why should the capacities that are constitutive of "moral personality" make all those who possess them one another's moral equals? For Rawls, the answer has to do with his belief that the principles of justice are grounded in a hypothetical contract. Thus he writes that "we use the characterization of the persons in the original position [that is, the hypothetical contractual situation] to single out the kind of beings to whom the principles apply. . . . Thus equal justice is owed to those who have the capacity to take part in and to act in accordance with the public understanding of the [contract]."[54] In short, duties of justice are owed to those with the capacities necessary for participation in the hypothetical contract. Again, however, we may ask why. Rawls's answer seems to be that this is required by "the principle of reciprocity": "Those who can give justice are owed justice."[55]

This account of the significance of the capacity for moral personality strongly suggests that this capacity is a necessary as well as a sufficient condition of moral equality. Indeed, when he comes to the discussion of animals, Rawls wavers on his earlier agnosticism as to whether the capacity for moral personality is a necessary condition for full equality. "While I have not," he notes, "maintained that the capacity for a sense of justice is necessary in order to be owed duties of justice, it does seem that we are not required to give strict justice anyway to creatures lacking this capacity."[56] But if this is right, Rawls's theory leaves various types of human being below his threshold and thus outside the scope of justice: fetuses, infants, the severely retarded, and perhaps even young children and moderately retarded adults. If we assume that Rawls's division of morality into the sphere of justice and the sphere of "compassion and humanity" corresponds to, or would map comfortably onto, the division between the morality of respect and the morality of interests, his suggested basis for superior status would of course exclude these same human beings from the scope of the morality of respect.

Rawls assumes, however, that these various types of human being are all *within* the scope of justice. Thus he amends his account of the basis of equality: "One should observe that moral personality is here defined as a potentiality that is ordinarily realized in due course. It is this potentiality that brings the claims of justice into play."[57] What Rawls says in defense of this revision is that "regarding the potentiality as sufficient accords with the hypothetical nature of the original position [that is, there is no actual contract from which infants and others would be debarred because of their lack of the capacities necessary for participation], and with the idea that as far as possible the choice of principles should not be influenced by arbitrary contingencies."[58] But this simply begs the question whether an individual's having not yet developed the relevant capacities is merely an arbitrary contingency, like the color of his skin, or whether it is a morally significant fact about him. In any case, it is obvious that Rawls's motive for shifting from the capacity to the potential to have the capacity is to preserve certain intuitions. "Since infants and children," he observes, "are thought to have basic rights. . . , this interpretation of the requisite conditions seems to match our considered judgments."[59] While I am sympathetic to Rawls's desire to accommodate strong intuitions, it would be nice to have a more principled rationale for extending the account in the way he does. It is also unclear that the extension he proposes captures our intuitions in the right way. While the stipulation that potential for moral personality is the basis of equality lets infants and children into the sphere of equal justice, it seems to let fetuses in as well, a consequence that it is doubtful that Rawls would welcome. And of course the focus on potential does nothing to bring the retarded within the scope of equality, as Rawls recognizes. But on this matter he is evasive, observing only that "those more or less permanently deprived of moral personality may present a difficulty. I cannot examine this problem here, but I assume that the account of equality would not be materially affected."[60]

Nothing I have said refutes Rawls's claim that the potential for moral personality is the basis of equality. But it also seem tolerably clear that Rawls offers no compelling reason for regarding the potential for moral personality, or even the capacity for moral personality, as the basis for the equal worth of persons, the worth that demands equal respect. This is particularly true for those of us who doubt that this area of morality has its foundations in a hypothetical agreement among hypothetical contractors.

The philosophical literature contains various other accounts of the bases of worth and respect. Avishai Margalit offers a recent example: "The trait I would like to suggest for justifying respect for humans is based on a capacity. The capacity is that of reevaluating one's life at any given moment, as well as the ability to change one's life from this moment on."[61] There is an affinity here with Kant, who, as I noted, held that the basis of our worth is our causally unconditioned autonomy in the noumenal realm. Margalit notes the parallel but stresses that he is concerned with human beings as they are in the "sensible world":

> Kant does indeed speak of Man as worthy of respect because he is free from the causal web of Nature, but Kant was not talking about "empirical Man." The present claim, however, is that a person who is really radically free is worthy of respect. Radical freedom means that, although a person's past actions, character, and environment constitute a set of constraints on her future actions, they nevertheless do not determine these actions. Every person is capable of a future way of life that is discontinuous with the past. The respect that people deserve for this is based precisely on the fact that Man does not have a nature, if a "nature" means a set of character traits that determine one's actions. Animals have natures, human beings do not.[62]

Margalit intends this as an account of "a trait . . . belonging to *all human beings, by virtue of which [they] are worthy of basic respect.*"[63] For the most part, however, he fails to discuss the marginal cases. He does not consider, for example, whether infants are supposed to be radically free. If it is implausible, as it seems to me to be, to suppose that infants have a power of acting in a way that is unconstrained by their nature, then it seems that Margalit, like Rawls, must retreat from the capacity for free action to the potential for it as the basis of respect. And even this will be insufficient to show that the retarded are worthy of respect. Indeed, the case of the retarded, which is the only marginal case he explicitly considers, prompts Margalit to reconsider his proposal. "The case of the retarded," he writes, "seems to me to constitute a serious reason not to base the attitude of respect for humans on a Kantian justifying trait such as rationality, moral capacity, or the like. This case also provides an important argument in favor of the skeptical justification"[64]—that is, an alternative justification for respect "based on the fact that in our way of life people believe that human beings deserve respect." According to the skeptical solution to the problem of justifying respect for human beings, "human beings have value because others value them, and not because of any prior characteristic that justifies such valuing."[65] In the end, Margalit does not decide between his positive account of the basis of respect and the skeptical justification, but instead appears to assume that, if one or the other is acceptable, that is sufficient.

Margalit's "skeptical" justification is no justification at all. Even if one can give clear content to the idea that "our" form of life includes a requirement of respect for all human beings, there is nothing in that that gives any individual a *reason* to adhere to or to continue to adhere to that requirement. The positive justification, in addition to raising unanswered questions about marginal cases, makes our moral status rest perilously on a controversial doctrine of free will. And this, I think, helps us to see the implausibility of the justification. If our reason to respect other human beings were that they have the power to act independently of any antecedently given nature, we would presumably have no reason to respect one another if it were to turn out that determinism is true—that is, if we were to discover that we do not in fact have that power. It seems clear, however, that the discovery that free will is an illusion would not compel us to conclude that there is nothing that separates us from animals, or that there is no reason to believe that killings of persons are equally wrong, or that we must abandon any of the other beliefs that seem most closely associated with the idea that people are equally worthy of respect.[66] If this is so, our alleged radical freedom is not the basis of our worth.

One lesson to draw from this is that, if we are to postulate certain properties as the basis of our worth, they had better be properties that we demonstrably have. Accounts of the morality of respect that base our worth on certain "metaphysical" attributes—such as that we possess a soul, or that we have been made in the image of God, or that we are endowed with free will—are always vulnerable to the possibility, or probability, that the favored attribute is in fact illusory.

Among the various accounts of the morality of respect with which I am familiar, the one that I find most suggestive is Warren Quinn's. The passage in which he sets out the core idea is worth quoting in full:

> [O]ne important part of morality is made up of constraints on our behavior toward others that spring from our recognition of others as mature agents on an equal moral footing with ourselves. The fundamental attitude underlying virtuous action of this type seems to be respect for what can be thought of as the moral authority of others. Defining the scope of this authority amounts to specifying the rights that mature moral agents have over each other. But what is characteristic, interesting, and important about these rights . . . is that they exert their force on others only in virtue of actual (or in some situations, counterfactual) exercises of will. Take, for example, the well-known rights of life, liberty, and the pursuit of happiness. Among the several moral reasons you may have not to kill me, take me captive, or subject me to your idea of the good life, perhaps the most important lies in the simple fact that I choose, or would choose were I to consider the matter, that you do not. Viewed in this way these rights are nothing other than equally distributed moral powers to forbid and require behavior of others, and violations of them are nothing more than refusals to respect the exercise of these powers.[67]

Sadly, Quinn never elaborated on these ideas in detail. In particular, he does not say what the properties are in virtue of which we have the rights that he believes to be the most notable features of the terrain within the morality of respect. But it is clear that the relevant properties must be those psychological capacities that enable us to have wills that assert their own moral authority—that is, autonomous wills. Thus Quinn would, I believe, agree with Robert Nozick that the basis of those rights that constrain our treatment of other persons but not our treatment of animals is the "ability to form a picture of one's whole life (or at least of significant chunks of it) and to act in terms of some overall conception of the life one wishes to lead."[68] The relevant capacity, in short, is simply autonomy itself: the capacity to direct one's life in accordance with values that one reflectively endorses. And respect for persons consists primarily, as Quinn says, in respect for their exercise of autonomy or self-determination. Autonomy does, of course, presuppose other capacities, such as self-consciousness and some degree of rationality. It does not, however, presuppose free will in Margalit's sense—that is, the ability to act in a way that is undetermined by any conjunction of antecedent conditions, such as one's nature, history, and circumstances.

These ideas are, as I noted, undeveloped in Quinn's work; and I have little to add. Among the many problems that need to be addressed is how the appeal to our capacity for autonomy can support the various intuitions that prompted our initial speculations about worth and respect. How, for example, does the fact that persons are autonomous make it more credible to suppose that all killings of persons are equally wrong, other things being equal? As Nozick puts it, we not only want to understand "in virtue of precisely what characteristics of persons are there moral constraints on how they may treat each other or be treated[.] We also want to understand *why* these characteristics connect with these constraints."[69]

One possibility is suggested by Quinn's claim that the main reason why killing a person is wrong is that this contravenes the autonomous and authoritative determination of the person's will that one not kill him. If this is so, and if the person's autonomous choice in this matter is all-or-nothing—that is, his choice is between being killed and not being killed—it would explain why the wrongness of killing does not ordinarily admit of degrees. For either the person's will is violated or it is not. If the wrongness consists primarily in the violation and the violation is all-or-nothing, then the wrongness should be all-or-nothing as well, if other things are equal.

Another way of putting this is to say that autonomy may be plausibly regarded as a range property, at least with respect to certain matters. If a person is sufficiently autonomous to know that being killed is incompatible with the plans he has for his own life, this is all that is necessary for his will to be autonomously set against his being killed. He is, where this matter is concerned, fully autonomous.

It has to be conceded, however, that the *intensity* of a person's autonomous preference for not being killed may vary. Moreover, autonomy presupposes an ability to recognize and to act on the basis of reasons. Autonomous choice is therefore normally a response to reasons. And some people—namely, those with a stronger time-relative interest in continuing to live—have a stronger reason to resist being killed than others. This explains how a person's autonomous preference for not being killed could *rationally* vary in intensity: it could vary with the strength of his reason to avoid being killed.

If we are to uphold the intuition that killings of persons are equally wrong, we must accept that the wrongness of violating a person's autonomous will not to be killed does not vary either with the intensity of his autonomous preference or with the strength of his reason to resist being killed. What matters is simply that his autonomous will is set against his being killed. This, however, exposes this understanding of the wrongness of killing to a serious objection. If killing a person is wrong because it is (or would be) opposed by the person's own autonomous will, and if neither the strength of the person's reason for opposing it nor the intensity of his opposition affects the degree to which the killing would be wrong, it is unclear why other acts that are also opposed by the person's autonomous will should not be equally wrong. Suppose, for example, that the person autonomously chooses that you should not tweak his nose. Your tweaking his nose would be just as much a contravention of his autonomous will as your killing him would be; therefore it should be as seriously wrong as killing him. But clearly it is not.

There are additional reasons for doubting that the wrongness of killing a person can be fully explained in terms of the violation of the person's autonomous will. Consider:

The Deluded Pessimist. A person autonomously prefers to die even though his future life would in fact be well worth living and his death would not be good for anyone else. (His desire to die must not be the product of an aberrant mental condition, such as depression, for that would compromise its status as autonomously formed. Perhaps he autonomously embraces a mistaken view of the value of life that has persuaded him, erroneously, that his life lacks value. A person's possession of capacities for rationality and autonomy does not guarantee that his autonomous preferences will be rational.)

It would clearly be wrong to kill the Deluded Pessimist despite the fact that this would be consistent with his own autonomous choice. Therefore there must be more to the explanation of why killing a person is wrong than just that it violates the person's autonomous will.

This, of course, is compatible with what Quinn says. His claim is only that the *most important* part of the explanation of why killing is wrong is that it violates the person's will. This is the part of the explanation that is concerned with considerations of respect. If it is a person's autonomous will that is the proper object of respect, and if the Deluded Pessimist autonomously prefers to die, the wrongness of killing him cannot be explained within the morality of respect. But killing him could still be wrong, on Quinn's view; it is just that the explanation of the wrongness must come from within the morality of interests. According to this explanation, one's reason not to kill the Deluded Pessimist concerns only his good or well-being, not his will. This explanation may be plausible, but only, it seems, on one condition: that killing the Deluded Pessimist would be less seriously wrong than killing a person whose autonomous will was set against his being killed. For it seems clear that an act of killing that involves a violation of the requirement of respect must be more seriously wrong than one that is wrong only because of considerations of interests or well-being. Part of the motivation for postulating an area of morality concerned with respect is, indeed, to acknowledge that offenses in this area are graver and less easily justified than offenses that merely affect an individual's interests or well-being. Thus, if we believe that killing the Deluded Pessimist would be just as wrong as killing any other person, other things being equal, it seems that the explanation of the wrongness must come from within the morality of respect rather than the morality of interests. It seems, in other words, that the proper object of respect cannot be just the autonomous determinations of a person's will, but must in some way include the person's good or well-being, as well. (I will return to this matter in section 2.3 of chapter 5.)

It is also unclear how Quinn's approach supports other intuitions that we might seek to capture through the notion of respect—for example, the intuition that in general it is wrong to kill one person in order to save another, or even in order to save a greater number of others. In these cases, the will of the potential victim is presumably set against his being sacrificed, but the wills of the potential beneficiaries may favor it. Why should the autonomous will of the one have priority over those of the others? For Quinn, the answer has to do with the sorts of rights people have within the morality of respect, where rights are sensitive to considerations of agency. According to Quinn, negative rights, such as the right not to be killed, normally have priority over positive rights, such as the right to be saved. This feature of the morality of respect is necessary, he argues, if we are to have moral authority over what may be done to us, which in turn is necessary if we are to recognize "our lives, minds, and bodies [as] really being ours."[70] Recognizing other people's authority over what one may do to them is essential to respecting them as one's own moral equals.

This is a suggestive interpretation of the Kantian notion that persons are ends-in-themselves. But it is not clear that it goes quite deep enough. A fully satisfactory account would have to explain why respect for persons does not require that they be recognized as having authority over what others may allow to happen to them as well as over what others may do to them. Quinn's account seems to presuppose that *doing* certain things to people may be incompatible with showing them due respect even when *allowing* those same things to happen to them would not be.

Certainly the common intuition is that what counts as respect for persons is sensitive to considerations of agency. I suspect that Quinn is right in thinking that the explanation of this has to do, at least in part, with the ways in which moral authority must be distributed among people in order for them to maintain their status as one another's moral equals. One person's moral authority over others can reach only so deep into their lives before it compromises their own authority. Thus, for example, a person's authority to forbid others to kill him is not substantially invasive of anyone else's sphere of autonomy, though it may have a disastrous effect on the well-being of certain others if his death is ever necessary in order for them to survive. If, by contrast, a person had the authority to demand that others should save him, they could become instruments of his will in such a way that his authority over their lives could exceed their own. And this, it seems, would be incompatible with their all being one another's moral equals.

There may, I believe, be other dimensions to the explanation of why certain forms of agency are compatible with what is required by respect for persons while others are not, even if they would both lead to the same outcome, such as the death of a person. It may be, for example, that certain modes of agency connect the agent more closely with the outcome than others. Thus an agent who kills a person is normally more intimately causally connected with the victim's death than an agent who lets a person die. In the latter case, but not normally in the former, the victim would have died in the same way at the same time even if the agent had not been on the scene at all.[71] Another possibility is that different forms of agency may sometimes differ in their moral significance for reasons that are conventional in nature. It may be that, for a variety of contingent reasons, deriving primarily from practices that have been socially necessary throughout much or all of human history, certain forms of agency have come to be regarded as signaling a failure of respect. And, if treating a person in a certain way is universally accepted as a failure of respect, then to treat a person that way *is* to fail to show proper respect.

This is not to suggest a relativist or conventionalist account of the requirement of respect for persons. I assume that the demand that one show respect for other persons as one's own moral equals is objective. But at least some of the forms that the requirement takes may be determined in part by historical or cultural contingencies. There is an analogy here with etiquette, or manners. It is compatible with the claim that the requirement to show proper manners is objective and universal that what counts as good manners may vary from culture to culture. If, moreover, a certain form of behavior is regarded as bad manners in a particular society, then anyone in that society who is aware of the code of manners but nevertheless engages in the behavior is guilty of bad manners, regardless of whether he is a member of the society and accepts its code. The social belief, together with the agent's awareness of it, makes the behavior an instance of bad manners.

I will not pursue this matter further here, though later, in section 9.4 of chapter 4, I will suggest that there may be an element of convention in the common view that, in general, killing involves a failure of respect in a way that letting someone die does not. But there too my claims will be merely speculative. What is required is a series of explanations: of why certain forms of respect are due to some beings but not to others, of what the basis of differentiation between the two sets of beings is, of how the basis of respect dictates the various requirements of respect, of why the requirements discriminate between various modes of agency, and so on. I join a distinguished tradition in failing to solve or even adequately to address these problems.[72] Like many others, I believe that morality, and in particular that area of morality concerned with killing, is divided between a region concerned with interests and well-being and a region concerned with respect; but, again like many others, I remain agnostic about the basis of the worth that demands respect. This much, however, seems clear: that the basis of worth is connected with our being *persons*—that is, with our possession of certain higher psychological capacities that distinguish us from most or all forms of animal life, and from some forms of human life as well. And I think that Quinn is right to this extent: that respect for a person is closely connected with respect for the autonomous determinations of that person's will; therefore, autonomy must be a significant element of the basis of the worth that demands respect.

Not much of substance follows unequivocally from this. One conclusion we may draw with confidence is that the congenitally severely retarded are below the threshold of respect. This, indeed, follows from the earlier discussion of Convergent Assimilation, where I concluded that there are no morally significant intrinsic differences between the severely retarded and animals with comparable psychological capacities. Because worth must be based entirely on intrinsic rather than relational properties, and because we are assuming that most if not all animals are below the threshold of respect, it follows that the severely retarded must be below the threshold as well. (If there are any animals above the threshold, they must be those, such as gorillas, with cognitive capacities considerably higher than those that define the severely retarded.)

This leaves most of the hard questions unanswered. For example, do fetuses and infants come within the scope of the morality of respect? The answer may seem obvious, in that they clearly lack the capacity for autonomy and, indeed, can scarcely be said to have wills at all. Yet it might be argued that their *potential* for autonomy makes them worthy of respect. And what about individuals who were once persons but, through brain damage or dementia, have lost their capacities for rationality and autonomy? It is arguable that they, too, are worthy of respect (or continue to be worthy of respect) by virtue of their *having been* autonomous.

I will return to these questions in chapters 4 and 5, respectively. Although they cannot be answered definitively without an account of the basis of the worth that demands respect, there is a surprising amount that can be said about them even in the absence of such an account.

There is another problem that ought to be considered. It concerns the status of children beyond early infancy. Of course, if the potential for autonomy is a sufficient basis for respect, all children except the severely retarded will come within the scope of the morality of respect. But let us suppose, provisionally, that potential alone is not a basis for respect: the relevant capacities are necessary. In that case, the question arises at what age children become worthy of respect. If autonomy is the basis of respect, at what point do children become sufficiently autonomous to merit respect?

When we consider this question, an awkward problem comes into view. Morally, the gap between those above the threshold and those below it is immense. The killing of an individual above the threshold seems to be a significantly more morally serious matter than the killing of one below it; indeed, the morality of killing those above the threshold seems to be governed by an entirely different set of considerations. Therefore the threshold separating those who command respect from those who do not is not so much a line as a chasm. Yet it seems that each of us must cross it with a single step. For we are assuming that all those above the threshold command equal respect. And if respect is all-or-nothing, a child cannot enter the sphere of respect by degrees—for example, by being initially worthy only of minimal respect but gradually becoming worthy of full or maximal respect. Each of us, therefore, must cross the chasm in a single leap.

This conclusion, however, coheres uneasily with the nature of human psychological development, which is gradual and slow, with few if any abrupt discontinuities. The basis of our worth, I have suggested, must be certain psychological capacities, the most important of which is probably autonomy (which presupposes self-consciousness and some degree of rationality). But if our moral status is determined by our psychological capacities, and if our transition across the threshold of respect is all-or-nothing and therefore not gradual, it seems to follow that our acquisition of the capacities that are the basis of respect must also be all-or-nothing. Yet this does not seem to be the case. Consider autonomy, for example. There is no moment in human development when an individual is suddenly transformed from a nonautonomous being into an autonomous person.

One response to this problem is to insist that autonomy may be understood as a range property. Admittedly, the various capacities that underlie autonomy—such as self-consciousness, rationality, analytical intelligence, and imagination—may be possessed by different people to varying degrees. But there is some minimum set of these capacities such that anyone who possesses the capacities to that degree counts as autonomous, while anyone who fails to meet this minimum condition does not. Therefore there really must be some point in human development at which a child develops the capacity for autonomy. It may, of course, be difficult to detect exactly when this occurs; but this, it might be argued, is unproblematic. We are also unable to specify the precise moment that a person becomes three feet tall; but that alone does not necessarily convince us that there is no such moment.

Even if it is correct, this response does not really eliminate the problem. For the problem is not simply that the acquisition of autonomy does not seem to be instantaneous. It is also that there is no discernable event in human development that is momentous enough for us to point to it and say, "*Now* that individual is worthy of respect." It simply does not happen that a child goes to bed one night as a being below the threshold only to wake the next morning sufficiently altered to be worthy of re-spect. For the alteration in moral status involved in crossing the threshold is momen-tous; but there is no event in human psychological development that is comparably momentous and thus suitable as a basis for explaining the shift in moral status. Even if autonomy is a range property, its acquisition consists only in a slight, incremental increase in one or more of the capacities that are its foundation.

We have several options. One is, of course, to accept that the potential for auton-omy is itself a sufficient basis of respect. That would enable one to retain the idea of the threshold but would obviate the problem of the abrupt transition across the threshold. For the threshold would be one that no one would ever cross: some would be permanently above it, the rest permanently below. Another option—one that I re-jected earlier—is to accept that there can be degrees of worth above the threshold. (A more extreme response would be to drop the idea of the threshold and thus abandon the Two-Tiered Account altogether. But this would leave us where we began, with compelling intuitions for which we could not account.) If an individual's worth varies with the degree to which he or she possesses the relevant psychological ca-pacities even above the threshold, people may command varying levels of respect. The moral transformation that occurs when a young child crosses the threshold of re-spect is thus minimized. Instead of making a quantum leap from being altogether un-worthy of respect to being worthy of the highest respect, the child goes from being unworthy of respect to commanding only minimal respect, and from there on to mer-iting ever-increasing levels of respect until its relevant psychological capacities are fully developed.

There are considerations that favor this view in addition to the fact that it would solve the problem of the abrupt transition across the threshold. For example, there is, as I noted earlier, a disturbing arbitrariness in the idea that a being's worth varies with the degree to which its psychological capacities are developed if the being is below the threshold but not if it is above it. It seems more consistent to suppose that, if cer-tain psychological capacities are the basis of our worth, and if we differ in the degree to which we possess those capacities, we should also differ in the degree of our worth. (As I noted earlier, even if the relevant capacities—such as autonomy—can be understood as range properties, they can equally plausibly be understood as vary-ing in degree. There is, for example, a sense in which competence is all-or-nothing; but there is also a sense in which, even among those who are competent, some are more competent than others—that is, more likely, in virtue of their capacities, to ar-rive at rational decisions.)

What would the moral implications be of recognizing different levels of worth above the threshold of respect? Presumably the wrongness of killing anyone above the threshold would be substantially greater—perhaps incomparably so—than the wrongness of killing of any being below it. (I leave the details of such comparisons—if indeed they are even possible—unexplored, as I have done in the case of the Two-Tiered Account as originally formulated.) But if we retain the assumption that the wrongness of killing above the threshold is determined, other things being equal, by the worth of the victim, the implication must be, as I noted earlier, that the killing of a person whose relevant capacities are higher is more seriously wrong, other things being equal, than the killing of a person with lower capacities. Beyond that, it is unclear whether there would be any other differences in what the Two-Tiered Account would imply. The idea that killing some people would be more seriously wrong than killing certain others would *not* necessarily imply that the lives of persons with lower worth could be sacrificed for the sake of those with higher worth. The idea that killing a person with higher worth is more seriously wrong, other things being equal, than killing a person with lower worth is in principle compatible with the view that *all* persons (that is, all individuals above the threshold) are inviolable. (The logic here is familiar and applies even among people acknowledged or assumed to be of equal worth. Intentionally to maim a person—for example, by breaking his arm—is of course gravely wrong. It seems less seriously wrong, other things being equal, than it is to kill a person. But it does not follow from this that it would be permissible intentionally to break one person's arm as a means of preventing another person from being killed.) Thus the threshold could still mark the boundary between those beings who in principle may be sacrificed for the greater good of others and those who may not.

Provided that it does not commit us to the view that persons with lower capacities may be sacrificed for the sake of those whose capacities are higher, some people may be willing to accept that there are, as Nietzsche says, "differences of worth between man and man."[73] Perhaps Albert Einstein, with his higher cognitive and emotional capacities, had a higher worth than I have, so that killing him would have been a graver offence against human worth, and therefore more seriously wrong, than killing me would be. Perhaps, if the practical significance of this claim is limited by an acknowledgement that I retain my inviolability, I can accept the idea that I am not Einstein's equal in worth. I suspect, however, that for most of us the claim that people differ in their intrinsic worth as persons is too profoundly at variance with deep egalitarian intuitions to be acceptable. We can accept that Einstein's achievements entitled him to much more of the sort of respect that can be earned than most of the rest of us deserve; but we cannot accept that he, or anyone else, had higher worth as a person, and therefore that it would have been more seriously wrong to kill him, because his cognitive and emotional capacities were higher than ours.

It seems, moreover, that even the idea that there are degrees of worth above the threshold will not entirely solve the problem of the abrupt transition across the threshold. For even if, when a child crosses the threshold, he is not transformed from a being unworthy of respect to one worthy of the highest respect, he does go from being in principle violable to being inviolable. For we are assuming that any degree of worth above the threshold is sufficient for inviolability. Thus there is still a significant discontinuity in moral status between those above the threshold and those below it; and a child must still undergo that shift in moral status on the basis of what can only be a comparatively minor enhancement of its psychological capacities.

There is, moreover, a further problem that I have yet to mention. I have suggested that it may be right to suppose that the capacity for autonomy is a necessary and sufficient condition of the worth that commands respect. Assume for the sake of argument that this is so. The capacity for autonomy presupposes a variety of abilities: for example, to project oneself imaginatively into the future, to envisage alternative possible futures, to evaluate and deliberate about the various possibilities, to act on the basis of reasons, and so on. It is reasonably clear that young children lack at least some of these abilities and therefore lack the capacity for autonomy. If a four-year-old lacks the capacity for autonomy and autonomy is the basis of the worth that commands respect, four-year-olds must fall below the threshold of respect. Since killing a being below the threshold is morally a less serious matter than killing an individual above it, it follows that the killing of a four-year-old must be less seriously wrong than killing an adult. Yet intuitively it is very clear that to kill a four-year-old is at least as wrong as it is to kill an adult, other things being equal.

One way of addressing both of these problems—the abrupt transition across the threshold and the exclusion of young children from the sphere of respect—is to reject the idea that the threshold of respect is a sharp line with clear cases on either side. We may instead believe that, while we all begin life lacking the kind of worth that commands respect, there is no point at which we instantaneously acquire it. Our worth is based on our psychological capacities—perhaps in particular our autonomy. But our psychological development and maturation is smoothly continuous and gradual, without abrupt discontinuities. This is true of our acquisition of autonomy. There is no point at which we are instantaneously transformed from nonautonomous beings into autonomous ones. During the earliest period of our lives—at least until we are more than a year or two old—we are indisputably nonautonomous. At some later point—for example, by the time we reach six or seven years of age—we are recognizably autonomous. Between these two points there may be a lengthy period of time in which it is simply indeterminate whether we are autonomous. During this period, we are neither determinately nonautonomous nor determinately autonomous: we are instead *becoming* autonomous. If this is right, parallel claims about our moral status will also be true. We begin life lacking the worth that commands respect, go through a period in which we are developing the bases of worth and in which it is indeterminate whether we are worthy of respect, and eventually emerge as beings worthy of full respect. Whether this conception of our transition across the threshold solves the two problems depends on two considerations. The first is how we are to understand the moral status of an individual during the period of indeterminacy. The second is roughly how long the period of indeterminacy lasts.

For the purpose of illustration, let us assume that the capacity for autonomy is the basis of our worth. Suppose, furthermore, that we insist that an individual is worthy of respect only if he clearly and determinately has the capacity for autonomy. In that case, the moral status of an individual during the period of indeterminacy will be the same as that of individuals below the threshold. Given this assumption, therefore, the problem of the abrupt transition remains. For it is only when an individual emerges from the range of indeterminacy—which must occur somewhere within a reasonably brief interval—that he becomes worthy of respect. And, because the shift in status occurs at the end of the period of indeterminacy, it seems that the problem of exclusion remains as well.

Suppose, then, that we assume that the moral status of individuals within the area of indeterminacy is the same as that of individuals above the threshold—that is, that they are worthy of respect. This is the conservative assumption. It could be defended by claiming that it is better, given the possibility of error, to err on the side of caution. Unless an individual clearly and determinately lacks the capacity for autonomy, it is safer to assume that he has the capacity and is therefore worthy of respect. This assumption also offers a reasonable response to the problem of exclusion, since it brings young children into the sphere of respect with the first indication that they are developing the rudiments of autonomy. It does not, however, address the problem of the abrupt transition, since the onset of the period of indeterminacy should itself be reasonably determinate. There is, moreover, a further worry about this proposal. If it lets very young children into the sphere of respect when they begin to possess the rudiments of autonomy, it may also let in certain animals, such as gorillas, that have cognitive and emotional capacities comparable to those of young children.

There is, perhaps, another alternative, which is that during the period in which it is indeterminate whether we are autonomous, we have an intermediate moral status. During that period, we are neither altogether unworthy of respect nor worthy of full respect; we are neither freely violable in the service of the greater good nor fully inviolable. This would go some way toward solving the problem of the abrupt transition, for an individual's elevation into the sphere of respect is no longer conceived to be instantaneous but is assumed to occur gradually, by stages. Particularly if the period of indeterminacy is assumed to be of substantial duration, the psychological differences between the very young child who is unworthy of respect and the older child who is clearly autonomous should be significant enough to justify the enormous difference in moral status we assign to them. In this way, our account of the moral status of children at different ages will map more comfortably onto the facts of human psychological development.

This proposal also helps to address the problem of exclusion. For the threshold is no longer a sharp line but is instead a broad band of indeterminacy. Only those very young children who clearly and determinately lack any capacity for autonomy are below it. Somewhat older children who are developing the capacity for autonomy are, as it were, within the threshold itself. Even if they are not fully within the sphere of respect, neither are they altogether excluded from it. Their status is, as I suggested, intermediate.

Certain animals—the higher primates, for example—may also fall within the area of indeterminacy and thus share the intermediate status of children in the process of becoming autonomous. This, I believe, is a welcome result. It seems plausible to suppose that the status of the higher primates is intermediate between that of lower animals that altogether lack self-consciousness and autonomy and that of persons.

What exactly is this intermediate status? How, in particular, are we to understand the morality of killing beings whose status is intermediate in this way? Presumably the killing of beings with intermediate status cannot be governed by the Time-Relative Interest Account, for that would fail to distinguish those beings from beings below the threshold. Possibly these cases could be governed by the Intrinsic Worth Account, if those with intermediate status are held to have a lower worth, and thus to be worthy only of a lesser degree of respect, than those above the threshold. But this is a merely formal description; we need to know what lesser respect would involve where killing is concerned. Possibly the killing of beings of intermediate status is governed by a different account that I have failed to identify. This is one of the many problems that this chapter has left unresolved. But the agnosticism to which I have frequently been driven in this chapter will not prevent us from arriving at decisive conclusions in the next, where we will begin to address certain important practical issues.

4

Beginnings

I. EARLY ABORTION

The Embodied Mind Account of Identity has immediate implications for the morality of abortion. For, according to that account, we do not begin to exist until our organisms develop the capacity to generate consciousness. Only then is there *someone* present rather than merely *something*. Let us define an *early abortion* as an abortion that is performed prior to that point—that is, the point at which the fetal brain acquires the capacity to support consciousness and at which one of us consequently begins to exist in association with the fetal organism. If the Embodied Mind Account is right, there is no one to be affected for better or worse by an early abortion other than the pregnant woman, her partner, and anyone else who might care about her or her possible progeny. An early abortion does not kill anyone; it merely prevents someone from coming into existence. In this respect, it is relevantly like contraception and wholly unlike the killing of a person. For there is, again, no one there to be killed.

It is not known with certainty at what point during gestation the fetal brain develops the capacity to generate consciousness. Most neurologists accept that the earliest point at which consciousness is possible is around the twentieth week of pregnancy, which is when synaptic connections begin to form among the cortical neurons. It is, however, unlikely that consciousness becomes possible until after at least another month—that is, until around the sixth month. Neurologist Julius Korein offers a representative sketch of the relevant aspects of fetal brain development:

> Neurons in the cortical plate first begin to form cortical synapses at about 20 weeks. These neurons then form synaptic connections between other intracerebral structures such as the thalamus and the brain stem, resulting in sensory reception and more patterned spontaneous and induced motor activity. Cortical EEG activity can be first recorded at about 21–22 weeks after fertilization; the blink-startle response, with eyes opening, to auditory stimuli can be demonstrated at 24 weeks; and *cortical sensory evoked potentials* appear at about 25–27 weeks. . . . Major components of cerebral function including aspects of consciousness (sentience) are unequivocally present in the fetus after 28 weeks of fetal age. The onset of the fundamental core of brain function . . . can be identified between the limits of about 20 to 28 weeks.[1]

Let us assume that the fetal brain develops the capacity to generate consciousness some time between the twentieth and the twenty-eighth week of gestation. It was during this period that each of us began to exist. This is, of course, a broad period in which to locate the beginning of our existence, but it does not seem possible as yet to be more specific by identifying a narrower interval. There are various reasons for this, not least of which is that our understanding of the neural basis of consciousness is still comparatively rudimentary. We do not, moreover, have a clear understanding of the nature of consciousness at lower levels. We are not even clear about what constitutes evidence of its presence at these levels, as is clear from the fact that there is no consensus, even among scientists who study the matter, whether houseflies or other insects are conscious. But, even if our understanding of these matters were considerably more advanced than it is, it would still be unlikely that we could determine with precision when the capacity for consciousness first arises. One reason for this is that the fetal organism may develop the *capacity* to generate consciousness before there is any actual consciousness. Thus, as Michael Lockwood has observed, we might begin to exist in a state of dreamless sleep—capable of consciousness but not yet actually conscious.[2] If so, we may begin to exist before there is any behavioral evidence that we are there. There may, moreover, be some genuine indeterminacy about when consciousness becomes possible. Assuming that consciousness is not possible in the absence of substantial synaptic connections among the cortical neurons, there must be some minimum degree of connectivity necessary for consciousness to occur. But it does not follow that there must be some precise number of synaptic connections such that the formation of only one more synapse would make consciousness possible where before it was not.

Our inability to identify a precise point at which we begin to exist is, I believe, of comparatively little practical significance. I will explain why later in this chapter. For the moment, let us pretend, for convenience of exposition, that there *is* an exact point at which we begin to exist—say, to make the most conservative assumption, at twenty weeks, or roughly five months after conception. An early abortion, therefore, is an abortion performed prior to twenty weeks. This is significant, for approximately 99 percent of all abortions in the United States are performed prior to twenty weeks.[3] If the Embodied Mind Account of Identity is right, these abortions merely prevent someone like you or me from existing. There is no one there to be killed.

There is, however, some*thing* that is killed in an early abortion—namely, a developing human organism. (I will assume for the present that abortion involves killing, though there are reasons to believe that some abortion techniques do not kill but merely allow the fetus to die. I will return to this in section 9.4 of this chapter.) How significant, in moral terms, is the killing of an unoccupied human organism? Three grounds of objection have been advanced. I will mention each briefly and suggest in a general way why I think it is mistaken. I will return to each in more detail later in the chapter.

First, some people believe that a fetal organism has a special sanctity or intrinsic value simply by virtue of being alive and human. I believe that this view is "speciesist"—that is, that it groundlessly attributes greater value to a *human* organism than to an otherwise comparable organism belonging to another biological species. I will explain this in more detail in section 7 of this chapter, in which I discuss the notion of the sanctity of human life.

Second, many people claim that the fetal organism, even if it is not one of us, nevertheless has the potential to become one of us (or, as it is more commonly put, to become a person). This, it is held, makes it seriously wrong to kill the fetal organism, even if one is not thereby killing someone like you or me. But the claim that the fetal organism has the potential to become one of us is ambiguous. Understood in one way, the claim is true but has little or no moral significance. Understood in another way, it is false, though it would have great moral significance *if* it were true. Again, I will explain and defend these assertions in detail in section 6 of this chapter on the relevance of potential.

Third and finally, it might be contended that the fetal organism merits protection because it is the vehicle through which someone like you or me, whose life would be worth living, may be brought into existence. The problem with this contention, however, is that it applies equally to any pair of sperm and egg.

In short, if the Embodied Mind Account is correct and the early fetal organism is not identical with the person who will later exist in association with it, it is hard to see how the organism can have a special moral status sufficient to make it seriously wrong to kill it. Apart from any effects it might have on the pregnant woman or on other preexisting people, an early abortion is morally indistinguishable from contraception. (I stress, again, that not all the argumentation for this conclusion has yet been given. It remains to be shown that the early fetal organism—that is, the organism prior to twenty weeks—cannot have a special sanctity that otherwise comparable nonhuman organisms lack and that it does not have the relevant sort of potential to become a person. These claims will be defended in later sections.)

2. LATE ABORTION

According to the Embodied Mind Account of Identity, an entity of our kind—one of us—begins to exist when a human organism develops the capacity to generate consciousness. If we assume that the capacity for consciousness arises at approximately twenty weeks after conception (an assumption that probably errs on the side of caution by a month or more), it follows that an abortion performed later than twenty weeks after conception involves the killing of some*one* rather than merely some*thing*. It involves the killing of one of us. Let us call such an abortion a *late abortion* and let us refer to the individual who is killed by a late abortion as the *developed fetus*—bearing in mind that the developed fetus is a distinct individual from the fetal organism that supports its existence. For, if we are not identical with our organisms, the developed fetus, being one of us, cannot be either.

How are we to understand the morality of killing a developed fetus? Before advancing the view that seems to me most plausible, I will briefly outline some of the other positions that might be defended. According to some views, late abortion is like early abortion in being morally indistinguishable from contraception. For example, as I noted in section 4.2 of chapter 1, the Psychological Account of Identity implies that we do not begin to exist until some time after birth, for only then does the mental life generated by the brain become sufficiently rich for there to be psychological continuity over time, and psychological continuity is, on this view, the criterion of our identity. If this view of our identity were correct, any abortion, whether performed early or late in the course of fetal gestation, would merely prevent one of us from existing. Of course, even on this view, an early abortion might be objectionable on the ground that the fetal organism would have a special sanctity, and a late abortion might be objectionable on the ground that it would frustrate the time-relative interest that the conscious pre-person might have in the future life of the person whose existence the abortion would prevent. But I will not pursue these possibilities here, since, for reasons given in chapter 1, I reject this account of personal identity.

One influential approach to abortion appeals to an understanding of the morality of killing that is very like what I have called the Harm-Based Account. This approach has been defended by Don Marquis. Although he does not invoke the concept of harm, he claims that what is essentially wrong with or objectionable about killing people is that it deprives the victim of a future that would have contained a great deal of good. He then notes that the killing of a human fetus normally has the same effect. "The future of a standard fetus," he writes, "includes a set of experiences, projects, activities, and such which are identical with the futures of adult human beings and are identical with the futures of young children. Since the reason that is sufficient to explain why it is wrong to kill human beings after the time of birth is a reason that also applies to fetuses, it follows that abortion is prima facie seriously morally wrong."[4] In short, the harm that killing inflicts on the fetus—namely, the loss or deprivation of all that future good—is sufficient to make the killing seriously wrong.

Marquis's argument is carefully qualified. He does not claim that it is a necessary condition of an act of killing being wrong that it should deprive the victim of a future that would have contained a great deal of good. There might, he concedes, be other reasons why killing is morally objectionable. Nor does he explicitly embrace or even consider what, in section 1.1 of chapter 3, I called the assumption of correlative variation—that is, the assumption that the wrongness of killing varies with the degree of harm caused to the victim. Thus the view he articulates does not imply that it is permissible to kill people whose futures cannot be expected to contain more good than evil; nor does it imply that, because the deprivation that an animal suffers in being killed is less, it is less objectionable to kill animals than it is to kill people. What Marquis does claim is that the fundamental reason why killing people is seriously wrong applies at least equally in the case of the fetus; hence abortion, which involves killing the fetus, must be seriously wrong, other things being equal.

There are at least three important objections to this argument, the first of which is that, because Marquis assumes that we begin to exist at conception, it fails to distinguish between early and late abortions. If, as I have argued, we do not begin to exist until approximately twenty weeks after conception, Marquis's argument does not apply to abortions performed before that point. But his position can, of course, be adjusted to accommodate the view that we begin to exist only after twenty weeks. It would then hold that only late abortions are wrong. For only in the case of a late abortion is there a victim who is deprived of a future like ours.

Revised in this way, Marquis's argument offers a distinctive view of the morality of late abortion. But it remains vulnerable to two other objections. The first is based on the claim that Marquis's position cannot remain noncommittal about the assumption of correlative variation. His understanding of the wrongness of killing requires an explanation of why it is more objectionable to deprive people of future goods through killing than it is to cause them lesser deprivations in nonlethal ways. And it should offer an explanation of why killing an animal is normally less objectionable than killing a person. The natural solution is to adopt the assumption of correlative variation. With that assumption, his view has an explanation of why killing a person is more seriously objectionable than either stealing his wallet or killing an animal: namely, the deprivation or loss inflicted is greater.

But if Marquis's view incorporates an assumption of correlative variation, it implies that a late abortion is more seriously wrong, if other things are equal, than the killing of an older child or adult. For in losing its future, the developed fetus suffers a greater loss—the whole of a human life. But scarcely anyone really accepts that the killing of a fetus is worse. On the contrary, even most opponents of abortion appear to accept that even an abortion performed relatively late in pregnancy is less seriously wrong than the killing of an older child or adult. If people really believed that the developed fetus has the same moral status as a normal adult, it would be difficult to explain why even most of those who are in general opposed to abortion are willing to recognize certain exceptions to what they regard as the general impermissibility of abortion—for example, in the case of pregnancies that result from rape or incest, or in cases involving fetal deformity, or when the continuation of the pregnancy poses a serious threat to the pregnant woman's life or health. It would also be difficult to explain why even most opponents of abortion strongly disapprove of the killing of abortionists and the bombing of abortion clinics. For if even the proportionally rather small number of late abortions performed each year were morally comparable to the murder of innocent children or adults, there would be a strong case for the permissibility of defending further innocent victims by violent means. The shootings and bombings might be reasonable responses to a practice of widespread, legally sanctioned murder.

Part of the reason why Marquis's view leads naturally to an implausibly strong condemnation of late abortion is that it presupposes that identity is what matters, both prudentially and morally. It presupposes that our moral concern should be with what is better or worse for individuals, taking account of their lives as wholes. It evaluates a late abortion in terms of its effect on the fetus's life as a whole, and thus finds no difference between the deprivation that abortion inflicts on a developed fetus and that which killing inflicts on an adult, except that the former is quantitatively greater. It fails, in short, to take account of the differences in the ways that fetuses and adults are related to their own future selves. This is the third objection to the view.

I will assume that these objections are decisive. I will also assume, from here on, that the Embodied Mind Account of Identity is correct and thus that there is no one present in the womb to be affected for the worse by an early abortion but that, after twenty weeks, there is someone present who would be killed by a late abortion. If this is the metaphysical situation, what should we believe about the morality of a late abortion? I suspect that many people would conclude that, while early abortion is innocuous because it merely prevents a person from existing, late abortion is murder because it involves the intentional killing of someone like you or me. It is not uncommon, after all, for people to want to draw a sharp line before which abortion is supposed to be permissible but after which it is not. The idea that the onset of the capacity for consciousness at twenty weeks marks the point at which one of us begins to exist offers a line that seems (in contrast to previously favored lines such as viability and quickening) to have obvious moral significance.

On reflection, however, it seems hardly plausible to suppose that there could be a sharp dividing line of this sort. Twenty weeks is 140 days. Is it really acceptable to suppose that an abortion performed 139 days after conception would be perfectly innocuous while an abortion performed a day later would be gravely wrong? Certainly it seems odd to suppose that abortion could go from being innocuous to being murder just as a result of the establishment of a few more synaptic connections in the fetal brain. As opponents of abortion often observe, fetal development is a smoothly continuous process in which it seems impossible to identify an event that is significant enough to make the difference between permissible killing and murder. Intuitively, the extent to which abortion seems morally objectionable increases slowly and gradually over time in a way that corresponds to the process of fetal maturation.

Of course, if I am right that the onset of the capacity for consciousness marks the beginning of the existence of an entirely new individual, the impression that fetal development is a process of merely incremental change is an illusion. For the onset of the capacity for consciousness is a momentous event, both metaphysically and, it seems, morally. Still, I find it difficult to believe that the moral status of abortion could shift radically overnight—or even (if there is genuine indeterminacy in the onset of the capacity for consciousness) over a period of a week or month. We should want, I think, an account of the morality of abortion that captures the sense that most people have, on reflection, that abortion becomes a morally more serious matter the later it is performed.

It is difficult for an account that assigns the developed fetus the same moral status as a normal adult to deliver that desired implication. For example, the Harm-Based Account, of which Marquis's view is a variant, draws a sharp line: before twenty weeks, no one suffers the loss of a future like ours; after twenty weeks, someone does. There will also be a radical moral difference between early and late abortion if the developed fetus comes within the scope of the morality of respect. For given that assumption, the killing of the developed fetus would be just as wrong as the killing of any adult person, if other things were equal. Yet an early abortion would not violate any requirement of respect, for, given that the early fetus is not one of us but is instead a mere unoccupied organism, it is uncontroversially not the sort of being that commands respect.

Is it reasonable to suppose that the developed fetus comes within the scope of the morality of respect? In chapter 3 I remained somewhat agnostic about the basis of the worth that demands respect. It is nevertheless possible to reach a conditional conclusion about whether the developed fetus is owed respect. The basis of respect must be some intrinsic property or set of intrinsic properties. These properties are what relevantly differentiate persons like you and me from animals. While many people believe that what distinguishes us from animals is that we but not they have souls—souls that are, perhaps, made in the image of God—I argued in section 2 of chapter 1 that this view is indefensible. The most plausible remaining candidates for the basis of respect are certain psychological capacities, such as self-consciousness, rationality, and autonomy. Our possession of these capacities does seem to distinguish us from animals in an importantly relevant way. But if the possession of certain psychological capacities is what relevantly distinguishes us from animals and so is the basis of respect, the developed fetus must fall outside the scope of the morality of respect, for it clearly does not possess the capacities that distinguish persons from animals.

There are, in fact, only two respects in which the developed fetus differs from an animal that might be thought to elevate the developed fetus above the threshold of respect while leaving the animal below it. One is the developed fetus's membership in the human species. But while many people believe that mere membership in the human species is a significant basis of moral status, I argued in section 2.2 of chapter 3 that this is a mistake. The other difference between the developed fetus and an animal is that the former, but not the latter, has the potential to develop the psychological capacities that distinguish us from animals. Although the developed fetus does not now have the capacities for self-consciousness, rationality, and autonomy, it will acquire these capacities during the normal course of its development. This, it might be claimed, is a sufficient basis for the worth that commands respect.

I will not pause here to consider whether the developed fetus's potential might be sufficient to bring it within the scope of the morality of respect. I will return to this issue later, in section 6.2 of this chapter. My conclusion there will be that potential alone cannot be a basis for respect. Anticipating that conclusion now, I will proceed on the assumption that the developed fetus lies below the threshold of respect.

It would, in fact, be rather problematic if the developed fetus did come within the scope of the morality of respect. For if that were the case, late abortion would be morally equivalent to the killing of a person, other things being equal. And while this is less implausible than the implication of the Harm-Based Account that late abortion is *more* seriously wrong than the killing of an adult, it is, as I suggested earlier, not what most people believe. Even most of those who believe that late abortion is wrong implicitly accept that it is less seriously wrong than the killing of an adult normally is.

It may, of course, be that the relation between a pregnant woman and the fetus she carries is such that abortion is relevantly different from, and substantially less objectionable than, paradigm instances of murder, even if the developed fetus has the same moral status as an innocent adult. It might be, for example, that abortion can be justified as a matter of self-defense, or that it is permissible for a pregnant woman to kill the developed fetus if that is the only way she can prevent it from appropriating her body as an instrument of life support. There are arguments that attempt to defend the permissibility of abortion on these grounds that grant that the fetus (and a fortiori the developed fetus) has the same intrinsic moral status as an innocent adult. I will explore these arguments in detail in sections 9 and 10 of this chapter. For now, it is sufficient to note that it is unlikely that the considerations identified in these arguments can explain the almost universal sense that even late abortion is quite different morally from the killing of an older child or adult. The main reason why this is so is that the vast majority of those who intuitively regard abortion as morally different from the killing of an adult have never thought of abortion in the ways suggested by these arguments. So, for example, if one has never conceived of pregnancy as a state in which a woman is compelled by the fetus's presence to submit to her body's being used as a means of life support, one is very unlikely to believe that abortion is different from murder *because* one believes that a woman has a right to prevent herself from being forcibly used as a source of life support for another person. Moreover, even if one of these arguments can explain how a late abortion could be permissible even if the developed fetus has the same moral status as an innocent adult, it cannot fully explain or support the common intuition that a late abortion becomes morally more serious the later it is performed. It is, of course, possible to argue that a later abortion is harder to justify because the burden to the pregnant woman of carrying the fetus to term diminishes as pregnancy progresses. But this fails to capture our intuitive sense that the explanation of why a later abortion is worse is that the fetus has by then undergone morally important changes. Only a view that recognizes that the developed fetus's moral status evolves along with its biological or psychological development can adequately explain and justify the common belief that a late abortion becomes morally more problematic the later it is performed.

It seems, therefore, that most people implicitly recognize that, even if the developed fetus is one of us, its moral status is different in certain critical respects from that of an adult. There are several possible views of late abortion that attempt to capture that recognition. One holds that, although the developed fetus is one of us, it is not harmed or affected for the worse by being killed. According to this view, an individual cannot have an interest in continuing to live, and therefore cannot be harmed by dying, unless it is capable of desiring to continue to live.[5] Call this the *Capacity Condition*. According to this view, although I once existed as a developed fetus, it would not have been bad for me to have died or to have been killed at that age. If we combine the claim that the developed fetus cannot have an interest in continuing to live with the Harm-Based Account of the wrongness of killing, we get the conclusion that, if there is any objection at all to a late abortion, it must have to do with the effects on individuals other than the fetus itself.

The Capacity Condition is vulnerable to a powerful objection, which is that there is a sense in which death would clearly be worse for a developed fetus even though the fetus is incapable of desiring to continue to live. If a developed fetus's future life would be worth living, the truncated life it will have if it dies will be a less good life than the longer life it will have if it does not die. Death would therefore be worse for it because it would cause it to have the less good of two possible lives. This insight of the Life Comparative Account seems undeniable; therefore a capacity to desire continued life is not necessary in order for death to be bad for an individual. We have seen, however, that while the Life Comparative Account states an obvious truth, it nevertheless gives a distorted account of the badness of death. It presupposes that identity is what matters and thus implies that the death of a developed fetus is worse, other things being equal, than the death of an adult. But fetal death seems less bad; somehow the loss does not seem fully ascribable to the fetus. One can interpret the Capacity Condition as a crude attempt to explain this intuition. It holds that what is missing in the case of the developed fetus is desire: only through desire can the goods of an individual's future have value for it now. We have seen, however, that the Time-Relative Interest Account offers a subtler and more plausible explanation. What matters is not all-or-nothing (that is, the presence or absence of a capacity to desire continued life); it is, rather, the extent to which the various prudential unity relations would hold. Desire is only one of many elements that relevantly bind an individual to its own future.

The Capacity Condition and the Time-Relative Interest Account both offer an explanation of why the death of a developed fetus is less bad. But the Capacity Condition implies that it is not bad at all. And it implies that death becomes bad for a human being abruptly, when that individual develops the capacity to conceive of and to desire its own future. The Time-Relative Interest Account, by contrast, has the more plausible implication that death becomes a more serious misfortune gradually as a human being's psychological capacities mature and it becomes more closely related to its future self in the ways that ground egoistic concern. (I will return to this in section 8.2 of this chapter.)

Another view that is perhaps more plausible than the Capacity Condition and seems to be more widely accepted is that, although the developed fetus is one of us, and although it suffers a significant loss in being killed, its loss matters less because the developed fetus as yet lacks the sort of status that would make it a proper subject of serious moral concern. According to a prominent variant of this view, personhood is the foundation of the high moral status that each of us now enjoys. But when we began to exist, and for some time thereafter, we were not yet persons. During that time—that is, before we became persons—our moral status was significantly lower. Our interests mattered less because we were not persons, in much the way that many people believe that the interests of animals matter less, not because they are lesser interests but simply because they are the interests *of animals*. So, even if our interest in not being killed was strong before we became persons, it would not have been as seriously wrong for someone to have killed one of us before he or she became a person.

This view is correct in claiming that it is significant that the developed fetus is not a person. But it misidentifies the significance of this fact. It is not that, because the fetus lacks the moral status of a person, its interests matter less. Rather, its not being a person means that it falls outside of the scope of the morality of respect, so that it is *only* its interests—or rather its time-relative interests—that significantly constrain our treatment of it. In short, it means that the morality of killing a developed fetus is governed by the Time-Relative Interest Account. (Again, part of the argument for this claim will come later, in section 6.2 of this chapter.)

According to the Time-Relative Interest Account, what is fundamentally wrong about killing is that it thwarts or frustrates the victim's time-relative interest in continuing to live; and the degree to which an act of killing is wrong varies, other things being equal, with the strength of the victim's time-relative interest in continuing to live. The strength of an individual's time-relative interest in continuing to live is itself a function of two factors: first, the amount of future good that the individual may rationally anticipate in an egoistic way, and second, the degree to which the prudential unity relations would hold between the individual now and itself in the future when the goods it may egoistically anticipate would occur. In the case of a developed fetus, the amount of good that lies in prospect is normally very great. But the prudential unity relations would hold only very weakly between the fetus and itself in the future. The developed fetus cannot envisage or contemplate its future and hence cannot have future-directed psychological states, such as intentions; it would, if it were to become a person, be unable to recall its life as a fetus; and it now has no psychological architecture—no beliefs, desires, or dispositions of character—to carry forward into the future. It is, in short, psychologically cut off or severed or isolated from itself in the future. Its future is, figuratively speaking, relevantly like someone else's future. It is for this reason that, despite the great good in prospect for it, the developed fetus has only a comparatively weak time-relative interest in continuing to live.

It is important to remember that the Time-Relative Interest Account is not a complete account of the morality of killing, but is instead just one component of the more comprehensive Two-Tiered Account. According to the Two-Tiered Account, the wrongness of killing beings who are above the threshold of respect is governed by a requirement of respect. Thus even if a person has a very weak time-relative interest in continuing to live because the amount of good in prospect for him is quite small, it would nevertheless be just as wrong to kill him as it would be to kill any other person, if other things are equal. For his worth as a person is a function of his intrinsic nature and is unaffected by the amount of good the future holds in prospect. It is only in the case of beings that fall below the threshold of respect that the morality of killing is governed by the Time-Relative Interest Account. Given the provisional assumption that the developed fetus is below that threshold, the morality of a late abortion should come within the scope of the Time-Relative Interest Account.

It is, I think, reasonable to believe that an act of killing that violates a requirement of respect for the victim must be more seriously wrong than an act of killing that merely frustrates the victim's time-relative interest in continuing to live. So a late abortion is in an altogether different moral category from an act of killing an older child or adult. There are forms of justification that are largely or wholly ruled out within the morality of respect but may be acceptable within the area of morality governed by the Time-Relative Interest Account. For example, it is generally held to be unacceptable intentionally to sacrifice one person for the greater good of others. But this constraint does not seem to operate below the threshold of respect. Thus even most of those who believe that animals matter morally accept that it may be permissible to kill an animal if that is necessary to prevent a greater amount of harm to people or other animals. If that is right, there will be a range of justifications for late abortion that appeal to considerations capable of outweighing the developed fetus's time-relative interest in continuing to live—for example, the interests of the pregnant woman.

The idea that the morality of a late abortion is governed by the Time-Relative Interest Account also supports the common view that a late abortion becomes increasingly morally objectionable the later it is performed. According to the Time-Relative Interest Account, the wrongness of killing varies with the strength of the victim's time-relative interest in continuing to live. As the developed fetus matures, its psychological capacities become more advanced, and the degree to which it would be psychologically continuous with itself in the future increases correspondingly. Assuming that its life in the womb contains little or no good, the amount of good in its future remains effectively constant until birth. Therefore, because the amount of good in prospect remains constant while the extent to which it would be relevantly related to itself in the future gradually increases, the developed fetus's time-relative interest in continuing to live becomes stronger as gestation progresses. And this means that killing it becomes increasingly objectionable, if other things are equal.

I claimed earlier that it may not be important, for practical purposes, to identify with precision when we begin to exist. I can now explain the basis for that claim.

Note that, immediately after the developed fetus begins to exist and for some time thereafter, its mental life, such as it is, is confined entirely to the present: its mental states do not refer forward or backward in time and there are no elements of its mental life, such as beliefs or desires, that persist over time. It is psychologically locked in the present. It has no psychological connections whatever to itself in the future. If it is right that psychological continuity is among the prudential unity relations, it seems reasonable to conclude that the developed fetus's time-relative interest in continuing to live is extremely weak, despite the amount of good its future can be expected to contain. According to the Time-Relative Interest Account, therefore, the moral objection to killing the developed fetus immediately after it begins to exist should be very weak. Thus there is no radical shift in the morality of abortion when the developed fetus begins to exist. It is not the case that, as soon as abortion comes to have a *victim* (that is, when the developed fetus appears), it shifts abruptly from being innocuous to being seriously objectionable. Rather, the moral status of abortion changes only incrementally. An early abortion, if it is morally objectionable at all, is objectionable only because of its effects on individuals other than the fetus. When the developed fetus begins to exist, there is then a victim who is affected for the worse by abortion, but the relevant effect, according to the Time-Relative Interest Account of the wrongness of killing, is minimal. At least initially, the developed fetus's time-relative interest in continuing to live is extremely weak and the moral objection to abortion is therefore correspondingly weak. As the pregnancy progresses and the developed fetus's time-relative interest in continuing to live increases in strength, a late abortion gradually becomes increasingly morally objectionable.

It is because the moral status of abortion changes incrementally over time that our inability to determine with precision when we begin to exist has relatively little practical significance. I have suggested that we begin to exist at some time between the twentieth and the twenty-eighth week of pregnancy, but that it is not at present possible to be much more precise than that. Just prior to twenty weeks, there is no one there to be affected by an abortion. After twenty-eight weeks, the developed fetus is definitely present and would be affected for the worse by an abortion. How strong its time-relative interest in continuing to live is at twenty-eight weeks depends on how long the developed fetus has existed. It will be stronger if the developed fetus began to exist shortly after twenty weeks and weaker if it began to exist closer to twenty-eight weeks. But unless the developed fetus matures psychologically at a rapid rate, it should not make a very great difference to the strength of its time-relative interest in continuing to live whether it is only a few days old or whether it is almost a couple of months old. Therefore the degree to which an abortion at twenty-eight weeks would be morally objectionable will be substantially the same whether the developed fetus began to exist at twenty weeks or closer to twenty-eight weeks.

If this is right, of course, it implies that the moral gravity of a late abortion does not substantially increase between the time that the developed fetus begins to exist and the time of birth. While a late abortion becomes a morally more serious matter as pregnancy progresses, the increase in gravity over the last three or four months of pregnancy cannot be very great. To suppose otherwise, one must (if one is being guided by the Time-Relative Interest Account) assume that the developed fetus's psychological capacities develop rapidly over that period, so that by the end of preg-

nancy its potential psychological connections to itself in the future would be significantly stronger than they were when it first began to exist. But this seems an unrealistic assumption.

Thus far I have sought to defend the common view that late abortion is morally
less objectionable than the killing of an older child or adult by appealing to two
claims: first, that the developed fetus's time-relative interest in continuing to live is
comparatively weak, and second, that, because the developed fetus falls below the
threshold of respect, the morality of late abortion is governed by the Time-Relative
Interest Account of the wrongness of killing. There is, however, an alternative but
closely related defense of this common view that appeals to a different understanding of the status of the developed fetus. It attributes to the developed fetus a rather peculiar metaphysical status. Because the metaphysical claims underlying this view are
obscure, my sketch of the view, though sympathetic, will be noncommittal.

When we note (as I did in section 6.1 of chapter 2) that the death of a developed
fetus is intermediate between nonconception and the death of a person, the intuition
we are seeking to capture is that there is somehow less of a victim than there is when
a person dies. The developed fetus seems too insubstantial—too psychologically insubstantial—to be a victim in the same way that a person would be. The idea that
there is less of a victim may seem a figurative way of articulating the sense that the
loss matters less; but there is also a quite literal understanding of this idea. It may be
that the developed fetus is not a fully real or fully existing individual of our kind.

Warren Quinn, to whose views on these matters I am much indebted, defends a
gradualist understanding of the coming into existence of entities of certain kinds.
According to gradualism, "the coming to be of substantial individuals may be a genuine process in time in the course of which the prospective individual comes into existence gradually, entering the world by degrees. The ontology in question thus involves the idea of the extent to which an individual has at a given time become fully
actual or real—or . . . the degree to which it already fully exists."[6] Quinn cites as an
example the building of a house. Materials are gathered, the foundation is laid, a
wooden skeleton is erected, plumbing and electrical wiring are installed, bricks are
laid, and so on until the house is completed. But in all this there is no point at which
a house suddenly begins to exist. Instead, the house seems genuinely to come into existence gradually. During much of the process by which the house is erected, the existence of the house is only *partial*. The degree to which it exists increases as the
work progresses.

According to Quinn, it is plausible to take an analogous gradualist view about the
beginning of our own existence. We may defensibly believe that we are essentially
human beings and that the fetus is a human being in the process of becoming—that
is, a partially real or partially existing human being. This view does not, he notes,
have the absurd implication that the fetus is in any way empirically indeterminate, or
that its existence is somehow ghostly or flickering. Again, the case of the house is illuminating: "A house under construction can, at a given moment, be characterized
with every bit as much precision as a fully built house. Its incompleteness lies only
in its relation to the special sortal that best indicates the kind of thing it is, namely
'house.' Thus there is no reason in the kind of full empirical reality that the fetus possesses to reject the claim that it is the human being in the making."[7]

Quinn does not say what he takes the essential properties of a human being to be or how he thinks a human being differs from a human organism. (He concedes that "a fetus is indeed a full-fledged organism, but this is quite consistent with the claim that such a full-fledged organism is not a fully real individual."[8] In the same way, a house in the making may be a full-fledged *construction* but not a fully real house.) According to the Embodied Mind Account of Identity, the substance sortal that provides the criteria of our identity is not "human being" but "mind" or "self." But a parallel gradualist account of the coming into existence of a mind or self can be given. There are, it might be claimed, the beginnings of a mind around the twentieth week of pregnancy, when (we are assuming) the capacity for consciousness first appears, but as the various psychological capacities characteristic of a human mind are being developed, the mind is relevantly like a house under construction: it is not yet fully present; it is only partially though increasingly present.

The gradualist view may be intuitively more compelling when applied to certain cases involving the ceasing to exist rather than the beginning to exist of a mind. In cases involving Alzheimer's disease or other forms of progressive dementia, for example, it is quite natural to think of the person as going out of existence gradually as the mind is increasingly eroded, with its constituent psychological states and capacities disappearing as the tissues of the brain atrophy and die. On this view, dying is not so much a process that occurs within life but an extended transition between life and total nonexistence in which the *existence* of the person gradually diminishes until it is extinguished altogether. I will return to this briefly in section 3.1 of chapter 5.

Suppose that the gradualist view is plausible and that the process by which we come into existence begins around the twentieth week of pregnancy. If we are essentially embodied minds, it seems reasonable to suppose that this process continues at least until birth and perhaps until some time after. If that is right, the developed fetus is not fully one of us; it is not a fully realized mind or self but a self in the process of becoming. It is a partially existing entity of the sort that you and I essentially are.

Recall the claim that the death of a newborn infant, and by extension the death of a developed fetus, is, intuitively, intermediate between the death of a person and nonconception, or the failure of a person to come into existence. That claim makes perfect sense if the developed fetus, and perhaps the newborn infant as well, is an only partially existing entity of our sort.

There are two ways in which the claim that the developed fetus is a partially existing member of our kind might support the permissibility of a late abortion. One appeals to the principle that the more fully real an individual is as a member of our kind, the higher its moral *status* must be, other things being equal. Quinn's view seems to be of this sort. He writes that because "the morally binding force of humane considerations varies according to various dimensions in which the object affected is nearer to or further from us, the fact that the fetus is to some extent already a human being, already to some extent one of us, can only make its loss, however qualified, count for more. And as the fetus becomes more fully human the seriousness of aborting it will approach that of infanticide."[9] According to this view, the more like one of us the fetus becomes, the stronger its rights will be.

The other approach, which seems to me more plausible, is to claim that the developed fetus's ontological status means that its loss in dying must be less than that which is normally suffered by a person who dies. For according to the gradualist view, the developed fetus is not fully identical with the person who will be the subject of future good if an abortion is not performed. (On the gradualist view, it seems that identity as well as existence must be a matter of degree.) The subject of the good that will be lost if the abortion is performed does not yet fully exist. The victim of that loss exists now only partially in the form of the developed fetus. Therefore the loss of future good that would be caused by a late abortion is only partially ascribable to the developed fetus. It is in this sense that the developed fetus is not a victim of loss in the same way as a person who dies is. The loss that is ascribable to it is less because the future that is lost is not fully *its* future (or, alternatively, it is not fully the same individual as the one who would have been the subject of the goods that are lost).

Is the gradualist view ultimately plausible? I will not attempt to judge. I mention it because it offers a particularly bold and striking way of accounting for our sense that, when a late abortion is performed and the whole of a human life is thereby lost, the developed fetus is nevertheless not a victim of loss in quite the same way that a person is when he or she dies or is killed.

3. PRENATAL HARM

I have suggested how the Time-Relative Interest Account of the morality of killing supports the permissibility of late abortion. There are, however, various objections to this understanding of the morality of late abortion. Some allege that the Time-Relative Interest Account simply leaves out or ignores the considerations that are morally most significant. Others claim that its implications are incompatible with our understanding of other matters. Among the objections of this latter sort is the challenge to reconcile the view that abortion can be permissible with our conviction that it is wrong to cause or inflict prenatal injury. There are, in fact, two challenges here, one quite general, the other addressed specifically to the Time-Relative Interest Account.

The general objection is familiar. It presupposes that the infliction of prenatal injury is seriously objectionable. Consider, for example, the following case:

> *Prenatal Injury.* A pregnant woman chooses to take a mood-altering drug, knowing that this will damage the reproductive system of the fetus she is carrying in way that will cause it to be sterile later in life.

Virtually everyone believes that the pregnant woman's action is seriously wrong—though many also believe that it nevertheless ought *not* to be illegal, on the ground that the enforcement of general laws forbidding prenatal injury would be excessively invasive of women's privacy. Nevertheless, if the infliction of this sort of prenatal harm would be *morally* wrong, and seriously so, this makes it puzzling how a late abortion could be morally permissible. For normally it is considerably more seriously wrong to kill someone than it is to inflict on someone a nonlethal injury—for example, an injury that causes sterility. How, then, could it be morally permissible to kill a developed fetus but not to cause it some nonlethal harm?

There is an equally familiar reply to this challenge. When a late abortion is performed, the victim is, at the time the relevant effect occurs, only a fetus. If a fetus's moral status is lower than that of a person, or if its time-relative interests are weaker, this may explain how a late abortion is relevantly different from the killing of a person and how it may therefore be permissible. But the victim of prenatal harm may be a person, and not just a fetus, at the time that at least some of the relevant effects occur.[10] In Prenatal Injury, for example, an injury is inflicted prenatally, but the relevant effect—sterility—becomes a burden or harm only after the victim has become a person. (Thus, if the affected individual had died in infancy or childhood from an independent cause, the woman's act would not, in the relevant sense, have caused any harm at all.) It is this difference in the nature of the victim at the time the relevant effect occurs that distinguishes late abortion from prenatal harm—though exactly how the difference is relevant depends on what one takes the important moral considerations to be. If one thinks that what matters is the victim's moral status, one may contend that the reason why late abortion may be permissible while the infliction of prenatal harm typically is not is that the victim of prenatal harm is a person while the principal victim of a late abortion is not. Or if one is guided by a concern for individuals' time-relative interests, one may contend that, while a late abortion frustrates only the weak time-relative interests of the developed fetus, prenatal harm frustrates the stronger time-relative interests of a person (for example, the time-relative interest in having children).

An explanation of this sort seems cogent, but it is not clear that it is available to those who believe that the morality of a late abortion is governed by the Time-Relative Interest Account. According to the Time-Relative Interest Account, a late abortion may be permissible because the developed fetus's comparatively weak time-relative interest in continuing to live may be outweighed by countervailing considerations, such as the time-relative interests of the pregnant woman. But if the developed fetus's time-relative interest in the goods of its own future is weak because of the great psychological distance there would be between itself now and itself later, this should affect not only the morality of abortion but also the morality of inflicting prenatal harm. (The Time-Relative Interest Account is, of course, an account of the morality of killing, but the considerations underlying it can be readily extrapolated to cover other cases, including cases of prenatal harm.) If the developed fetus's future good matters less in the case of abortion, it should matter less in general, and thus in the case of prenatal harm as well. If its time-relative interest in continuing to live to enjoy the goods of its future is weak, its time-relative interest in later being fertile rather than sterile, or in being able rather than disabled, must be correspondingly weak. It seems, therefore, that if we conclude on these grounds that a late abortion is less seriously objectionable than killing a person, other things being equal, we should also conclude that the infliction of prenatal injury, where the relevant effect is delayed, is less seriously objectionable than inflicting the same harm on a person.

To illustrate this objection, let us compare the act of the pregnant woman in Prenatal Injury with the action in the following case:

> *Involuntary Sterilization.* Agent is confined to bed in a hospital room she shares with another patient, a young adult who is unconscious and cannot be moved. To amuse and console herself, Agent smokes an exotic drug knowing that the fumes will cause the patient in the other bed to become sterile.

While the act of the pregnant woman in Prenatal Injury affects a fetus with only a weak time-relative interest in later being fertile rather than sterile, Agent in Involuntary Sterilization frustrates the much stronger time-relative interest of a person in not becoming sterile. The person's time-relative interest in being fertile is stronger than that of the fetus because he will be much more closely psychologically continuous with himself later, when the bad effects of sterility will be felt. But the harm is exactly the same in both cases: namely, being sterile rather than fertile. The only difference is that in Prenatal Injury the act that causes the harm is done while the victim is a fetus and thus well before the bad effect occurs, whereas in Involuntary Sterilization the act that causes the harm immediately precedes the bad effect. And it is difficult to see how this could be morally significant. If an act causes a person to be sterile, it hardly seems to matter whether the act was done early in the victim's life or later, when the victim would be more closely psychologically connected to himself at the time that he might desire to have children. Therefore if the Time-Relative Interest Account implies that it would be less objectionable to cause a person to be sterile by injuring him when he was a fetus than to cause him to be sterile by injuring him later, say at age fifteen, this is seriously damaging to the account's credibility.

This objection can be extended. In cases in which a later harm is caused prenatally, the Time-Relative Interest Account seems to imply that it matters less whether the victim has more future good rather than less. By parity of reasoning, the Time-Relative Interest Account should also imply that, in other cases involving the developed fetus, it matters less whether it will later have less of what will be *bad* for it. Consider:

> *Prenatal Therapy.* Unless a developed fetus is administered a certain treatment in utero, it will later, in middle age, develop a condition that causes episodes of severe pain that cannot be relieved with analgesics.

Because of the great psychological distance there would be between the developed fetus now and the middle-aged person it will become, its present time-relative interest in avoiding the later pain must be comparatively weak—much weaker, certainly, than the time-relative interest in avoiding the pain that it will later have at the time the pain will occur. The Time-Relative Interest Account therefore seems to imply that it matters much less now whether the therapy is administered. And that seems false.

The reply to this objection parallels the reply to the more general objection cited earlier. Whereas abortion affects its victim only when the victim is a fetus with weak time-relative interests, prenatal harm affects its victim later, when the victim is a person whose time-relative interests are much stronger. In the case of a late abortion, the only time-relative interest that can be satisfied or frustrated by one's action is the comparatively weak time-relative interest the developed fetus has now in continuing to live. For if an abortion is performed, the fetus will not have any future time-relative interests. If the abortion is not performed, of course, the developed fetus will later have numerous time-relative interests that can then be satisfied. But the question one faces now, where those hypothetical time-relative interests are concerned, is simply whether or not they will exist. And if one has reason now to ensure that they will exist, it must be (if one is being guided by a respect for time-relative interests) because the developed fetus has a *present* time-relative interest in the formation and satisfaction of future time-relative interests. But any present time-relative interest it has in having strong time-relative interests in the future must be weak for the same reason its time-relative interest in continuing to live is weak. (Indeed, its time-relative interest in forming and satisfying future time-relative interests is surely subsumed within its time-relative interest in continuing to live.)

In the case of prenatal injury, by contrast, one's action affects not only the weaker time-relative interests concerning its own future that the developed fetus has now, but also the stronger time-relative interests it will have later as an older child or adult. If our concern is with individuals' time-relative interests, we must take account of all the time-relative interests affected by our action. The important consideration is whether one's action frustrates a time-relative interest; it does not matter whether the act is done before the time-relative interest exists. Admittedly, the notion of a time-relative interest is supposed to indicate what an individual has egoistic reason to care about *at the time the interest is present*—so the notion itself is implicitly temporally relativized. But that does not mean that a concern for time-relative interests must be similarly restricted to presently existing time-relative interests.

In short, the objection assumes that, if we are to explain why the infliction of prenatal injury is wrong by reference to the victim's time-relative interests, we must focus on only those time-relative interests that the victim has prenatally, at the time the act is done. But that restriction is arbitrary; we must evaluate the act in terms of its effect on all those time-relative interests it affects, present or future.

This response raises a further problem, a problem of consistency. The idea that one must give equal weight to all the time-relative interests, present and future, that are affected by one's action is incompatible with what many people believe about prudential rationality, and in particular with the way that the notion of a time-relative interest is supposed to function in prudential deliberation. Recall that the notion of a time-relative interest differs from the traditional notion of an interest in that the latter presupposes that identity is the basis of rational egoistic concern about the future. If a future good would come within the boundaries of one's own life, the strength of one's present interest in that good is determined entirely by the magnitude of the good. (The magnitude of the good need not be wholly a matter of its intrinsic features, but may be affected by such considerations as whether it has been an object of desire, whether investments have been made in its realization, how it fits in the overall narrative structure of one's life, and so on.) But one's time-relative interest in some future good is a function both of the magnitude of the good and of the extent to which the prudential unity relations would hold between oneself now and oneself in the future at the time the good would occur. And this, it is normally supposed, has implications for one's present prudential rationality. If, in particular, the prudential unity relations would hold only weakly, it may be rational (or not irrational) for one *now* to give less weight to that future good—*even* if one knows that one will later have a much stronger time-relative interest in having it.

A parallel claim holds for future evils—for example, future suffering. Consider:

The Alzheimer's Patient. A woman is in the early stages of Alzheimer's disease. She knows that, for reasons peculiar to her case, she will later, after the disease has considerably advanced, suffer episodes of severe pain that will not be controllable by analgesia.

Because the progression of the disease will gradually destroy various areas of her brain involved in the generation of consciousness, the prudential unity relations will hold only weakly between herself now and herself in the later stages of the disease when the suffering will occur. Consequently, it may be rational for her now to care less about, or to give less weight to, her own future suffering. This is true even though she will later have a strong time-relative interest in avoiding that suffering. She may, in short, give less weight now to her future time-relative interests than to her present time-relative interests.

The problem is that parallel claims may seem to hold in the case of a fetus. If a fetus could deliberate about such matters, it would, like the Alzheimer's Patient, be justified in giving less weight to its own future interests—and for the same reason: namely, because the prudential unity relations between itself now and itself in the future would be weak. But, if a fetus could rationally give *its own* future interests less weight, and if the justification for abortion is that *we* are justified in giving less weight to the fetus's future because it would be only weakly related to itself in the future in the ways that matter, it seems that we can be justified in giving the fetus's future interests less weight now. If, however, we are justified in discounting the fetus's future interests, the objection to prenatal injury may be no stronger, and may even be less strong, than the objection to abortion. And that is counterintuitive. Even those who believe that abortion is permissible typically believe that the infliction of prenatal injury is seriously objectionable.

This challenge involves two errors that it is important to expose. First, the defense of abortion does not depend on discounting the fetus's *future interests*. It appeals only to the fact that the fetus's *present* time-relative interest in continuing to live is weak. Abortion cannot be contrary to the fetus's future interests because it effectively prevents them from ever arising.

Second, the claim that an individual may rationally discount *her own* future interests when the prudential unity relations would be weak does not imply that *others* would be justified in discounting them as well. For example, even though the Alzheimer's Patient can rationally discount her own future interests, it would be morally wrong for others to do so. This is because the bases of prudential concern and moral concern are different.

The foundation of prudential or egoistic concern is *relational*. It is because one will be related in an important way to some future person that it is rational for one now to care about that person in a special, egoistic way. According to the traditional view, the relation is identity. But according to the Embodied Mind Account of Egoistic Concern, it is not identity but a set of relations, most of which are constitutive of identity in the normal case. When they would be weaker, as in the case of the Alzheimer's Patient, it is not irrational *for that person* to care less about her own future.

But the core basis of moral concern is different; it is not relational but has to do with an individual's intrinsic nature. And this need not vary with time. Thus the basis of our moral concern for the Alzheimer's Patient's future interests need not be any different from the basis of our moral concern for her present interests. Her future suffering should, for example, matter just as much to a disinterested third party as her present suffering should, other things being equal.

There may be exceptions to this—that is, there may be certain cases in which at least part of the basis of moral concern about an individual diminishes over time along with the basis of egoistic concern. This might be true, for example, if some part of the basis of egoistic concern (such as psychological continuity) were also a critical component of a special relation between individuals. Consider friendship, for instance. This is regarded by most people as the sort of relation that grounds both special responsibilities and special privileges. There are various things that one may be morally required to do for a friend that one is not required to do for others. But friendship, as a special relation between two people, may require a certain stability of character in each. If one of the friends alters in ways that are detrimental to the basis of the friendship (for example, if one person's character changes in ways that are destructive of the affinities and sympathies on which the friendship is based), the friendship may weaken or collapse. Something of this sort might happen in the case of the Alzheimer's Patient. As the disease progresses and the basis of the victim's egoistic concern about the future diminishes, her character is correspondingly eroded in ways that may undermine the basis of her friendships. And as the relations that are constitutive of the friendship diminish, the special moral reasons that those who have been her friends have had to be unusually attentive to her interests may diminish in strength as well.

This conception of the special responsibilities of friendship may nor may not be plausible. Most people, I suspect, believe that friendship demands loyalty, especially in periods of great misfortune, and even when—as in the case of the Alzheimer's Patient—the misfortune involves the destruction of those aspects of a friend's character that were the principal basis for the friendship. They believe, with Shakespeare, that "love is not love which alters when it alteration finds." I cite this conception only to acknowledge the possibility that *some* dimensions of the complex bases of moral concern coincide with *some* of the bases of egoistic concern, so that there may be cases in which the basis of moral concern about a person's future well-being becomes weaker, if other things are equal, along with the basis of the person's own egoistic concern about the future.

The implications for the case of the fetus should be obvious. If it were capable of deliberating about its own future life, the developed fetus could rationally give significantly less weight to its future interests than to its present interests. This, however, is not the basis of the argument for abortion. The case for abortion does not depend on discounting the fetus's future interests, though it does appeal to the fact that abortion cannot be opposed by possible interests that it would prevent from existing. Moreover, the claim that it could be rational for the fetus to discount its own future interests does not entail that others would be justified in doing so. If other things (such as special relations) are equal, a third party must give the developed fetus's future interests as much weight as its present interests or, for that matter, anyone else's present interests. Hence—again if other things are equal—a third party has as much reason not to injure the developed fetus in a way that will later cause it to suffer a certain harm as he has not to inflict a comparable harm on another person now. For, again, the third party's reason to be morally concerned about the developed fetus's future well-being is unaffected by the fact that the developed fetus will be only weakly related, in the ways that ground *egoistic* concern, to itself in the future.

Could special relations make a difference here, as they might be thought to do in the case of the Alzheimer's Patient? I do not see how they could. We have to imagine a special relation that holds between a developed fetus and an agent capable of causing it a prenatal injury but that will systematically diminish in strength as the developed fetus matures and develops into a person. If there were such a relation, the agent's reason not to inflict the prenatal injury might be weaker the later in the victim's life the harmful effect would occur. But I can think of no special relation that has this character. Moreover, even if there were such a relation, and even if it would have disappeared entirely by the time the harmful effect of the prenatal injury would occur, the agent's primary reason not to cause harm to others—which is independent of any special relations—would still forbid the infliction of the prenatal injury. The primary moral reason the agent would have not to inflict the prenatal injury would be just as strong as his reason not to inflict a comparable harm on another person now.

This seems a reasonably plausible explanation of why an individual may rationally give his own future time-relative interests less weight than he must give to his present ones, while other people are required to give his future time-relative interests the same weight they must give his present ones. But it leaves an important question unanswered. I will pose this question by reference to the case of the Alzheimer's Patient. It seems that prudence permits the Alzheimer's Patient to care less about her future well-being than she is rationally required to care about her present well-being, and to act accordingly. But morality requires others to care equally about her present and future well-being, if other things are equal, and to act accordingly. Why, then, does *morality* not also require the Alzheimer's Patient herself to give equal weight to her future well-being? Why is she exempt from the demands that morality imposes on others, where her own future is concerned?

These questions may seem clear, but they involve a crucial ambiguity. To see the ambiguity more clearly, let us phrase the question this way: "Is the Alzheimer's Patient morally required to give equal weight to her own future well-being?" The ambiguity is in the implied comparison. The question posed *might* be whether *morality* requires the Alzheimer's Patient to give her own future well-being the same weight she is *rationally* or prudentially required to give to *her own present well-being*. If that is the question, the answer is that it does not. Morality does not require that people should give as much weight to the future well-being of others as prudence requires that they give to their own present well-being. Indeed, morality does not require that people should give that much weight to the *present* well-being of others. It does not require that we should care as much about what happens to others as prudence requires that we care about what happens to ourselves now. Therefore, if morality does not require *others* to give as much weight to the Alzheimer's Patient's future well-being as she is rationally required to give to her own present well-being, and if morality therefore does not require *her* to give as much weight to the present or future well-being of others as she is required to give to her own present well-being, it seems to follow that it also does not require her to give that much weight to her own future well-being. For it would be very odd to suppose that morality requires that we give more weight to our own future well-being than to the present well-being of others. It would, in other words, be a highly peculiar conception of morality that held that our self-regarding duties are stronger than our duties to others.

But the question I have posed might imply a different comparison. It might be understood as asking whether morality requires the Alzheimer's Patient to give her own future well-being the same weight she is morally required to give to *the future well-*

being of others (or, what comes to the same thing, the same weight that others are morally required to give to her future well-being). The answer to that question might well be, "Yes." It could be that morality imposes this limitation on the extent to which prudence permits a person to be guided by his present time-relative interests to the detriment of his own future well-being. Morality might step in at this point to take up some of the slack allowed by prudence, preventing a person from utterly disregarding the well-being of his future self in cases in which he would be almost entirely unrelated to himself in the future in the ways that ground egoistic concern.[11] And this might be supported by appealing to the idea that, when an individual would be only weakly related to himself in the future in the ways that ground egoistic concern, his future may seem, figuratively speaking, to be as much like someone else's future as it is his own. To the extent that his future seems relevantly like someone else's future, it makes more sense to suppose that any action that he now takes that will affect that future should be governed by moral as well as prudential considerations.

Suppose that, in cases in which a person would be only weakly related to himself in the future in the ways that ground egoistic concern, he is nevertheless required by morality to give his own future well-being as much weight as he is required to give to the present or future well-being of others, if other things are equal. This still allows the person to give substantially less weight to his future well-being than the traditional conception of prudence insists that he give. For, according to the traditional conception, a person is rationally required to give his future well-being the same weight as his present well-being (after discounting for uncertainty), and he is rationally required to give his present well-being substantially greater weight than the minimum weight that morality requires him to give to the well-being of others, if other things are equal.

It is also worth noting that morality may permit one to sacrifice one's own present or future interests, *for a sufficient reason,* even when one would not be permitted to sacrifice the comparable interests of *another* for the same reason. That one has this prerogative is compatible with the demand that one give one's interests at least as much weight as the interests of others. One is morally permitted to sacrifice one's interests *only* when they are outweighed. Thus it remains morally objectionable to sacrifice them for an insufficient reason.

We should be careful at this point not to confuse claims about what a person is morally or prudentially required to do with questions about whether those requirements are enforceable. Even if a person is morally required to give her future well-being as much weight as she is morally required to give to the well-being of others, this requirement may not be legitimately enforceable in the way that her duties to others often are. For acts that are entirely self-regarding (however rare such acts may be) are traditionally held to be beyond the scope of legitimate forcible intervention, at least in the case of individuals capable of autonomous choice. Thus paternalism— forcing a person to do what is best for her and therefore what is rationally required by traditional prudence—has generally been regarded as wrong. Respect for people's autonomy requires that they sometimes be allowed to do what will predictably be worse for them, even when this would not be better for others. But what about those cases (if any) in which a person is required *by morality* to give a certain weight to his own future well-being when he is not required *by prudence* to do so? There is some reason to think that in these cases the requirements of morality are not legitimately enforceable. Traditional commonsense morality has always recognized a limited range of moral duties that people owe to themselves—for example, duties to embody certain virtues even when doing so has no effect on others—but has seldom treated these duties as externally enforceable. Perhaps the moral requirement to give one's own future well-being a certain minimal weight should be regarded as similarly unenforceable. But the justification cannot be simply that it is more important to respect the person's autonomy than it is to protect his future well-being—for that justification would apply equally to acts that cause harm to others. The justification must, it seems, appeal to the fact that the harmful effects of the person's action would be confined within his own life. But this is problematic as well, given that the explanation of why the person is not required *by prudence* to avoid these effects is that he is psychologically cut off from his own future in a way that makes it seem, from his point of view now, relevantly like *someone else's* future. To the extent that his future is relevantly like someone else's future, the case against the permissibility of enforcement is weakened.

I will not pursue this matter further, as it is only tangentially related to our present concerns. I will instead turn now to another objection to my argument.

4. IS A LATER ABORTION WORSE?

Most people believe that abortions performed late in pregnancy are morally more problematic than those performed earlier. In a poll taken in the United States in 1998, 61 percent of the people polled favored having abortion legal during the first trimester of pregnancy; but only 15 percent approved of legally permitting abortions during the second trimester, and the figure dropped further to 7 percent for third trimester abortions.[12] This pattern of belief is manifest in legislation, both in the United States and in other countries, that permits abortions on demand before a certain point but subjects abortions after that point to various restrictions, which in some jurisdictions are quite stringent. An awareness that people tend to believe that later abortions are worse is also what has led activist opponents of abortion to focus their campaigns in recent years on late-term abortions, such as the notorious "partial birth abortion." I have argued that the Time-Relative Interest Account of the wrongness of killing (which is a component of the more comprehensive Two-Tiered Account) offers a plausible explanation and defense of this common belief. Of course, because I claim that abortions performed prior to twenty weeks from conception have no victim, my defense of the idea that abortion becomes morally more serious the later it is performed applies only to abortions performed after twenty weeks (that is, to what I refer to as "late abortions"). But even such a restricted defense of the common view that abortion becomes increasingly objectionable as pregnancy advances should be welcome. (For the remainder of this section, I will, for the sake of brevity, generally refer to late abortion simply as "abortion" and to the developed fetus simply as "the fetus." Thus the phrase "an earlier abortion" will, in this section, mean a late abortion that occurs earlier rather than later during the period between twenty weeks and the time at which birth would normally occur.)

According to the Time-Relative Interest Account, abortion is objectionable prima-rily on the ground that it frustrates the fetus's time-relative interest in continuing to live. Because the fetus's time-relative interest in continuing to live becomes stronger as its psychological capacities develop, the moral objection to abortion becomes stronger as pregnancy progresses. There is, however, something odd about this view. Given that the developed fetus is the kind of entity that has a time-relative interest in continuing to live, it seems highly peculiar to suppose that one would be doing what would be better *for it* to kill it earlier rather than later. Insofar as we are concerned about the fetus for its own sake, it seems that a later abortion would be preferable to an earlier one; for a longer life is preferable to a shorter one, other things being equal.

There is, therefore, a tension between these two commonsense moral beliefs:

1. Abortion is morally more acceptable when it is performed earlier rather than later.

2. Abortion is worse for the fetus when it is performed earlier rather than later.

This problem is not specific to the defense of abortion I have developed. Any account of the morality of abortion that supports the commonsense view that abortion be-comes a morally more serious matter as the fetus matures must explain how this can be so given that it seems better for the fetus to live longer rather than less long.

Can claims 1 and 2 be reconciled? One possibility might be to argue that, al-though it would be better for the fetus to die later rather than earlier, a later abortion, *as an act of killing,* is morally more objectionable because the fetus's moral status is progressively enhanced as it matures psychologically. This would be a plausible re-sponse if the moral objection to abortion were based on an assessment of the fetus's *status.* But the Time-Relative Interest Account, to which I have appealed, does not make the morality of abortion a matter of the fetus's status. It instead implies that the objection to abortion derives from the effect that abortion would have on the fetus's time-relative interests—that is, on what someone who cares about the fetus would have most reason to want for its own sake now. By this standard, the effect of an abor-tion on the fetus *at the time* is less bad if it is performed earlier rather than later.

A more promising response to this problem is simply to deny claim 2. The idea that it is better for the fetus to die later in pregnancy rather than earlier presupposes that the life it has in utero is worth living, so that more of it is better than less. This, however, is doubtful. The fetus's level of consciousness appears to be extremely rudi-mentary. Whatever experiences it might have are almost certainly dim and colorless, with no emotional content. There is no evidence to suggest that it experiences any-thing remotely resembling pleasure (for example, contentment or serenity). If this is right, the fetus's life in utero is most plausibly thought of as neutral in value: it is neither positively worth living nor intrinsically bad. The fetus therefore has no time-relative interest in its continued life in the womb, except insofar as this is necessary for the good life it may have beyond the womb. If the pregnancy is going to be aborted at some point, it will not be worse for the fetus if the abortion is performed earlier rather than later. There is therefore no conflict, for an earlier abortion is both less morally objectionable and no worse for the fetus itself.

I suspect that this response to the problem is correct. But suppose, for the sake of argument, that it is wrong. Suppose that the developed fetus's life in utero is worth living, so that it would be worse for it to die earlier in pregnancy rather than later. Or suppose, alternatively, that its moral status increases as it matures and that it is better for it to become a higher and more valuable kind of being. Either way, there would be a reason, for the fetus's own sake, to prefer a later abortion to an earlier one. Could we still maintain the commonsense view that abortion becomes morally more problematic the later it is performed?

The problem here is parallel to a problem discussed earlier, in section 7 of chapter 2—namely, the Paradox. Recall, in particular, the Choice between Deaths. As I stated it earlier, that case involved a newborn infant. For the sake of parallelism, let us now make it a developed fetus. This fetus has a condition that will very soon be fatal unless it receives a treatment that will prolong its life—in which case it will live to be thirty-five, which is the longest that anyone with this condition can live. If we consider the two possible deaths—in utero and at age thirty-five—there is a clear sense in which the earlier death would be less bad. For the individual's time-relative interest in continuing to live, which would be frustrated by death, would be substantially weaker at the time of the earlier death. Yet it is clear that, if we must choose between saving the fetus and allowing it to die, we ought to save it. And this is because there is another sense in which the earlier death would be worse. It would be worse for the fetus to die earlier rather than later if its life would be worth living.

The parallel with abortion is obvious. The reason why an earlier abortion is less bad is the same as the reason why the earlier death in the Choice between Deaths is less bad: the time-relative interest that is frustrated is weaker. But, in both abortion and the Choice between Deaths, there is also a sense in which an earlier death would be worse for the fetus: for it is better to live longer rather than less long if life would be worth living. So the resolution of the conflict between claims 1 and 2 should mirror the solution to the puzzle posed by the Choice between Deaths.

In the Choice between Deaths, two seemingly conflicting claims seem true: first, that the earlier death would be *less bad* than the later death and, second, that the earlier death would be *worse* than the later death. I suggested earlier that the conflict is at least mitigated if we see that these two claims as presupposing different forms of evaluation. The first claim—that death as a fetus is less bad than death as an adult—is about the effect that death has on the victim at the time. It is, more specifically, about the impact of the death on the victim's time-relative interests. It is this form of evaluation that naturally guides our thinking about the other case on which the Paradox is based—namely, the Choice between Lives. In this case one must choose between saving a developed fetus and saving an adult. If one chooses to save the adult on the ground that death would be worse for her than it would be for the fetus, one is being guided by one's recognition that the adult's time-relative interest in continuing to live is stronger than that of the infant.

The second claim about the Choice between Deaths—that it would be worse for the individual to die earlier rather than later—is, I suggested in chapter 2, a claim about the effect that death has on the value of the individual's life as a whole. If the individual dies as a fetus rather than later as an adult, this earlier death will have a much worse effect on the value of the individual's life as a whole than the later death would have. The individual's life as a whole will be much better if he dies at age thirty-five rather than as a fetus.

I suggested earlier that the Paradox arises from our failure to distinguish explicitly between these two forms of evaluation: evaluation by reference to time-relative interests and evaluation by reference to what would be best for an individual's life as a whole. If that is right, we can explain our beliefs about what ought to be done in the two cases in the following way. In the Choice between Lives, we ought to be guided by the comparative strengths of the different individuals' time-relative interests. But in the Choice between Deaths, we ought to be guided by what would be best for the individual's life as a whole.

This resolution of the Paradox is, however, incompatible with the argument I have advanced in support of the permissibility of abortion. For the difference that saving the fetus will make to the value of its life as a whole is enormous; therefore, if one's reason to save the fetus is based on this consideration, the reason should be correspondingly strong. But if, in the Choice between Deaths, one has a strong moral reason to save the fetus that is based on the difference that saving it will make to the value of its life as a whole, then one must have a reason that is at least that strong not to kill a fetus by aborting it. For killing a fetus would make the same enormous difference to the value of its life as a whole as letting it die would.

The reason to save the fetus in the Choice between Deaths is no stronger than the reason not to abort a fetus, if other things are equal. I have argued that the strength of the reason not to abort a fetus is commensurate with the strength of the fetus's time-relative interest in continuing to live, which is comparatively weak. It follows that, if, in the Choice between Deaths, one is concerned about the fetus for its own sake now, one's reason to save it must be comparatively weak.

If we accept this conclusion, we would seem to have two options. One is to retain the view that the reason to save the fetus is based on the difference that saving it would make to the value of its life as a whole. But we must then accept that the reason is weak even though the difference that saving it would make is very great. And this failure of correspondence between the strength of the reason and the magnitude of the difference in value seems to undermine the plausibility of this explanation of the reason. For if the reason to save an individual is weak even when the difference that saving him would make is great, it seems that the reason must be even weaker when the difference would be less. And this implies that the reason to save a middle-aged person is very weak, for the difference that saving him would make to the value of his life as a whole is arguably less than the difference that saving a fetus would make to the value of its life as a whole. But this is implausible. The reason one might have to save a middle-aged person, for his own sake, is quite strong, and in any case is certainly stronger than the reason one might have to save a fetus, if one were concerned about it for its own sake.

The other, more plausible option is to accept that the reason one has to save the fetus in the Choice between Deaths has the same source as the reason one has, in general, not to kill a fetus (for example, by aborting it). And that reason cannot be grounded in the difference that killing or letting die would make to the value of the life as a whole; otherwise there would be a stronger reason to save the life of a fetus than there is to save an adult. The argument I advanced in defense of the permissibility of abortion presupposes that one's reason not to kill the fetus derives from a more basic reason to respect its time-relative interests. The objection to killing it is therefore that this would frustrate its time-relative interest in continuing to live. And, obviously, the same objection applies to letting the fetus die in the Choice between Deaths. The objection is comparatively weak because its time-relative interest in continuing to live is weak. But even if the reason to save the fetus is comparatively weak, it is nevertheless decisive in the Choice between Deaths because it is unopposed by any conflicting reason.

Or perhaps one should say that the fetus's present time-relative interest in continuing to live does not conflict with anyone *else's* interests. For there is a sense in which the fetus's present time-relative interest conflicts with the time-relative interest in continuing to live that it will later have if it is saved. If we respect the fetus's present time-relative interest by saving it, we thereby ensure that it will suffer a *worse* death later, in the sense that when it dies later, as an adult, its time-relative interest in continuing to live will then be much stronger. If we regard the Choice between Deaths as precisely that—a choice of which death the fetus is to suffer—it may seem that a concern for its time-relative interests will dictate that we choose the death that will frustrate the weaker time-relative interest in continuing to live—that is, that we should choose for it to die at the time when it has a weaker egoistic reason to go on living. If so, we should choose for it to die as a fetus rather than as an adult—that is, we ought not to save the fetus.

This, however, cannot be right. It is highly counterintuitive to suppose that we should let the fetus die in order to spare it a worse death later. Indeed, if it is a reason to let the fetus die that this would enable it to avoid a worse death later, it must equally be a reason to kill it. But it is preposterous to suppose that there is a reason—even a reason that is always outweighed—to kill any fetus because this would prevent it from having to suffer a worse death later. But can we defend the option of saving the fetus in the Choice between Deaths by appealing solely to its time-relative interests and not to the value of its life as a whole? As I argued in the earlier discussion of the Paradox, we can. Recall that the fetus's present time-relative interest is to continue living, to be saved. And if it is saved, it will never have any time-relative interests that would have been better served by allowing it to die. Provided that its remaining life will be on balance worth living, it will never have egoistic reason to regret one's having chosen to save it. It is true, of course, that saving it will cause it (or enable it) to have a strong time-relative interest in continuing to live that will inevitably be frustrated. But a respect for the fetus's time-relative interests, present and future, does not require that we avoid the frustration of that time-relative interest by ensuring that it never exists. I said a little about this at the end of chapter 2; I will say a little more now.

Recall that death is bad primarily because it involves the loss of future goods to which one would have been related in the right way (that is, by the relations that are the basis of rational egoistic concern). It is not a sensible way of avoiding that loss to avoid getting in the right relation to the goods. That would be to avoid the *loss* of goods by precluding any possibility of having them. It would be to avoid suffering a loss by ensuring that there is nothing to lose. The reason this is not a sensible strategy is that it is a condition of having any good at all that one be vulnerable to the loss of future good. In other words, the price one pays for being the kind of being that experiences goods and stands in the right relation to further goods in the future is that one will eventually, as long as death remains inevitable, suffer the loss of goods to which one would have been related in the right way. If what is bad about death is that it prevents one from having *more* good, it makes no sense to avoid that evil by ensuring that one gets *even less*. Just as it makes no sense to prevent a person from existing on the ground that this will spare him the evil of death, so it makes no sense to prevent a fetus from continuing to exist on the ground that this will prevent it from developing and eventually suffering the frustration of a stronger time-relative interest in continuing to live.[13]

If this is right, it is unnecessary to appeal to what would be best for the fetus's life as a whole in order to explain why one ought to save its life in the Choice between Deaths. One ought to save the fetus because that is what is most in its time-relative interests. The fact that saving it will ensure that it will later suffer a worse death—in the sense that its later death will frustrate a stronger time-relative interest in continuing to live—provides no reason not to save it now.

This does not mean that the Paradox cannot be resolved in the way I suggested in chapter 2, by distinguishing what is in an individual's time-relative interests from what would be best for the individual's life as a whole. That explanation of the apparent contradiction remains valid and plausible. But I have also argued, both in chapter 2 and at greater length here, that there is an alternative and equally valid explanation that appeals only to individuals' time-relative interests. And it is this alternative explanation that is more closely linked to our reasons for action.

Return now to the case of abortion. The problem we are addressing is that there is a tension between the common view that abortion is less objectionable when it is performed earlier and the view that an earlier abortion is worse for the fetus than a later abortion, since the latter would allow the fetus to live longer. The resolution of this tension parallels the resolution of the Paradox that I have just sketched. We can concede that, if the fetus's life in utero is worth living (an assumption I think is mistaken but that I am granting for the sake of argument), it is worse for the fetus to die earlier rather than later. And this can be explained by reference to its time-relative interests. At the time that an earlier abortion might be performed, the fetus's time-relative interest is to go on living. That explains why it would be worse for it to die then rather than to continue to live and then die at some point later. (It is also true that the value of the fetus's life as a whole will be greater if it is aborted later rather than earlier; but it is unnecessary to appeal to this fact to explain why the earlier abortion would be worse for it.)

How, then, can the earlier abortion be *less* objectionable morally? The answer lies in the fact that the fetus's time-relative interests are in conflict with those of the pregnant woman. If one were guided solely by a concern for the fetus's time-relative interests, one would not abort it earlier—indeed, one would not abort it at all. Whether an abortion is justified, and, if so, at what point during pregnancy the justification would be strongest (that is, at what point the considerations favoring abortion would most decisively outweigh those opposing it), is determined by how the time-relative interests of the pregnant woman weigh against those of the fetus. Given this criterion, an abortion performed earlier is more likely to be justified, or to be more strongly justified, than one performed later. For, assuming that it would be better for the woman to have the abortion as soon as possible, her time-relative interest in having an abortion will be stronger in the case of an earlier abortion. And the time-relative interest of the fetus that is opposed to an abortion—its time-relative interest in continuing to live—will be weaker in the case of an earlier abortion. It is therefore likely that the woman's time-relative interests will outweigh those of the developed fetus *by more* the earlier the abortion is performed. And it is for this reason that, all things considered, a late abortion becomes more difficult to justify, and therefore more problematic morally, the later it is performed.

5. TIME-RELATIVE INTERESTS AND ADAPTATION

I have argued that it is a mistake to suppose that one's reason to save the fetus in the Choice between Deaths is that this would be better for its life as a whole. If one's reason had to do with the effect that saving it would have on the value of this life as a whole, the reason would be considerably stronger than in fact it is. By parity of reasoning, it is a mistake to suppose that one's reason not to kill a fetus has to do with the effect that killing it would have on the value of its life as a whole. It does not follow, however, that we ought never to be guided, morally, by a concern for the effect that our action would have on the value of an individual's life as a whole. And there are cases that suggest that we must be guided by just this concern. To see this, we need to reconsider the problem of prenatal injury.

I argued in section 3 of this chapter that we can explain why the infliction of prenatal injury is objectionable by noting the effect that it has both on the fetus's present time-relative interests and on its future time-relative interests. But there are certain cases in which it seems that our intuitions cannot be supported in this way. I will discuss two such cases (the Fetus with Cerebral Deficits and Prenatal Retardation) in section 6.3 of this chapter. For the moment, I will focus on a different type of case, one that raises a different problem.

> *Prenatal Blinding.* A pregnant woman will develop a moderate but permanent disability unless she takes a certain drug. When taken by a pregnant woman, however, this drug predictably causes a more severe disability—congenital blindness—in the fetus. In spite of this, the woman takes the drug.

Most of us believe that the woman's act in this case is wrong. She knowingly causes her own child to have a severe disability in order to avoid suffering a lesser disability herself. According to the argument presented in section 3 of this chapter, the reason why it is wrong for her to take the drug is not just that her doing so frustrates the fetus's present time-relative interest in later being sighted rather than blind; it is also that it dooms to frustration the much stronger time-relative interests that the fetus will later have when it becomes a person. The assumption is that these interests of her child will outweigh her own interest in avoiding the lesser disability.

There is, however, a reason for doubting that this assumption must be true. For, as her child grows older, he may adapt to his actual life of blindness. He may form bonds with other blind people, develop musical abilities that he otherwise would not have had, shape his identity around his blindness—for example, by becoming an activist on behalf of the blind, and so on. Thus the period in which he would *rationally regret* being blind may be comparatively brief. During his adult life, he may rationally prefer to have been born blind.[14] I call this phenomenon *adaptation*.

The mere fact that he would prefer to have been born blind would not necessarily show that having been born blind was not against his later time-relative interests. His preference might be irrational. It would be irrational, for example, if it derived from a knowledge of certain studies that suggest that congenitally blind people who are later enabled to see have more trouble orienting themselves in the world than they did when they were blind.[15] This fact is irrelevant to whether the person should prefer to have been *born* with the ability to see.

Suppose, however, the person quickly adapts to his blindness and that his preference for having been born blind is rational—perhaps because the life he has is better, *in terms of the values that he has within it,* than the life he would have had if his mother had not taken the drug. In that case, it may be that the woman's interests over time in not having the moderate disability will outweigh her child's conflicting time-relative interests, both present and future, in being sighted rather than blind. For the child's time-relative interest in being sighted would be confined to the early parts of his life, while the woman's interest in not having the moderate disability would extend over a considerably longer period—assuming, of course, that she would adapt to it less well. In spite of this, however, it seems clear that her action was wrong.

This problem is quite general. Even though they are usually unaware of it at the time, people often face choices that will determine which of certain very different alternative lives they will have. And it is often true that a person would prefer *each* alternative future *from within it.* For a person's preferences tend to adapt to his or her actual circumstances. It is, for example, undoubtedly true of most people who are married and have children that they could have been happier had they married a different person and had different children. But even if a person had the knowledge that he would have been happier if he had married someone else and had different children, it is likely that, deeply embedded in his actual life, he would not prefer to have had that alternative, happier life. His attachments are to the people who make up his actual life. Let us say that adaptation has occurred when a person prefers his actual life to an alternative life that he might have had and in which he would have been better off or have had a higher level of well-being.

The phenomenon of adaptation threatens to undermine the solution I proposed in section 3 to the problem of prenatal injury. For it is sometimes true that a person whose life has been greatly affected by a prenatal injury may rationally prefer that life, from within it, to an alternative life without the injury in which he would have been better off. When this is the case, the act that caused the injury cannot be criticized for its adverse impact on the person's later time-relative interests.

(It is worth noting that this problem also threatens to undermine a more familiar but parallel response to the problem of prenatal injury that appeals to the fetus's future *interests.* As we have seen, many people who argue for the permissibility of abortion do so on the ground that the fetus—at least up to a certain point—is not the sort of entity that can have interests, or not the sort of entity that can have interests in a future life of which it can now form no conception and about which it can therefore have no desires.[16] In order to explain the wrongness of inflicting prenatal injury, these people appeal to the impact that prenatal injury will have on the later interests of the person the fetus will eventually become. They claim, for example, that, although the fetus can have no present interest in later being sighted rather than blind, it is nevertheless wrong to injure it in a way that will cause it to be born blind, because this will frustrate the interest it will later have in being able to see. But just as the adverse effect of prenatal injury on an individual's time-relative interests may be short-lived because of adaptation, so the effect on his interests may likewise be only temporary—for, in the case of normal adults, interests and time-relative interests tend to coincide. Thus those who appeal to this familiar objection to the infliction of prenatal injury must, it seems, revise their views.)

It may seem that the best we can do, if we insist on trying to solve the problem of prenatal injury by appealing only to people's time-relative interests, is to claim that an act that would cause prenatal injury would *probably* frustrate the victim's future time-relative interests. That may well be true in most cases. But in those cases in which it turns out, because of adaptation, that the person rationally prefers his actual life with the injury to the better life he would have had without it, his actual later time-relative interests may not provide a sufficient basis for objecting to the act that caused the injury. Should we concede that, while it may have been reasonable to believe that the act was wrong, it turns out that it was not?

That would be a mistake. At the time it was performed, the act that caused the injury was wrong, and this judgment is not overturned by the person's later preferring his actual life with the injury. It may, indeed, have been entirely predictable that he would. The judgment that the infliction of prenatal injury is wrong seems to be based instead on the assumption that a life without the injury would be *a better life as a whole* than a life with the injury. Prior to the person's forming attachments within any of the possible alternative lives, one surely ought to choose for him the best life among those that are possible for him, insofar as these matters are predictable and other things are equal.

It seems, in short, that in deliberating about choices that may cause or risk causing prenatal injury, one should be guided, other things being equal, by the effect that one's choice will have on the fetus's life as a whole. Yet I have argued that, in determining whether abortion is permissible, one ought to be guided, not by the effect an abortion would have on the value of the fetus's life as a whole, but by the effect it would have on the fetus's time-relative interests. Are these claims consistent or are we inconsistently switching theories in mid-argument in order to get intuitively plausible results across a range of different cases?

If our intuitions are to be trusted, it seems that there are some contexts in which one's treatment of a particular individual is appropriately guided primarily by a concern for the individual's time-relative interests. Yet there are other contexts in which it seems appropriate to be guided instead by a concern for what would be better for the individual's life as a whole. If this is right, we must have a principled criterion for determining in which cases we should focus on time-relative interests and in which we should focus on what would be best for the life as a whole.

Given the way the terms are ordinarily used, whatever would be best for an individual's life as a whole is also what would be most in that individual's interests. Thus our question can be rephrased this way: "In which cases should we be guided by a concern for an individual's *interests* and in which should we be guided by a concern for his *time-relative interests?*" As I have noted earlier, an individual's interests and time-relative interests normally coincide. But there are two ways in which an individual's time-relative interests may diverge from his interests. There is *strong divergence* when one option or outcome would be in an individual's best interest while a different and incompatible option or outcome would be in his best time-relative interest. The case of Spontaneous Division, cited in section 1.1 of chapter 3, provides an example of strong divergence. In that case, an individual will spontaneously divide unless we prevent her from doing so. If she does not divide, she will die in a year; if she divides, her successors can expect to live for many years. Because dividing would cause her to cease to exist now rather than in a year, it would be against this person's interest to divide. But she has a strong time-relative interest in dividing, for she would be strongly related in the ways that ground egoistic concern to *both* of the long lives of her successors. Strong divergence may also occur in cases involving *fusion*. If, for example, a person would die in a month if he were not to fuse with another person now, it would be against his interest to undergo fusion (because that would cause him to cease to exist now), but it might be in his time-relative interest to do so.

There is *weak divergence* between an individual's interests and his time-relative interests when both favor the same option or outcome but are of different strengths. For example, a fetus whose future life would be well worth living has both an interest and a time-relative interest in continuing to live. But while its interest in continuing to live is very strong, its time-relative interest in continuing to live is comparatively weak. For the strength of its interest is commensurate with the value of the life it will have if it survives; but its time-relative interest reflects the value that its future life has for it *now,* and that value has to be discounted for the fact that the fetus would be only weakly related to itself in the future in some of the ways that ground egoistic concern.

There can be strong divergence between one's interests and one's time-relative interests only when it is rational for one to be egoistically concerned about some good (or evil) that would be outside the boundaries of one's own life. (In such a case, one's time-relative interest in one option might be stronger than one's interest in another, either because the amount of good outside one's life about which one might be egoistically concerned would exceed that within one's life, or because the relations that ground egoistic concern would be stronger between oneself and someone else than they would be between oneself now and oneself later.) According to the Embodied Mind Account of Egoistic Concern, there are only two such types of case— namely, cases involving division and cases involving fusion—and both of these are merely hypothetical. (Other accounts of the basis of egoistic concern may recognize other cases in which it can be rational for one to be egoistically concerned about events outside one's own life. The Psychological Account of Egoistic Concern, for example, implies that teletransportation and cases involving pre-persons and post-persons may be cases of this sort.) In all actual cases, the only goods (or evils) about which it can be rational for one to be egoistically concerned are ones that will fall within the boundaries of one's own life. In these cases, there can be only weak divergence. And the only form the divergence can take is that one's time-relative interest in a certain future good may be *weaker* than one's interest in it. The strength of one's interest in the good is commensurate with the value that it would contribute to one's life as a whole. One's time-relative interest, by contrast, may be of comparable strength only if the prudential unity relations would hold maximally between oneself now and oneself at the time the good would occur. Otherwise, the strength of one's time-relative interest in having the good must be diminished for any reduction in the strength of those relations—though presumably only substantial reductions are of practical significance.

In short, the cases in which significant divergence is possible between an individual's interests and his time-relative interests are hypothetical cases in which an individual may rationally be egoistically concerned about goods (or evils) outside the boundaries of his own life and cases in which the prudential unity relations would hold to an unusually weak degree between an individual and himself at some later point in his life. Cases of this latter sort involve significantly diminished physical or functional continuity of an individual's brain or significantly diminished psychological continuity within his life—for example, cases of people who suffer brain damage or dementia or cases involving fetuses or infants. The divergence between interests and time-relative interests tends to be less when the weakened base for egoistic concern is the result of damage or deterioration in the brain, for these phenomena tend to reduce the amount of good in a person's future as well as weakening the basis for egoistic concern. Hence the person's interests weaken along with his time-relative interests. But the amount of good that lies in prospect for a fetus or an infant is normally very great; thus its interest in having that good is very strong, while its time-relative interest is relatively weak. It is therefore in cases involving fetuses and infants that the most significant instances of weak divergence occur.

I have suggested that, in general, we should be guided in cases of divergence by a concern for individuals' time-relative interests rather than for their interests, if other things are equal (particularly, of course, if there are no issues of respect for persons or for their autonomy). There is, however, at least one possible exception: namely, cases involving a possibility of prenatal injury followed by adaptation. Most of us believe that prenatal injury is seriously objectionable even if it would be followed by adaptation—even, perhaps, if the victim would *never* actually regret that he had been injured and would indeed prefer his life with the injury to an alternative life in which it would never have occurred. To defend this intuition, it seems that we cannot appeal to the effect that prenatal injury would have on the victim's present and future time-relative interests. We must instead appeal to the effect that the injury would have on the value of the victim's life as a whole—that is, on the victim's *interests*.

Is there a basis for distinguishing between this case and the others? One suggestion is to appeal to the following principle:

> *The Criterion.* In cases in which there is a divergence, whether strong or weak, between an individual's interests and his time-relative interests, one should be guided by a concern for his time-relative interests *if* one's choice will determine whether the individual will continue to exist; otherwise, if the individual will exist in all the outcomes of one's choice, one should be guided by a concern for his interests, or the effect one's choice will have on the value of his life as a whole.

The Criterion appears to sort the cases in a way that conforms to our intuitions. In cases in which there is strong divergence—that is, cases involving division or fusion—it requires that we be guided by a concern for the time-relative interests of those involved. For although an individual who divides or undergoes fusion does not literally die, he does cease to exist. Abortion, the Choice between Deaths, and the Choice between Lives are all cases involving weak divergence in which one's choice will determine whether an individual will continue to exist; thus, according to the Criterion, these cases, too, should be decided by reference to the time-relative interests of the individuals concerned. But cases involving a possibility of prenatal injury (or perhaps neonatal injury) are different. In these cases, there is weak divergence between the fetus's interests and its time-relative interests. But since the fetus will exist in both outcomes of one's choice—that is, whether one causes the prenatal injury or not—the Criterion implies that one ought to be guided by the effect that one's choice will have on the interests of all concerned (that is, by the effect that it will have on the values of individuals' lives as wholes).

Intuitively this all seems right. Is there a principled rationale for distinguishing among the cases in this way? Why should it be a reason for focusing on an individual's time-relative interests that one's choice will determine whether or not he will continue to exist? One suggestion is that, if one's choice will determine whether an individual will continue to exist, the goods of that individual's possible future life should count in favor of the option in which he will continue to exist only if he has a significant time-relative interest in having those goods. For suppose we were to insist that, even when the individual has no significant time-relative interest in those goods, they should nevertheless count as much in favor of preserving his life as they would if he did have a strong time-relative interest in having them. This would be too much like insisting that the goods that a person's life would contain *if he were to come into existence* count in favor of causing him to exist in the same way and to the same extent that the goods of a person's future count normally in favor of saving his life. And no one believes that.

The basic point is that causing or allowing a fetus to continue to exist is, in moral terms, relevantly analogous to causing or allowing someone to come into existence; for in neither case is there anyone now who would be significantly related in the ways that matter to the goods of the future life that is in prospect. If this analogy is valid, then, just as the fact that an individual's life would contain certain goods if he were caused to exist does not provide a significant moral reason to cause or allow him to exist, so the fact that an individual's future life would contain certain goods does not provide a significant moral reason to cause or allow him to *continue* to exist *unless* he now has a significant time-relative interest in having those goods. In short, there is no significant moral reason, if other things are equal, to ensure the existence of future goods unless there is someone to whom the existence of those goods matters in an egoistic way—in particular, someone with a significant time-relative interest that would be frustrated if the goods were not to exist.

In suggesting these claims, I am colliding head-on with a range of problems in an area that I once referred to as "population theory."[17] As Derek Parfit has shown, there are cases in which we seem to have a moral reason to ensure the existence of certain goods even when the absence of those goods would not frustrate anyone's time-relative interests or, indeed, be worse for anyone in any way.[18] Impersonal considerations have a role in our moral thought.[19]

Furthermore, in appealing to the commonsense conviction that the expectation that an individual's life would contain certain goods provides no significant moral reason to cause that individual to exist, I am raising the problem of justifying what I have elsewhere called the *Asymmetry*.[20] The Asymmetry is the view that, while the expectation that a person's life would be worth living provides no moral reason to cause that person to exist, the expectation that a person's life would be worth *not* living *does* provide a moral reason *not* to cause that person to exist. Most of us are strongly committed to this view. But it is notoriously difficult to defend. For it seems, in the abstract, that there should be a perfect symmetry here. If the goods in a person's possible life provide little or no reason to cause him to exist, it seems that the evils in his life should provide little or no reason not to cause him to exist. The presumption of symmetry here means that, if one wants—as I do—to appeal to the claim that the goods in a person's possible life provide little or no reason to cause him to exist, one must be prepared to show that this does not commit one to the parallel claim about possible evils. But I cannot show this.

One suggestion that may seem obvious at this point is that, whereas failing to cause a person to exist does not necessarily frustrate anyone's time-relative interests, causing someone to exist when the contents of his life are predominantly bad is to cause him to have numerous frustrated time-relative interests. There are, however, various objections to this. I will note only one. If the fact that someone would have time-relative interests that would be frustrated counts against causing him to exist, then the fact that he would also have time-relative interests that would be satisfied must count in favor of causing him to exist. Otherwise it would never be permissible, if we confine ourselves to the effect our action would have on the people themselves, to cause people to exist. For everyone has time-relative interests that go unsatisfied. If that fact could not be counterbalanced by the fact that people also tend to have even stronger time-relative interests that do get satisfied, it would always be presumptively wrong to cause people to exist. Since it is not wrong to cause people to exist, even when the net impact on existing people is neutral, it follows that the fact that a person would have time-relative interests that would be satisfied counts in favor of causing him to exist. But this contradicts the claim to which I have appealed in support of the Criterion.

This is just one example of the difficulties one faces when one attempts to defend the seemingly obvious and compelling belief that there is no significant reason to cause the existence of goods whose absence would not frustrate any significant time-relative interest—no reason, in particular, to cause people to exist just because their lives would contain sufficient good to outweigh any bad. Yet my limited defense of the Criterion has appealed to precisely this belief. That there is no strong moral reason to sustain an individual's life, even if it would contain much good, unless the individual has a strong time-relative interest in its continuation, is an idea that has the same source, I believe, as the view that there is no strong moral reason to cause a person to exist just because his life would contain much good. The latter view is deeply intuitive and probably impossible to dislodge; but it is, as I have suggested, notoriously difficult to defend. Similarly, and for similar reasons, the Criterion seems to account well for our intuitions about the various cases; but it may be on unstable theoretical ground.

The real problem, it may be objected, is not so much to justify the appeal to time-relative interests as it is to justify the Criterion's insistence that, in cases of weak divergence in which the individuals affected will exist in all the outcomes of one's choice, one must be guided by a respect for their interests rather than their time-relative interests. According to this objection, we can readily understand why in cases such as Spontaneous Division or abortion we should be guided by a concern for time-relative interests rather than interests. For to do otherwise would be to assume that identity is what matters—that is, that identity is the basis of egoistic concern. In Spontaneous Division, for example, the person's own future life would contain only a year's worth of further good; but the lives of his two possible successors, to whom he would be related in the ways that are normally constitutive of identity, would each contain a great deal of good. If other things are equal, it simply makes no sense to opt for the lesser good unless identity itself, rather than the relations that are constitutive of identity in the normal case, is the basis of egoistic concern. But, according to the Criterion, we ought to be guided by a concern for the fetus's interests—that is, for the value of its life as a whole—in cases involving a possibility of prenatal injury. And does not that presuppose that identity is what matters? For if what matters is the set of relations identified by the Embodied Mind Account of Egoistic Concern, the strength of one's reason to avoid causing prenatal injury should be determined by the strength of the fetus's time-relative interests, both present and future, not by the difference one's action would make to the value of its life as a whole. Only if identity is the basis of egoistic concern should a concern for the sake of the fetus as it is now give us a reason to do what would be best for the value of its life as a whole.

The phenomenon of adaptation appears, therefore, to pose an extremely difficult problem. If the Embodied Mind Account of Egoistic Concern is correct and identity is not the basis of egoistic concern, there can be only a relatively weak reason, for the sake of a fetus *now,* not to injure it in a way that would be worse for it only later in its life. And if one could be confident that adaptation would occur, there may also be only a relatively weak reason, or no reason at all, not to injure the fetus because of a concern for what would *later* matter to it in an egoistic way. For if adaptation occurs, it will rationally prefer its actual life with the injury to the possible life it would have had if the injury had not been inflicted. In short, if our concern for the fetus is only for what it has or will have egoistic reason to care about, we may have only a comparatively weak reason not to injure it in ways that would make its later life worse. This, however, is hard to accept. The common intuition is that our reason not to cause prenatal injury is quite strong. I suggested that one way of trying to defend that intuition is to appeal to the Criterion. But the Criterion appears to presuppose that, in cases in which those affected by our action would exist in all the possible outcomes of our choice, we should act as if identity were the basis of egoistic concern. Since I have argued that identity is not the basis of egoistic concern, I seem to be denied the option of appealing to the Criterion. An alternative way of trying to defend the common intuition is to note that the infliction of prenatal injury would be worse *impersonally,* in that the overall state of affairs will contain less good if the injury is inflicted than if it is not. But this response to the problem is incompatible with the approach that I have taken to the problem of abortion. In general, it would be impersonally worse for a woman to have an abortion than to carry the fetus to term, for the outcome in which the fetus lives a long life is almost certain to contain more good than the outcome in which it is killed before it is born.

Perhaps it is not unacceptable, after all, to be guided by a concern for individuals' time-relative interests rather than by their interests in cases, such as Prenatal

Blinding, in which prenatal injury would be followed by adaptation. Suppose that, in Prenatal Blinding, it was predictable that the woman's interest in not having a moderate disability would, over time, outweigh the limited time-relative interests, present and future, that her child would have in being born sighted rather than blind. In that case, the reason she has, at the time, to take the drug would seem to be stronger than the sum of the reasons that her child would ever have for wishing that she had not taken it—even though her taking the drug would make the child's life as a whole worse *by more* than her not taking it would be worse for her life as a whole.

It may be easier to accept this if we recognize how rare such cases must be. They are rare for several reasons. First, it is always uncertain whether adaptation will occur. Second, in cases involving significant disability, even if adaptation does occur, it remains possible that the person's preference for his life with the disability is misguided. He may simply fail to recognize that the life he would have had without the disability would have been better, not only in terms of the values he would have had within that alternative life, but also in terms of the values that inform his actual life. Third and finally, it typically takes a long time for adaptation to occur. Thus an act that causes prenatal injury will be opposed not only by the weak time-relative interest of the fetus but also by the time-relative interests it will have as a child before the process of adaptation is completed. These will usually be substantial enough in strength and duration to weigh heavily against any interests that might be served by the infliction of prenatal injury.

Perhaps, however, the solution to the problem of adaptation lies beyond considerations within the morality of interests. I have claimed that the developed fetus does not come within the scope of the morality of respect. Thus the killing of a fetus, like the killing of an animal, cannot be criticized on the ground that it violates a requirement of respect. But, unlike the victim of an abortion, the victim of prenatal injury is not just a fetus. That victim is, admittedly, a fetus at the time that the injury is caused; but if the act has delayed or continuing harmful effects, it also harms the victim when he is a person—assuming, of course, that adaptation is not completed until after the victim becomes a person (which, in the nature of the case, is bound to be true). This fact seems sufficient to bring prenatal injury within the scope of the morality of respect. If so, it is not a sufficient justification for causing prenatal injury that the present and future interests served by causing it would outweigh the present and future time-relative interests of the fetus in avoiding it. For one of the distinctive features of the morality of respect is that it imposes constraints on sacrificing the interests of an individual as a means of promoting or protecting the greater interests of others. Given that prenatal injury inflicts harm on a person, it seems to be ruled out, even in cases involving predictable adaptation, not because it sacrifices greater interests for lesser, but because it violates the requirement of respect for persons.

6. POTENTIAL

6.1. *Potential and Identity*

It is frequently claimed that, even though abortion is not *murder*, because it does not involve the killing of a *person*, it is nevertheless seriously objectionable because it thwarts the fetus's potential. The focus is often on the fetus's potential to become a person. It is, for example, often claimed that abortion is wrong because the fetus is a potential person and it is seriously wrong to kill potential persons, even if it is not quite murder. In this section I will seek to understand exactly what sort of potential the fetus has and what its moral significance is.

The claim that the fetus is a potential person, or has the potential to become a person, is ambiguous. There are at least three ways in which it might be interpreted. I will try to elucidate these three interpretations by noting what each asserts about the relation between me and the fetus from which I developed.

First, the claim might mean that the fetus from which I developed was not me but had the potential to become me. One might make this claim if one believed that we are essentially persons—that is, that we cannot exist except as persons.

Second, the claim that the fetus is a potential person is perhaps more commonly understood to mean that, although I once existed as a fetus, I was not then a person and, consequently, my moral status was different from what it is now. Understood in this way, the claim presupposes that we are *not* essentially persons. On this view, "person" is a phase sortal—that is, a predicate that may apply to us only during a certain phase, or certain phases, of our existence.

Third, the claim is sometimes interpreted to mean that the fetus in its *present* state is an uncompleted person, a person in the process of becoming, a being whose essential nature is to evolve into a full-fledged person.[21] The person is understood to be somehow latently or even occultly present in the potential person. This is thought to explain why whatever is morally due to a person is also due to a potential person.

Whether the claim that the fetus is a potential person—however that claim is interpreted—can ground a forceful objection to abortion depends, in part, on what is meant by "person." Let us assume for the sake of argument that "being a person" is shorthand for the possession of properties that are the basis of a high moral status—so that, for example, persons come within the scope of the morality of respect, or possess rights such as the right to life. I will continue to use "person" to refer to any being with a comparatively highly developed set of psychological capacities. But this is compatible with the assumption that personhood is a basis of high moral status, for it is plausible to suppose that the possession of the relevant psychological capacities is a sufficient basis for commanding respect or possessing rights.

The claim that the fetus is a potential person has to be examined in relation to the distinction that I have drawn between the early fetus and the developed fetus. If the Embodied Mind Account of Identity is correct, the developed fetus—but not the early fetus—is identical with (that is, is the same individual as) the person into whom it might develop. Thus the first interpretation of the claim that the fetus is a potential person can apply only to the early fetus, while the second interpretation can apply only to the developed fetus. (The third interpretation, which is rather more obscure, might be thought to apply to either. I will return to it later.) It will therefore be helpful to consider separately the potential of the early fetus and that of the developed fetus.

Consider first the claim that the early fetus has the potential to become a person. This must mean that, while the early fetus is not the same individual as the person, it can nevertheless become or develop into that person. As I indicated in section 1 of this chapter, I believe that this claim is false when understood in a way that would make it clearly morally significant, and true only when understood in a way that seems largely morally insignificant. To see why this is so, we need to distinguish between two understandings of the notion of potential.[22]

There is a sense in which X has the potential to become Y only if X and Y would be identical—that is, only if X and Y would be one and the same individual entity. Or, rather, since what an individual has the potential to become is normally a thing of a certain *sort,* perhaps we should say that X has the potential to become a Y in this first sense only if X will continue to exist as a Y. It is in this sense that Prince Charles has the potential to become the king of England, since he would continue to exist as king. If he realizes his potential to become the king, he and the king will be one and the same individual. I will call this kind of potential *identity-preserving potential.* (Notice that if X has the identity-preserving potential to become a Y, it seems that "Y" must be a phase sortal. X cannot become an entity of a different substantial kind and continue to exist.)

Identity-preserving potential contrasts with what I will call *nonidentity potential.* Nonidentity potential may take a variety of forms, which are unified by two features: first, when X has the nonidentity potential to become Y (or a Y), Y will not, when it exists, be identical with X (or Y will not just be a phase in the history of X); but, second, we nevertheless employ the idiom of "becoming" in describing the transition from X to Y. In the commonest case, when X has the nonidentity potential to become Y, X gives rise to, or causally contributes to the production of Y when its constituent matter is transformed in such a way that, while X itself ceases to exist, a new and different individual, Y, is formed out of that same matter. We say, for example, that the sperm and egg together have the potential to become a zygote. This is a paradigm of nonidentity potential, for when the sperm and egg fuse, they both cease to exist but the zygote is created out of the matter of which they were composed. Or, to take another example, consider the possibility of running my wooden desk through a wood chipper, which grinds wood into sawdust. We have no hesitation in saying that my desk would become a pile of sawdust and therefore that it is now potentially a pile of sawdust or has the potential to become a pile of sawdust. But this is a deviant form of *becoming,* since it would involve the ceasing to exist of the desk. The desk's constituent matter would continue to exist and would take a new form, but the desk itself would no longer exist. Thus the desk's potential to become a pile of sawdust is nonidentity potential.

Not all forms of nonidentity potential conform to this paradigm. In some instances in which X has the nonidentity potential to become Y, X does not cease to exist when it is causally involved in the production of Y but coexists with Y without being identical to it. An example is the potential a lump of bronze has to become a statue. When the lump of bronze is shaped in a certain way, we say that it becomes a statue. But the common view is that the statue is a new and distinct individual entity: it is not identical with or the same thing as the lump of bronze. Thus the lump of bronze continues to exist when the statue begins to exist; they coexist, both sharing the same constituent matter.

(Some might challenge this example on the ground that the lump of bronze in fact has the identity-preserving potential to become a statue, since the statue is really not a distinct substance but is only a phase in the history of the lump of bronze, in the same way that a child is not distinct from the person but simply *is* that person during a certain phase of his or her life. But, to show that the lump of bronze and the statue are distinct substances, Derek Parfit has suggested that we imagine that the statue is hollowed out, with all the bronze removed from the interior collected in a single lump, leaving the surface material unaffected.[23] The bronze that has been extracted would be the original lump of bronze—since a lump of bronze can continue to exist if it loses only a tiny proportion of its constituent matter. But suppose the lump was then destroyed, by being turned into coins. The statue would nevertheless continue to exist, although it would now be hollow—or alternatively, it might be filled back in with a cheaper iron ore. That the statue could continue to exist after the lump of bronze had ceased to exist shows that they are distinct substances.)

Of the two types of potential, it is normally only identity-preserving potential that is capable of grounding an interest in its own realization. That is, it is normally only if X's potential to become Y is identity-preserving that X can have an interest in becoming Y, or that it can be good for X to become Y. In the commonest case, if X has the nonidentity potential to become Y, the realization of the potential involves the ceasing to exist of X. And it is seldom in an individual's interest to cease to exist— though of course there are comparatively rare cases when it is. Thus a person whose life has ceased to be worth living may have an interest in the realization of his nonidentity potential to become a corpse. In the case of nonidentity potential whose realization does not involve the ceasing to exist of the original entity, it is in principle possible that X could have an interest in "becoming" Y because the existence of Y would somehow benefit X even though Y would be a different individual from X. But I cannot think of any instances in which this would be true.

Return now to the issue of fetal potential. Let us first consider the early fetus, then the developed fetus. Having distinguished between identity-preserving and nonidentity potential, we can now see why the early fetus cannot have an interest in becoming a person. Most previous discussions have assumed that the potential of the early fetus to become a person is identity-preserving. But if, as I have argued, we are not identical with our organisms, this assumption is false. The early fetus is simply the human organism in its early stages. It therefore has the identity-preserving potential to become a mature or adult human organism. But the adult human organism will not be the same individual as the adult person or self. Therefore the early fetus does not have the identity-preserving potential to become a person. It has only the nonidentity potential to become a person. Its nonidentity potential is of the second sort described above: that is, as it matures, the fetal organism causally gives rise to the existence of the individual who will become a person but it does not thereby cease to exist. Rather, it continues to exist as a mature organism that coexists with the person.

Because the early fetus has only the nonidentity potential to become a person, it lacks an interest in the realization of that potential. It could have an interest in becoming a person if it would actually *be* that person, but that is what we must deny if we accept that we are not identical with our organisms. Assuming that the early fetus has only the nonidentity potential to become a person, the only way it could have an interest in the realization of that potential would be if the later existence of the person would somehow benefit the organism. But, as I noted earlier, a mere organism lacks the capacity for consciousness (or has it only derivatively) and therefore is not the kind of entity that can be benefited in the morally relevant sense.

It is, of course, strange that we describe the organism's giving rise to the existence of the person as its *becoming* that person. But the same sense of "becoming"—that is, one that does not presuppose the continued existence of the entity that becomes something else—also appears in other contexts: for example, when it is said that the sperm and the egg become a zygote. The basis for this locution is probably the persistence, in the same region of space, of the constituent matter of the original entity, as if the thing that does the becoming were the matter itself rather than the entity it composed.

I have argued that the early fetus cannot have an interest in the realization of its potential to become a person, for that potential is not identity-preserving. Yet those who believe that even the early fetus has significant potential could argue that there are ways in which potential can be morally significant other than by an individual's having an interest in the realization of its potential. We should distinguish three ways in which potential might be morally significant:

1. X's potential to become a Y might be morally significant because it would be good for X, or in X's interest or time-relative interest, to become a Y.
2. X's potential to become a person might be morally significant because it would be good or valuable, either for others or impersonally (though not for X), for there to be a Y, or more Ys than there already are.
3. X's potential to become a person might be morally significant because it would give X an enhanced moral status.

I will discuss the third of these in the following section. For reasons that I will give there, this way in which potential may be valuable is not relevant to the case of the early fetus. But the second of these ways in which potential might be valuable may well apply to the early fetus. For the early fetus has the nonidentity potential to develop into (that is, to give rise to the existence of) a person. To the extent that it is good or desirable that new people should exist with lives worth living, the early fetus's potential is instrumentally important. In order for the early fetus's potential to be important in this way, it is not necessary that the early fetus should benefit from its realization; hence it does not matter that the early fetus's potential to become a person is not identity-preserving. For, on this view, the value lies in the *outcome,* not in the effect on the early fetus itself.

There are, however, two points that should be noted. First, the moral significance of the early fetus's potential lies wholly in the value of what it is a potential *for*—that is, the existence of the person. If there is a reason to respect the early fetus's potential, it has nothing to do with any alleged interests, good, or status of the early fetus itself. It has to do instead with the desirability of a person's coming into existence with a life worth living. Second, any healthy pair of sperm and egg has the same nonidentity potential that the early fetus has to become a person. Thus, making allowances for differences in the probability that their potentials will be realized, whatever reason there is to promote the early fetus's potential is equally a reason to ensure that the potential of the sperm and egg is also realized. So if the early fetus's potential counts against an abortion, the potential of the sperm and egg counts equally in favor of conception and against contraception.

The claim that a sperm and egg together have the potential to become a person is quite commonly advanced as a reductio ad absurdum argument against appeals to fetal potential. The contention is that if one objects to abortion on the ground that the fetus is a potential person, one must oppose contraception as well, since that, too, actively thwarts the potential that the sperm and egg have to become a person. While this argument has force, its scope is narrowly restricted. It is a plausible response to anti-abortion arguments that appeal to the fetus's potential when the only relevant potential the fetus has is nonidentity potential. For that is the sort of potential that the sperm and egg have. The argument is therefore quite forceful in exposing the limited moral significance of the early fetus's nonidentity potential to become a person. But it has no force against the claim that late abortion is wrong because it frustrates the potential of the developed fetus to become a person. For the developed fetus's potential to become a person is identity-preserving, and is therefore completely different in kind from the potential of the sperm and egg.

Because the developed fetus's potential to become a person is identity-preserving, the developed fetus itself can have an interest in its realization. Its potential, in other words, may be morally significant in the first of the three ways I distinguished. The claim that it is wrong to thwart the developed fetus's potential to become a person might be based on the assumption that it is wrong to frustrate its *interest* in becoming a person. And to say that it has an interest in becoming a person is just to say that it would be better for it to be a person, either because its acquisition of the attributes constitutive of personhood would enable it have a much higher level of well-being, or because in becoming a person it would become a higher form of being, or both.

I accept that the developed fetus has an interest in becoming a person and that the strength of this interest is commensurate with the extent to which it would be worse for the fetus never to become a person. I have argued, however, that the morality of a late abortion is not determined by the effect that abortion has on the developed fetus's interests—that is, by the extent to which abortion makes the fetus's life as a whole worse than it would otherwise have been. Rather than focusing on what would be better or worse for the fetus (where the value of its life as a whole is concerned), we should weigh the reasons that favor an abortion against the effect that an abortion would have on the fetus's *time-relative interests*—that is, on what there is most reason to care about *for its own sake now.* It might, of course, be held that the moral significance of the developed fetus's identity-preserving potential to become a person just is that it has a present time-relative interest in becoming a person. That time-relative interest, however, is subsumed within its time-relative interest in continuing to live. Thus this claim about the developed fetus's potential adds nothing to the objection to late abortion that is implied by the Time-Relative Interest Account of the wrongness of killing.

Before concluding this section, we should briefly consider the idea that a human fetus has the potential to become a person in the third of the three senses distinguished at the beginning of the section. I have included this third interpretation of the notion that a fetus is a potential person because I have found it gestured at in the literature; but it is not clear that it is really a distinct interpretation. Although those who appeal to this notion of potential often say such things as that the fetus is an uncompleted person or that it somehow contains the person in inchoate form within itself, what is normally meant seems to be only that the fetus is an entity whose essential nature is to unfold itself into a person. And this, I take it, is just a dramatic way of emphasizing that the fetus's potential is suitably internal or intrinsic—that is, that it is *not* that the fetus becomes a person by having the elements of personhood added from without; rather, they develop from within. Understood in this way, the third interpretation is equivalent to the claim that the fetus has the identity-preserving potential to become a person; thus it is true of the developed fetus but false of the early fetus. There is, however, a way in which the third interpretation could be a distinctive claim. It might claim that the fetus (or, more specifically, the developed fetus) is a potential person because it is a *partially existing* person, a person in the making or in the process of coming into existence. This, as I suggested in section 2 of this chapter, is an interesting and intuitively appealing claim. But it does not, as I also argued earlier, offer a strong argument against abortion. Its implications for abortion seem instead to coincide closely with those of the Time-Relative Interest Account of the morality of killing.

In summary, then, the early fetus's potential to become a person is not identity-preserving but is only nonidentity potential. It therefore has no interest, and no time-relative interest, in becoming a person. If it would be good if another person were to come into existence, the early fetus's nonidentity potential could have instrumental value. But that could not ground a strong objection to early abortion, because the potential of any pair of sperm and egg would have a similar nonidentity potential and thus a similar instrumental value. The developed fetus, by contrast, does have the identity-preserving potential to become a person, and thus has an interest in its realization. But we should not be guided by the developed fetus's interests. Rather, we should be guided by a respect for its time-relative interests, and its time-relative interest in realizing its potential to become a person is weak for the same reason that its time-relative interest in continuing to live is weak.

6.2. *Potential as a Basis for Moral Status*

We have yet to consider the idea that potential may be a source of moral status. It is sometimes claimed that, because the fetus has the potential to become a person, it therefore already has the moral status, or perhaps the rights, that persons have. This, surely, is excessively crude. The possession of the potential, whether identity-preserving or otherwise, to become a Y does not normally give one the rights of a Y. A tennis player, for example, may have the potential to be a Wimbledon champion, but he does not have a right to the trophy unless he realizes this potential. And Prince Charles's potential to become the king of England does not give him the rights of a king.[24]

Even if this crude view is certainly false as a general claim, there may be special instances in which X's having the identity-preserving potential to become a Y confers on it a special moral status—perhaps not exactly the status of a Y but something approximating it. It might be, for example, that an individual that has the identity-preserving potential to become a person thereby also has a high moral status, one that entails certain moral protections. People often have something like this in mind when they claim that abortion is wrong because the fetus is a potential person.

The idea that the potential to become a person confers a special moral status is plausible, if at all, only if the potential is identity-preserving. (It makes little sense to suppose that X's potential to become a Y confers a special status on X now if X will never actually *be* a Y, and especially if the transition to Y involves X's ceasing to exist. In these conditions, if X had a high moral status, that might be a reason to *prevent* the realization of its potential, thereby preventing its ceasing to exist.) In the following discussion, therefore, I will use the term "potential person" to refer only to individuals that have the identity-preserving potential to become a person. I have argued that, among fetuses, only developed fetuses are potential persons. Hence the subsequent discussion will apply only to developed fetuses. For convenience, however, in the remainder of this section I will drop the cumbersome term "developed fetus" and refer simply to "the fetus." Those who believe, on whatever basis, that the early fetus also has the identity-preserving potential to become a person may take my references to fetuses to apply to whatever it is they believe has the relevant identity-preserving potential: the fetal organism, the fetal soul, or whatever, at any point in its career as a fetus.

Our question, then, is whether the fetus's identity-preserving potential to become a person confers on it a special moral status that constrains the permissibility of abortion. Of particular importance for our inquiry is the more specific question whether the fetus's potential to become a person brings it within the sphere of the morality of respect—or, as I will say, whether its potential is a basis for respect. For if its being a potential person makes it worthy of respect, killing it must be as seriously wrong as killing an innocent person, if other things are equal. Aborting it may therefore be seriously wrong even if its time-relative interest in continuing to live is comparatively weak (just as it would be seriously wrong to kill a very elderly person without her consent, even if her time-relative interest in continuing to live was weak because there was little prospect of further good in her life). For if the fetus's potential makes it worthy of respect, the morality of abortion is not governed by the Time-Relative Interest Account of the morality of killing, as I have suggested, but by the morality of respect.

Recall that the property or properties that are the basis of respect must be intrinsic rather than relational. These properties must be what morally differentiates us from animals, making us worthy of respect in a way that animals are not. I have suggested that the most plausible candidates are certain psychological capacities, arguably those capacities that are constitutive of personhood: primarily self-consciousness, but perhaps minimal rationality and autonomy, as well. Fetuses lack these capacities, but they differ from animals in having the potential to develop these capacities—that is, to become persons. Perhaps, then, the basis of the worth that commands respect is the possession of the relevant psychological capacities *or* the potential to develop those capacities. The main aim of this section is to determine whether the fetus's potential can plausibly be regarded as a basis for respect—though for the most part I will refer more generally to the possibility that its potential is a basis for moral status.

What exactly do we mean when we say that the fetus has the potential to become a person? What is it about the fetus now that is the ground for our ascribing that potential to it? If its potential is to be a basis for moral status, and if the basis for status must be a property or set of properties that are intrinsic, there must be something intrinsic about the fetus now that justifies the claim that it is a potential person.

We can approach this question by considering the following three cases:

The Normal Fetus. This is a developed fetus that is in every way normal and healthy.

The Fetus with a Chemical Deficit. This is a fetus whose brain is developing normally—in that it will have a typical array of cortical neurons and synapses—except that it is deficient in a certain chemical (perhaps a neurotransmitter) that is important for the proper functioning of the cerebral cortex. In the absence of this chemical, its brain will never function above the level of a chimpanzee's brain. Without this chemical, the fetus will never be a person.

The Fetus with Cerebral Deficits. This is a fetus whose brain is developing abnormally, in that it is developing fewer than the usual number of cortical neurons and synapses. If it continues on its present developmental path, its cerebral cortex will be underdeveloped in certain regions, so that its cognitive capacities will never be higher than those of a chimpanzee.

Most people, I believe, want to say that all three of these fetuses are potential persons. I have conceded that this is true in the case of the Normal Fetus, but the claim is more contentious in the cases of the Fetus with a Chemical Deficit and the Fetus with Cerebral Deficits. On what basis might it be claimed that these latter two fetuses are potential persons?

One response is simply that these fetuses are both the sort of entity that normally becomes a person. If they never actually become persons, that is simply because of the absence of some condition necessary for the actualization of the potential (the chemical or certain cerebral structures that failed to develop). But to point out that these two fetuses are entities of a kind whose normal members tend to become persons is not to show that they have the potential to become persons. It is only to note that *normal* members of the kind have that potential. But *these* two members of the kind are not normal members. And their abnormality is precisely that they lack something that is necessary for them to become persons.

It seems a truism that, in order for X to have the potential to become a Y, it must be *possible* for X to become a Y. It seems to make no sense to say that X is a potential Y if it is literally impossible for X to become a Y. Yet there are forms and degrees of possibility. There is a sense in which it is impossible in the midst of a severe drought for a seed to become a plant; yet there is another sense in which it is clearly possible for the seed to become a plant: all that is necessary is that it should be supplied with water. It is this second kind of possibility that is necessary for potential, for we accept that the seed has the potential to become a plant, even when there will in fact be no rain. Similarly, in a time of famine the probability may be zero that a normal fetus will become a person, yet we accept that it is possible for it to become a person and thus grant that it is a potential person. Perhaps we should treat the case of the fetus with a chemical deficit in the same way, claiming that its lack of the necessary chemical is compatible with its having the potential to become a person in the same way that the normal fetus's lack of nutrition in a time of famine is compatible with its being a potential person.

Is it similarly possible for the fetus with cerebral deficits to become a person? The difference between this fetus and the fetus with a chemical deficit does not seem significant: the one lacks a certain chemical necessary for normal functioning of the brain; the other lacks certain tissues in the brain that are necessary for normal functioning. Yet the claim that it is possible for the fetus with cerebral deficits to develop the cognitive capacities necessary for personhood seems deeply problematic.

Compare the case of a child born without eyes a thousand years ago. Did this child have the potential for sight? I think most people would find it hardly credible to suppose that it did. Now imagine a child born without eyes in a world in which eye transplants are routinely performed. This second blind child clearly has the potential for sight. Certainly if he receives a transplant and is thereby enabled to see, that demonstrates that all along he had the potential to see. Next suppose there were a form of genetic therapy that, if administered to the fetus with cerebral deficits, would cause it grow the cerebral tissues necessary for normal cognition; and suppose that the growth of these tissues would be identity-preserving. If such a therapy existed, it is clear that the fetus with cerebral deficits would have the potential to become a person, just as the child born without eyes would have the potential for sight if the technology existed for the transplantation of eyes.

Notice, however, what this implies. Suppose that we accept that a child born without eyes a thousand years ago did not have the potential for sight, but that a relevantly similar child born in a world in which eye transplants are performed would have that potential. If this is what we believe, it seems that we should also believe that the fetus with cerebral deficits does not have the potential to become a person in a world, such as ours, in which cerebral augmentation is not possible, but that it would have that potential in a world in which cerebral augmentation could be achieved through genetic therapy. But if there is no intrinsic difference between the fetus with cerebral deficits in our world and the fetus in the world in which cerebral augmentation is possible, the difference in their potentials cannot be a matter of their intrinsic properties. The basis for ascribing to the one fetus the potential to become a person must be wholly extrinsic. Hence its potential to become a person cannot be a basis for moral status, for it is not grounded in its intrinsic properties.

One might adopt a more radical view. One might hold that, as long as it is *physically possible* for the fetus with cerebral deficits to develop the cognitive capacities that are constitutive of personhood in a way that is identity-preserving, that fetus counts as a potential person. And surely it is physically possible for such a fetus's brain to develop further in a way that would give it the relevant capacities. If, as seems likely, a genetic therapy is ever devised that can promote cerebral growth in fetuses that would otherwise be profoundly cognitively impaired, that will decisively show, on this view, that all along fetuses with cerebral deficits have had the potential to become persons. It is just that our science has so far been insufficiently sophisticated to enable us to elicit it.

According to this view, moreover, the basis of the fetus's potential is not extrinsic. The potential is not supplied by the genetic therapy. It is present in fetuses with cerebral deficits that live and die long before the advent of the therapy. For what the potential essentially consists in is an intrinsic receptivity to an identity-preserving transformation into a person. This is a fact about the fetus itself: that it is the sort of thing that can in principle be transformed into a person while continuing to exist.

There are, however, two objections to this understanding of the fetus's potential. First, because it is virtually impossible to identify the full range of identity-preserving transformations that it is physically possible for an entity to undergo, we can in practice have only a limited appreciation of any given entity's potentials. Second, and more important, if it is physically possible, through some as-yet-undiscovered form of genetic therapy, to augment a defective fetus's brain in a way that will enhance its future cognitive capacities, it is surely physically possible to achieve the same result in an animal—for example, a dog. If, therefore, we claim that a fetus with cerebral deficits is a potential person on the ground that it is physically possible for its brain to develop in ways that would be identity-preserving and would overcome or repair the deficits, we must concede that a dog is a potential person for the same reason. And if we claim that the fetus's potential to become a person is a basis for moral status (because it is grounded in a suitably intrinsic receptivity to transformation), we must concede that a dog has an equivalent status, other things being equal. Since, however, no one would (or should) accept that dogs are potential persons with a moral status appropriate to their nature as such, we must abandon the broad conception of potential that implies that they are.

One might seek to distinguish between the potential of the fetus with cerebral deficits and that of a dog by claiming that the way the genetic therapy would work would be to stimulate some dormant gene that the fetus has but a dog lacks. But even if that were true, all it would mean is that the form of genetic therapy necessary to transform a dog into a person would have to be different: it would have to work, not by stimulating a preexisting but dormant gene, but by inserting a gene that would have the same function. There is no reason to suppose that this would be physically impossible.

There is, I believe, no basis for claiming that the fetus with cerebral deficits has the potential to become a person that does not also imply that a dog has that potential. (Recall that the fact that such a fetus is a member of a kind whose normal members are potential persons does not entail that it is a potential person. And for any mechanism that could cause the fetus to develop into a person, there should be an analogous mechanism whereby a dog could be transformed into a person.) If that is right, we should abandon the ambition to include fetuses with cerebral deficits within the category of potential persons. Perhaps we can settle for the more modest conclusion that the normal fetus (and perhaps even the fetus with a chemical deficit) is a potential person.

What we require, it seems, is a distinction between *intrinsic* and *extrinsic* potential, where intrinsic potential to become a Y involves more than mere receptivity to being transformed into a Y in an identity-preserving manner. (Recall that such a distinction seemed necessary earlier, in section 5.1 of chapter 2.) For surely the normal fetus's potential to become a person is in some sense intrinsic, while any potential that a dog might have to become a person is wholly extrinsic. If we can draw the distinction in a way that is principled and that provides an intuitively plausible division of the various cases, we can then claim that it is not the potential to become a person that is the basis of moral status, but the *intrinsic* potential to become a person. It might be argued, for example, that the developed fetus is worthy of respect because it has the intrinsic potential to become a person.

How is the distinction between intrinsic and extrinsic potential to be drawn? One suggestion is that X has the intrinsic potential to become a Y if all it requires from the outside in order to become a Y is its normal environment. In its normal environment—namely, the womb with its various amenities—the normal fetus can develop into a person. Hence it has the intrinsic potential to become a person. The same is not true, of course, of a dog. This view also explains how it can be that an individual can have the potential to become a Y even if the probability is zero that it will actually become a Y. A seed has the potential to become a plant even in a time of drought, because the drought is an abnormal condition. In its normal environment, which includes periodic rainfall, the seed would become a plant. (In this connection, consider the claim of Rabbi Elliot N. Dorff, quoted in the *New York Times,* that embryos "have no legal status whatever in Jewish law when they are outside the womb, because they have no potential for becoming a human being."[25] According to this view, an embryo created in vitro is not a potential human being even if it will actually become a human being if it is implanted in a surrogate womb. If that implication strikes us as implausible, we can explain the mistake by appealing to the view that an entity's potential is determined by what it can become in its normal environment. According to this view, the embryo is a potential human being if it can become a human being when situated in its normal environment, which is the womb. The fact that it will not become a human being if it remains outside the womb is irrelevant.)

I have been deliberately vague about a certain element in this understanding of intrinsic potential. In order for X to have the intrinsic potential to become a Y, must it be the case that, when placed in its normal environment, it *will* become a Y, that it is *likely* to become a Y, or that it is merely *possible* that it will become a Y? Jeffrey Reiman, from whose analysis of the concept of potential I have borrowed the notion of a normal environment, insists on the second of these three options. He claims that, "if the normal environment were such that zygotes did not *usually* develop into human beings, they would not be potential human beings."[26] From this, together with the observation that "fewer than one third of conceptions result in live births," he draws the conclusion, which he welcomes, that "the newly conceived zygote is [not] even a potential human being."[27] I will not dispute the truth of this conclusion, since much depends on exactly what one means by "human being." But if, as seems clear, Reiman accepts that *some* zygotes do in fact become human beings (in the identity-preserving sense), it is doubtful that he can consistently claim that these zygotes were never potential human beings. It would seem to be more reasonable to claim that it is at least sufficient for X to have the intrinsic potential to become a Y if it is possible for it to become a Y in its normal environment, with no external intervention beyond what is part of that environment.

But now a more embarrassing question arises. What constitutes an entity's normal environment? It seems that what counts as normal varies with, among other things, time and technology. A hundred years ago, the normal environment was such that it was not possible for babies born with certain heart conditions to become adults. With the advent of transplant technology, the environment changed in a way that now makes it possible for babies with the same defects to become adults. It seems to follow, on the proposal we are considering, that babies born a hundred years ago with certain heart defects did not have the intrinsic potential to become adults, whereas babies born now with the same defects do have that intrinsic potential. But it is clearly incompatible with the notion of intrinsic potential to suppose that an entity's intrinsic potential varies with the state of technology. It is the essence of intrinsic potential that it is independent of wholly extrinsic factors.

Of course, all potential—including intrinsic potential—requires certain external conditions for its realization. If there is such a thing as intrinsic potential, the potential of a seed to become a plant is surely a paradigm example. Yet the seed requires water, nutrients from the soil, carbon dioxide in the atmosphere, and sunlight in order to realize this potential. The challenge is to determine *how much* of what is necessary in order for X to become a Y can come from external sources compatibly with X's having the *intrinsic* potential to become a Y.

Since personhood is a matter of the possession of certain capacities, let us focus on the potential for having a certain capacity, such as the capacity to see. An intuitively appealing suggestion is that X has the intrinsic potential to have the capacity for sight only if X has an inherent tendency, or is internally programmed, to develop the physical basis for sight, given an environment in which this tendency or program can operate. If, however, the physical basis for the capacity to see (for example, the eyes or the relevant parts of the brain) has to be added from the outside (for example, through an eye transplant or a brain graft) in order for X to have the capacity to see, X has only an extrinsic potential to be able to see. According to this proposal, the normal fetus has the intrinsic potential to see, for it is genetically programmed to develop eyes and a brain with a visual cortex. But a baby born without eyes has at most the extrinsic potential to see, for it must be externally supplied with eyes, which are part of the physical basis of sight.

Attractive though it is, this proposal contains a good deal of indeterminacy. The distinction between intrinsic and extrinsic potential is based on the contrast between an internally programmed tendency to develop the physical basis for a certain capacity and the external addition of the physical basis for that capacity. But consider again the fetus with a chemical deficit. Its internal program does not provide for the production of the chemical necessary for higher cognitive functions. Is the chemical it needs analogous to a vital nutrient—that is, something that can be regarded as external to the physical basis of the capacities constitutive of personhood—or is the chemical a part of the physical basis of personhood? It is unclear how this question should be answered, but the answer will determine whether, according to this proposal, the fetus's potential to become a person is intrinsic or extrinsic.

Or consider the fetus with cerebral deficits. If genetic therapy could stimulate the growth of new brain tissue that would enable the fetus to develop the capacities constitutive of personhood, would that mean that the fetus had the intrinsic potential to become a person? In support of an affirmative answer, one could claim that the physical basis of personhood—the brain—would be developed from within rather than being supplied externally. Yet it could also be argued that the program for the development of critical parts of the brain would have an external source: the genetic therapy. Whether this contention is plausible might depend, in turn, on whether the therapy would activate a preexisting but dormant gene or whether it would supply the gene and thus the program itself.

It is important to remind ourselves that our concern here is with potential as a basis of moral status. Yet it is hard to see how an entity's moral status could depend on considerations of this sort. Let us, however, press on. There are several other problems with this attempt to distinguish between intrinsic and extrinsic potential. The case of the fetus with cerebral deficits reveals a critical ambiguity in the proposed understanding. Suppose the fetus receives the therapy and its brain is stimulated to develop new tissues in which the capacities essential for personhood will eventually develop. Prior to receiving the therapy, its potential to become a person was, intuitively, extrinsic. As I have noted, it is not clear that the proposed way of drawing the distinction can capture that. But now there is a further question. After the therapy has been applied and the fetus's brain has grown new tissues, is its potential to become a person intrinsic or extrinsic? It seems that, according to the proposed understanding, its potential must now be intrinsic, for the physical basis for the capacities constitutive of personhood is now in place. It no longer needs to be supplied externally, but merely requires the usual forms of stimulation and support (nutrition, contact with people, exposure to language, etc.) in order for the relevant capacities to develop. If that is right, the application of the therapy has converted the fetus's potential from extrinsic to intrinsic. If only intrinsic potential is a basis for high moral status, the therapy has profoundly altered the fetus's moral status. But if what is relevant to status is potential, and if it was equally true both before and after the therapy that the fetus was going to become a person, is it really plausible to suppose that its moral status is radically altered at the point at which its potential shifts from extrinsic to intrinsic?

Let us run the process in reverse. Suppose a normal fetus suffers brain damage that destroys various areas of the brain necessary for the development of certain cognitive capacities necessary for personhood. When this happens, the fetus loses its intrinsic potential to become a person and thus, presumably, its moral status as a potential person. But suppose the relevant areas of the brain can, and will, be restored via genetic therapy. And suppose that enough of the fetus's brain would remain unaffected that the same mind would persist throughout: thus the processes of loss and regeneration would both be identity-preserving. Is it really plausible to suppose that during the interval between the occurrence of the brain damage and the restoration of the relevant tissues, the fetus's moral status is significantly lower, even though the fact that it will eventually become a person is unaffected by the processes that change the character of its potential from intrinsic to extrinsic and then to intrinsic again?

These brief remarks should indicate both how difficult it is to draw a distinction between intrinsic and extrinsic potential and also how problematic it is to treat that distinction as critically relevant to an individual's moral status. Let us assume, however, that we have a clear distinction between intrinsic and extrinsic potential and that it implies that, while the normal fetus's potential to become a person is intrinsic, that of the fetus with cerebral deficits is extrinsic. In that way, the distinction avoids the implication that the existence of a genetic therapy for cognitive enhancement would give dogs an intrinsic potential to become persons. Potential derived from this source would, we can assume, count as extrinsic.

It is obvious that even the normal fetus's intrinsic potential to become a person requires considerable external input for its realization. In the absence of physical protection, nutrition, and, later, exposure to language and culture, and so on, even a normal human fetus will not become a person. There are, indeed, many forms of intrinsic potential that must be elicited by human intervention. It seems, for example, that the potential for language is intrinsic in human beings, but a human child will not realize this potential unless it is exposed to language by other people. It is possible, therefore, that certain forms of intrinsic potential may pass unrecognized and may therefore never be elicited. Suppose that we were to discover that this has hitherto been the case with dogs. Suppose that we were to discover that dogs have the intrinsic potential for self-consciousness and rationality but that until now we have failed to recognize this because the potential has never been realized. For suppose that, in order to elicit this potential, it is necessary for someone to cultivate and nurture the relevant cognitive capacities through an intensive and highly structured program of "cognitive therapy." Only through years of patient work, taking virtually every waking moment of the dog's life from earliest puppyhood on, can the relevant mechanisms latent in the dog's brain be activated and developed. For the first few years there are no perceptible results (which is part of the explanation of why the process was not discovered earlier), but after five or six years, dogs subject to this program develop cognitive capacities comparable to those of a normal four-year-old human child.[28]

Suppose that all this were true. What we would have discovered is that, on any remotely plausible conception, dogs have the intrinsic potential to become persons. Assuming we were to discover this, ought we to conclude that all dogs have a high moral status—in particular, that all dogs are above the threshold of respect, so that killing a dog is just as wrong as killing a person, if other things are equal? Indeed, ought we to conclude that we and our forebears have been guilty of monstrous wrongs to dogs, who have always been within the scope of the morality of respect though we have been unaware of it? I doubt that anyone would draw these conclusions. While we would (or should) accept that respect would be owed to any dog whose potential to become a person had been realized, the knowledge that all dogs had this potential would not require us to reassess our estimation of the actual worth of all those dogs whose potential was never cultivated or never would be cultivated. But if we would not accept that all dogs, in these circumstances, would be worthy of respect, we do not really believe that the intrinsic potential to become a person is a basis for respect, or for high moral status generally.

To drive home the point, we can consider a variant of this example. Suppose that the plasticity in the canine brain that allows for this intrinsic potential is transient unless it is exploited; thus, unless the intensive cognitive therapy is begun within the first year of a dog's life, the potential fades and is unrecoverable. In this respect it would be analogous to the human capacity for language acquisition, which steadily diminishes after the first few years of life—except that in this case the potential would not just diminish, but would vanish altogether. If this were the case, all puppies would intrinsically be potential persons, but those that failed to receive the therapy within a year would lose the potential and therefore, presumably, the moral status that goes with it. Puppies would initially be within the scope of the morality of respect, but those that failed to receive the therapy would then drop below the threshold of respect even though, as adult dogs, their actual psychological capacities might be more highly developed than those of puppies that had so far retained their intrinsic potential. This, I believe, is utterly implausible.

6.3. Potential, Cognitive Impairment, and Animals

Even if a human fetus has the intrinsic potential to become a person, that does not affect its moral status. It does not make it worthy of respect. In fact, it seems morally irrelevant whether an entity's potential is intrinsic or extrinsic. An entity's potential is simply what it can become through the full range of possible transformations that would be identity-preserving. We do not need to quibble about different forms and degrees of possibility. The real relevance of possibility is practical. For the important question in each particular case is not how X's potential affects its moral status but how strong a moral reason, if any, there is to try to realize X's potential. And this may be affected by "how possible" it is to realize or to elicit the potential. (The possibility of an eye transplant, for example, would be remote if they were rarely performed and seldom succeeded even when they were.)

If dogs had the potential to become persons—whether through genetic therapy that would stimulate the growth of new cerebral tissues or through cognitive therapy that would activate mechanisms latent in the dog's brain—the crucial question would be how important it would be, morally, to try to ensure that dogs became persons. I believe that the strength of one's moral reason to try to realize X's potential to become a Y depends in great measure on the strength of X's time-relative interest in becoming a Y. (There are, of course, many other considerations that are relevant—for example, one's relation to X, the costs one would be likely to incur, the possibility of undesirable side effects, the probability of success, and so on. But these considerations come into play only if there is a reason to try to realize the potential that is grounded in X's own time-relative interest in its realization. Otherwise, these other considerations simply do not arise.)

How strong a moral reason one has to try to realize X's potential to become a Y is, it seems, completely unaffected by whether the potential is intrinsic or extrinsic. Consider, for example, two children, one whose ability to see has been thwarted from birth by the presence of microbes that block the action of the optic nerve, and another born without eyes. It is reasonable to suppose that the first of these children has the intrinsic potential for sight, since it possesses a complete visual apparatus whose functions are externally impeded, while the second child's potential for sight is extrinsic, since a critical component of its potential visual apparatus has to be externally provided. Yet it is obvious that, if other things are equal, there is just as strong a moral reason to try to realize the second child's potential as there is to realize that of the first.

To repeat: the important question raised by an individual's potential is how much it matters, for the individual's own sake, that he should fulfill that potential—that is, that he should become what it is possible for him to become, or have what it is possible for him to have. In the case of abortion, the moral importance of the fetus's potential is therefore entirely captured by the Time-Relative Interest Account. Whatever reason there is to ensure the realization of the fetus's potential to become a person is subsumed by the reason to respect its time-relative interest in continuing to live. The good of becoming or being a person is one dimension of the good that its future might contain and that it has a present time-relative interest in having. I argued earlier, however, that its present time-relative interest in having the goods of its own future is relatively weak, given the virtual absence of psychological connections between itself now as a fetus and itself later as a person. What this means is that it matters comparatively little, for the fetus's own sake now, whether it realizes its potential or not.

Consider three possible scenarios. Consider first a fetus with cerebral deficits in a world in which there is no possibility of cognitive enhancement. This fetus, if it lives, will be severely cognitively impaired. Its time-relative interest in continuing to live is, therefore, considerably weaker even than that of the normal fetus. For not only would its future contain substantially less good than that of a normal fetus, but also, if its psychological capacities are abnormally low even at this early age, it will be less closely connected to itself in the future psychologically than the normal fetus.

Second, consider a fetus with cerebral deficits that has the potential to become a person (perhaps because a genetic therapy exists that could enhance its cognitive capacities in an identity-preserving way). If this potential would never in fact be realized, its existence may make little difference to the morality of abortion. For the strength of the fetus's time-relative interest in continuing to live seems to depend on the character of the life that it would be likely to have, not on the character of a life that it could conceivably have but in fact will not. (One qualification is necessary here. It may matter *why* the fetus would not realize its potential to become a person. It would seem illegitimate for a pregnant woman to defend her decision to have an abortion by claiming that the life her child would have if it were to live would be of low quality, when the reason it would be so is that *she* would refuse to provide her child with the therapy it would need in order to have a better life.)

Third and finally, consider a fetus with cerebral deficits whose potential to become a person would be realized, or would be very likely to be realized. In that case its time-relative interest in continuing to live would be comparable in strength to that of a normal fetus; but that would still be relatively weak.

My claims about these cases presuppose that, if an abortion is performed, the only time-relative interest that would be opposed to the action is that of the fetus at the time. For the abortion itself would effectively preclude the existence of any later time-relative interests. But suppose, for whatever reason, that abortion was not an issue. Suppose that a fetus with cerebral deficits was going to live and that the only question was whether to administer the genetic therapy that would enhance its cognitive capacities, thereby enabling it to become a person. How strong would the moral reason be to administer the therapy? How important is it that the fetus should realize its potential to become a person rather than living its life as a nonperson?

In practice, the interests of the fetus's parents will be strongly engaged in favor of administering the therapy, as will those of any others who might be required to help meet the costs of caring for an individual who would be severely cognitively impaired. But let us put these considerations aside. Alternatively, we might imagine that the parents are wealthy activists on behalf of the disabled who believe that it would be unjustly discriminatory, or would implicitly devalue the lives of the cognitively impaired, to insist that their child should have genetic therapy for cognitive enhancement. Our question might then be whether there would be a moral objection to their not providing the therapy when they would have ample means of doing so. The important question, in short, is whether—and, if so, to what extent—it is important, for the sake of the fetus itself, that it should realize its potential to become a person.

The obvious response, suggested earlier in the section on prenatal harm, is that we must be guided not just by the fetus's present time-relative interests but also by those time-relative interests that it will have in the future that might be affected by whether or not it fulfills its potential. A baby born with a neurological defect that, if untreated, would later prevent it from being able to walk has a present time-relative interest in later being able to walk; but that time-relative interest may be comparatively weak because of the relative weakness of the psychological relations that would bind the baby to itself in the future. But when it becomes older, and closely psychologically related to itself in the future, its time-relative interest in being able to walk may be quite strong (assuming that adaptation does not occur, or occurs only incompletely). It is therefore an important reason to enable the baby to realize its potential that to fail to do so would be to doom to frustration its later, stronger time-relative interests.

Perhaps a similar claim can be made on behalf of the fetus with cerebral deficits. This, in fact, is one case in which adaptation will assuredly not occur. A severely mentally retarded adult will certainly not prefer his actual life with severe cognitive impairment to the life he might have had if the impairment had been corrected. For the severely retarded adult will lack the cognitive resources to entertain *any* preferences about his life as a whole. But whatever the explanation is of why the fetus's cerebral deficits ought, if possible, to be corrected, it is clear that the commonsense view is that there is a strong moral reason to enable to fetus to realize its potential to become a person. There is, however, a problem here—one that many people will not be inclined to take seriously, though it is, in my view, a serious problem indeed. Again, suppose that the fetus with cerebral deficits lacks a certain gene that directs the growth of various areas of the brain necessary for the cognitive capacities that are constitutive of personhood. If the gene is introduced via therapy, it will stimulate the growth of the relevant areas and the fetus will eventually become a person. Next imagine, as I suggested earlier, that the insertion of a functionally equivalent gene into the body of a canine fetus would stimulate the growth of comparable cerebral tissues, thereby causing the dog eventually to become a person—that is, a being with capacities for certain minimum levels of self-consciousness, rationality, and autonomy. It seems that whatever reasons we have for administering the therapy to the fetus with cerebral deficits that appeal in some way to its own good would apply equally to administering the therapy to the dog. Their potential, after all, appears to be the same: both would rely on the same form of identity-preserving genetic therapy in order to be enabled to become persons.

Of course, extrinsic considerations, such as effects on other people, would normally weigh heavily in favor of administering the therapy to the human fetus but would not do so in the case of the canine fetus. But if we put those considerations aside for the moment and focus just on the reason we would have to administer the therapy *for the sake of the individual who would receive it,* it is difficult to see why we would have more reason to administer it to the fetus with cerebral deficits than to a canine fetus. (Let us assume, for the sake of argument, that a dog with human intelligence could have a life that would be well worth living even in a society in which it would be a freak, would have no acceptable mate, and so on. In short, let us put those contingent problems aside, as well.)

I know of no one who believes that it would be morally important to enable canine fetuses, or even adult dogs, to become persons if it were possible to do so. There are also, I think, relatively few people who accept that there is comparatively little moral reason, for a defective fetus's own sake, to give it a genetic therapy that would enable it to become a person rather than a severely retarded adult. But there seem to be no intrinsic properties that differentiate the human fetus with cerebral deficits from a canine fetus in a way that would make it important to realize the extrinsic potential of the human fetus but not that of the canine fetus.

It is worth emphasizing the nature of the problem we face. We must adopt one of the following three options:

1. We can accept that there is no strong reason, for a dog's own sake, to enable it to become a person; that there is no significant intrinsic difference between a dog and a human fetus that, if unaided, will develop cognitive capacities no higher than those of the dog; and that there is therefore no strong moral reason, for the defective fetus's own sake, to enable it to become a person rather than a severely retarded adult.

2. We can accept that it is morally important that a fetus with cerebral deficits should be enabled, if possible, to become a person; that there is no significant intrinsic difference between such a fetus and a dog; and, therefore, that there is a strong moral reason, for dogs' own sakes, to enable them, if possible, to become persons rather than retaining the cognitive capacities characteristic of dogs as they are now.

3. We can argue that there is an important intrinsic difference between a dog (or other animal) and a cognitively impaired human fetus that explains why, even if both have an equal extrinsic potential to become a person, we have a strong moral reason in the case of the fetus—but not in the case of the animal—to enable it to fulfill its potential to become a person.

As I have noted, both of the first two options are highly counterintuitive; therefore virtually everyone will want to adopt the third. But it is highly problematic. The problem is to identify a relevant intrinsic difference; but, as I tried to argue at length in section 2.2 of chapter 3, there is in fact no relevant difference to be found. There are no intrinsic differences of psychological capacity or potential, and therefore no difference in capacity for well-being. The only intrinsic differences are physical: differences of physical constitution and morphology traceable to, or equivalent to, the fact that the human fetus and the canine fetus or adult dog are members of different biological species. And these differences are without moral significance. That a human fetus with cerebral deficits has certain physical properties that a canine fetus lacks provides no reason for thinking that it is more important to realize its potential than it is to realize the equivalent potential of the canine fetus.

One way to proceed is to consider why there appears to be little or no moral reason to enable an animal to become a person via cognitive enhancement. It is hard to deny that, if a dog were to receive a genetic therapy that would enhance its cognitive capacities in an identity-preserving way, thereby enabling it to become a person, that would be good for the dog. For it is hard to deny that its capacity for well-being would thereby be expanded and that there would be a high probability that its life as a whole would be better—by as much as the lives of persons are typically better, or more worth living, than the lives of animals. These considerations fail to impress us, however; we do not accept that the fact that an animal's life as a whole would be better if it were to become a person provides a reason to enable it to become a person. Of course, our failure to be impressed might be just the result of prejudice; for there is certainly no shortage of that in our beliefs about the morality of our treatment of animals. Yet our response is consistent with the tendency of my argument in this chapter, which has been to move away from considering the effect that one's action has on the value of an individual's life as a whole and to focus instead on the effect one's action has on the individual's time-relative interests.

One striking reflection is that it does not seem that it would be a *misfortune* for a dog to retain its own low cognitive capacities rather than to become a person. This may seem odd. How could it not be a misfortune for an individual to fail to receive a great benefit? A moment's reflection reveals, however, that there is really nothing odd about this and that certain conditions must be met in order for a missed benefit to count as a misfortune. It would, for example, be good for me to discover a vein of gold in my back yard worth millions of dollars. But it is not a misfortune for me that there is in fact no vein of gold there.[29] It seems, however, that the explanation of why it would not be a misfortune for a dog not to become a person is different from the explanation of why it is not a misfortune for me to fail to discover gold on my property. For there is an important difference between the two cases.

I noted just now that the tendency of my argument has been to replace the concern for individuals' interests, or for the value of their lives as wholes, with a concern for their time-relative interests. And it is where time-relative interests are concerned that the difference between the two cases lies. Whatever else is true, I have a strong egoistic reason for wanting to own large amounts of gold. But someone who cares about a dog for its own sake would seem to have little or no reason to want, for the dog's own sake now, for it to become a person—even if its becoming a person would mean that its life as a whole would be better. Another way of making this point is to note that there is no point in the dog's life at which it would have a serious time-relative interest in becoming a person. Even assuming that the transformation would be identity-preserving and that being a person would be a very great good, the nature of the transformation would be so radical as to exclude certain conditions of egoistic concern. I have argued that, in addition to physical and functional continuity in certain areas of the brain, psychological continuity is among the conditions of egoistic concern—not in the sense that it is *necessary* in order for egoistic concern to be rational, but in the sense that the *degree* to which it is rationally appropriate to be egoistically concerned about oneself in the future varies, other things being equal, with the degree to which one would be psychologically continuous with oneself in the future. This, I believe, applies in the case of animals as well. For conscious animals are, like ourselves, essentially minds; therefore the conditions of identity and of egoistic concern are the same for animals as they are for us. But if this is right, the psychological distance between a dog now and itself as it would be if it were to become a person would be too great for the dog to have a serious time-relative interest in being thus transformed. And this, I suspect, is the main reason why it would not be a misfortune for a dog to fail to become a person: it has no time-relative interest that would thereby be frustrated. Even though the prospect of becoming a person would be a prospect of a great good, a dog simply cannot be related to that good in a way that makes it important for it to have or to achieve it.

To make this point intuitively clearer, one might imagine the prospect of becoming like a god. Imagine the possibility of becoming vastly more intelligent and developing a vastly richer and deeper range of emotions, including emotions of which one cannot now form any conception. One would be as different from oneself now, in terms of psychological capacities, as one is now from a dog (or, more to the point, as different from oneself now as a dog would be from itself if it were to become a person). One would be, in short, so utterly psychologically remote from oneself as one is now that one may now have little or no egoistic reason to want to become that way. Even if the transformation would be identity-preserving and would lead to a state that would be clearly superior to one's present state, it would be too much like becoming someone else—and, of course, losing oneself in the process—to be very desirable from an egoistic point of view.

I have argued that the psychological distance between a normal fetus and the person it might later become is too great for it to have a strong time-relative interest in realizing its potential to become that person. I have suggested, furthermore, that the same is true, mutatis mutandis, of a dog with the potential to become a person, and of a person with the potential to become a god. But if this is right, the same must be true of a fetus with cerebral deficits that has the potential to become a person. Like a normal fetus, the fetus with cerebral deficits cannot have a strong *present* time-relative interest in becoming a person. For the psychological relations that would hold between itself now and itself much later, when it would be a person, are too weak. But notice that the fetus with cerebral deficits will, as long as it remains retarded, *always* be distantly psychologically related to itself in the future. In this respect it is like an animal rather than a normal fetus. Its relation to itself in the future will always be comparable to the relation that a normal fetus bears to itself in the future, or the relation that an animal bears to itself in the further future. This is because the mental life of the fetus with cerebral deficits will, as long as it remains retarded, never develop much beyond that of a fetus or an animal. Even as the fetus with cerebral deficits develops and grows, therefore, there will never be a point at which it will have a strong time-relative interest in being a person rather than remaining what it is: a severely cognitively impaired human being.

Because of this, the reasoning that may condemn many forms of prenatal injury, and may support the correction, when possible, of fetal impairments, does not apply in the case of the fetus with cerebral deficits. For this reasoning appeals to the time-relative interests that a fetus will *later* have. The reasoning is that, in the case of a fetus *without* cerebral deficits, it is wrong, if other things are equal, to inflict an injury that causes disability, or to fail to correct a condition that causes disability, because this will frustrate the strong time-relative interest that the individual will later have, when he becomes a person, in having certain abilities rather than being disabled (assuming that adaptation does not occur). But the fetus with cerebral deficits is different. It is relevantly like an animal in that, even as it develops physically, it will remain psychologically cut off from itself in the future and thus will never have a strong time-relative interest in being or becoming a person. Thus we cannot appeal to any later time-relative interest it will have in being or becoming a person in order to defend the view that it is important for it to become a person. Like an animal that fails to receive a genetic therapy that would enable it to become a person, the fetus with cerebral deficits never has a strong time-relative interest that would be frustrated by its failure to become a person.

If this is right, it suggests that, just as it is not a significant misfortune for an animal that could become a person to fail to do so, so, too, it is not a serious misfortune for the fetus with cerebral deficits if it fails to become a person. While it may be a serious misfortune for either to have a level of well-being well below the higher levels of which it is capable, it is not a significant misfortune, in itself, for either to have limited cognitive capacities or a limited range of well-being. Individuals who are not persons are not necessarily unfortunate for that reason.

It seems, therefore, that we cannot defend the commonsense intuition about the fetus with cerebral deficits by appealing to its time-relative interests. If we are guided by a concern for time-relative interests, we will have little reason, apart from that deriving from a concern for the time-relative interests of others, to try to ensure that a fetus with cerebral deficits, or even a congenitally severely cognitively impaired adult, is transformed into a person, if that becomes possible.

The problem, of course, is that these conclusions about fetuses with cerebral deficits and congenitally severely retarded adults are highly counterintuitive. Almost no one would accept them. And there is worse to come. The case of the fetus with cerebral deficits is parallel to cases involving prenatal injury, except that it involves allowing an individual to be harmed rather than causing it to be harmed. Thus the claims that I have made about the case of the fetus with cerebral deficits should also apply to a case in which one causes a normal fetus to have cerebral deficits. Consider:

> *Prenatal Retardation.* Unless she takes a certain drug, a pregnant woman will develop a moderate disability. The drug would, however, cause the fetus she is carrying, which she intends in any case to put up for adoption, to be severely mentally retarded. Her present interest in not having the disability is stronger than the time-relative interest the fetus presently has in becoming a person rather than being retarded (which must be comparatively weak because of the weakness of the prudential unity relations), and indeed is stronger than any time-relative interest the fetus will ever have in being or becoming a person. She therefore takes the drug.

Intuitively, the woman's action seems clearly wrong. But how can we explain why it is wrong?

It is worth repeating why her interests may outweigh the combined present and future time-relative interests of the fetus. This fetus, like every other normal fetus, has only a very weak present time-relative interest in realizing its potential to become a person. And if it is caused to have cerebral deficits sufficient for severe retardation, it will *never* have a significant time-relative interest in being a person. If, therefore, the woman is guided only by a concern for its time-relative interests, both present and future, she will have only a weak moral reason not to cause this normal fetus to be retarded rather than allowing it to become a person. This will be true even if *doing* what is against an individual's time-relative interests is significantly worse than *allowing* what is worse for the individual's time-relative interests to occur. For this asymmetry can yield a strong objection to causing the fetus to become retarded only if its *being* retarded would be a seriously adverse condition. But, as long as we focus only on its time-relative interests, there is no reason to suppose that that is true.

This, therefore, is another form of prenatal injury that cannot be adequately objected to by appealing to the fetus's present and future time-relative interests. But the explanation of why the appeal to time-relative interests will not work in this case is different from that in cases involving adaptation. It is not that the fetus with cerebral deficits may later rationally prefer its life with retardation; it is, rather, that its cognitive capacities do not allow for the possession of *any* significant time-relative interests, except perhaps ones that are both negative and concerned only with the immediate future, such as a time-relative interest in the avoidance of great suffering now or in the near future.

It is important to note that what seemed to be the best solution to the problem of adaptation cannot apply in the case of Prenatal Retardation. That solution was to claim that, because prenatal injury harms the victim when he is a person, it comes within the scope of the morality of respect. Because of that, it is not a sufficient justification for the infliction of prenatal injury that the interests it serves outweigh those it frustrates. In the case of Prenatal Retardation, however, the fetus that is caused to be severely retarded is thereby prevented from ever becoming a person. The act that we wish to condemn has the effect of preventing itself from coming within the scope of the morality of respect.

One option is, of course, to appeal to what in section 5 of this chapter I called the Criterion. Both the cases with which we are now concerned—the fetus with cerebral deficits and the normal fetus that might be caused to have cerebral deficits—are cases in which the fetus will exist in all the possible outcomes of one's choice; therefore, according to the Criterion, one ought to be guided by a concern for the effect that one's choice will have on the value of its life as a whole. Since a fetus would have a substantially better life if its cognitive capacities would be those of a person rather than comparable to those of an animal, an appeal to the Criterion supports the common intuition that one has a strong moral reason to administer the genetic therapy to the fetus with cerebral deficits and, if anything, an even stronger reason not to cause a normal fetus to have cerebral deficits. But the Criterion is problematic in various ways. It seems, in its application to cases of this sort, to presuppose that identity is what matters—that is, that identity is the basis of egoistic concern. This is not only implausible in itself, but is also incompatible with the argument I have advanced concerning abortion. Even more important for present purposes, the Criterion does not appear to offer any ground for differentiating between a fetus with cerebral deficits and a comparably endowed animal. If it were possible to enable an animal to become a person, it seems that one would have the same reason to enhance its cognitive capacities as one would have to enhance those of the fetus with cerebral deficits— namely, that this would make its life as a whole much better. The only way to avoid this implication, if one appeals to the Criterion, is to deny that an animal's life would be better if it were to become a person. One would have to deny, for example, that the Superchimp has a better life than a normal chimpanzee. And that is hard to do.

It is tempting to think that it is *obvious* why there is reason not to cause, or if possible to cure, mental retardation in a human fetus, while there is no reason to try, if possible, to enhance the cognitive capacities of an animal. The explanation, it might be thought, is simply that mental retardation in a human being is a pathological condition, a defect or impairment, while the possession of comparable cognitive capacities by an animal cannot be regarded as a defect or disability, for it is entirely normal. A retarded human being is therefore unfortunate in a way that a normal animal is not. It is clear, however, that this explanation involves an implicit appeal to what is normal for the members of a particular species as a standard of evaluation—that is, it simply resurrects the Species Norm Account. And although this account may fairly accurately reflect common ways of thinking about these matters, it is vitiated by its attribution of decisive evaluative significance to an evaluatively neutral artifact of biological taxonomy—namely, species categories. As the example of the Superchimp demonstrates, what counts as fortune or misfortune is not determined by species membership.

The fundamental problem is to understand how the exact same intrinsic state could be bad or unfortunate for one individual but acceptable or even fortunate for another. It is obvious that this is often the case. A person who suffers brain damage that reduces him to a condition of contented idiocy, with cognitive capacities and a mental life comparable to those of a contented dog, is clearly in a dreadful condition. It may not be dreadful *experientially*—that is, it may not be dreadful because of the subjective character of the individual's experiences—but it is dreadful nonetheless *for this individual.* But the same state would not be dreadful for a dog. It might, indeed, be a comparatively fortunate state for a dog. Thus the explanation of why this condition is bad for the former person cannot be that it is intrinsically bad, in the way that suffering is intrinsically bad. The condition is bad only in a certain context, against a certain background, or relative to some norm or standard. The Species Norm Account claims that it is bad for the former person because it is bad by comparison with the range of conditions possible for normal human beings—that is, because it is at the low end of the scale of states that are possible for one endowed with psychological capacities that are normal for members of the human species. But while it seems right that a condition must be evaluated by comparison with what is possible given a certain set of psychological capacities, it seems a mistake to suppose that the relevant capacities are those typical of the members of the individual's own biological species. In the case of the Superchimp, for example, how it is faring depends not on how its condition compares with the condition of typical members of its species but on how its condition compares with what is possible for it, given the psychological capacities that are constitutive of its own actual nature.

These reflections led me, in section 5.1 of chapter 2, to consider an account of fortune and misfortune that I called the Peak Capacity Account. According to this view, how well or badly off an individual is depends on how its condition or level of well-being compares with the spectrum of states of well-being accessible to it, given the peak psychological capacities it has so far possessed. This explains why the person who suffers brain damage is unfortunate: his condition is very bad by comparison with the range of states that were possible for him when his psychological capacities were at their peak. But the Peak Capacity Account conflicts with intractable intuitions about retardation. Recall the case, also presented in section 5.1 of chapter 2, of the Brain-Damaged Individual. In this case, a newborn infant suffers brain damage that arrests its psychological development at its present level. Most of us strongly believe that this infant has suffered a misfortune and that, as it grows, its condition will be an unfortunate one (despite the fact that it does not have and never will have a strong time-relative interest that will be frustrated by its loss). If, however, we assess misfortune relative to the range of well-being made possible by the peak psychological capacities that an individual has achieved, the infant's condition may never count as unfortunate at all. For it may well fare, both now and in the future, as well as possible relative to the highest capacity for well-being that it has ever possessed.

What I have called the Intrinsic Potential Account was intended to remedy the deficiencies of the Peak Capacity Account. It seems that what is unfortunate about the newborn infant that suffers brain damage is that for most of its life it will fare very poorly relative to the range of well-being that it once had the intrinsic potential to achieve. This reflection prompted me to propose that whether a being is well or badly off depends on how its level of well-being compares to the range of well-being made possible by the highest psychological capacities it has actually achieved *or* that it had the intrinsic potential to achieve. This is the Intrinsic Potential Account.

This account allows that the Brain-Damaged Individual is unfortunate, because its level of well-being will forever fall dramatically short of the higher levels it once had the intrinsic potential to achieve. Thus it explains how it can be a misfortune to suffer cognitive impairment even if the victim never has more than a marginal time-relative interest in avoiding retardation or becoming a person. It therefore has the resources to condemn the woman's taking the drug in Prenatal Retardation. And it offers its explanation of the misfortune involved in cognitive impairment by evaluating an individual's condition by comparison with what the individual's own nature or constitution makes possible rather than by reference to characteristics typical of the individual's species. Thus it also allows that the Superchimp is unfortunate in its brain-damaged condition, since its level of well-being then falls well short of the levels it was once capable of achieving.

Yet, as I noted in chapter 2, the Intrinsic Potential Account seems incapable of supporting our intuition in the case of the Fetus with Cerebral Deficits. Because of its congenital cerebral deficits, this fetus lacks the intrinsic potential to become a person; therefore the Intrinsic Potential Account cannot deem its failure to become a person a misfortune; nor can it, therefore, support our intuitive conviction that it is important, for the fetus's own sake, to administer to it a genetic therapy that would cause it develop the areas of the brain that it congenitally lacks.

There is, moreover, another, equally disturbing problem with the Intrinsic Potential Account. Recall that earlier, in section 6.2 of this chapter, I sketched a scenario in which dogs are discovered to have the intrinsic potential to become persons—a potential that has until now remained undiscovered because it requires intensive external stimulation to be elicited. If this were to happen—that is, if dogs were discovered to have this potential—the Intrinsic Potential Account would imply that we have all along been mistaken in believing that dogs are not, in general, unfortunate beings. According to the Intrinsic Potential Account, what we would have discovered is that dogs have all along been unfortunate because the levels of well-being they have actually achieved have consistently fallen well below the levels that they have had the intrinsic potential to achieve. In this respect they are comparable to a human being who suffers brain damage in early infancy, except that they retain a potential that continues unrealized, whereas the infant's potential goes unrealized because it is lost. The dogs and the Brain-Damaged Individual are equally pitiable because they are condemned to live at a level far below that which they have or once had the potential to achieve. These implications, however, strike most of us as utterly implausible. While we believe that an infant that suffers brain damage would be unfortunate, we would not conclude that dogs are, and have always been, unfortunate if we were to discover that they have the intrinsic potential, which they have never realized, to become persons. The Intrinsic Potential Account delivers the wrong conclusion in this case.

I must end this section inconclusively. I began by suggesting that the strength of one's moral reason to facilitate the realization of an individual's potential is determined primarily by the strength of the individual's time-relative interest in becoming what it has the potential to become or having what it has the potential to have. Whether the individual's potential is intrinsic or extrinsic seems not to matter. I was immediately confronted, however, by an apparent counterexample: the fetus with cerebral deficits. If it were possible to enable this fetus eventually to become a person—for example, by administering a genetic therapy that would cause it to develop the missing areas of its brain—it seems intuitively that one would have a moral reason of considerable strength to do so. Yet this fetus has at present only a very weak time-relative interest in becoming a person and, as long as it remains severely cognitively impaired, it will *never* have more than a weak time-relative interest in being or becoming a person. The Criterion, I noted, supports the commonsense intuition in the case of the fetus with cerebral deficits, but it seems to presuppose the mistaken view that, in this case at least, identity is the basis of egoistic concern; and, more importantly, it appears to imply that there would be equal reason to administer a genetic therapy for cognitive enhancement to an animal.

The various accounts of fortune (that is, of what it is for an individual to be fortunate or unfortunate) appear to fare no better. The Species Norm Account does distinguish in the desired way between the fetus with cerebral deficits and an animal with comparable intrinsic potential, but it does so in a way that is arbitrary. It implies that the fetus is worthy of cognitive enhancement, while the animal is not, simply because the fetus is a member of the human species. Because it arbitrarily makes fortune dependent on species norms, the Species Norm Account has wholly implausible implications in the case of the Superchimp.

The Peak Capacity Account supports the view that there would be little or no reason to provide cognitive enhancement for animals but, by parity of reasoning, fails to support the view that there would be a strong reason to provide genetic therapy for the fetus with cerebral deficits. Indeed, because it implies that it would not be a misfortune for a fetus or neonate to suffer severe brain damage, it offers no basis for objecting to *causing* a fetus or newborn infant to become severely retarded. The Intrinsic Potential Account, by contrast, implies that it can be a misfortune to lose the potential to become a person; hence it can condemn the act of causing a normal fetus to have cerebral deficits, as the woman does in Prenatal Retardation. It also supports the view that there would be little or no reason to provide cognitive enhancement for an animal; but, like the Peak Capacity Account, it cannot justify our intuition that there would be a strong reason to provide genetic therapy for the fetus with cerebral deficits. And it has implausible implications in the case in which dogs are discovered to have the intrinsic potential to become persons.

It is worth noting that the Intrinsic Potential Account draws a distinction that is not captured by an exclusive focus on time-relative interests. It implies that both the Brain-Damaged Individual and the fetus in Prenatal Retardation that is caused to have cerebral deficits are unfortunate because they fare poorly relative to the kind of life they had the intrinsic potential to have. Yet it also implies that the fetus with cerebral deficits may hardly be unfortunate at all. As I noted in section 5.1 of chapter 2, this may initially strike us as arbitrary. One reason why this may be so is that, at every point, the Brain-Damaged Individual's time-relative interest in becoming a person may be no stronger than that of the fetus with cerebral deficits. Similarly, the Intrinsic Potential Account implies that if dogs had the intrinsic potential to become persons (even if intensive "therapy" were necessary to elicit it), they would be unfortunate to remain ordinary dogs. But it also implies that dogs as they actually are would not be unfortunate not to become persons, even if it were possible to enable them to do so via genetic therapy. In both cases, however, the dogs would have an equivalent time-relative interest in becoming persons.

This discrepancy would be minimized if the Intrinsic Potential Account were to acknowledge that both the Brain-Damaged Individual and dogs with intrinsic potential would be only slightly unfortunate. And this seems possible. As I noted earlier, animals and human beings whose psychological capacities never rise above those of animals seem psychologically too insubstantial to be the victims of *tragic* misfortune. Thus, as I also noted, the Intrinsic Potential Account must recognize that it is a substantially more serious misfortune to fare badly relative to levels of well-being one is or has been *capable* of achieving than it is to fare badly relative to levels of well-being one has, or had, only the intrinsic *potential* to achieve.

The problem with this response, however, is that it applies equally to the fetus in Prenatal Retardation that is knowingly caused to be severely retarded. If the Intrinsic Potential Account can recognize only that this individual suffers a slight misfortune, it fails to provide the basis of a strong condemnation of the woman's act.

It is important to realize that the problem here is quite general. It is not just a problem for the Intrinsic Potential Account of fortune or for the view that, within the morality of interests, our concern should be with time-relative interests rather than with interests. There do not seem to be any considerations that plausibly explain and justify our intuitions about these various cases. We believe, for example, that there would be a significant moral reason to employ genetic therapy to enable the fetus with cerebral deficits to become a person but that there is no corresponding reason to enable an animal with comparable psychological capacities to become a person. Yet there seems to be no fundamental difference between their intrinsic natures (hence we cannot claim that the fetus is above the threshold of respect while the animal is below it), they both have the same extrinsic potential to become a person, they each have an equal (and quite weak) time-relative interest in realizing their potential to become a person, and their lives as wholes would both be better if they were to become persons. They are distinguished only by their species membership, and that seems an insufficient basis for claiming that it is very important for one, but not the other, to become a person. Similarly, we believe strongly that the woman acts wrongly in Prenatal Retardation. The Intrinsic Potential Account offers an explanation—namely, that her act causes her child to fare poorly relative to the sort of life it had the intrinsic potential to have. Yet there seems to be nearly as strong a reason to provide genetic therapy for the fetus with cerebral deficits as there is not to cause a normal fetus to become retarded. Hence it is unlikely that the appeal to potential can be the full explanation of why the woman's act is so objectionable.

These reflections may compel us to reconsider our understanding of the importance of cognitive enhancement in the case of congenitally severely mentally retarded human beings. While it is incontestably important to correct (and, a fortiori, not to cause) severe cognitive impairments in human fetuses and infants, the foregoing discussion calls into question the assumption that it is important to do so *for the sake of the fetus or infant.*

It may be that the main reason that people in general have to correct the impairment of a fetus with cerebral deficits has to do with the interests and concerns of human beings other than the fetus itself. ("People in general" embraces all those who might be affected by whether the impairment is corrected other than those who are specially related to the fetus. The latter presumably have a much stronger reason to care about the fetus for its own sake; hence any reason there would be to correct the impairment for the fetus's own sake will apply with considerably greater force to them—for example, the fetus's biological parents—than to others.) Our reason— that is, the reason that people in general have—is similar to the reason we have to ensure that, if a human being is going to come into existence, it should be one with normal cognitive capacities rather than a different one that is severely retarded. While it is preferable that an individual with normal cognitive capacities should exist, it is not better *for that individual* to exist than not to exist. It is not for that individual's sake that we ought to ensure that he exists. Rather, our reason to ensure that the one individual exists rather than the other may be primarily that that is better for *us*—that is, for people in general.

Of course, another relevant consideration is *impersonal:* it is simply a better outcome—that is, the world is a better place overall—if the individual with higher capacities (and therefore, presumably, a better life) exists. This is the better outcome even if there is *no one* for whom it is better. Similarly, it is impersonally better if a fetus with cerebral deficits has those deficits corrected. In neither case, however, can impersonal considerations provide a complete account of our moral reason for bringing about the better outcome. Just as it is impersonally better to cause a human being with higher cognitive capacities to exist rather one with lower capacities, so it is impersonally better to have a child rather than to breed an animal. But surely breeding an animal rather than having a child (if one cannot do both) is less objectionable (if it is objectionable at all) than causing a severely retarded human being to exist rather than a person with normal cognitive capacities. Similarly, it would also be better impersonally if an animal were enabled to become a person; but, as we have seen, no one believes that we would have a significant moral reason to transform an animal into a person if that were possible, though most believe that we would have a strong moral reason to enable a fetus with cerebral deficits to become a person. If these cases cannot be differentiated on impersonal grounds, it is likely that a regard for our own interests is a significant part of our reason to bring an individual with higher capacities into existence rather than a different individual with lower capacities, and also a significant part of our reason to correct cerebral deficits in a fetus.

7. THE SANCTITY OF HUMAN LIFE

I have thus far argued for several claims about the morality of abortion: that the early human fetus is a mere unoccupied organism and as such has no interest in continuing to live and cannot be harmed by being killed; that, although the developed fetus can be harmed by being killed, its time-relative interest in continuing to live is comparatively weak; that the developed fetus falls below the threshold of respect; therefore, if its time-relative interest in continuing to live is outweighed by a conflicting interest of the pregnant woman, its life may be sacrificed for the sake of the woman. These claims presuppose that the morality of abortion is determined within the framework of interests and rights—that is, that if abortion is wrong, the objection to it must be that it harms the fetus, frustrates its time-relative interest, or violates a duty owed to the fetus as a matter of respect, or in virtue of its rights.

Some have argued, however, that the morality of abortion cannot be understood within the framework of interests and rights. Most notably, Ronald Dworkin has argued that most people's views about the morality of abortion cannot be adequately explained within that framework. He claims, for example, that the views of most people who oppose abortion are not really views about the interests or rights of the fetus. If they were, they could be easily refuted; for rights presuppose interests and the capacity for consciousness is a necessary condition for the possession of interests. It is clear, therefore, that the early fetus (the victim of most abortions) can have neither interests nor rights. Moreover, most people who oppose abortion allow for certain exceptions: they accept that abortion may occasionally be permissible, for example, in the case of rape or incest, or when the pregnancy imperils the woman's life. But these exceptions, Dworkin contends, are incompatible with the idea that the fetus has the same rights as the rest of us. If people really believed that the fetus has a right to life of the sort that normal adult human beings have, they would not accept that the fetus could permissibly be killed because of the conditions of its conception or as a means of saving the life of its mother. (Here he places himself in opposition to a prominent line of thought among philosophers who believe that abortion can be justified even if the fetus is a person with the full panoply of rights. I will consider this line of thought in section 9 of this chapter.)

What best explains the views that people actually hold, Dworkin contends, is a belief in the sanctity of human life. The value of a life, according to Dworkin, is multidimensional. A life has *instrumental* value insofar as it contributes to the interests or well-being of others. It has *personal* value to the extent that it is good for the person whose life it is—that is, to the extent that it is worth living. But it may also have *intrinsic* or *impersonal* value—value that is independent of its being valued by or good for anyone, whether its possessor or others. Dworkin cites several examples of things that many people believe have intrinsic value: works of art, biological species, and human cultures. The destruction of a work of art, or the extinction of a species, may be instrumentally bad—bad for people who would have benefited from experiencing the work, or bad for the members of other species that depended in certain ways on the presence of the now extinct species—but it is also bad impersonally, bad because something wonderful or marvelous has been forever annihilated.

Within the category of intrinsic value, Dworkin draws a further distinction. A thing that is intrinsically valuable is also *incrementally* valuable if it is better for there to be more of it. Knowledge, for example, is incrementally valuable (in addition to being, in most cases, instrumentally valuable). That which is intrinsically but not incrementally valuable is *sacred* or *inviolable.* "The hallmark of the sacred as distinct from the incrementally valuable is that the sacred is intrinsically valuable because— and therefore only once—it exists."[30] Human life has, according to Dworkin, sanctity rather than incremental value. We do not believe that it is better the more lives there are; but once a human life exists, its preservation becomes a matter of moral significance. "The life of any human organism, including a fetus, has intrinsic value whether or not it also has instrumental or personal value . . . [A]ny form of human life [is] something we should respect and honor and protect as marvelous in itself."[31]

Dworkin himself never explicitly endorses the claim that human life is sacred in this sense; he is reporting what he thinks other people believe. The idea that human life has sanctity is, he contends, the common foundation of the various competing positions that have been staked out in the debate about abortion. His claim is that the conflict over abortion is really a dispute about the proper interpretation of the notion of the sanctity of human life. This lays the foundation for his legal argument, which is that, if the abortion debate is really about what is required by respect for the sanctity of human life, the competing views are essentially religious in nature and none may therefore be endorsed or enforced by the government.

My concern here is not with the legal status of abortion, or the constitutionality of legislation regulating abortion. The relevant question for our purposes is whether the notion of the sanctity of human life provides the basis for a serious challenge to the *moral* permissibility of abortion. Might abortion be seriously wrong even if there is no compelling objection to it within the framework of interests and rights? Is it really true that "the life of a human organism has intrinsic value in any form it takes, even in the extremely undeveloped form of a very early, just-implanted embryo"?[32]

It is important to stress that the idea that human life has intrinsic value is distinct from the various related ideas that we have previously considered: for example, that it is good for human beings to continue to live, that human beings may have a time-relative interest in continuing to live, that human beings have a worth that commands respect, that human beings have the right to life, and so on. The intrinsic or impersonal value of a human life is different from its personal value—that is, the value it has for the individual whose life it is. Even though a life may have impersonal value in part or even entirely for the same reasons that it has personal value, the two types of value are distinct. Similarly, respect for the sanctity of human life is different from respect for the worth of the person. Respect for the worth of a person is not distinct from respect for the person himself. Respect for a person arguably has two dimensions: concern for his good and respect for the determinations of his autonomous will. But the intrinsic value of a person's life may be independent both of the personal value of the life and of what the person himself autonomously desires his life to be like. Thus what is required by respect for the intrinsic value of the life may be different from what is required by respect for the person. (I will defend this claim in greater detail in sections 2.2 and 2.3 of chapter 5.) Moreover, the duties that are constitutive of respect for a person are *owed to* that person; thus a failure to fulfill such a duty constitutes a wrong done to the person. By contrast, the duty to respect the sanctity of a person's life is an *impersonal* duty. It is not owed to anyone, and therefore a failure to fulfill it wrongs no one: a violation of the sanctity of life is a wrong without a victim. (An act that violates the sanctity of life may also wrong the victim, but not *by virtue* of its violating the sanctity of life.)

These differences are in fact essential if the appeal to the sanctity of human life is to ground an objection to voluntary euthanasia. By hypothesis, voluntary euthanasia is in the best interest of the individual who dies and is also in conformity with the dictates of his autonomous will. It therefore cannot be opposed on the ground that it harms or is worse for that individual, or—arguably—on the ground that it is incompatible with respect for that person. (Again, I will return to this is section 2.3 of chapter 5.) Nor does voluntary euthanasia violate the individual's right to life; for in requesting to be killed or allowed to die, the individual waives his right. Only if the life has a value that is distinct from its value to the person whose life it is, and only if this value exerts its force even in opposition to the autonomous will of the person, can the sanctity of life ground an objection to voluntary euthanasia. And in fact this is the way that the notion of the sanctity or intrinsic value of human life is sometimes understood. Thus, as Dworkin notes, Supreme Court Justices William Rehnquist and Antonin Scalia have both argued, in opinions concerning the right to die, that the state may legitimately prevent both suicide and euthanasia in order to protect the intrinsic value of human life, even in cases in which a person autonomously desires to die and in which it is acknowledged that it would be better for him, or in his interests, if he were to die.[33]

If the intrinsic or impersonal value of a human life is distinct from both the instrumental and the personal value of the life, and if respect for that value is different from respect for the person whose life it is, what is the basis of this special value? There are various possibilities, some religious, others essentially secular. By far the commonest religious view is that what makes human lives sacred and sets them apart from the lives of animals is that human beings possess (or *are*) immortal souls made in the image of God. If it were true that all human beings differ from animals in this respect, the doctrine of the sanctity of human life would have a solid foundation. But I have argued in section 2 of chapter 1 that the view that we are incorporeal souls is untenable.

There are other religious views that may invoke the notion of the sanctity of human life. It is often said, for example, that human beings are specially beloved by God and that the fundamental difference between human beings and animals is that God, because of his love for us, granted us dominion over animals. It is important to see, however, that this is not a claim about intrinsic value. What makes human beings special, on this view, is not an intrinsic property they share but a relational one: they are favored by God. Some people claim that it is because human beings are favored by God that their lives have sanctity. They are sanctified simply by virtue of being favored. That may be a coherent claim, but it invokes a wholly different notion of sanctity. Given this different notion, if God had favored rocks over human beings, rocks would have greater sanctity; but that would be compatible with their being inferior to human beings in intrinsic value.

One secular reason why human lives might be thought to have intrinsic value is that most human beings are endowed with uniquely high capacities. Our cognitive and emotional capacities, it might be argued, set us wholly apart; they give us an intrinsic value incomparably higher than that of animals. Another reason for thinking that human lives have intrinsic value is that they are made up of experiences and activities of which a great many are intrinsically good. Most things that have personal value have impersonal value as well. The two types of value often coincide. It is, for example, good for me if my life contains pleasure; but it is also good in itself for there to be pleasure in the world. (This, however, may be a reason for thinking that human life has incremental value: for it may be that the more pleasure the world contains, the better it is.) A third ground for the intrinsic value of human lives is the extraordinary biological complexity of the human organism. The human brain, in particular, is surely the most intricate and complex biological structure in the known world.

Dworkin, however, does not discuss any of these possible bases for the intrinsic value or sanctity of human life. He focuses instead on the notion of "creative investment"—on the idea that things derive their intrinsic value through the time, energy, resources, effort, and so on invested in their creation and development. He distinguishes three sources of investment in a human life: divine, natural, and human. Religious people, he suggests, regard human beings as "the highest achievements of God's creation"—each one of us "a creative masterpiece."[34] Secular thinkers marvel at the natural processes involved in the genesis of each human life and thus "assign. . . the masterpiece to nature." Finally, the life of each human being is initially nurtured and guided by the efforts of countless others, who draw on the resources of their culture, a process that continues throughout the individual's life and is increasingly supplemented, and soon overshadowed, by the individual's own increasing investment in the shaping and structuring of his life. Thus, Dworkin contends,

> the life of a single human organism commands respect and protection, . . . no matter in what form or shape, because of the complex creative investment it represents and because of our wonder at the divine or evolutionary processes that produce new lives from old ones, at the processes of nation and community and language through which a human being will come to absorb and continue hundreds of generations of cultures and forms of life and value, and, finally, when mental life has begun and flourishes, at the process of internal personal creation and judgment by which a person will make and remake himself.[35]

Differences of view about abortion, Dworkin suggests, are at bottom disagreements about the relative importance of the different forms of investment. Opponents of abortion tend to believe that the killing of the fetus constitutes a waste of the natural or divine investment in the life. But proponents of abortion tend to think of human investment as the primary source of intrinsic value. Thus they believe that "it may be more frustrating of life's miracle when an adult's ambitions, talents, training, and expectations are wasted because of an unforeseen and unwanted pregnancy than when a fetus dies before any significant investment of that kind has been made."[36]

This analysis of the abortion debate bears little fidelity to the beliefs that people actually hold. It is revealing, for example, that Dworkin fails to cite a single religious thinker who appeals to the notion of divine investment in a life in order to explain the basis of the sanctity of human life. When pressed to explain why they believe that it is wrong to take human life, most religious thinkers contend that to take human life is to usurp God's prerogative or to violate his will. Deliberately to end a human life is something that human beings lack the authority to do. To the question of why God reserves the authority to end human life for himself alone, there are many possible answers: for example, that we are his property, or that he has purposes for our lives (connected, perhaps, with our fate as immortal souls) that we cannot fathom but that would be thwarted by our intervening to end a life before its appointed time.

It would, nevertheless, be a mistake to dismiss the idea that human life has intrinsic value, or sanctity, simply because people do not seem to hold the sorts of views that Dworkin attributes to them. It is, I believe, entirely plausible to suppose that human lives have intrinsic or impersonal value. The question is how significant that value is, particularly in the case of lives whose personal value is neutral (a category that arguably includes human fetuses) or negative (as is true of those who are candidates for euthanasia).

Let us here confine our attention to the case of the human fetus. (I will return to the question whether an appeal to the sanctity of human life can support an objection to euthanasia in the next chapter.) In most cases in which an abortion is at issue, the fetus is unwanted and therefore has no positive instrumental value. I have argued, furthermore, that it lacks the worth that commands respect. Let us also assume, for the sake of argument, that the life of a human fetus lacks personal value. For the reasons given earlier, I believe that this is true in the case of the early fetus. Whether it is true of the developed fetus as well depends on how the notion of personal value is understood. Even in the case of the developed fetus, there may be nothing about its *present* life that is good *for it*. That might be a sufficient reason for denying that its present life has personal value. I have argued that the fetus does have a present time-relative interest in its future life or, in other words, that its future life has personal value. But let us put that aside and assume that the only consideration militating against the abortion of a fetus is that its life has impersonal value. How strong an objection is posed by that consideration alone?

In order for an appeal to the sanctity of human life to support the beliefs of those who oppose abortion, the impersonal value of fetal life must greatly exceed the impersonal value (if any) of an animal. For those who oppose abortion generally believe that the killing of a human fetus is substantially more seriously objectionable than the killing of an animal, other things being equal. So if the fetus lacks worth, and if its life lacks both instrumental and personal value, its impersonal value must greatly exceed that of an animal if killing it is to be significantly more objectionable morally than the killing of an animal.

For each possible basis for impersonal value that I have mentioned, it is clear that the impersonal value of a normal adult human being must greatly exceed that of an animal. (Since neither human beings nor animals have souls, we can ignore this frequently asserted basis for the sanctity of human life.) Normal adults have significantly higher cognitive and emotional capacities, their lives (consequently) generally contain more and higher goods, their biological complexity is unrivaled, and they have made enormous investments of time and effort in planning and preparing for their futures. By all measures, then, the life of a normal adult human being should have substantially higher impersonal value than the life of any animal.

What about a human fetus? A fetus's present capacities—including the cognitive and emotional capacities of the developed fetus—are inferior to those of an adult nonhuman mammal. Nor does its present life contain experiences or activities more valuable than those of an animal. And, in its present state, it is no more biologically complex than an adult animal. This leaves the matter of investment. Certainly there is no greater natural investment in the life of a fetus than there is in the life of an adult animal—in fact, the reverse seems true, as natural investment seems necessarily to increase as a life develops biologically. Nor is there necessarily any more human investment. A trained domestic animal, for example, embodies considerably more human investment than an unwanted fetus. Divine investment—assuming, for the sake of argument, that there is such a thing—is difficult to measure; but there seems to be no reason to suppose that God has put more into the making of a fetus than he has into the making of an animal. If all human beings had souls while no animals did, that might be a reason for thinking that the divine investment was greater; but, as we have seen, there is good reason to believe that this assumption is false.

What other differences are there between a fetus and an adult animal? The fetus, of course, is a member of the human species, but that, as I argued in chapter 3, provides no basis for attributing to it a higher intrinsic value. The other major difference between the fetus and an animal is that the developed fetus has significantly greater potential. Perhaps this potential—the potential to become a person, with highly developed psychological capacities and a life filled with higher goods—gives the fetus a higher intrinsic or impersonal value than an animal.

It is unclear, however, whether potential alone is ever a basis for the attribution of intrinsic value to an entity. Doubtless it is tempting to believe that a developed fetus has intrinsic value by virtue of its identity-preserving potential to become a person. The fetus is, after all, itself the first stage in the existence of the entity that will later have highly developed psychological capacities, great biological complexity, and so on.

In section 6.1 of this chapter, I conceded that the developed fetus has an interest in the realization of its potential to become a person—though I also questioned the moral significance of this fact. But it is not the personal value of the developed fetus's potential—the value that the potential and its realization have for the developed fetus itself—that is at issue here. The question is whether its potential to become a person has *intrinsic* or *impersonal* value. Is there something valuable in itself, independently of any value that it might have for the fetus or others, in the fetus's potential to become a person? It is hard to see what it could be. Even if the outcome of the realization of the potential—that is, the presence of another person—would have impersonal value, it seems that all that would follow about the developed fetus's potential to become a person is that it would have instrumental value—that is, it would have value insofar as it was instrumental in bringing about what would have impersonal value. It seems, in fact, that claims about the intrinsic value of fetal potential are really misdirected claims about the intrinsic value of properties that the fetus would later have, if it were to become a person (for example, highly developed psychological capacities, great biological complexity, and so on). Consider, by way of analogy, the first few brush strokes that Rembrandt applied to a certain canvas in 1669. These strokes constituted the initial stage of the existence of his self-portrait of that year. The canvas, at that point, may have had the identity-preserving potential to become the great painting that we now know. But it did not, at that point, have great intrinsic value. For that it had to await further work; and it did not achieve its full intrinsic value until it reached completion. This suggests that potential alone has merely instrumental value; it is only when the potential is realized that there may be something of intrinsic value.

But suppose that this is wrong. Suppose that the potential of a human fetus has impersonal value. Even so, the appeal to fetal potential cannot support the position of those who believe in the special sanctity of all human life. Recall that among the intuitions that Dworkin's analysis is intended to capture is that "the life of a human organism has intrinsic value in any form it takes." The basis of this sanctity must therefore be something that *all* human beings share—and, presumably, that few, if any, animals possess. While the potential to become a person satisfies the second of these conditions, it does not satisfy the first. Many human embryos and fetuses—those that are defective in certain ways—lack the potential to become, or to give rise to the existence of, a person. Indeed, some—for example, those genetically destined to develop into anencephalic infants—lack the potential to become *anything* fundamentally different from, or anything with a higher intrinsic value than, the sort of the thing they already are. They have, in short, no morally significant potential at all. If, therefore, there is something that gives *all* human beings an intrinsic value or sanctity that animals lack, it cannot be potential.

It seems that there is no reason to suppose that a human fetus, in its present state, has an intrinsic or impersonal value that exceeds that of a higher animal. But because most people will find it very difficult to accept that conclusion, let us assume, for the sake of argument, that the life of every human fetus has a special sanctity that is not present in the lives of animals. Can that assumption ground a strong objection to abortion?[37]

If, as Dworkin claims, people's opposition to abortion is, at bottom, grounded in their beliefs about the sanctity of human life, the appeal to the sanctity of life will have to carry a great deal of weight. For people who object to abortion typically do not think that the killing of a fetus is a comparatively minor form of wrongdoing. It is, for example, considered to be a far graver matter than the killing of an animal. So the sanctity or intrinsic value of the fetus's life must be a weighty or highly significant moral consideration.

Just how important it is must, however, be variable. As Dworkin explicitly recognizes, most people believe that abortion becomes more seriously objectionable the later in pregnancy it is performed. If the objection to abortion is that it violates the sanctity of the fetus's life, the explanation of why a later abortion is worse should be that the intrinsic value of the fetus's life increases as it matures. On Dworkin's analysis, this is because the investment in its life increases with time. Thus, according to Dworkin, "there are degrees of the sacred."[38]

If, however, the sanctity or intrinsic value of life is variable, the life of a normal adult human being must have considerably greater value than the life of a fetus. This will be true whatever the variable basis of the sanctity of life is supposed to be—investment, psychological capacity, biological complexity, or whatever. Thus the killing of an adult human being must be a significantly more serious offense against the sanctity of life than the killing of a fetus. And, since the sanctity of life poses a strong objection to abortion, it should pose a significantly stronger objection to the killing of a person. In short, the idea that killing violates the sanctity of the victim's life should be a significant part of the explanation of why the killing of a person is wrong.

But if the sanctity of life is a significant part of the reason why killing a person is wrong, and if people's lives vary in sanctity or intrinsic value, it seems to follow that some killings of persons must be more seriously wrong than others. It should, for example, be more seriously wrong, if other things are equal, to kill a person with highly developed cognitive and emotional capacities who has received unusually high levels of care and education than it would be to kill a person with lower endowments who has suffered from neglect. This conclusion, however, conflicts with the Equal Wrongness Thesis, to which most of us are strongly committed.

If the sanctity of life is variable, not only should some killings of persons be more seriously wrong than others, but also it should be permissible, or perhaps even required, to sacrifice some persons for the sake of others. Although Dworkin often uses the term "inviolable" to mean "possessing intrinsic value," it is clear that he does not really believe that things that have sanctity or intrinsic value cannot in general be sacrificed for the sake of protecting or preserving other things that have greater intrinsic value.[39] He claims, for example, that works of art can have intrinsic value. Presumably a painting by Rembrandt has greater intrinsic value than a painting by Wyeth. And it seems clear that, if a Rembrandt will be destroyed unless we deliberately destroy a Wyeth instead, we ought to destroy the Wyeth. Similarly, if there are three Rembrandts of comparable quality and two will be destroyed unless we deliberately destroy the third, we ought to destroy the third: for there is a lesser loss of intrinsic value if one Rembrandt perishes than there is if two equally great Rembrandts do so. By parity of reasoning, the doctrine of the sanctity of human life should imply that, if a highly cultivated person will be destroyed unless we kill a less-well-endowed and neglected person, we ought to kill the neglected person; and, if two cultivated persons will be destroyed unless we kill a third, equally cultivated person instead, we ought to kill the one to save the two—if, in both cases, other things are equal. But if this is what is implied by respect for the sanctity of life, we should conclude that the appeal to the sanctity of life cannot be a significant part of the explanation of why killing people is wrong.

Should we conclude, further, that the sanctity of life is also incapable of grounding a strong and plausible objection to abortion? Dworkin would reject this inference. He accepts—or at least acknowledges that most people accept—the Equal Wrongness Thesis. He notes that "most people think (and our laws certainly insist) that people have an equal right to life, and that the murder of a depressive handicapped octogenarian misanthrope is as heinous, and must be punished as seriously, as the murder of anyone younger or healthier or more valuable to others. Any other view would strike us as monstrous."[40] He also observes, however, that "these judgments about murder . . . belong to the system of rights and interests, the system of ideas I said could not explain our most common convictions about abortion."[41] These passages suggest that Dworkin's explanatory framework must attribute to people a two-tiered understanding of the morality of killing analogous to that which I have defended. The claim that all human life has intrinsic value or sanctity is a significant consideration in determining the morality of abortion. But even though the life of a normal adult must, by any measure, have greater intrinsic value than the life of a fetus, the intrinsic value or sanctity of human life cannot be a significant factor in determining the morality of killing children or adults—that is, persons. For if it were, the killing of people with lower intrinsic value would be less seriously objectionable than the killing of people with higher intrinsic value, and would in principle be permissible if it were necessary in order to save those with higher value. Dworkin, in short, seems to attribute to us the view that, while the sanctity of life is a major factor in determining the morality of killing a fetus, it is not a significant factor, or not a factor at all, in determining the morality of killing persons. The morality of killing persons is governed instead by "the system of rights and interests."

The parallel with the Two-Tiered Account is obvious. In chapter 3, I suggested that the central moral objection to the killing of animals is that this harms the animals—or, more precisely, frustrates their time-relative interest in continuing to live. Thus the wrongness of killing animals varies, other things being equal, with the strength of the victim's time-relative interest in continuing to live. But the wrongness of killing persons does not vary with the strength of the victim's time-relative interest in continuing to live. It seems reasonable to conclude, therefore, that the fact that killing a person frustrates that person's time-relative interest in continuing to live is not a significant part of the explanation of why killing persons is wrong. Our account of the wrongness of killing persons must be fundamentally different from our account of the morality of killing animals. Dworkin suggests, similarly, that the central objection to killing a fetus is that the fetus's life has intrinsic value or sanctity, and that the degree to which an abortion is objectionable therefore varies, other things being equal, with the intrinsic value of the life of the fetus. But because his account must accommodate the Equal Wrongness Thesis, he seems committed to accepting that the sanctity of life has little or no role in explaining the wrongness of killing persons. The explanation of why killing a person is wrong must appeal to different considerations—considerations drawn from the system of rights and interests.

Because I have defended the Two-Tiered Account, I cannot object to a view that has a parallel structure. But it is worth emphasizing the dilemmas that most people who are tempted to invoke the notion of the sanctity of life are likely to face. If the sanctity of life is variable, it cannot be a significant element in the explanation of why killing people is wrong unless the Equal Wrongness Thesis is mistaken and some killings of persons are more seriously objectionable than others. One can, of course, accept a two-tiered view according to which the sanctity of life poses a strong objection to the killing of a fetus but is no part of the objection to the killing of persons. But this view carries a heavy cost: one forfeits the ability to appeal to the sanctity of life in contesting the permissibility of euthanasia in the case of persons. Dworkin cites convincing evidence to show that beliefs about the sanctity of life are a significant ground of many people's opposition to euthanasia. But, if the sanctity of life is variable, these people must either abandon their objection to euthanasia or accept a highly inegalitarian account of the wrongness of killing. I will consider whether there is a coherent way of evading this dilemma in section 2.2 of chapter 5.

Another option is deny that the sanctity of life is variable. But this, too, has its costs; for example, the objection to abortion based on the sanctity of life no longer has the resources to explain why a later abortion seems more seriously objectionable. More importantly, it seems impossible, as I have argued at length, to identify any intrinsic properties that could constitute a plausible basis for the sanctity of life that are possessed equally by all human beings, including fetuses, but are not possessed by any animals.

8. INFANTICIDE

8.1. *Abortion and Infanticide*

Although it raises deep issues (some of which have been explored in sections 4 and 5 of this chapter), the position I have developed on the morality of abortion is in essence quite simple. Early abortions, which constitute approximately 99 percent of the abortions actually performed in the United States, do not kill one of us but merely prevent one of us from existing. Other things being equal, these abortions are morally indistinguishable from contraception. Late abortions, by contrast, involve the killing of someone who, in most cases, would otherwise have had a long life that would have been well worth living. But because the developed fetus is almost totally isolated psychologically from the person it might later become, its time-relative interest in continuing to live is very weak, despite the magnitude of the good that lies in prospect for it. Moreover, because the developed fetus's rudimentary cognitive capacities are significantly lower even than those of various animals, it is outside the scope of the morality of respect; hence the killing of a developed fetus is properly governed by the Time-Relative Interest Account of the morality of killing. These two claims—that the central moral objection to killing a developed fetus is that this would frustrate its time-relative interest in continuing to live and that this time-relative interest is comparatively weak—together imply that the killing of a developed fetus is substantially less seriously objectionable than the killing of a person, and perhaps not seriously objectionable at all, if other things—such as the effects on the biological parents—are equal. Because the killing of a developed fetus is not governed by the morality of respect, the fetus's time-relative interest in continuing to live may permissibly be weighed and traded off against the time-relative interests of others in the manner approved by consequentialists. The act of killing is not, as some would express it, directly subject to or opposed by a deontological constraint.

It should be obvious that the two claims that support the argument for the permissibility of abortion apply equally to a newborn infant. If it is the actual possession of certain psychological capacities (and not just the potential for having those capacities) that is the basis for inclusion within the morality of respect, newborn infants must be excluded from the realm of respect just as surely as developed fetuses are. And because the prudential unity relations would hold only weakly between a newborn infant and itself later as a child or adult, its time-relative interest in continuing to live is also comparatively weak. Therefore the same considerations that may permit the killing of a fetus in order to protect a pregnant woman's interests should also permit the killing of a newborn infant if there are comparably weighty reasons for doing so.

This, of course, is anathema to most of us. Most people draw a sharp moral distinction between abortion and infanticide, regarding infanticide as just as seriously wrong, if other things are equal, as the killing of an adult person. As I noted earlier, most people, however they vote and whatever they profess through stickers displayed on their cars, recognize that abortion is somehow different. If it were not, there would, as I noted earlier, be a serious moral case in favor of the bombing of abortion clinics and the killing of those who perform abortions. But virtually everyone, including the vast majority of those who oppose abortion on moral grounds, condemns these acts—not because they are ineffective or counterproductive, but because they are immoral. Most believe that these acts would be immoral even if they were the only means of trying to stop the practice of abortion. If, however, there were a legally sanctioned practice that involved the killing of many thousands of healthy newborns, people who oppose abortion, and a great many of those who support it, would almost certainly approve of the use of violence against those responsible for the practice if that were necessary to bring it to an end.

If this is right, most of us face a challenge in showing that our beliefs about infanticide are consistent with our beliefs about abortion. The challenge is particularly acute for those, like myself, whose reasons for believing abortion to be generally permissible seem directly to imply that infanticide may be permissible as well. But there is a challenge to anyone who believes that abortion is often morally permissible and ought therefore to be legally permissible, while infanticide is normally wrong and therefore ought to be legally prohibited. Indeed, even those who oppose abortion but nevertheless implicitly accept that it is less seriously wrong than infanticide—and, as I have suggested, this includes the great majority of those who oppose abortion—must be able to explain the moral difference between the two.

The reason why common beliefs about infanticide present a challenge even to most of those who would reject the argument I have developed about the morality of abortion is that the intrinsic differences between a developed fetus and a newborn infant are comparatively slight. Indeed, a developed fetus approaching birth at the normal due date or whose birth has been delayed beyond the due date will be chronologically older and therefore in general better developed, both physically and psychologically, than an infant born prematurely. And, as has often been pointed out, it may be difficult to see how birth, which involves only a change in the fetus's location, could significantly affect the fetus-cum-infant's moral status, which ought instead to be determined entirely by its intrinsic properties.

It is perhaps worth noting, at the outset, that although people typically profess a profound horror of infanticide, our intuitions about the killing of infants are in fact quite mixed. Certainly the killing of babies in some contexts seems to us even more fiendishly evil and repulsive then the killing of adults. Anyone who followed the various wars in Central America in the 1970s and 1980s at all closely will recall with special repugnance the lurid reports of soldiers, usually government forces supported by the United States, smashing the heads of infants against a wall or tossing babies into the air to spear them with bayonets. Although there is usually little reason to doubt the veracity of such tales of atrocities against babies, it is clear that one reason they are often recounted is that they stir our passions against the perpetrators and thus make powerful propaganda. This is partly because the killing of an infant by a soldier is so glaringly a wanton, gratuitous, pointless, and cowardly act. But it is also because we have an overwhelmingly poignant sense of the innocence, purity, vulnerability, and helplessness of the victim, which arouses our protective and nurturing tendencies, making it almost unthinkable that these very characteristics would excite sadistic impulses in others. Thus when Dostoyevsky set out to state the problem of evil as forcefully as possible, he had his character Ivan Karamazov narrate stories of exactly the sort that have become depressingly familiar in reports of modern wars:

> These Turks, among other things, have also taken a delight in torturing children, starting with cutting them out of their mothers' wombs with a dagger, and ending with tossing nursing infants up in the air and catching them on their bayonets before their mothers' eyes. But here is a picture that I found very interesting. Imagine a nursing infant in the arms of its trembling mother, surrounded by Turks. They've thought up an amusing trick: they fondle the baby, they laugh to make it laugh, and they succeed—the baby laughs. At that moment a Turk aims a pistol at it, four inches from its face. The baby laughs gleefully, reaches out its little hands to grab the pistol, and suddenly the artist pulls the trigger right in its face and shatters its little head . . . Artistic, isn't it?[42]

The infant's sweetness, its complete lack of familiarity with evil and its consequent inability to recognize the danger, even its littleness, all conspire to elicit our most profound revulsion at its killing.

We have, however, a rather different set of intuitive responses that coexist uneasily with our deep abhorrence of cruelty to infants. In the recent past it was common practice in developed countries such as the United States and Britain to allow certain infants with Down's syndrome to die. Down's syndrome is not itself fatal, but there are other congenital conditions that often occur in conjunction with it that, if untreated, are rapidly fatal. In one such condition, the esophagus is unconnected to the back of the throat. This defect can be repaired by comparatively minor surgery, but if it is not corrected, the infant cannot eat and will eventually starve. In the case of otherwise normal infants, this defect is of course routinely repaired. But when this condition occurred in conjunction with Down's syndrome, the decision was frequently made not to operate. At least in many such cases, the motivation cannot have been to spare the child a life that would not have been worth living; for most individuals with Down's syndrome lead contented lives, provided that they are well cared for. Indeed, they tend to be unusually cheerful. Therefore the main motivation in many cases was presumably to spare the parents the burden of supporting the child, given the assumption (perhaps no longer as plausible as it once was) that the child would be an unlikely candidate for adoption. The practice cannot, of course, be called infanticide because the infants were not killed but were merely allowed to die. It is clear, however, that the intention was to ensure that the infant did not survive and that many of those who participated in the practice would have greatly preferred the more humane option of painlessly killing the infants with a lethal injection, since even with the use of analgesics it was likely that the infants suffered during the slow process of starvation. But a lethal injection would have risked a charge of murder.

Although efforts were made to conceal this practice, it enjoyed sufficient support among physicians and parents of newborn infants with Down's syndrome to become fairly common. This is rather surprising, given the largely self-interested character of the motivation. For, while self-interest is of course a powerful source of motivation, it certainly seems that one's conscience would be less troubled about allowing one's own child to die if one could convince oneself that one was acting for the benefit of the child—which doubtless many of the parents were able to do, though not without considerable self-deception.

The point of calling attention to this practice is not just to note that it was accepted by decent people, though that alone reveals that common intuitions about the moral status of newborn infants are mixed. What is equally significant is that the people who participated in the practice—physicians, parents, and hospital staff—did not have, and would not have even considered having, a comparable practice of allowing older children with Down's syndrome to die of easily correctable conditions in order to relieve the parents and others of the burden of caring for them. In short, the practice was a psychological possibility only because those involved in it believed, whether or not they acknowledged the fact to themselves, that the moral status of newborn infants is different. They accepted that it was permissible to allow a newborn infant to die, even when its life could have been worth living, though they would have found it unthinkable to withhold similar forms of treatment from *the same child* had it been a few years older, or even perhaps a few months older.

It is common in discussions of infanticide to note that many previous cultures, including ancient Athens at the height of its civilization, have practiced infanticide, in particular the exposure of defective newborns; yet we do not necessarily regard them as barbarous for that reason.[43] Even today, there are many societies in which infants are not recognized as members of the community, and are not even given names, until they reach a certain age. Only then are they regarded as having moral status in their own right. Again, we do not perceive these societies as wicked or morally obtuse. We understand that, just as a practice of exposing defective newborns may be necessary in a society with limited resources, so a practice of withholding recognition from infants may be necessary to the maintenance of emotional and social stability in a society in which a high proportion of infants die within the first year of life. Without such a practice, a significant proportion of the adult population would at any given time be paralyzed or disabled with grief at the loss of a child. Emotional distancing from newborn infants can, in harsh circumstances, be a necessary self-protective mechanism both for societies and for individuals within those societies.

One must be careful, however, in interpreting the significance of our relatively tolerant attitude to these practices. Some commentators contend that our reluctance to condemn these practices, or at least to judge them severely, reflects an intuitive recognition that the moral status of infants is lower. Others claim that the prevalence of these practices throughout human history exposes our contemporary Western condemnation of infanticide as a parochial aberration.[44] I believe, by contrast, that to draw such conclusions is unwarranted. We can accept that infanticide and the withholding of moral recognition from infants are comprehensible and excusable social practices in extremis without conceding that infants have a different moral status from adults. After all, we take a similarly tolerant view of the practice of leaving very elderly people to die in societies whose material circumstances are precarious; yet there is no reason to suppose that this indicates that we intuitively accept that killing elderly people is in general a morally less serious matter than killing people who are younger. Nonetheless, the prevalence of infanticide throughout most of human history and, in particular, its acceptance within civilizations that unquestionably had high moral standards do suggest that we are not entitled to a high degree of confidence in our intuitive sense that infanticide is just as wrong as the killing of adults.

It is, however, virtually impossible to believe that infanticide is morally indistinguishable from abortion. A plausible account of the ethics of killing must have the resources to discern the relevant differences between them. I believe that the Time-Relative Interest Account of killing is capable of recognizing those differences that there really are. These differences, however, do not support the commonsense conviction that there is a deep and radical gulf between abortion and infanticide. While the differences are sufficient to make infanticide in general more seriously objectionable than abortion, they are only differences of degree rather than kind. I believe, therefore, that commonsense beliefs about the morality of infanticide have to be revised. Because the newborn infant differs only slightly in nature and status from the developed fetus, there is no basis for a radical moral distinction between abortion and infanticide.

Of the relevant differences between abortion and infanticide, the first is that infanticide normally frustrates a stronger time-relative interest in continuing to live than abortion does. The reason why the newborn infant's time-relative interest in continuing to live is normally stronger than that of a developed fetus is quite simple. Given that the developed fetus's time in utero is relatively brief, and assuming that the life it has there is largely neutral in value, the good that lies in prospect for it is only marginally greater than that which remains in prospect when it has become an infant. But because at birth it begins to be bombarded with stimuli, its mind is impelled to a higher level of activity and its psychological development thereby accelerates accordingly. As its psychological capacities develop and its mental life becomes richer, the degree to which it would be psychologically continuous with itself in the future sharply increases. In short, while the amount of good in prospect for it remains almost constant, the strength of the relations that bind it in the relevant ways to itself in the future is increasing at a rapid and accelerating pace; therefore the newborn infant's time-relative interest in continuing to live is stronger than it was when the infant was a fetus, and it will continue to increase in strength as the infant continues to mature psychologically.

It has to be conceded, however, that the strength of an individual's time-relative interest in continuing to live cannot be significantly greater immediately after birth than it was immediately prior to birth. Yet at birth another important process begins: the newborn infant begins to form bonds with those around it. In the typical case, a process of mutual bonding begins to occur between the infant and its parents; and the ties that are formed strengthen with incredible rapidity. The newborn infant is a participant, and not an entirely passive one, in a network of special relations with others.

This point should not be confused with the related observation that we feel differently about an infant once we can see and touch it from the way we feel about a fetus that is necessarily removed from certain forms of contact with us. While it is true that infants engage our sentiments in ways that fetuses do not, this consideration is largely irrelevant—in the same way that it is irrelevant to the constraints that govern our treatment of puppies and pigs that puppies engage our affections in ways that pigs do not. Our sentiments are not a reliable guide in determining a being's moral status. The relevant point is therefore not about the feelings that infants evoke but about the objective nature of the relations that infants form with others (which of course involve the evocation of various feelings). The special relations that quickly develop between a newborn infant and its parents and others may magnify the reason those people have not to frustrate its time-relative interest in continuing to live. Moreover, the infant's participation in special relations with others means that the side effects of infanticide will normally be worse than those of abortion. Because an infant may be specially related to others in ways in which it is not possible for a fetus to be, the death of an infant may have more serious adverse effects on the lives of others than the death of a fetus.

Again, however, it has to be conceded that a newborn infant may not become significantly specially related to anyone in cases in which infanticide is contemplated. If, for example, the infant is unwanted, or if its life is judged not to be worth living, or if for some other reason the parents would prefer to try to have a different child instead, people are likely to draw back from the infant and refrain from forming close personal connections with it. In these cases, special relations and potential adverse side effects may not count against infanticide any more than they typically do against abortion.

There remains one other significant difference between abortion and infanticide. Given that the differences I have so far cited may be of comparatively minor significance in certain cases, this last difference may be the most important of all. It is this. The reasons that may favor killing a fetus are usually considerably stronger than those that may, on occasion, favor infanticide. For the fetus is lodged inside the pregnant woman's body and is dependent upon the continued use of her body for its survival; therefore the burden it imposes is particularly onerous and invasive. Moreover, there is usually no way of relieving the woman of the burden that does not involve killing the fetus (or, perhaps, letting it die). But because infants exist independently, the sacrifices that they may require from others in order to survive and flourish are of a fundamentally different and usually less burdensome kind. And there are typically ways in which those to whom the burden initially falls can evade it without having to kill the infant—for example, by giving it up for adoption. The burden of caring for an infant can be much more widely distributed than the burden of supporting a fetus. Hence the possible justifications for infanticide are more limited and tend to be substantially weaker than the possible justifications for abortion. This may be the principal reason why infanticide is, in general, more objectionable than abortion.

The point about the fetus's dependency on the pregnant woman for life support has been expanded into a powerful argument for the permissibility of abortion—originally and most famously in a justly celebrated article by Judith Jarvis Thomson.[45] This argument offers a defense of abortion that is independent of any claims about the nature or moral status of the fetus. It purports, for example, to provide a defense of abortion even if it is true that the fetus has the same moral status as a normal adult human being. It is possible, therefore, that one could accept that both fetuses and infants lie above the threshold of respect (or are persons, have the right to life, or whatever) and yet consistently believe that abortion is often permissible. But because the justification for abortion would appeal to claims about the nature of the fetus's *relation* to the pregnant woman that would not apply to any relation that an infant bears to another, the justification would apply only to abortion; it would not extend to infanticide as well. This is an argument, in short, that promises to demonstrate the permissibility of abortion without implying the permissibility of infanticide. It is therefore exactly what is needed to support the commonsense intuition that, while abortion is somehow very different from the killing of an adult, infanticide is not.

This argument, which I will refer to as "the Thomson argument," can, if it is persuasive, enable us to defend abortion while categorically condemning infanticide—but only if we reject my two earlier claims, namely, that infants fall below the threshold of respect and that the morality of infanticide is therefore properly governed by the Time-Relative Interest Account of the morality of killing. There are therefore reasons for exploring this argument in detail. If my earlier arguments about the nature and moral status of the early fetus and the developed fetus turn out to be mistaken, the Thomson argument may provide an alternative explanation and defense of the commonsense conviction that abortion is morally different from, and less seriously objectionable than, most other acts of killing human beings. And even if my earlier arguments are right, the Thomson argument serves to illuminate certain important differences between abortion and infanticide. Thus my arguments might be combined with the Thomson argument to yield an exceptionally strong defense of abortion. My arguments would show why the moral considerations that oppose abortion are comparatively weak, while the Thomson argument would show that there are positive considerations that favor abortion that are extremely strong. This in turn would enable us to see more clearly why infanticide is morally more problematic. For although my arguments would suggest that the considerations that oppose infanticide are weaker than most people have supposed, the fact that the considerations to which the Thomson argument appeals are absent in the case of infanticide allows for the possibility that the positive case in favor of infanticide may often, or even in almost all cases, be insufficient to outweigh the considerations that oppose it. Finally, one further reason for examining the Thomson argument is that it may help to explain the relevance to the morality of abortion of certain factors that the approach that I have developed fails to explain. Many people, for example, believe that whether a pregnancy is the result of rape or of voluntary sex can affect the permissibility of abortion. Yet it seems clear that facts about the fetus's provenance cannot affect its moral status. So there is a problem of explaining how the conditions in which a pregnancy arose may affect the morality of abortion. I believe that, even if the Thomson argument is not fully successful as a general defense of abortion, it nevertheless provides a persuasive explanation of why abortion may be easier to justify when the pregnancy is a result of rape.

8.2. *Are Infants "Replaceable?"*

I will examine the Thomson argument in the next section. For the moment, let us consider what can be said about the morality of infanticide on the assumption that my earlier claims about the nature and status of fetuses and newborn infants are true. The cases in which infanticide is most likely to be justifiable are those in which an infant's anticipated future life can reasonably be expected not to be worth living—or, more precisely, those in which an infant's life can be expected, on balance, to be *worse* than merely neutral in value, or worse than no life at all. This might be true, for example, if the bad aspects of the life could be expected clearly to outweigh the good. In these circumstances, the case in favor of infanticide would be a case for nonvoluntary euthanasia. I will consider this issue in section 2.4 of chapter 5. In this section, I will confine the discussion to cases in which an infant's future life could reasonably be expected to be worth living. Can it ever be morally justifiable to kill a newborn human infant whose future life promises to be worth living?

I have suggested three reasons why infanticide is, in general, more difficult to justify than abortion: the infant normally has a stronger time-relative interest in continuing to live than a fetus can have, the infant is normally a participant in special relations that are not possible for a fetus, and the positive reasons favoring infanticide could seldom if ever be as potent as those that may favor abortion. In spite of this, the considerations that I have claimed make abortion fundamentally different from the killing of an older child or adult, must make infanticide fundamentally different, as well. For if developed fetuses fall below the threshold of respect, so must newborn infants. Whether a being is worthy of respect is a matter of its intrinsic properties; and by any measure a premature infant is less developed in its intrinsic nature than a chronologically older and biologically more mature fetus. Indeed, assuming that the basis of respect is ultimately some psychological capacity or complex of such capacities, we cannot accept that newborn infants are above the threshold without also accepting that a great many animals are as well, for there are numerous types of adult animal whose present psychological capacities are in every respect more advanced than those of a newborn human infant.

But if a newborn infant is below the threshold of respect, that means that, apart from considerations of effects on others, such as the parents, the strength of our reason not to kill it is determined by the strength of its own time-relative interest in continuing to live. And this, I have claimed, is weak, at least in comparison with the time-relative interest that an adult typically has in continuing to live. The infant's time-relative interest is weak, despite the magnitude of the good that lies in prospect for it, because it would be only weakly psychologically related to itself in the future. Moreover, because newborn infants fall outside the scope of the morality of respect, the various constraints that drastically limit the permissibility of sacrificing some persons for the sake of others do not appear to apply to our treatment of infants. Their time-relative interests, including their time-relative interest in continuing to live, can appropriately be weighed against, and therefore be outweighed by, the competing interests of others. The central question, then, is whether the interests of others that might favor the killing of an infant whose life would be worth living are ever sufficiently strong to outweigh the infant's own time-relative interest in continuing to live.

This is a question that, in a great many cases, it may be difficult to answer with confidence. It is, of course, more likely that infanticide could be justified in this way when an infant's time-relative interest in continuing to live is more than usually weak—for example, because the infant's prospects in life are exceptionally poor as a result of severe congenital defects, particularly cognitive defects. In such cases, the weighing up of competing time-relative interests must be a matter of judgment; there are no agreed methods of quantifying the strengths of the different time-relative interests that are at stake. It would, however, be unwarranted to assume that an infant's time-relative interest in continuing to live (together with any other interests that might coincide with it) could never be outweighed by the conflicting interests of others. It must therefore be conceded that the reasons I have given for thinking that abortion may often be permissible also imply that infanticide can in principle be justified. Given that our intuitions about the moral status of infants are mixed in the ways I indicated earlier, and given that the belief that infanticide is seriously wrong is far from universal, it should not be surprising if careful reflection on the issue of infanticide forces us to modify our previous beliefs.

Reconsideration of the morality of infanticide in recent years has generated considerable controversy, culminating in a storm of vigorous public opposition to the appointment of Peter Singer, a philosopher who has argued for the permissibility of infanticide, to an endowed chair in bioethics at Princeton.[46] Singer's views on infanticide have exposed him to an extraordinary amount of public vilification, often based on a deliberate misrepresentation of his position.[47] I will consider his arguments in some detail. In addition to clarifying both the nature of his own position and the differences between his views and mine, an examination of his arguments should serve to illuminate some of the deeper issues in the public debate about infanticide.

Perhaps the most notorious feature of Singer's view is that he explicitly claims that newborn human infants are *replaceable*—by which he means that it can be permissible to kill an existing infant if that is necessary in order to bring a different infant, whose prospects would be better, into existence. The killing of the existing infant might be necessary in order to make the "replacement" child possible if, for example, the existing infant were so badly handicapped that no one would adopt it and caring for it would consume too much of the parents' time and resources to allow for the possibility of raising another. In support of the claim that infants are replaceable, Singer advances a general argument that appeals to considerations of consistency.[48] Certainly, he notes, we regard possible people as replaceable—or, more accurately, "intersubstitutable." If, for example, a woman who intends to have a child has a choice between conceiving a child whose life would predictably be well worth living and conceiving a child who would be less well off, it seems clearly preferable, if other things are equal, for her to decide in favor of the better-off child. Many people accept a parallel view about fetuses. It is quite common, Singer observes, to screen fetuses for certain abnormalities in order to enable women who are pregnant with a defective fetus to have an abortion and then try again to conceive a normal, healthy child. This is commonly done even in the case of abnormalities that almost always allow for a life that is worth living. But if fetuses are replaceable in this way and there are no deep intrinsic differences between a fetus and a newborn infant, it seems that newborn infants must be replaceable in the same way.

This is a powerful challenge. Anyone who accepts the legitimacy of late-term prenatal screening with an option of abortion in the event that an abnormality is detected will find it extremely difficult to reject the legitimacy of early infanticide when significant abnormalities are discovered only at birth. But Singer's argument cannot end here. For he concedes that older children and adults are not similarly replaceable; therefore he has to explain why fetuses and infants are replaceable when older human beings are not. In order to understand his explanation of why fetuses and infants are replaceable, we have to examine his general account of the morality of killing.

Singer's account, like the account I have defended, is two-tiered. It has one account of the morality of killing persons, or self-conscious beings, and a different account of the morality of killing beings who are conscious but not self-conscious. The fundamental objection to killing persons is that it typically violates or dooms to frustration virtually every preference the victim has—not only his countless preferences for specific future states of affairs but also, and more importantly, his preference for continued life itself. In developing this view, Singer presents and endorses Michael Tooley's argument for the claim that only self-conscious beings can have the right to life.[49] According to Tooley, one can have a right to something only if the violation of that right would frustrate some corresponding desire. So, as Singer puts it, paraphrasing Tooley, "if the right to life is the right to continue existing as a distinct entity, then the desire relevant to possessing a right to life is the desire to continue existing as a distinct entity. But only a being who is capable of conceiving herself as a distinct entity existing over time—that is, only a person—could have this desire. Therefore only a person could have the right to life."[50] In short, Singer contends that,

because only persons are capable of desiring to continue to live, they are the only beings who can be seriously harmed or wronged by being killed.

The objection to killing non-self-conscious beings is different. These beings are
incapable of desiring to continue to live. Thus, according to Singer, "these beings are,
in a sense, 'impersonal.' Perhaps, therefore, in killing them, one does them no personal wrong, although one does reduce the quantity of happiness in the universe."[51]
Singer is here assuming that identity alone is not a sufficient basis for having a present interest in one's own future life. He appears to assume that having desires for the
future, or at least the capacity for having such desires, is the basis of egoistic concern
about the future. His point here might be expressed by claiming that, because non-
self-conscious beings cannot desire their own continued existence, and cannot even
have desires for states of affairs beyond the immediate future, they are unrelated to
their own futures in the way that provides the basis for concern about their future for
their own sake now. Thus their future cannot matter for their sake now. (This is the
view, which I called the Capacity Condition, that I criticized in section 2 of this chapter.) But if their future lives would be good (for example, if they would be on balance
pleasurable), it seems that something valuable is lost when they die—namely, good
experiences. Singer concludes that the death of a non-self-conscious being can be
bad *impersonally,* if it prevents the occurrence of good experiences. The loss of these
experiences is bad, in that the state of the world is worse without them, but it cannot
be bad for the non-self-conscious being itself.

Singer initially advances these claims with reference to animals that lack self-
consciousness. It is in this context that the notion of replaceability is introduced. Because these animals' possible future experiences matter only impersonally, it does
not matter how they are distributed among different possible animal lives. Thus the
wrong involved in killing non-self-conscious animals, "if it is wrong, can be counterbalanced by bringing into existence similar beings who will lead equally happy
lives."[52] Singer captures the intuitive force of this idea with the following illustration:

> We can presume that if fish become unconscious, then before the loss of conscious-
> ness they would have no expectations or desires for anything that might happen sub-
> sequently, and if they regain consciousness, they have no awareness of having pre-
> viously existed. Therefore if the fish were killed while unconscious and replaced by
> a similar number of other fish who could be created only because the first group of
> fish were killed, there would, from the perspective of fishy awareness, be no differ-
> ence between that and the same fish losing and regaining consciousness.[53]

In the case of fish, this idea has genuine intuitive plausibility. But the argument can
be readily extended to encompass infants as well, and most people's intuitions will
not happily follow the argument through that extended application. Before I examine
the plausibility of the extended replaceability argument, there are two possible
sources of confusion that I should clarify. One concerns a couple of assertions that
Singer makes that are inconsistent with his general position and that provoke unnecessary opposition to his position by exaggerating its implications. Thus he claims at
one point that we should "accord the life of a fetus no greater value than the life of a
nonhuman animal at a similar level of rationality, self-consciousness, awareness, capacity to feel, etc."[54] And later he makes a parallel claim about infants: "the life of a

newborn baby is of less value to it than the life of a pig, a dog, or a chimpanzee is to the nonhuman animal."[55] (This second claim may trade on an ambiguity in the phrase "value to," which can mean either "valued by" or "valuable or good *for*." What is critically relevant to the morality of killing, it seems to me, is the second of these two senses.) These claims suggest that, apart from considerations of side effects, the killing of a fetus or infant can be no more morally objectionable than the killing of a comparably endowed animal. But according to Singer, the central objection to the killing of non-self-conscious beings is that the consequent loss of good future life is impersonally bad. And if this is so, the killing of a human fetus or infant should be very significantly worse in impersonal terms than the killing of an animal, since the quality and quantity of good life that is thereby lost is substantially greater. (For this reason, a newborn human infant could not, on Singer's view, be adequately "replaced" by causing an animal to exist in its stead. As we will see, the positive justification that Singer gives for replacing an infant appeals to the *greater* impersonal value that a different, better-off individual's life would have.)

The second point of clarification concerns the reason Singer gives for thinking that an infant cannot have an interest in its own future life. Usually the reason he gives is simply that it cannot have preferences about its future life. But on occasion he suggests a different reason. He sometimes suggests that an infant cannot have an interest in the life of the person it would become because the infant is literally *not the same individual* as the later person. If that is true, the life that is lost when an infant is killed would not have been that infant's life at all, but someone else's. In the relevant passages, Singer appears to presuppose that we are essentially persons. If we are essentially persons and infants are not persons, then infants are merely the vehicles through which we come into existence. To replace one infant with another is literally to substitute one possible person for another, just as in a preconception choice among possible people.

This view is strongly suggested when Singer asserts that "to kill a new-born infant is no more—and no less—the prevention of the existence of an additional person than is a decision not to produce [a child]."[56] "Admittedly," he concedes,

> when we refrain from reproducing, there is no being whose life has already begun. Intuitively, this makes a difference. We must recall, however, that when we kill a new-born infant there is no *person* whose life has begun. When I think of myself as the person I now am, I realize that I did not come into existence until some time after my birth. At birth I had no sense of the future, and no experiences which I can now remember as "mine." It is the beginning of the life of the person, rather than of the physical organism, that is crucial so far as the right to life is concerned.[57]

Singer is aware that the idea that infants are not identical with the persons they become is different from the idea that self-consciousness is necessary for having an interest in one's future life. For he explicitly attributes the claim about identity—"I am not the infant from whom I developed"[58]—to Michael Tooley (and in a way that suggests agreement), noting that it constitutes a departure from the argument he has already endorsed from Tooley's earlier work.

The idea that we begin to exist with the onset of self-consciousness is plainly counterintuitive—so much so that it is difficult even to articulate without incoherence (of the sort, for example, that appears in the claim that "I did not come into existence until some time after my birth"). It may even be incoherent in itself. For the onset of self-consciousness is marked by the appearance of a second-order awareness of an ongoing stream of consciousness. But the preexisting consciousness of which there begins to be a higher-order awareness cannot, at least in the first instance, be the consciousness of the person who begins to exist when he becomes aware of it. For it must have been going on before he became aware of it. Therefore what seems to be the onset of self-consciousness cannot, on the view that the onset of self-consciousness marks the beginning of our existence, literally be *self*-consciousness. It must be instead be the beginning of a higher-order awareness of the consciousness of a different, non-self-conscious being. But presumably the higher-order awareness then appropriates the preexisting stream of consciousness as its own, so that self-consciousness soon involves the self's awareness of its own consciousness. This entire description, however, is barely intelligible and, even if intelligible, is certainly implausible. Self-consciousness arises when a conscious entity develops a higher-order, reflexive awareness of its own experiences. The onset of self-consciousness in the world as we know it presupposes the prior existence of the conscious subject.

I do not think that Singer needs to worry about this. For it becomes clear in his subsequent writing on the notion of brain death that he does not accept that we are essentially persons.[59] He assumes, instead, the common view that we are organisms and goes on to conclude that we can continue to exist and to be alive not only after we have ceased to be persons, and not only after we have lost the capacity for consciousness, but even after we have undergone brain death. We can therefore read the claim that the life of a person begins only with the advent of self-consciousness as a hyperbolic expression of the idea that we do not become persons and therefore do not acquire an interest in our own future life until we develop the capacity for self-consciousness.

Having now clarified the two possible sources of confusion about Singer's position, I will return to the examination of the replaceability argument as it applies to human infants. In human development, the threshold that separates those who are in principle replaceable from those who are not is the onset of self-consciousness. Thus Singer writes that "perhaps the capacity to see oneself as existing over time, and thus to aspire to longer life (as well as to have other non-momentary, future-directed interests) is the characteristic that marks out those beings who cannot be considered replaceable."[60] Exactly when this capacity arises may affect the intuitive plausibility of Singer's view. At one point he suggests that it probably arises within the first year of life; but elsewhere he speculates (mainly in order to illustrate the difficulty of establishing when it does arise) that it may not develop until the third or fourth year of life.[61] Certainly the idea that a three-year-old child is in principle replaceable will be deeply repugnant to almost everyone. But I will not pursue this possible line of objection.

Instead, let me draw attention to the fact that there are two basic components to Singer's replaceability argument: the *negative case* and the *positive case*. The negative case states the reason why infanticide is less seriously objectionable than the killing of persons and thus may be more easily justified. The positive case states the considerations that may favor infanticide and thus weigh against the considerations that oppose it.

It is crucial to understand that the essence of the negative case is that the central moral objection to killing non-self-conscious beings is substantially weaker than the corresponding objection to killing persons. Singer is explicit about this, as he must be.[62] For it is only if the objection to killing non-self-conscious beings is weaker that it can be outweighed by the considerations cited in the positive case, thereby making these beings replaceable. Persons are not replaceable because, even though the same considerations that sometimes favor replacing a non-self-conscious being may also, on occasion, favor replacing a person, they are insufficient to outweigh the much stronger moral objection to killing persons. This much stronger objection is that killing a person affects the person for the worse, by frustrating his preferences. The assumption here seems to be that this *kind* of objection—the kind that focuses on the effect of an act on the victim—is in general stronger than an objection that is merely impersonal. In short, killing persons is more seriously objectionable than killing non-self-conscious beings because the effect of killing a person is *worse for the victim,* whereas the effect of killing a non-self-conscious being is not *worse for* anyone, but is worse only impersonally. (It is perhaps worth noting, in order to avoid misunderstanding, that the assumption that effects on individuals for better or worse are uniformly more important than impersonal considerations is not one that I would accept. I believe that, in some instances, an effect is worse when it is worse for someone than it would be if it were bad only impersonally. Yet there are other instances in which there is just as strong a reason to prevent an effect that is bad only impersonally as there is to prevent a corresponding effect that would be bad for someone.)

So the core of Singer's negative case is that, because infants are non-self-conscious beings, the central objection to killing them—namely, that doing so reduces the amount of good there would otherwise be—is comparatively weak. The essence of his positive case for the replaceability of infants is that the value of creating what he sometimes call "the next child"—that is, the child who will exist if and only if the existing infant is killed—more than makes up for the loss involved in killing the existing infant. (That this is the crucial element of the positive justification is implied by the notion of *replacement.*) Thus he notes that, "when the death of a disabled infant will lead to the birth of another infant with better prospects of a happy life, the total amount of happiness will be greater if the disabled infant is killed. The loss of happy life for the first infant is outweighed by the gain of a happier life for the second."[63] The reason one has for creating a better-off child may, of course, be impersonal in character. For at the time one acts to cause the child to exist, there is as yet no child for whose sake one could be acting. (However, some people—though not many—believe that to be caused to exist can be *good for* the one who comes into existence; and if that is so, one might have a reason to cause a child to exist for its own sake—that is, a reason that is not impersonal. But I will not pursue this here. I will assume that the reason Singer recognizes to cause the better-off "replacement" child to exist is impersonal in character.) But notice that, even if the reason to cause the better-off child to exist is impersonal, it is perfectly suited to outweighing the reason not to kill the existing infant—for that reason, according to Singer, is impersonal as well. The impersonal badness of the loss of the good life that the one infant would have had is more than made up for by the greater impersonal value of the better life that the replacement child will have.

I believe that both components of Singer's replaceability argument—both the negative case and the positive case—are highly problematic. It will be obvious that I reject the negative case. I believe it is a mistake to suppose that the only reason one has not to kill an infant, apart from reasons connected with possible effects on others, is impersonal. The infant itself has a stake, a time-relative interest, in its own future life. I have conceded—or, rather, contended—that an infant's time-relative interest in continuing to live is comparatively weak. But if I am right that it has such a time-relative interest, killing it must be worse for it. Recall, moreover, that it seems to be a presupposition of Singer's argument that killing is more seriously objectionable when it is worse for the victim than when it is bad only impersonally. But if this is right and if killing an infant is bad for it and not just bad impersonally, the central moral objection to infanticide is stronger than Singer acknowledges.

I do not think that Singer's view of the wrongness of killing an infant can be sustained, for the reasons I gave earlier in section 2. The main reason is this. Singer accepts that the infant and the person into whom it might develop would be one and the same individual. The life that will be lost if it is killed would have been *its* life. Assuming that the life it might have would be worth living, it follows that its life as a whole will be better if it is not killed than if it is killed; therefore, to kill it would be worse for it; therefore, it has an interest in not being killed, or in continuing to live.

In places, Singer seems to acknowledge this. He concedes, for example, that "as long as sentient beings are conscious, they have an interest in experiencing as much pleasure and as little pain as possible."[64] It seems to follow from this that a sentient being, such as an infant, has an interest in continuing to live in order to have as much pleasure as possible—or, in other words, that death would be against its interests because it would limit the amount of pleasure it can experience. But he immediately goes on to assert that the fact that it has these interests "does not mean that the being has a personal interest in continuing to live."[65] The only way to make sense of this is to interpret the earlier claim to mean only that a non-self-conscious being can have an interest at time t in having as much pleasure as possible at t, though it cannot have an interest at t in having pleasure at any time subsequent to t. But, again, that final clause seems to be refuted by the fact that the being's life would be better if it were to contain more pleasure; hence, if other things are equal, it must be worse for that being, or against its interests, not to experience that pleasure.

One can make sense of Singer's view if one assumes that identity is not the basis of egoistic concern about the future. His argument could then be reconstructed as follows. Identity is a necessary but not a sufficient condition of rational egoistic concern about the future. In addition to having a future that would be its own, a being must have desires for that future, or at least the capacity for having such desires, in order to have a time-relative interest in continuing to live. The central objection to killing persons is that it frustrates their time-relative interest in continuing to live, which is grounded in their future-directed desires. But because non-self-conscious beings, including newborn infants, are incapable of having desires about their own future lives, they can have no time-relative interest in continuing to live. Hence the objection to killing them must be impersonal and therefore considerably weaker.

Given this reconstruction of Singer's position, the dispute between us concerns the basis of rational egoistic concern about the future, or the basis for having time-relative interests in one's future life. According to the view I am attributing to Singer, it is necessary for a being to have the capacity to have desires about its own future in order for it to be reasonable for anyone to care, for the being's own sake now, whether it continues to exist. According to the view that I hold, it is reasonable to care, for a being's own sake now, whether it continues to live if there would be continuity of mind between itself now and itself in the future (which there will be necessarily, according to the account of personal identity I accept). Moreover, the strength of the being's time-relative interest in continuing to live will vary, other things being equal, depending on the extent to which the prudential unity relations would hold between itself now and itself in the future. And these relations *would* hold, if only weakly, between an infant and the person it might become, despite its present inability to conceive of itself in the future. According to my view, therefore, an infant has a time-relative interest in continuing to live, although it is comparatively weak.

As I noted earlier in section 2, the account I have given of the prudential unity relations is more consistent with the gradual nature of human development than the account that seems implicit in Singer's argument. Singer and I agree (on this reading of his view) that a being's time-relative interest in continuing to live depends on the psychological relations between itself now and itself in the future. But he focuses on one feature of psychological life—future-directed desire—and claims that it cannot be present before the onset of self-consciousness. He must therefore conclude that when a human being achieves self-consciousness, it goes from having *no* present stake in its own future to having a time-relative interest in continuing to live that is presumably commensurate in strength with the magnitude of the expected good in its future. It is implausible to suppose that so momentous a change occurs just with the onset of self-consciousness. For even if self-consciousness is a matter of degree, the transition from being non-self-conscious to having sufficient self-consciousness to have future-directed desires occurs over quite a short period. It is more reasonable to see the human being's present stake in its own future as increasing gradually over a substantial period of time along with the strength of the psychological connections between itself now and itself later in the future.

Let us turn now from Singer's negative case for the replaceability of infants to the positive case. The positive case appeals to the importance of causing a better-off child to exist. Most people, on considering the positive case, would reject it out of hand. The commonsense view is that the expectation that a child would have a life that would be well worth living provides no moral reason at all to cause it to exist. If this is correct, the prospect of being able to bring a better-off child into existence will contribute nothing to the case for infanticide.

The commonsense view is, however, deeply problematic. First, as I noted in section 5 of this chapter, it is difficult to reconcile this view with the equally commonsensical belief that the expectation that a child's life would be *bad*, or worse than no life at all, provides a strong reason not to cause it to exist, or even to prevent it from existing. The imperative to show that these two beliefs (which together constitute what I have called the Asymmetry) are mutually consistent is one of the major challenges faced by those who wish to defend the central pillars of commonsense morality. I believe that this challenge has not been met, and that there is ample reason to doubt that it can be. I strongly suspect that the need for consistency will force us to accept that the mere fact that a person would have a life worth living constitutes a reason, though not necessarily a decisive or even very strong one, to cause that person to exist.

There is a further tension within commonsense morality that supports Singer's appeal to the value of creating a better-off child. When someone intends to have a child and has a choice between having a well-off child and a less well-off child, we believe that there is reason for the person to choose to have the better-off child. Part of the reason may be that this would be better for those who already exist; but there is another dimension to the reason that is independent of effects on others. The reason is impersonal: it is simply better, even if it is not better *for* anyone, that a better-off child should exist rather than a less well-off child. And this reason is sufficiently strong that we believe that a person should make certain sacrifices, within limits, to ensure the existence of the better-off child. This demonstrates, I think, that impersonal considerations do play a role in commonsense moral thought. We do accept that it is impersonally better for a better-off child to exist than for a less well-off child to exist, and we accept that this consideration is sufficiently important to require existing people to accept certain sacrifices of their own well-being.

Singer appeals to these intuitions about the importance of impersonal considerations in preconception choices among possible lives. He rightly perceives that they provide support for the claim that there is reason to cause the better-off child to exist. He concedes that, if we recognize the value of causing the better-off child to exist, this will commit us to accepting that there is a moral reason to cause new people to exist if their lives would be worth living. But he believes that this reason can usually be outweighed by the various considerations that motivate people not to have children (or additional children). He writes:

> unless we are prepared to hold that people ought to reproduce whenever possible, we cannot give *overriding* value to the creation of additional life; but we can give *some* value to it, so that it counts as an important factor in decisions about killing new-born infants. The value of creating additional life would then still be a factor in decisions about reproducing, but it would be much less significant, because it would often be outweighed by reasons which point in the opposite direction.[66]

It is, of course, awkward to have to embrace the view that there is a moral reason to cause new people to exist just because their lives would be worth living. Singer's position would be more appealing if we could accept that there is a moral reason to have a better-off child *rather than* a less-well-off child and yet deny that there is a general moral reason to cause new people to exist if their lives would be worth living. But are the two claims consistent? Some have claimed that they are. Jonathan Glover, for example, contends that "a principle that did not tell us to create extra happy people" could nevertheless imply that, "when we are going to add to the population, where the choice arises we must always prefer to add a happier rather than a less happy person. . . . A policy of always choosing the best ones when picking apples does not commit us to picking as many as possible"—or, he might have added, to picking any at all.[67]

While Glover's analogy with picking apples is suggestive, it is also misleading. One's reason for picking the best apples is entirely instrumental in character (as is one's reason for picking apples in the first place). The analogous reason in Singer's replaceability argument—the reason to have a better-off child rather than a less-well-off child—is not like this. If creating new people were like picking apples, there would indeed be a reason, in general, to create a better-off child rather than a less-well-off child if one were going to have a child. That reason would have to do with the desires and interests of the prospective parents. As such, it would obviously not imply the existence of a further reason to create additional happy people when this would *not* be in the interests of potential parents. But the reason cited in Singer's argument is different: it is *impersonal,* not instrumental. This impersonal reason to have a better-off child rather than a less-well-off child would apply even if, for some reason, the interests of existing people favored the creation of a less-well-off child instead. Because of this difference in the nature of the reasons, the analogy with picking apples fails. One can accept that the instrumental reason to have a better-off child rather than a less-well-off child does not imply a reason to have a well-off child rather than no child at all—just as the reason to pick the best apples does not imply that there must be a reason to pick apples in the first place. But one cannot infer from this that the *impersonal* reason to have a better-off child rather than a less-well-off child does not entail an impersonal reason to cause people to exist if their lives would be worth living.

We are considering whether it is coherent to suppose that the impersonal reason to have a better-off child rather than a less-well-off child could be conditional on a prior determination to have a child. That is, we are asking whether there might be an impersonal reason to have a better-off child *rather than* a less-well-off child even if there is *no* impersonal reason to have a well-off child rather than no child at all. For, if there could be, Singer could claim that the prospect of being able to create a better-off child could count in favor of infanticide without committing us to the counterintuitive view that there is a general moral reason to cause new people to exist if their lives would be worth living. There is another analogy, suggested by Derek Parfit, that might be thought to show that the reason to have a better-off child does not entail a general reason to cause new people to exist.[68] Parfit supposes that I have three alternatives:

A. At some great cost to myself, saving a stranger's right arm.
B. Doing nothing.
C. At the same cost to myself, saving both the arms of this stranger.[69]

Most of us believe that, if these are the alternatives, it is permissible to do B—that is, to save neither arm. But if one has decided to help the stranger, it would be wrong to do A—that is, to save one arm rather than two. If one has decided to accept a certain cost to help the stranger, and the cost will be the same whether one saves one arm or both, it would be perverse not to do what would achieve the greater good. In short, while there is no duty to do C rather than B, there *is* a duty to do C rather than A.

Now alter the values of the variables so that one's alternatives are:

A. Having a less-well-off child.
B. Having no child.
C. Having a well-off child.

Again, the common view is that, if these are the alternatives, it is permissible to do B—that is, it is permissible not to have a child. But if one has decided to have a child, it would be wrong to do A—that is, to have a less-well-off child rather than a well-off child. As in the first set of alternatives, there is no duty to do C rather than B, though there is a duty to do C rather than A. This is the commonsense conception of the morality of procreation. The parallel with the first set of alternatives suggests that this conception is defensible. It suggests that, even if there is a reason to have a well-off child rather than a less-well-off child, this does not imply that there is also a reason to have a well-off child rather than no child.

The analogy does not *show* this, however. The reason why there is no duty in the first set of alternatives to do C rather than B is that the great cost to the agent of doing C makes it permissible not to do it. If there were no cost to the agent involved in any of the alternatives in the first set (or, alternatively, if the cost to the agent of each alternative, *including B,* were the same), there would be a decisive reason to do C rather than B. If, therefore, we assume that the second set of alternatives is relevantly parallel to the first, so that A and C, but not B, involve great costs to the agent, the same considerations would explain why it is permissible to do B rather than C. In other words, if we tighten the analogy between the two sets of alternatives, we find that it does not show that, in the second set of alternatives, there is no reason to do C (have a well-off child) rather than B (have no child). It shows only what is already obvious: that the great cost of having a child can make it permissible not to have a child. But what needs to be shown is that there is no impersonal reason to have a child just because its life would be worth living, not that such a reason could be outweighed by considerations of cost.

Let us try one more tactic. It might be argued that the reason to cause a better-off child to exist rather than a less-well-off child is essentially *comparative.* If one causes the less-well-off child to exist, he will be *worse off* than the better-off child would have been. If, however, one simply fails to cause a well-off child to exist, no such comparison is possible. There is no one who is worse off than a different person might have been. The problem with this response, however, is that it is irrelevant from the *impersonal* point of view. The claim, "The less-well-off child is worse off than the better-off child would have been," is, in impersonal terms, reducible to, "The outcome in which the less-well-off child exists contains a lesser amount of good than that in which the better-off child exists." From the impersonal point of view, the references to individuals are eliminable without loss. If the outcome in which no child exists contains less good than the outcome in which a well-off child exists, then having no child is worse than having a well-off child for the same reason that having a less-well-off child is worse than having a well-off child.

It seems likely that, if there is an impersonal moral reason to have a better-off child *rather than* a less-well-off child, the principle that is the source of that reason will also imply that there is in general an impersonal reason to cause people to exist if their lives would be worth living. Singer's positive case for the replaceability of newborn infants therefore seems to commit him to the view that there is always a moral reason to cause a new person to exist if that person's life would be worth living. Singer in fact accepts this, but claims, as we have seen, that this reason is usually outweighed by the considerations that motivate people not to have children (for example, considerations of personal cost). Hence he believes that he need not accept that there is a general obligation to have children, or additional children. How can he be confident that the reason to cause well-off people to exist can be generally outweighed by the preferences of existing people? The answer, it seems, lies in the assumption I identified earlier: that effects on people for better or worse are, in general, more significant morally than impersonal considerations. (This, it will be recalled, appears to be the basis of Singer's view that the killing of persons is more seriously objectionable than the killing of non-self-conscious beings.) Since the reason to cause people to exist with lives worth living is impersonal, while the reasons people typically have for wanting to avoid having children appeal to those people's own preferences and interests, it is not surprising that Singer believes that the latter will generally outweigh the former.

The appeal to this assumption—that effects on people for better or worse matter more than impersonal considerations—imperils the replaceability argument. The argument may seem secure as long as the negative case is sound—that is, if it is true that the central objection to infanticide is impersonal in character. For if that is true, this impersonal objection to killing the existing infant can be outweighed by the impersonal reason to cause a better-off child to exist (for the impersonal loss involved in killing the infant can be more than made up for by the impersonal value of the better-off child). And this will be compatible with the absence of a general obligation to reproduce. But if I am right that infanticide is objectionable because of the effect on the infant itself—because it is *bad for* the infant to be killed, bad because it frustrates the infant's time-relative interest in continuing to live—then the replaceability argument seems to fail. For if the impersonal reason to cause a well-off child to exist can generally be outweighed by the effects for the worse on existing people—as it must be if people are in general not obliged to have children—then it seems that this reason should also be outweighed by the effect for the worse on an infant of killing it.

Even if Singer's negative case were sound, the argument would prove too much—that is, it would have implications that are impossible to accept. The negative case is that the fundamental objection to killing an infant must be impersonal in character. According to Singer, however, impersonal considerations are generally weaker than, and therefore readily outweighed by, the effects on actual individuals for better or worse. This claim about the comparative strengths of impersonal considerations and considerations concerning effect on individuals seems necessary in order for Singer to claim that the impersonal reason to cause happy people to exist is often outweighed by the conflicting interests and preferences of existing people (for example, by the interest a potential parent might have in avoiding the burden of caring for an unwanted child). But, if the reason not to kill an infant is impersonal, and if impersonal considerations are generally outweighed by conflicting considerations of effects on existing people, it may seem that infanticide could be justified, other things being equal, whenever it would be favored by an interest or preference of an existing person that would be at least as weighty as those capable of justifying a decision not to have a child. In short, Singer's argument seems to imply that the kinds of consideration that can justify a decision not to have a child would also be sufficient, other things being equal, to justify infanticide. And that is impossible to believe.

Let me briefly recapitulate and summarize my critique of the replaceability argument. First, Singer may overstate the positive case. The impersonal reason to create the better-off child may be weaker than he supposes. (Many people will be tempted to deny that there is any such reason at all—though it will be difficult for them to reconcile this view both with the view that there is a reason not to cause a person to exist if his life would be bad and with the view that there is a reason, in preconception cases, to have a better-off child instead of a less-well-off child.) But even if Singer does not overstate the positive case, his negative case seems mistaken. Provided that its life would be worth living, an infant does have a time-relative interest in continuing to live. Killing it would therefore be worse not only for its life as a whole but also for it as it is now—that is, for its present sake. If effects on individuals for better or worse are generally more important morally than impersonal considerations, it seems that the reason not to affect an infant for the worse by killing it must outweigh the impersonal reason to cause a better-off child to exist. In short, the impersonal value of creating a better-off child cannot justify the killing of an existing infant. Finally, even if the negative case were persuasive, the argument as a whole would have implications that are plainly unacceptable.

Suppose one were to believe that the impersonal reason to have a better-off child could be strong enough to outweigh the bad effect on the infant of killing it. If the impersonal reason were that strong, it seems that it would also be sufficiently strong, at least in many cases, to outweigh the considerations of personal cost that often motivate people not to have children. In that case, we would have to conclude that a great many people do wrong in failing to have children, or in failing to have additional children. The strong impersonal reason to cause people to exist if their lives would be worth living would also weigh heavily against the interests of women burdened with an unwanted pregnancy. It would, in short, weigh heavily against the permissibility of abortion. And these are implications that I think very few people would be willing to accept.

Although I believe that Singer's replaceability argument fails, the view for which I have argued appears to have implications that are similar to, though rather weaker than, those of his argument. Reconsider the common practice of prenatal screening. I believe that the common practice of screening for fetal deformities and aborting defective fetuses—particularly in order to allow people to try again to conceive a healthy child—is defensible. According to the view for which I have argued, the justification is that the interests of the prospective parents in avoiding the burden of caring for an unwell child and in having a normal, healthy child outweigh the fetus's comparatively weak time-relative interest in continuing to live. (I refer to the interests of the parents rather than to their time-relative interests because I assume that the two coincide and are of roughly equivalent strength.) Because the fetus falls below the threshold of respect, the "deontological constraints" that limit what may permissibly be done to persons do not apply to our treatment of it; therefore its weaker time-relative interests may justifiably be sacrificed for the sake of the stronger interests of the potential parents. (There is also, I believe, an impersonal reason to have a better-off rather than a less-well-off child, and this impersonal reason may combine with the reason deriving from the interests of the parents to support infanticide. But the impersonal reason may be comparatively weak; the main focus of the positive case, according to the view I accept, is the interests of the parents.)

Unless there is a significant intrinsic difference between a developed fetus and a newborn infant—and it seems clear that no such difference exists—it seems that the same form of reasoning can be deployed to justify infanticide in certain cases. Suppose, for example, that an infant is discovered to have a defect that could not have been detected prenatally, and suppose further that the defect is sufficiently serious that it is unlikely that anyone can be found who would be willing to adopt the infant. If the interests of the parents that favor infanticide are strong—for example, if the burden of caring for the defective child would be so great as to preclude the possibility of their having a further, healthy child—it is not unreasonable to believe that they could outweigh the infant's time-relative interest in continuing to live.

Whereas Singer's replaceability argument focuses primarily on impersonal considerations—both in the negative case and the positive case—the argument I have stated focuses primarily on the effects that the different options would have on the interests or, where there is a divergence, on the time-relative interests of those concerned. But there is an important point of similarity between Singer's argument and mine. Singer treats the choice between the existing infant and the hypothetical better-off child as morally exactly like a preconception choice between possible people. On his view, the infant has *no* present stake in its own future life as a person. Morally and prudentially, its relation to its own future is no different from its relation to anyone else's future. According to my view, a similar though not so categorical claim holds. An infant is a barely constituted self whose psychological relations to itself in the future are extremely tenuous. Its relation to its own future is therefore *relevantly like* its relation to someone else's future. Thus, while the choice between allowing a defective infant to live and killing it in order to conceive a different, healthy child is not exactly like a preconception choice between two possible people, it is *more like* such a choice than people have hitherto supposed.

The justification for infanticide implied by the view I have defended is less decisive than Singer's replaceability argument would be, were it persuasive. According to Singer's argument, if the amount of good that a replacement child's life would contain exceeds that which an existing infant's life would contain, impersonal considerations favor infanticide. According to the argument implied by my view, it is much more a matter of judgment whether the interests of the parents and others outweigh the existing infant's time-relative interest in continuing to live.

Given the furor that has erupted over Singer's defense of infanticide, I expect that many readers will regard the fact that my position supports the permissibility of infanticide in certain conditions as a reductio ad absurdum of the position itself. But the implications of the view are in fact even more shocking to common sense than I have so far acknowledged. Let me cite the worst-case example. Suppose that a woman who wants to be a single parent becomes impregnated via artificial insemination, but dies during childbirth. She has no close friends and no family—no one to claim the child. The newborn infant is healthy and so is an ideal candidate for adoption. But suppose that, in the same hospital in which the infant is born, there are three other children, all five years old, who will soon die if they do not receive organ transplants. The newly orphaned infant turns out to have exactly the right tissue type: if it were killed, its organs could be used to save the three ailing children. According to the view I have developed, it ought to be permissible, if other things are equal, to sacrifice the newborn orphaned infant in order to save the other three children. For if the infant is below the threshold of respect, its time-relative interests can legitimately be weighed and traded off against the interests of others. And its time-relative interest in continuing to live is much weaker than that of each of the three older children; it is only one individual, whereas they are three; and it has no parents or relatives, while each of them, we may suppose, is cherished by its parents and others. It might, of course, be argued that the interests of the potential adoptive parents must be weighed and counted along with the infant's own time-relative interest in continuing to live; but, even in combination, these interests are clearly outweighed by those of the other three children and their parents. And for potential adoptive parents there are usually other options. (It might be suggested that the ideal solution to the problem would be to wait for one of the three ailing children to die so that its organs could be used to save the other two. But it seems that this would be a worse outcome: for the ailing five-year-old has a stronger time-relative interest in continuing to live than the infant, and the interests of its parents are also engaged on its behalf.) It therefore seems difficult, within the framework I have sketched, to avoid the conclusion that it would be permissible (and perhaps even morally required, if other things are equal) to kill the healthy, orphaned newborn in order to use its organs to save the three other children. (It should, of course, be obvious that Singer's understanding of the morality of killing has the same implication.)

Most people will find this implication intolerable, and I confess that I cannot embrace it without significant misgivings and considerable unease.[70] It is interesting and perhaps revealing that we are similarly reluctant to accept that abortion could be permissible for the purpose of using the aborted fetus's tissues or organs for transplantation. Most people accept that it can be permissible to kill a perfectly healthy fetus in order to spare the pregnant woman the inconvenience of carrying it to term; but most of these same people would be scandalized by the thought that a pregnant woman might wish to abort and kill her fetus in order for its tissues or organs to be used to benefit, or even to save the life of, some existing person (her own older child, for example). Of course, we often object to *using* people for very important purposes even when we would think it justifiable to do the very same thing to them for a much less important reason, provided that we are not using them as a means to an end. For example, commonsense morality accepts that one may allow a stranger to die if it would cost one, say, a thousand dollars to save him; but it forbids one to allow that same person to die *in order that* his organs may be available for transplantation. Doubtless it is this sort of intuition, carried over into the context of abortion, that disposes us to reject the use of abortion as a means of procuring tissues or organs for transplantation. Yet, if I am right, this intuition is appropriate only within the morality of respect. Most people would accept, for example, that it would be permissible to kill a healthy baboon if its organs could be used to save the life of a human child. Most, of course, would accept this because their views are implicitly speciesist; but the claim that it would be permissible to sacrifice the baboon need not be speciesist. It could instead rest on the fact that the child's time-relative interest in continuing to live is considerably stronger than the baboon's, together with the claim that the baboon's psychological capacities place it below the threshold of respect. But if a baboon is below the threshold of respect, and thus outside the scope of deontological constraints, and if whether a being is above or below the threshold depends on its intrinsic properties, it is difficult to see how a human fetus could be above it. And, as I have already noted, if a fetus is below the threshold, it is difficult to see how a newborn infant could be above it.

I doubt, therefore, that it is defensible to believe that it could be permissible to kill a baboon to use its organs to save a human child, but impermissible in principle to kill a human fetus—or a newborn infant—for the same reason. Of course, the value of the life that would be lost if a human fetus or infant were killed is typically much greater than the value of a baboon's life; and the side effects of killing a fetus or infant would also be worse. For these reasons, the killing of a baboon might be justified in a much wider range of circumstances than the killing of a fetus or infant. But these differences are differences of degree rather than kind.

This is not just a problem for my view. It is a problem that anyone must face. Suppose one believes that it would be permissible to kill a baboon in order to use its organs to save the life of a human child. If one believes this, one believes that baboons are below the threshold of respect: deontological constraints do not apply to our treatment of them. I have argued, however, that if baboons are below the threshold, human fetuses must be, as well. For whether a being is above or below the threshold is determined by its intrinsic properties. But the only conceivably relevant differences of this sort between a baboon and a fetus are species membership and potential, and I have argued that neither the fetus's membership in the human species nor its potential (and only the developed fetus has a significant form of potential in any case) is a sufficient basis for the worth that demands respect. Therefore fetuses—and, by extension, newborn infants—must in principle be sacrificeable as well. To deny this, one must either reject the permissibility of killing animals such as baboons in order to save the lives of children, or one must show that fetuses and infants are above the threshold even though animals with higher psychological capacities are below it—and, for reasons that I have given earlier, I do not believe that this can be done.

It is worth noting that, although until recently it would have been unthinkable to kill any living human organism in order to use its organs for transplantation, there is now increasing acceptance of the permissibility of killing anencephalic infants for this purpose, provided of course that the parents give their unforced consent. Some people have no doubt worried that such a practice would constitute the first lunge down a very slippery slope. I think perhaps they are right.

I will conclude this section by briefly noting the implications of the foregoing reflections for the morality of killing non-self-conscious animals. The main point is that, just as Singer is mistaken to suppose that the central objection to killing infants is impersonal, so he is mistaken to think that the only objection (other than those that appeal to side effects) to killing non-self-conscious animals is impersonal. It is surprising to note that, according to his view, the objection to killing non-self-conscious animals is vanishingly weak. If the objection is impersonal, there can be no more reason not to kill a non-self-conscious animal than there is reason to cause an animal of the same sort to exist. For one's reason not to kill it is simply not to prevent certain good experiences from occurring, while one's reason to cause such an animal to exist is to cause the same sorts of good experience to occur. But how much reason is there to cause a chicken to exist in order that there might be more good chicken-experiences? Virtually none. Therefore, according to Singer's view, there is virtually no reason not to kill a chicken, provided one thereby causes it no pain.

Assuming that the killing would be painless, the impersonal objection to killing a chicken could be outweighed, it seems, by virtually any interest or preference of a self-conscious being. His view may, therefore, attribute even less moral significance to the painless killing of a chicken than does orthodox opinion about these matters. I believe, by contrast, that the principal objection to killing a non-self-conscious animal is that this would violate its time-relative interest in continuing to live. Because this objection focuses on the effect on the victim, it is a stronger form of objection.

9. ABORTION AS THE DENIAL OF LIFE SUPPORT

9.1. *The Argument*

Let us turn now to the Thomson argument. Because this argument focuses on the nature of the relation between the fetus and the pregnant woman and not on the fetus's metaphysical or moral status, it could, if successful, show that abortion can be permissible even if the argument I have developed is mistaken. It is, moreover, more congruent with commonsense morality because it claims to justify abortion without offering any support for infanticide. But while the Thomson argument may be viewed as an alternative to the argument I have developed, the two are also compatible with one another. As I noted earlier, the Thomson argument might be invoked to show how, even on the view I have defended, infanticide is more difficult to justify than abortion; for what the Thomson argument purports to show is that there is a positive case for abortion—one that does not apply to infanticide—that is remarkably strong.

The thrust of Thomson's argument is that abortion is a permissible refusal by a pregnant woman to allow her body to be requisitioned as an instrument of life support for the fetus. Her central claim is that the fetus does not (at least in many cases) have a moral right to the use of the woman's body; therefore the pregnant woman is not morally required to allow the fetus the continued use of her body. For according to Thomson, "no person is morally required to make large sacrifices to sustain the life of another who has no right to demand them."[71] Thus, in the case of pregnancy, "except in such cases as the unborn person has a right to demand it"—and Thomson leaves open the possibility that there are such cases—"nobody is morally *required* to make large sacrifices, of health, of all other interests and concerns, of all other duties and commitments . . . to keep another person alive."[72] Even if the fetus has the right to life, that in itself "does not guarantee having either a right to be given the use of or a right to be allowed continued use of another person's body—even if one needs it for life itself."[73]

As these remarks indicate, Thomson believes that, if other things are equal, a woman can be morally *required* to carry a fetus to term only if the fetus has a *right* to be carried to term. (There is some ambiguity about this. At one point, she notes that if a woman is pregnant as a result of rape and the fetus needs the use of her body for only an hour in order to survive, "we should not conclude that [it] has a right to do so; we should conclude that she is self-centered, callous, indecent, but not unjust, if she refuses. The complaints are no less grave; they are just different."[74] But if these complaints are insufficient to ground a *requirement* that she allow the fetus the use of her body for an hour, they *are* less grave than the charge that she has violated the fetus's right.) For the most part, however, I will discuss the Thomson argument in a way that avoids questions specifically about rights. There are really two questions that we must answer. First, does a pregnant woman have a special moral reason—one that other people (except perhaps the biological father) do not have—to provide support for the fetus? It may be that the woman has no reason to support the fetus other than the reason that anyone would have to save its life, if that were possible. But, if the woman does have a special reason to support the fetus, then a second question arises: is the special reason decisive in the circumstances? It might not be. The woman could have a reason beyond that which others might have, and yet that reason might be insufficient to ground a requirement to support the fetus. Or the special reason might be decisive: it might require her to support the fetus, even at considerable cost to herself. I believe that the important question is whether she is morally required to support the fetus. Whether it would follow from her being required to support the fetus that it had a right to the use of her body is a question I will leave open.

What I am calling the Thomson argument appeals to an analogy that is now well known. The analogy between the following case and unwanted pregnancy is intended to help us to recognize that a pregnant woman is not morally required to make her body available to the fetus in order to enable it to survive:

> *The Involuntary Benefactor.* A person wakes up to discover that she has been kidnapped in the night and hooked up to an unconscious violinist whose blood must be filtered through her kidneys for a certain period if he is to survive. The director of the hospital concedes that it was wrong of the violinist's admirers to have hooked her up to him without her consent; nevertheless, he observes, "To unplug you would be to kill him," and "A person's right to life outweighs your right to decide what happens in and to your body."[75]

This case is intended to elicit the intuition that, in spite of what the director of the hospital says, the woman is not morally required to allow the violinist to remain hooked up to her, particularly if the cost to her of doing so would be comparable to the burden typically involved in continuing an unwanted pregnancy. Thomson concludes that, if this case is otherwise analogous to an unwanted pregnancy, a pregnant woman is also not morally required to allow the fetus to remain hooked up to her.

One initial question is why the analogy is necessary at all. Why is it not just intuitively obvious in the case of pregnancy itself that the woman is not required to make her body available as a means of life support for the fetus? Possibly Thomson wishes to eliminate or abstract from a feature of pregnancy that may seem important but is in fact morally irrelevant: namely, the naturalness of the fetus's presence in the womb. But whatever Thomson's reason for introducing the analogy, there is an important reason for testing our intuitions by reference to some analogy of this sort. This is that our intuitions about the case of abortion itself are very likely to be affected by the sense, however deeply buried in our minds it may be, that the fetus is different, that its moral status cannot be quite the same as that of a person. If we seek to understand the moral significance of the relation between the pregnant woman and the fetus in a way that is unaffected by our sense that the fetus is different, it may be necessary to probe our intuitions about cases in which the same sort of relation is present but in which the dependent individual is unambiguously a person with the same moral status that you and I have. The case of the Involuntary Benefactor can be regarded as a test for our intuitions of just this sort.

Admittedly, however, if the nature of the relation were the same in the two cases and we were disposed to find the killing of a fetus less serious because of the fetus's uncertain moral status, we ought to find abortion more obviously justifiable than unplugging the violinist in Involuntary Benefactor. But we do not. The explanation of this, I think, is that the analogy between Involuntary Benefactor and a case of unwanted pregnancy is imperfect in several ways. Exploring the various failures of analogy can aid our understanding of the factors that are relevant to determining whether a pregnant woman has a special reason to support the fetus, assuming for the sake of argument (as Thomson does) that the fetus has the same moral status that you and I have.

There is a well-developed literature on the Thomson argument in which at least four seemingly significant failures of analogy have been noted.

1. Whereas the involuntary benefactor is in no way responsible for the fact that she is hooked up to the violinist, a pregnant woman bears some measure of responsibility for the fact that she is connected to the fetus—unless, of course, the pregnancy is a result of rape.
2. Whereas the involuntary benefactor is in no way responsible for the fact that the violinist needs her aid in order to survive, a woman whose pregnancy is the result of her having voluntarily engaged in sexual intercourse does bear some responsibility for the fact that the fetus requires her aid in order to survive.
3. Whereas the involuntary benefactor is not specially related to the violinist in any way, a pregnant woman is the biological parent of the fetus she carries (unless, of course, she is merely the surrogate mother).
4. Whereas the involuntary benefactor would merely be allowing the violinist to die if she were to unhook herself from him, a woman who has an abortion kills the fetus.

Many of Thomson's critics have thought that the first of these four failures of analogy undermines her case for abortion. They have suggested that, when a woman becomes pregnant by voluntarily engaging in sexual intercourse, she thereby gives the fetus a right to the use of her body by tacitly consenting to its being there. I will not pursue this objection. It seems to me manifestly false that a woman consents to support a fetus simply by having sex. Those who do not find this obvious can consult the extensive discussions of the objection in the literature.[76]

9.2. Responsibility for the Fetus's Need for Aid

The second failure of analogy is more significant. In cases in which a pregnancy arises as a result of a woman's voluntary behavior—as a direct result of what she *chose* to do—it may seem that she is to some degree *responsible* for the fetus's dependency on her, or for its need for her aid, and that this fact gives her a special moral reason to provide that aid. This objection to the Thomson argument is generally referred to, in the literature, as the *Responsibility Objection*.[77] Thomson in fact considers this objection, arguing in effect that the extent of the pregnant woman's responsibility may be insufficient to give the fetus a right to the use of her body.[78] Even in most cases of rape, Thomson observes, there are precautions the woman could have taken that would have made the rape less likely (such as staying at home behind locked doors); yet we do not conclude that a woman who is pregnant as a result of rape is even partially responsible for the fetus's dependence upon her support. Surely we should reach a similar conclusion when pregnancy is, for example, the result of contraceptive failure. Nevertheless, Thomson concedes that there may be some cases in which a pregnant woman's responsibility for the fetus's predicament is sufficient to give it a right to the use of her body.

On the general point it seems that Thomson is right: whether a pregnant woman has a special reason to aid the fetus, and if so how strong that reason is, depends on the degree of her responsibility for its need for her aid. But there seems to be a significant difference in a woman's responsibility for a pregnancy that results from rape and her responsibility for a pregnancy that results from contraceptive failure. It is not just that the probability that the woman will become pregnant is much higher when she has sex while using contraception than it is, say, when she goes for a walk; it is also that, in the case of rape, full and undivided responsibility seems to lie with the rapist. He alone is responsible for what he does; thus the fetus's dependency on the woman when pregnancy is the result of rape is attributable entirely to his action and not at all to her not having taken every possible precaution to minimize the probability of being raped. (There are, presumably, cases in which the victim of a rape has deliberately engaged in provocation or incitement; but I will ignore these comparatively rare cases here.)

To say that a woman who becomes pregnant as a result of having voluntarily engaged in sex bears some responsibility for her fetus's need for aid is not to imply that she is blameworthy or even in any way at fault. Compare a case in which, while one is driving a car, the steering column breaks, unavoidably causing the car to collide with another vehicle parked on the side of the road. One is not to blame for what has happened; nor has one done anything wrong or objectionable; but one is nevertheless responsible for the damage to the other vehicle by virtue of having chosen to drive knowing that there is always some minuscule risk that the activity may inadvertently cause harm. One's responsibility is, moreover, sufficient to make one liable to pay compensation to the owner of the damaged vehicle. If indeed a pregnant woman is responsible for her fetus's need for aid, her responsibility will typically be of the same sort: she has done nothing wrong, but is merely a victim of bad luck, in that her innocent activity has had the unlikely effect of making her responsible for someone else's plight.

One response to the Responsibility Objection has been to point out that having caused an innocent person to need aid is not always sufficient to give one a special reason to provide that aid. This can be seen in the following case:[79]

Imperfect Drug. Ten years ago an unconscious cellist was brought to a physician who discovered that he was suffering from a condition that, if untreated, would have been rapidly fatal. The only treatment for this condition was a drug that, although effective, has the side effect of causing the patient ten years later to develop the same kidney ailment that afflicts Thomson's violinist. Knowing that she alone would have the right tissue type for being hooked up to the cellist, the physician administered the drug, thereby saving the cellist's life. As a consequence, the cellist now needs to be hooked up to the physician in order to survive.

In this case it is clear that, although the physician's earlier action is the cause of the cellist's present need for aid, that action does not now give her a special reason to provide that aid. Why not? Harry Silverstein, who originally devised this example, claims that the explanation is that, although the physician is responsible for the fact that the cellist now *exists,* she is not responsible for his need for her aid. For according to Silverstein, in order for the physician to be responsible for the cellist's need for aid, it must have been possible for her to make it the case that the cellist would exist but *not* require her aid.[80]

Silverstein claims that an unwanted pregnancy arising from voluntary sex is relevantly analogous to the Imperfect Drug case. Although the pregnant woman bears some responsibility for the fetus's existence, she is not responsible for its being dependent on her, or for its need for her aid, for there is nothing she could have done that would have enabled it to exist without needing her aid. But if she is not responsible for the fetus's need for aid, the Responsibility Objection fails.

This is not, however, the right explanation of why the physician in the Imperfect Drug case does not have a special reason to aid the cellist. It is not necessary, in order for the physician to be responsible for the cellist's need for aid, that she should have been able to ensure that the cellist would exist without needing her aid. It is enough that she deliberately administered the drug that she knew would cause the cellist's present condition. Had she not done this, the cellist would not now need her aid. Of course, he would also not now exist. And preventing an individual from existing is, admittedly, an unusual way of ensuring that he is not in an undesirable state, such as a state of dependency. But it is certainly possible to be responsible for an individual's being in an undesirable state, even if the only way one could have prevented the individual from being in that state was to prevent him from existing. Sometimes, in other words, the only way to prevent an individual from being in an undesirable state is to prevent his existing, or his continuing to exist. Suppose, for example, that a person knows that, because of a defective gene he carries, any child he might conceive would inevitably have a very short life filled with agony. If he nevertheless conceives a child, he will be responsible for its agony even though it was not possible for that child to exist but not be in agony. Similarly, suppose that a person will die unless I save him and I know that, if I do save him, he will inevitably suffer from constant pain. If, unable to consult his preferences, I decide to save him, I will be responsible for his being in pain even though it was not possible for him to exist and not be in pain. In the same way, a pregnant woman can be responsible for the fact that the fetus needs her aid even though it was not possible for the fetus to exist without needing her aid.

In order to make it reasonable to deny that the woman is responsible for the fetus's need for her aid, what Silverstein requires is the claim that there was nothing the woman could have done to prevent the fetus from needing her aid. But that claim is false: she *could* have prevented it from needing her aid by not causing it to exist. What Silverstein actually says is that the woman "is *not* responsible for the fact that, given that the fetus exists at *t,* it needs the use of her body at *t,* for she had no alternative which would have avoided that result."[81] But as we have seen, in order for one to be responsible for an individual's being in a certain state, it does not have to have been possible for the individual to exist without being in that state. All that is necessary is that one could have ensured that the individual would not be in that state. Silverstein's explanation, it seems, conflates the impossibility of preventing an individual from being in a certain state with the impossibility of preventing the individual from being in that state, *given that he exists* (or, in other words, the impossibility of ensuring that the individual exists without being in that state).

What, then, is the explanation of why the physician in the Imperfect Drug case does not have a special reason to aid the cellist? I believe the explanation is that the act by which the physician caused the cellist to need her aid will, on balance, have been better for the cellist *even if* the cellist fails to receive the aid he needs. To see why this is important, we need to consider why responsibility for a person's need for aid normally *does* give one a special reason to provide that aid. Consider:

The Accidental Nudge. A number of people are gathered for a party on a dock. One guest accidentally bumps into another, knocking him into the water. The guest who has plunged into the water cannot swim and will drown if no one rescues him.

I assume that each of the guests who are capable of swimming has a moral reason to dive in to save the drowning man. But the guest who is responsible for the drowning man's need for aid has an additional, special reason to save him. This is that, if the drowning man is not saved, the responsible man will not only have failed to save him but will also have *harmed* him, or caused him to die. For the earlier act of knocking him into the water will then have caused his death. Thus the responsible man's special reason for aiding the drowning man is that this may be necessary in order to ensure that he—the responsible man—will not have harmed the drowning man or caused him to die. This is a reason that none of the other guests on the dock has.

In the Imperfect Drug case, by contrast, even if the physician does not aid the cellist, so that he dies, her earlier act of causing him to need her aid will not have harmed him or been worse for him. Her giving him the drug enabled him to live ten years longer than he otherwise would have. *That* can hardly be a ground of liability to make a sacrifice now in order to enable him to benefit even more.

Before moving on, let us briefly consider a variant of the Imperfect Drug case.

Malpractice. The situation is the same as in the Imperfect Drug case except that, when the physician administered the imperfect drug, there was in fact an alternative drug available that would have cured the initial condition without later causing the kidney ailment.[82]

It seems that, in this case, the physician *does* have a special reason to aid the cellist now. But in this version, as in the original version, it seems that her earlier act of administering the imperfect drug would have been better for him even if she now fails to provide the aid she has caused him to need. So what can be the basis of her special reason? To answer this, we must resolve an ambiguity. Even if the physician does not aid the cellist, her having given him the imperfect drug was better for him *than her doing nothing* would have been (assuming that no one else would have administered the better drug); but it was worse for him *than what,* other things being equal, *she ought to have done.* Assuming that she ought to have administered the better drug, she now has a special reason to prevent her earlier act from being worse for him than what she ought to have done instead. She has a special reason to ensure that the ultimate outcome of her earlier act is no worse for him than the outcome would have been if she had instead done what she ought to have done.

Return now to the problem of abortion. Is a pregnant woman's responsibility for the fetus's need for aid relevantly like the physician's responsibility for the cellist's need for aid in the Imperfect Drug case? If so, her responsibility should not entail a special reason to support the fetus. Or is her responsibility relevantly like the guest's responsibility for the drowning man's need for aid in the Accidental Nudge? If it is like this, it should entail a special reason to support the fetus.

The answer seems to depend on whether, if the woman does not aid the fetus, the act by which she caused it to need her aid (that is, the act of conceiving it) will have been worse for it, better for it, or neither. If her having caused it to exist in its dependent state will have been on balance worse for it if she fails to support it, it seems that the case is relevantly like the Accidental Nudge. For she will then have a special reason to support it in order to prevent her earlier act from having harmed or been worse for the fetus. If, by contrast, her having caused it to exist in its dependent state will have been on balance better for it even if she fails to support it, it seems that the case is relevantly like the Imperfect Drug case and she has no special reason to allow the fetus the continued use of her body.

It is worth noting here, parenthetically, that if the pregnant woman has a special reason to aid the fetus based on her responsibility for its need for aid, and if (as in most actual cases of pregnancy) the biological father shares this responsibility with her, he must have an equal reason to aid the fetus, if it were possible for him to provide the aid it needs. Since this is not possible, he is presumably morally required to share the burden of responsibility indirectly by compensating the woman or by taking a correspondingly greater share of the responsibility for the care of the child after it is born. There would, of course, be formidable problems in enforcing the biological father's duty to provide compensation—for example, problems in determining paternity, determining how much compensation would be due and what form it should take in particular cases, and so on. I will not pursue these problems here, but they will be important if it turns out that parents acquire a special moral reason to aid the fetus through their joint responsibility for its need for aid.

It is important to be clear about the question we are asking. What we want to know is whether a pregnant woman who is responsible for her fetus's need for aid has a *special* reason to provide that aid. The relevant question is *not* whether her failing to aid the fetus would be worse for it than her aiding it would be. The answer to that is obvious; but it tells us only that she has *a reason* to aid the fetus—a reason that anyone who *could* aid the fetus would also have. Nor is it quite right to ask whether her failing to aid the fetus would be worse for it than its never existing would have been.[83] The relevant question seems instead to be this: if the pregnant woman refuses to aid the fetus, so that it dies, will the act by which she caused it to need her aid then have been worse for it, better for it, or neither?

Posing the question this way raises yet another question: better or worse than what? When we considered the Malpractice case, this question was crucial; for in that case, the act by which the physician caused the cellist's need for aid was better for the cellist than doing nothing would have been, but worse for the cellist than administering the better drug. But the case of pregnancy is not like this. The only alternative that the pregnant woman had to causing the fetus to need her aid was not to cause it to exist at all. Therefore the relevant question must be whether, if she fails to aid the fetus, her having caused it to exist in a dependent state will have been better or worse for it than if she had not caused it to exist at all.

When phrased this way, the question remains problematic. For the claim that to exist is, for example, *better for* an individual than never to exist at all implies that never to exist at all would have been *worse for* that individual: "better for" is comparative. But never to exist cannot be worse for an individual, for by hypothesis there is no one for whom not existing could be bad. The solution to this problem, I believe, is to abandon the comparative form of the evaluation.[84] The relevant question should be rephrased in noncomparative terms. Our question, then, should be: if the pregnant woman refuses to aid the fetus, so that it dies, will the act by which she caused it to need her aid then have been on balance bad for it, good for it, or neither? If the answer to this question is that her earlier act would have been bad for the fetus, it is reasonable to conclude that she has a special reason to aid it. Her special reason to provide the aid will be to prevent her earlier act from harming or being bad for the fetus.

Many people believe that to cause a fetus to exist in a dependent condition *is* bad for it if it is not then given the support it needs to survive. For they believe that it is bad for an individual to be caused to exist if its life will inevitably be very brief. There are four different arguments that might be advanced in support of this belief.

First, it might be held that it is bad to get only a fleeting glimpse of life, to be teased by the prospect of so much good only to be denied anything more than the glimpse itself. This suggestion, however, covertly and illegitimately assimilates the case of the fetus to the more familiar case in which an individual has the prospect of some good dangled before him only to be denied it, thereby contaminating his life with disappointment and bitter regret. A fetus, by contrast, is not teased by the prospect of life for the obvious reason that it is incapable of having the slightest conception of the future life that it might or might not have.

Second, some have argued that causing the fetus to exist without then doing what is necessary to enable it to survive is bad for it because it makes it inevitable that it will suffer the harm of an extremely premature death.[85] Michael Lockwood, for example, claims that "death is, other things being equal, a misfortune for an individual and . . . therefore, by [causing or] allowing . . . a being to come into existence, under circumstances in which it cannot ultimately survive, one is responsible for bringing about such a misfortune."[86] Of course, all human lives end in death, yet we do not regard this as a reason not to cause people to exist. But the difference, it might be argued, is that in most cases death, even if premature, comes sufficiently late that the life contains enough good to outweigh the badness of death. In the case of fetal death, however, the magnitude of the loss is especially great while the life has been especially short; hence the good that the life has contained is insufficient to outweigh the badness of the loss.

This, however, is a mistake. As we have seen, when death is bad, it may be bad for a variety of reasons, principal among which is that it deprives its victim of further good life. But the evil of being deprived of further life is not appropriately avoided by ensuring that the possible victim gets *no* life at all. It is not that kind of evil. Intrinsic evils, such as suffering, may reasonably be avoided by ensuring that the potential victim does not exist. It may, for example, be morally right to prevent some-one from ever existing if his life would be filled with agony, or it may be prudentially rational to end one's life in order to avoid great suffering that would not be counter-balanced by compensating goods. But death is not an intrinsic evil. It is bad only by comparison with continued life. Thus it is irrational to seek to prevent a potential per-son from suffering the loss of *continued* life by preventing him from having any life at all. The failure to get *more* good life cannot negate the value of having *some*. That a life could in principle contain more good than it will in fact contain if it is created does not, therefore, provide a reason not to create it. Even if causing a fetus to exist condemns it to a tragically premature death, it does not follow that causing it to exist is bad for it. (The argument of this paragraph echoes the claim I made earlier, in sec-tion 4 of this chapter, that it would be absurd to allow a fetus or infant to die now on the ground that that would spare it a worse death later—or at least a later death that would frustrate a stronger time-relative interest in continuing to live.)

A third reason for thinking that causing the fetus to exist will have been bad for it unless the woman supports it is that the refusal to support it—that is, abortion—involves *killing* it, and to be killed is bad independently of the badness of death. Thus Michael Davis, in discussing the Responsibility Objection, contends that "to be killed is bad, so bad that merely being brought into existence for a time is not neces-sarily enough to make up for it. We would not, I take it, allow a scientist to kill a ten-year-old child just because the scientist had ten years ago 'constructed' the child."[87]

This claim, too, is mistaken, for several reasons. First, even if there is something bad about being killed over and above the badness of dying, it cannot be seriously bad. It is not, for example, significantly worse *for a person* to be pushed over a precipice than to stumble over it. Thomas Nagel has remarked that he would "not re-ally object to dying if it were not followed by death."[88] I think one should take a sim-ilar view of being killed. But, even if it were significantly worse to be killed than to die in some other way, it is not obviously true that abortion must involve killing. In section 9.4 of this chapter, I will contend that abortions could be performed in a way that would merely involve allowing the fetus to die. If this is right, then, even if Davis's objection were valid, a pregnant woman could avoid having a special reason to aid the fetus simply by denying it her aid in a way that would not involve killing it. But the real problem with Davis's objection is that causing the fetus to exist is not what causes it to be killed. Therefore one cannot ascribe the badness of its being killed to the act of causing it to exist. Recall that whether the pregnant woman has a special reason to aid the fetus depends on whether her having caused it to exist will be bad for it if she does not aid it. If she kills it, that may be bad for it over and above the badness of its dying; but the fact that it is *killed*, over and above the fact that the woman has not provided the aid she caused it to need, does not retroactively make it bad for the fetus that she caused it to exist and to need her aid. While the woman's failing to aid the fetus may retroactively make her previous act of causing it to need her aid bad for it, her inflicting the alleged additional harm involved in *killing* it does nothing to make the previous act turn out to have been bad for it.

There is one more possible reason for supposing that the pregnant woman must support the fetus if she is to prevent her previous act of causing it to need her aid from being bad for it.[89] This is that extreme brevity makes a life objectively bad. This claim has been advanced by Frances Kamm, who draws an analogy between an extremely short life and a life of mild mental retardation. Of the latter she says that it meets "an objective standard of defectiveness," a fact that may make it bad to cause a retarded child to exist even when the alternative is to have no child at all.[90] Many of us will reject that judgment, but that is not the point here. The point is that, even if the life of a retarded individual seems good from the inside, Kamm claims that there may be an objectively bad dimension to the life that outweighs the subjectively good aspect, making it overall a bad life to have. Analogously, she claims, extreme brevity is an objective defect in a life that may outweigh any subjectively good features that the life might have.

It is interesting to note that Kamm's claim that a very short life is objectively bad seems to presuppose that death in these cases has a retroactive effect on the value of the life that precedes it. Consider a life that lasts from t_1 to t_2. If the interval is very short, the life is bad. But, if the death at t_2 were not to occur, so that the life would be of normal length, the period from t_1 to t_2 would then not be bad; it would simply be the initial phase of a good life. Thus, whether or not death occurs at t_2 may determine the value of the period from t_1 to t_2.

How plausible is the claim that a very short life, simply by virtue of its brevity, is objectively bad? I can think of no reason to accept this claim. Suppose it were claimed that a life that ends six months after birth is so brief as to be objectively defective and therefore bad for the infant whose life it was. But if the infant lived a normal, contented life before dying unexpectedly at six months, I see no reason to suppose that its life must have been objectively unworthy of a human being, so that we should conclude that it was bad for it to have existed at all. If one were to consult those with the strongest reasons for being concerned about the infant for its own sake—namely, its parents—it would be surprising if they were not glad, for the infant's sake, that it had existed, experienced life, and enriched their own lives. Naturally they would regret their own grief, but it is unlikely that they would wish, for its own sake, that the infant had never existed.

There remains the possibility that a very brief life is bad *impersonally*—that is, not bad for the individual whose life it is but bad in that it detracts from the overall value of the world. Again, however, I fail to see the force of this suggestion. And, in any case, even if we grant that a short life is bad impersonally, this will support only a very weak version of the Responsibility Objection. For it would mean that the woman would have a special reason to aid the fetus, not to prevent her earlier act from harming it, but to prevent her earlier act from detracting from the impersonal value of the world. And this, I think, would not be a compelling reason for her to accept the burden of an unwanted pregnancy and birth.

We have now considered four reasons for thinking that a pregnant woman's refusal to support the fetus makes it bad for the fetus that she caused it to exist in a dependent state. I have argued that none of these reasons is persuasive. If it is bad to cause someone to exist whose life will inevitably end prematurely, that must be either because the inevitability of early death would poison the life itself (for example, because the person would be morbidly obsessed with or terrified by the prospect of an impending death) or because of the effects the life would have on others—for example, because of the anxiety and grief that those who would care about the person would suffer. (It is worth noting here an interesting asymmetry. Most people, if they knew that any child they might have would inevitably die at age three, would take care not to have a child. They would want to avoid the great suffering they would inevitably experience. But people who have a child that dies at age three typically and emphatically do not wish that they had never had the child. They suffer, but their love for the child makes it unthinkable for them to wish that he or she had never existed.)[91]

We must conclude, therefore, that the situation of a pregnant woman is not analogous to that of the guest in the Accidental Nudge case who has knocked a person into the water. It is not a reason for the woman to aid the fetus that this is necessary to prevent her earlier act of causing it to need her aid from being bad for it. Even if she fails to aid it, it will not have been bad for it to have been caused to exist in a dependent state. (This explains why it is not an acceptable response to the Responsibility Objection to alter Thomson's violinist analogy by making the involuntary benefactor responsible for the violinist's need for aid. The case would then be relevantly analogous to the Accidental Nudge case but not to the case of an accidental pregnancy.)

Is a pregnant woman's situation instead analogous to that of the physician in the Imperfect Drug case? I think the answer must be: *only if* the short life she has caused the fetus to have is *good* for it. It is, of course, highly controversial whether it can be good or bad for an individual to be caused to exist.[92] Thus far in this section I have been assuming, for the sake of argument, that it can be bad to be caused to exist. So let us make the parallel assumption that it can be good to be caused to exist. Even if we make this assumption, however, it seems, as I noted earlier, that the life that a fetus has in utero is neither good nor bad: it is a life of bare consciousness with virtually no possibilities for good, a life in which little is experienced and nothing is done. If that is right, the life a fetus has in utero is neutral in value, and we should therefore conclude that, if a pregnant woman refuses to support the fetus that she has caused to need her aid, the earlier act by which she caused it to need her aid will turn out to have been neither good nor bad for it. For the effect of her act will simply have been to cause the fetus to have a life of neutral value.

It seems, therefore, that the Responsibility Objection fails. For even if a pregnant woman is responsible for the fetus's need for her aid, that fact alone does not give her a special reason to provide that aid—at least not for the usual reason, which is to prevent the act by which she caused the fetus to need her aid from harming or being bad for it.

It may be worth noting, however, that there is one way in which the situation of the pregnant woman differs from that of the physician in the Imperfect Drug case that may be significant. In the Imperfect Drug case, the act by which the physician causes the cellist to need her aid prevents the cellist from suffering a great harm, and she therefore has a decisive moral reason to do the act. That she was morally required to do the act for the cellist's own sake makes it exceedingly unlikely that the act could make her liable to make sacrifices to benefit the cellist again. In the case of pregnancy, by contrast, the woman had no moral reason to do the act that caused the fetus to need her aid, and a fortiori no moral reason connected with the well-being of the fetus. It is therefore conceivable that there is a basis for liability to provide aid in the case of pregnancy that is absent in the Imperfect Drug case.

9.3. *Parental Responsibility*

In Thomson's case of the Involuntary Benefactor, the unconscious violinist and the person who gets hooked up to him are complete strangers to one another. There are no special relations between them. But in the case of an unwanted pregnancy, the fetus is the biological offspring of the pregnant woman. Does this difference matter?

As I noted in the discussion of special relations in section 2.1 of chapter 3, the parent-child relation is widely viewed as a paradigmatic instance of a special relation that grounds a range of special responsibilities that the parent has for the child. In particular, a parent may have a special duty to provide aid and support for his or her child—a duty that he or she may not owe to others. It is certainly arguable that the fact that a pregnant woman is the biological parent of the fetus she carries gives her special reason to support it. Because the same special relation does not hold between the involuntary benefactor and the unconscious violinist, Thomson's analogy fails to capture what may be a crucial feature of the relation between the pregnant woman and the fetus.

There is, of course, a question as to whether the parent-child relation has any significance in cases in which the biological offspring is a *fetus*. It might be argued that the parent-child relation has moral significance only when there is really a *child* (or, later, a *person*) present. But for the moment, following Thomson, we are putting aside questions about the status of the fetus and are assuming that it has the same status as, for example, an older child. At the end of this section, I will offer a few reflections on the relevance of the parent-child relation to the issue of abortion, given a realistic understanding of the nature and status of the fetus.

Thomson anticipates this objection to her argument, noting that critics may contend that the fetus " is a person for whom the woman has a special kind of responsibility issuing from the fact that she is its mother."[93] Her response is to claim that parental responsibilities must be voluntarily assumed: "Surely we do not have any such 'special responsibility' for a person unless we have assumed it, explicitly or implicitly."[94] If a pair of parents "have taken all reasonable precautions against having a child, they do not simply by virtue of their biological relationship to the child who comes into existence have a special responsibility for it."[95]

It seems true that, in certain conditions, one's consenting to accept parental responsibilities is sufficient for one to have them. If, for example, the natural parents of a child are eager to transfer their parental rights and responsibilities through the process of adoption, one may acquire the full panoply of parental responsibilities by consenting to adopt the child. But it does not seem to be true that the voluntary assumption of parental responsibilities is *necessary* in order for one to have them. Consider the situation of a young couple in a premodern society in which contraception and induced abortion are unknown, infanticide is severely punished, and there is no social provision for adoption. Suppose they live in a remote area and have no extended family to help them. The woman gives birth to an unwanted infant that they allow to live only because they fear the penalty for infanticide. After they have lived with the child for a year in total isolation, they realize that no one would know if they were to abandon it, or cease to support it. I assume that they have done nothing that involves consenting, even tacitly, to take responsibility for the child: they have supported it, grudgingly, only out of fear. Yet most of us believe that they must take responsibility for this child. They are responsible for it, moreover, in a way in which they would not be responsible for an unrelated one-year-old that they might find abandoned in the woods (or that they might hear about having been found in the woods). While they would surely have *some* reason to take responsibility for the abandoned child, their reason to support and care for their *own* child seems considerably stronger. (In order to ensure that our judgment about this case is not affected by the sense—which I have suggested has a rational basis—that the moral status of a newborn infant is lower than that of an older child, I have set up the case so that the child is a year old when the question of abandonment is raised. For those with traditional, commonsense intuitions about infants, the question could be simpler: if the couple give birth to a child and there is no one but the two of them to support it, do they have any more reason to care for it than they would have to care for an unrelated infant whose parents had died and who will certainly die itself unless they take responsibility for it? If one believes they do, one must believe that there is a nonvoluntary basis for parental responsibility.)

One might supplement these reflections by noting that most of us believe that the father of a child may have certain duties to it even if he has done everything possible to avoid or renounce responsibility for the child.[96] Suppose, for example, that a man conscientiously uses contraception but that his wife becomes pregnant despite his precautions. He urges her to have an abortion or to agree to put the child up for adoption. His aversion to having a child is so profound that, when she initially rejects his suggestions, he threatens to leave her if she insists on keeping the child. This, clearly, is a man who does not voluntarily accept parental responsibilities. But most of us believe that, if the woman elects to keep the child, he must share the burden of caring for it, that he acts wrongly if he leaves his wife to evade those burdens, and that the legal system will be functioning to enforce his moral obligations when it requires him to share at least the financial costs of caring for the child.

These examples show that most of us accept that there is a basis for parental responsibilities that is nonvoluntary. Since we know that adoptive parents can acquire parental responsibilities simply by agreeing to accept and fulfill them, it seems that there must be multiple independent sources of parental responsibility, some voluntary, some nonvoluntary. Some sources—such as consent—may be sufficient for the full range of parental duties. Other sources may be insufficient for the full range but may nevertheless give the parent a special reason to provide certain forms of support or assistance for the child beyond what he or she owes to other people. To say that one source is sufficient for the full range of duties is, of course, to imply that the absence of other possible sources does not diminish the strength or scope of one's responsibilities and that the presence of additional sources does not increase one's responsibilities. Thus if, for example, consent is a sufficient basis of the full range of duties, the responsibilities of adoptive parents will be as strong and as extensive as those of natural parents, even if the duties of natural parents are based on both consent and other factors not present in the case of adoption.

In order to explain why parents cannot simply abandon their children and why fathers cannot simply renounce their ties to their children, we must identify the nonvoluntary sources of parental responsibility. We can then attempt to determine whether those sources are present in the relation that a pregnant woman bears to her fetus. Given the centrality of parental obligation in our understanding of the moral life, it is surprising how little thought this issue has received in the history of philosophy.[97] There is comparatively little serious literature to draw on.

One source of parental responsibility that can be ignored for present purposes is the set of personal relations that typically develops between parent and child. Parents typically form strong emotional bonds with their children and establish a history of shared experience and reciprocal benefit. But these relations require time and personal contact and therefore cannot be present at birth or in the relation that an unconsenting father bears to a child he has never met. Nor, of course, can they be present in the relation that a pregnant woman bears to her fetus. (Some people believe that the ways in which a pregnant woman may bond with the fetus she carries establish a special relation between them. It is difficult to know what to make of this. If this alleged special relation is thought to be a source of parental responsibility, it seems that surrogate mothers must have certain parental responsibilities for the children they bear.)

Apart from consent and the various personal dimensions of the parent-child relation, there are only two possible sources of parental responsibility that I can think of. One of these is the purely biological or genetic connection. Some have objected that this alone cannot be a source of parental responsibility; otherwise a sperm donor, or even someone whose reproductive material was taken without his or her knowledge (for example, if a woman were surreptitiously to preserve and impregnate herself with the contents of her lover's discarded condom), would have parental responsibilities to any children conceived from the donated or stolen genetic material.[98] Yet it seems that the only other possible source is the parent's responsibility for the child's need for aid, and I have suggested that that does not seem to be a plausible basis for the attribution of special duties when the alternative was for the child never to exist at all.

We are, however, quite firm in our conviction that, even when a child's parents have in no way consented to care for it, if there is no one else available to care for it, the parents are not free to abandon it but must instead take responsibility for it. We are also confident that a child's biological father cannot free himself from all parental responsibilities simply by refusing to accept them and by avoiding forming any relations with the child. Unless we are to dismiss these convictions as illusions, we must find a basis for parental responsibility in these cases. I think we must reconsider the significance of both the genetic connection and the parents' responsibility for the child's need for aid.

Consider first the relevance of responsibility for the child's need for aid. It is significant that, once there is a *child* present (whether one takes this to occur immediately at birth or at some slightly later time), we believe that it must be supported; it cannot simply be allowed to die from lack of care. If there is no provision for adoption and if, for whatever reason, there is no mechanism for distributing responsibility for the child throughout the entire society (for example, by having state-supported orphanages for unwanted children), responsibility seems to lie with the parents. Our thought may be this: *someone* must care for the child; they caused it to exist and to need support through their own voluntary action; therefore they must bear at least the major part of the burden of its care. It is, of course, true that their situation is different from that of the responsible guest in the Accidental Nudge: it is not necessary for them to support the child now in order to prevent their earlier act of causing it to need aid from harming it. It may be, however, that there is another explanation of how their responsibility for its existence and its need for aid gives them a special reason to support it—one that is different from the explanation that applies in the Accidental Nudge. I do not know what that explanation might be, but it seems reasonable to attempt to discover such an explanation, given the intuitive cogency of the thought that the parents' responsibility singles them out from the rest of humanity as having a special reason to accept the burdens of the child's care.

It may also seem relevant that the child is genetically their progeny. Yet, as I noted, the genetic component of the parent-child relation is present in the relation between a sperm donor and any children conceived from the donated sperm, and even in the relation between someone whose reproductive materials have been taken without his or her knowledge and any children conceived from those materials. Surely, some have argued, it is absurd to suppose that the bare genetic relation could be sufficient in these cases for the biological parent to have parental responsibilities for the child. But, while it does seem absurd to suppose that the genetic relation alone could be sufficient for the full range of parental responsibilities, it is not absurd to believe that it could give the biological parent some special reasons to care for his or her biological child that an unrelated stranger would not have. In short, we need to remember that parental responsibility is not necessarily all-or-nothing. While some sources of parental responsibility may be sufficient for the full range of parental duties, others may, on their own, be the basis for only a limited degree of special responsibility. In the case of the Sperm Donor as I presented it in section 2.3 of chapter 3, a child conceived from the sperm a man previously donated will die unless it receives a bone marrow transplant; and the donor is the only person known to have the right blood type. I suggested that many people believe that the donor has a special reason to aid the child—a reason he would not have in the absence of the genetic relation. My own intuition—and it is really nothing more than that—is that the bare genetic relation does give him a special reason to help the child. This reason may not be decisive in the circumstances. And certainly his genetic relation to the child does not by itself entail that he has extensive responsibilities for the child. But the genetic relation does seem to have some significance.

This should not be surprising, given the tremendous importance that people attribute to the genetic relation in their aspirations for parenthood. Many couples who experience problems of fertility will go to extraordinary lengths and accept enormous financial costs in order to be able to have a natural child, even when the option of adoption is readily available and there are numerous children desperately in need of care. The significance that people attribute, whether consciously or unconsciously, to the genetic relation is also evident in the grim statistics on child abuse, which show that adopted children are at significantly higher risk of physical violence from their parents than natural children are. Of course, the fact that most people attribute profound significance to the genetic component of the parent-child relation does not entail that the genetic relation is by itself a basis of special responsibilities. On the other hand, it would be odd, and would require explanation, if we felt that the genetic connection is a deeply significant (though not absolutely necessary) element of the parent-child relation, and yet also accepted that in some cases, such as that of the Sperm Donor, the presence of this connection in the absence of other elements of parenthood has no significance whatsoever.

It might help to focus our thinking to consider the rare cases in which babies are switched at birth—that is, cases in which one set of parents (parents *A*) are mistakenly given the wrong baby (child *B*) by the hospital staff, while their baby (child *A*) is mistakenly given to the other set of parents (parents *B*). In such a case, parents *A* take home child *B,* and otherwise do those things that indicate that they tacitly consent to care for it. There is also reciprocal bonding between parents *A* and child *B.* So two relatively uncontroversial sources of parental responsibility bind parents *A* closely to child *B.* But suppose that, after a number of years, the mistake is discovered. Typically, each pair of parents will feel strongly bound to both children. Suppose, further, that the mistake is discovered because child *A* requires a bone marrow transplant in order to survive, and when parents *B* are both tested for tissue compatibility it is found that they cannot be child *A*'s biological parents. Would parents *A* have a special moral reason to donate bone marrow for the sake of child *A?* I suspect that most people would believe that they would, even though the less contested sources of parental responsibility bind them to child *B* rather than to child *A.* If both parents *A,* including the biological father, would have a special reason to donate, it seems that it must derive from their genetic connection to child *A.*

In sum, even in cases in which the parents of a child do not consent to care for it and have developed no personal relations with it, they nevertheless seem to have special responsibilities for it that they must fulfill if no one else can or will take over for them. If this is right, it must be because of either their responsibility for the child's existence and need for aid, or their genetic relation to it, or both. Because both of these dimensions of the parent-child relation are present in the relation between a pregnant woman and her fetus when the pregnancy is the result of voluntary sex, and given that we are assuming that the fetus has a moral status no different from that of a child, it is reasonable to conclude that these factors give the woman a special reason, though not necessarily a decisive one, to support the fetus.

Before concluding this section, I should briefly address two questions that are relevant here. First, what is the significance of the parent-child relation if the fetus is not a person (or whatever) but instead has the sort of status I suggested earlier? I believe the answer is that whatever reasons there are to protect the fetus's life and to promote its present or future well-being are magnified in their application to its parents. They are not magnified by the full force of the parental relation, for only some of the various dimensions of that relation are present; but they are magnified somewhat. This is, after all, the main way the parental relation has an effect morally: it does not so much create reasons where otherwise there would be none, but functions to strengthen reasons that would be present though much weaker in the absence of the relation. The effect of the parental relation is most salient in strengthening positive reasons to promote the child's well-being; but it also strengthens the reasons there are not to harm the child. Thus we have a special horror of those who abuse or kill their own children—for example, the notorious Susan Smith, mentioned earlier, who drowned her two sons. In that case, of course, all the dimensions of the parent-child relation were present, and the reason not to kill the two children was already overwhelmingly strong even in the absence of that relation. If I am right, our reasons for concern about the fetus are in general considerably weaker. Nevertheless, whatever reasons people in general have not to injure the early fetus apply with somewhat greater force to the biological parents. Where the developed fetus is concerned, I have argued that the primary moral reason either to sustain or to refrain from ending its life is comparatively weak because of the comparative weakness of its time-relative interest in continuing to live. But even this reason is strengthened somewhat in its application to the parents because of the presence of certain dimensions of the parent-child relation.

Second, why is it that people generally believe that once a child has been born it *must* (barring unusual circumstances) be supported and thus the parents must take responsibility for it if no one else will, while very few people have a comparably strong conviction about the necessity of supporting a fetus? As I indicated earlier, it seems likely that a crucial part of the explanation is the widely shared intuitive sense that the fetus is relevantly different. But we are now, following Thomson, trying to screen out the effects of that sense. The other possible explanation, on which Thomson focuses, is that the circumstances of pregnancy are unique in that the burden of supporting a fetus necessarily falls exclusively on the pregnant woman, and that burden is distinctively onerous in that it involves a sacrifice of the woman's bodily integrity. It is worth noting—and this is the reason that I have raised this second question—that those who take this second explanation to be exhaustive (because they believe that a fetus has the same moral status as a child) must be prepared to concede that, if advances in technology make it possible for fetuses to be supported in other ways, the reasons we recognize for believing that even an unwanted child must be supported will also be reasons for providing alternative forms of support for unwanted fetuses. This could prove awkward. Suppose, for example, that it becomes possible to support a fetus in an artificial uterus from shortly after conception.[99] If the reasons we have to provide public support (such as orphanages and adoption agencies) for unwanted children apply with equal force to unwanted fetuses, it might be incumbent upon us to provide costly artificial uteruses for unwanted fetuses that would otherwise die from being aborted.

9.4. *Killing and Letting Die*

The standard methods for performing abortions clearly involve killing the fetus: the fetus dies by being mangled or poisoned in the process of being removed from the uterus. In the case of the Involuntary Benefactor, Thomson has the director of the hospital say to the woman that "unplugging you would be directly killing an innocent violinist"; and Thomson herself later addresses the reader as if the reader were hooked up to the violinist: "we have to notice that in unplugging yourself, you are killing him."[100] If this is right—that to disconnect the violinist would be to kill him—disconnecting the violinist and aborting a fetus may involve the same mode of agency. But it may seem that the woman's disconnecting herself from the violinist would not be to kill him but merely to allow him to die. If that is so, there is a further failure of analogy between Thomson's case and a case of abortion. Moreover, most people believe that, if other things are equal, it is generally (though not necessarily always) more seriously morally objectionable to kill a person than it is to let a person die. If that is right, and if the woman's disconnecting herself from the violinist would be to let him die, we cannot infer from the fact that it is permissible for the woman to disconnect herself from the violinist that it is permissible for a pregnant woman to kill her fetus.[101]

It is, perhaps, instructive to consider a variant of the Involuntary Benefactor in which, in order to disconnect herself, the woman must first unambiguously *kill* the violinist, for example by dismembering or poisoning him. Even if we would still think it permissible for her to disconnect herself, most of us would have greater qualms about reaching this conclusion here than in the original version of the case. And this remains true even when we remind ourselves that the violinist is unconscious, so that it is no worse for him to be killed than to be allowed to die.

If the woman simply disconnects the violinist from her circulatory system, as in the original version of the case, is it plausible to suppose that she does not kill him but merely allows him to die?[102] Some would argue that the woman merely lets the violinist die because it is the underlying kidney ailment that kills him. By removing the source of aid that protects him from the effects of the disease, she merely "lets nature take its course."[103] But this cannot be all there is to it, as is shown by the following variant of the case of the Involuntary Benefactor:

> *The Enemy.* The circumstances are the same as in the Involuntary Benefactor except that the woman has agreed to remain hooked up to the violinist until he can survive on his own. But late one night, the violinist's enemy steals into the hospital and surreptitiously disconnects him from the woman.

In this case, the enemy merely removes a source of aid that has been protecting the violinist from the effects of his condition; so, when the aid is removed, the violinist dies of his underlying kidney condition. But here it seems absurd to say that the enemy merely allows him to die.[104]

It is sometimes held, alternatively, that, if the woman in the Involuntary Benefactor case disconnects herself, she does not merely allow the violinist to die, for the violinist dies as a direct result of what she *does*. If the woman were not to *act* as she does, the violinist would survive. And that, surely, shows that she kills him.

But this cannot be right either, as the following example shows:

> *The Aborted Rescue.* Two persons are in the water when one begins to drown. The other attempts to haul the drowning man to shore but the latter, in a panic, begins to claw and encumber his rescuer in a way that threatens to drown him as well. To extricate himself from this peril, the erstwhile rescuer has to push the drowning man off and swim away, leaving the drowning man to his fate.

In this case, too, the erstwhile rescuer does something to the drowning man that results in the latter's death—namely, he shoves the drowning man away in order to prevent him from trying to save himself at the rescuer's expense. Yet it seems clear that he does not kill the drowning man but merely lets him die. (He *does* let the drowning man die, for there was a chance that he could have saved him had he continued to try.) The drowning man faced a threat for which the rescuer was in no way responsible. The rescuer intervened to save the drowning man but was compelled to abandon the attempt. He began to save him, thereby holding the threat at bay; but then, through an active process of disengagement, he stopped his efforts to save the drowning man, thereby allowing the threat to continue as it would have had he not intervened at all. If he had never intervened at all, that would clearly have been to allow the drowning man to die. It seems absurd to suppose that his initial efforts to effect the rescue could make him a killer.

Some cases in which an agent removes a barrier to a person's death are instances of killing: for example, the act of disconnecting the violinist in the case of the Enemy. Other cases involving the removal of a barrier to death are instances of letting someone die, even when the withdrawal of the barrier requires strenuous action, as in the Aborted Rescue. Our question is: into which of these two categories does the woman's act of disconnecting the violinist in Involuntary Benefactor fall? To answer this question, we must determine why some instances of withdrawing life-supporting aid are killings and why others are instances of letting someone die.

Let us call someone who provides life-supporting aid or protection the *Provider,* and someone who removes or withdraws life-supporting aid or protection the *Remover.* I claim, subject to certain qualifications to be noted presently, that when a Remover withdraws the source of a dependent person's life support and as a consequence the dependent person dies, he merely lets the person die if he is also the Provider of the aid he withdraws. For in that case, he is simply stopping himself from saving the dependent person, which is simply an instance of *not saving* the person— in short, an instance of letting the person die. This is true, for example, in the Aborted Rescue, in which the would-be rescuer temporarily intervenes to avert the threat to the drowning man but then withdraws, thereby allowing the threat to continue. The situation is completely different, however, when the Remover is not the Provider. In that case, it is not the Remover who has been keeping the dependent person alive; therefore when the Remover withdraws the source of the dependent person's life support, he is not stopping saving or failing to save him. He is, rather, intervening in a way that ensures that the person will die when otherwise, in the absence of this intervention, he would have survived. And this, in most instances, is killing—as it is, for example, in the case of the Enemy.

These two claims require qualification. The claim about letting die must be qualified in at least two ways. First, even when the Remover is also the Provider, the act of withdrawing the aid he has been providing may make him a killer if he was responsible for creating the threat to the dependent person's life from which he has subsequently been shielding him. In this kind of case, the agent acts to create a threat to another's life but then intercedes to hold that threat at bay. If the agent then withdraws his protection of the victim from the threat he created, so that the threat then brings about the victim's death, the agent will have killed the victim. It is not, however, that the act of withdrawing the aid-in-progress constitutes an act of killing; in itself that is an instance of letting die. Yet that act retroactively makes it the case that the earlier act that created the lethal threat now counts as an act of killing. For it allows that earlier act to eventuate in the victim's death. Only by continuing to protect the victim from the threat he created earlier could the agent have prevented himself from becoming the victim's killer.

Second, the Remover's act of withdrawing aid he has himself provided will count as an instance of letting die only if the aid is in some sense continuing or in progress, so that the victim remains dependent on him at the time it is withdrawn. For only then is the withdrawal of support an instance of ceasing to save. Aid that was provided in the past and has subsequently become self-sustaining, requiring no further contribution from the Provider, has become a fixed part of the background against which the Remover's act takes place, as in the following case:

> *The Pipe Sealer.* Some years ago, an earthquake cracked a pipe at a factory, threatening to release toxic chemicals into the local water supply. Before any harm was done, a worker sealed the pipe. Now, however, the worker returns and removes the seal, thereby releasing the industrial poisons, which this time kill a person before the problem is rectified.[105]

Although the person who died was dependent on the seal for her safety, and although the worker was the Provider of the seal, he was no longer providing it when he removed it. The barrier that he had interposed between that person and the lethal threat posed by the toxic chemicals did not require continuing provision; thus at the time the barrier was removed, the person did not depend for her safety on any aid, assistance, or protection from the worker. In the absence of any intervention by him, she would have been safe. Therefore, in removing the seal, he did not merely let her die. The case of the Pipe Sealer is relevantly analogous, not to the Aborted Rescue, but to a variant in which the rescuer brings the drowning man to shore but then carries him back out into the water and leaves him there to drown. In each case, the agent effectively eliminates a threat but then, having saved a life, recreates the threat—or, rather, creates a new threat that is just like the original one—by undoing what he has previously done.

The idea that the Provider's aid must be in some sense continuing in order for his withdrawing it to count as letting die does not imply that any further *action* is required from him on the dependent person's behalf. That is, one may let a person die even if there is nothing that one must *do* in order for the person to survive. As long as the dependent person's continued survival depends on resources that properly belong to the Provider (where "resources" are understood liberally to include action, physical possessions, political power, and so on), it can be appropriate to see the dependent person as being kept alive by the Provider, so that the withdrawal of the life-sustaining resources by the Provider will count as an instance of letting die.[106]

With this as background, let us return to the Involuntary Benefactor. If the woman disconnects herself from the violinist, she is withdrawing life-supporting aid-in-progress that she herself has been providing. Although she has been doing so involuntarily and unintentionally, without acting or exercising her agency on his behalf, and, during the initial phase when she was still unconscious, even without *knowing* she was doing so, *she* has been keeping the violinist alive. She is, of course, not the cause of the threat from which she has been shielding him. If, therefore, she decides to stop keeping him alive, she will simply be failing to save him—that is, she will be letting him die.

This implication of the analysis I have offered seems intuitively compelling. Most people, I think, would see the woman's disconnecting herself from the violinist as letting him die. Suppose, however, that the woman is connected to the violinist in such a way that she cannot simply yank the tubes out of her body: that would cause irreparable injury to her kidneys. Only a qualified physician can safely disconnect her. So she asks a physician present to disconnect her. If the physician were to disconnect her, however, *he* would be a Remover who was not the Provider. It seems to follow from the analysis I have given that he would kill the violinist. But this seems implausible. Suppose the disconnection could be accomplished simply by flipping a switch but that the woman, being tethered to the bed by various tubes, cannot reach the switch and so asks a doctor to flip it for her. It is surely arbitrary to suppose that, if she were to flip the switch herself, she would be letting the violinist die, while if a doctor were to flip it for her, he would be killing him.

This reflection indicates that a further refinement is necessary in the account of when the withdrawal of aid counts as killing and when it counts as letting die. It suggests that a Remover who is not also the Provider may nevertheless, in withdrawing a dependent person's life support, merely let that person die *if* he does not act in a personal or private capacity but instead somehow takes over or continues the agency of the Provider. In the variant of Involuntary Benefactor in which the woman asks the physician to disconnect her, the physician is her agent, acting vicariously on her behalf, and it is for this reason that we intuitively apprehend that he merely lets the violinist die. Because he is simply implementing the woman's will, it is *as if* she were acting; therefore we see this as a case in which *she* is disconnecting herself via his action.

Another instance of this general phenomenon occurs when a person acts to provide aid in a role-based capacity—that is, in his capacity as the occupant of a particular role—and then a different person, acting as the Provider's successor in that role, later withdraws the aid. In this kind of case too, the Remover merely lets the dependent person die if his withdrawal of the life-supporting aid is properly understood as a continuation of the agency of the Provider by virtue of his continuity with the Provider in the role. Suppose, for example, that two doctors, working in shifts, are responsible for a certain patient. One of these doctors, on admitting the patient, connects her to a life-support machine. Later, the other doctor decides to disconnect her. Assuming that, if the first doctor had disconnected her for the same reason, that would have counted as letting her die, it seems that the second doctor's disconnecting her should also count as letting her die, even though he was not the Provider. The reason is that both doctors act in their capacity as occupants of the same role: "physician in charge of the case." (Alternatively, imagine a variant of this case in which the doctor who admits the patient and connects her to the life-support machine unexpectedly dies. A colleague then takes over the case and later decides to disconnect the patient from the machine. Assume that, if the first doctor had lived and had later decided to disconnect the patient, that would have counted has letting her die. If that is so, the second doctor's disconnecting her should also count as letting her die, even though he was not the Provider.)

These observations about the withdrawal of life-supporting aid reflect a more general understanding of what it is for an agent to let someone die. I suggest that Agent does not kill Victim but instead lets Victim die if: (1) there is, independent of anything that Agent might do, some antecedent probability that Victim will die within a certain period; (2) Agent is not responsible for the fact that Victim is thus at risk of death; (3) Victim dies; and (4) Victim could have survived if Agent had provided, or had continued to provide, some form of aid, support, assistance, or protection that it was possible for him to provide—if, in effect, Agent had saved Victim.

This analysis may seem straightforward, but it is not. The main problem is that there is considerable vagueness about what would count as Victim's surviving via Agent's provision of help, aid, support, or protection. It seems clear that the "provision" can be involuntary and even unwitting. If I am swimming to shore and a drowning man clutches onto me with a grip I cannot disengage, so that I am forced to haul him to shore, I have saved him, though not voluntarily. If he is floating unconscious and, without my knowing it, the prow of my boat gently pushes him to shore, I have saved him without being aware that I was doing so. (Thus, if I had noticed that I was pushing him toward shore but then decided to drop anchor for a spot of fishing, I would have let him die. And I would also have let him die if I had shoved him aside because he was retarding the progress of my cruise.) As I noted earlier, the provision, or continued provision, of aid or protection does not necessarily require action on the agent's part. It can be sufficient if the vulnerable individual is shielded from death by the agent's *resources,* which include his body, his physical possessions, his money, his power or influence, and so on. These two facts—that one can provide aid or protection involuntarily, unintentionally, and even inadvertently or unwittingly, and that aid can consist entirely in the vulnerable individual's drawing on one's resources for his or her survival—introduce substantial vagueness into the analysis of what it is to let someone die, thereby generating equally substantial gray areas in which it is unclear whether a certain act or failure to act counts as letting someone die. I will not pursue these complications here, though I have elsewhere indicated in greater detail what some of the problems are.[107]

In any case, I will take it as established that the woman in the Involuntary Benefactor case merely lets the violinist die if she disconnects herself from him (or if she orders her physician to disconnect her). But if that is right, the violinist analogy is flawed in yet another respect: for abortion as it is normally practiced involves killing the fetus rather than merely letting it die. Thus, if—as most people believe—killing is generally more seriously objectionable than letting die, then letting the violinist die could be permissible while killing a fetus would not be, even though in both cases the agent would be disconnecting herself from someone who has been drawing life support from her body.

Defenders of the Thomson argument might respond by denying that the distinction between killing and letting die has moral significance. Although many philosophers would accept that response, I believe that we should not reject the strong and widespread intuition that the distinction does have significance unless there are compelling reasons for accepting that it does not. An alternative and more plausible response is to see the Thomson argument as establishing (if we put aside, for the moment, the two other failures of analogy previously noted) a strong presumption that abortion is permissible in cases in which the fetus is not killed but is merely allowed to die. Of course, the central question raised by this response is whether there are or even could be any such cases. Is there a method of abortion that merely involves allowing the fetus to die?

There are possible methods of abortion that closely parallel the woman's disconnecting the violinist in Involuntary Benefactor.[108] For it is certainly possible to remove a fetus from a pregnant woman's body without injuring or damaging its body in a way that would cause its death. One procedure that would work this way is hys-

terectomy, in which the entire uterus, with the fetus inside, would be surgically removed. Another, less radical method is hysterotomy, in which the fetus is surgically
extracted, alive and intact, from the womb. These are both instances of what I call
merely extractive abortions. (Abortifacients that prevent the implantation of the embryo—for example, the IUD—work even more clearly by letting the embryo die.
They operate in a way that is analogous to preventing the violinist from being hooked
up in the first place.) If a merely extractive abortion is performed prior to the fetus's
becoming viable, it will necessarily die. And, of course, it will also die if a merely extractive abortion is performed after the point of viability and nothing is then done to
keep it alive. Nevertheless, the analysis I have offered seems to imply that in either
case the procedure would merely allow the fetus to die. In each case the pregnant
woman would be withdrawing life-supporting aid-in-progress that she herself had
been providing, albeit involuntarily. The process would be relevantly different from
the standard procedure in which the fetus's death is caused by injuries inflicted in the
course of removing it. In this case its death would be the result of the woman's ceasing to save it from its own inherent vulnerability.

Again, exploring the Thomson argument has forced us to confront important
questions. Does a merely extractive abortion really involve only allowing the fetus to
die rather than killing it? If so, would such an abortion be less objectionable than a
method that involves killing—so that, if abortion can be justified at all, there would
be a moral case for switching to merely extractive methods?

Let us consider the first question first. I maintain that to perform a merely extractive abortion—in which the woman does nothing to cause the fetus's death other than
to remove it from the protective environment through which she has been sustaining
its life—is not to kill the fetus but only to allow it to die. In removing it, she is simply ceasing to protect it from the consequences of its inability to survive on its own.
Many people, however, find this conclusion counterintuitive. I am aware of five distinct objections to the claim that merely extractive abortions allow the fetus to die. I
will address each in turn.

1. Even in a merely extractive abortion, something is *done to* the fetus that directly causes its death. If this were not done to it, it would survive. Surely this counts
as killing it.

This objection has already been answered. When the provision of life-supporting
aid is in progress, the Provider is sometimes required, as in the Aborted Rescue, to do
something quite specific to the beneficiary of the aid in order to disengage himself
from the process of providing the aid. If we insist that *doing* something to a person
that results immediately in his death must count as killing, we will be committed to
the absurd conclusion that one would kill a person if one were actively to resist his
efforts to save himself at one's own expense (for example, if one were to resist a person's attempt to use one's body as a shield against a lethal threat).

2. A woman cannot perform a merely extractive abortion on herself. It is a third
party—a doctor—who must remove the fetus from the source of its life support. In
depriving it of life support that the fetus had independently of him, the doctor kills
the fetus.

This objection, too, has already been answered. In order for the withdrawal of
aid-in-progress to count as letting die, it is sufficient that the Provider should deter-

mine that the life-supporting aid should cease. The status of the act of withdrawal is not affected if the actual implementation of the decision is done by proxy, or through an agent. Thus, provided that a merely extractive abortion is undertaken at the initiative of the pregnant woman, she and the doctor through whose agency she vicariously implements her decision both allow the fetus to die.

3. Philippa Foot has argued that the relevant distinction that lies behind the distinction between killing and letting die, and gives it whatever moral significance it has, is the distinction between, on the one hand, initiating a threatening sequence of events or keeping it going (or, one might add, redirecting it) and, on the other hand, allowing a threatening sequence that is already in train to continue.[109] She then distinguishes between two ways of allowing an existing sequence of events to continue, one of which involves "forbearing to prevent" a sequence from continuing while the other involves "the removal of some obstacle which is, as it were, holding back a train of events."[110] In one respect this analysis seems clearly wrong. Foot's claim is that to unblock or release a threat by removing a barrier to it is always merely to allow the threatened harm to occur. But, as we have seen, while this may be true if the barrier is one that the agent has herself been providing, it is not true if the barrier was in place entirely independently of her. Still, even though this part of Foot's analysis seems mistaken, there is a further component that may well be correct— namely, her assumption that in order for one to allow a harm to occur, there must be a preexisting threatening sequence that is either in progress or being held back by some obstacle. On the basis of this assumption, Foot contends that to have an abortion cannot be merely to allow a fetus to die, for there is no threat to the fetus that the abortion allows to continue either by failing to arrest it or by unblocking it. She therefore concludes that the abortion itself "originates the sequence which ends in the death of the fetus, and the destruction comes about 'through the agency' of the mother who seeks the abortion."[111] This is, of course, obviously true in the case of the usual abortion methods. (Hence, Foot observes, abortion is relevantly different from unplugging the violinist, which does not create a threat but instead unblocks a preexisting threat.) But it is also true in the case of a merely extractive abortion, for in that case as well there is no threat to the fetus other than that created by the action of the woman and her doctor. Therefore, even a merely extractive abortion kills the fetus rather than allowing it to die.

It may seem obvious that, in order for one to allow a person to die, there must be an antecedent threat to that person that one allows to continue. Otherwise, where does the person's death come from? There is, however, an ambiguity in the notion of a person's being under threat of death. When Foot observes that the fetus is not under threat when it is in the womb, she means that it is not imperiled by a sequence of events that constitutes a deviation from normal background conditions in which people are able to ensure their own safety and survival. This is the usual sense of being "under threat": one is at risk of harm because some deviant chain of events— for example, an accident or disease—has compromised the ability one has hitherto had to ensure one's own security. There are, however, some individuals who are chronically unable to satisfy their essential needs without aid or assistance from others. These individuals are "under threat" in a different sense: they are threatened by their own inherent helplessness and dependency. The threat to these individuals is latent. It does not stand out as a distinct causal sequence but is instead a chronic, background condition of their lives. This is most pronounced in the case of the fetus, whose utter dependence on aid from the pregnant woman begins with the beginning of its own existence and is a natural and universal feature of its stage of life. Thus it is not under threat in the sense that Foot invokes, but it nevertheless faces a latent threat of death by virtue of its own inherent vulnerability.

Foot's claim that all abortions kill the fetus rather than allowing it to die presupposes that, in order for one to allow an individual to die, that individual must already be under threat of death in the first and stronger of these two senses—that is, that he must be in the path of a threatening sequence of events that is already in train and is external to his own natural state. I believe, by contrast, that it is possible for an agent to allow an individual to die when the only threat the individual faces is a threat latent in his own inherent dependency on aid from the agent. Foot herself supplies an example: "The fetus is not in jeopardy [i.e., under threat] because it is in its mother's womb; it is merely dependent on her in the way children are dependent on their parents for food."[112] Foot assumes that parents "murder" their baby if it dies of starvation when they could have fed it.[113] They cannot, she thinks, merely be allowing it to die, for it is not under threat in the strong sense. But notice that they also do not create or initiate a threatening sequence of events. When an abortion is performed—even if it is a merely extractive abortion—there is something that the pregnant woman and her doctor *do* that can (though I believe mistakenly) be understood as the creation of a threat—namely, actively removing the fetus from its source of life support. But parents may fail to feed their baby simply by lying inert, or by going off on holiday to Acapulco. There is nothing they do that initiates a threatening sequence, in Foot's sense. So, since they neither initiate a threatening sequence nor allow one that is already in train to continue, it seems that by Foot's analysis they neither kill the baby nor allow it to die. But surely, since they could prevent its death, they do one or the other.

It is clear that by failing to feed it, the parents let their baby die—just as they might let a baby that was not their own die if they found it starving on their steps but simply ignored it. If that is right, it is not necessary that an individual be under a threat of death in the strong sense that Foot intends in order for one to allow that individual to die. Hence a merely extractive abortion may allow a fetus to die even though it is not antecedently under threat in this sense.

There is, of course, a temptation to say that parents who fail to feed their baby thereby kill it. But as I argued in section 3.1 of chapter 3, this can be readily explained by reference to our desire to condemn the parents in the strongest possible terms. Because killing is generally worse than letting die, so that one who kills generally deserves harsher condemnation than one who merely allows another to die, we want to say that parents who let their baby die have killed it. In short, our classification of the act may be guided by moral considerations—as is evidenced by Foot's choice of the term "murder." But this is a mistake. The reason that the failure to feed one's own baby is at least as seriously wrong as typical instances of wrongful killing is not that it is itself an instance of killing, but is instead that the wrongfulness of allowing the child to die is magnified by the way in which one is related to the child.

4. A fourth objection to the idea that a merely extractive abortion merely allows the fetus to die is that, at least in cases in which the pregnancy has arisen from vol-

untary intercourse, it is the pregnant woman herself who is responsible for the fetus's being in its vulnerable, dependent state. And, as Michael Levin has written, "when one is completely responsible for dependence, refusal to continue to aid is indeed killing."[114] To appreciate the force of Levin's claim, consider again the agent's conduct in the Accidental Nudge. When he fails to rescue the man he has knocked into the water, he cannot plead that he has merely allowed the man to die. Because he created the threat from which he failed to rescue the man, and from which the man died, he killed him (albeit accidentally). He caused the man to drown. It was to accommodate this kind of case that I included the second condition in my earlier analysis of what it is to let a person die rather than kill him.

This objection, like the previous three, rests on a mistake. In the case of the Accidental Nudge, when the agent fails to aid the drowning man, he is *then* merely allowing the man to die, even though he was the cause of the man's peril. It is not that his failure to save the man itself constitutes an instance of killing. Rather, his failure to save the man allows his earlier act of knocking him into the water to become an act of killing. By failing to save the man, the agent ensures that his earlier act has become the act that caused the man's death rather than being merely an act that exposed the man to a risk of death. It is, in short, that *earlier* act that constitutes the killing.

In the case of a merely extractive abortion, the woman's refusal to aid the fetus is also just an instance of letting it die. But does her letting it die convert the earlier act by which she caused its dependency into an act of killing—in the way that the agent's failure to save the drowning man converts the earlier act by which he caused the man's peril into an act of killing? The act by which she caused the fetus to be in a dependent was the act of causing it to exist—that is, the act of conception. And whatever else is true, it cannot be that her subsequent failure to support the fetus could retroactively convert *that* act into an act of killing. Even if the cause of a person's death is somehow traceable to or inherent in the conditions of his being caused to exist, one cannot cause the person's death, or kill him, by causing him to exist. Thus even if a pregnant woman is responsible for her fetus's need for aid, she will not have killed it if she refuses to provide that aid and instead has a merely extractive abortion.

It is an interesting question why knocking a person into the water and then failing to save him counts as killing him, while causing a person to exist in a dependent condition and then failing to support him does not. The answer may have to do with the fact that, in cases such as the Accidental Nudge, the agent initiates a threatening causal sequence in Foot's strong sense, whereas in causing a person to exist in a dependent state one does not create a threat but only the conditions in which there is a probability of death—conditions that are inseparable from a person's existing at all. But I will not pursue this further here.

5. The fifth and, I believe, most serious objection to the claim that a merely extractive abortion allows the fetus to die takes the form of an analogy. In 1879, an Italian theologian, Daniel Viscosi, noted that if one takes a fish out of the water, one kills it; this is precisely analogous to removing a nonviable fetus from the womb; therefore, in removing the fetus, even in a merely extractive abortion, one kills it.[115]

The analysis I offered earlier suggests an initial reply to this objection. In taking a fish out of the water in which one finds it, one removes it from a source of life support that it has had independently of oneself. One's action is analogous, not to that of

a woman who removes a fetus from her own body, but to that of the agent in the
Enemy who disconnects the violinist from a source of life support that he has not
himself provided.

The obvious response to this, of course, is to change the terms of the analogy.
Surely, it might be said, even to take a fish out of a tank of water that one has oneself
supplied would be to kill it.

Again, however, this may be because the fish was initially secure independently
of oneself. Before one put the fish in one's tank, it did not require any provision of
water by oneself in order to survive. If one has removed it from an environment in
which it could have survived independently of oneself and then established it in a
condition of dependence, and if one then fails to provide the resources one has
caused it to become dependent on one for, one will of course have done more, overall, than merely to allow it to die.

Let us, therefore, alter the analogy once more. Suppose the fish was hatched in
one's own aquarium, in water one has always supplied. If one now removes the fish
from the water one has supplied, it seems, intuitively, that one will have killed the fish.
But how is this different from a pregnant woman's removing the fetus from the life-
sustaining environment that she has so far provided since it began to exist? If the one
act counts as killing, surely the other must as well.

What makes this challenge so forceful is that the act of removing a fish from
one's own aquarium falls in the gray area, mentioned earlier, that is a product of
vagueness in our notion of providing life-sustaining aid or support. If removing the
fish seems to be an instance of killing, that may be because we do not see one's providing it with water as a case of providing continuous life-supporting aid—for much
the same reason, perhaps, that we do not think of a man who has a pond on his property as providing life support for the fish that inhabit it.

Alternatively, perhaps we are misled into believing that to remove the fish is to kill
it by the fact that removing it involves *doing* something *to it* that results in its death.
That, as we have seen, is not sufficient to make an act an instance of killing, but it
may affect our intuitions nonetheless. If, instead of removing the fish from the tank,
one were simply not to replenish the water, so that it would evaporate, leaving the fish
in exactly the state it would be in if it had been taken out, most people would regard
this as letting the fish die. The difference between removing the fish and not replen-
ishing the water is just the difference between doing something and not doing something. But that difference, in this kind of case, does not make the difference between
killing and letting die. If I have been keeping someone alive by allowing him to use
my life-support machine, I will let him die (rather than kill him) if I terminate my
support, and this is so whether I actively disconnect him from the machine or simply
fail to recharge the machine's battery. (The claim that I merely let him die assumes,
of course, that other things are equal—for example, that my allowing him the use of
my machine has not caused him to forfeit access to alternative sources of support .)

It seems, therefore, that it is not unreasonable to conclude that to remove a fish
from one's own aquarium is in fact to let it die—though, because removing it is an
act that results in its death, we are strongly inclined to believe that it counts as killing.
It is well to recall, however, that this case lies in a rather murky gray area; for it is not
obvious that one's provision of an aqueous environment for the fish counts as sus-

taining its life. There is less room for doubt, I think, that a woman who bears a fetus in her womb is sustaining its life by supplying it with oxygen, nutrition, and so on. Thus the principal source of uncertainty about the classification of the act of removing the fish from the water arises with considerably less force, if it arises at all, in the classification of a merely extractive abortion as an instance of letting die.

None of the five objections to the claim that a merely extractive abortion allows the fetus to die seems to succeed. I will therefore assume that the claim is correct. It is, I believe, well supported by the analysis I gave earlier of what it is to allow someone to die. The next question, then, is what the significance of this claim is. Among other things, it establishes parallelism, in this one respect, between disconnecting the violinist and having a merely extractive abortion. The parallel is presumptively significant, since it is widely accepted that to let someone die is, in general and if other things are equal, less seriously objectionable than to kill someone. We should therefore expect that a merely extractive abortion would be less objectionable than an otherwise comparable abortion performed by one of the traditional methods that involve killing. Surprisingly, however, there does not seem to be an intuitively detectable difference between a merely extractive abortion and an abortion that directly kills the fetus (unless, of course, the latter would cause the fetus pain while the former would not—a merely contingent difference that I will assume, for simplicity, does not arise). It is doubtful that anyone who opposes abortion on moral grounds would even find it an improvement if all abortions began to be performed by merely extractive methods.

Why is this—that is, why does it seem not to matter morally whether an abortion kills the fetus or merely allows it to die? One explanation, which I believe has considerable plausibility, is that the distinction between killing and letting die derives its significance from the requirement of respect for persons. In those instances in which an act of killing is more seriously objectionable than an otherwise comparable act of allowing someone to die, this is because killing, but not letting die, involves a particular kind of failure of respect for the victim. If that is so, the distinction should lack significance in cases in which the victim of an act of killing or letting die falls below the threshold of respect. It may well be, therefore, that the reason we do not find that a merely extractive abortion would be less objectionable than an abortion by a method that kills the fetus is that we implicitly recognize that the fetus is below the threshold of respect. It may be that our sense that letting a fetus die is no less objectionable than killing it reflects our intuitive sense of the lesser status of the fetus. Because it is not the kind of entity that commands respect, it is no worse to kill it than it is to let it die. The outcome is the same and, since considerations of respect do not arise, that is all that matters.

Those who are skeptical of the significance of the distinction between killing and letting die have pressed for an explanation of why killing is supposedly more seriously objectionable, and their challenge has been notoriously difficult to answer.[116] If it is right that the significance of the distinction is connected to the requirement of respect for persons, the skeptical question is why we should suppose that killing involves a different and graver violation of the requirement of respect, or why killing constitutes a more serious offense against the worth of persons. One possibility, which I suggested earlier in section 3.3 of chapter 3, is that what counts as respect for a person and, correspondingly, what counts as an egregious failure of respect may in some instances be conventionally determined. If it is universally accepted that, in general, killing a person involves a failure of respect that is not necessarily involved in letting a person die, that by itself may be sufficient to make killing a more serious offense against the requirement of respect than letting a person die. For it may be a sufficient indication of disrespect if a person does what he and others *believe* to involve a failure of respect. Consider, for the sake of comparison, the more familiar, non-Kantian notion of respect. It is important to show people respect in this sense when it is merited, and one's reason to do so may have nothing to do with social convention; but the ways in which one is required to act—the signs and tokens of respect that one is required to show—are in some instances determined by convention. Similarly, the Kantian requirement of respect for persons does not have its basis in convention, but the manifestations of respect and disrespect may in some instances be shaped by convention, or by what we all believe that others owe us.

If this is right, the various debunking explanations of our intuitive conviction that killing is worse than letting die could be true, and yet it could also be true that killing *does* in general involve a failure of respect that is not involved in allowing someone to die. We might have come to believe that killing is worse than letting die for a variety of reasons that have nothing to do with the truth of the belief. Thus, for example, the distinction between killing and letting die is, in most cases, an instance of the more general distinction between harming and failing to prevent harm; and the belief that harming someone is worse than failing to save someone from harm might be the product of a convention that has evolved as a tacit compromise between the insistence of the powerful on a norm of nonintervention and the insistence of the weak on a norm of mutual aid.[117] If so, our belief that killing is worse than letting die is, in the first instance, a product of our conditioned or learned acceptance of norms that are necessary for social stability. Yet once we all believe that killing is a different and graver kind of wrong from letting someone die, our believing it may make it so; for it seems incompatible with respect for a person to do to him what he and others believe to be a particularly egregious offense against his worth as a person.

This suggestion is highly speculative; and, even if it is plausible, it cannot be more than a part of the full explanation of why killing is, in general, more seriously objectionable than letting die. The significance of the distinction is not, I believe, entirely conventional. Even the suggestion that the distinction lacks significance when the victim of an act of killing or letting die is below the threshold of respect is controversial. One way to test this suggestion is to compare cases of killing and letting die in which the victim is an animal. Such a test would, however, be no more reliable than our intuitions, which suffer from a notable speciesist bias. It would, for example, prove nothing if we judged that killing animals is not worse than letting them die because killing them is hardly objectionable at all. (It is, perhaps, worth mentioning one possible counterexample. Most pet owners, if they felt that their pet's life had ceased to be worth living, would greatly prefer for the animal to die naturally than to have it euthanized. They would feel guilty about killing the pet, or having it killed, but not about merely allowing it to die. Of course, if the pet's suffering is great, most pet owners overcome their reluctance to be the agent of their pet's death. But most would be greatly relieved if the pet were to die naturally en route to the veterinarian's office.

This seems to be an instance in which people believe that there is something objectionable about killing an animal that does not apply to letting it die. Perhaps it is that beliefs about the wrongness of killing that are normally restricted to the killing of persons become engaged in this kind of case because the special relation between the owner and the pet gives the pet something like the status of a person in the eyes of the owner. Note, moreover, that there is here a curious inversion of the significance normally attributed to the distinction between doing and allowing. The pet owner believes that it would be better for the animal to die, but is reluctant actively to do what would bring about that outcome. This suggests the influence of a taboo mentality about killing—one that severs the significance of the distinction between killing and letting die from its roots in the distinction between doing harm and allowing harm to occur. I will discuss this feature of common attitudes to euthanasia—both in the case of animals and human beings—in chapter 5.)

If the distinction between killing and letting die has significance only within the morality of respect, and if the fetus is outside the scope of the morality of respect, this would imply that, if it is permissible to let the fetus die, it is also permissible to kill it. That would explain why there is no intuitive difference between an abortion that kills the fetus and a merely extractive abortion. For the moment, however, we are trying to screen out any intuitive sense that the fetus has a moral status different from that of a person. So we must not try to determine whether the distinction between killing and letting die is relevant to the morality of abortion by exploring our intuitions about abortion itself. We must instead follow Thomson by exploring analogous cases in which the individual who is killed or allowed to die is unambiguously a person, or an individual with full moral status.

Return to the case of the Involuntary Benefactor. Suppose that, if the woman is disconnected while the violinist's body is still drawing support from hers, her kidneys will be damaged. In order for her to be disconnected unharmed, the violinist must be killed before being disconnected. This procedure, in which the violinist is first killed and then disconnected, corresponds to an abortion by one of the traditional methods. Disconnecting the violinist without killing him corresponds to a merely extractive abortion: both merely let someone die but both involve a significant cost to the agent (kidney damage in the one case, abdominal surgery in the other). Some commentators on Thomson's argument have suggested that, if it would be permissible to let the violinist die, it should also be permissible to kill him if two further conditions are satisfied: (1) it would not be worse for the violinist to be killed than to be allowed to die, and (2) the cost to the agent of letting the violinist die would be significantly higher than the cost of killing him.[118] In the case as I have just presented it, both these conditions are met (the first because the violinist is unconscious). Even if killing the violinist would violate a requirement of respect, this may be outweighed by considerations 1 and 2.

This may seem intuitively compelling. If so, it suggests that, if a merely extractive abortion would be permissible, so would an abortion that kills the fetus, provided that killing the fetus would not cause it more pain than merely allowing it to die. The problem, of course, is that the case of the violinist still suffers from certain failures of analogy that may be relevant—in particular, the woman is not responsible for the violinist's need for aid and she is not his biological parent.

We have explored the significance of each of the three respects in which the original case of the Involuntary Benefactor differs from a case of unwanted pregnancy. But we have examined each factor on its own. We should not ignore the possibility that, in combination, these factors may have a significance that could not be extrapolated or predicted from the significance that each has in isolation. Is there a case in which the various potentially significant features of an unwanted pregnancy are combined, but in which the dependent individual is not a fetus but is uncontentiously and unambiguously a person, an individual with full moral status?

9.5. *The Dependent Child Case*

As the literature on Thomson's case of the Involuntary Benefactor abundantly attests, it is difficult to devise an analogue of unwanted pregnancy that combines all the potentially relevant features, does not introduce significant features that are not present in pregnancy, and is sufficiently realistic to engage our intuitions. It is, nevertheless, worth trying. The following example offers, I believe, a revealing test of our intuitions:

> *The Dependent Child.* A woman has a condition that will cause any child she conceives to have a defect that manifests itself only during the child's fourth year of life and that is rapidly fatal unless the child receives life-supporting aid by being connected to the mother's body for a certain period. For reasons of tissue compatibility, no one else's body will do: it has to be the mother. As a consequence, this woman and her sexual partner are highly scrupulous in their use of contraception. But, despite their precautions, she becomes pregnant. In her society, abortion is not a possibility; however, a couple are found who are willing to adopt the infant when it is born, despite their knowledge of its condition. The adoption procedure legally absolves the biological mother of all responsibility for the child. The adoptive parents take the child immediately after birth and nurture it for a little over three years, when it becomes seriously ill. Its condition deteriorates rapidly. When it lapses into a coma, the adoptive parents approach the biological mother with a plea to allow herself to be hooked up to the child in order to save its life. The burden to her of doing so would be roughly comparable to the burden of being pregnant. As with the burden of pregnancy, there is uncertainty about how severe the effects would be (for example, it is uncertain how long she would need to be hooked up, whether she could be disconnected at intervals, whether there would be any lasting physical effects, and so on).[119]

In this case, it is certain that, if the woman has a child, it will be dependent upon her aid for its survival. This parallels the inevitable dependency of a fetus on the woman who is pregnant with it. The child exists as a result of the woman's having voluntarily engaged in sexual intercourse, knowing that there was a risk of pregnancy. This parallels a common cause of unwanted pregnancy. It also makes the woman partially responsible for the child's need for her aid. But as in the case of pregnancy as a result of voluntary sex, the act by which the woman caused the child to exist and to need her aid was entirely permissible and will not have been bad for the child even if she fails to aid it, so that it dies. For it is not bad to exist for only a comparatively short time, provided that one's life is worth living while it lasts. Because the woman is responsible for the child's need for aid, the Dependent Child case is more closely analogous in this respect to most cases of pregnancy than Involuntary Benefactor is. (One can, of course, consider variants of the case in which the woman becomes pregnant for different reasons.)

In the Dependent Child case, the potential benefactor is the biological mother of the child. So in this respect as well the Dependent Child case is more closely analogous to an unwanted pregnancy than the Involuntary Benefactor case is. Furthermore, because abortion is not possible and the child is given up for adoption immediately after birth, the biological mother cannot be said to have consented to be responsible for the child; nor does she have any personal relation with it. Thus two possible bases for parental responsibilities are entirely absent, just as they are in the relation that a pregnant woman bears to the fetus she carries.

Finally, the dependent individual—the one who requires aid in order to survive— is not a fetus but a child: a three-year-old child who uncontroversially has the moral status of a person.

We should distinguish two relevant questions about this case. One is whether the woman has a *special moral reason* to aid the child—a reason that someone who is in no way related to the child would not have. The other is whether it is morally *obligatory,* all things considered, for the woman to aid the child by allowing herself to be connected to him. The answers to the two questions may be different. It is possible that the woman could have a special reason to aid the child but that the reason would not be decisive in the circumstances. There might be countervailing considerations, such as the great personal cost of aiding the child, that would make it permissible for her to refuse to provide the necessary aid.

Most people, on considering this case, believe that the biological mother would have a special moral reason to aid the dependent child. This is significant, for it suggests that, if the case is relevantly analogous to an unwanted pregnancy, a pregnant woman must also have a special moral reason to provide support for her fetus. Defenders of abortion will, therefore, wish to find failures of analogy between the Dependent Child case and the case of unwanted pregnancy. And there are indeed several significant differences. In each instance, however, the difference suggests that, if the mother in the Dependent Child case has a special reason to aid the child, then a pregnant woman should have an *even stronger* special reason to support her fetus.

The relevant differences between the Dependent Child case and an unwanted pregnancy are, in other words, significant in exactly the opposite way from the differences between the case of the Involuntary Benefactor and an unwanted pregnancy. In the Involuntary Benefactor, we judge that the woman has no special moral reason to aid the violinist and that it is permissible for her to withdraw her support for him. But the differences between this case and an unwanted pregnancy prevent us from being able to infer that a pregnant woman also has no special reason to aid the fetus or that it would be permissible for her to withdraw her support for it. In the Dependent Child case, by contrast, we judge that the woman does have a special moral reason to aid the child. And the relevant differences between this case and an unwanted pregnancy, rather than blocking our ability to extrapolate our judgment from the one case to the other, suggest that the judgment that there is a special reason to provide aid in the one case is even more likely to be true in the other.

Let us consider each of the relevant differences in turn. In the Dependent Child case, if the biological mother refuses to aid the child, she does so by simply not getting hooked up to him. This is a clear instance of letting die. In a case of pregnancy, if the woman refuses to aid the fetus, she must either have a merely extractive abortion or an abortion by one of the traditional methods. I have contended that, if she has a merely extractive abortion, she thereby lets the fetus die. But even if actively withdrawing aid-in-progress counts as letting die, some people believe that it is more difficult to justify, other things being equal, than simply failing to offer aid in the first place. If a woman has an abortion by one of the traditional methods, she thereby kills the fetus; and in general killing is more difficult to justify than letting die. If, therefore, the woman in the Dependent Child case has a special reason to support the child when the alternative is simply not to aid him, it seems that the case for thinking that a pregnant woman has a special reason to aid her fetus must be *at least* as strong, if other things are equal. For the alternative to supporting the fetus is either actively to withdraw its life support or to kill it, and each of these is at least as difficult to justify as simply failing to provide support.

To see this, we might imagine a variant of the Dependent Child case in which the alternatives to supporting the child are similar to the alternatives to supporting a fetus. Suppose that the adoptive parents have, in desperation, kidnapped the biological mother and hooked her up to the child while she was unconscious. Suppose that, as in the variant of the Involuntary Benefactor we considered earlier, the mother's kidneys will be damaged if she disconnects herself without first killing the unconscious child. In this variant, her alternatives to supporting the child are to allow him to die by withdrawing her support for him, though at a significant cost to herself, and to kill the child in order to disconnect herself at minimal personal cost. These options are analogous to a merely extractive abortion and a traditional abortion, respectively. It seems clear that, if the biological mother in the original Dependent Child case has a special reason to *become* hooked up to the child, she should have at least as strong a reason to *stay* hooked up in the variant.

I have found, in fact, that when I present these two versions of the Dependent Child case to students, most of those who believe that it is permissible, in the original version, for the woman not to get hooked up to the child also believe that, in the alternative version, it is *not* permissible for her to kill the child in order to disconnect herself at minimal cost. This is important because it suggests that the distinction between killing and letting die has intuitive significance in this context—which makes it all the more interesting that it does not seem to have significance in the context of abortion.

Why have two versions of the case? Why not just present the version that is more closely analogous to pregnancy and abortion? The answer is that in the second version the woman is forcibly hooked up to the child, and this introduces into the case a complication that has no parallel in the ordinary case of pregnancy and that might therefore distort our intuitive response.

Turn now to the second relevant difference. In the Dependent Child case, the woman is responsible for the fact that the child exists and needs her aid—responsible in the sense that the cause of the child's existing in a dependent state was an act she did voluntarily as a responsible agent. Similarly, in most instances of unwanted pregnancy, the pregnant woman is responsible in the same way for the fact that the fetus exists in a dependent state. As we noted, however, the act by which the woman caused the fetus to need her aid will not have been bad for the fetus even if she fails to aid it. I argued that her act will have been neither bad nor good for the fetus because the life it has in utero is neutral in value. The Dependent Child case is arguably different in this respect. In that case, it is plausible to suppose that the child's life has been worth living. If so, it is arguable that the act by which the woman caused the child to need her aid will have been *good* for him even if she fails to provide the aid. (It is, as I noted earlier, controversial whether it can be good or bad for a person to be caused to exist. If it cannot, there is no failure of analogy of the sort I am discussing. For the sake of argument, therefore, let us assume that to cause a person to exist can be good or bad for that person.) The upshot is this. Suppose we believe that the woman in the Dependent Child case has a special reason to aid the child even though the act by which she caused him to need her aid will have been good for him even if she does not provide the aid. *If* her responsibility is part of the explanation of why she has this special reason, and if the cases are otherwise relevantly analogous, then a pregnant woman should have at least as strong a special reason to aid her fetus. For if an act that was *good* for an individual can ground a special reason to aid that individual, surely an act that was otherwise similar but was merely *not bad* for an individual can also ground such a reason.

The third difference between the two cases is that the biological mother in the Dependent Child case has already provided considerable aid to the child by carrying him the full term of pregnancy, whereas a woman considering abortion has normally supported the fetus for only a short time and at relatively little personal cost. The fact that the woman in the Dependent Child case has already done so much may seem to diminish the strength of her reason to do even more. Therefore, if this woman nevertheless has a special reason to aid the child, we should expect that a pregnant woman would have a special reason to support her fetus that would be at least equally strong, assuming that her situation is relevantly analogous except that she has done less in the past to help the one who now needs her aid.

If the woman in the Dependent Child case has a special reason to aid the child, what is its source? Earlier, in section 9.2, I expressed skepticism about whether one's responsibility for a person's need for aid could ground a special reason to provide that aid unless the act by which one caused the need for aid would be worse, or bad, for the person if one did not provide the aid. In the Dependent Child case, however, it seems intuitively that the biological mother does have a special reason to aid the child even though, if she does not, she will not have harmed the child by doing what caused it to need her aid. Is there any reason to think that her responsibility for its need for aid is nevertheless part of the basis of her special reason? I believe there is. If we vary the circumstances in which her pregnancy arose, I believe we will find that, intuitively, the strength of her special reason to aid the child varies with the degree of her responsibility for its need for aid. In the case as I stated it, her pregnancy arose from voluntary intercourse. If we change that feature and instead make the pregnancy a result of rape, so that the woman bears no responsibility for the child's need for aid, I think most of us will agree that her reason to aid the child is appreciably weaker. It is, perhaps, puzzling that an act (engaging in sexual intercourse) that was not wrong or impermissible and that will not, whatever happens, have been bad for the child—it is puzzling that such an act could give the woman a special reason to make a further and significant sacrifice of her well-being for the sake of the child. But I think that most of us find, intuitively, that the act does engender such a reason.

That the woman is the biological parent of the child also seems significant. This will be especially evident to those who found a basis for a special reason to provide aid in the case of the Sperm Donor. Many people, of course, hold that parental responsibilities must be voluntarily assumed; thus there can be no basis for parental responsibility in this case. But while it is true that the biological mother has done everything possible to avoid or renounce parental responsibilities, I argued earlier that there are bases of parental responsibility that are nonvoluntary. Nevertheless, it might be argued that, even if there are nonvoluntary bases of parental responsibility, the mother in the Dependent Child case has transferred to the adoptive parents whatever responsibilities she may have nonvoluntarily acquired. For that is what adoption involves: the transfer to the adoptive parents of all of the natural parents' rights and responsibilities regarding the child.

In a general way, this is of course true. But when we descend to particulars, there is a complication. In the Dependent Child case, there is one possible responsibility that the adoptive parents cannot possibly fulfill: the provision of life support to the child during its fourth year. Thus, if the biological mother had a special reason to aid the child, she still has it when the child comes to need her aid; for she cannot transfer to someone else a responsibility that no one else can fulfill. A child's natural parents cannot, for example, transfer their duty to feed their child to another couple who cannot afford to feed it. It seems, therefore, that the fact that the child was successfully given up for adoption does not release the biological mother from any responsibility she might have nonvoluntarily acquired to aid her child and that only she can fulfill.

It seems, in short, that the biological mother in the Dependent Child case has a special reason to aid the child and that among the sources of this reason are her responsibility for the child's need for aid and the fact that she is his biological parent. Given the very close parallels between this woman's situation and that of a woman who is pregnant as a result of voluntary intercourse, this conclusion strongly suggests that the pregnant woman, too, has a special reason to support her fetus—assuming, of course, that the fetus has full moral status. While there are several significant failures of analogy between the two cases, the differences tend to strengthen rather than weaken the case for thinking that the pregnant woman has a special reason to support the fetus.

The question remains, however, whether this reason is decisive. Does a woman who is pregnant as a result of voluntary intercourse have not just a special moral reason but an *obligation* to support the fetus? If we look to the Dependent Child case for guidance, we must ask whether the woman in that case is morally *required* to aid the child (which, of course, is not the same as asking whether she can permissibly be compelled to aid him). It seems that there is unlikely to be intuitive agreement about this, which suggests that it is a matter about which people may reasonably disagree.

The central components of the case for saying that it is permissible for the biological mother *not* to aid the child are: that she took all reasonable precautions against becoming pregnant, the cost to her of being certain to avoid becoming pregnant (that is, abstaining from sex) was too high to be demanded of her, she therefore acted permissibly in having sex in the circumstances, she has renounced or transferred her parental responsibilities to the maximum degree possible, she has previously supported the child at considerable cost to herself, and aiding the child would be enormously and invasively burdensome to her.

The main elements of the case for claiming that she is obligated to aid the child are: that, knowing that there was a risk that she would become pregnant with a child who would later need her aid to survive, she nevertheless voluntarily and for her own benefit engaged in sex, she is the child's biological mother, and the harm that the child will suffer if she does not aid it greatly exceeds the likely cost to her of aiding it.

In weighing up these various considerations, some people may reasonably give greater weight to certain considerations than others do. Frances Kamm, for example, in discussing pregnancy in general, contends that the cost to a woman of abstaining altogether from sexual intercourse is too high for her to be required to abstain in order to avoid causing a fetus to exist. But if she is not required to avoid the act that might cause a fetus to exist, then (provided she takes all reasonable precautions, such as practicing contraception) she cannot be held liable to accept the high cost of supporting the fetus on the ground that she has done the act.[120] This claim applies equally to the Dependent Child case. Others may, however, emphasize instead the fact that the woman is this child's *mother.* How can she, they might ask, stand by and let *her own child* die?

It is important to recall the relevance of the various respects in which the Dependent Child case differs from an ordinary case of pregnancy resulting from voluntary intercourse. If it is not unreasonable to suppose that the woman in the Dependent Child case is obligated to aid the child, it is even more likely to be true that a woman who is pregnant as a result of voluntary intercourse is obligated to support her fetus. For—to note only one of the relevant differences—the alternative to aiding the child is simply not to aid it; but the alternative to supporting a fetus is normally (that is, as abortions are actually performed) to *kill* it. Thus, in the variant of the Dependent Child case in which the woman becomes hooked up to the child, many people intuitively find that it is *not* permissible for her to kill her own child in order to avoid the burden of helping him. Our intuitions are, admittedly, swayed by the fact that it is a *child* she might kill. But it is supposed to be a virtue of the Thomson argument that its support for abortion does not depend on controversial assumptions about the status of the fetus. Thus it is a virtue of the Dependent Child case that it makes us vividly aware that the dependent individual is a *child.*

One critical source of reluctance to accept that the biological mother is morally required to aid the child, or that a woman is required to support her fetus, is that the personal cost to her of doing so is very high. If, in either case, the cost were significantly lower, we would, I think, be strongly inclined to accept that the woman ought, all things considered, to support her biological offspring (assuming, of course, that we also accept that the fetus has full moral status). It is therefore important to note that, in the Dependent Child case and in most cases of pregnancy as well, the bases of the woman's special reason to provide aid apply at least equally to her sexual partner. He is equally responsible for the child or fetus's need for aid and is also the child or fetus's biological parent. Anyone who takes the Thomson argument seriously must therefore accept that whatever sacrifices must be made must be shared equally between both responsible parents. Since the man cannot directly aid either the child or fetus, he must, as I observed earlier, do his share by somehow compensating the woman. If we assume that he would comply, or could permissibly be compelled to do so if the woman does her part, that should reduce the overall burden on the woman roughly by half. And that should, as I noted, diminish our reluctance to accept that she is required to provide the necessary aid.

The conclusion I believe we should draw from all this is that it is doubtful that the Thomson argument offers an adequate defense of abortion on its own. The Dependent Child case is more closely analogous, in the relevant respects, to an unwanted pregnancy than the case of the Involuntary Benefactor is. And in the Dependent Child case, it is not implausible to believe that the biological mother ought, all things considered, to aid her child, even at considerable cost to herself. While the considerations that the Thomson argument stresses may well suggest that abortion is permissible in cases in which there is no responsibility for the fetus's need for aid, or in cases in which the cost of supporting the fetus is abnormally high, they are less persuasive in cases in which pregnancy is the result of voluntary sex, and particularly when the alternative to supporting the fetus is to kill it. For, again, it is hard to believe that it is permissible to kill one's own child in order to avoid the burden of providing the aid one has caused it to need.

This conclusion, however, is premised on the assumption that the fetus has the same moral status that you and I have—an assumption of which the Dependent Child case is intended to make us vividly aware. I have argued at length that this assumption is indefensible. If that is right, the considerations that favor aiding the fetus are substantially weaker than we have been assuming in this discussion of the Thomson argument. If the fetus is not a person and the reason to sustain its life is, in the first instance, commensurate only with the strength of its time-relative interest in continuing to live, that reason is comparatively weak. Thus even if the pregnant woman's reason to support the fetus is magnified both by her responsibility for its need for aid and by the special way in which she is related to it, it remains relatively weak. It is readily outweighed by the considerations to which the Thomson argument draws our attention, such as that we are not normally morally required to make great sacrifices, particularly of our bodily integrity, in order to help another. In short, even if the Thomson argument does not provide an adequate defense of abortion on its own, it can be combined with the argument I have advanced; and the two arguments together seem wholly decisive.

10. ABORTION AND SELF-DEFENSE

10.1. Self-Defense against a Nonresponsible Threat

In this section, I will consider whether abortion may be justified by appealing to a woman's right of self-defense. I will assume, for the sake of argument, that my previous claims about the nature and status of the fetus are mistaken. I will assume that, from conception on, the fetus has the same moral status that you and I have. I will assume that it is a person, that its worth is equal to our own, and that it is therefore above the threshold of respect and comes within the scope of the morality of respect—or, alternatively, that it has a right to life equal to yours or mine.

It is often claimed that abortion may be justified as an exercise of a woman's right to defend herself against the threat posed by the fetus.[121] Call this the *self-defense argument* for abortion. An immediate problem with this argument is that its scope may be extremely limited. For abortion normally involves *killing,* and it seems clear that killing in self-defense is justified only in response to a limited range of serious threats—for example, when a person is threatened with being killed, tortured, raped, or kidnapped. One is not permitted to kill in response to lesser threats, even if the person who poses the threat satisfies all the other standard conditions for liability to self-defensive violence: for example, he intends the threatened harm, his action is unjustified, he is fully culpable, and so on. If, for example, someone maliciously threatens to give me a hard pinch and the only way I can prevent him from doing so is to kill him, I must submit to being pinched. For to kill my assailant would be to violate the requirement of proportionality, which holds that the amount of harm one inflicts in self-defense must not be disproportionate to the harm one thereby averts. (This is not a simple requirement that the amount of harm caused must not exceed the amount averted, taking probabilities into account. Whether a defensive harm is proportionate may depend on various considerations, such as whether the individual who poses the initial threat is morally innocent. I will return to this shortly.) It may seem, therefore, that the appeal to the pregnant woman's right of self-defense cannot provide a justification for abortion except, perhaps, in cases in which the continuation of the pregnancy poses a serious threat to the woman's life or, possibly, to her health.

This conclusion seems, however, to ignore the nature of pregnancy. Pregnancy, of course, is often desperately sought and greatly welcomed when it occurs. But when it is unwanted, it can plausibly be regarded as a form of *bodily invasion.* In these respects, it is like the act of sex itself. And, in some respects, pregnancy is even more invasive than rape. Another individual's entire body becomes lodged within the pregnant woman's body and draws sustenance from it. And, unlike rape, the invasive process continues for nine months unless it is forcibly arrested. If, therefore, the threat to bodily integrity from rape is sufficiently serious to warrant a lethal defensive response, it seems that the more deeply invasive and enduring threat from pregnancy should be as well.

This raises another problem. If we assume that the threatening feature of an unwanted pregnancy is bodily invasion itself, then it may seem that abortion cannot be regarded as an act of *defense,* strictly speaking. Consider the analogous case of national self-defense. When an invasion by an aggressor is imminent or in progress, defense is possible. But once an invasion has been successfully completed and the invaded country is under foreign occupation, defense is no longer possible. The conquered people may, of course, continue to fight against the invaders, but their aim is no longer defense but liberation or recovery of rights that have been lost. Similarly, it might be argued, once pregnancy has begun, the bodily invasion is a fait accompli and self-defense is not longer possible. Abortion must be regarded as an act that frees a woman from a burden that has already been unjustly imposed (as Thomson's argument contends) rather than an act of self-defense.

Although this objection is more than merely pedantic, it does not undermine the self-defense argument. It seems that the moral considerations that justify self-defense should also, if other things are equal, justify action to recover that which has been lost when justified self-defense has failed. So, for example, if one would be justified in knocking down a pickpocket to prevent his seizing one's purse, it seems that one would be equally justified, and for the same reasons, in knocking him down to recover one's purse if he has just seized it by force. So even if an abortion is not literally defensive in the way that acts that attempt to avert imminent harms are, it may nevertheless come within the scope of the principles that govern the morality of self-defense.

I will, in any case, avoid this problem by focusing my discussion on the case in which the continuation of a pregnancy threatens the pregnant woman's life. Call this the *Extreme Case*. In the Extreme Case, the self-defense argument need not presuppose that an unwanted pregnancy itself constitutes a form of bodily invasion. It can instead appeal to a woman's right to defend herself from the lethal threat posed by the fetus's continued presence in her body. Because the harm is imminent rather than already realized or ongoing, it is conceptually unproblematic to regard an abortion in the Extreme Case as an act of defense. But the real reason for focusing on this case is that this is the case in which the self-defense argument should be strongest. I will argue, however, that it has doubtful cogency even in this case. If that is correct, we can safely ignore the self-defense argument altogether. For, if it fails in the Extreme Case, in which the pregnant woman's life is at risk, it is almost certain to fail in cases in which the relevant harm is not death but the bodily invasion involved in unwanted pregnancy.

It is obvious that, even in the Extreme Case, an abortion is far from being a paradigm instance of an act of self-defense. Perhaps the most salient difference is that virtually all intentionally induced abortions are carried out not by the pregnant woman herself but by a physician. Assuming that the abortion defends the woman against a threat, it is an act of *other-defense* rather than self-defense. Although this may seem unimportant, it is actually of considerable significance. I will return to this feature of abortion later. For the moment let us focus on the fact that the fetus is quite anomalous as an attacker. In the paradigm case of self-defensive action, the individual who poses the initial threat (1) poses the threat through his present action, (2) intends the threat he poses, (3) acts in a way that is morally unjustified, and, because (4) he is a morally responsible agent and (5) there is no excuse that exculpates him, (6) he is morally culpable for posing the threat. The fetus, by contrast, cannot be characterized in any of these ways. The fetus has no intentions, does not act, and indeed is not an agent at all. It is not morally responsible for the threat it poses and therefore cannot be culpable. Do these differences between the fetus and a typical attacker have any moral significance? The answer depends on whether the characteristics I have listed figure importantly in the justification for self-defense in the paradigm case.

I believe that several of these characteristics are critical to the justification for self-defense in the paradigm case. Before I attempt to defend that claim, it will be useful to draw some relevant distinctions. I have noted that the fetus is not an agent and therefore does not pose an active threat. An individual who poses an initial threat to another through his action is, I will say, an *Attacker*. (As I use it, this is a technical term, in that an Attacker may pose a threat inadvertently or accidentally. In ordinary use, an "attack" must be intentional.) An individual who poses a passive threat—that is, a threat that derives not from his action but from his mere existence or presence or from the movement of his body—is a *Threat*. An individual who is threatened by an Attacker or a Threat is a *Victim*. (I will, in general, use masculine pronouns to refer to Attackers and feminine pronouns to refer to Victims. This reads quite naturally given that, in those actual situations in which self- or other-defense is possible, the overwhelming majority of Attackers are male.)

An individual who poses a threat to another and is morally at fault for doing so—because he has neither justification nor excuse—is a *Culpable Attacker* or a *Culpable Threat*. By contrast, an individual who poses an unjustified threat to another but is not morally at fault or blamable for doing so is an *Innocent Attacker* or an *Innocent Threat*. An individual who justifiably poses a threat that, if realized, would nevertheless wrong the Victim is a *Justified Attacker* or a *Justified Threat*. Finally, an individual who justifiably poses a threat that would not wrong its Victim is a *Just Attacker* or a *Just Threat*. I include Justified and Just Attackers and Threats merely for the sake of completeness: they will not figure in the subsequent discussion.

Innocent Attackers and Innocent Threats threaten without justification, but are nevertheless morally innocent because they have an excuse. There are three commonly recognized forms of excuse: nonculpable ignorance, duress, and diminished responsibility. The last of these is sufficiently important, for reasons I will explain presently, to warrant a further distinction. An Attacker who is innocent because he is not morally responsible for his conduct is a *Nonresponsible Attacker*. Examples include individuals who are insane, mentally underdeveloped or impaired (for example, young children and individuals who are severely retarded or demented), and (in science fiction) individuals subject to deep hypnosis or mind control. Similarly, a Threat who is not morally responsible for the fact that he poses a threat is a *Nonresponsible Threat*. Examples include the Nonresponsible Projectile (someone whose body has been hurled, by forces beyond his control, at another), the occupants of a lifeboat that contains too many people to remain afloat, and a fetus growing inside a woman's body.

Although Nonresponsible Attackers and Threats are, according to the definitions I have given, Innocent Attackers or Threats, their moral status is, as I will argue, different from that of other Innocent Attackers and Threats. Because of this, it will be useful, for the sake of clarity, to treat Nonresponsible Attackers and Threats as belonging to entirely separate categories. Hence for the remainder of this section on self-defense, when I refer to Innocent Attackers and Threats, I will mean to exclude Nonresponsible Attackers and Threats. When I use the label "innocent" to describe an Attacker or Threat, I will mean that to imply that he is a morally responsible agent.

Return now to the paradigm case of justified self-defense, in which a Culpable Attacker poses a threat to an Innocent Victim. There are, I believe, several facts about the Attacker that contribute importantly to the justification for engaging in self-defensive action against him. These are that the threat he poses is unjustified, that he is a morally responsible agent, and that there are no conditions that excuse his conduct. These are the three conditions that make him a *Culpable* Attacker. And it is precisely his culpability that justifies the use of violence against him. For in cases in which a person's culpable action has made it inevitable that someone must suffer harm, it is normally permissible, *as a matter of justice,* to ensure that the culpable person himself suffers the costs of his own wrongful action rather than to allow those costs to be imposed on the innocent. And at least part of the reason why justice demands that the culpable person should suffer the costs of his own wrongdoing is that he has had the opportunity to avoid those costs (by refraining from engaging in the wrongful action) but refused to accept it, whereas the Innocent Victim has had no choice at all.

I call this understanding of the moral foundations of self-defense the *Justice-Based Account* of the right of self-defense.[122] It treats the morality of self-defense as a matter of justice in the distribution of harm. It is important to note that, although the account holds that it is a person's culpability that makes him liable to self-defensive violence, it is not the person's culpability in general that does this but only his culpability in bringing about conditions in which someone must be harmed. Thus one may not normally harm a culpable person, even in self-preservation, if his culpability is unrelated to the threat to oneself. For, *relative to that threat,* the culpable person is an Innocent Bystander. His culpability engenders liability only to those harms that are necessary to prevent his culpable action from harming the innocent.

According to the Justice-Based Account, it is the Culpable Attacker's moral culpability that establishes a strong moral asymmetry between him and his potential Victim, an asymmetry that makes it permissible, as a matter of justice, to ensure that he rather than the potential Victim suffers any harm necessitated by his culpable action. There can, however, be weaker asymmetries that do not involve culpability. Although culpability presupposes responsibility, there are two types of case in which there can be moral responsibility for a threat in the absence of culpability. First, a morally responsible individual may pose a threat to another by acting in a way that is unjustified or wrong and yet not be culpable for doing so because of the presence of some excusing condition. Consider, for example:

> *The Mistaken Attacker.* A notorious mass murderer who has thus far evaded capture has a little-known identical twin brother. On a lonely road in the middle of the night and during a terrible storm, the twin brother's car breaks down. Seeking shelter, the bedraggled twin knocks on the door of the nearest house. On opening the door, the resident, thinking that the murderer has come to kill him, panics and kills the twin before the latter even has time to speak and identify himself.

The resident certainly acts wrongly in killing the twin, who is entirely innocent. Yet he acted on the basis of the reasonable belief that the person he killed was a mass murderer who posed a lethal threat to him and his family. This excuse may be fully exculpating. If so, the resident is an Innocent Attacker. Yet it seems reasonable to believe that there is nevertheless a moral asymmetry between the Innocent Attacker and his Innocent Victim, which is that the resident is morally responsible for creating a situation in which someone must be harmed. Suppose that the only way the twin could have prevented himself from being killed was preemptively to kill the resident. Most people believe that it would have been morally acceptable for him to do so, despite the resident's moral innocence. The Justice-Based Account can, it seems, accommodate this intuition by claiming that the resident's responsibility for the fact that the twin faced a forced choice between his own life and that of the resident made it permissible, as a matter of justice, for the twin to kill the resident. For the resident acted freely and voluntarily in creating the situation of forced choice; he knew, or could have known if he had reflected, that there was a possibility of mistaken identity. Justice, therefore, seems to require that he rather than the twin should die; for it was his own voluntary action that has made it inevitable that one of them must die. The resident, in short, must take responsibility for the risks he himself voluntarily creates.

There is a further, even weaker moral asymmetry between Attacker and Victim that may nevertheless be sufficient to justify self-defensive killing as a matter of justice in the distribution of harm. Just as one can be at fault in the creation of a threat without being culpable (as in the case of the Mistaken Attacker), so one can be morally responsible for the creation of a threat without being in any way at fault. Here is an example:

> *The Inadvertent Attacker.* This driver always exercises reasonable caution in driving and in maintaining the safety of his vehicle. But on this occasion an improbable mechanical failure causes him to lose control both of the brakes and the steering. His vehicle veers out of control in the direction of a pedestrian.

The vehicle that this man is driving now poses a lethal threat to the pedestrian. But the driver is an Innocent Attacker. He is, moreover, not only not culpable for the threat he poses; he is not even at fault. His driving the vehicle was neither wrong nor in any way unjustified. Yet he *is* morally responsible for the threat he poses. He chose to drive knowing that there was a small risk that he would lose control of his vehicle and imperil the lives of others. This, I believe, constitutes a sufficient asymmetry between him and the pedestrian to make it permissible, as a matter of justice, for the pedestrian to kill him in self-defense, assuming that that is the only way the pedestrian can prevent herself from being killed.[123]

In summary, there are, according to the Justice-Based Account, three independent conditions for the permissibility of killing in self-defense. In order to state these conditions succinctly, I will define a couple of phrases. When a person makes it inevitable that someone must be harmed, but there is a subsequent possibility of choosing who the victim will be, I will say that the person creates a *forced choice* among harms. When the harm that is made inevitable is death, the person creates a *forced choice among lives.*[124] With these definitions as background, the three conditions may be stated as follows:

1. *Culpability:* the creation of a forced choice among lives in a way that is neither justified nor excused.
2. *Fault without culpability:* the creation of a forced choice among lives by a responsible individual in a way that is unjustified but excused.
3. *Responsibility without culpability or fault:* the creation of a forced choice among lives by a responsible individual who has not acted impermissibly.

Although each of these conditions may justify killing in self-defense, the justification is stronger in case 1 than in case 2, and stronger in case 2 than in case 3. What this means in practice is that the restrictions on killing in self-defense are weakest when the Attacker or Threat is culpable, stronger when he is at fault but not culpable, and strongest when he is responsible but neither culpable nor at fault.

The restrictions that may apply to the exercise of one's right of self-defense take various forms. I will describe several here, some of which are relevant to the problem of abortion, as I will note in the following section.

1. *Retreat.* In some instances, a potential Victim may be morally required to retreat from a confrontation with an Attacker or Threat, if she can do so in comparative safety, rather than exercise her right of self-defense.

2. *Division of the burden.* In many cases, either the Attacker or the Victim must suffer a serious harm. But in some cases there is a third alternative, which is for each to suffer a less serious harm. Call this third option "sharing the burden." In some cases the Victim may be required to share the burden with the Attacker rather than to impose the full burden on the Attacker. Another way of sharing the burden involves a trade-off between the degree of force employed and the probability of success. In some cases a Victim may be required to share the burden by using lesser force even if this entails a lower probability of successfully evading the threat.

3. *Proportionality.* The self-defensive response must be proportionate to the threatened harm. In order for self-defensive *killing* to be justified, the threat must, as I noted earlier, be of a certain level of gravity. This applies both to the nature of the threatened harm itself and to the probability of its occurrence in the absence of self-defensive killing. Proportionality may also restrict the number of Attackers or Threats that it is permissible to kill in self-defense.

4. *Third-party intervention.* In certain cases, a Victim's right of self-defense is sufficiently strong or well grounded to make it permissible for third parties to engage in other-defense on her behalf. In other cases the permission to engage in defensive violence may not extend to third parties.

5. *Forfeiture.* In certain cases, a Victim's right of self-defense is sufficiently strong or well grounded to make it impermissible for the Attacker or Threat to use violence to resist the Victim's own self-defensive violence. In other cases, however, the Attacker or Threat may permissibly defend himself against the Victim's legitimate self-defensive violence.

These various possible restrictions may apply differently in the three kinds of case, distinguished earlier, in which the Justice-Based Account implies that self-defense may be permissible. First, there is generally no requirement to retreat in the face of a Culpable Attacker, but there may be in the case of an Innocent Attacker, particularly one who is without fault, or a Nonresponsible Attacker. Second, there is generally no requirement to divide the burden with a Culpable Attacker, though there may be with an Innocent or Nonresponsible Attacker. Third, the gravity and probability of the threat must be greater in order to justify the killing of an Innocent or Nonresponsible Attacker than is necessary to justify the killing of a Culpable Attacker. Fourth, third-party intervention on behalf of the Victim is less likely to be justified when the Attacker is innocent or nonresponsible rather than culpable. Fifth and finally, the Attacker is more likely to retain a right of self-defense against the Victim's justified self-defensive action if the Attacker is innocent or nonresponsible rather than culpable.

Despite the fact that more stringent restrictions may apply to self-defense against an Innocent or Nonresponsible Attacker or Threat than to self-defense against a Culpable Attacker or Threat, the scope of permissible self-defense implied by the Justice-Based Account is quite extensive. It seems to apply to cases involving Innocent Attackers and Threats. It does not, however, extend to cases involving Nonresponsible Attackers or Threats. Whether or not a Nonresponsible Attacker or Threat is in an objectively unjustifiable position in posing a threat, his lack of moral responsibility for the situation in which he finds himself seems to exclude any liability to self-defensive violence as a matter of justice. In the cases covered by the Justice-Based Account, even if the reason that the Attacker or Threat poses a threat is simply that he has had bad luck (as in the case of the Inadvertent Attacker), it is still true that *he* is morally responsible for the fact that there is a forced choice between his life and that of the Victim. That seems to constitute a decisive asymmetry between him and the Innocent Victim, at least in cases in which the burden cannot be shared between them. But the same cannot be said of the Nonresponsible Attacker or Threat. There seems to be no moral asymmetry, at least where considerations of justice are concerned, between the Nonresponsible Attacker or Threat and the Innocent Victim. Neither bears any responsibility for the forced choice between their lives.

If this is right, the Justice-Based Account provides no justification for self-defense by a pregnant woman against a fetus, even in the Extreme Case. For the fetus is neither culpable, nor at fault, nor even in any way morally responsible for the threat it poses. Of course, it may be that the Justice-Based Account is only one component of a complex, more comprehensive account of the right of self-defense. In that case, a justification for killing the fetus in self-defense might be implied by some other part of the more complex account. There is, however, a reason for doubting that this is the case. For there is a positive argument for the view that there is no right of self-defense against a Nonresponsible Threat.

The argument is quite simple. It is, in general, impermissible to kill an Innocent Bystander as a means of self-preservation. Because there is no morally relevant difference between a Nonresponsible Threat and an Innocent Bystander, it follows that it is impermissible to kill a Nonresponsible Threat as a means of self-defense.[125] (This succinct statement of the argument requires two parenthetical comments, one substantive and one merely terminological. First, the argument presupposes only that the killing of an Innocent Bystander *as an intended means* of self-preservation is wrong. It does not claim that it is impermissible foreseeably to kill an Innocent Bystander as a side effect of action aimed at self-preservation. That may be wrong as well but, because most people are intuitively ambivalent about that claim, it is best for the argument not to depend on it. Second, the killing of an Innocent Bystander may be self-preservative, but it cannot be literally self-defensive. Because an Innocent Bystander does not, by definition, pose a threat, it is conceptually impossible to *defend* oneself against him.)

The most controversial claim in the argument is that there is no relevant difference between a Nonresponsible Threat and an Innocent Bystander. I will attempt to support that claim by appealing to an intermediate case.

> *The Trapped Miners.* Two miners are working in a mine shaft when a slight tremor from a distant earthquake pitches one of them against a support beam. His body dislodges the beam, causing a collapse. The miners are then trapped, each in a separate chamber. They are, however, able to communicate with each other and with people on the surface by means of walkie-talkies. They learn that rescuers will reach them in five hours. But their instruments reveal distressing information about the oxygen supply. In the chamber occupied by the miner whose body caused the collapse, there is enough oxygen for one person to survive for six hours. But in the smaller chamber where the other miner is trapped, there is only enough oxygen for a person to survive for two hours. Therefore breaching the wall between the chambers cannot save them both, for the combined oxygen supply would enable them together to sur-

vive for only four hours. In short, only one can survive. And the only way that the one in the smaller chamber can be the survivor is to break through the wall and kill the miner whose body caused the collapse.

The miner who was tossed against the shaft is what I call a *Cause* of a threat—that is, someone whose previous action, movement, or presence is the cause of a present threat to another but who is no part of the threat now, while it is occurring. There can be Culpable Causes, Innocent Causes, and Nonresponsible Causes. If the case were different and the miner who caused the collapse were a Culpable Cause, the Justice-Based Account would imply that the other miner would be justified in breaking through the wall and killing him. For, in culpably causing the collapse, the miner would have culpably created the forced choice between his life and that of the other miner. As a matter of justice, he should pay the price of his own culpable action. The same might be true (though this is more controversial) if the miner were an Innocent Cause—that is, if he had caused the collapse by means of action for which he was responsible but which was either excused or not at fault. But in the case as I have presented it, the miner who caused the collapse is a Nonresponsible Cause. He is in no way morally responsible for the predicament in which he and the other miner find themselves. And he is presently no part of the threat to that other miner. Indeed, relative to the threat that the miner in the smaller chamber faces, he is an Innocent Bystander.

(It might be argued that the miner in the larger chamber cannot be an Innocent Bystander because he is in fact a Nonresponsible *Threat;* for his presence is draining the oxygen that the other miner needs to survive. In order to eliminate this possible complication, we can assume that, were it not for the presence of the miner in the larger chamber, the other miner would not know that the other chamber was intact or that there was oxygen in it. Given that assumption, the one miner's presence in the larger chamber does not make him a Threat, for it does not prevent the other miner from saving himself by gaining access to the air in that chamber.)

Recognition that the Nonresponsible Cause is also an Innocent Bystander serves to confirm our strong intuitive sense that it would be wrong for the miner in the smaller chamber to kill him, even though that is the only way the other miner can save himself. It also supports the idea that there is no right of self-defense against a Nonresponsible Threat. For there seems to be no relevant difference between a Nonresponsible Threat and a Nonresponsible Cause. The only real difference between the two is a difference of timing: while it is the Nonresponsible Cause's movement *in the past* that is the innocent cause of a present threat, the Nonresponsible Threat innocently causes a present threat by his movement or presence *now.* And it is hard to see how this mere difference in timing—the difference between *having caused* a present threat and *causing* a present threat—could *by itself* make a decisive moral difference, making it permissible to kill one who is the present cause of a present threat (that is, the Nonresponsible Threat) when it is clearly impermissible to kill one who is the past cause of a present threat (that is, the Nonresponsible Cause).

If, however, there is no relevant difference between a Nonresponsible Threat and an Nonresponsible Cause, and if a Nonresponsible Cause is also an Innocent Bystander, then it follows that there is no relevant difference between a Nonresponsible Threat and at least this kind of Innocent Bystander. Thus if killing this kind of Innocent Bystander as a means of self-preservation is wrong, then killing a Nonresponsible Threat in self-defense should be wrong for the same reason.

Michael Otsuka has defended this same argument—namely, it is wrong to kill an Innocent Bystander in self-preservation; there is no relevant difference between an Innocent Bystander and a Nonresponsible Threat or Attacker; therefore it is wrong to kill a Nonresponsible Threat or Attacker in self-defense. But Otsuka offers a different defense of the critical premise that there is no relevant difference between an Innocent Bystander and a Nonresponsible Threat or Attacker. I will briefly discuss his defense of this premise, which I believe has considerable plausibility but is not decisive.

Otsuka presents three cases:

> *Case 1.* A runaway trolley is headed in one's direction. One will be crushed by it unless one destroys it by hurling a bomb. If one blows up the trolley, however, the explosion will also kill a nearby Innocent Bystander.

> *Case 2.* In this case, the Innocent Bystander is, through no fault of his own, trapped inside the runaway trolley. If one blows it up, one will blow her up as well.

> *Case 3.* A person's body is hurtling towards one. Unless one blows her up, one will be crushed and killed by her body. (Assuming that she is not responsible for the threat her body poses, she is what I have called a Nonresponsible Projectile, which is one kind of Nonresponsible Threat.)

Otsuka claims that it would be wrong to kill the Innocent Bystander in Case 1. Since the change of the Innocent Bystander's location in Case 2 from beside the trolley to inside it does not seem to make a moral difference, it seems that it would be wrong to kill the Innocent Bystander in that case as well. Finally, there seems to be no reason to suppose that it is impermissible to kill the Innocent Bystander in Case 2 but permissible to kill the Nonresponsible Projectile in Case 3. The difference between them is that the one is *aboard* the mass that threatens to crush one while the other *is* that mass. But this is a trivial difference. Indeed, because the Nonresponsible Projectile is in no way responsible for the movement of her body, she may appropriately be regarded, in Alec Walen's revealing phrase, as an Innocent Bystander "aboard her own body."[126] (Otsuka himself explicitly denies that the Nonresponsible Projectile is distinct from her body—or at least sufficiently distinct that one could intend to destroy her body without intending to destroy her.[127] According to the Embodied Mind Account of Identity, she *is* distinct. But metaphysical distinctness is not necessary for her to be a bystander to her body in the morally relevant sense—that is, the sense that establishes the parallel with the Innocent Bystander in Cases 1 and 2.)

There is, in fact, reason to believe that the self-defensive killing of the Nonresponsible Projectile in Case 3 would be *more* seriously objectionable than the self-preservative killing of the Innocent Bystander in either Case 1 or 2. For in Case 3 the killing seems to be intended as a means of saving one's life, whereas in Cases 1 and 2 the killing of the Innocent Bystander is merely an unintended side effect of action aimed at self-preservation. And killing someone as an intended means of achieving some goal is, in general, more seriously objectionable than killing someone in a way that is unintended, though foreseen. But if killing the Innocent Bystander in Cases 1 and 2 is wrong, and if killing the Nonresponsible Projectile in Case 3 is more objectionable in one respect than the killings in Cases 1 and 2 and no less objectionable in others, it seems to follow that killing the Nonresponsible Projectile in Case 3 must be wrong.

I am skeptical of this argument as it stands. For it presupposes that it is wrong to kill the Innocent Bystander in Cases 1 and 2. But many people feel intuitively that killing would be permissible in these cases. And there is support for this intuition in the moral tradition to which Otsuka appeals—namely, the tradition of deontological morality. For the killing of the Innocent Bystander would be an unintended effect of action intended to produce a good effect (the agent's own survival), and the harm caused to the Innocent Bystander would be proportionate to the harm that would be prevented. (Because the act of killing would satisfy these conditions, it would be permitted by the traditional Doctrine of Double Effect.) If, however, killing the Innocent Bystander in Cases 1 and 2 is permissible, Otsuka's argument fails to show that killing the Nonresponsible Projectile is wrong. For if it is not wrong to kill the Innocent Bystander, then, even if killing the Nonresponsible Projectile is objectionable in a way that killing the Innocent Bystander is not, it does not follow that killing the Nonresponsible Projectile is wrong. If an act is worse in some respect than a different, permissible act, it does not follow that the act is wrong. An act can be objectionable in a way in which some permissible act is not and yet still be permissible.

As might be expected, Otsuka has an argument for the impermissibility of killing an Innocent Bystander even as a side effect. (The argument is restricted, appropriately I think, to cases in which the killing occurs via the creation of a threat rather than via the redirection of a preexisting threat.) He cites with approval Philippa Foot's claim that "you may not drive over one innocent recumbent person even if that is necessary for you to arrive in time to save five others."[128] But if it is impermissible to kill an Innocent Bystander as an unintended effect of saving five other people, it surely cannot be permissible to kill an Innocent Bystander as an unintended effect of saving one, even if the one is oneself.

The problem with this argument is that there seems intuitively to be a moral difference between the mode of agency in Foot's case and that in Cases 1 and 2. Running over a person on one's way to save the five seems different from, and worse than, killing a person by setting off a bomb that also saves five lives. If that is so, one cannot infer the impermissibility of killing the Innocent Bystander in Cases 1 and 2 from the impermissibility of running over the person in Foot's example. It is therefore important to consider whether there really is a difference and, if so, what exactly it is. Both killings are unintended, neither is a means of saving the five, and both are necessary if the five are to be saved. They are, in short, alike in the obviously relevant ways. One possibly relevant difference is that the person who is run over is killed on the causal path to the saving of the five, whereas the one who is killed by the explosion is killed as a further effect of the event that saves the five. The former killing is, to borrow Jonathan Bennett's phrase, causally upstream from the saving of the five, while the latter is causally downstream. Whether this difference is morally relevant, and if so why, are matters that I will not take up here.[129]

Despite the problems I have noted, Otsuka's argument is important. For its main point is to reveal the insignificance of the difference between an Innocent Bystander and a Nonresponsible Threat. And in this I think he succeeds. The Innocent Bystander in Case 2 and the Nonresponsible Projectile in Case 3 really do seem morally indistinguishable. The Innocent Bystander is *part* of the threat without literally *being* the threat. If this is insufficient to strip him of his moral immunity to being killed, surely the same is true of the Nonresponsible Projectile, who differs only in that her body *is* the threat rather than being contained within the threat.

Given that Otsuka's cases succeed in revealing the triviality of the difference between an Innocent Bystander and a Nonresponsible Threat, it seems that his argument could be reconstructed in a way that avoids the objection I have urged. What is needed is a version of Case 2 in which the killing of the Innocent Bystander would be intended as a means of self-preservation, as the killing of the Nonresponsible Projectile is in Case 3. Here is such a case. Like many other examples in contemporary moral philosophy, it is quite silly; but it seems impossible to avoid an absurdly contrived case while preserving the necessary similarity to the Nonresponsible Projectile.

> *Case 4.* A villain who delights in forcing people to act against their conscience has tied one to the tracks and set a trolley in motion on the track. He has, however, provided a means of escape. He has given one a gun, strapped an Innocent Bystander to the trolley, and rigged up a device that will cause the trolley to explode if, but only if, it detects that the Bystander's heart has ceased to beat. (Note that this does not make the Innocent Bystander a threat. It is not her beating heart that keeps the trolley going.) One can therefore save oneself from being crushed by the trolley only by shooting and killing the Bystander.

In this case the Bystander is on board the threat in the same way as in Case 2, so the relevant parallel with Case 3 is maintained. And it seems much clearer in this case than in Case 2 that it would be wrong to kill the Innocent Bystander. For in this case the Bystander must be killed as a *means* of self-preservation. So, unless there is some critical difference between the Innocent Bystander lashed to the trolley and the Nonresponsible Projectile who is, in effect, lashed to her own body, it seems that it must also be wrong to kill the Nonresponsible Projectile as a means of self-preservation. And unless, improbably, there is something peculiar about Nonresponsible Projectiles that distinguishes them morally from other Nonresponsible Threats, this conclusion can be extrapolated to apply to Nonresponsible Threats generally.

I have now advanced two arguments for the claim that there is no right of self-defense against a Nonresponsible Threat: my own argument based on the absence of a relevant difference between an Innocent Bystander who is also a Nonresponsible Cause and a Nonresponsible Threat, and a revised version of Otsuka's argument based on the absence of a relevant difference between an Innocent Bystander aboard a lethal projectile and a Nonresponsible Threat who *is* a lethal projectile. If it is right that these arguments demonstrate the impermissibility of killing a Nonresponsible Threat as a means of self-preservation, then it seems that there can be no right to kill a fetus in self-defense, even in the Extreme Case. For a fetus is incapable of posing a threat except as a Nonresponsible Threat.

One response to this argument is to note that I have conceded that it may be permissible to kill an Innocent Bystander in self-preservation provided that the killing is not intended as a means of self-preservation but is instead a proportionate side effect of action aimed at self-preservation. If that is right, the claim that there is no relevant difference between a Nonresponsible Threat and an Innocent Bystander leaves open the possibility that it may be permissible to kill a Nonresponsible Threat in self-defense provided that the killing is not intended as a means of self-defense. Where abortion is concerned, therefore, we need to ask two questions. First, is it possible to kill the fetus in self-defense without intending to kill it as a means of self-defense? Second, if this is possible, might it be morally permissible?

There is an ambiguity in the idea that a killing is intended as a means. There is a narrow conception of an intended means, according to which an effect, as specified by a certain description, is intended as a means only if the agent is motivated to bring it about because he believes that it will be instrumental, *under that description,* in achieving his desired end. If we understand "intended as a means" in this narrow way, it is certainly possible to kill a fetus in self-defense without intending the killing as a means of self-preservation. A woman might intend only that the fetus be re-moved from her womb, but foresee that the act of removing it will also cause its death. Yet showing that a killing is not intended as a means *in this narrow sense* does very little to establish its permissibility. As Jonathan Bennett has pointed out, it is possible even to drop bombs on innocent people without intending in the narrow sense to kill them; for one may intend only (for example) to render them inoperable long enough to cause their leaders to believe them dead, foreseeing of course that one's action will have the further unintended effect of actually rendering them *dead.*[130] This kind of action is obviously a paradigm of wrongful killing despite the fact that the killings would not be intended as a means in the narrow sense.

There is, however, a broader sense of "intended as a means" that people normally have in mind when they condemn an act as an instance of intentional killing. In this sense, a killing is intended as a means when one acts with the intention of affecting an individual in a way that one believes will either be causally sufficient for his death or have a high probability of causing his death. This, I believe, is the best way to un-derstand the intuition behind the traditional prohibition of intentional killing (though, given that probability has a role in the definition and that the notion of a "high prob-ability" is vague, the prohibition cannot be absolute in the way the traditional prohi-bition has often be understood to be).

Instances of the *wrongful* killing of an Innocent Bystander in self-preservation are often intentional only in this broad sense. To take one commonly cited example, suppose that one is being shot at and one therefore seizes an Innocent Bystander to in-terpose as a shield between oneself and one's attacker. If the Innocent Bystander is, as a consequence, killed by a bullet, it is natural to say that one has caused her to be killed as a means of self-preservation. But one certainly did not intend that she be killed in the narrow sense. One did, however, intend to affect her, or use her, in a way that one believed would have a high probability of causing her to be killed.

Instances of the *permissible* of killing of an Innocent Bystanders are seldom, if ever, intended as a means in the narrow sense. But that consideration scarcely figures at all in the explanation of why these killings are permissible. What is significant is that they are not intended in the broad sense. So, for example, what is significant about the killing of the Innocent Bystander in Cases 1 and 2 is that the Bystander is not an intentional object of the agent's action at all. The agent intends nothing for her, and a fortiori nothing harmful or lethal: she is simply in the way.

So the relevant question where abortion is concerned is not whether killing the fetus in self-defense would be intended as a means in the narrow sense. I have conceded that it often need not be, but that is unimportant. The important question is whether it would be intended as a means of self-preservation in the broad sense. And the answer to this is that it must be. When the fetus is killed in self-defense, it is killed because it is a Nonresponsible Threat. The self-defensive action is therefore necessarily directed against the fetus. The fetus must be the intentional object of the action. But if the self-defensive action is intended to affect the fetus, and in a way that will foreseeably cause its death, then the action is necessarily intended, in the broad sense, to kill the fetus as a means of self-preservation. Thus if killing an Innocent Bystander as a means of self-preservation is wrong—and commonsense intuition strongly affirms that it is—then killing a Nonresponsible Threat as a means of self-defense should be wrong as well. So the earlier conclusion stands: abortion cannot be justified by appeal to the pregnant woman's right of self-defense, even in the Extreme Case.

10.2. *Proportionality, Third-party Intervention, and Forfeiture*

The claim that there is no right of self-defense against Nonresponsible Threats and Attackers is difficult to accept. Commonsense morality seems to distinguish morally between Innocent Bystanders on the one hand and Innocent and Nonresponsible Threats and Attackers on the other. Most people believe that, while it is wrong to kill an Innocent Bystander as a means of self-preservation, it is nevertheless permissible to kill a Nonresponsible Threat or Attacker as a means of self-defense. Although I have argued against this belief, I recognize that it is difficult to reject. The suspicion remains that there is a morally significant asymmetry between the Nonresponsible Threat and the Innocent Bystander that I have failed to detect. Because of this, it would be unwise to leave the self-defense argument without exploring it a bit deeper. Therefore I will assume, for the sake of argument, that my reasoning thus far has been wrong and that there is, in fact, a morally significant asymmetry between the Nonresponsible Threat and the Innocent Bystander that I have failed to identify, and that killing the fetus as a means of self-defense is therefore not ruled out along with the killing of an Innocent Bystander as a means of self-preservation.

My claim in this section will be that, even if there is a right of self-defense against a Nonresponsible Threat, it is so hedged about by restrictions that it is doubtful that it can justify abortion except in a very limited range of cases; and even in those cases it may have further implications that would be repugnant to those who believe that abortion is morally permissible. Hence those who wish to defend the permissibility of abortion would be unwise to attempt to do so by appealing to the pregnant woman's right of self-defense.

I noted earlier that there are various restrictions that may apply to the exercise of one's right of self-defense. These include restrictions having to do with the possibility of retreat, the division of the costs of confrontation, proportionality, third-party intervention, and the retention of the right of self-defense by the initial Attacker or Threat. Because our concern here is with the threat that a fetus may pose to a pregnant woman, we can ignore the first two types of restriction. For there is no possibility of a pregnant woman's retreating from a conflict with the fetus or of her sharing the burdens of the conflict with it. Thus in cases in which the fetus constitutes a threat, either the woman or the fetus must suffer a harm; there is no other alternative. (The one possible exception is the rare case in which, if nothing is done, both the woman and the fetus will die—though, if the fetus is aborted, the woman will live. Allowing both to die is, I suppose, a way in which the two might share the burden, though a way that increases the overall amount of harm rather than reducing it.)

In general, the restrictions governing the exercise of one's right of self-defense become stronger as the justification for engaging self-defense becomes weaker; and the justification becomes weaker the less pronounced the moral asymmetry is between the Threat or Attacker and the Victim.[131] Consider, for example, how the requirement of proportionality applies in the range of cases covered by the Justice-Based Account. The requirement of proportionality holds, roughly, that the harm inflicted in self-defense must not be excessive in relation to the threatened harm one seeks to avoid. But what counts as excessive depends on the strength of the justification for self-defense, which in turn may depend on the status of the Attacker or Threat. Consider killing in self-defense. That is certainly an excessive or disproportionate response to a threat of being pinched, even by a Culpable Attacker. But as I noted earlier, there is a range of threats from a Culpable Attacker to which killing would be a proportionate response: for example, the threat of being killed, tortured, raped, kidnapped, and so on. The range of threats to which killing would be a proportionate response is narrower, however, in the case of an *Innocent* Threat or Attacker. For in that case one of the considerations that favors the Victim over the Threat or Attacker as a matter of justice—namely, culpability—is absent. Thus, while it might be permissible to kill a Culpable Attacker to prevent him from breaking one's arms, that would be a disproportionate response to the same threat from an Innocent Attacker. Of course, a moral asymmetry remains between the Innocent Threat or Attacker and the Innocent Victim: for an Innocent Threat or Attacker is, by definition, morally responsible for the threat he poses, and may also be at fault (though excused) for posing that threat. And these considerations are relevant to how the inevitable misfortune ought to be distributed as a matter of justice. Yet they constitute a weaker case for self-defense than there would be if the Threat or Attacker were also culpable for posing the threat.

Suppose that a Threat or Attacker threatens one's life but that the probability that one will be killed, even if one takes no action in self-defense, is quite low. Imagine, for example, that one's attacker is a long way off and cannot get closer, is firing an inaccurate rifle with bad sights, and suffers from intention tremor, which causes his hands to shake uncontrollably while he fires. His bullets are consequently hitting ten to twenty feet away and he will soon run out of ammunition. Suppose that the probability of one's being killed if one does nothing is about 1 in 200 and that one must either kill him or take a chance of being killed, for there are no other alternatives. Again, whether killing in self-defense would be proportionate depends on the strength of the considerations favoring the Victim over the Attacker. If the Attacker is culpable, one may permissibly kill him; but if he is an Innocent Attacker, it is reasonable to believe that one may not kill him but must instead accept the small chance of being killed.

Finally, suppose that one's life is threatened by a number of Attackers—say, ten—acting in concert and that the probability of one's being killed if one does not kill them all in self-defense is close to one. If they are all Culpable Attackers, killing them does not seem disproportionate. (There does not, in fact, seem to be *any* proportionality restriction on the number of Culpable Attackers one may kill, if killing them is necessary to preserve one's life.) But if they are Innocent Attackers, it is less clear that it would be permissible to kill them. It must be conceded, I think, that the commonsense intuition is that it can be permissible to kill a number of Innocent Attackers in self-defense—though the grip of this intuition weakens as the numbers increase.

These various dimensions of the proportionality restriction must be even stronger in the case of self-defense against a Nonresponsible Threat or Attacker. Consider the Nonresponsible Threat. He is like the Innocent Threat except that he lacks one property—moral responsibility for the threat he poses—that makes the Innocent Threat liable to being killed in self-defense as a matter of justice, and therefore brings the Innocent Threat within the scope of the Justice-Based Account. This suggests that the justification for self-defense is weaker in the case of a Nonresponsible Threat than in the case of an Innocent Threat. There are two reasons for thinking this, one more plausible than the other. The less plausible reason presupposes that the considerations that may justify self-defense are additive, and that the case for self-defense is therefore stronger the more considerations there are that favor it. Given that self-defense against an Innocent Threat is supported by considerations of justice while self-defense against a Nonresponsible Threat is not, and assuming that any considerations that support self-defense against a Nonresponsible Threat also support self-defense against an Innocent Threat, it follows that there are fewer considerations supporting self-defense against a Nonresponsible Threat. This, however, implies that the moral case for self-defense against a Nonresponsible Threat is weaker only if the various considerations that may favor self-defense are additive—that is, only if the strength of the case for self-defense is the sum of the strengths of the considerations favoring self-defense. And that, I think, is a dubious assumption.

Rather than criticize that assumption here, however, I will move on to the second, more cogent reason for thinking that the case for self-defense against a Nonresponsible Threat is weaker. This is that the principal, and strongest, justification for self-defense is that it is permitted as a matter of justice in the distribution of harm—or, in other words, that the strongest justification for self-defense is given by the Justice-Based Account. If that is right, then the fact that the justification for self-defense against an Innocent Threat appeals to considerations of justice, while the justification (whatever it may be) for self-defense against a Nonresponsible Threat cannot, suggests that the former justification must be stronger.

It is, perhaps, conceivable that there might be numerous converging justifications for self-defense against a Nonresponsible Threat that together are stronger than the justification that the Justice-Based Account provides for self-defense against an Innocent Threat. But that is most unlikely. There is, after all, only one serious rival to the Justice-Based Account in the literature, and it is doubtful whether it offers any support for self-defense against a Nonresponsible Threat at all.[132] According to this rival account, self-defense is justified, other things being equal, when the Threat or Attacker would otherwise violate the Victim's rights. But rights operate to constrain only the actions of morally responsible agents. Thus, just as a right cannot impose a duty on a tiger not to charge or on a boulder not to fall, so it cannot impose a duty on a person not pose a threat in a way that involves neither agency nor responsibility. A

Nonresponsible Threat, therefore, can no more violate a right than a charging tiger or a falling boulder can.[133] This alternative account of the morality of self-defense seems, in short, to provide no support at all for a right of self-defense against a Nonresponsible Threat. There are, of course, other efforts in the literature to justify self-defense against a Nonresponsible Threat, but the asymmetries they identify between the Nonresponsible Threat and his Victim are of doubtful moral significance—or, more modestly, they are certainly less morally significant than the asymmetry identified by the Justice-Based Account between the Innocent Threat and his Victim.[134] (I will note some of the more credible of these attempts at justification below.) I think, therefore, that it is safe to conclude that the justification for self-defense against a Nonresponsible Threat is weaker than that for self-defense against an Innocent Threat; hence the restrictions on self-defense against a Nonresponsible Threat must be stronger.

Recall that the restrictions governing the killing of an Innocent Threat in self-defense are already quite stringent. Thus the restrictions governing the killing of a Nonresponsible Threat must be very stringent indeed. Consider, for example, the proportionality restriction on killing in self-defense. It is, of course, difficult to apply this restriction with precision. But in the case of self-defense against a Nonresponsible Threat, it seems reasonable to suppose that the range of threats sufficiently serious to justify killing the Threat must be very small, the probability that the threatened harm will occur unless the Threat is killed must be very high, and the number of Nonresponsible Threats that may be killed in self-defense must be very low—presumably no more than one.

The implications of these claims for the justification of abortion as an act of self-defense are similarly difficult to infer with precision. But it seems likely that the only threat to the pregnant woman that is sufficiently serious to justify her killing the fetus, given its status as a Nonresponsible Threat, is a threat to her life. That is, while abortion may be justifiable in the Extreme Case, it is unlikely to be justifiable in the case of lesser threats, such as the threat of continuing bodily invasion that is present in all unwanted pregnancies. Moreover, not only must the pregnant woman's life be under threat, but the probability of her dying if the abortion is not performed must also be quite high. If that is so, the number of abortions that might be justified by appealing to a woman's right to self-defense is very small. For cases in which an abortion is necessary to avert a high probability of a woman's dying from complications arising in pregnancy are now very rare. Finally, it is worth noting that the proportionality restriction on the number of Nonresponsible Threats that may be killed in self-defense may well rule out abortion in the cases in which a woman is carrying more than one fetus, *even* if the continuation of the pregnancy threatens her life.[135]

Turn now to the restriction on third-party intervention. When the justification for self-defense appeals to considerations of justice in the distribution of harm, it applies equally to the Victim and to third parties. In these cases, other-defense is justified for the same reason that self-defense is. The outcome of the conflict between the Threat or Attacker and the Victim is a matter of justice, and anyone who is in a position to ensure that justice prevails is permitted (and, in some instances, required) to do so. So, for example, when an Innocent Victim is threatened by a Culpable Attacker, third-party intervention on behalf of the Victim is clearly permissible and, if it would involve little or no risk for the intervening agent, may even be morally required.

Two points of clarification are necessary here. First, it certainly seems that the Victim's reason to engage in self-defense is considerably stronger than the third party's reason to intervene on her behalf. How could that be, if they both have essentially the same reason—that is, a reason grounded in considerations of justice? One answer—and there may be others—is that the Victim's *moral* reason is reinforced by a powerful *prudential* reason, whereas third parties normally have no prudential reason to intervene (though they might if they were specially related to the Victim, could expect a reward, or something of that sort). Indeed, the risk that is normally involved in intervening against a Culpable Attacker may give third parties a strong prudential reason *not* to intervene, one that is often sufficient to release them from any obligation they would otherwise have to come to the aid of the Victim. Hence there is not necessarily any difference between the *moral* reasons that the Victim and suitably situated third parties have to engage in self- or other-defense against the Culpable Attacker. (I should note one possible exception. Special relations sometimes magnify the strengths of certain duties that we have to others. Thus a third party specially related to the potential Victim of a culpable attack might have a *moral* reason to intervene on behalf of the Victim that is not only stronger than the moral reason that other third parties have, but is also stronger than that which the Victim herself has.)

A second point of clarification is that self-defense is normally morally optional—even self-defense against a Culpable Attacker. Morality appears to grant people the right to permit injustice if they alone would be the victims of it. There is thus one restriction on third-party intervention in cases involving Culpable Attackers, and this is that it must not be carried out in contravention of the autonomous preference of the Victim. If the Victim autonomously prefers to sacrifice herself rather than to defend herself or be defended, that is a preference that third parties ought to respect, other things being equal.

Return now to the general question of the permissibility of third-party intervention. I have claimed that third-party intervention against a Culpable Attacker is permissible. The general principle that explains why this is so is that third-party intervention is justified whenever the explanation of why self-defense is justified provides anyone with a moral reason for preferring the survival of the Victim to the survival of the Threat or Attacker. And this will be so only if there is a moral asymmetry between the Threat or Attacker and the Victim that is recognizable from a neutral point of view.[136]

On the basis of this principle, Ann Davis has argued that abortion cannot be justified by appealing to the pregnant woman's right of self-defense. She contends that, from a neutral point of view, there is no moral asymmetry between an Innocent Victim and what I call a Threat (which she calls a *passive threat*—that is, "someone whose mere movements *qua* physical object or mere presence constitutes a threat to our life").[137] There is therefore no neutral justification for self-defense against a Threat. (She believes that it is the Threat's lack of agency that precludes a relevant moral asymmetry. This, I think, is a mistake; for absence of agency while the threat exists is compatible with moral responsibility, and indeed culpability, for the existence of the threat arising from previous action. This is why my earlier argument focused on Nonresponsible Threats and Attackers rather than on Threats generally. Perhaps Davis assumes that absence of agency necessarily precludes responsibility.) Davis does not conclude, however, that one may not defend oneself against a passive threat. She claims that an Innocent Victim is permitted to kill a Threat in self-defense, but only because, in the circumstances, the Innocent Victim is entitled to give a certain priority to her own life, simply because it is hers: "Because of the greater value that each of us understandably attaches to the continuation of his or her own life, we are (in certain circumstances) permitted to kill another person to preserve our own life, even though we acknowledge that the other person's claim to life is not weaker than our own."[138] Note that this applies universally: thus the Nonresponsible Threat may give priority to his own life as well. The Innocent Victim and the Nonresponsible Threat may therefore both be justified in trying to kill the other in self-defense. But this justification applies only to the parties involved in the conflict; it does not extend to third parties, for the mere fact that each values his or her own life more does not give third parties a moral reason to favor one or the other. (There is a possible exception. If the relevant permission is not just to give priority to one's own life but to give priority to those things that one reasonably cares specially about, a third party who is specially related to the Victim might also be permitted to give priority to her life and to intervene on her behalf.) Applied to the case of abortion, Davis's argument implies that, *if* the justification for abortion appeals to the right of self-defense, a woman (the Innocent Victim) may be permitted to perform a self-induced abortion, but a doctor (a third party who is not specially related to her) is not permitted to intervene on her behalf. And this rules out most actual abortions, the possible exceptions being those induced by the "abortion pill," RU-486.

Davis's argument is plausible. (Her most questionable claim is that the self-defensive killing of a Nonresponsible Threat can be justified by appealing to the permissibility of assigning priority to one's own life when all else is equal. Unless this claim is appropriately restricted, it implies that it is permissible to kill an Innocent Bystander as a means of self-preservation.)[139] Although I am inclined to agree with her, as my argument in the previous section (10.1) indicates, that there is no moral asymmetry between a Nonresponsible Threat and the Innocent Victim, I am nevertheless now assuming, for the sake of argument, that there *is* such an asymmetry. But, while the absence of an asymmetry seems sufficient to rule out the permissibility of third-party intervention, the presence of an asymmetry is not necessarily sufficient to make third-party intervention permissible. If the moral asymmetry is very weak, it may be just sufficient to make it justifiable for the Innocent Victim to kill the Nonresponsible Threat in self-defense (though only, perhaps, in the Extreme Case) but insufficient to justify third-party intervention on her behalf.

I have suggested that, if there is a moral asymmetry between the Nonresponsible Threat and the Innocent Victim, it is not a highly significant one. For there are very few differences between the two, and those there are seem doubtfully morally significant. Here, for example, are the main differences that have been cited in the literature as allegedly making it permissible for the Innocent Victim to kill the Nonresponsible Threat in self-defense: that the Nonresponsible Threat is in a morally inappropriate position vis-à-vis the Innocent Victim, that the threat he poses is objectively unjustified, and that he causes the problem or brings the problem to the Innocent Victim rather than vice versa.[140] These suggestions are all, I believe, open to objection. (It seems, for example, that the position of a Nonresponsible Threat cannot be *morally* inappropriate any more than that of a charging tiger or a falling boulder can.) More importantly, even if the suggested differences are real, they cannot plausibly be regarded as deeply morally significant.

I believe it is doubtful that so weak an asymmetry can justify third-party intervention on behalf of the Innocent Victim. But I have no argument to show that it cannot. It is nevertheless worth pointing out an unsettling possibility. Recall that one way that an individual's right of self-defense may be restricted is that it may not be well enough grounded to make it impermissible for the target of the defensive action (that is, the initial Threat or Attacker) to fight back. In some cases, in other words, the Threat or Attacker retains a right of self-defense and thus may be justified in engaging in self-defense against the Victim's justified self-defensive action. I suggest that this must be so in the case of the Nonresponsible Threat. Whatever else is true, the Nonresponsible Threat's unfortunate position in the causal matrix does not involve the forfeiture of his right to life. Suppose, then, that the asymmetry between the Nonresponsible Threat and the Innocent Victim is such that the Victim is justified in killing the Threat in self-defense, and third parties are also justified in intervening on the Victim's behalf. But the Nonresponsible Threat is also justified in defending himself against the Victim's defensive action by killing the Victim. (In other words, while the Nonresponsible Threat *initially* poses a merely *excused* threat, the threat he poses *in response* to the victim's defensive action is *justified*.) But, if the Innocent Victim and the Nonresponsible Threat are each justified in trying to kill the other in self-defense, and if a third party would be justified in intervening on behalf of the Innocent Victim, it may well be that a third party would be justified in intervening on behalf of the Nonresponsible Threat as well. That is, the Nonresponsible Threat's right of self-defense might legitimize third-party intervention on his behalf in the same way that the Victim's does.

If this is right, the implications for abortion are disturbing. Normally, a pregnant woman is unable to defend herself from a threat posed by the fetus. To eliminate the threat by terminating the pregnancy, she must normally enlist the assistance of a third party: a physician. But the fetus is, of course, also incapable of exercising its right to defend itself against the physician who is acting on behalf of the woman. If its right to self-defense transfers to third parties in the way we are supposing the woman's does, then, just as it may be permissible for a physician to try to defend the woman from the threat posed by the fetus, so it may also be permissible for another third party to try to defend the fetus from the threat posed by the physician. But this cannot possibly be right; otherwise it provides a justification for those who have killed abortion providers (assuming that the killings met certain conditions, such as being necessary to prevent the physicians from performing abortions). If the self-defense argument has the intolerable conclusion that the killing of abortion providers may be justified, this shows that there must be something wrong with the argument.

Suppose we believe that there is a moral asymmetry between a Nonresponsible Threat and an Innocent Victim that is strong enough both to justify the Innocent Victim's killing the Nonresponsible Threat in self-defense, and also to justify third-party intervention on behalf of the Innocent Victim. These assumptions make abortion justifiable as a matter of self-defense, at least in the Extreme Case. I have claimed, however, that we cannot accept that the fetus's being a Nonresponsible Threat entails that it forfeits its own right to life or its right of self-defense. In order, therefore, to avoid the intolerable conclusion that it can be permissible to kill those who perform abortions in order to save women's lives, we must accept all four of the following claims. We must accept that the moral asymmetry between a Nonresponsible Threat and an Innocent Victim is:

1. strong enough to justify the self-defensive killing of the fetus by the pregnant woman in the Extreme Case,
2. strong enough to justify the killing of the fetus by a physician on the woman's behalf,
3. strong enough to forbid a third party from forcibly intervening to save the fetus,
4. but *too weak* to deprive the fetus of its own right of self-defense—or, in other words, too weak to forbid the fetus to kill the woman in self-defense, if it were able to do so.

Although there is no incompatibility among these claims, it is odd to suppose that the asymmetry could be insufficiently significant to forbid the fetus to defend itself (if it could), but sufficiently significant to forbid others to defend it.

10.3. *The Decisive Asymmetry*

In the preceding section, I granted the assumption that there is a moral asymmetry between a Nonresponsible Threat and the Innocent Victim that is sufficient to justify the killing of the Threat in self-defense—though earlier, in section 10.1, I had suggested that there is in fact no such asymmetry. For I argued there that there is no morally relevant difference between a Nonresponsible Threat and an Innocent Bystander; and since an Innocent Victim is in effect an Innocent Bystander, it follows that there is no relevant difference between the Nonresponsible Threat and the Innocent Victim. In this section, I will argue that, in the case of abortion, there is in fact a morally relevant asymmetry between the pregnant woman (the Innocent Victim) and the fetus (a Nonresponsible Threat), though not the sort of asymmetry that I granted for the sake of argument in the previous section.

In the previous section, I assumed that there is an asymmetry between the woman and the fetus, but not one that is based on considerations of justice. I assumed that, although the Justice-Based Account must form the core of any plausible understanding of the morality of self-defense, there may nevertheless be grounds for self-defense other than the appeal to considerations of justice in the distribution of harm and that some such ground might justify the woman in killing the fetus in self-defense. But these other grounds, if any, are weaker than the justification for self-defense provided by considerations of justice. If considerations of justice apply in any particular case, they are dominant, or overriding.

I also suggested, in section 10.1, that there are three conditions for liability to self-defensive violence as a matter of justice. In descending order of importance, they are: (1) culpable responsibility for the creation of a forced choice among harms ("culpability"), (2) moral responsibility for the creation of a forced choice in a way that involves fault but, because there is an excuse, not culpability ("fault without culpability"), and (3) moral responsibility for a forced choice without either culpability or fault ("responsibility without culpability or fault").

I can now state the central claim of this section, which is that, in most cases in which a woman is threatened by the continuation of pregnancy, she is morally denied the option of self-defense because the last of these three conditions of liability applies to her. In most cases in which a woman is threatened by the continuation of pregnancy (whether the threat is to her life or is a lesser threat, such as that of continued bodily invasion), the pregnancy is the result of voluntary sexual activity on her part. She is therefore morally responsible for the fact that there is a forced choice between her suffering a harm and the fetus's suffering a harm. For she voluntarily chose to engage in sexual activity knowing both that it carried a risk of pregnancy and that pregnancy can be an onerous or threatening condition. Thus although she is an *Innocent* Victim, she is *not* a *Nonresponsible* Victim. For she bears some responsibility for the fact that she is threatened by the presence of the fetus. (She is an *Innocent Cause* of the threat to herself.) The degree of her moral responsibility is, admittedly, quite weak. She is certainly not culpable; indeed, she is presumably not at fault in any way—that is, she presumably acted entirely permissibly in doing what brought about the forced choice. Nevertheless, she is to a degree morally responsible for the situation of forced choice, whereas the fetus bears no responsibility whatever. And that is, according to the Justice-Based Account, a morally critical asymmetry between them.

It may be, as I assumed for the sake of argument in the previous section, that there is also another moral asymmetry that favors the woman over the fetus—for example, that the fetus is in a morally inappropriate position vis-à-vis the woman. But as I suggested earlier, considerations of justice are dominant or overriding. And we can see, intuitively, that that is so in the present case. The fetus may be in an inappropriate position or pose an unjustified threat, but it is the woman who put it in that position. Her responsibility for its being in an inappropriate position, or posing an unjustified threat, clearly shifts the liability for any consequent harm from it to her.

When the pregnant woman is thus morally responsible for the forced choice between her being harmed by the presence of the fetus and the fetus's being harmed by an abortion, considerations of justice favor the fetus. Even in the Extreme Case, justice prefers its life to hers. She would therefore be acting wrongly if she were to abort it, even to save her own life. For that would be to impose the cost of her own voluntary action on it. Assuming that the fetus will survive if it is not aborted, she must acquiesce in dying rather than kill it.

This, I believe, is a grotesquely harsh and implausible conclusion. Even most opponents of abortion would reject it. But there is worse to come. Given that the pregnant woman is not permitted to kill the fetus in self-defense, it is clear that a third party is not permitted to kill it on her behalf. Suppose that the woman nevertheless hires a physician to abort it for her. The fetus would then face a lethal threat from a responsible agent acting wrongly. (And, while it might be plausible to regard the woman as excused by duress, no such excuse would apply to the physician.) Its right to self-defense would therefore be supported by considerations of justice. It could not, of course, defend itself; but the moral asymmetry between itself and its Attacker would be grounded in considerations of justice and would therefore give anyone a moral reason to defend it. Third-party intervention on its behalf and against the physician would seem to be permissible.

Again, this conclusion is intolerable. Admittedly, it does not apply in cases in which a threatening pregnancy arises from rape (or, perhaps, in those very rare cases in which a woman—or more likely a girl—voluntarily engaged in sex but was nonculpably and non-negligently unaware that it might result in pregnancy)—for in those cases the pregnant woman bears no responsibility for the threat she faces. But this limitation to the appalling implications of the self-defense argument is small consolation for those who expected implications of quite a different sort.

One cannot, of course, evade these conclusions simply by not appealing to the self-defense argument. Those who wish to defend the permissibility of abortion must find a flaw in the reasoning that has led to these conclusions. In my case this is simple, for I reject the assumption that the fetus—even the developed fetus—is a person with full moral standing, full moral rights, or whatever. And without some such assumption, the fetus presumably has no right to kill in self-defense and, a fortiori, third parties would not be permitted to kill in its defense. For, in the absence of a certain status—personhood or whatever—the fetus would fall outside the scope of principles of justice.[141] (Although the comparison is inexact, it is instructive to note that, even when the killing of a certain animal would be wrong, and would wrong the animal itself, it would still be impermissible for a third party to kill the culpable human Attacker, even if that were the only way to save the animal's life.)

Those who accept the permissibility of abortion but grant that the fetus is a person with full moral status are in a more awkward position. Although they may not wish to rest their case on an appeal to the self-defense argument, and may even reject that argument, they must find a reason for denying the permissibility of third-party intervention on behalf of a fetus threatened by abortion. One possibility is to appeal to the consideration I noted in responding to the Responsibility Objection to the Thomson argument. Even though the pregnant woman is morally responsible for the fact that she is threatened by the fetus, the act by which she created the threat will not have been worse for the fetus even if she (or a third party acting on her behalf) kills it in order to avert the threat to herself. In other words, it is not worse for the fetus for her to cause it to be a threat and then kill it in self-defense than it would have been if she had never done what caused it to be a threat. This is because the act that caused the fetus to be a threat also caused it to exist. If she had not caused it to be a threat, it would never have existed at all.

Is this consideration sufficient to nullify the injustice that would otherwise be involved in the woman's killing the fetus in self-defense? It can be argued that there is no injustice. For there is a sense in which her killing the fetus would not force it to pay the cost of the action by which she created the forced choice. Overall, that act has *no* cost for the fetus. For as I noted, even if she kills the fetus, that will not be worse for it than if she had never done the act that created the forced choice. We can perhaps imagine the woman justifying herself to the fetus: "I know my voluntary act created the condition of forced choice. But if I had not done that act, you would never have existed at all. So how can that act be cited as a reason why I should be harmed rather than you?"

On the other hand, it can also be argued that there is injustice. If she kills the fetus, that is certainly worse for it than her not killing it would have been. Killing it imposes a grave cost on it in that sense. We can perhaps imagine the fetus arguing against the woman: "Your killing me would inflict a terrible harm on me. I recognize, of course, that if you do not kill me, my presence will cause you to suffer a terrible harm. But that predicament is entirely the result of your voluntary action. That I would never have existed if you had not done that act is irrelevant. You certainly did not do the act with any intention of benefiting me. The fact is that I do exist and have an interest in continuing to exist that is at least as strong as yours. You have no right to kill me to save yourself from the consequences of your own action."

I am uncertain which of the two has the better argument.

5

Endings

1. WHEN DO WE DIE, OR CEASE TO EXIST?

1.1. *Two Concepts of Death*

I have argued that the view that best captures our intuitions about our own survival and persistence is that we are essentially embodied minds. If that is right, we begin to exist when our brains begin to support the existence of a mind—that is, when they develop the capacity to generate consciousness and mental activity. Since the capacity for consciousness is the defining essential property of a mind, we must cease to exist when we lose the capacity for consciousness in a way that is in principle irreversible.

It is quite commonly believed that we cease to exist, or at least cease to exist *here,* in association with our organisms, when our brains lose the capacity to support consciousness. When the body of Nancy Cruzan died in 1990, after spending almost eight years in a persistent vegetative state (PVS), her family, who had gone to the Supreme Court in their efforts to terminate the body's life support, engraved on her tombstone: "DEPARTED JAN 11, 1983 / AT PEACE DEC 26, 1990."[1] This is not an isolated phenomenon. In the late 1960s and early 1970s, the highly successful efforts to persuade medical bodies and legislatures that brain death marks the death of a human being focused largely on the fact that brain death is sufficient for the irreversible loss of the capacity for consciousness. Thus Alan Shewmon, a pediatric neurologist who has written extensively on brain death, observes that "the introducers of the concept [of brain death] intended to *redefine* death in terms of unconsciousness rather than diagnose it as the cessation of biological life of the human organism."[2] Significantly, the title of the report that was most influential in gaining support for the concept of brain death was "A Definition of Irreversible Coma," implying that what the tests for brain death actually test for is not death but the irreversible loss of the capacity for consciousness—that is, that brain death indicates when a coma is genuinely irreversible.[3] For death and coma are mutually exclusive states.

Perhaps initially many people believed that only with a diagnosis of brain death could one be confident that an individual had lost the capacity for consciousness irreversibly.[4] It soon became obvious, however, that in certain conditions there is a near certainty that the capacity for consciousness has been destroyed even though brain death has not occurred. Most neurologists agree, for example, that this is true in most instances of PVS. Some of those who had been motivated to accept brain death as the criterion of death therefore obeyed the promptings of consistency by rejecting brain death and embracing instead a criterion that they took to be more tightly connected with the irreversible loss of the capacity for consciousness. Some contended that the proper criterion of death is *neocortical death,* defined by the neurologist Julius Korein as "the destruction of cortical neurons bilaterally while deep structures of the cerebral hemispheres such as the thalamus and basal ganglia may be intact along with the brainstem and cerebellum."[5] Others, slightly more conservative in their estimation of what is sufficient for the irreversible loss of the capacity for consciousness, defended the notion of *cerebral death,* defined by Korein as the "irreversible destruction of both cerebral hemispheres exclusive of the brainstem and cerebellum."[6] According to these views, a person dies when he or she suffers the destruction of those areas of the brain in which consciousness is realized, whether these areas are confined to the cortex, as some believe, or include other parts of the cerebral hemispheres as well.

These revisionist proposals for a "higher-brain" criterion of death continue to enjoy strong support in certain quarters, but they have been unsuccessful in dislodging brain death as the orthodox criterion of death in most parts of the world.[7] The main reason why this is so is that both cerebral death and neocortical death are compatible with the survival and continued functional integrity of the brainstem, and thus with continued spontaneous respiration and heartbeat in the organism. A human organism that has suffered neocortical death or cerebral death can continue to breathe and to maintain other vital functions with a minimum of external support—in some cases with little more than intravenous nutrition and hydration and basic nursing care. It has seemed to most observers to be preposterous to say of such an organism that it is *dead.*

We can escape this impasse if we accept that we are not identical with our organisms. Recognition that we are embodied minds distinct from our organisms allows us to embrace the intuition behind the revisionist higher-brain proposals—namely, that we cease to exist when we irreversibly lose the capacity for consciousness—while at the same time recognizing that an organism that has suffered neocortical or cerebral death is nevertheless a living organism. For if we are not identical with our organisms, one of us can cease to exist even if his or her organism remains in existence and, indeed, even if it remains alive.

If a person and his organism are distinct substances, and if both can die or cease to be alive, it seems that we need two concepts of death—one for the person and one for the organism. Following most writers in the area, I accept that the death of a human organism is a biological phenomenon that consists in the irreversible cessation of integrated functioning in the major organs and subsystems (respiratory, circulatory, immune, and so on) of the body. Perhaps this is not exactly right; I do not pretend to any particular expertise in the matter.[8] But for our purposes it is close enough. If we were human organisms, it might be important to be able to determine precisely what the death of an organism essentially involves, and to be able to identify precisely when it occurs. But we are not organisms. We die or cease to exist when our brains lose the capacity for consciousness in a way that is in principle irreversible.

Many people believe that the concept of death is univocal and belongs to biology. Charles M. Culver and Bernard Gert, for example, assert that "death is a biological concept. Thus in a literal sense, death can be applied directly only to biological organisms and not to persons. We do not object to the phrase 'death of a person,' but the phrase in common usage actually means the death of the organism which was the person."[9] This view is echoed by David Lamb, who claims that "the concept of 'death' can only be applied to organisms, not persons."[10] As the passage quoted indicates, Culver and Gert take "person" to be a phase sortal rather than a substance sortal. It is therefore unsurprising that they believe that a person can die only in a way that is supervenient upon the death of an organism. A person dies only if an organism dies while it is a person, just as a child dies only if an organism dies during its childhood phase. Just as no child dies when an organism ceases to be a child by becoming an adult, so no one dies when a living organism ceases to be a person by losing certain psychological attributes that are constitutive of personhood.

While it is often asserted that death is a univocal biological concept, the assertion is never, to my knowledge, argued for. People seem to have no difficulty in understanding the idea that I may die before my organism does. I have been telling my students this for years and am pretty confident that they have not suspected me of talking nonsense. Even if the primary sense of the notion of death is biological, people are able to grasp an extended sense in which a person—a psychological rather than a biological substance—dies when he loses the capacity for consciousness. For it is entirely natural to say that a person dies when he ceases to exist, even if his organism remains alive. (Thus James Rachels quotes the wife of a man who some years previously had lapsed into a PVS: "He died back in 1970. We know that.")[11] A person who is first alive and then ceases to exist thereby also ceases to be alive; and normally ceasing to be alive is a sufficient condition of dying. (There are exceptions. An amoeba ceases to exist when it divides but arguably does not die. Similarly, two embryos in the same womb may fuse, thereby also ceasing to exist but not necessarily dying.) In any case, I propose to say that when a person ceases to exist by losing the capacity for consciousness, he dies. If this is a technical sense of the notion of death, so be it.

The two concepts of death correspond to two concepts of life, or of being alive. To say that a human organism is alive is just to say that its various organs and subsystems are functioning together in a coordinated and harmonious way. To say that a person is alive is just to say that she exists—for which, at present, it is a necessary but not a sufficient condition that her organism be biologically alive.

These two concepts of life should not be confused with the distinction James Rachels has drawn between *being alive,* which involves only life in the biological sense, and *having a life,* which involves life "in the biographical sense" and requires a conscious subject.[12] Rachels believes that in the normal case both types of life, biological and biographical, can be predicated of one and the same thing: the human organism or human being. Thus he also believes that there are cases—for example, cases of PVS—in which a human being ceases to have a life in the biographical sense but does not die because he remains alive in the biological sense. In my view, by contrast, the organism is the primary bearer of biological life, and only the mind (or self or person) has a biography. Thus most of the cases that, according to Rachels, involve an individual's remaining alive only in the biological sense are, in my view, cases in which the self or conscious subject dies (and thus has no life of any sort) while his or her organism continues to live. (There is one type of case in which I would agree with Rachels that a person remains biologically alive but ceases to have a biographical life. I will return to this in the following two subsections.)

1.2. Brain Death

If we need two concepts of death—one for ourselves and one for our organisms—we presumably also need two corresponding criteria. A criterion of death enables us to determine when death has occurred. The orthodox criterion of the death of a human being, virtually everywhere in the world, is *brain death:* the death of the brain as a whole. Is brain death really death—and, if it is, what is it the death of?[13]

There are two powerful intuitions that have informed the debate about brain death from its inception. One is that death involves, and perhaps consists in, the annihilation of the self through the irreversible loss of the capacity for consciousness. (This same intuition is what motivates some people to embrace the Embodied Mind Account of Identity.) The other is that death is a biological phenomenon that involves the cessation of integrated functioning in the organism as a whole. I believe that the perennial appeal of brain death as the criterion of death is that it seems to capture both of these seemingly disparate dimensions to, or aspects of, human death. When the brain as a whole dies or ceases to function, all traces of the self are gone: there is no longer any possibility of the organism's again being able to support consciousness or mental activity. And the death of the brain also heralds the immediate disintegration of the organism as a self-regulating system of interconnected parts. Therefore, if brain death is death, it may seem that the loss of biological life and the annihilation of personal life must coincide. There is, perhaps, no need to distinguish between the person and the organism. We can do justice to both intuitions about the nature of death without having to embrace a controversial dualism that treats the person and the organism as distinct substances.

This is not to say, of course, that these considerations are what motivated people to accept brain death as the criterion of death in the first place. It is now commonly accepted that the major factors that prompted the shift from the traditional cardio-pulmonary criterion of death to brain death were primarily practical in nature. New life-sustaining technologies—in particular, mechanical respirators—were causing hospital wards to become increasingly congested with the bodies of patients in whom all capacity for consciousness had been lost, but who could not be declared dead until their circulation had stopped despite the continuous provision of mechanical ventilation. In many cases, externally supported respiration will prompt the heart to continue to beat even after the brain has died. Only after the heart itself has deteriorated beyond a certain point will it cease to respond to the signals generated by respiration. By declaring that brain-dead patients were dead, hospital staff no longer had to wait for these patients' hearts to stop beating to disconnect them from respirators, thereby freeing the hospital's resources for use on patients who could benefit from them. Patients who were brain dead but whose hearts continued to beat as a result of mechanical ventilation also tended to have healthier organs than patients whose hearts had ceased to function despite the provision of mechanical ventilation. Thus the ability to declare a brain-dead patient dead enabled surgeons to secure a larger supply of healthy organs for transplantation. It was therefore hardly a coincidence that the acceptance of brain death as death occurred just as transplant surgery was becoming a more effective and therefore more common mode of treatment for conditions that had once been invariably fatal.

But, however convenient it may have been to declare brain-dead patients to be dead, there had to be a convincing philosophical case for treating brain death as death. As I noted, the main arguments focused initially on the fact that brain death necessarily involves the loss of selfhood through the irreversible loss of the capacity for consciousness. These arguments later tended to be supplemented or displaced by a focus on the brain as the regulator of the organism's integration. But both claims were influential. Together they led people to believe that both dimensions of death—the loss of consciousness and the loss of bodily integration—occur when brain death occurs.

I will argue, however, that the notion of brain death does not do justice to either of our intuitions about death. Brain death is not an acceptable criterion of either the ceasing to be of the mind or the biological death of the organism. There is, in fact, no single criterion that can capture both dimensions of death. This is because the two critical functions of the brain—the generation of consciousness and the regulation of integrated functioning in the organism—are localized in different areas. The preponderance of the evidence indicates that it is in the "higher brain"—and in particular in the cortex, which is the outer layer of the cerebrum—that consciousness and mental activity are realized. And it is primarily the "lower brain," consisting mainly of the brainstem, that coordinates the functioning of various organs and subsystems throughout the organism. (Functioning in one particular region of the lower brain—the *ascending reticular activating system,* or *reticular formation*—is necessary for the *activation* of the capacity for consciousness. I will discuss the significance of the reticular formation at the end of this section.) Because these two functions are localized in different regions of the brain, each can be lost while the other is retained. It is, for example, quite common for the cerebral cortex to be destroyed while the brainstem remains intact and functional. This is because the cortex is more sensitive to the effects of anoxia. When the brain is deprived of oxygen, the tissues of the cortex begin to die quite quickly. If the oxygen supply is soon restored, however, the tissues of the brainstem may survive undamaged. Thus it often happens that people lose the critical functions of the higher brain—including consciousness and cognition—while retaining the regulatory functions of the brainstem. When this happens, the person has lapsed into a PVS.

It is an accepted tenet of neurology that a patient in a PVS occasioned by the destruction of the cerebral cortex altogether lacks the capacity for consciousness or mental activity. If this is true—and one can be reasonably confident, though not certain, that it is—then brain death cannot be the criterion for the loss of the capacity for consciousness. For a human organism in a PVS has lost the capacity for consciousness, and is therefore without a mind or self; but it is not brain dead. While the death of the brain as a whole is certainly *sufficient* for the irreversible loss of the capacity for consciousness, the phenomenon of PVS shows that it is not *necessary* for this. Thus if the capacity for consciousness is essential to our existence—as the Embodied Mind Account of Identity holds—brain death cannot be the criterion of *our* dying or ceasing to exist. If the capacity for consciousness is essential to us and PVS involves the irreversible loss of that capacity, it follows that we cease to exist in PVS. And this, of course, is the view of those whose fidelity to the idea that the capacity for consciousness is essential to us led them to embrace one of the revisionist "higher-brain" criteria of death.

Another option, obviously, is to reject the intuition that the capacity for consciousness is essential to our existence. This is the alternative embraced by those who have continued to accept brain death as the criterion of death. It has considerable intuitive support: many people believe that they could continue to exist in a PVS.

The idea that brain death is death goes naturally with the view that we are essentially human organisms, or living human organisms. Indeed, the advocates of brain death (to whom I will refer as the "brain death theorists") soon muted their initial appeal to the relation between brain function and consciousness and instead concentrated on the case for brain death as the criterion for the biological death of the human organism. If we are essentially human organisms, and brain death is the right criterion for the biological death of the human organism, then brain death is the right criterion of death, period. (Brain death would have the same significance if we assume, not that we are organisms, but that we are incorporeal souls that cease to exist in association with our organisms when, and only when, those organisms die or cease to be alive biologically.)

I have argued that we are not human organisms. Therefore, even if brain death is the right criterion for the biological death of a human organism, it does not follow that it is the right criterion for determining when one of *us* dies. But many people will be unpersuaded by my arguments against the view that we are essentially human organisms. It is therefore worth considering whether brain death is the proper criterion for determining when a human organism has died.

It is, perhaps, a little puzzling why brain death should seem so obviously the right criterion to so many people. Recall that most brain death theorists hold that the concept of death is univocal—that death is the same in whatever kind of life it occurs: plant, animal, or human. (Thus David Lamb writes that "the death of a man is no different from the death of a dog or cat.")[14] This highlights the oddity of taking brain death to be death: for many—perhaps even most—living things that die do not have brains at all. And even in human organisms the brain is only one organ among many. Why should the death of this one organ be treated as equivalent to the death of the organism as a whole?

The answer that most brain death theorists have given is that brain death marks the irreversible cessation of coordinated functioning in organisms that have brains because, as a presidential commission mandated to study the problem put it, "the brain is the regulator of the body's integration."[15] Without the brain to integrate the functions of the various parts of the organism, integrated functioning ceases and the organism is dead. Thus, according to Lamb, "the centrality accorded to the brain is . . . bound up with its role as supreme regulator and co-ordinator." "That structural disintegration follows brain death," he claims, "is not a contingent matter; it is a necessary consequence of the death of the critical system. The death of the brain is the point beyond which other systems cannot survive with, or without, mechanical support."[16] Similar claims underlie the more recent pronouncement of James L. Bernat that "permanent cessation of the clinical functions of the entire brain is the criterion of death because it is the only condition that is both necessary and sufficient for death"—which he understands as "the permanent cessation of the *critical* functions of the organism as a whole."[17]

I believe that all of these claims are mistaken. Brain death is neither necessary nor sufficient for the cessation of integrated functioning in the organism as a whole.

That brain death is not necessary for the death of an organism is shown by the case, discussed in section 3.3 of chapter 1, of brain transplantation. If one's entire brain were surgically removed and transplanted into the cranium of one's identical twin, from which the brain had just been removed, one's brain would remain alive and functional in the body of one's twin. But one's original organism, from which one's brain had been removed, would certainly die unless it were provided with external life support. Its various component parts would cease to function and soon begin to decompose. In that case, an organism would die but without having suffered brain death. For, even though the organism would no longer be governed by the operations of a brain, its brain would not have *died:* its brain would be alive and well, albeit housed in a different organism.

In that earlier discussion, I mentioned an alternative interpretation of this case. According to this interpretation, what happens in this case is that, although a lot of the original matter composing one's organism is cut away, one's organism survives alive in the form of the living brain. What I described as the transplantation of one's brain into the organism of one's identical twin is actually, on this view, the grafting onto one's original organism of a new assembly of parts. The original organism does not die: it merely has one set of parts cut away and a different set grafted on. Given this interpretation, the example is not a counterexample to the idea that brain death is death. If the living organism can be pared down to the functional brain, or perhaps even to a functional part of the brain, it does seem that brain death must be a necessary condition of the death of the organism.

I advanced several objections to this interpretation. The claim that the organism survives in the form of the brain is based on the idea that the brain is the control center of the organism. Thus Bernat says of such a case, "the capacities for spontaneous breathing and control of circulation are retained [by the brain] although they cannot be implemented."[18] But this is not the case. The isolated brain has no more capacity to breathe or to circulate blood than a man whose hands have been amputated has the capacity to play Beethoven on the piano. Once the brain has been separated from the rest of the organism, it no longer has any claim to be the control center of anything. It therefore has no more claim to be the organism than the heart would have if it were extracted and kept alive. It is true that an isolated brain would retain some of its distinctive capacities, such as consciousness and cognition; but the same is true of the heart. That the isolated brain could continue to support consciousness is no more reason to suppose that it would be the original organism than the isolated heart's retention of the ability to pump blood would be reason to regard it as the surviving organism.

Hence the original conclusion stands: brain death is not necessary for the death of a human organism. Nor is it sufficient. Recall Lamb's claim, quoted earlier, that "the death of the brain is the point beyond which other systems cannot survive with, or without, mechanical support." This, too, is simply false—indeed, spectacularly false. With mechanical ventilation and the provision of nutrition, hydration, and a daily injection of a hormone to prevent diabetes insipidus, human organisms that have been reliably diagnosed as brain dead have been able to maintain integrated functioning for considerable periods of time—in some cases for many months and in several cases for longer than a year. In these cases, the level of systemic functioning is high: the organisms circulate blood, metabolize food, maintain immune response to infection, excrete wastes, and so on. There have even been cases in which the bodies of brain-dead women who were discovered to be pregnant were able to function sufficiently well to support the growth of the fetus for several months, thereby enabling it to be delivered alive by caesarian section.[19]

In one instance, a boy of four was diagnosed as brain dead from intracranial edema caused by meningitis. The physicians recommended discontinuation of life support, but the mother refused. Eventually the boy's body was transferred home where, with only mechanical ventilation, tube feeding, and little more than basic nursing care, it has remained comprehensively functional for the last fourteen and a half years. Alan Shewmon was recently allowed to perform an examination. He reports that "evoked potentials showed no cortical or brain-stem responses, a magnetic resonance angiogram showed no intracranial blood flow, and an MRI scan revealed that the entire brain, including the stem, had been replaced by ghost-like tissues and disorganized proteinaceous fluids." Yet Shewmon also observes that, "while 'brain-dead' he has grown, overcome infections and healed wounds."[20]

Brain death theorists are obliged to describe these externally supported organisms as ventilated *corpses* whose functions present only a simulacrum of life. The mere functioning of the various organs and subsystems of the organism is insufficient for the presence of life. In claiming that these brain-dead but externally supported organisms are biologically dead, the brain death theorists effectively make it a condition of life not only that the organism should function in normal ways, but also that the functions should be regulated by the brain. An organism in which comprehensive functioning has irreversibly ceased is definitely dead; but according to the brain death theorists, the presence of comprehensive functioning is not sufficient for a human organism to be alive. In order for an organism to be alive, the functions of its parts and subsystems must be genuinely *integrated*, and they cannot be integrated unless they are controlled by the brain.

Because new technologies can replace the regulatory functions of the brain to varying degrees, an awkward question arises for those who claim that integrated functioning has to be regulated by the brain in order to be constitutive of life. *To what extent* do the somatic functions of the organism have to be regulated by the brain in order for the organism to count as alive? The brain death theorist cannot say that the organism remains alive as long as *any* somatic functions are regulated by the brain. For the continuation of certain forms of regulatory activity by the brain is compatible with a reliable diagnosis of brain death. Shewmon observes: "some residual hypothalamic function, manifested by absence of diabetes insipidus, occurs fairly commonly in 'brain death.' . . . Some primitive autonomic functions can remain (mediated perhaps by the hypothalamus or lower medulla), such as temperature and blood pressure autoregulation or rise in heart rate and blood pressure in response to skin incision for organ retrieval."[21] The last two functions, he notes, are "typically attributed to the spinal cord, but debatably might involve some lower brain-stem contribution."[22]

On discovering these facts, why did the brain death theorists not revise their clinical criteria for pronouncing brain death, so that an organism could not be considered brain dead until these various residual brain functions had ceased? No doubt part of the explanation is pragmatic. If a patient could not be declared dead until all such functions had ceased, our ability to procure usable organs for transplantation under the "dead donor rule"—the convention that insists that organs may not be removed from a live body—would be imperiled. This is not, however, a motivation that any brain death theorist is likely to acknowledge. What the brain death theorists in fact tend to say is that the presence of some few residual functions is compatible with the death of the brain as a whole. But once this is conceded, how are we to determine which brain functions, and how many, are compatible with the death of the brain as a whole? Recall that the death of the brain is supposed to be equivalent to the cessation of functioning in the organism as a whole. Thus the dimensions of brain function that would have to be absent in order for the state of the brain to be indicative of the death of the organism should be those directly associated with somatic functioning. Brain death, in other words, need not exclude certain brain functions whose presence is not necessarily indicative of life in the organism. It would, however, be more than serendipitous if our current notion of brain death, which is partly dictated by our current capacities for testing, were to discriminate precisely between those brain functions that are sufficient for the presence of life in the organism and those that are not. It seems that there are forms of brain function, such as consciousness, that are unconnected with somatic functioning but whose presence now precludes a diagnosis of brain death. (I will shortly indicate how the brain might continue to generate consciousness while ceasing to perform any regulative functions.) This suggests a need for a revision of the notion of brain death, as well as for a correspondingly revised set of clinical criteria for diagnosing brain death.

While brain death theorists thus cannot say that the presence of *any* regulative function in the brain is sufficient for life in the organism, they also cannot say that a human organism remains alive only if *all* somatic functions normally regulated by the brain continue to be so regulated; for there are many forms of selective brain damage that eliminate a single regulative capacity that can then be replaced by a mechanical substitute. For example, a lesion affecting the respiratory center in the brainstem may destroy a person's capacity for spontaneous respiration, but no one doubts that the person remains alive if he is given mechanical ventilation. So what brain death theorists have to say is that a human organism remains alive if and only if *enough* of its functioning is integrated by the brain. But how much is enough?

This question can be explored by considering patients who suffer from *locked-in syndrome*. In this comparatively rare but horrific condition, damage to the brainstem, which may leave the cerebral hemispheres unaffected, causes two types of deficit. First, the transmission of signals between the cerebrum and the rest of the organism is impeded. As a result, the patient may be fully conscious but unable to move any part of his or her body (except perhaps the eyes), unable to receive sensory information from most parts of the body, and so on. Second, various of the brainstem's regulatory capacities may be lost. In order for the patient to survive, these regulatory functions have to be taken over by external mechanisms.

How does the locked-in patient compare to a brain-dead organism whose characteristic functions are maintained with external support? For convenience, let us focus on the case of a brain-dead pregnant woman whose organism is maintained in a sufficiently functional state to be capable of supporting fetal gestation. The first point to note is that the locked-in patient may require exactly the same forms of external support that the brain-dead pregnant woman requires. But locked-in syndrome may involve varying degrees of damage to the brainstem, and even in the worst cases *some* areas of the brainstem are preserved and at least potentially functional. The question is whether it is really the presence of these capacities that constitutes the difference between life and death. In order to determine whether the locked-in patient is alive, do we have to count the number of regulatory functions still carried out by the brainstem? If the patient were losing brainstem functions gradually, one by one, would there be some critical point at which the loss of one more regulatory function would be equivalent to death—even if that function could be taken over by an external source of support?

I think the answer to this last question is obvious. Provided that each regulatory function of the brainstem could be taken over by an external replacement, the patient could in principle remain conscious throughout the entire process by which *all* the regulatory functions of the brainstem were lost. He would therefore clearly remain alive.

It might be objected that the replacement of the brainstem by mechanical substitutes is impossible. Brain death theorists often claim that the brain is irreplaceable. Bernat, for example, asserts that "the final proof of the validity of the whole-brain criterion centers on the criticality and irreplaceability of the brain."[23] It usually turns out, however, that such claims about the irreplaceability of the brain are overgeneralized claims about the irreplaceability of the those areas of the brain in which consciousness and mental activity take place. Thus, in elucidating his general claim, Bernat asserts that, "although some of the brain's regulatory functions may be replaced mechanically, the brain's functions of awareness, sentience, and sapience, and its capacities to experience and communicate cannot be reproduced or simulated by any machine."[24] I would agree with this, not because I believe that consciousness could never be generated by anything other than a brain, but because, as I indicated in chapter 1, I think that at least a certain core of the areas of the brain in which consciousness is realized is essential to our identity. Thus even if a person's cortex could be replaced by an exact duplicate, the original person would have ceased to exist and been replaced by a replica. But the hypothetical replacement of the brainstem that I am envisaging need involve only areas of the brain devoted to regulatory functions and not areas, such as the cortex, whose replacement is in principle incompatible with our continued existence. We could, of course, imagine that the entire brainstem is destroyed, including the areas concerned with consciousness—namely, the reticular formation, which functions as a sort of "off-on" switch for consciousness, and those areas that appear to modulate the emotional hue of certain experiences. But because these are not areas in which consciousness is directly realized, and are in any case areas that make only a marginal contribution to determining the contents of consciousness, it is plausible to suppose that we could survive their replacement—that is, that they are, unlike the cerebral cortex, not essential to our continued existence. Thus it seems that Michael B. Green and Daniel Wikler are right when they write that the brainstem "could conceivably be replaced by an artificial aid which performed its function. The respirators and other life-supports which maintain body functioning after lower brain death collectively constitute a sort of artificial lower brain, and development of a more perfect mechanical substitute is merely a technological problem."[25]

The proof that the total replacement of the integrating functions of the brain is possible appeals to the traditional metaphysical principle that what is actual must also be possible. For there are actual cases in which people have survived the complete blockage of the regulatory action of the brain. Shewmon has pointed out that in rare, extreme instances of Guillain-Barré Syndrome (acute inflammatory demyelinating polyneuritis), the cranial and spinal nerves are so badly affected that "no information can enter or leave the central nervous system, creating a total locked-in syndrome externally mimicking 'brain death.' Such patients appear completely comatose, even though they have essentially normal electroencephalograms and are quite conscious inwardly."[26] In these cases, the person may survive for several weeks in the absence of any regulation of the organism by the brain. Of course, no part of the brain is actually dead; but the brain is functionally completely disconnected from the rest of the organism. Patients thus require all the forms of external life support that are necessary to sustain a brain-dead pregnant woman. Hence, where somatic regulation is concerned, these instances of Guillain-Barré Syndrome are indistinguishable from brain death. But the patients are undeniably alive.

The brain death theorist might contend that the relevant difference between the patient with severe Guillain-Barré Syndrome and the brain-dead pregnant woman is that the former's brain retains the *capacity* for somatic regulation while the latter's does not. It is, in short, the capacity for somatic regulation by the brain that makes the difference between a living human organism and a dead one. This, however, is completely arbitrary and implausible. Retreat to this position is tantamount to defeat.

Brain death theorists do not have to retreat to this position. They acknowledge that all locked-in patients are alive—even the hypothetical locked-in patient whose entire brainstem has died and been replaced by an array of mechanical substitutes. For in all locked-in patients, most or all of the upper brain is intact and functional. They retain cortical function. Therefore they are not brain dead. Brain death theorists can claim that it is because the locked-in patients have some significant brain function, while the brain-dead pregnant woman has none, that the former are alive, while the latter is not.

But what exactly is it about the locked-in patients' retention of certain brain functions that makes them alive, while the brain-dead pregnant woman is not? It cannot be that the presence of brain function in the locked-in patients ensures that integrated functioning continues in the organism, for in these patients the brain contributes nothing to somatic integration, at least for a significant period of time. These cases demonstrate that coordinated functioning in a human organism does not have to be regulated by the brain to any degree whatever in order for the organism to be alive. Thus the brain death theorists' principal rationale for claiming that the brain-dead pregnant woman is a corpse—a dead human organism—collapses. They are left without any principled explanation of why coordinated functioning in this organism cannot count as life. They will, of course, say that it is because there is no significant brain function present. But this seems inadequate, given their assumption that the concept of death is univocal for all living beings, together with the fact that there are many types of organism in which integrated functioning is sufficient for life in the absence of brain function, and indeed in the absence of a brain.

Return to the comparison between the patient who is wholly locked-in and the brain-dead pregnant woman. Suppose the locked-in patient's brainstem is dead, though its vital regulatory functions are being maintained externally, as in the case of a patient with severe Guillain-Barré Syndrome. Brain death theorists claim that because the locked-in patient has cortical function, while the brain-dead pregnant woman has no significant brain function at all, the locked-in patient is a living human organism, while brain-dead pregnant woman is not. The difference between the two cases is certainly profoundly important; but is it really the difference between a living organism and a dead organism? Suppose that the locked-in patient irreversibly loses cerebral functions as well. She is now brain dead; but, if the external life-support systems continue to operate as they have, the physical state of the organism as a whole will be unaltered. One part of the organism—the cerebrum—has ceased to perform one isolated function, namely, the generation of consciousness and cognition. But, to repeat, the loss of this one function is insignificant where the overall physiology of the organism is concerned. (In clinical terms, the only detectable difference would be that the electroencephalogram would cease to register cortical activity.) As the brain death theorists' own understanding of PVS shows, the mere loss of the capacity for consciousness cannot be what the biological death of a human organism consists in. It is simply not credible to suppose that the cessation of cortical or cerebral function alone marks the death of the organism as a whole, when the organism itself goes on *exactly* as it did before except that consciousness has ceased to occur.

I think we must conclude that, in the case of the locked-in patient, if there was a living organism present prior to the loss of cerebral function, there is still a living organism present afterward, provided that the functional integration of the organism continues to be maintained at a level comparable to that which was sustained prior to the loss of cerebral function. But the locked-in patient's organism is now brain dead. It is a living organism, but it is also brain dead. Brain death, therefore, is not sufficient for the biological death of a human organism.

I have claimed that brain-dead organisms whose functions are maintained with external support should be considered living organisms. The argument for this conclusion appeals to considerations of consistency. I have claimed that we should accept that these organisms are alive if we believe that a wholly locked-in patient who requires the full panoply of life-support systems is alive and if we believe that the mere loss of the capacity for consciousness cannot constitute the biological death of a human organism. It is important to realize, however, that, like the question when a human organism begins to exist, the question whether a brain-dead but externally sustained human organism is alive is not a scientific question. It is not a question that might be answered by further empirical investigation or experimentation. It seems, rather, to be a *conceptual* question—a question about the boundaries of our concept of a living organism. For we know all of the relevant basic facts—for example, that a brain-dead but externally sustained organism cannot breathe on its own but that, with mechanical ventilation and a few other forms of support, it will circulate blood, digest food, excrete wastes, fight infections, heal wounds, and even retain the capacity for reproduction. Whether it is alive is a *distinct* fact, but not one that obtains independently of these other facts we already know. If it is alive, that is *because* of these other facts. That is, its being alive is a property that supervenes upon other properties, such as having circulating blood and so on. So the question is whether our concept of a living organism is such that an organism with certain characteristically vital properties (e.g., having various coordinated functions) but lacking certain others (e.g., brain functions, spontaneous respiration, etc.) falls within the scope of the concept. This is a prima facie puzzling question because our concept of a living organism arose over a period of time in which there simply were no instances of human organisms that lacked the capacity for spontaneous respiration but nevertheless retained a host of other coordinated functions. So the concept does not come, as it were, with instructions as to whether or how it is to be applied in these cases. If it is to cover these cases, it has to be extended. And to determine whether it should be extended, we have to ascertain whether the extended concept coheres better with our other beliefs than the narrower concept presupposed by the brain death theorists. What I have argued is that the extension of the concept of a living human organism to cover cases of brain-dead but externally sustained organisms is more consistent with our other beliefs—for example, about the status of locked-in patients.

We can see now that the notion of brain death does not correspond to any single conception of what it is for a human organism to be alive. Although brain function of some sort is held to be the sine qua non of human life, the brain death theorists have no clear conception of why brain function is essential to life. The relevance of brain function cannot be that it is necessary for the capacity for consciousness, for a living organism can survive the destruction of those areas of the brain necessary for the generation of consciousness (as happens in PVS). Nor can it be that brain function is necessary for the integration of somatic functioning, for a living organism can also survive in the absence of any integrating action on the part of the brain (as happens in severe instances of locked-in syndrome).

It seems that the notion of brain death implies that there are two distinct and unrelated criteria of life in a human organism. And these two criteria are asserted disjunctively. The idea that brain death is death presupposes that a human organism is alive *either* if there is a mind with the capacity for consciousness (as in locked-in syndrome) *or* if the functioning of the organism's various organs and subsystems is integrated (to a sufficient degree) by the brain (as in PVS). It is also alive, of course, if both conditions are fulfilled.

Just as brain death does not correspond to any single conception of what it is for a human organism to be alive, so also it does not seem to correspond to any coherent conception of the kind of thing we essentially are. For what kind of thing can have these disjunctive criteria for its own continued existence? What kind of thing can survive *either* as an organism that lacks a mind *or* as a mind associated with an organism that, were it not for the presence of the mind, would not be considered a living organism? Most brain death theorists would say that we are human organisms and that a living human organism is one that retains significant brain function. But as we have seen, they have no explanation of why brain function is necessary in order for a human organism to be alive. The truth seems to be that nothing necessarily dies with brain death except the brain itself. For the mind can cease to be even when brain death has not occurred, and the organism can continue to live even when brain death *has* occurred.

The case against brain death is strengthened when we consider the criterion of when we begin to exist that corresponds to the view that we cease to exist at brain death. Any understanding of the conditions of our ceasing to exist, or ceasing to be alive, implies a corresponding understanding of the conditions of our beginning to exist, or beginning to be alive. The beginning to exist and the ceasing to exist of a certain kind of thing should be symmetrical, mirror-images of one another. The reason for this is that, for each kind of thing, there are essential properties without which a thing of that kind cannot exist. Thus a thing of a certain kind begins to exist only when all the essential properties of a thing of that kind have come to be present, and it ceases to exist when it ceases to be the case that all the essential properties are still present—that is, when one or more of the essential properties are lost. A similar condition holds for a thing's beginning to be alive and its ceasing to be alive.

The idea that brain death is death presupposes that the possession of significant brain function is an essential property of a living human organism. For when all significant brain function is lost, the organism ceases to be alive. This implies that a human organism cannot begin to be alive until significant brain function is present. Recognizing that there must be this symmetry between the beginning and end of life, some proponents of brain death have explicitly endorsed the conclusion that we begin to be alive only when significant brain function develops. Drawing on the parallel with brain death, they have designated the point at which brain function begins as *brain life*. Some have then gone on to argue that abortion, embryo experimentation, and other practices that may destroy the embryo or fetus are permissible prior to the onset of brain life.

When does brain life occur—that is, at what point does significant activity in the brain begin to occur? Some contend that this occurs at around eight weeks after fertilization; but this is controversial.[27] The important point, as a matter of principle, is that brain death theorists seem committed to the view that brain life occurs with the initial appearance of any form of brain function or activity the continued presence of which, later in life, would preclude a diagnosis of brain death.

In general, brain death theorists do not distinguish, as I do, between ourselves and our organisms. If they did, they might claim that *we* begin to exist, and to be alive, when brain life occurs, though our organisms began to exist, and to be alive, at an earlier point—for example, at syngamy or around two weeks after fertilization. But brain death theorists tend to believe that we *are* organisms. Thus brain death is supposed to mark the death of the human organism. Therefore brain life has to be understood by the brain death theorist as the point at which the human organism becomes alive. And presumably it becomes alive at the same point that it begins to exist. Although organisms normally continue to exist as dead organisms after they cease to be alive, it does not seem that there is a corresponding period during which they exist *prior* to becoming alive. There is no pre-vital form that an organism takes that corresponds to the post-vital corpse.

What the brain death theorist seems committed to believing, therefore, is that the human organism begins to exist (and, simultaneously, to live) when brain life occurs—that is, with the onset of significant brain activity. But consider what this claim really means. Suppose, for the sake of argument, that brain life occurs at eight weeks after fertilization. (Most of those who accept the notion of brain life but dispute this estimation of when it occurs believe that it occurs later than this rather than earlier.) If the human organism begins to exist at eight weeks after fertilization, there must be something else that exists in the womb during the two-month period prior to brain life. What is it? Certainly from at most two weeks after conception there is *something* there. We use the term "embryo" to refer to it. It appears to be an individual, not just a collection of unconnected tissues and organs. And it seems to be alive. Moreover, it seems that it must, on this view, cease to exist when the organism begins to exist. That is, it is somehow replaced or supplanted by the organism, with which it is physically continuous. It vanishes when the brain it has been developing begins to function. And at that point the organism pops into existence in its stead.

This is clearly absurd. The only alternative for the proponent of brain life is to claim that, for the first eight weeks following fertilization, the womb contains a collection of living tissues and organs that do not constitute an individual. There are cells, tissues, and organs present, but nothing else. Only when the brain is sufficiently formed to begin to function in significant ways do these tissues and organs somehow become united to form a single individual—a living human organism. This view is, however, no more plausible than the idea that the embryo is a living precursor of the organism. It is obvious that the constituent tissues and organs of the six- or seven-week-old embryo are sufficiently integrated and sufficiently distinct from their environment to constitute a single living entity.

In summary, if the beginning and end of life must be symmetrical, the idea that an organism dies when brain death occurs implies that it begins to be alive (and, therefore, begins to exist) when brain life occurs—that is, with the onset of significant brain function. But given that there does not appear to be any capacity for significant brain function until at least eight weeks after fertilization, it follows that the human embryo from two to eight weeks after fertilization either must be a precursor of the organism that ceases to exist when its brain begins to function, or cannot be an individual at all, but is instead a mere bundle of physically contiguous but otherwise isolated tissues and organs. Since neither of these views is even remotely plausible, we should conclude that the onset of significant brain function does not mark the beginning of the life of a human organism. Therefore, if the beginning and end of life are symmetrical, we should also conclude that the cessation of significant brain function does not necessarily mark the end of the life of a human organism either.

This should have been obvious all along. The crux of the brain death theorists' view is that significant brain function is essential to the life of a human organism. This is a logical corollary of the idea that a human organism ceases to be alive when it irreversibly loses significant brain function. But a human embryo is universally acknowledged to be a living human organism, and yet it has no capacity for significant brain function. Indeed, in the earliest stages of its development, it has no brain at all. But if a human organism can be alive prior to the onset of significant brain function, it can surely remain alive after the cessation of brain function, provided that its various parts continue to function in an coordinated way.

Brain death theorists might argue that the embryo's vital functions are spontaneously generated and internally integrated—in contrast to the functions of a brain-dead organism, which require external stimulation and regulation. And even if severe cases of locked-in syndrome show that spontaneous internal integration is not necessary for the presence of life, it is arguably sufficient. This is why the embryo is alive while a brain-dead organism with external support is not.

This response cannot rescue the notion of brain death, for it concedes that a human organism can be alive even in the absence of any capacity for brain function. Moreover, the assumption that the embryo's functions are spontaneously generated is false. The embryo's functions are sustained and regulated by the maternal body in much the way that, for example, a brain-dead pregnant woman's functions are maintained by the ventilator and other forms of external life support. The maternal body, in short, serves as an external life support system for the embryo.

We can, I believe, do justice to our intuitions about these matters only if we distinguish between ourselves and our organisms. Consider first the human organism. Assume that it begins to be alive at the same time that it begins to exist. There should then be a symmetry between its beginning to exist and its dying, or ceasing to be alive. If it is an essential property of a living human organism that its various parts should function together in an integrated and coordinated way, we can say that an organism begins to exist when the cells that form its constituent matter begin to be differentiated and to function in a coordinated and counter-entropic manner. Prior to that point, as I argued in chapter 1, the cluster of proliferating cells that originated in the fertilization of the egg are simply a collection of contiguous but uncoordinated cells that do not together constitute an individual. Given the symmetry between the beginning and the end of life, the organism must die, or cease to be alive, when its constituent parts irreversibly cease to function in an integrated way—or, rather, when they together lose the capacity to function in an integrated way. (The insistence that the loss of integrated function must be irreversible—or that the capacity for integrated functioning must be lost—is necessary in order to accommodate the possibility of suspended animation via cryogenics. A frozen but intact human organism would have ceased to function and hence would no longer be alive; but it would also not be dead. Life and death are apparently not jointly exhaustive of the possibilities.)

It should be stressed that integration requires a significant degree of *internal* coordination, with certain parts responding directly to the action of others. If each organ or part were maintained alive in isolation from the others, so that the functioning of each part was coordinated with that of the others entirely by external means, there would be no *systemic* functioning at all. There would therefore be no life in the organism, even though each part might be alive. There are, however, as yet no actual cases of organisms in which the action of each living organ or part is directed entirely by external means so that there is no autonomous interaction among the parts themselves. Human embryos manifest substantial internal integration—and so do brain-dead organisms that are sustained by external life support. The modes of functioning in, for example, a brain-dead pregnant woman are indefinitely extensive, yet the external assistance necessary to maintain these functions is quite limited. In addition to circulating blood, digesting food, clearing wastes, healing wounds, maintaining body temperature, and so on, the body of a brain-dead pregnant woman will gain weight, redistribute blood flow to increase the supply to the uterus, restrain its immune response to the fetus, and respond in various other ways to the presence of the fetus.[28] Yet none of these functions is directed or directly triggered externally.

In summary, the life of the human organism begins when the cells of which it is initially composed begin to function together in an organized, integrated manner; and the organism dies when its various parts irreversibly cease to function together in this way. If, as I have argued, *we* are not organisms, it is not necessary that we begin to exist when our organisms do, or that we die, or cease to exist, when our organisms die. I have argued that we are embodied minds and that our existence is supported by the operations of our brains. We begin to exist when our brains develop the capacity to generate consciousness and mental activity—that is, when a mind first begins to exist in association with the organism—and we cease to exist when our brains lose that capacity in a way that is in principle irreversible.

If I am right that we must have two distinct *concepts* of death—the death of the organism and the death of the person (or, more precisely, of the mind or self)—then we also need two *criteria* of death—one to enable us to determine when a human organism has died and another to determine when one of *us* has died. How can one tell when a human organism has irreversibly lost the capacity to function in an integrated way? Shewmon has advanced what seems a reasonable proposal. He contends that "the almost universal context" in which the death of a human organism becomes imminent and inevitable is "a terminal cardiac arrest, after which all major organs rapidly become increasingly damaged by anoxia and ischemia. A thermodynamic 'point of no return' is soon passed, beyond which the body's entropy-resisting dynamic unity is irretrievably lost and decomposition (unopposed progression to entropy) will inexorably proceed. . . . The exact timing of this thermodynamical turning point cannot be empirically determined with unlimited precision." Nevertheless, "perhaps 20 to 30 minutes following circulatory arrest would be a reasonable guess."[29]

There is perhaps some vagueness in this proposal, a bit more clinical indeterminacy than is desirable. But if we are not organisms, this is of little practical significance. What is important is being able to determine when one of us dies. Of course, the death of one's organism is, in the world as it is, sufficient for one's own death. But it is not necessary and, particularly if organisms typically do not die until half an hour after the cessation of circulation, a person's death will often, and perhaps usually, precede that of his organism. If that is so, it may not matter much whether we can ascertain the moment at which a human organism dies with great accuracy. For, again, what matters is being able to determine when one of us—the person—dies or ceases to exist. And if this usually occurs before the organism dies, there will usually be little reason to care about the exact timing of the death of the organism.

Let us now consider the more important question, which is what the appropriate criterion is for determining when one of us dies. What we are looking for is an accurate indicator that an individual's brain has lost the capacity for consciousness in a way that is in principle irreversible. In general terms, it seems that the appropriate criterion must be the destruction of those areas of the brain in which consciousness is realized. The problem is that as yet no one knows exactly which areas those are. As I have noted, the consensus in neurology is that the relevant areas are in the cerebral hemispheres—perhaps in the cerebral cortex alone. If consciousness is realized in the cortex only, the death of the cortex ("cortical death") would be a sufficient criterion of the death of a person. Some believe, however, that consciousness is generated in other areas of the cerebral hemispheres as well. If that is right, the death of the cortex would not be sufficient for the death of the person, although the death or destruction of the cerebral hemispheres ("cerebral death") would be. But even cerebral death might not be a completely accurate criterion. If there are areas of the hemispheres that are not involved in the generation of consciousness, the survival of just those areas would be compatible with the death of the person.

The upshot is that I cannot offer a precise criterion for the death of a person—that is, of one of us. This is an inevitable consequence of our present lack of knowledge about the way in which consciousness is generated by the operations of the brain. But, because we require a criterion for purposes of public policy, we should adopt the one that can be most reasonably regarded as both a necessary and a sufficient condition of the irreversible loss of the capacity for consciousness. Brain death, or the death of the whole brain, is certainly sufficient, but is almost certainly not necessary. Cortical death is certainly necessary, but there seems to be insufficient evidence that it is sufficient. Cerebral death, on the other hand, may reasonably be regarded as necessary, even though it is possible that residual function in some areas of the cerebral hemispheres is compatible with the irreversible loss of all capacity for consciousness. This latter possible discrepancy could result in a certain number of false negative diagnoses of the death of a person (that is, finding that a person is alive who is in fact dead), but at least one would be erring on the side of caution. It would be more seriously worrying if the criterion carried a significant risk of false positive diagnoses (that is, finding that a person is dead who is in fact alive). But it seems reasonable to believe that the death or destruction of the cerebral hemispheres is sufficient for the loss of the capacity for consciousness in a way that is in principle irreversible, and thus that there is no significant risk of false positive diagnoses, provided that the clinical tests for cerebral death are themselves accurate. It would, however, be mendacious to pretend that there is *no* risk of false positive diagnoses. I will consider the morality of accepting this risk in section 1.3.

For the moment, I want to clarify the significance of my insistence that the loss of the capacity for consciousness should be *in principle irreversible*. The point of this insistence is to acknowledge that, if a person has lost the capacity for consciousness but it remains possible, even if only in principle, to restore that capacity in such a way as to revive the *same mind,* then the person has not ceased to exist. Consider, by way of illustration, two distinct forms of irreversible coma. In a common form of PVS, cerebral death has occurred, but the brainstem remains intact and functional. Thus, although the organism remains alive, the person has died or ceased to exist. Because the tissues in which consciousness and mental activity were realized have atrophied and died, they cannot be revived or restored. The original mind cannot, therefore, be revived; for a mind is individuated by reference to its physical substrate. If new, functional cerebral tissues were somehow grafted onto the PVS patient's brainstem, the conscious subject who would then exist in association with the organism would be a different individual from the original person whose cerebral hemispheres had been destroyed. This would be so, in my view, even if the original person's hemispheres were replaced by exact functional duplicates, thereby creating a mental life that would be qualitatively continuous with that of the original person.

Suppose it were possible that, after the person had suffered cerebral death, consciousness could begin to be generated in certain tissues of the brainstem, areas in which consciousness had not previously been realized. There are in fact documented cases in which consciousness has been realized in the tissues of the brainstem following the destruction of the cerebral hemispheres. In the condition know has hydranencephaly, the fetus develops cerebral hemispheres that are then destroyed prenatally by a pathological process such as vascular occlusion.[30] Although hydranencephalic infants normally live longer than anencephalic infants (in whom the cerebral hemispheres are never formed, or never fully formed), they usually die soon after birth or live for a short period in a wholly vegetative—that is, nonconscious—condition. Recently, however, an erstwhile pediatric nurse adopted and scrupulously cared for three hydranencephalic infants, two of whom have subsequently developed unmistakable signs of consciousness. Because in both children the cerebral hemispheres are entirely absent, consciousness must be being generated in the complex consisting of the brainstem and the diencephalon. The most likely explanation of what has happened in these cases is that the remarkable plasticity of the developing brain made it possible for certain functions normally assigned to the cerebral hemispheres to be "taken over" by the brainstem.[31] Despite the gradual decline in the brain's plasticity, a similar phenomenon is observed in the adult brain—for example, when the area of the cortex that receives signals from a limb gets "colonized" by an adjacent area after the limb has been amputated, thereby creating the illusion of a phantom limb.[32]

The reason I mention these cases of hydranencephaly at this point is to note what my understanding of personal identity implies about them. Assume that in these cases the cerebral hemispheres were initially sufficiently formed to be capable of supporting consciousness. They were then destroyed, but structures capable of supporting consciousness were subsequently developed in the brainstem. If this is what happened, I believe that one mind, supported by the cerebral hemispheres, began to exist but was soon destroyed. Thereafter a new and different mind began to exist, supported by apparently unique structures in the brainstem. In short, these are cases in which two different and distinct minds were generated serially by one and the same brain, and in which two different conscious subjects serially inhabited the same body. To the best of our knowledge, nothing comparable to this has ever occurred in the case of an adult, for by the time that adulthood is reached the plasticity of the brain has presumably become degraded to such a degree that it is no longer possible for the brainstem to take over any of the characteristic functions of the cerebral hemispheres. But if this could happen in the case of an adult brain, the Embodied Mind Account of Identity would have the same implication: the original person whose hemispheres had been destroyed would have ceased to exist and would have been succeeded or supplanted in the same body by a different conscious subject (whose level of cognitive function would presumably be too low to warrant the label "person").

In summary, in cases of irreversible coma in which the cerebral hemispheres have been destroyed, the capacity for consciousness has been lost in a way that is in principle irreversible. For the mind cannot in principle be revived. Even if consciousness can later be generated in the same body (for example, through transplantation of new cerebral tissues), or even in some remnant of the original brain, the subject of this consciousness will not be the original individual who existed before the destruction of the cerebral hemispheres. The original mind has been destroyed beyond any possibility of revival or recreation.

This form of PVS contrasts with another form of coma that is treated as irreversible. This latter type of coma is caused by damage to the reticular formation, which, as I have noted, is an area primarily in the brainstem that controls arousal in the cerebral hemispheres. When the reticular formation fails to function, arousal does not occur and coma ensues: consciousness and mental activity cease to occur. But the functioning of the reticular formation does not appear to affect or contribute to the contents of consciousness. In particular, it does not appear to be a region of the brain in whose tissues consciousness and mental activity are directly realized. The locus of consciousness and mental activity instead appears to be the cerebral hemispheres. If that is right, then in an irreversible coma caused by damage to the reticular formation only, the physical substrate of the mind is preserved intact and potentially functional in the cerebral hemispheres. It is just that the absence of function in the reticular formation impedes the activation of the mind. Moreover, because at present we do not know how to repair or replace a damaged reticular formation, there is a sense in which the loss of the capacity for consciousness that occurs in this type of coma is in practice irreversible.

Here a qualification is necessary. These comas do appear to be temporarily reversible, as was demonstrated in a series of experiments performed in the mid-1970s. The experiments have been described as follows: "By means of surgically implanted electrodes, stimulation of the reticular formation above the level of the lesion caused these patients to awaken from coma sufficiently to recognize their families and exhibit appropriate emotional responses, only to lapse back into unconsciousness immediately upon cessation of the stimulation."[33] For reasons that I fail to understand, these experiments have not been repeated and patients in this form of coma are not treated by applying continuous electrical stimulation to the relevant area of the reticular formation.

These experiments demonstrate that, although in clinical practice these comas are treated as irreversible, they are, in some cases, at least temporarily reversible. It therefore seems clear that these patients retain the capacity for consciousness. They continue to exist, albeit in a state of deep unconsciousness. There might be cases, though, in which the reticular formation was completely destroyed and there was no possibility of achieving arousal in the cerebral hemispheres via external electrical stimulation. (These cases may or may not be merely hypothetical; I am not sure.) There are two ways of describing such cases. It might be said that patients in such as state had irreversibly lost the capacity for consciousness. For there is a perfectly intelligible sense in which they would not longer be capable of consciousness. There would be nothing anyone could do that would enable them to regain consciousness, even temporarily. But if the relevant consciousness-generating structures in their cerebral hemispheres were preserved, their brains would lack the capacity for consciousness only *in practice*. The lack of capacity would be contingent rather than necessary. If we were to discover how to repair or replace the reticular formation, these patients' capacity for consciousness could be restored. Hence their loss of the capacity for consciousness would not be irreversible *in principle*. I therefore believe that these patients would remain alive, qua persons, even though there would be a sense in which they had irreversibly lost the capacity for consciousness. It is because this seems an intelligible way of describing these cases that I earlier insisted that the death of a person must be understood to involve the loss of the capacity for consciousness in a way that is irreversible in principle.

There is, however, an alternative way of describing these cases, which is to say that these people would retain the capacity for consciousness, but would be unable to exercise it. Because the consciousness-generating structures in their brains would be preserved, they would be in a condition relevantly similar to that of a person who is unconscious as a result of having been administered a powerful form of anesthesia. Even if the anesthetized person could not be roused to consciousness until the action of the drug had ceased, we would certainly say that he retained the capacity for consciousness throughout the period of unconsciousness. He had the capacity, but its exercise was impeded by the action of the drug. Similarly, it might be said, a patient whose cerebral hemispheres were preserved, but whose reticular formation had been destroyed, would also retain the capacity for consciousness; but the exercise of that capacity would be permanently impeded by the absence of function in the reticular formation.

It seems that either of these two descriptions is acceptable. If we describe these cases in the second way, it is unnecessary to stipulate that the loss of the capacity for consciousness must be *in principle* irreversible in order for a person to be dead. For the second way of describing these cases presupposes that the genuine loss of the capacity for consciousness is always in principle irreversible. If there is any possibility, even if only in principle, that an unconscious person could be restored to consciousness, it follows that he has not lost the capacity for consciousness but only the ability to exercise that capacity. If, however, we describe these cases as ones in which people lose the capacity for consciousness, then we will need to insist that the loss of this capacity must be irreversible in principle, and not just in practice, in order for a person to be dead.

1.3. *Persistent Vegetative State and Deep Coma*

In order to distinguish between irreversible comas caused by cerebral death and those caused by damage to the reticular formation, I will refer to the former as "PVS" and to the latter as "deep coma." It will be well to bear in mind that these are stipulative uses of these terms; other writers may use the terms "PVS" and "deep coma" differently. I will also use the term "patient" ambiguously to refer either to a person or to a human organism. Often when I use "the patient" to designate a human organism, that organism may be "unoccupied"—that is, it may be a mere organism that does not support the existence of a conscious subject.

In this section, I will continue the discussion of the metaphysical and moral status of patients in PVS and in deep coma. I will begin by reviewing some of the views that have been defended or might be defended. The orthodox view is, of course, that we continue to exist and retain our full moral status in both PVS and deep coma; therefore it would be murder to kill a patient in PVS or deep coma (for example, in order to obtain his organs for transplantation) and might also be wrong to allow such a patient to die—unless, perhaps, the patient has previously expressed an autonomously formed preference to be allowed to die in such circumstances. The reason this view is so common is that it combines one or the other of the two most common views of what we essentially are—that is, the view that we are souls and the view that we are organisms—with an equally common though usually vaguely apprehended sense of the sanctity of human life. As long as there is still an innocent human being present, it would be wrong to kill him, particularly as an intended means of benefiting others.

A second view appeals to a revisionist, "higher-brain" criterion of death. According to this view, cerebral death, or cortical death, or some other higher-brain criterion marks the biological death of a human organism. If the persistently vegetative patient meets the relevant criterion, PVS is equivalent in that case to the death of the organism. Since most of those who accept this view believe that we are human organisms, they conclude that when one lapses into a PVS, one thereby dies. Most advocates of this view also go on to claim that, once one is dead (even if one's organism continues to function spontaneously in a way that mimics life), it may be permissible to remove one's various organs for purposes of transplantation.

Advocates of this view differ, however, about the way in which a patient's prior consent is relevant to the permissibility of taking his organs once he is dead. Some believe that the organs may be taken only with prior consent. Others believe that all that is necessary is that consent should not have been denied—that is, that it is permissible to take the organs unless the patient has explicitly denied permission to take them. Finally, a small minority believe that consent is irrelevant: organ donation should, on this view, be compulsory. A similar division of views about the relevance of consent will be found among the proponents of other views about the status of patients in PVS and deep coma.

This second view, which appeals to a higher-brain criterion of the death of a human organism, distinguishes radically between PVS and deep coma. In most instances, at least, it deems patients in a PVS to be dead. But it holds that patients in deep coma, whose cerebral structures are intact but cannot be aroused (at least not more than temporarily), are alive. Proponents vary in their beliefs about the moral status of these patients; but it seems that most believe that they retain their full moral status, so that it would be seriously wrong to kill them to obtain their organs for transplantation.

Most proponents of a higher-brain criterion of death appear to believe that whether or not a patient is still alive is the crucial consideration in determining whether it would be permissible to remove his organs for transplantation. There is, however, a third view, whose most prominent advocate is Peter Singer, that directly challenges that assumption. Because his aim is to challenge common beliefs on grounds of consistency, he makes the common assumption that we are organisms. But, for reasons that overlap with those I presented earlier, he explicitly rejects the view that brain death constitutes the death of a human organism. He claims, in fact, that, "if we choose to mark death at any moment before the body goes stiff and cold (or to really be on the safe side, before it begins to rot) we are making an ethical judgment."[34] He therefore believes that we remain alive both in PVS and deep coma. He goes on to say, however, that "the fact that a being is human, and alive, does not in itself tell us whether it is wrong to take that being's life."[35]

As I explained in section 8.2 of chapter 4, Singer defends a two-tiered account of the wrongness of killing. The killing of a self-conscious being is seriously wrong if it violates the individual's preference for continued life. The killing of a being capable of consciousness but not self-consciousness is less seriously objectionable, and can be objectionable only impersonally, because it reduces the amount of good in the world. In both types of case, however, it is necessary for the victim to have the capacity for consciousness in order for killing to be wrong (at least for reasons other than those having to do with side effects—that is, effects on individuals other than the victim). "Without consciousness," Singer notes, "continued life cannot benefit" an individual; nor can it be a source of experiences the occurrence of which would add to the quantity of good in the world.[36] Hence, when the capacity for consciousness is irreversibly lost, as in PVS and deep coma, the individual's life ceases to be worth living and the central objections to killing cease to apply (though killing may still be objectionable for reasons having to do with side effects). According to Singer, therefore, even though a person continues to exist and to be alive in a PVS or deep coma, there is no general, principled reason why it would be wrong to kill him in order to obtain his organs for transplantation. The main constraints on the procurement of organs from persons in PVS or deep coma are of two sorts. The first concerns side effects—for example, consideration of the feelings of family members. The second is that, "if a patient in a persistent vegetative state has previously expressed wishes about what should happen to her or him in such circumstances, they should also be taken into account."[37] If, however, killing a person in a PVS or deep coma would not have adverse side effects and would be compatible with (or at least not incompatible with) the person's own autonomous wishes, then, according to Singer's view, it could be permissible to kill the person in order to obtain his organs for transplantation.

A similar view has been defended by James Rachels. Rachels believes that in many cases there may be no fact of the matter as to exactly when a person dies. "Empirical considerations," he claims, "only establish limits within which a decision must be made. The final decision [as to when death occurs] is determined by moral considerations."[38] He therefore thinks that it is a mistake, at least in many circumstances, to ask when a potential organ donor is *really* dead. "Instead, we may ask, 'At what point is it morally all right to declare him dead?'—or even, 'At what point is it morally all right to remove his organs?' "[39] In some cases, in short, we should not claim that it is permissible to take a person's organs because he is dead; rather, we may conclude that he is dead because it is morally permissible to remove his organs.

Rachels believes that the relevant moral considerations are roughly the same as those Singer identifies. He distinguishes, as I noted in section 1.1 of this chapter, between one's *biological* life and one's *biographical* life. To be biologically alive is just "to be a functioning biological organism," whereas to be alive in the biographical sense is to *have* a life, to be the subject of a life that can be described from the inside.[40] Rachels then makes two claims: that consciousness is necessary for biographical life and that biological life is valuable only insofar as it supports biographical life. "From the point of view of the living individual," he writes, "there is nothing important about being alive except that it enables one to have a life. In the absence of a conscious life, it is of no consequence to the subject himself whether he lives or dies."[41] It follows that, when a person has permanently lost the capacity for consciousness, his biographical life is concluded and any biological life that remains is morally irrelevant. "At that point," Rachels claims, "we cannot possibly be harming him by removing his heart or kidney or whatever."[42] Therefore, according to the Harm-Based Account of the wrongness of killing, which Rachels accepts, the fundamental moral objection to killing fails to apply in this case. Unless there is some other objection to killing (based, for example, on considerations of side effects or on the autonomous preference of the person prior to his losing consciousness) that is sufficient to outweigh the reason for taking his organs, it should be permissible on Rachels's view to remove a person's organs for transplantation as soon as it is clear that he has permanently lost the capacity for consciousness.

Curiously, Rachels takes brain death as the point at which consciousness is permanently lost: "Studies show that consciousness is possible when and only when certain sorts of brain activity are possible. This means that 'brain death' precludes any restoration of consciousness: at that point, we can be sure the donor's organs are no longer of any use to him. So, it is morally all right to fix the time of death at that point."[43] This, however, appears to be a mistake. If, as is generally accepted, the capacity for consciousness is permanently lost in PVS and deep coma (although it may not be *irreversibly* lost in the latter case), it ought generally to be permissible, on Rachels's view, to remove the organs of individuals in those conditions, even if this involves ending those individuals' biological lives. Perhaps the reason that Rachels does not explicitly acknowledge this implication of his view is that he is skeptical of the claim that a patient in a PVS or deep coma altogether lacks the capacity for consciousness. Or even if he accepts that the capacity for consciousness has been lost, he may be skeptical of the idea that the capacity cannot in practice be restored. I will return to these suggestions later.

The basic point that Singer and Rachels are making is that, even if a person still exists in a PVS or deep coma, there is no possibility of good in prospect for him. There is therefore no point in preserving his life and indeed no reason, where he alone is concerned, not to end his life. We may add to this the further thought that, in the case of a person in a PVS, there seems to be no basis for egoistic concern about the future—or, what is perhaps more germane, no basis for third parties to be concerned, *for the sake of the PVS patient now,* about what will happen to him later (except, perhaps, insofar as what will happen in the future might affect the value of the life he had previously). For there will be no functional continuity of the relevant areas of the brain and therefore no psychological continuity, however weak. Of course, those who accept an account of personal identity that implies that a person still exists in a PVS may well accept a corresponding account of egoistic concern—or its third-person analogue—that implies that the relevant basis is present even in a PVS. Some may find such an account credible. But even if they do, Singer's point remains: there will be nothing in the PVS patient's future—at least nothing *good*—for those who care about him for his own sake to be concerned about. There is no reason to want, *for his own sake now,* for him to continue to live.

Having noted the foregoing three accounts of the status of PVS patients and patients in deep coma, I turn now to the implications of the views that I favor. Consider first the patient in a PVS. Let us assume that the orthodox view in neurology is correct—that is, that there is no capacity for consciousness in a PVS and that the loss of the capacity is irreversible. If that is right, the Embodied Mind Account of Identity implies that *we* cannot exist in a PVS. When a person lapses into a PVS, he ceases to exist. What remains is a living but unoccupied human organism. If this is right, then, other than objections that appeal to considerations of side effects, there are only two possible objections to removing the organs from an organism in a PVS. One appeals to the idea that the organism—as a living human organism—has a special moral status even if it no longer supports the existence of a person. I believe that there is something to this idea, though I also think that the common views of what this special status is are mistaken. It seems fundamentally confused, for example, to suppose that a mere organism could have interests or rights. In order for a being to have interests or rights, it must have the capacity for consciousness.[44] The other, perhaps more common, objection is that the organism, simply by virtue of being alive and human, has a special sanctity or intrinsic value. In chapters 3 and 4, however, I have argued, following other writers, that mere membership in the human species has no intrinsic moral significance. But if an unoccupied human organism does not have interests, rights, or sanctity, what kind of special status can it have?

I propose that we should assign the living organism in a PVS much the same status we now assign a dead human organism. Even though we do not believe that human corpses have interests or rights, or that they are sacred or have intrinsic value that requires that they be preserved as long as possible, we nevertheless accept that they must be treated with appropriate respect. The bodies of the dead are not to be mutilated, degraded, ridiculed, or even neglected—a belief that has been constant in human cultures since antiquity. In Homer's *Iliad,* for example, warriors undergo great risks to retrieve the bodies of fallen comrades from the battlefield in order that the appropriate rites may be performed. And in the *Odyssey,* when Odysseus visits the kingdom of the dead, he is confronted by the ghost of Elpenor, a member of his crew who had recently died and whose body had been left behind, who beseeches him: "Don't sail off and desert me [i.e., my body], left behind unwept, unburied, don't, or my curse may draw god's fury on your head. No, burn me in full armor, all my harness."[45] It is important to note, however, that what counts as respectful treatment of a dead body varies from one culture to another. In a celebrated passage in his history of the Persian wars, Herodotus relates how King Darius of Persia found that a company of Greeks were horrified at the suggestion that they might eat the bodies of their dead fathers rather than burn them, while a company of Callatians were equally scandalized by the thought that they might burn their dead fathers' bodies rather than eat them.[46] In short, both cultures agreed that dead bodies must be treated with respect, but differed in their beliefs about how respect was to be manifested. In contemporary western cultures, it is not considered inappropriate to perform an autopsy on a dead body, or to remove its organs for transplantation, or to cremate or bury it. We ought, I contend, to extend the criteria governing the respectful treatment of a corpse, perhaps modifying them in relevant ways, so that they apply as well to the treatment of a living organism in a PVS. For, according to the Embodied Mind Account of Identity, a living organism in a PVS is, in relevant respects, just like a dead body: they are both instances of the physical remains a person leaves when he or she ceases to exist.

According to this view, a living organism in a PVS has a special moral status that excludes various forms of treatment as inappropriate. But the removal of the organism's organs should not be regarded as a desecration, even though it involves the termination of the organism's biological life. It must be conceded, of course, that much depends on the prior wishes of the person whose body it was. If the person had a preference about how his body should be treated in a PVS, there is a presumption that the preference should be honored. This, then, is the second possible objection to the removal of organs from an organism in a PVS: that to do so would be a failure of respect, albeit a posthumous one, *for the person,* if he preferred that the organs not be removed. It is, I think, largely irrelevant what a person's reasons might have been for preferring that his organs not be taken. Even if the reasons were bad ones, there is a strong presumption that they must be respected. Suppose, for example, that a person believes that he would continue to exist in a PVS and that his life would continue to have value to him in that state. Even if I am right that he is mistaken on both counts, his preference is probably decisive. Even if a person demands that his organs not be taken because he actively desires that potential beneficiaries should die rather than be saved, his preference cannot be disregarded.

While a person's prior desires can require that we abstain from treating his vegetative organism in certain ways, it cannot morally compel us actively to care for it in certain ways. Suppose that someone believed that he would continue to exist and to be alive even after brain death, provided that his organism would receive external life support that would ensure that blood would continue to circulate, food continue to be metabolized, and so on. While the wishes he entertained prior to brain death may morally prohibit our taking his organs even after he has suffered brain death, they lack the authority to compel us to provide costly life support for his organism after brain death has occurred. Similarly, the beliefs and desires a person had when competent cannot, other things being equal, require us to provide life support in order that his organism should survive indefinitely in PVS.

While respect for a person who has ceased to exist may require that we refrain from removing the organs from his vegetative organism, it may also, in other circumstances, exert strong moral pressure to kill that organism or, in particular, to kill it *in order to* remove its organs. If a person autonomously wishes, prior to lapsing into a PVS, that he should not be significantly outlived by his own vegetative organism, or that his organs should be used to benefit others after he has ceased to exist, there is a presumption that these preferences should be honored. We have seen, of course, that a person's autonomous preference cannot morally compel us to act if the act desired is excessively demanding or costly. But neither the desire that, should one lapse into a PVS, one's organism should be killed, nor the desire that its organs should be removed for transplantation, is excessively demanding in terms of time, effort, or resources. It must be conceded, however, that either of these desires may be excessively demanding in a different way if it would require a person to act against his or her conscience. Respect for another person's autonomous wishes stops short of requiring that one kill his organism if, for whatever, reason, one believes that to do so would be wrong.

Having conceded this, I hasten to add that, if my understanding of the relevant metaphysics is credible, there is nothing here for a person's conscience to be exercised about. Most of the qualms or inhibitions that people may feel about euthanasia, for example, would be inappropriate in this case. For the killing of a human organism in a PVS is not euthanasia: there is no one there to be benefited by being killing. Nor, a fortiori, is there anyone there to be harmed. Apart from effects on others (which will presumably favor the removal of the organs), the central consideration is what the person whose organism it was preferred should be done with it. If he preferred that it should be killed or that its organs should be used for transplantation, it seems that all relevant considerations favor the removal of the organs: existing people are likely to benefit, and one would also be showing appropriate respect for the person whose organism it was.

Turn now to the case of deep coma. As I have noted, the Embodied Mind Account of Identity distinguishes radically between deep coma and PVS. In deep coma, there is physical, functional, and organizational continuity of the areas of the brain in which consciousness and mental activity are realized. Not only does the patient remain alive, but the basis for egoistic concern is preserved as well. It is as if the person is asleep but cannot be waked. All aspects of his mind are preserved intact in the tissues of his cerebral hemispheres, but their arousal is impeded by a defect in a critical support system.

Although deep coma is fundamentally different from PVS in metaphysical terms, it may not be much different prudentially or morally. While the person in a deep coma remains alive, his life has altogether ceased to be worth living, for the future holds no prospect of good. Indeed, continued life in such a state, while having no subjective character at all, may be regarded as objectively degrading. Dworkin's description of an individual as "an unthinking yet scrupulously tended [or] . . . manicured vegetable" aptly conveys the sense of horror that many of us experience in contemplating the possibility of continued existence devoid of consciousness—an existence in which one would be reduced, in effect, to an object whose most salient active function would be the excretion of wastes.[47]

Is there any positive reason to try to sustain the life of a person in a deep coma? There is, of course, a strong reason to keep such a person alive if there is any serious prospect of his being revived. If someone one cared about were in a deep coma, one would surely insist that everything be done to keep that person alive if there was the slightest possibility that he might be revived. But suppose there is really no possibility that a person in a deep coma could be revived—as at present seems to be the case. Even then, if the person had expressed an autonomous wish to be kept alive in such a state, that would constitute a more or less decisive reason not to kill him and would certainly count in favor of sustaining his life—though there are limits to the costs that others would be required to incur in order to honor his preference.

Suppose that, prior to lapsing into a deep coma, a person expressed both a horror of being in such a state and an autonomous preference for being killed or being allowed to die once he had lost consciousness. At present it is possible to issue a binding advance directive insisting that one be allowed to die if one lapses into a deep coma, though it is not possible to demand that one be killed. Our concern, however, is with morality rather than the law. Ignoring legal issues for the moment, might it be permissible to kill such a person if that would be in accordance with his own autonomous preference? The life in prospect for him would at best be of neutral value, and might be intrinsically bad, because it would be degrading to him or incompatible with his own conception of personal dignity. In these circumstances, it seems that both his autonomous preference and consideration of his personal well-being would coincide in favoring killing him. To kill him for his own sake would be an act of voluntary euthanasia, and might serve other important purposes as well—for example, making his organs available for transplants that could save others whose lives could be worth living. Nevertheless, there is a serious question whether to kill such a person, even in these circumstances, would violate the sanctity of life or be incompatible with respect for the person. I will address these issues in the following sections.

My provisional conclusion, then, is that, if a deep coma is genuinely irreversible, and if voluntary euthanasia can be permissible, patients in a deep coma should be treated in much the same way that we ought to treat patients in a PVS. Perhaps the major difference is that the previously expressed preferences of a person in a deep coma would carry more weight, since those preferences would concern his own life rather than merely the fate of his surviving organism. This conclusion narrows the gap between the understanding of PVS that I have advanced and that defended by Singer. If Singer were right to make the assumption that a person still exists in a PVS, I think his view of the morality of killing such a person or allowing him to die would be substantially correct.

1.4. *Anencephalic Infants*

Anencephalic infants are infants born without cerebral hemispheres. Often they have functional brainstems and so are capable of surviving for an extended period but, mainly because aggressive life-sustaining therapies are rarely administered to them, they usually die within a few days or weeks after birth. The consensus in neurology is that, because they lack cerebral hemispheres, they altogether lack either the capacity or the potential for consciousness.

How should we understand the metaphysical and moral status of anencephalic infants? For obvious reasons, there are parallels with the various ways of understanding the status of a patient in a PVS. According to the most common view, an anencephalic infant is a living human organism, a human being. Thus it is assumed that an anencephalic infant is essentially the same kind of being as you and I, only profoundly disabled. For it is assumed either that we are essentially human organisms or that, because an anencephalic infant is a human being, it must have a soul. But if an anencephalic infant is essentially the same sort of entity as you and I, it must have the same fundamental moral status as you and I. Therefore to kill it—for example, in order to use its organs for transplantation—would be wrong, for it would be to kill an innocent human being, without his or her consent, as a means of benefiting someone else.

This is the orthodox view, and it has had tragic consequences for thousands of children who have needed organ transplants in order to survive. Because an anencephalic infant is regarded as a living human being, its organs cannot be removed for transplantation until it is diagnosed as brain dead. But, as I noted in section 2.1 of chapter 3, the processes that terminate in natural death for an anencephalic infant almost always involve reduced blood flow to the infant's organs, causing them to deteriorate and to become unsuitable for transplantation by the time that death occurs. On several occasions, the parents of an anencephalic infant have sought to have their infant's organs removed while it was still alive so that, in their view, something good could come of its life. But the courts have always denied the parents' request on the ground that to remove the organs from a living human being would be murder. The consequence of this legal situation is that, over the years, thousands of children whose lives could have been saved by an organ transplanted from an anencephalic infant have died instead. It is true that the number of anencephalic infants born alive each year is small and growing smaller all the time, because the condition is more frequently detected by prenatal screening, which is followed by abortion when the condition is found. And it is also true that the organs of many of those born alive are already defective in ways that make them unsuitable for transplantation. So the number of children who could have been saved each year by taking organs from living anencephalic infants is comparatively small. But, over the years, these numbers add up. And anyone who has had (or been) a seriously ill child will know how important even one life can be.

One view that challenges the orthodox view is that of Peter Singer. Singer accepts, at least for the sake of argument, the common understanding of the metaphysical status of an anencephalic infant as a living human being, but argues that, because an anencephalic infant is incapable of having a life worth living and is also incapable of desiring to continue to live, it cannot have an interest in remaining alive. Therefore, according to Singer, one would neither harm nor wrong it if one were to kill it in order to obtain its organs for transplantation.

A third view of the status of anencephalic infants is that taken by those who advocate the revisionist, higher-brain criterion of death. According to this view, which has in fact been adopted by the courts in Germany, an anencephalic infant cannot be a living human being because it lacks any higher-brain function. It can be regarded as a collection, itself inanimate, of living human organs. Since it is not itself alive, to take its living organs for transplantation cannot count as killing or, a fortiori, murder.

It seems absurd, however, to deny that a functional anencephalic infant is a living human organism. It has all the biological functions and capacities that an ordinary human infant has except those involving consciousness or mental states. According to the view that I have defended, it is indeed a living human organism, but one that never supports the existence of a mind or conscious subject. Since you and I are essentially minds and are not identical with our organisms, an anencephalic infant is a fundamentally different sort of thing from us. It is simply an organism—a permanently unoccupied human organism. Whereas in a normal infant's crib there are two distinct things—a human organism and the infant mind or self that will eventually become a person—there is only one individual in the crib of an anencephalic infant. This organism may well be alive, but it will never support the existence of a mind, self, or person.

Because an anencephalic infant has neither the capacity nor the potential for consciousness, it is not a bearer of interests. Nothing can matter, or be good or bad, for its sake. Nor can it have rights or be an appropriate object of respect. If, therefore, the view for which I have argued is correct, it is difficult to see what objection there could be to taking the organs from a living anencephalic infant for transplantation— apart, of course, from objections based on the interests and rights of the parents. There are, in fact, fewer possible objections to taking the organs of an anencephalic infant than there are to taking those of a patient in a PVS. For, in the latter case, the organism once belonged to a person who may have a surviving interest in what is done to it or may have expressed preferences about what should be done with it. But in the case of an anencephalic infant, there is never anyone whose organism it is. The only people whose interests or preferences can be affected by what is done with the infant organism are its parents and those who might benefit from the use of its organs or tissues.

It is worth noting the tension between the orthodox view of the moral status of anencephalic infants and the quite general acceptance of the practice of aborting fetuses discovered through prenatal screening to be anencephalic. The only difference between an anencephalic fetus and an anencephalic infant is the greater physical maturity of the latter; there is no psychological maturation at all. There seems, therefore, to be no relevant intrinsic difference between the two, as there is between a normal developed fetus and a newborn infant. Yet we allow the killing of an anencephalic fetus in order to spare the pregnant woman and her partner the burden of carrying it to term and caring for it as an infant, but prohibit the killing of an anencephalic infant even for the considerably more important purpose of saving the life of a child. I doubt, however, that these two views can be coherently combined.

These claims are, of course, highly controversial. Even more controversial is the idea that it might be permissible intentionally to create anencephalic infants in order to use their organs for transplantation. But, again, it is difficult to locate the source of the revulsion that most people feel at this idea. It is, perhaps, easier to dismiss the possibility by noting the practical obstacles—for example, that "growing" anencephalic infants as organ sources would require the cooperation of women willing to endure the costs and risks of pregnancy in order to bring into the world an infant organism that would immediately be carved into a little collection of transplantable organs. But objections of this sort are contingent rather than essential and may, in any case, be overcome sooner than one thinks, since an effective artificial uterus is already on the horizon.[48]

Moreover, by starting from relatively uncontroversial practices and proceeding by a series of small steps, no one of which seems to cross the barrier between permissibility and impermissibility, one can reach the conclusion that it is permissible to grow anencephalic infants as organ sources. It is at present a common practice for veterinary surgeons to kill a perfectly healthy animal—say, a dog—in the process of taking an organ for transplantation into another animal of the same species. Usually the "donor" animal is in any case slated for "convenience euthanasia"—that is, it is scheduled to be painlessly killed instead of being allowed to live as a stray. If one accepts that this practice can be permissible, one surely ought to approve of xenotransplantation—that is, the use of healthy animals as sources of organs for transplantation into human beings. While most of the purposes for which animals are routinely sacrificed are comparatively trivial, the saving of the life of a person is clearly a very important purpose. If there are any instances in which it could be justifiable to kill an animal as a means of serving the interests of persons, xenotransplantation is surely among them. If, for example, one could save the life of a child by giving it a vital organ taken from a baboon, most of us believe that this goal would be sufficiently important to justify the painless killing of the baboon.

There are, however, technical obstacles to xenotransplantation—for example, problems in the rejection of animal tissue by the human immune system. As we saw in section 2.2 of chapter 3, one response to these problems is the breeding of transgenic animals—for example, pigs with a single human gene intended to moderate the human immune response to the transplanted porcine liver. Very few people think that the insertion of a single human gene into an animal is morally wrong, or that it would make it impermissible to kill the animal in order to use its organs for xeno-transplantation.

There is, however, certainly an objection to killing an animal in order to make its organs available for transplantation, especially if the animal is a higher animal such as a baboon or chimpanzee. This is, of course, that the killing frustrates the animal's time-relative interest in continuing to live, which may be moderately strong—the more so the higher the animal. It would surely be desirable if the needed organs could be obtained without causing this harm.

There is in principle a way to do this, which is to suppress the action of the genes responsible for the growth and development of an animal's cerebral cortex. One might, for example, make several genetic alterations to an animal zygote: some intended to make the animal's organs less vulnerable to the human immune system and others intended, in effect, to make the animal anencephalic. There is every reason to believe that both such alterations are possible. By suppressing a gene involved in the growth of the head, scientists have already produced living but headless mouse fetuses. While most die at midgestation, a few have survived until birth.[49] Once the genome is better understood, it should be equally possible to create animals lacking only the upper brain. These animals would have a much higher probability of surviving to birth and beyond, but they would be equally lacking in any capacity or potential for consciousness. To kill such an animal in order to use its organs for xenotransplantation would not be to harm it in any way. Surely that would be preferable to killing an animal that has a significant time-relative interest in continuing to live.

Some people will doubtless object to the deliberate creation of an anencephalic animal. They could not object, however, for the sake of or on behalf of the animal. For to create an anencephalic animal would not be to deny that animal a mental life that it would otherwise have. The Embodied Mind Account of Identity applies to conscious animals as well: they are no more identical with their organisms than we are. Thus in creating an anencephalic animal, one would merely be preventing a conscious subject from existing in association with a particular animal organism. And there is certainly very little to object to in preventing a conscious nonhuman individual from existing. So if there is an objection to creating an anencephalic animal organism, it cannot be because of the effect on the organism itself. And the other effects of the action—principally the saving of a human life through xenotransplantation—should be emphatically positive. I suspect that some people would be opposed to the deliberate creation of an anencephalic animal organism because they sense that the manipulation of the genome in this way would be unnatural or involve some sort of cosmic impiety. But these complaints make sense, if at all, only in the context of a set of theological assumptions that there is no space to challenge here.

Suppose, next, that xenotransplantation is more likely to succeed if the transgenic anencephalic animal has two human genes rather than just one. Surely the addition of one further human gene would not make a moral difference. But now we have the possibility of a spectrum of the sort suggested in section 2.2 of chapter 3: a series of cases in which each succeeding individual in the series has one more human gene than the preceding one. At one end of the spectrum there is a transgenic anencephalic animal with a single human gene; in the middle, anencephalic human-animal chimeras; and, at the other end, an anencephalic human infant with a single nonhuman gene. Suppose, for the sake of argument, that the probability of a successful transplant would be greater the more human genetic material the "donor" individual has. It seems, as I have suggested, that it would be permissible to create, and to take organs from, an anencephalic animal with a single human gene. Is there some point along the spectrum such that it would be impermissible to use individuals beyond that point as organ sources, so that one would be morally compelled to accept a lower probability of success by using the organs of an individual with fewer human genes? Or, alternatively, are there objections to creating and killing individuals in the spectrum that increase in strength along with the number of human genes that an individual possesses, so that there might be a point at which the objections would outweigh the higher probability of success afforded by the greater number of human genes?

There is, I believe, no basis for moral differentiation among the various individuals in the spectrum. Ordinarily, of course, the introduction of increasing numbers of human genes would result in morally significant differences, such as differences of cognitive and emotional capacity. But in this spectrum of cases, all the individuals are anencephalic. None has properties that could ground the ascription of interests or rights; none has properties that could plausibly be seen as a basis for the worth that demands respect. The differences among the cases are necessarily purely physical. These differences are presumably such that individuals at one end of the spectrum are nonhuman, while those at the other end count as members of the human species. But this alone is just a matter of biological classification. As I argued earlier, it is devoid of moral significance.

It may well be that, with only slight genetic modifications, animal organs will eventually be as effective for transplantation as, in general, human organs are. But there is one sort of human organ that would be better for transplantation than any animal organ: namely, an organ that is genetically identical to the organ it is intended to replace. There is, therefore, a powerful practical reason for using a certain type of anencephalic human infant rather than a transgenic animal as a source of transplantable organs or tissues. This is an anencephalic infant that is a clone of the person who requires a transplant. If it could be permissible, as our spectrum of cases suggests, to grow an anencephalic infant from genetic material from an anonymous source, it should also be permissible for a person needing a transplant to grow an anencephalic infant from his or her own genetic material via cloning technology. This would assure perfect compatibility between the tissue of the transplanted organ and the tissues of the recipient, thereby eliminating the need for immuno-suppressant drugs.

Again, most people regard with horror the possibility of growing a clone of oneself—even an anencephalic clone—as a source of transplantable tissues or organs. Most people would, however, have far fewer scruples about growing a single living organ—a possibility that seems increasingly likely to be realized. Human stem cells are pluripotent—that is, capable of developing into any type of tissue in the body. It may soon be possible to take a stem cell from an adult and to direct the processes of division and growth in such a way as to produce a living organ, such as a liver. This liver would, of course, be genetically identical to the liver of the person from whom the stem cell was taken and thus would be ideal for transplantation into that person.

Suppose, as I think most people would agree, that it would be permissible to grow a single organ in this way in order to save a person's life. If it would be permissible to grow one organ this way, it should also be permissible to grow two—for example, if the person needed two organ transplants rather than just one. But, if it would be acceptable to grow two organs separately, it should be acceptable to grow three, or four, or five. Imagine that a person has a rare disease that can be cured only by a series of tissue grafts to most parts of his body. To cure him, it would be necessary to use the techniques of stem-cell-based biosynthesis to grow organic replicas of most of his body parts and then graft a small amount of each replica into the corresponding part of his body. It is hard to see how it could be wrong to grow a set of separate organs and body parts in this way. It would be macabre, certainly, but it is hard to see how the organs themselves could have a moral status that would make it wrong to create them for instrumental purposes, or to use or even to destroy them once they were created. But if there is no objection to creating each organ or body part separately, it ought equally to be acceptable to grow them all together in the form of an anencephalic clone. It would, of course, make a difference if they were grown together as an organism with a functional brain, for that would involve the existence of a further, distinct entity with interests and rights. But if the clone is anencephalic, the only difference is that the organs and parts would be physically integrated and mutually supporting rather than maintained separately, each on its own scaffolding of combined organic and inorganic support systems. And it is hard to believe that this could make the difference between permissibility and impermissibility. It seems, rather, that the intrinsic moral status of an anencephalic clone—that is, the moral status it has based on its intrinsic rather than relational properties—is no different from that of a collection of separately grown organs.

2. EUTHANASIA AND ASSISTED SUICIDE

2.1. *From Suicide to Euthanasia*

"Suicide" and "euthanasia" are concepts with blurred edges. It is often unclear whether a certain act counts as suicide or whether an act is an instance of euthanasia. These conceptual problems merit discussion, but only a rather brief discussion here. In the past, some of these questions were thought to have profound significance. For example, when it was widely accepted that suicides were excluded from heaven, it seemed of the utmost importance to be able to determine whether a particular act was an instance of suicide. Here, by contrast, the main point of the conceptual preliminaries is simply to delimit the subject matter of this section of the book.

Let us say that an agent commits suicide if he dies as a consequence of acting with the intention of bringing about his own death. This allows that suicide can be either by act or by omission. It thus treats as an instance of suicide the act of a person who dies as a result of refusing a life-saving medical treatment on the ground that he wished to die rather than to continue to live. Yet the definition's reliance on the notion of intention introduces substantial unclarity. It is clear that a person who accidentally or inadvertently causes his own death does not commit suicide; and it is equally clear that a person who deliberately kills himself (for example, by putting a gun to his head and pulling the trigger) does commit suicide. Whether, in the latter case, the agent intends his own death as an end or whether he intends it as a means to an end (for example, the punishment of his wife or, perhaps, the relief of his own suffering) is immaterial. I believe, though others have disputed this, that it is also immaterial whether the agent acts under duress or coercion.[50] There is nothing paradoxical about the notion of a coerced suicide. It is also reasonably clear that, when a person does something that he merely foresees may or will result in his death (such as playing Russian roulette), he does not necessarily commit suicide. But what about cases in which a person intentionally *uses himself* in a way that he believes will result in his own death? Examples include the soldier in a foxhole who flings himself on a live grenade to shield his comrades, and the man who deliberately attracts the attention of a deadly wild animal to himself in order to allow his child to escape. Have such people, when they are killed, committed suicide?

Our inclination is to deny that they have. And certainly it is reasonable to see these deaths as foreseen but unintended; for, in each case, if the act had accomplished the person's aim without resulting in the person's death (for example, if the grenade had merely maimed the soldier or if the animal had mauled but not killed the parent), none of his intentions or plans would thereby have been thwarted. Yet there is another sense, associated with traditional readings of the Doctrine of Double Effect, in which these people's deaths *are* intentional. To see this, we need only to imagine variants of the cases in which the agent sacrifices someone else rather than himself. If, for example, the soldier were to fling someone else on the grenade, most people would see this as an instance of intentional killing—that is, an instance of killing one person as a means of saving others, hence a paradigm of the sort of act that the Doctrine of Double Effect ought to condemn. Perhaps we should say that, even though the death would not be an intended effect in the narrow sense distinguished in section 10.1 of chapter 4, it nevertheless has, because of its relation to the agent's intentions, the same significance as an intended effect. If so, the question is then whether, in the original cases, the presence of this same relation between the agent's death and his intentions makes it appropriate to count these cases as instances of self-sacrificial suicide.

I will not pursue these complications here, though I have discussed the analysis of intention elsewhere.[51] Because our concern is primarily with euthanasia, we can confine our brief discussion of suicide to cases that are relevantly parallel—that is, cases in which an agent brings about his own death because he believes that his subsequent life would not be worth living, and hence that death would be better for him than continued life. In these cases, the death is an intended effect on any account.

Next, a few words about the concept of euthanasia. An act of euthanasia, as I will understand the term, is an act of killing or of letting someone die that satisfies two conditions: first, that death benefits, or is good for, the individual who dies and, second, that the agent must be motivated to do what is good for that individual and must intend to benefit the individual in bringing about his death. Even if an act that brings about a person's death is intended thereby to benefit the person, it does not count as euthanasia if it is not in fact good for that person. If it would have been better for the person to continue to live, the act may be an instance of intended euthanasia or attempted euthanasia, but it is not actually euthanasia. Similarly, if an act of killing or letting die is not intended to benefit the individual who is killed or allowed to die, it does not become an act of euthanasia if, fortuitously, it turns out to have been better for the individual to die rather than to continue to live.

There is an interesting conceptual question that I have never seen discussed in the literature on human euthanasia. This question arises from a problem frequently encountered in veterinary medicine. Suppose that a man brings his dog to the vet and requests that it be "put to sleep." When asked why he wants the dog killed, the man replies that he and his family are going on a long trip and cannot afford to have the dog kept in a kennel (or that the dog wets the carpet, that the children have lost interest in it, or whatever). Although killing an animal in circumstances such as these is commonly known as "convenience euthanasia," it may seem that this is just a euphemism, for it cannot be good for an animal to be killed when it is perfectly healthy. But there may be more to it than this. The vet may have reason to believe that, if she does not kill the animal painlessly, its owner will take it away and kill it himself, in a manner that would not be painless, or that he will turn it loose to starve or be hit by a car. Suppose, in fact, that the man has credibly threatened to do something of this sort. The vet might, of course, offer to take the animal and give it a home herself. But suppose that she gets two cases of this sort every week—far more animals than she herself could care for or even find homes for. In each individual case, then, the situation is that there is an animal whose life could in principle be worth living but no one is willing, nor perhaps obliged, to do what is necessary to make it worth living. The vet therefore has the choice, in practice, between painlessly killing the animal and allowing it to live a life that she has good reason to believe will in fact be worth not living. A parallel case could arise in the case of a human being—for example, if a person's life will be worth not living unless he has a surgical procedure that he cannot afford and that would be so expensive that no one else is willing or obliged to provide it for him. In these circumstances, would it count as euthanasia to kill him and could it be permissible to do so?

Again I raise these questions only to put them aside. I will restrict my attention here to cases in which it is not possible to change an individual's life in a way that would make it worth living.

I will briefly note a few common distinctions and then turn to substantive matters. Euthanasia is said to be *voluntary* when a person freely and autonomously requests or consents to be killed or allowed to die for his own good. It is *nonvoluntary* when it is not possible for the individual who is killed or allowed to die either to give or to withhold consent. This category, therefore, encompasses all cases of euthanasia in which the individual killed or allowed to die is a fetus, an infant, an animal, a congenitally severely cognitively impaired human being, or a human being who has ceased to be competent to form autonomous preferences about life and death, and who has not previously expressed his will on the matter. Euthanasia is said to be *involuntary* when an individual who is competent to give or withhold consent is killed or allowed to die either contrary to his expressed will or when his consent has not been sought. (There may be cases in a gray area between nonvoluntary and involuntary euthanasia in which an individual, though capable of expressing a preference, lacks the competence to have an informed, autonomous preference.) Finally, killing an individual for his own good is commonly referred to as *active* euthanasia, whereas letting an individual die when that is in his best interests is referred to as *passive* euthanasia.

It has sometimes been remarked that it is difficult to accept that suicide can be morally permissible without accepting that euthanasia can be as well.[52] And indeed there are only a few short steps between the premise that suicide can be permissible and the claim that euthanasia can be.

Consider a case in which a person's life is worth not living: it is and will remain dominated by pain and suffering that cannot be alleviated and that are not counterbalanced by compensating goods. Some people, of course, claim that life is always worth living, or at least that it always can be made to be worth living. But if it is true that pain and suffering are in themselves bad, it seems that a life that contains little or nothing but pain and suffering—one, moreover, that is neither redeemed by its good effects on others nor elevated, ennobled, or enlightened by the experience of suffering—cannot be worth enduring. I will assume that, when a life is bad in this way for the one whose life it is, and when that individual's death would not be worse for anyone else, it can be prudentially rational for that individual to commit suicide. Most people accept that, in these circumstances, suicide would also not be immoral. Certainly few people now accept that someone who commits suicide in such circumstances is guilty of *murder.*

Let us assume, conditionally, that, when suicide is rational and not worse for others, it is also morally permissible. Most people also accept that there are circumstances in which it is permissible to assist someone to commit suicide. Consider, for example, a case in which a person's suicide would be rational and not worse for others but in which the person cannot easily bring about his own death because he is tethered to a battery of life-support machines from which it would be difficult to extricate himself. Most of us believe that, in these circumstances, it would be permissible for the person's physician to accede to his request to collaborate with him in withdrawing the life-support systems—for example, by assisting the person to remove the various pieces of apparatus from his body. Indeed, most of us believe that, provided that the person is competent, the physician *ought* to enable him to free himself from the machines. Given that the withdrawal of the life-support systems will lead immediately to the person's death, we should regard the person's removal of them as an act of suicide, albeit an instance of "passive suicide," since he does not create the cause of his death but instead allows himself to die by removing the protections that have thus far been saving him from a preexisting threat. In assisting him to remove these protections, the physician assists him to commit suicide.

I have described a case in which a person chooses to die "passively" by ceasing to resist a threat of death that is not of his own making. In most cases, people commit suicide actively, by creating the threat that results in their death. Many people regard it as impermissible to assist someone in actively committing suicide, and it is at present illegal in most areas of the United State for physicians to assist their patients in actively killing themselves—for example, by prescribing a lethal dose of some medicine. Yet it is hard to see how it could be permissible to provide assistance to a passive suicide but not to an active suicide. How could the permissibility of assistance by a third party depend on whether the person bent on suicide chooses an active or a passive means, particularly when either would be equally permissible?

It is tempting to appeal here to the general claim that, if it is permissible for a person to do something, it must also be permissible for others to assist him. But that claim seems false. There are, for example, rare circumstances in which one wholly innocent person will be killed by another wholly innocent person unless the one kills the other first. In these circumstances, it may be permissible for each to try to kill the other but not permissible for a third party to assist either. For while it may be permissible for each agent to give priority to himself, a neutral third party may be required to treat both principals equally and impartially and may therefore be forbidden to provide assistance to either at the expense of the other.[53] But it seems that this restriction on the permissibility of assistance by third parties applies only in cases in which what an agent is permitted to do may prevent others from doing what they are permitted to do or otherwise have adverse effects on others. In the case of a rational suicide that would not be worse for others, these complications do not arise; therefore there is no reason to suppose that a third party may not assist the agent in doing what it is permissible for that agent to do.

There are, moreover, positive reasons why, in the case of a rational suicide, assistance from others is desirable. People who set out to kill themselves sometimes fail, leaving themselves not only alive but disabled, disfigured, humiliated, and in pain. As Arthur Koestler, "speaking in the name of many . . . who tried and failed," once observed, "there is only one prospect worse than being chained to an intolerable existence: the nightmare of a botched attempt to end it."[54] And even when people succeed in committing suicide, they are often forced to quit life alone, in terror, without the support or validation of others, and with greater pain and mess than is necessary. If it is prudentially rational and morally permissible for a person to seek death, how much better it would be if he could be assured assistance from others that would enable him to die with as much comfort, reassurance, and certainty as possible.

Thus far we have passed by short steps from the permissibility of rational suicide to the permissibility of assisted passive suicide and assisted active suicide. But we have also, perhaps without noticing it, taken another step as well: to passive euthanasia. In the case I cited of assisted passive suicide, the physician assists the patient to disconnect himself from the life-support systems. But by refusing to collaborate, or by actively preventing the patient from disconnecting himself, the physician could have kept the patient alive. Therefore this is a case in which the physician allows the patient to die. If the physician is motivated to do this at least in part by the true belief that death would be in the best interest of the patient, her action constitutes an instance of passive euthanasia. It seems, in fact, that this is a case in which the categories of assisted suicide and euthanasia overlap: the patient commits suicide, with the physician's assistance, by refusing to continue to be saved, or kept alive; yet the physician also allows the patient to die, and does so with the intention of thereby benefiting him.

It would, perhaps, be a more obvious case of passive euthanasia if the physician alone turned off or disconnected all the life-support systems. Assuming that the systems she withdrew were all ones that she had herself been providing, this would be an instance of allowing the patient to die and not a case of killing—in short, a case of *passive* euthanasia, despite the fact that allowing the patient to die required action rather than inaction. Still, in either case—whether the physician assists in the withdrawal of the life-support systems or removes them entirely by herself—most of us acknowledge the permissibility of her action. We accept, in short, the permissibility of at least some instances of voluntary passive euthanasia. For it is widely accepted that a physician not only may but must comply with a patient's competent request for the termination of life-supporting medical aid. And it would seem absurd to suppose that, while the physician could permissibly remove the patient from life-support systems, she could *not* permissibly do so *with the intention* of benefiting the patient by enabling him to die.

Passive euthanasia is, however, as far as we as a society have so far been willing to go. Many people, at least when they consider the matter in the abstract, think that there is a sharp moral line—one that must not be crossed—between allowing someone to die when it is in his interest to die and actually *killing* him. But when one considers the matter closely, it seems that the step from passive to active euthanasia is again a very short one. Consider, for example, the activities of the notorious Dr. Jack Kevorkian. (Let us put aside whatever reservations we may have about his character and methods: his publicity seeking, megalomania, insufficient knowledge of his "clients," and so on.) His earlier cases were instances of assisted suicide: he hooked people up to a device containing a lethal chemical, but the people themselves actually pressed the button that released the chemical into their bloodstream. By contrast, in a more recent case, the person—a man named Youk—suffered from amyotrophic lateral sclerosis and was so disabled that it was difficult for him to push the button. He therefore asked Kevorkian to push it for him, which Kevorkian did, with a video camera rolling all the while. Most of us, on reflection, find it difficult to believe that it could make a momentous moral difference whether Youk pushed the button himself or whether Kevorkian pushed it for him. Yet that is all that the difference between assisted suicide and killing amounts to.

In addition to the fact that it seems insignificant who pushes the button, provided that the person whose death it causes autonomously wants it to be pushed, there is another feature this case that supports the inference from the permissibility of passive euthanasia to the permissibility of active euthanasia. This is Youk's apparent inability to press the button himself. Most people who desperately want to die are capable of killing themselves and thus seek the assistance of others only in order to ensure that their own action is painless, minimally shocking to others, and successful. If we accept the permissibility of rational suicide (subject, of course, to certain constraints), and in particular if we accept the permissibility of assisting in the commission of rational suicide, we are acknowledging that people have a right to die when life has become an intolerable burden and when continued life is not demanded by consideration of others. If, however, we reject the permissibility of active euthanasia, we are effectively denying that right to those who are so disabled that they cannot take their own lives, even with assistance from others. In order for those people to escape from an intolerable existence, it is necessary for someone else to kill them. If we forbid others to kill them, when there are others who are willing to do so, we are exacerbating the already quite terrible hardships these people have had to bear. Thus some advocates of the rights of the disabled have claimed, with considerable plausibility, that a policy that permits suicide but forbids active euthanasia unfairly discriminates against the disabled.

Despite these considerations, many people are unable to evade the nagging sense that killing another person is fundamentally different from allowing him to die or even assisting him to kill himself. Yet how can they explain why, intuitively, it seems to make no difference whether Youk pressed the button himself or whether Kevorkian pressed it at Youk's request? Some philosophers have contended that cases of this sort—in which the distinction between killing and letting die seems to have no moral significance—show that the distinction is, in these cases and all others, devoid of significance. They argue that, because we are wrong to suppose that the distinction has moral significance, we must acknowledge that, in the absence of contingent differences, active euthanasia must be permissible when passive euthanasia would be—particularly in cases in which merely allowing a person to die would prolong his agony.[55]

I believe that there is a different and more plausible explanation of why it is no worse for Kevorkian to press the button, thereby killing Youk, than it is for Youk to press it himself. This explanation is compatible with, and indeed presupposes, the belief that the distinction between killing and letting die is, in general, morally significant. It assumes that, if the distinction has moral significance, that must be because it is an instance of the more general distinction between doing and allowing. Most people believe that a person's actively bringing about an outcome that would not have occurred without his intervention has a different moral significance from a person's allowing that outcome to occur. Perhaps the active causing of the outcome ties the agent more closely to it, making him more responsible for it than he would have been if it had occurred even in his absence. I will not attempt to defend any particular explanation of the moral significance of the distinction between doing and allowing. If, however, this broad distinction does have a general significance, it offers an explanation of why killing is in general more seriously wrong than letting someone die. If, in general, the mode of agency involved in actively intervening to bring about an outcome is morally more significant than that involved in allowing an outcome to occur, it seems that doing harm must in general be more seriously morally objectionable than allowing harm to occur. Because death is normally harmful to those who die, it follows that killing must in general be more seriously objectionable than letting die.

Notice, however, that the significance of the distinction between doing and allowing should be reversed in cases in which the outcome is good rather than bad. If doing harm is worse than allowing harm to occur, actively *benefiting* someone should, in general, be *better* than merely allowing someone to be benefited, even when all other things (such as motive, intention, cost to the agent, and so on) are equal. If that is right, it explains why it was not worse for Kevorkian to press the button, thereby killing Youk, than it would have been for him to have allowed Youk to die by allowing him to press the button instead. For Youk's death was unusual in not being harmful to him. It was instead beneficial; hence, if benefiting someone is better than merely allowing him to be benefited (for example, allowing him to benefit himself), Kevorkian's actively bringing about that death was, if anything, better or more praiseworthy than merely allowing or enabling Youk to bring it about would have been.

Because, in cases of euthanasia, death is beneficial rather than harmful, active euthanasia should in general be better or more imperative than passive euthanasia.[56] To suppose otherwise is to divorce the distinction between killing and letting die from its source in the distinction between doing and allowing, and to treat the general proscription of killing as a taboo rather than as a rational moral requirement to which there are intelligible exceptions. It is, of course, desirable that each of us should be profoundly averse to killing other human beings and that this aversion should be sed- ulously inculcated as a fundamental element of each person's moral education. But the aversion should retain its grounding in the reasons we have for refraining from killing; it should not degenerate into an indiscriminate squeamishness. If, for example, the reason not to kill persons derives from a requirement of respect for persons, we should seek to prevent our aversion to wrongful killing from spilling over into cases in which killing is compatible with, and perhaps even required by, respect for a person. I will consider presently whether voluntary active euthanasia is a case of this sort.

The argument from suicide to euthanasia starts from cases in which suicide is both prudentially and morally justified. Often, of course, suicide is either pruden- tially or morally unjustified, or both. A great many people commit suicide in the mis- taken belief that their lives are not or will not be worth living. This is an easy mistake to make: one's predictions about the character and content of one's future life may be faulty; and, even if they are accurate, one may inadequately imagine what such a life would be like or fail to appreciate one's ability to adapt oneself to it. Thus even if one accepts that suicide and euthanasia can in principle be justified, one should recognize that there will be cases in which it will be justified to restrain a person from commit- ting suicide, or to deny a person's request for assistance in committing suicide or for "euthanasia," on the ground that the person is mistaken in believing that his life is worth not living. The difficulty of discriminating between these cases and those in which the person's life is genuinely not worth living is, of course, one of the major problems with accepting the legitimacy of assisted suicide and euthanasia.

Let us, however, confine our attention to cases in which it is true, and all those in- volved can agree that it is true, that a person's life is worth not living. Even in these cases, suicide or euthanasia may be unjustified because of its effects on others. There are individual cases in which a person's death would be so harmful to others that the person ought morally to endure a miserable existence for the sake of those others. These cases are, however, comparatively rare. For those who care enough about a person to be devastated by his death are normally motivated by love to give that per- son's interests priority over their own. Still, there remain some cases in which a pru- dentially rational suicide is morally unjustified because of its effects on others—for example, a suicide by a single parent that would leave small children emotionally maimed and physically and socially vulnerable.

Even if suicide or euthanasia can be prudentially and morally justified in individ- ual cases, there are various objections, based on a consideration of possible side ef- fects, to accepting the legitimacy of either as a matter of social policy. I will consider some of these objections very briefly in section 2.4. First, we should consider whether there are convincing fundamental objections to these practices—objections that claim that either suicide or euthanasia is an instance of wrongful killing for rea- sons that are independent of such contingencies as possible effects on others and the possibility that a person's evaluation of his own life is mistaken.

I have suggested that, if there are cases in which suicide is prudentially rational and morally permissible, we should conclude that, if other things are equal, voluntary active euthanasia is permissible in such cases as well. Some people, however, believe that, even when suicide is permissible, euthanasia is not. They believe that who brings about the death is fundamentally important. I believe that this is a perversion of certain deontological intuitions about agency. Deontologists rightly recognize that there is a sense in which it matters who does a certain act: for example, it may be wrong for *me* to do a certain act (such as an act of killing) even if this would prevent *others* from doing *more* acts of exactly the same sort. But when it is *permissible* for a person to do a certain act, it should also be permissible for a third party to do that act for him, at his request, provided that in doing the act the third party would not be unfairly favoring the one person over another. Thus if it would be prudentially rational for a person to kill himself and his death would not be worse for others, it should be permissible for a third party to kill him at his request. To believe otherwise is, it seems, to treat the killing of another as a taboo, an act that taints the soul of the agent irrespective of the conditions in which the act is done.

There are two other possible views. One is that, while suicide is wrong, euthanasia can be permissible. Like the previous view, this view assumes that it is of decisive importance *who* performs the act of killing. But because it attributes to third parties a prerogative with respect to the lives of others that it denies to the individuals themselves, it is a view that no one accepts. The final possibility is that there is a fundamental objection to both suicide and euthanasia that shows that both are wrong. If correct, this view obviously undermines the conditional argument I have given for the permissibility of voluntary active euthanasia. It is therefore important to consider whether there really is a plausible fundamental objection to suicide and euthanasia.

My strategy here will be to argue for the permissibility of suicide and euthanasia by negation or exclusion—that is, I will try to show that, of the various accounts of the wrongness of killing, those that have some plausibility fail to condemn suicide and euthanasia. There are, I will claim, no good reasons for thinking that suicide and euthanasia are fundamentally wrong—that is, wrong for reasons other than those concerned with merely contingent effects. This kind of strategy can never, of course, be decisive, for one can never be certain that one has taken account of all the plausible objections or all the plausible accounts of the wrongness of killing. But because there are comparatively few accounts of why killing is in general wrong, the strategy may have considerable force in this particular context.

I will limit my discussion to broadly secular accounts of why killing is wrong. There are various objections to suicide and euthanasia that are necessarily theological in character—that is, that make sense only in the context of a set of theological beliefs. (Thus I do not include among these arguments those that claim that God prohibits suicide or euthanasia for reasons that can be understood and justified independently of claims about God's will, preferences, or plans.) Among the arguments that are necessarily theological are those that claim that only God has the right to determine when a human life should end, that human suffering serves God's purposes in ways we cannot understand, that how we respond to the burdensome aspects of life may in part determine our destiny in the afterlife, and so on. I believe that all of these objections fail even in their own terms: they imply, for example, that it is wrong to save people's lives or to alleviate their suffering, or they attribute motives and intentions to the deity that would be shameful in a human being (for example, a parent).[57] Still, to do full justice to these arguments, one would have to challenge their theological underpinnings, and that would take us too far afield here. So I will leave these arguments aside.

The more obvious objections to killing that are secular in character seem simply not to apply to rational suicide and voluntary active euthanasia. When most of us begin to reflect about the morality of killing, our initial thought is that killing is wrong because of the dreadful effect it has on the victim: it deprives him of the whole of the good life he would otherwise have had. This intuition is the foundation of the Harm-Based Account of the wrongness of killing and also, when suitably refined, of the Time-Relative Interest Account. I have argued that neither of these is ultimately successful as an account of the wrongness of killing persons; but the relevant point here is that neither condemns rational suicide or euthanasia. For in these cases death is by hypothesis not bad for, or against the time-relative interests of, the person who is killed.

Another common objection to killing is that it overrides the autonomy of the victim, usurping a literally vitally important prerogative that is properly the victim's own. This, I believe, is a critical part of the explanation of why killing persons normally involves a violation of the requirement of respect for persons: for respect for a person consists in part in a proper deference to the determinations of his autonomous will in matters within his own rightful sphere of control. (What the boundaries of that sphere are is, of course, a controversial question; but, if we put aside theological claims about God's dominion, choices that determine how a person's life will go and that do not affect the rights of others must surely lie at the very center of that sphere.) Again, however, neither rational suicide nor euthanasia that is genuinely voluntary can possibly violate the autonomous will of the person killed. Nor, for that matter, can nonvoluntary euthanasia: for, by definition, that involves the killing or allowing to die of an individual who lacks an autonomous will. (Involuntary euthanasia, by contrast, does involve a violation of the autonomous will of the person who is killed or allowed to die, and it is precisely for this reason that it can never, in practice if not also in principle, be justified.)

Another way in which people frequently articulate their opposition to killing is to claim that it violates the victim's right to life. But, as many rights theorists have pointed out, rights can be waived. A person who kills himself or autonomously requests to be killed clearly waives his right not to be killed. Hence suicide and voluntary euthanasia cannot be objectionable on the ground that they violate the right to life.

Because these familiar objections do not apply, those who have objected to suicide and euthanasia on grounds that are neither theological nor concerned merely with side effects have tended to appeal to one of the other of two notions: the sanctity of life and the notion of respect for the worth of persons. I will begin with the former.

2.2. *The Sanctity of Life, Again*

It is sometimes held that life—or human life—has a special value or sanctity that is independent of the value that it has either for the individual whose life it is (its personal value, in Ronald Dworkin's terms) or for others (its instrumental value). Because it is not value *for* anyone, this value is *impersonal*. It is sometimes held, therefore, that this form of value can be present—indeed, *is* present—in a life even when the continuation of the life is *bad for* both its possessor and others. When in 1990 the Supreme Court ruled on the Cruzan case, in which the state of Missouri claimed the right to keep the body of a young woman in a PVS alive against the wishes of her parents, Chief Justice William Rehnquist, writing for the majority, and Justice Antonin Scalia, in a concurring opinion, both appealed to the idea that the state has an interest in protecting the value of human life *even* when this is contrary to the interests of the individual whose life it is. As Dworkin paraphrases his view, Scalia held that "a state has the constitutional power to prohibit suicide in any circumstance, . . . even for someone dying in terrible pain who would plainly be better off dead, because it has the power to protect human life for its own sake."[58] Similarly, John Finnis holds that those who accept the legitimacy of euthanasia or suicide erroneously suppose that "human life in certain conditions or circumstances retains no intrinsic value or dignity."[59] He then argues that human life *always* has intrinsic value or dignity, and that respect for this value requires that human life must never be intentionally terminated, no matter how wretched it may be for the person condemned to live it and irrespective of whether that person autonomously desires to die.

How are we to understand the basis of this alleged impersonal value or sanctity of life? As I noted earlier in section 7 of chapter 4, Dworkin contends that it is implicit in a range of widely held beliefs that the impersonal value or sanctity of a life derives primarily from the investment that has been made in the life. If, however, that is the basis of the sanctity of life, the appeal to the sanctity of life cannot plausibly sustain an objection to rational suicide or euthanasia. For the fact that an investment has been made in a life does not make it important that the life should be preserved irrespective of what its character will be. The significance of investment derives from the value of the outcome in which the investment is realized or redeemed. Thus Dworkin frequently refers to the *waste* of investment that occurs when a human being dies. Yet there are cases in which death does not involve a waste of investment. When, for example, a person dies at a very old age having fully realized his potential, the investment made in his life is not wasted because it has already been redeemed. When the investment has already yielded all the good that can come of it, its significance is ended and there is no possibility of its being wasted. In such a situation, there is no sense in the idea that the person should be kept around for the sake of the investments that were once made in his life (though, of course, there may be other reasons for preserving or extending his life). Similarly, there is also no sense in the idea that the investments that were once made in a person's life make it important to extend his life when, for whatever reasons, there is no prospect of those investments yielding any further good. The person's death would not involve a waste of investment, because the investment is already doomed to frustration. The death would not prevent the investment from being made good; thus keeping the person alive would do nothing to redeem the investment.

Indeed, the failure of an investment in a life is even more tragic when the investment not only fails to yield an expected good, but ultimately results in a life of misery and degradation. Thus the more the wretched outcome is prolonged, the worse the waste or spoliation of the investment is. And it only makes the situation even worse if, in such circumstances, one continues to squander further investments when it is impossible that they should yield anything of value. Yet this is what one does when one devotes energy, effort, and resources to the prolongation of a life that can no longer be worth living. As the metaphor from economics suggests, it is irrational to increase rather than to limit one's losses.

There is a reply to these claims implicit in Dworkin's contention that "we believe . . . that a premature death is bad in itself, even when it is not bad for any particular person."[60] It is true, I think, that many people believe that death is bad even when further life would be worth not living. (Recall, for example, Richard Wollheim's remark, quoted in section 4.3 of chapter 2: "That there are circumstances in which we would prefer to die rather than to live is . . . compatible with death being a misfortune because there are circumstances in which life has become a yet greater misfortune.") Dworkin can claim that this shows that we believe that a life can continue to have impersonal value or sanctity even when it has become *bad* for the person whose life it is. And if investment is the basis of this value, it must be that the death somehow undermines or defeats the investment, even if it does not literally waste it. Or, alternatively, it may be that there is a further dimension to the impersonal value of such a life that is independent of any investment that has been made in it.

There is, however, a different and better explanation of our sense that death can be bad even when the life the person would otherwise have had would have been bad for him. It is not so much that we believe that the death is impersonally bad, in that it ends a life that would otherwise have contributed to the value of the world even though it would have been bad for its possessor; rather, as I noted in chapter 2, the death seems bad because we compare it not only with the life the person would *actually* have had (relative to which the death seems good), but also with other, more desirable futures that the person *could* have had but would not *in fact* have had. It is not obvious that such an evaluation is rationally defensible. But I suspect that it is the source of the sense of loss we experience even when someone dies whose life has ceased to be worth living.

Thus far I have assumed, with Dworkin, that the principal basis of the sanctity of life is the investment that has been made in a life. But many will find this assumption implausible. So, for the moment, let us put this aside and make no assumptions about the basis of the sanctity of life. And let us grant, for the sake of argument, that all human life does have an impersonal value of this sort. In order for this impersonal value to stand in opposition to suicide and euthanasia, it must be present even when the personal value of a life is negative—that is, even when the life is bad for the individual whose life it is. This assumption is, as we have seen, explicit in the arguments of Justices Rehnquist and Scalia. But this raises an obvious question: when the two dimensions of the value of a life—the personal and the impersonal—are in conflict, which has priority? Can the sanctity of life be outweighed by the negative value of the life for its possessor?

There is reason to believe that most proponents of the sanctity of life accept that it can be outweighed. Most of those who appeal to the sanctity of life in objecting to suicide and euthanasia accept that there are certain other cases in which the killing of a human being can be permissible: for example, in self-defense, war, or for the purpose of punishment. But how can killing in these cases be compatible with respect for the sanctity of life? One possibility is that the life of the victim in these cases has, because of something he has done, lost its sanctity or impersonal value. Persons who may permissibly be killed in self-defense, in war, or as punishment are in some sense relevantly noninnocent, and it might be held that what they have done to compromise their innocence has also negated or nullified the impersonal value or sanctity of their lives.[61] But this suggestion seems incompatible with the usual assumptions about the basis of the sanctity of life. If our lives have sanctity simply by virtue of our being human, or because we have certain psychological capacities or potentials, of because certain investments have been made in our lives, then they cannot lose this sanctity simply because we compromise our innocence through our action. Moreover, people whose action compromises their innocence and thus lowers the moral barriers to their being killed often recover their innocence once they desist from the action. For example, a person may be relevantly noninnocent while he unjustifiably threatens the life of another, but may then fully regain his status as innocent, and thus his moral immunity to being killed, as soon as he ceases to pose the threat. But it would be absurd to suppose that the sanctity or impersonal value of a person's life could similarly fluctuate, or come and go, in response to considerations of this sort. It therefore seems more reasonable to conclude that in cases such as those in which killing is justified in self-defense, the sanctity of the victim's life is not forfeited but is simply outweighed by countervailing considerations, such as justice in the distribution of harm.

But if the sanctity of an individual life can be outweighed by such considerations as distributive or retributive justice, it should be susceptible of being outweighed by other considerations as well, including the interests and autonomous preferences of the person whose life it is. There is, of course, no guarantee that a person's interest in (and preference for) avoiding a future life that would be bad for him will always outweigh the impersonal value or sanctity of his life. Nor is it obvious that the two forms of value can even be rendered fully commensurate on a single scale of value. But it does seem that, if other values can outweigh the sanctity of an individual's life, that person's own good can, in some cases at least, outweigh it as well.

Many of those who believe in the sanctity or impersonal or intrinsic value of human life reject this inference, as indeed they must if they are to resist the conclusion that suicide and euthanasia can be morally permissible. Some hold that the sanctity of human life is such that it can never be permissible intentionally to kill an innocent human being. On this view, the intentional killing of a human being may be justified *only* if that human being is relevantly noninnocent. It is usually left unclear whether, in these cases, the noninnocent individual's life is supposed to have lost its sanctity or whether its sanctity is retained but overridden. But whatever is supposed to happen to the sanctity of human life in these cases, the important point is that *only* noninnocence is supposed to be sufficient to nullify or override it, thereby making the intentional killing of a human being permissible. Exactly why the sanctity of life is supposed to yield to noninnocence but not to any other consideration has never, to my knowledge, been adequately explained.

A purer form of absolutism holds that the sanctity of human life is such that it is never permissible intentionally to kill *any* human being. According to this view, killing in self-defense may on occasion be permissible, but only if one's intention is not to kill one's assailant but only, for example, to incapacitate him. Some acts of killing in war might be justified in a similar manner, but killing itself could never be justified as a mode of punishment.

Both of these views imply that suicide and euthanasia are ruled out because they involve the intentional killing of an innocent human being. (The first view may allow for one exception: an act of suicide intended as in instance of self-punishment by a person who is noninnocent.) Each, however, permits a limited range of acts that are quite close to suicide or euthanasia. Each, for example, may permit a physician, in certain circumstances, to administer a lethal dose of an analgesic to a patient, provided that the intention is only to alleviate suffering and not to end the patient's life— though the physician may, of course, foresee that the drug will also kill the patient.[62]

These absolutist views raise many questions. Why, for example, does the sanctity of life have absolute priority over all other considerations? Why does the sanctity of life absolutely rule out only intended killing and not killing that is foreseen, and to that extent deliberate, but not intended? Most important, these views require that a sharp line be drawn between those who may never be intentionally killed (unless, perhaps, they act in ways that compromise their innocence) and those who may in principle be intentionally killed if there is sufficient reason for doing so. Where is this line to be drawn, and why? Virtually all those who object to suicide and euthanasia by appealing to the sanctity of life are in fact proponents of the sanctity of *human* life—that is, they draw the line at the boundaries of the human species. But as I have argued at length in chapter 3, there is simply no basis for drawing any moral line, much less one freighted with as much significance as the absolutist line has, at that point.

It has occasionally been suggested that all human beings, and only human beings, have certain morally significant properties that are different from the purely biological properties that define our species. But these claims either are plainly false or else seem unintelligible. John Finnis, for example, claims that every living human being is "a person, a being with the radical capacity to deliberate and choose"—in short, a being with free will.[63] It is clear, however, that an anencephalic infant, or even a congenitally severely retarded human being, does not have the capacity for deliberation and choice. Indeed, neither has even the potential to be able to deliberate and choose. But Finnis distinguishes between capacity and *radical* capacity. What, then, is the radical capacity to deliberate and choose? Finnis writes: "The living principle (dynamic and constitutive inner source) which actively animates, organises and informs every aspect of one's existence from conception to one's death establishes, constitutes, one's radical capacity to metabolise, feel, move, notice, understand, respond, want, choose and carry out choices all in a human way."[64] Thus even when a human being lacks "the capacity (ability) to think and feel," as in the case of an anencephalic infant, that individual still has "the humanity, the *human* life, which until his death goes on shaping, informing, and organising his existence *towards* the feeling and thinking which are natural to human life (i.e. which human life is radically capable of and oriented towards)."[65]

These remarks do not, however, seem to tell us anything that would enable us to discriminate morally between an anencephalic human infant and a chimpanzee. There are references to capacities for deliberation, choice, thinking, and feeling, and it is certainly plausible to suppose that these capacities endow their possessor with a certain moral status; but there is nothing here that tells us how an anencephalic infant is somehow closer to having the capacity for deliberation and choice than a chimpanzee is. Perhaps the suggestion is that, because an anencephalic infant is a member of the human species, it is somehow directed by an inner human essence or "living principle" toward the development of capacities for deliberation and choice, but is frustrated in the realization of these capacities. But there is no clear indication of what this essence or principle might be. There are, it seems, human beings, or members of our species, in whom the genes that direct the development of those regions of the brain necessary for the capacities for deliberation and choice are either absent or defective. In these cases, in which there is no genetic coding for the development of the physical basis of the relevant psychological capacities, there is no reason grounded in the biology of the organism to suppose that that human individual is shaped or organized or oriented toward the possession of those capacities.

These reflections lead to my final reason for concluding that suicide and euthanasia cannot be ruled out by an appeal to the sanctity of life. Some of the elements of this argument were stated in section 7 of chapter 4, but they are worth repeating here. As I have argued, there is no plausible basis for the sanctity of life that is such that all human beings possess it and, moreover, possess it equally, while no nonhuman animals possess it at all. It remains a possibility, however, that there is a basis for attributing a special sanctity or impersonal value to most or all human lives. If this basis is present in *all* human lives, it must be present in some nonhuman lives. A fortiori, if it is not present in any nonhuman lives, it must be absent in some human lives. One or the other of these two alternatives may well be acceptable to those who believe that suicide and euthanasia involve an insult to the sanctity of life, but who are not wedded to the idea that there is an unbridgeable gulf between all human life and all nonhuman life. Some may accept that the killing of certain nonhuman animals also involves an offense against the sanctity of life. Others may hold instead that, although not all human life has sanctity, anyone capable of deliberately killing himself or of autonomously requesting euthanasia necessarily has the properties that give a life sanctity; hence to kill such a person intentionally is to violate the sanctity of life.

It is reasonable to suppose that, on both these views, the basis of the sanctity of life must be variable—that is, some individuals must have it to a greater degree than others. According to the first view, the sanctity of life opposes suicide and euthanasia but also opposes the killing of certain animals. But if human and animal lives all have sanctity to the same extent, the objection to suicide and euthanasia should be no stronger than the objection to killing certain animals. Most opponents of suicide and euthanasia will therefore want to conclude that most human lives have greater sanctity than most animal lives. According to the second view, not all human lives have sanctity and few, if any, nonhuman lives do. So the basis of the sanctity of life must be some property or set of properties that are not universal within the human species. Yet there do not seem to be any properties that are possessed by some but not all human beings, are clearly morally significant, but do not come in degrees (that is, are either possessed fully or not at all). The various candidates for the basis of the sanctity of life, on this view—for example, certain psychological capacities, certain forms of experience or activity, investment, and so on—are instead matters of degree. Some human beings have them in higher forms or to a higher degree than others.

If, however, the sanctity of life is variable among human beings, and if the explanation of why killing is wrong is that it violates the sanctity of life, it seems that killing those persons whose lives have greater sanctity or impersonal value should be more seriously wrong, if other things are equal, than killing those whose lives have a lower degree of sanctity. Most of us find this inegalitarian implication disturbing. (As I noted earlier, the view may have other disturbing implications as well—for example, that it may be permissible to kill a person with a lesser degree of sanctity in order to save a different life with a higher level of sanctity. Whether this implication holds depends on whether the sanctity of life is assumed to provide an exhaustive explanation of the wrongness of killing.) There is, I think, only one alternative, other than giving up the idea that the sanctity of life is relevant to understanding the morality of killing. This is to adopt a two-tier view that explains the wrongness of certain acts of killing in terms of the violation of the sanctity of life, but offers a wholly different account of why killing is wrong in certain other cases. This, as we have seen, is the strategy that Dworkin appears to adopt. He notes that we accept that "people have an equal right to life," so that killing one person is as wrong as killing another (provided that such factors as intention, the guilt or innocence of the victim, and so on are equal). But, he observes, "these judgments about murder . . . belong to the system of rights and interests."[66] This suggests, as I noted in section 7 of chapter 4, that Dworkin believes that we have one account of the wrongness of killing certain beings (principally *persons*) that appeals to rights and interests, and a different account of the wrongness of killing beings that lack rights (and perhaps interests as well) that appeals to the sanctity of life. This sort of two-tier view has the advantage of enabling us to preserve our egalitarian intuitions about the killing of persons (that is, to retain the Equal Wrongness Thesis) and at the same time to recognize that killing various other types of being (such as fetuses or animals) may also be morally objectionable, though less so and for a different reason. If, however, we accept this sort of view, according to which the sanctity of life is no part of the explanation of why killing persons is wrong, then we cannot object to suicide or euthanasia, as practiced by or on persons, by appealing to the sanctity of life.

It seems, however, that we must be missing something. Although Dworkin distinguishes between the sanctity of life and the "system of rights and interests," he also assumes that beliefs about the sanctity of life underlie much of the opposition to euthanasia. And it seems that this should be an option. Suppose we accept a two-tier view of the sort Dworkin suggests. According to this view, the reason why killing persons is normally wrong is that it violates the victim's right to life. (Let us assume, for convenience, that this is correct. But we could equally hold that the reason is that killing normally constitutes an egregious failure of respect for a person.) But there are, let us suppose, some cases in which even the intentional killing of a person would not violate the right to life. For example, it might be that some people forfeit the right to life through wrongful action while others waive it by requesting or consenting to be killed. Surely it is possible to hold that, even in these cases, the person's life retains its sanctity and that this consideration opposes the permissibility of, say, capital punishment or euthanasia. After all, if a fetus's life has sanctity, this is not something that is lost when the fetus later develops into a person. It is, on the contrary, reasonable to believe that the sanctity of an individual's life *increases* with the transition from fetus to person.

To try to make sense of this, let us distinguish three variants of the two-tier view. According to the *pure two-tier view*, the wrongness of killing certain sorts of being, including persons, is *exhaustively* explained within the framework of rights and interests (which, for present purposes, we may assume to encompass the morality of respect), while the wrongness of killing beings of certain other sorts is explained by reference to the sanctity of life. This variant excludes by hypothesis the possibility that the sanctity of life could ever be relevant to the morality of killing of a person. But this, as I noted, seems implausible if the lives of persons are conceded to have sanctity.

A different variant that avoids this objection is the *mixed two-tier view*. According to this view, the sanctity of life is *no* part of the explanation of why killing a person is wrong when killing would violate the right to life. When killing would violate the right to life, that fact exhaustively explains why the killing would be wrong. But, in cases in which killing a person would *not* violate the right to life, the sanctity of life reemerges to oppose the killing. On this view, capital punishment and euthanasia are opposed by the sanctity of life even if those forms of killing would not violate the victim's right to life. The problem with this view, of course, is that it is utterly mysterious why the sanctity of life should exert moral force only when the force exerted by the right to life is in abeyance. If the lives of persons have sanctity, and if this consideration opposes killing in cases in which killing would not violate the right to life, surely it should also be part of the explanation of why killing is wrong even in cases in which there is another dimension to the explanation: namely, that killing violates the victim's right to life.

The third variant—the *additive two-tier view*—responds to this objection. It holds that the sanctity of life opposes killing in all cases in which it is present. In the case of beings that lack the right to life but whose lives have sanctity—Dworkin cites fetuses as an example—the sanctity of life may be the only consideration that opposes killing. But, in the case of persons, while the sanctity of life opposes killing, the normative force it exerts is overshadowed by that exerted by the right to life. That the lives of persons have sanctity is part of the explanation of why killing people is wrong, but it is a comparatively insignificant part of the explanation. The dominant element in the explanation is that killing persons normally violates the right to life.

It seems that, formally, the additive two-tier view is incompatible with the Equal Wrongness Thesis. We are assuming that the sanctity of life may vary in degree from person to person. Thus if persons A and B both have equal rights to life but A's life has greater sanctity than B's, and if the right to life and the sanctity of life combine in opposition to killing, it seems that the objection to killing A must be stronger than the objection to killing B. For the array of considerations that oppose the killing of A are stronger than those that oppose killing B.

The additive two-tier view thus has the kind of inegalitarian implications we have sought to avoid—assuming, as it seems we must, that the basis of the sanctity of life is variable, or present in different people to varying degrees. There are two possible responses to this problem. One is to claim that different considerations can combine to condemn some acts of killing as worse than others without this being *objectionably* or *offensively* inegalitarian. Consider, for example, the way that side effects affect the morality of killing. Suppose that person A has no one who cares about him or depends on him, whereas B is loved by many and contributes to the well-being of many others as well. Because of this difference, there is a sense in which it would be worse to kill B than to kill A. Yet it does not seem objectionably inegalitarian to acknowledge this. For we can concede that the *fundamental* objection to killing each is the same (for example, each has an equal right to life). There is no suggestion that B is, in himself, a more worthy or more intrinsically valuable person. Rather, the difference between the two cases is that, while to kill A would be to commit only one wrong (namely, the wrong to him), to kill B would be to wrong him *and* to commit various other wrongs as well (the wrongs done to all those who care about or depend on him). That is the sense in which it would be worse to kill B.

The problem with this response is that the claim that killing violates the sanctity of life is, unlike the appeal to side effects, a fundamental objection to killing. Thus to say that to kill B would be worse than to kill A because B's life has greater sanctity does seem objectionably inegalitarian. It implies that the fundamental objection to killing A is weaker because his life has less intrinsic value.

The second response to the charge that the additive two-tier view has inegalitarian implications is to claim that, because the violation of the right to life is the dominant part of the explanation of why killing a person is wrong, whatever variations there may be in the sanctity of people's lives will make very little difference to the degree to which killing is wrong. If the violation of the sanctity of life is a comparatively insignificant part of the explanation of why killing a person is wrong, variations in the degree of sanctity among persons may have little or no effect on our practical judgments. (This, of course, will be particularly true if the variations in the sanctity of life among persons are small.) In this way the *formally* inegalitarian character of the additive two-tier view might not matter in practice. The differences in the degree to which different acts of killing are wrong are, on this interpretation, so slight as to be unworthy of attention.

I suspect that this is our best option if we want to accept both the Equal Wrongness Thesis and the claim that the lives of persons have sanctity to varying degrees. Although we would have to reject the Equal Wrongness Thesis as I have stated it, we could accept a claim that would be sufficiently similar to it to satisfy our egalitarian intuitions—namely, that, if other things are equal, variations in the degree to which different acts of killing persons are wrong are too slight to be of practical significance. Notice, however, that on this interpretation of the additive two-tier view, the sanctity of life is a comparatively insignificant element in the explanation of why killing people is wrong. Therefore in cases in which the dominant part of the explanation (which we are assuming, for convenience, to be that killing violates the right to life) does not apply, the objection to killing will be comparatively weak. If, for example, a person has forfeited or waived his right to life, it may still be that killing him would be objectionable because it would violate the sanctity of life. But this consideration alone would constitute only a relatively weak objection—one that could plausibly be outweighed or overridden by countervailing considerations, such as, perhaps, considerations of retributive justice or the interests or autonomous preferences of the person himself.

It seems reasonable to conclude, therefore, that, even if the lives of persons do have sanctity, this alone is insufficient to rule out suicide or voluntary euthanasia. For unless the sanctity of life is variable, it cannot ground a strong objection to killing most human beings without also grounding an equivalent objection to killing many animals. But if the sanctity of life is variable, we must either accept an objectionably inegalitarian view of the morality of killing or else conclude that the sanctity of life is a comparatively minor consideration that cannot support a decisive objection to rational suicide or euthanasia.

2.3. *Respect for the Worth of Persons*

I turn now to what I believe to be a more promising objection to suicide and euthanasia. This objection appeals to considerations that are integral to what, in chapter 3, I referred to as the Two-Tiered Account of the wrongness of killing. That view, one will recall, holds that there is a threshold on the scale that measures cognitive capacity such that the morality of killing beings below that threshold is governed by a concern for their time-relative interests, while the morality of killing beings above the threshold is governed by a requirement of respect. Earlier I assumed that the threshold divides persons from nonpersons and that, although persons vary in the degree to which they possess the psychological capacities that are the basis of the worth that commands respect, their worth does not vary but is equal. Killing a person is wrong, I suggested, because it violates a requirement of respect for the worth of the person. Since persons have equal worth, acts of killing a person are equally wrong, if other things (such as the agent's intentions, the guilt or innocence of the person killed, and so on) are equal.

It has been argued that suicide, even when it is rational (in the sense that the person's continued life would not be worth living), and euthanasia normally violate the requirement of respect for the worth of the person killed. This was the view of Kant himself and it has subsequently been defended by various writers in the Kantian tradition. In stating the argument, I will follow the presentation given by David Velleman, which is the clearest, subtlest, and most plausible articulation of the Kantian view of these issues of which I am aware.[67]

Velleman distinguishes between what is good for a person and the value of the person himself. This distinction corresponds to the one I drew in section 3.2 of chapter 3 between the value of a person's life (or, more narrowly, the value *for the person* of the contents of his life) and the worth of the person. According to Velleman, a person's good matters, or makes a claim on us, only if the person himself matters for his own sake, or has a value that is independent of what is good for him. For how, he asks, could what is good for a person matter if the person himself did not matter? Moreover, unlike the value of the person's life, the value of the person is not a value *for* him or, for that matter, for anyone. It is an impersonal value. "A value of this kind," Velleman writes, "which a person has *in* himself but not *for* anyone, is the basis of Kantian moral theory. Kant's term for this value is 'dignity', and he attributes dignity to all persons in virtue of their rational nature. What morality requires of us, according to Kant, is that we respect the dignity of persons."[68] Velleman continues to use the term "dignity" where I have used "worth." Both are used in translations of the relevant passages in Kant's writings, and I will assume that they are, in this context, synonymous. Velleman also follows Kant in identifying "rational nature" as the basis of the worth that commands respect. By contrast, I wish to remain agnostic on the exact nature of the psychological capacities that are the basis of the worth of persons. I will, however, in the remainder of this section, use "rational nature" as shorthand for whatever those capacities are (for example, self-consciousness and autonomy).

According to Kant and Velleman, to kill a person, or for a person to kill himself, in order to spare him a future that would be worth not living, is to violate the worth of the person. It is to assume that the value or worth of the person is commensurable with and outweighed by what is good *for* him. But these values are not commensurable: "the value of what's good for a person is only a shadow of the value inhering in the person, and cannot overshadow or be overshadowed by it."[69] Therefore to kill a person out of a concern for the person's own good, even if the person is oneself, is to make the mistake of giving the person's good priority over the worth of the person himself. It is to sacrifice the person for the sake of his good, thereby treating the person as a means rather than as an end-in-himself. (It is worth noting that there are other latter-day Kantians who believe that the worth of a person, while distinct from his good, is in principle commensurable with it. Thomas E. Hill, Jr., for example, proposes that "one should treat humanity [that is, a person's rational nature] as a special intrinsic value, independent of but not always overriding considerations of pleasure and pain," or, more broadly, the person's good.)[70]

If we assume, as the Two-Tiered Account asserts, that the fundamental moral objection to killing a person is that this violates the person's worth, the Kantian view I have described implies that suicide and euthanasia are normally wrong for the same reason and to the same degree that other acts of killing persons are normally wrong. Unlike the appeal to the sanctity of life, therefore, the Kantian view supports a strong objection to most acts of suicide and euthanasia. It also supports the Equal Wrongness Thesis. It simply extends the Two-Tiered Account, which implies the Equal Wrongness Thesis, by including most instances of suicide and euthanasia among those acts of killing persons that are equally wrong if other things are equal.

It is also worth noting that the Kantian view, as interpreted by Velleman, takes rational nature to be a characteristic of persons rather than human beings as such. Thus we need not suppose that, for example, fetuses come within the scope of the requirement of respect. "What secular morality must regard as sacrosanct," Velleman writes, "is not the human organism but the person, and a fetus may embody one but not the other."[71] (Whether all persons have rational natures in the Kantian sense *in the sensible world* is a question I will not pursue. Kant thought not. He believed that respect for persons must be respect for the rational natures possessed by people's noumenal selves. I will assume, by contrast, that the rational nature that is the basis of the worth of persons is characteristic of persons as they actually are.)

The Kantian view also seems to support the common view that, while euthanasia is morally problematic as applied to persons, it is clearly permissible when applied to animals. For the Kantian claim is that euthanasia is normally wrong because it violates the worth that is grounded in a person's rational nature—an objection that does not apply in the case of beings, such as animals, that lack a rational nature. Yet the matter is actually rather more complicated than this. Recall that Velleman claims that an individual's good cannot matter unless that individual matters, or is valuable in himself. If this is true, then, in order for an animal's suffering to matter in a way that would provide a reason for euthanasia, the animal itself must matter or have a value that is distinct from its good. This value cannot be equivalent to the worth that persons have, and it may vary in degree from animal to animal; but, as long as it is an intrinsic value that is distinct from the animal's good, it ought—at least according to the Kantian view—to count against the killing of an animal for the sake of its own good.

Kant himself avoided this problem by assuming that an individual cannot have a value below the level of worth. On this view, animals lack worth and therefore have no intrinsic value. They do not matter; therefore their interests do not matter. Just as there is no reason for their own sake not to harm them, so there is no reason to benefit them. Therefore there can be no reason to practice euthanasia on an animal, unless doing so would have an important effect on a person.

Most people, however, will rightly part company with Kant at this point. Most people accept that an animal's suffering matters—even if they typically underestimate the extent to which it matters. But if the view that an animal's suffering matters implies that the animal itself matters, or has an intrinsic value (albeit a lesser value than worth), and if a being's having intrinsic value counts against killing it, even for the sake of its good, then euthanasia for animals should be objectionable in the same way that, though to a lesser degree than, euthanasia for persons is.

There are several responses to this problem. For the sake of clarity, I will distinguish them by number.

1. One response, which few will find plausible, is to accept that euthanasia for animals is ruled out, even when it is clear that it is in the interests of an animal to die, because it would violate the value of the animal itself to sacrifice it for the sake of its good.
2. Another possibility is to hold that, unlike the worth of a person, the intrinsic value or importance of an animal is commensurable with its own good. On this view, euthanasia can be justified in the case of an animal if its interest in avoiding suffering outweighs its own intrinsic value.
3. Thomas E. Hill, Jr.'s view, which I mentioned parenthetically at the beginning of this section, extends the claim of commensurability to embrace the worth of persons as well. On his view, euthanasia may be justified if a person's interest in dying outweighs his worth as a person.
4. A further possibility is that killing an individual for the sake of its own good can be compatible with respect for the value of that individual, provided that the individual's value is below the level of worth. On this view, euthanasia for animals can be compatible with respect for their value as individuals, though euthanasia for persons is, in general, incompatible with respect for their worth.
5. Alternatively, it might be true quite generally—that is, in the case of animals and persons—that it can be compatible with respect for the value of an individual to kill him for the sake of his own good.

While either the second or the fourth of these possibilities seems best to support the commonsense discrimination between euthanasia for persons and euthanasia for animals, I will later argue that the fifth and last possibility is correct.

Let us now examine the plausibility of the Kantian view. Consider, first, Velleman's claim that an individual's good cannot matter unless the individual matters *as an individual*. There are reasons for doubting this. Recall the hypothetical sentient creature discussed in section 5.2 of chapter 1. That creature's mind is so simple that it altogether lacks either synchronic or diachronic psychological unity. That is a reasonable basis for claiming that the creature, as an individual, does not matter at all. It is, as Singer would say, replaceable without loss by another creature of its sort whose experiences would be equally good. But does it follow that it cannot matter whether the creature's experiences are pleasurable or painful? While it may follow that the quality of the creature's experiences cannot matter *for its sake,* it seems wrong to suppose that the sequence of the creature's mental states cannot matter at all. It matters impersonally whether, for example, the creature's experiences are pleasurable or painful.

More importantly, if an individual's good matters only if the individual matters, it seems reasonable to assume that an individual's good also matters only *to the extent* that the individual matters. If animals matter less than persons (because persons have worth, while nonpersons have only some lesser and varying form of intrinsic value), it follows that their good or interests matter less than the comparable interests of persons. On this view, it matters less if an animal suffers than it does if a person experiences a comparable amount of suffering. But that is not obviously right. It is certainly true that animals in general matter significantly less than persons do, but it does not seem to follow that an animal's interest always matters less than the comparable interest of a person.

We can waive these doubts for present purposes. Whether or not it is true quite generally that an individual's good cannot matter unless the individual matters, it is reasonable to believe that persons do matter, that they have a value in themselves that is independent of their good. If we grant this, as I think we should, the relevant questions are how exactly we should understand this value and whether it stands in opposition to rational suicide and voluntary active euthanasia.

We can begin by asking how it affirms or upholds a person's worth for that person to endure a life of suffering rather than to commit suicide. How is his worth being served, or respected, by his simply enduring a life that has ceased to be worth living, or by our refusing to facilitate or bring about his death for the sake of his good? It is doubtful that anything positive is thereby being achieved. But perhaps that is not the point. Perhaps the point is essentially negative: namely, that a person's merely suffering through a life that is worth not living, or our refusing to end his life for him, affirms his worth simply by refusing to violate it.

So we should perhaps pose a different question. What reason is there to suppose that killing a person violates his worth? It is, of course, obvious that, if persons have worth, killing them normally violates that worth. But there are different possible explanations of why killing a person violates his worth, only some of which imply that suicide and euthanasia typically violate the worth of the person killed, while others do not. One suggestion, for example, is that, in destroying the person, suicide and euthanasia destroy his rational nature, which is the basis of his worth; and this must be tantamount to destroying his worth itself, which is hardly compatible with respect for that worth.

This is not a particularly plausible explanation. The claim is that killing destroys a person's worth. But we need to recall what it is for a person to have worth: it is for him to matter in a special way. Does killing a person cause him to cease to matter? Consider, for the sake of comparison, another way of eliminating a person's worth. One may destroy a person's rational nature (assuming that this is a feature of his empirical self) by inflicting on him a degree of brain damage that leaves him conscious but lacking in self-consciousness and rationality. If one destroys his rational nature, one destroys the basis of his worth; but does one destroy his worth—that is, does one cause him to cease to matter, or to matter less? A plausible response is to say that he still matters in the same way, but there is now not much that we can do for him. But we should still respect the prior determinations of the rational will he has now lost—

for example, by honoring his advance directive concerning the kind of care he should receive in a demented state. On this view, one does not lose one's worth even if one loses the properties that gave one one's worth in the first place. And perhaps this is true even of persons who have died. They may still matter in a special way, even though there is little we can do for them beyond honoring the autonomous wishes they expressed before they died.

Even if to kill a person is not to *destroy* his worth, it is usually to *violate* it in that it is to treat him in a way that would be appropriate only if he did not matter or if he mattered less. But is the killing of a person, and the concomitant destruction of his rational nature, *always* a violation of his worth? Velleman suggests that it is not. He concedes that, "when a person cannot sustain both life and dignity, his death may indeed be morally justified. One is sometimes permitted, even obligated, to destroy objects of dignity if they would otherwise deteriorate in ways that would offend against that value."[72] Thus if the conditions of a person's life threaten to undermine his rational nature while leaving him alive, suicide or euthanasia may not violate his worth. For it could be compatible with respect for his worth to kill him for the sake of avoiding the insult to his worth that would be involved in his living on in the degraded state of having lost his rational nature.

Velleman is here conceding an important point: namely, that "respecting . . . people is not necessarily a matter of keeping them in existence; it is rather a matter of treating them in the way that is required by their personhood—whatever way that is."[73] This fact helps to distinguish worth from other forms of impersonal value that persons might be thought to have. The idea that persons have worth is different, for example, from the idea that it is good in itself that beings as exalted as persons should exist—that is, that the world is better for having persons in it, and the more persons there are, the better it is, other things being equal. According to this view, there is reason not only to preserve those persons who already exist but also, if other things are equal, to cause new persons to exist. This is an intelligible view, but it is not what lies behind our beliefs about the morality of killing. It is, however, quite closely related to the idea that human life has sanctity. The difference is that the idea that life has sanctity does not imply that it is good to create more of it. But it does imply that, once a human life exists, it has a value that is independent of the value the life has *for its possessor* and that supports the preservation of the life. Thus Dworkin claims that the idea that human life has sanctity implies that "it is *intrinsically* regrettable when human life, once begun, ends prematurely" and "that a premature death is bad in itself, even when it is not bad for any particular person."[74] If a person's life has sanctity, in other words, it follows that there is a moral reason to keep the person in existence—though, as I suggested earlier, that reason may be outweighed by competing considerations. (Dworkin suggests that euthanasia may be compatible with respect for the sanctity of life.[75] But it is not clear that his reasons for making this claim cohere with other things he says about the notion of sanctity. It seems more plausible to see the cases he mentions either as cases in which the sanctity of a life is outweighed by considerations of personal value or as cases in which a life has lost the properties that are the basis of its sanctity. But I will not pursue this here.)

Velleman invites us to see the notion of worth as essentially equivalent to the notion of sanctity when he writes that "such talk [of dignity or worth] is a secular version of religious talk about the sanctity of human life."[76] But it seems to me that they should be distinguished, and not just because one is a religious notion while the other is secular. The claim that an individual's life has sanctity does seem to imply that there is necessarily a reason to preserve the life, though the reason may be outweighed by competing considerations. But worth is different. Just as the claim that persons have worth does not imply that it would be better to create more persons, so it does not imply that it would always be better to preserve the lives of existing persons. All it implies is that persons matter in a special way, a way that demands our respect. This leaves it open what counts as respect for a person's worth. And one possibility, explicitly noted by Velleman, is that "respect for an object may sometimes require its destruction."[77]

Velleman is in fact insistent that worth makes different demands from those made by other sorts of value. He contends that, "insofar as we regard rational nature as something for us to promote, preserve, or facilitate, we regard it no differently from happiness, and our motive toward it is no different from desire."[78] He then advances an alternative understanding:

> When considering the motivational force of respect, [Kant] says that its object "must . . . be conceived only negatively—that is, as an end against which we should never act, and consequently as one which in all our willing we must never rate *merely* as a means." In other words, respect can motivate us, if not by impelling us to produce its object, then by deterring us from violating it; and the violation from which we are thus deterred can be conceived as that of using the object as a mere means to other ends."[79]

According to this view, when suicide and euthanasia are wrong, it is not because they destroy a person's rational nature, but because they sacrifice the person's rational nature for the sake of his good, thereby treating the person's rational nature as if it were an instrument of the person's good rather than as an end-in-itself. To commit suicide or to request euthanasia on the ground that one's life has ceased to be worth living is to "trad[e] one's person in exchange for . . . relief from harm," and this is incompatible with respect for one's worth as a person.[80]

This is Velleman's (and Kant's) understanding of why killing a person normally constitutes a violation of his worth as a person. To kill a person for a reason other than to respect his rational nature is to treat his rational nature as commensurable in value with, and sacrificeable for, some other value—and this is to violate the person's worth. There is, however, an alternative understanding of respect for a person's worth. To respect a person, on this understanding, is a matter of respecting both his good and the determinations of his autonomous will. It is to accept that a person's good matters in the same way that any other person's good matters, and that the person's own autonomous will is authoritative with respect to how his own life should go. According to this understanding, the reason why killing a person is normally a violation of the requirement of respect for his worth is that it is contrary both to his good and to his will. There are, of course, cases in which the two criteria of respect diverge: namely, cases in which a person autonomously wishes to die even though his future life would in fact be worth living, and cases in which a person wishes to continue to live even though his future life will not be worth living. These cases are difficult, primarily because neither criterion seems to be uniformly dominant. There are cases in which a person's good seems to have priority over his will—for example, a case in which a person has considered the matter at length and in a calm state of mind, but persists in wanting to kill himself because he is convinced (as the members of the Heaven's Gate cult were) that extraterrestrial beings will then carry him off to a better life. In such a case it would seem permissible to attempt to prevent the person from committing suicide. But there are also cases in which a person's will seems to be decisive—for example, when a prisoner of war who faces inevitable torture and death refuses to kill himself or to allow his comrades to kill him painlessly, because he believes that it would be ignoble to evade torture in a way that would affirm the enemy's power over him. For present purposes, however, it is not necessary to resolve these issues. Our concern is with the permissibility of prudentially rational suicide and voluntary euthanasia, and in these cases the person's good coincides with his autonomous will. In these circumstances, therefore, rational suicide and voluntary euthanasia are compatible with respect for the worth of the person, according to the alternative understanding of respect.

Which of these two understandings is more plausible—Velleman's or the one I have suggested? I readily concede that Velleman's understanding is more faithful to Kant. The question is whether Kant's own view is really plausible. Is Kant's view the best version of Kantianism?

There is, I believe, a tension in Velleman's view. Following Kant, Velleman contends that "to destroy something just because it no longer does one more good than harm is to treat it as an instrument of one's interests."[81] This is the basis of the claim that to kill oneself in order to avoid a future life that would not be worth living is to treat oneself as a means, or as an instrument in the service of one's good. Yet Velleman's own understanding seems to treat the person as an instrument of his rational nature: it treats the person, in effect, as a mere housing for his rational nature, or the medium in which the rational nature is manifest. This emerges in the implication that, if a person's life ceases to be worth living, he is required simply to suffer through it if the alternative to enduring it involves the sacrifice of his rational nature. If told by a Kantian that he must not sacrifice his rational nature for the sake of his good, a person who desperately wants to die could reasonably conclude that he was being subordinated to the value of his rational nature.

It seems, in short, that the Kantian view takes the person's rational nature to be the proper object of respect. Indeed, Kant himself is quite explicit about this. There might be no serious distinction between respecting the person and respecting his rational nature if the rational nature were an essential property of the person. And Velleman seems to attribute such a view to Kant when he notes that Kant refers to a person's rational nature as the "person's true or proper self."[82] But while a person may be identifiable with his rational nature *in the Kantian noumenal realm,* it is clear that in the world as we find it a person may continue to exist (though perhaps not as a person) in the absence of his rational nature, as happens in cases involving dementia or brain damage. Therefore a person's rational nature is not an essential property. And the person is, of course, more than just his rational nature. Thus it seems a mistake to take the rational nature as the object of respect. It is the person who matters. It may be that he matters because he *has* a rational nature; but it does not follow that he matters because his rational nature does.

It is, of course, also true that a person is more than his good. The Kantian might therefore reply that, in insisting that a person not kill himself for the sake of his good, Kant is not subordinating the *person* to his rational nature; he is, instead, subordinating the person's *good* to his rational nature. But a parallel reply is open to those who doubt Kant's claim that a self-interested suicide subordinates himself to his good. They can claim that such a person merely subordinates his rational nature to his good. And because a person is more than his rational nature, to sacrifice his rational nature for the sake of his good is not necessarily to sacrifice *himself* for the sake of his good. It is, of course, to destroy himself, but whether this counts as sacrificing himself or treating himself as an instrument of his good is precisely what is at issue.

The issues here—for example, whether a person is treated as a mere means if he is killed, by himself or by another, for the sake of his good—are admittedly obscure. I will return to them shortly. For the moment, let us grant that to kill a person for the sake of his good is to treat him as a mere instrument of his good. Let us assume that to sacrifice a person's rational nature for the sake of his good is to violate that person's worth. For it is to treat his rational nature as if it were an instrument in the service of his good, and is therefore to act against "an end against which we should never act." This is sufficient to rule out self-interested suicide and euthanasia. But if we make these assumptions, what else is ruled out as well?

There are various ways of acting against a person's rational nature. One may annihilate a person's rational nature by killing the person. Or one may utterly destroy his rational nature while leaving the person in existence, though no longer as a person—for example, by causing him to suffer brain damage that obliterates his capacities for self-consciousness and rationality. Another possibility is to *impair* a person's rational nature in a way that is compatible with his remaining a person. There are several ways of doing this. One may permanently impair a person's rational capacities in a way that is compatible with his remaining a person—for example, by inflicting on him some minor form of brain damage. Or one may temporarily diminish a person's rational capacities in such a way that for a while he loses the ability to function as a person—for example, by causing him to become severely intoxicated, delirious, or unconscious. Or one may temporarily diminish a person's rational capacities in a way that does not undermine his ability to function as a person—for example, by causing him to become moderately intoxicated. Finally, one may also act against a person's rational nature in a way that leaves his rational capacities unimpaired but impedes his exercise of them—for example, by enslaving him.

Velleman accepts that certain of these states may count as insults to a person's rational nature even when they are not inflicted via the agency of another. He accepts, for example, that the threat to a person's rational nature posed by progressive dementia may be sufficiently grave that it would be justifiable for the person to kill himself, or to request to be killed by another, in order to avoid it.[83] Thus the Kantian view, as interpreted by Velleman, treats the prospect of a condition such as dementia as a threat to a person's worth (not because it threatens to undermine it, but because it threatens to violate it). By parity of reasoning, it should also treat states of intoxication or stupefaction as insults to a person's rational nature, and therefore to his worth; for these are, in effect, temporary forms of dementia, in which a person's rational capacities are dulled, blunted, subdued, or suppressed. It seems to follow that the Kantian view must condemn the use of analgesics or anesthetics that impair, even temporarily, a person's rational capacities. For to take a stupefying analgesic, or to accept total anesthesia, for the purpose of avoiding suffering is to sacrifice one's rational nature for the sake of one's interests. It is to trade one's rational capacities, albeit temporarily, for relief from suffering. It is to treat one's rational nature instrumentally, as commensurable in value with and sacrificeable for the sake of one's good. In short, the Kantian objection to suicide and euthanasia seems to apply equally to the use of analgesics or anesthetics that impair one's rational capacities.[84]

The Kantian will naturally seek to avoid this embarrassing implication, and the most obvious line of resistance is to contend that impairments of a person's rational capacities that are temporary and reversible are not insults to his worth in the way that the destruction or permanent impairment of his rational nature is. Perhaps one could say that, in the case of temporary impairment, one's rational *nature* is preserved, whereas in the case of death or permanent impairment, the nature itself is sacrificed. Yet it is doubtful that the distinction between the temporary and the permanent can bear this much weight. Consider, for example, what Velleman says about slavery. To illustrate his general claim that there are offenses against persons that are not reducible to offenses against their interests, Velleman contends that "people have no right to sell themselves into slavery, . . . but the reason is not that they would thereby be harming themselves; the reason is that they would be violating their personhood."[85] This contention has considerable plausibility, but its plausibility seems unaffected by whether the state of enslavement would be temporary or permanent. If to sell oneself into permanent slavery in order to avoid an even graver harm would be to violate one's worth as a person, the same should be true of selling oneself into slavery temporarily. Similarly, whether a state of stupefaction, dementia, or unconsciousness is temporary or permanent should not determine whether it is compatible with one's worth as a person to accept that state as an alternative to suffering.

It should be conceded that there is a problem here even for those who reject Velleman's understanding of respect for persons. It seems true that it is incompatible with one's worth as a person to sell oneself into slavery in exchange for benefits. Yet it seems permissible to take a stupefying analgesic for relief from suffering. In at least one respect, however, the analgesic seems an even greater affront to one's rational nature: it directly impairs one's rational capacities, while enslavement, though it impedes the exercise of one's rational capacities, leaves one's rational nature unimpaired. So it is not obvious how the use of stupefying forms of analgesic or anesthesia is compatible with respecting one's worth as a person, while the acceptance of enslavement is not. Possibly it has to do with the fact that slavery, as Frances Kamm observes, involves giving one's rights "over to someone else who then has power over one."[86] But I will not pursue this further here.

If it is compatible with respect for one's worth as a person to impair one's rational capacities temporarily for the sake of relief from suffering, this should also be true of eliminating one's rational capacities through death. If in the one case there is no violation of one's worth in sacrificing one's rational nature for the sake of one's good, the same should be true in the other case as well.

I have suggested that, as interpreted by Velleman, the Kantian view condemns those forms of analgesia and anesthesia that impair, even temporarily, a person's rational capacities. It also, I believe, condemns another practice that is widely accepted as permissible: namely, the refusal to accept or to continue to accept life-sustaining treatment on the ground that one's life has ceased to be worth living. If one's intention in refusing life-sustaining treatment is to avoid a future life that would be worth not living, this seems as clear an instance of sacrificing oneself for the sake of one's good as active suicide or euthanasia. In this case, admittedly, the act of suicide is passive: one does not kill oneself, but instead allows oneself to die. It might be thought, therefore, that this would be compatible with respect for one's worth as a person. For the Kantian injunction is stated "negatively"—that is, the person, or his rational nature, is "an end against which we should never act." But on Velleman's interpretation, which is faithful to the text, this is not an endorsement of an asymmetry between doing and allowing. Rather, to "act against" an end is to treat it "*merely* as a means," and one may do this either by doing or by allowing. Hence, even if refusing treatment is merely to allow oneself to die, it should count as an instance of treating oneself as an instrument of one's good *if,* as Velleman claims, to kill oneself for the same reason is to treat oneself merely as a means. For in both cases one's intention is to avoid suffering by ceasing to exist.

It is, however, important to note the limited scope of the implication. My claim is that the Kantian view condemns the refusal to accept life support when one's aim is to die in order to avoid a life that would not be worth living. It does not necessarily condemn the refusal of life support if one's aim is only to reject the invasive nature of the treatment. In the latter case, one rejects bodily invasion; in the former, one rejects life itself. And it may be that it is only the explicit rejection of one's own continued existence that is incompatible with respect for one's worth. If so, those who accept the Kantian view of suicide and euthanasia may well accept as plausible the limited claim that it is impermissible to refuse life-sustaining treatment if one's intention is to use one's death as a means of avoiding suffering. Still, most people will find this hard to accept.

Given that Velleman's interpretation of the Kantian notion of respect seems to rule out considerably more than just most instances of self-interested suicide and euthanasia, it is worth considering the alternative I noted earlier. According to this interpretation, to respect a person is to show appropriate acknowledgment that his good is important in the same way that any other person's is, and to defer to his autonomous will in certain matters, principally those concerning how his own life should go. As I noted earlier, this interpretation does not condemn rational self-interested suicide or euthanasia in cases in which these acts are not bad for other people. Rather, it suggests that we honor or show appropriate respect for the person's worth precisely by ministering to his good, provided that this is also what he autonomously wills, even when what is required by a concern for his good is that his life should be ended.

According to this alternative interpretation, to commit suicide or to practice euthanasia is not to give a person's good priority over his worth. For in these cases, respect for his worth and fulfillment of his interests are not opposed. Recall Velleman's claim that it is only because a person matters, or has worth, that his good matters. This concedes a connection between a person's worth and the importance of ministering to his good. If a person's good matters *because* he does, it is natural to conclude that respect for his good is at least part of what is enjoined by respect for his worth. In a case of voluntary euthanasia, for example, respect for a person may require that we defer to the determination of his autonomous will, thereby giving his will and his good priority over the preservation of his rational nature (*not* over his worth). Even though we destroy the rational nature, we respect the *person.*

This is not to collapse the distinction between a person's worth and his good. They remain distinct forms of value. This is shown by the fact that a person retains his worth even when his life has lost its value, or ceased to be good. To acknowledge the independence of the person's worth from his good is just to assert that, even when his life has ceased to be worth living, *he* still matters as much as he ever did, that how he is treated and what happens to him still matter as much as they did previously.

There are two responses to Velleman's charge that this interpretation treats the person as an instrument of his interests, thereby violating the Kantian imperative to treat the person as an end-in-himself.[87] Velleman's claim is that to kill a person, even when this is what is demanded both by the person's will and by his good, is nevertheless to violate his worth as a person. The stronger response to this claim is that it conflates the worth of the person with the notion of the sanctity of life as I elucidated it earlier. For it appears to presuppose that the mere continued existence of the person has value in itself. On what other basis can it be claimed that ending the person's existence is to treat him instrumentally, or to give priority to his good over his worth? Suppose, for the sake of comparison, that it would be best for a person to sleep, but that he cannot fall asleep and so requests a sedative. And suppose that a doctor then administers a sedative to him. *This,* it seems, is not to treat the person as an instrument of his good. But why not, given that the doctor manipulates him for the sake of his good? It must be because his being asleep is not impersonally bad or, in other words, because his remaining awake at that time is not impersonally good. If it is not good in itself that he should remain awake, there is simply no basis for the claim that giving him a sedative uses him in a way that is incompatible with respect for his worth. Similarly, if ending a person's existence is compatible with his will and with his good, it cannot count as a violation of his worth unless it is assumed (as the notion of the sanctity of life assumes) that there is impersonal value in his mere continued existence that is necessarily violated when his existence is ended. But this is an assumption that Velleman rightly denies.

A weaker response concedes that there is a sense in which to kill a person in these circumstances is to sacrifice him in deference to his will and in support of his good, and is therefore to treat him instrumentally; but it also denies that this violates the Kantian imperative. Earlier I cited the passage in which Velleman quotes Kant's claim that a person is an end "which in all our willing we must never rate *merely* as a means."[88] Velleman here omits the end of Kant's sentence: "but always at the same time as an end."[89] This reemphasizes what Kant has already stressed by underscoring the word "merely"—namely, that it may be permissible to treat a person instrumentally provided that what one does is compatible with his status as an end. This should in fact be obvious, for, as others have pointed out, we regularly treat people instrumentally without denying their worth. We do this when we use them for our purposes, but in ways that are compatible with the acknowledgment that they matter in themselves just as we ourselves do—that is, in ways that are respectful of their good, their autonomous will, and their status as rational beings. If, for example, I pay someone to do a job for me, I certainly treat him instrumentally, but I do not violate his worth as a person provided that I take appropriate account both of his good and his autonomous will. Similarly, even if to kill a person when this is both what is best for him and what he autonomously desires is to treat him instrumentally in the service of his good, it is also at the same time to treat him as an end. We defer to his will and secure his good precisely because we recognize that he matters in himself. If we kill him precisely in order to promote his good in accordance with his autonomous desire, it is hard to see how we could be treating him *merely* as a means, as if he did not matter in himself.

There is a further suggestion in Velleman's discussion that is worth noting. Velleman seems to regard this suggestion as just an alternative formulation of the claim that to cause a person's death for the sake of his good is to treat him instrumentally. Yet it seems to me rather different. The suggestion is that what is missing "in so many discussions of euthanasia and assisted suicide" is "a sense of a value in us that makes a claim on us—a value that we must *live up to*." There is, he claims, more at issue than whether "one may end one's life simply because one isn't getting enough *out* of it. One has to consider whether one is doing justice *to* it."[90] This, I believe, is an important idea, though I think its range of application is limited. It helps us to understand why suicide is wrong, and possibly even contemptible, in those cases in which it might be condemned as "the easy way out." The narrator in Samuel Butler's *The Way of All Flesh* observes that suicide "is universally condemned as cowardly."[91] This is a rather surprising claim, especially as it was written in the late nineteenth century, when many people believed that a person who commits suicide thereby dooms himself to eternal damnation. But the attitude described is nonetheless familiar. Those who judge suicide to be cowardly typically have in mind a limited range of cases, which are nevertheless not uncommon, in which one's aim in committing suicide is to avoid exposure, imprisonment, financial ruin, or some other form of humiliation, rejection, abasement, disgrace, or defeat. These are not cases in which life has irremediably ceased to be worth living; they are instead cases in which, in order to restore one's life to a state in which it will be worth living, one must endure some ordeal, all the while devoting oneself sedulously to remaking one's life in a way that will redeem one's previous errors or misfortunes. This is hard work, but to shrink from it is certainly to treat oneself as a paltry and disposable thing, unworthy of serious effort or commitment. Still, it is a mistake to suppose that to commit suicide in these circumstances is to sacrifice oneself for the sake of one's good. It is, rather, to exchange oneself *and* one's good for release from the burden of confronting the ruins of one's life and rebuilding a life worthy of a person.

In these circumstances, in short, both one's worth and one's good coincide in demanding continued life. Suicide would be prudentially irrational and euthanasia a conceptual impossibility. The question, then, is whether Velleman's suggestion also applies in cases in which life has genuinely and irretrievably ceased to be worth living. Is there a sense in which one lives up to or does justice to one's status as a person by enduring such a life rather than committing suicide or requesting euthanasia? I find it hard to make sense of this. I cannot see how one lives up to or does justice to one's worth as a person by merely persisting through suffering.

I have argued in this section that if, when all dimensions of the good are taken into account, a person's life has ceased to be worth living, and if he consequently prefers death to continued life, neither suicide nor euthanasia is incompatible with respect for that person's worth. We can concede that persons have a value that is independent of their good, yet hold that respect for that value is nevertheless manifested in an active concern for their good, at least when that coincides with respect for their autonomous will. There is simply no sense in which a person's worth is upheld or affirmed by his mere persistence through suffering.

2.4. *Nonvoluntary Euthanasia*

The discussion has thus far been confined to voluntary euthanasia. It is generally agreed that nonvoluntary euthanasia is more problematic, and more difficult to justify. There are two types of case in which the question of nonvoluntary euthanasia might arise: first, cases involving individuals that have never been self-conscious and thus have never been able to have or to express a rational preference between death and continued life; and, second, cases involving individuals who were once persons (that is, self-conscious and minimally rational) but have irreversibly lost the capacity to deliberate competently about whether it would be better for them to die or to continue to live. Cases of this second sort raise particular difficulties. It is arguable, and probably true, that former persons remain within the scope of the requirement of respect for persons. Their former preferences, at least, continue to exert their moral authority over us. An individual who has lost the capacity to deliberate about life and death and whose life now seems, to third parties, to have ceased to be worth living, may formerly, when competent, have been opposed to being euthanized in these circumstances. Or he may have expressed a desire to be euthanized. Or, finally, he may have had or expressed no view at all. If he was formerly set against being euthanized, that seems to constitute a decisive reason not to kill him, though there are limits to what others may be required to do to sustain his life. If, by contrast, he earlier expressed an informed preference to be killed if his condition were to become as it is now, to kill him might be an instance of permissible voluntary euthanasia. Yet a preference formed in advance of the situation may, for various reasons (some of which I will explore in section 3), have less authority than a contemporaneous one.

Matters are even more complicated if an incompetent individual whose life now seems to be a burden to him never, when competent, expressed a preference about what should be done to him in his present condition. It is arguable that to kill him could be compatible with the requirement of respect. For his rational nature, having already been subverted, would not be sacrificed, his will is silent, and his good seems to demand that his life should cease. Yet there are nagging worries about the possible consequences of permitting the killing of former persons in these circumstances. The commonest fears are that mistakes would be made, that abuses would occur, and that the acceptance of killing in these cases would erode our sensitivity to the value of life and engender an increasingly callous and promiscuous attitude toward killing.

These same fears are often expressed about voluntary euthanasia. But, when euthanasia would be fully voluntary, they seem exaggerated. Doubtless some mistakes would occur: occasionally someone would be killed who was misdiagnosed or would have been among the tiny minority who recover against the odds or for whom a cure is unexpectedly found. Yet rational people must decide for themselves whether to take this risk—as we recognize when we allow people to decline certain treatments despite the risk that the best predictions about the outcomes of accepting or rejecting treatment may be mistaken. Moreover, even if mistakes are statistically certain, the costs of permitting voluntary euthanasia have to be weighed against the equally certain and probably much greater costs of denying people a release from great suffering.

The risk of abuse is also real but the rational response is the one we have adopted in the case of the even greater risk of abuse in permitting killing in self-defense. Our acceptance of the permissibility of killing in self-defense offers significant opportunities for people to perpetrate wrongful killings under the guise of self-defense—for example, by provoking a person to violence and claiming that killing him was necessary to save oneself, or by killing, in a secluded spot, a person with a known history of violent aggression and then claiming that one killed in self-defense. Although we are aware of these possibilities of abuse, we do not respond by forbidding killing in self-defense. Instead we erect safeguards against the abuse.

The same response is available to the problem of the "slippery slope." If we know where the line between permissible and impermissible killings lies, we can take precautions to prevent ourselves from being seduced into crossing it. We seem to have managed this in the case of killing in self-defense, even though the motives and forms of justification for self-defensive killing (for example, "he was at fault and it was him or me") easily blur into rationalizations for wrongful killing. It seems, moreover, that resistance to euthanasia has its own slippery slope. If those who advocate euthanasia are in danger of becoming less sensitive to killing, it seems equally true that those who seek to deny others the option of euthanasia are in peril of becoming inured and desensitized to the suffering of others and more willing to tolerate it in all areas of life.

The requirement to obtain a person's unforced consent before he can be euthanized constitutes a powerful safeguard against these various problems. When that safeguard is removed, however, as it is in nonvoluntary euthanasia, the scope for these problems is increased. These problems are, however, less serious if the subject of nonvoluntary euthanasia is not a former person but an individual that has never been a person—for example, an animal, a fetus, or a newborn infant. In these cases, the problems are somewhat less likely to arise: for there are fewer incentives for abuse, lines are easier to draw with precision (for example, age limits), and so on. Perhaps more importantly, even if these problems would arise with the same frequency as they would if euthanasia were permitted for former persons, they would nevertheless be less serious when they occurred. This is because individuals that have never been persons are, if my earlier arguments were sound, below the threshold of respect. So, for example, instances of killing that would be abuses of a policy allowing nonvoluntary euthanasia would not involve a violation of the requirement of respect, as they very likely would if the victim had once been a person. For these reasons, it is at best highly speculative to object to permitting nonvoluntary euthanasia for individuals that have never been persons on the ground that it would have pernicious side effects.

If, therefore, there are strong moral reasons for permitting nonvoluntary euthanasia for individuals that have never been persons, those reasons are likely to outweigh concerns about possible side effects. Yet, if the account I have developed of the morality of killing is correct, there are doubts about whether there can actually be strong reasons that favor euthanasia in these cases. In the remainder of this section, I will explain why this is so and discuss the problems it raises for the position I have developed.

In order to explain the problem, I will focus on nonvoluntary euthanasia for animals. I do this because most people accept the permissibility, and desirability, of euthanasia for animals. It seems obvious that there can be strong reasons for euthanizing animals in some cases. It is important to realize, however, that most aspects of the following argument also apply to euthanasia for human beings that have never been persons—for example, fetuses and newborn infants. But, because their membership in our species makes us think of fetuses and infants differently, and to doubt the permissibility of subjecting them to euthanasia, it will be easier to bring out the problems I want to discuss by focusing on the case of animals.

It will help to recall the discussion in section 1.2 of chapter 3 of what I called the view that suffering matters more—that is, the view that animals differ from human beings in that, although their *suffering* may matter considerably, their *lives* cannot. I suggested that this view draws support from the fact that an animal's time-relative interests are, in general, strongest with respect to the character of its present experience. Thus its time-relative interest in avoiding present suffering can be quite strong. But, because the prudential unity relations within its life are weak, the strength of its present time-relative interests in its own possible future states declines as the objects of those interests recede into the future. Because its present time-relative interest in having the goods of its own future life is comparatively weak, its present time-relative interest in continuing to live is correspondingly weak. I argued, however, that these facts do not support the conclusion that it can often be justifiable to kill an animal as a means of preventing it from suffering. To the extent that euthanasia may be more often rational in the case of an animal than in the case of a person, this is because there is ample scope for suffering within the life of an animal though only limited scope for good, since an animal's capacity for well-being is limited by its psychological nature. Thus it may more often be true of an animal's future life than of a person's that the expected good is outweighed by the expected suffering, so that the individual's present time-relative interest is in avoiding rather than having that future.

To this earlier discussion we can now add a further consideration that emerged in the discussion of prenatal injury in chapter 4. This is that our concern for an individual's time-relative interests should include a concern for its *future* time-relative interests. Thus, even though an animal's *present* time-relative interest in avoiding suffering in the distant future may be very weak, the time-relative interest it *will* have at that later time may be quite strong, and that interest can ground a strong reason *now* not to do what would cause that suffering to occur, or to do what would prevent it from occurring.

This further consideration yields a rather stronger asymmetry than I acknowledged in chapter 3 between one's reason for concern about an animal's life and one's reason for concern about its suffering. One's reason not to kill an animal (or to save it) *for its own sake* derives from its present time-relative interest in continuing to live, which is comparatively weak, for the reasons given earlier. But one's reason not to cause it to suffer (or to prevent its suffering) in the future derives both from its present time-relative interest in avoiding future suffering and from the stronger time-relative interest it will have, if it lives, at that later time. If the future suffering would be great—that is, intense and protracted—one's reason not to cause that suffering may actually be stronger than one's reason not to kill the animal.

This asymmetry is, in part, a result of the fact that, although one's reason not to cause future suffering is strengthened by the animal's future time-relative interest in avoiding suffering, one's reason not to kill it cannot be strengthened by the time-relative interests it might have in the future in having goods at those later times. For to kill an animal is to ensure that it will have no future time-relative interests. Thus one can prevent possible later time-relative interests from constraining one's present action by preventing them from arising—in this case by killing their potential bearer now. (This is compatible with the recognition that an animal's future time-relative interests in having goods can ground present reasons to ensure the satisfaction of those interests *if the animal will live.*) The idea that one can avoid being constrained by possible later time-relative interests by preventing them from arising has little application, of course, in the case of persons—both because persons have strong present time-relative interests in their future lives (including interests in whether they will later have and be able to satisfy further interests) and because there are reasons not to kill persons other than those that derive from respect for their time-relative interests. In the case of animals, however, we are constrained only by their interests, and the only interest that an animal can have independently of whether or not one kills it that is relevant to whether it is permissible to kill it is its present time-relative interest in continuing to live.

With these considerations as background, let us now examine the case in favor of euthanasia for animals. Suppose one discovers a wild animal in the early stages of an incurable disease that, after a few months, will begin to cause it agonizing pain that will then continue unabated for several months until the animal finally dies. The only way to prevent that future suffering is to kill the animal now. If one has the means to kill it painlessly, one would seem to have a strong moral reason to kill it to spare it those months of agony. But notice that the animal's *present* time-relative interest in avoiding that future suffering may be comparatively weak because the prudential unity relations between itself now and itself several months from now would be weak. Thus, if one's only reason to euthanize the animal derives from its present time-relative interest in avoiding future suffering, that reason should be comparatively weak. Yet it seems that the reason would be quite strong.

In short, the appeal to an animal's present time-relative interest in avoiding future suffering seems insufficient to explain our sense of the importance of euthanasia in a case of this sort. The problem of explaining and justifying the common view is even more acute for those numerous philosophers who accept what, in section 2 of chapter 4, I called the Capacity Condition—that is, the view that something can be intrinsically good or bad for an individual only if that individual is capable of desiring it or caring about it in some way. These philosophers embrace the implication of the Capacity Condition that death cannot be bad for individuals that are incapable of desiring either continued life itself or the goods that their lives might contain in the future. Hence they claim that death cannot be a misfortune for a non-self-conscious animal or a fetus. But their claim also has a parallel implication that death cannot be good, or better than continuing to live, for individuals that are incapable of desiring to die or to avoid future suffering, even if these individuals can avoid a prospect of great future suffering only by dying. If, therefore, one accepts this view, it seems that one must accept that there can be *no* reason, for an animal's own sake, to kill it in order to prevent it from experiencing great suffering in the future.

How can we defend the plausible view that there can be a strong reason to kill an animal painlessly if that is the only way to prevent it from experiencing intense and protracted suffering in the future, suffering that would greatly outweigh any good that its future might also contain? It might be suggested that, just as an animal's *future* time-relative interests in avoiding suffering can ground a reason not to do now what would cause it to suffer later, so those same interests can ground a reason to kill the animal now if that is the only way to prevent those interests from being frustrated. The problem with this suggestion, however, is that if one kills the animal now, it will never have any future interest in avoiding suffering. The interest to which this suggestion appeals is not, in other words, a *future* interest relative to the agent deliberating about whether to kill the animal. It is, instead, a merely *possible* interest, for whether it will exist depends on the outcome of the agent's deliberation—that is, on whether or not the agent kills the animal.

It seems, therefore, that if one has a reason to euthanize an animal that is based on considerations other than the animal's *present* interests, it must appeal, not to the animal's *future* interests, but to its *possible* future interests. But this raises a different problem. If an individual's possible future interests can ground present reasons for action that are independent of reasons generated by the individual's *present* time-relative interests, its possible interests in having goods should, it seems, matter in the same way that its possible interests in avoiding suffering do. In particular, if one can have a reason to *prevent* the existence of a possible interest in avoiding suffering if that is the only way to prevent it from being *frustrated,* it seems that, by parity of reasoning, one can also have a reason to *ensure* the existence of a possible interest in having goods in order to enable it to be *satisfied*. Possible interests in avoiding suffering and in having goods should be treated symmetrically. But this means that, if an individual's possible future interests in avoiding suffering can ground a reason to kill that individual, its possible future interests in *having goods* can similarly ground a reason *not* to kill it, or even a reason to save it.

To concede this latter point would, however, be fatal to my earlier argument for the permissibility of late abortion. For that argument hinges on the claim that the only significant reason not to kill a developed fetus for its own sake derives from its present time-relative interest in continuing to live. If the interests in having goods that a fetus would later have if it is not killed can ground a reason not to kill it (in the same way that the interest in avoiding suffering an animal would later have if it were to live can ground a reason to kill it), there would then be strong reasons not to kill a developed fetus whose future life could be expected to be worth living.

This is not a problem only for my argument in support of abortion. There are wider implications. If it is true that an individual's possible future interests in having goods can ground a strong reason to preserve its life despite its having only a weak time-relative interest in continuing to live, it seems that we should have a strong reason to preserve the lives of fetuses by preventing spontaneous abortions and miscarriages. We should do this, not just for the sake of the potential parents, but for the sake of the fetuses themselves. For their possible future interests, according to this view, make demands on us now. Given that more than two-thirds of the conceptions that occur result in spontaneous abortion, those who believe that we begin to exist at conception would have to accept that these demands are quite extensive. If the possible future interests of a fetus make its life matter now, the death prior to birth of two-thirds of those conceived must surely constitute a continuing holocaust.

It seems that we face a dilemma. If interests that an individual will later have only if it continues to live cannot ground present reasons either to preserve or to terminate its life, it seems that one's only reason to euthanize an animal, for its own sake, must derive from its present time-relative interest in avoiding future suffering. But that interest may be insufficiently strong to account for the strong reason it seems there would be to euthanize an animal whose future would otherwise consist mainly of intense and protracted suffering. Alternatively, if an individual's possible interests *can* ground a reason either to end or to preserve its life, we could appeal to an animal's possible future interest in avoiding suffering to strengthen the case for euthanasia. But the idea that these interests are relevant seems not only to exaggerate the importance of preserving animal lives but also to oppose the permissibility of abortion and to demand significant efforts to prevent the deaths of fetuses in utero. It seems, therefore, that the common sense view must reconcile two claims: first, that an individual's possible future interest in avoiding suffering can ground a reason to end its life now, if that is the only way to prevent the suffering, and, second, that an individual's possible future interests in having goods cannot ground a reason not to end or to preserve its life now.

One possible defense of the commonsense view appeals to the idea that there is an asymmetry between the importance of preventing suffering and promoting the good.[92] It would, of course, be implausible to suppose there is *no* reason to promote an individual's good. But it could be maintained that one's reason to promote an individual's good is in general substantially weaker than one's reason to prevent that individual from suffering. If this claim were conjoined with the claim that an individual's merely possible interests can ground present reasons for action, that would support a view similar to the commonsense view. But, while this conjunction of claims would mitigate our problem, it would not solve it. For the two claims still imply that an individual's merely possible interests in having goods ground a reason to preserve its life, though not so strong a reason as the reason one has to prevent its suffering.

Another possibility is to claim that, although merely possible interests count, our concern should always be to prevent the frustration of interests rather than to ensure their satisfaction.[93] Provided that we treat the *elimination* of an interest as tantamount to its frustration, this claim implies that we always have reason to satisfy existing interests in order thereby to prevent their frustration. But, with regard to merely possible interests, it implies that, while there is a reason to prevent them from arising if they would otherwise be frustrated, there is no reason to cause or to allow them to arise just so they could be satisfied (unless, of course, the individual has an existing interest in having new interests arise).

This may seem promising. It allows that an individual's present time-relative interest in continuing to live grounds a reason not to kill it or to save it. But it denies that this is true of merely possible future interests in having goods, even if they would be satisfied if the individual were to live. Finally, it accepts that, if certain interests (whether in avoiding suffering or in having goods) would be frustrated if they were to arise, this grounds a reason to prevent their existence, if necessary (and if other things are equal) by preventing the future existence of the individual whose interests they would be. In short, this view seems to support the commonsense view: it implies that an individual's possible future interests can strengthen the case for euthanasia but cannot ground a reason not to kill or to save that individual.

This view seems, however, to be vulnerable to a decisive objection. Consider any individual that has never been a person—an animal or fetus, for example. If this individual has a time-relative interest in continuing to live, this grounds a reason not to kill it. But, no matter how many interests it might have in the future and no matter how many would be likely to be satisfied, these possible interests do not, on the view we are considering, add to the case against killing this individual. But any interests it might later have if it were to continue to live that would unavoidably be frustrated— and there are likely to be many of these—*do,* on this view, count against allowing the individual to continue to live. If the combined strengths of these interests would outweigh the individual's present time-relative interest in continuing to live, this view implies that it would be better, for this individual's own sake, to kill it now, *even if its future life would on balance be well worth living.* This is clearly unacceptable. (It is worth noting that the claim that there is an asymmetry between the importance of preventing suffering and the importance of promoting an individual's good may have similar implications.)

One could, of course, stipulate that, while the prospect of satisfying an individual's possible future interests does *not* by itself provide a positive reason to cause or allow that individual to continue to exist, it *is* capable of weighing against and potentially canceling out the reason to prevent the individual from continuing to exist that derives from the expectation that many of its possible interests would be frustrated. This suggestion seems, however, essentially ad hoc. It is hard to imagine how it might be defended. If the prospect of satisfying possible future interests can weigh against the reason to prevent the frustration of possible interests, why can it not also ground a reason not to kill the individual whose interests they would be?

I know of no satisfactory solution to the problem discussed in this section. This should not be surprising. For this problem precisely parallels an intractable problem in the area of ethics concerned with causing people to exist—a problem that has perennially defeated the many attempts to solve it. This problem is also concerned with possible future interests—not those of existing individuals but of individuals who do not now exist but might exist in the future. The question we have considered in this section is whether an individual's possible future interests can ground a reason to prevent or to cause that individual's *continued* existence. The parallel question in population ethics is whether an individual's possible future interests can ground a reason to prevent or to cause that individual's *existence.*

Suppose we are deliberating about whether to cause a person to exist. If we can predict that the person's life would be filled with suffering that would greatly outweigh any good the life might contain, it seems that we have a strong reason not to cause that person to exist. This parallels the reason we might have to euthanize an animal whose future life would similarly be filled with uncompensated suffering. One difference, however, is that in the case of the possible person, our reason to prevent the possible suffering cannot be grounded in *any* present interest (time-relative or otherwise) of the victim—for the victim does not exist. Our reason may, therefore, derive from the possible person's possible interests. Our reason may be to prevent those interests from arising in order to prevent their frustration. Or our reason may be impersonal in character: for example, a reason not to cause an increase in the amount of suffering in the world. (The reason to euthanize an animal could also be impersonal in the same way. The reason that I have not invoked this explanation will soon become obvious.)

The problem here is that, whether our reason derives from the possible person's possible interests or from impersonal considerations, it seems that the same considerations should ground a moral reason *to cause the person to exist* if his life would be worth living. If, for example, there is an impersonal reason to prevent suffering, there should be a corresponding impersonal reason to promote the good. Thus, if the expectation that a person would have a life that would be bad for him, or worth not living, grounds a reason not to cause him to exist, it should also be true that the expectation that a person would have a life that would be good, or worth living, grounds a reason to cause him to exist. But most of us reject this second claim. It is not that we believe that the reason to cause a person to exist because his life would be good is normally outweighed (for example, by considerations of cost to the agent); rather, we believe that there is no such reason.

In short, we believe that the suffering that a person would experience grounds a reason not to cause, or to prevent, his existence. This reason may be decisive if the suffering would not be outweighed by compensating goods. But we also believe that the good that a person's life would contain does not ground a reason to cause him to exist. Earlier, in section 5 of chapter 4, I referred to this conjunction of beliefs as the "Asymmetry" and noted that it is very difficult to defend. If we say that a person's suffering, or the frustration of his possible future interests, counts against causing him to exist, but his possible good, or the satisfaction of his possible interests, does not count in favor of causing him to exist, it seems that there will always be a strong moral presumption against causing people to exist. And that is surely wrong. If we were to say, instead, that a person's possible good *does* count in favor of causing him to exist, though less strongly than his possible suffering counts against it, we would have to conclude that it is generally objectionable to cause people to exist, if other things are equal, though it may be morally required to cause people to exist if their lives would be unusually well worth living, again if other things are equal. This too is implausible.

The idea that there can be a strong reason to euthanize an animal that is independent of its present time-relative interest in avoiding future suffering parallels the view that there is a strong reason not to cause a person to exist if his life would be dominated by suffering. And the idea that there is not a strong reason to prevent a spontaneous abortion that is independent of the fetus's time-relative interest in continuing to live (and of the interests of others) parallels the view that there is no reason to cause a person to exist just because his life would be worth living. These views run parallel because the prudential unity relations that would bind an animal or a fetus to itself in the future are very weak. Its relation to its own future is, figuratively speaking, almost wholly impersonal. For this reason, as I argued in section 6.1 of chapter 2, the death of a fetus (or an animal) is intermediate between the death of a person and the failure of an individual to come into existence. Indeed, the future lives of animals and fetuses seem to matter more in the way the possible futures of possible people matter, and less in the way that the possible futures of existing people matter.

The positive justification for animal euthanasia therefore remains elusive. An animal's possible future suffering clearly matters but exactly how or why it matters is hard to say. For the obvious claims have other implications that are difficult to accept. There is, however, some consolation in the fact that parallel problems beset our efforts to defend the view that there is a strong reason not to cause a person to exist if his life would contain so much suffering as to be worth not living. This view, too, simply must be right. But an adequate defense continues to elude us.

3. THE WITHERING AWAY OF THE SELF

3.1. *The Metaphysics of Progressive Dementia*

There are various forms and causes of progressive dementia.[94] The most common cause is Alzheimer's disease, which involves progressive degenerative changes in the brain that, over a period of years, result in the gradual erosion of the victim's mental life and psychological capacities. The disease usually presents with a deterioration of memory, which continues relentlessly through the later stages. As the disease progresses, comprehension, reasoning, and judgment are increasingly impaired, elements of character become unstable, linguistic abilities decline, recognition of other people becomes problematic and eventually impossible, and ultimately even self-awareness is lost. The final stage of the disease has been characterized as follows: "All language skills have been lost, and there seems to be very little left of the patient's 'self.' . . . Motor skills decline until it is no longer possible for the person to walk, sit up, chew and swallow food, or control bowel and bladder. . . . As the brain shuts down, the patient becomes unresponsive, and finally coma ends in death."[95]

Let us refer to a person in the very early stages of progressive dementia as the *Patient at Onset,* and the individual in the later stages of the disease as the *Demented Patient.* As I noted in chapter 1, the Psychological Account of Identity has the surprising and implausible implication that the Patient at Onset and the Demented Patient are not the same individual. For as the day-to-day psychological connections within the victim's life become progressively fewer, a point is eventually reached at which the Demented Patient is no longer psychologically continuous with the Patient at Onset. I speculated that the point at which psychological continuity ceases to hold coincides roughly with the point at which the individual loses those psychological capacities that are constitutive of personhood. According to this view, then, the Demented Patient is a post-person who succeeds the Patient at Onset in the latter's own body. The person who contracts progressive dementia may thus cease to exist well before the disease has run its full course. (There are very few, if any, actual cases in which the Psychological Account implies that a person has been supplanted by a different *person* in his own body. The only kind of case in which this might occur is a case in which brain damage causes total amnesia and a radical transformation of character, but in which the psychological capacities constitutive of personhood are preserved.)

According to the Embodied Mind Account of Identity, by contrast, there are no cases in which progressive dementia results in a different individual, much less a different person. As long as the victim remains a person, he is the same person as the Patient at Onset. And even when the Demented Patient's psychological capacities have dropped below the level of personhood, he is nevertheless the same individual as the Patient at Onset. As long as the victim's brain retains the capacity to support consciousness, however minimal, the same individual remains in existence.

Perhaps it would be more accurate to say that there is no new or different individual. For what remains may not in any robust sense be the same individual but merely a fragment of that individual. The losses one suffers in progressive dementia are more than ordinary losses. As the description I cited of the late stages of the disease indicates, progressive dementia gnaws away unrelentingly at the core of the self, eventually stripping it to the vanishing point. One way of understanding this process appeals to the notion introduced in section 2 of chapter 4 that the existence of the self may be partial, so that the self may come into existence or cease to exist gradually, by degrees. I have argued that we are essentially embodied minds. In progressive dementia, the elements of the mind and their physical bases in the brain are steadily worn away. It is possible to see this process as the gradual fading from existence of the individual himself.

Consider, for the sake of comparison, a complex physical object such as a car. A car may be dismantled piece by piece. The process of disassembly may be gradual and continuous. At the beginning there is a car; at the end there is no longer a car but merely a collection of parts. But there is no point at which the car suddenly ceases to exist, no point at which the removal of one further part makes the difference between the existence and nonexistence of the car. It is sometimes claimed that, as the car is dismantled, there is a period during which its existence is *indeterminate*—that is, a period during which it is not true either that the car continues to exist or that it has ceased to exist. As I suggested earlier, however, there is another possibility, which is that during this period the car does not fully exist yet continues partially to exist. On this view, it goes out of existence gradually, by degrees.

Analogous claims could be made about the victim of progressive dementia. During the early phases of the condition, the person fully exists. But as the dementia progresses, the individual himself begins to fade from existence. In the late stages, he is barely there at all. If we distinguish, as I have argued we should, between the biological death of the human organism and the death or ceasing to exist of a person, we could say that progressive dementia is a protracted process of dying—not dying in the traditional sense in which dying precedes and ends in death, but dying understood as a process in which death itself occurs by degrees.

If this is a coherent and accurate conception of progressive dementia, it seems that the Patient at Onset ought rationally to care less, in an egoistic way, about what will happen to him in the later stages of the disease—less, at least, than he ought to care if he were going to be fully preserved. Although the Demented Patient will not be a different individual, he will be only a ghostly remnant of the Patient at Onset. While the Patient at Onset will continue to exist as the Demented Patient, his existence then will be only partial; therefore he ought now to discount his egoistic concern for his future self for the extent to which his own existence will be diminished.

As I conceded earlier, the notion that existence may be partial is problematic. But the same intuitions that tempt us to see the Demented Patient as slowly fading from existence may be expressed and defended differently by noting that the basis for the Patient at Onset's egoistic concern about the Demented Patient is radically attenuated. According to the Embodied Mind Account of Egoistic Concern, the prudential unity relations include physical, functional, and organizational continuity of the brain as well as the mental correlate of organizational continuity—namely, psychological continuity. All of these relations may hold to varying degrees, and all hold much less strongly between the Patient at Onset and the Demented Patient than they do over a comparable period of time within the life of a cognitively normal adult person. For, with progressive dementia, areas of the brain involved in the generation of consciousness and mental activity gradually atrophy and die: the brain itself shrinks, its capacities diminish, and the neurological bases of the victim's psychological capacities and mental states, which are the elements of psychological continuity, gradually disappear. Between the Patient at Onset and the Demented Patient in the very final stages of the disease, all of the various prudential unity relations are present to only a very weak degree. Because of this, the Patient at Onset may rationally be only minimally egoistically concerned about what will happen to him in the final stages of dementia.

It is important to be clear about the precise nature of this claim. It should not be confused with the profoundly mistaken claim that the Patient at Onset ought to be only minimally egoistically concerned about the prospect of progressive dementia itself. About this he should now be intensely egoistically concerned. For the prospect of progressive dementia is figuratively, and perhaps literally, a prospect of gradual extinction. It involves the gradual erosion of the basis of egoistic concern about the future—the very foundations for having anything to care about in the future. In the absence of the prospect of dementia, a great deal of good would lie in prospect for this person, and the person would be related to that future good in the right way. But the prospect of dementia excludes most of these goods that he could otherwise look forward to, and greatly reduces the extent to which he can rationally look forward to those few goods that will be accessible to him in his demented state. Thus the threat that progressive dementia poses to the Patient at Onset's time-relative interest in having a good future is almost as grave as the threat posed by death itself. But the prospect of dementia also means that the Patient at Onset should be less fearful of any positive evils that he will later suffer in his demented state. If, for example, he expects to suffer a certain amount of physical pain when he is in the later stages of dementia, he should now anticipate that pain with less dread or fear than it would be rational to feel if his basis for egoistic concern about the future were stronger.

Among those who accept that identity is not the basis of egoistic concern about the future and who also believe that the prudential unity relations between the Patient at Onset and the Demented Patient are very weak, most accept only that it is *not irrational* for the Patient at Onset to be egoistically concerned to a weaker degree about his own future than would be rationally required in the absence of dementia. Derek Parfit, for example, claims that, while it is "not irrational" for one to "have a discount rate with respect to the degrees of psychological connectedness" between oneself now and oneself in the future, one is "not rationally required to have this discount rate."[96] I believe, however, that a stronger claim is warranted. We should accept that, insofar as the concern is egoistic in character, it is rationally required for the Patient at Onset to be less concerned about his own future when the relations that ground egoistic concern—the prudential unity relations—are weaker. It is, in other words, *irrational* for the Patient at Onset to have the same degree of egoistic concern about his own future as he would have in the absence of the prospect of dementia.

Parfit's claim is weaker and more congruent with common sense. Why insist on the bolder and less plausible claim that discounting for diminished psychological connectedness is rationally mandatory? One reason is that this seems to be demanded by consistency. Recall that progressive dementia is, in a rough way, a mirror-image of our early psychological development. In both cases, the prudential unity relations are weak between a given individual at different times. The difference is that the physical and psychological discontinuities between a fetus or infant and the person it will later become are the products of growth and development, while those between the Patient at Onset and the Demented Patient are the results of deterioration. I have claimed that it is rationally mandatory for third parties to be less concerned about the fetus or infant's future *for its own sake now*. Assuming that the fetus or infant is going to continue to live, I believe, as I argued in section 3 of chapter 4, that third parties should be equally concerned about its future time-relative interests. But *if* their concern were only for the fetus or infant as it is now, they would be rationally required to discount the importance *to it now* of its own future life—that is, they would have to recognize that its time-relative interests in its own future life are greatly weakened by the weakness of the prudential unity relations between itself now and itself in the future. But if we are rationally required to discount the fetus's or infant's time-relative interests in its own future because of the weakened prudential unity relations, it seems that we should maintain this insistence in the case of the Patient at Onset as well— particularly given that the weakness of the prudential unity relations is in this case a result of deterioration rather than development. If discounting for weakened prudential unity relations is mandatory rather than optional in cases involving growth and development, it seems it should be mandatory as well in cases involving deterioration.

It is important to bear in mind, however, that discounting for weakened prudential unity relations is rationally mandatory in cases of progressive dementia only insofar as the form of concern is *egoistic*. My claim is only that, *if* he is thinking egoistically from his present point of view, the Patient at Onset ought rationally to be less concerned about the particular goods and evils in his own future life. It does not follow that he must be less concerned simpliciter. If, for example, the basis of his concern is moral rather than egoistic, he may rationally care as much about his future, demented self as he cares about himself now, in the same way that he may rationally care as much about another person as he cares about himself.

3.2. *The Moral Authority of Advance Directives*

This understanding of the prudential significance of progressive dementia has certain implications for an unusually puzzling problem, which emerges in the following case:

The Advance Directive. A woman whose life has been devoted to creative intellectual work finds herself in the very early stages of Alzheimer's disease. Given her nature, her values, and the character of her previous life, she believes that for her to continue to live in a demented state would be horribly degrading, worse than simply ceasing to exist. She accepts, however, that her life will continue to be worth living as long as she remains competent; therefore to commit suicide now would be bad for her. But, once she becomes incompetent, she will no longer be able to recognize and act on her reasons for preferring death to dementia. She therefore settles on a compromise. She signs an advance directive stipulating that, if she contracts a potentially fatal condition once she has ceased to be competent, no life-supporting treatment is to be administered. (She would prefer to stipulate that, on passing a certain threshold of dementia, she should be painlessly killed. But given the present state of the law, such an advance directive could not be honored.) Later, when she has in fact become incompetent, she develops pneumonia, which is almost certain to prove fatal unless she is administered penicillin. At this point, however, she is quite contented, cannot remember the advance directive, and, when asked, says that she wants to live.

In this section, let us use our generic labels—"Patient at Onset" and "Demented Patient"—to refer to this woman in the early and late stages, respectively, of Alzheimer's disease. The question is what her physicians should do when the Demented Patient develops pneumonia. The advance directive she signed when competent demands that she be allowed to die. Yet it may seem unconscionable to allow a patient to die when she is contented and expresses a desire to continue to live.

We should distinguish two questions. What, if anything, is required by respect for the person? And what would be best for, or in the best interests of, the Demented Patient? If respect for a person involves both a deference to certain of her preferences and an appropriate concern for her good, the two questions may not be clearly separable. But before determining whether the questions can be answered independently, there is an antecedent question that must be considered. This is whether the Demented Patient, who has ceased to be a person, is an appropriate object of respect at all. If a human being does not come within the scope of the morality of respect prior to becoming a person with an autonomous will, should we not conclude that an individual who irreversibly ceases to be a person thereby also ceases to be within the scope of the morality of respect?

This inference is unwarranted. There is an important asymmetry between individuals who have not yet become persons and individuals who once were but have ceased to be persons. For the latter once had autonomous preferences that may still make a claim on us. Most people have preferences that extend beyond the boundaries of their lives—for example, preferences concerning the posthumous disposition of their property or the treatment of their dead bodies. If we regard it as a failure of respect for the person to disregard these preferences—and most of us do—then we should also accept that respect for a person can require that we honor the autonomous preferences she previously expressed concerning how she is to be treated after she ceases to be competent.

In the case of the Advance Directive, the Patient at Onset articulates an autonomous preference to be allowed to die once she becomes demented. It is true that, as the Demented Patient, she later has a different and conflicting preference. But the preferences of the demented are notoriously arbitrary, whimsical, and ephemeral. And respect for an individual does not demand the honoring of preferences that are not autonomously formed. Thus, because the new, nonautonomous preference does not countermand or supersede the earlier autonomous preference, the Demented Patient's physicians have a reason grounded in respect for the preference of the person the Demented Patient once was to allow her now to die.

This reason will be decisive if there is no conflict with the Demented Patient's good, or best interest. Thus an earlier advance directive will be decisively authoritative if what it demands is that life-saving treatment not be administered if the person becomes permanently unconscious in what I have called a deep coma. It will also be decisive if it demands the withholding of treatment if the person both becomes incompetent and has a life that is clearly intolerable from any perspective. But what if we conclude that it is in the best interest of the Demented Patient to continue to live? In that case, we believe that there is a conflict between this individual's earlier autonomous preference and her present good. Sometimes when a person's good conflicts with her autonomous will, respect requires deference to the will—for example, when a Christian Scientist whose life would be worth living refuses life-saving medical treatment. But in other cases we accept that it is compatible with respect for a person to override her autonomous will—for example, when we restrain a teenager who, after serious reflection, attempts to commit suicide. In short, it is not obvious what respect for a person requires when it is in her interest to live, but her autonomous preference is to die. And the uncertainty is exacerbated in the case of the Advance Directive by the Demented Patient's inability to reconsider her earlier preference.

Is it in the Demented Patient's best interest to continue to live? Ronald Dworkin claims that it is not. He claims that her best interest coincides with her earlier autonomous preference. This is because what he calls her "critical interests" are in large measure *determined by* her autonomous preferences. Dworkin distinguishes our critical interests from our "experiential interests." We have experiential interests in those things that we find "pleasurable or exciting as experiences."[97] Our critical interests, by contrast, "represent critical judgments rather than just experiential preferences."[98] (Critical interests are not, however, entirely subjectively determined, for people "would be mistaken, and genuinely worse off, if they did not recognize" their own critical interests.)[99] Critical interests are, moreover, closely tied to the value of a life as a whole. "Convictions about what helps to make a life good on the whole," Dworkin writes, "are convictions about those more important interests."[100] Because the Patient at Onset's life has been devoted to creative intellectual activities rather than passive pleasures, so that a period of dementia at the end would be jarringly inharmonious with what has gone before, and because she autonomously desired to maintain the integrity of her life by avoiding a protracted period of dementia at the end, her critical interest—what would be better for her life as a whole—is to be allowed to die. And her critical interest, Dworkin assumes, has priority over the Demented Patient's experiential interest in continuing to live.

Is Dworkin right? Is the present best interest of the Demented Patient determined by what would be best for her life as a whole? Or is it possible that her present good diverges from what would be best for her life as a whole? Normally, of course, what is best for a person at a time coincides with what is best for her life as a whole. The obvious exception is when what would be best for a person now, considering the moment in isolation from the remainder of the life, would exclude some greater good in the future, so that to have the greater good—and thus the better life as a whole—the person must accept a lesser good now. But this is not an issue in the case of the Demented Patient. There is, however, another possible form of divergence. In the case of the Advance Directive, the period of dementia is isolated from the rest of the life by the dramatically weakened prudential unity relations. Because of this, how good the period is for the Demented Patient—that is, how strong a time-relative interest she has in having it—is only weakly affected by its lack of coherence with the rest of the life. It may be good in its own terms even if it is worse for the life as a whole. (By contrast, when the prudential unity relations are strong, a person's time-relative interests coincide with her interests, so that what would be best for her life as a whole will also be in her present time-relative interest.)

What is good for an individual at a time, or in his best time-relative interest, may vary with a number of factors, among which is the individual's nature at the time. Thus what is good for an individual as a child is different from what is good for her when she becomes an adult. What is good for a child is not determined by reference to the nature she will later have as an adult; nor is it much affected by how it fits into the narrative structure of the life that is established primarily by choices made in adult life. What is good for the child is instead determined primarily by the child's nature at the time. What is good for the Demented Patient might be similarly dependent on her nature at the time.

The comparison with childhood is, however, intended only to be suggestive. There are important asymmetries between a childish period at the beginning of a life and a childish period at the end. By the nature of the case, there are no prior autonomous preferences that might partially determine the nature of a child's good. Nor do people typically regret that they once had a childish nature or believe that their childhood, so altogether alien in character from their adult life, mars the overall unity or integrity of their life as a whole. The natural progression from childhood to adulthood is regarded as an acceptable narrative or normative structure for a life. Yet while a life may appropriately begin with a childish phase, it is a tragic decline if a mirror-image childish phase follows maturity. (It is difficult to say to what extent these evaluations of the narrative patterns that a life may follow simply track our perception of what is normal or natural. One does not regret the childish bit at the beginning of one's life although one may dread a comparable childish bit at the end. But would one take the same view if a period of dementia were universal after a certain age and were generally pleasant and contented the way childhood normally is? Some people, of course, do not regard a contented phase of dementia as degrading for them and, if contented passivity is consistent with the way they have lived hitherto, there is no reason to suppose that they are wrong.)

What is good for a person depends, to some extent, on what kind of person he is, what he cares about, and what his personal ideals or values are. Consequently, what is good for a person can change over time along with his character and values. If, for example, a person is committed to egalitarian ideals and as a consequence wishes to lead an ascetic life, the acquisition of expensive possessions might not be good for him at all. But if, after time, his ideals change and he becomes materialistic and self-

interested, it may then be in his interest to accumulate these same expensive possessions. As this example suggests, what is good for a person may change with his character even when the change of character is a corruption, or a change for the worse.
This suggests that it is necessary to distinguish between forms or levels of personal
good. We must distinguish between, first, what is better for a person given, or conditional upon, his actual nature and values, and second, what nature and values it would
be better for a person to have. But I will not pursue this complication here.

The relevant point here is that an individual's good may change along with his
nature, character, values, and preferences. And this is the basis for claiming that it
would be better for the Demented Patient now to continue to live. The dementia has
caused a profound alteration in her nature. She was once devoted to creative intellectual endeavors. For a person like that, the plunge into dementia could be deeply degrading. Yet now that the dementia has already occurred, the elements of her nature
that opposed or were hostile to a state of contented dementia have been eradicated.
Now that she is demented, the good that seems appropriate to her present nature is
contentment.

It remains true, however, that the Demented Patient now is one and the same individual as the person whose personal values condemned a condition of bovine contentment as degrading and unworthy. (I say "personal values" to allow for the possibility that she recognized that a state of contented dementia would not necessarily be
degrading for everyone.) And given that her life was shaped by those values, we
should accept, as Dworkin insists, that her life as a whole would be better without a
protracted period of dementia at the end. This is true even though she is and would
continue to be contented in her demented state. For part of what she found repellent
about dementia, we may suppose, was precisely the prospect of becoming capable of
being content with personal vacancy.

It seems, in short, that there are conflicting criteria for determining what is best
for the Demented Patient now. For an individual with her present nature, it is better
to continue to live. But continued life with her present nature would make her life as
a whole worse. Can these two claims be combined to yield a single answer to the
question whether it would be better for her to be treated or to be allowed to die?
Which has priority in determining her present good or best interest—what would be
best given her present nature, or what would contribute most to the value of her life
as a whole?

Recall that the destruction wrought by Alzheimer's disease has radically weakened the various prudential unity relations between the Patient at Onset and the Demented Patient. My suggestion is that, when the prudential unity relations are weak
between an individual now and herself during most of the rest of her life, what is
good for her now is determined less by the way in which her present life contributes
to the value of her life as a whole and more by her nature and preferences at the time.
Her present good is less a matter of how the present moment fits into the overall pattern of her life and more a function of the intrinsic features of the moment. This is because the less prudential unity there is within the life, the less the life matters *as a
whole*. For it is the prudential unity relations that make the life a significant whole
rather than just a series of "discreet and mutually irrelevant episodes" (Huxley's description, quoted earlier, of the life of a lower animal). In the case of the Demented

Patient, it may indeed be appropriate to regard her prudentially unified life up to the onset of dementia as forming something of a whole, with the period of dementia being rather an excrescence dangling at the end—a period alien to and sufficiently distinct from the earlier unified life to have its own independent good.

An alternative way of making essentially the same point is to claim that the Demented Patient's present time-relative interests are more authoritative in determining her present and future good than the time-relative interests she previously had, when competent, in what would happen to her now. For the latter were time-relative interests that she had during a period when she was only distantly connected via the prudential unity relations to the individual she is now.

For these reasons, I believe we should conclude that what is best for the Demented Patient now is determined primarily by her present nature and preferences rather than by what would make her life as a whole better. In ascertaining her present good, we should give more weight to the intrinsic rather than the relational features of her present life. This means that her overall present good is more a function of what Dworkin calls her experiential interests and less a function of her critical interests. In short, what is best for her as she is now is to be treated and to continue to live.

What is best for the Demented Patient now thus diverges from what would be best for her life as a whole. This raises new questions. Should her physicians do what would be best for her now, or ought they instead to do what would give her the best life as a whole? Assuming that her present good diverges from the previous autonomous preference that she has never actually renounced (and which itself gives priority to the value of her life as a whole), what does respect for her require? Although he does not accept that there is a conflict between the Demented Patient's present good and the value of her life as a whole, Dworkin does accept that there is a conflict between her experiential and critical interests. And he believes that this must be resolved in favor of the critical interests. He writes: "when we consider how the fate of a demented person can affect the character of his life, we consider the patient's whole life, not just its sad final stages, and we consider his future in terms of how it affects the character of the whole."[101] If we disregard the earlier autonomous preference for the sake of the present experiential interest, "that would not be compassionate toward the whole person, the person who tragically became demented."[102]

Dworkin is presumably assuming that identity is what matters. If identity were the basis of egoistic concern, there could presumably be no conflict between what is best for the Demented Patient now and what is best for her life as a whole. What would be best for *her,* as a temporally extended individual, would necessarily be what would be best over time, or for her life as a whole. But I have argued, following Parfit, that identity is not the basis of egoistic concern. It is instead the prudential unity relations that ground egoistic concern within a life and give the life significance as a whole. When these relations are weak, as they are between the Patient at Onset and the Demented Patient, the life as a whole matters less. For when the basis of significant unity within a life is weak, the life, *considered as a unit or whole,* has less significance, and the different moments or periods that together constitute the life have greater significance, independently of their relation to the whole.

This last claim has most force when *all* the parts of a life are relatively weakly connected to one another via the prudential unity relations, as in the life of a lower animal. The life of the Demented Patient is not, however, like that. It divides into two major parts, the predementia period and the period of dementia. While the prudential unity relations hold only weakly between these two parts of the life, so that they together do not constitute a tightly unified whole, the earlier predementia period was deeply unified in the ways that matter. Because it is overwhelmingly the dominant part of the life, there is a genuine unity to *most* of the life. The life does, after all, constitute a significant whole, though the Demented Patient now is, as it were, dangling outside the unified part of that whole, and the longer she continues to exist, the more the integrity of the whole is compromised or degraded.

One way to conceive of the problem, then, is as a conflict between the good of two distinct parts of the life—or, alternatively, between the good of the earlier competent self and that of the later demented self. The later segment, considered independently of its relation to the whole, will be better if it is extended. And given that the Demented Patient's physicians must make their choice now, there is a presumption that they should give priority to the present part of the life, or the present self. On the other hand, this same individual, when she was competent, had a time-relative interest in preventing her life as a whole from being marred by a period of dementia at the end. It might be argued, however, that the strength of this earlier time-relative interest must be heavily discounted for the weakened prudential unity relations between herself then and herself now. If, for example, she had less reason, when competent, to care about her future pain, it should also be true that she had less reason to care about the degrading nature of her future dementia.

This claim misses an important point. The concern that the Patient at Onset had about her future dementia is different from her concern about her future pain. It was, as I have argued, rational for her to be less concerned in an egoistic way about her future pain. Her future pain would, she knew, affect only her future self, to whom she would be only rather distantly related in the ways that ground egoistic concern. But her future dementia mattered to her more directly. For whether and how long she would live in a demented state would in part determine what kind of life as a whole the earlier segment would be a part of. And that could affect the meaning and value of her life at the earlier time. For the meaning and value of a certain period within a life can be affected by the nature of the life as a whole of which it is a part. So whether the Demented Patient continues to live can retroactively affect the meaning and value of her life prior to the onset of dementia.

I believe that, in this situation, the Demented Patient's physicians ought to give priority to the earlier part of her life, or to her earlier self. They ought, in other words, to allow her to die. So my practical conclusion coincides with Dworkin's, though my reasons for accepting this conclusion are different. Unlike Dworkin, I do not believe that the Demented Patient's present good is determined by what would be best for her life as a whole. It is, on the contrary, in her present time-relative interest to continue to live. But her continuing to live would, as Dworkin rightly emphasizes, be worse for her life as a whole, which in turn would be worse for the earlier life, making it a component or constituent of a lesser whole. Because the earlier part of the life is overwhelmingly the dominant part, its good should have priority. The earlier part was, in itself, a reasonably full and complete life with its own deep prudential unity. It was the life of the individual in her higher state, when she was a rational and autonomous person. Its good—which is the good of that earlier, higher self—is therefore more significant than the good of the shallow and necessarily rather brief period of dementia dangling at the end of the life. And its good—the good of the dominant part of the life—coincides with what would be best for the life as a whole. So the Demented Patient's present good ought to be sacrificed for the greater good of her earlier self, which is also the greater good of her life as a whole.

It is true that to allow the Demented Patient to die would be bad for her in a way that is more direct and immediate than the way in which her death would be better for her former self. But it is important to appreciate how comparatively weak the Demented Patient's time-relative interest in continuing to live actually is. There is very little good—even of the lower sort that remains accessible to her—in prospect. And the prudential unity relations that would bind her to herself in the future are extremely weak and growing weaker all the time. Her present and prospective future life are unhappily but aptly describable as a series of "discreet and mutually irrelevant episodes." Just as the prospect of this sort of life does not normally make a strong claim on us in the case of an animal, so it does not offer a strong reason for sustaining the Demented Patient's life. It would, of course, be a different matter if, when she was competent, this woman had autonomously preferred that her life should continue in this way. But, in the Advance Directive, her present time-relative interest in sustaining her sadly diminished life is actually opposed by her former autonomous will.

There is a further consideration, contingently present in many cases, that reinforces the conclusion that the Demented Patient ought to be allowed to die. It is often the case that, when a person stipulates in an advance directive that she should not be given life-supporting treatment in the event of dementia, her reasons are only partly self-interested. She may also be motivated by a desire to ensure that her life in a demented condition should not be prolonged at the expense of her family members. Her values may be such that, however she evaluates the prospect of dementia from an egoistic point of view, she is powerfully averse to becoming an emotional and financial burden on those she cares about. There is no reason to suppose that this reason for allowing her to die is in any way weakened if it comes to be in her time-relative interest, when demented, to continue to live. There is, indeed, often reason to believe that many of an individual's values persist well into dementia, even when the individual loses the capacity to be guided by those values in her behavior.[103] In such a case, one may honor a demented individual's present values by allowing her to die, even if she professes to want to live. For it may be that the values remain and what she has lost is the ability to understand that her continued existence is incompatible with them.

NOTES

Preface and Acknowledgments

1. For a slightly more extensive discussion of the morality of practices involving the killing of animals, see McMahan (2002).

1. Identity

1. Walker Percy, "A View of Abortion, With Something to Offend Everybody," in Percy (1991), p. 341.

2. Carter (1982), p. 77.

3. The distinction between reductionist and nonreductionist accounts of personal identity is carefully developed in Parfit (1984) and Parfit (1995).

4. Here I follow Lockwood (1985), p. 14.

5. These notions are elucidated in Wiggins (1980), p. 24.

6. Parfit (1984), p. 202.

7. Locke (1894), bk. 2, xxvii, sec. 7, pp. 444–45. A comparable argument is advanced in Kant (1964), p. 342, note a. The observations by Locke and Kant are elaborated in Parfit (1984), pp. 223 and 228; Shoemaker (1984), pp. 123–24; and Mackie (1976), pp. 194–95.

8. Mencken (1982), p. 87.

9. Williams (1986), p. 197.

10. Ibid., pp. 195 and 197.

11. Ibid., pp. 196–197.

12. Shewmon (1997), p. 74.

13. Finnis (1995c), p. 69. Emphases added.

14. Shewmon (1997), p. 74.

15. Ford (1988), p. 75.

16. Donceel (1984), p. 18.

17. Ford (1988), pp. 27–28 and 41–43.

18. Descartes (1991), pp. 189 and 336.

19. Swinburne (1984), p. 34. Emphasis added.

20. Descartes (1991), p. 189.

21. Descartes (1985), pp. 171–72.

22. Quoted in Huxley (1952), p. 159.

23. Matthews (1979), pp. 153–154.

24. William Shakespeare, *Hamlet, Prince of Denmark,* 5.1.137.

25. The idea that we are souls, understood to be essentially mental substances, entails a nonreductionist account of personal identity. An attack on nonreductionism is therefore an attack on the idea that we are souls. The most thorough and devastating critique of nonreductionism is developed in Parfit (1984), esp. ch. 11, and Parfit (1995).

26. These experiments and their philosophical implications are reviewed in Nagel (1979c), pp. 147–64; Parfit (1984), pp. 245–52; Jonathan Glover (1988), ch. 2; and Wilkes (1988), ch. 5.

27. This conclusion has been challenged. See, for example, Robinson (1988), pp. 325–27.

28. My abbreviated presentation of these thought-experiments follows the more detailed and convincing account given in Parfit (1984), pp. 253–61, although I have broken down the series of cases into a couple more than Parfit presents. The basic idea first appears in Wiggins (1967), p. 52.

29. Parfit (1984), p. 253.

30. See, for example, Swinburne (1984), p. 20.

31. Compare Parfit (1984), p. 259.

32. Among those who have defended this view are Carter (1982), Quinn (1984), Snowdon (1991), van Inwagen (1990), and, most recently and thoroughly, Olson (1997).

33. McMahan (1995b), p. 98.

34. Oderberg (1997), pp. 270–71.

35. See, for example, Kuhse and Singer (1990), p. 67.

36. The first interpretation is defended in Holland (1990) and Oderberg (1997), the second in Ford (1988), p. 137 and Olson (1997), pp. 90–93.

37. Parfit (1984), pp. 211–12.

38. Locke (1894), bk. 2, xxxvii, sec. 5, p. 443.

39. Olson (1997), p. 136. An animal is, according to Olson, one kind of organism.

40. See van Inwagen (1990).

41. This is the response recommended in Snowdon (1991).

42. Van Inwagen (1990), sec. 15.

43. Compare van Inwagen (1990), p. 173.

44. Van Inwagen (1990), pp. 177–78.

45. Ibid., p. 179.

46. Ibid., p. 172.

47. Van Inwagen actually develops his view via a discussion of a cerebrum transplant rather than a brain transplant. There is a footnote, however, apparently added as an afterthought, in which he recognizes that a cerebrum, "the thinking part of a brain," supported by an external life-support system, would not constitute an organism, and hence that one could not survive as a detached cerebrum. See van Inwagen (1990), pp. 169 and 291–92.

48. See, for example, Wilkes (1988), Baillie (1993), and Rovane (1994).

49. The argument here extends the discussions of dicephalus in McMahan (1998a), pp. 254–55, and McMahan (1999), pp. 82–83.

50. Miller (1996).

51. There is some reason to believe that van Inwagen might be tempted by this option. See his discussion of the imaginary double-brained creature called Cerberus in van Inwagen (1990), sec. 16.

52. Twain (1996), pp. 323 and 431. The case of the Tocci twins is discussed in Monestier (1987), pp. 146–48.

53. Van Inwagen (1990), p. 189.

54. I owe this example to Mark Reid.

55. Parfit (1984), p. 206. Emphasis in the original.

56. Ibid. Emphasis in the original.

57. See Thomson (1987), pp. 226–27.

58. The general form of this claim is challenged in White (1989), esp. pp. 315–16.

59. Schechtman (1996), p. 52.

60. For an indication of what might be lacking, see White (1989).

61. Parfit (1984), p. 262.

62. Parfit (1971).

63. Parfit (1984), p. 313.

64. See Parfit's discussion of reductionism in Parfit (1984), secs. 79, 84, 85, and 86.

65. Ibid., p. 206. Strictly speaking, Parfit should say "many fewer than *half* the number of direct psychological connections. . . ."

66. Ibid., p. 202.

67. This claim is challenged, though not in my view persuasively, in Bermúdez (1996).

68. Parfit (1984), p. 212. The claim is retracted in Parfit (1999).

69. Parfit (1984), p. 313.

70. Williams (1970) and Unger (1990).

71. Parfit (1984), p. 208.

72. Rovane (1994), p. 123.

73. Parfit (1984), p. 205.

74. Cp. Parfit (1984), p. 220.

75. This account has affinities with the accounts advanced in Mackie (1976), ch. 6, Nagel (1986), ch. 3, Johnston (1987), and Unger (1990).

76. Lockwood (1985), pp. 22–23.

77. Lockwood (1988), p. 206.

78. Green and Wikler (1980), pp. 126 and 127. There is, however, some ambiguity in their account. Their use of the word "normally" leaves it open that the relevant processes might be preserved in the absence of continuity and connectedness. On occasion they also refer to "mental traits *and capacities*" (125, emphasis added), suggesting that the retention of certain psychological capacities alone, in the absence of any continuity in the contents of a person's mental life, might be sufficient for identity.

79. Parfit (1984), p. 474.

80. Ibid., p. 475.

81. Ibid., p. 476.

82. Ibid., sec. 85.

83. Ibid., p. 313.

84. Ibid., p. 341.

85. Singer (1993a), p. 121.

86. Sacks (1987), p. 27.

87. Ibid.

88. Wilson and Wearing (1995), pp. 15 and 26.

89. Ibid., pp. 17 and 19.

90. Sacks (1987), p. 29.

91. Bayley (1999), p. 275.

92. Bate (1975), p. 473.

93. Huxley (1939), p. 53.

94. Cases of fusion are discussed in Parfit (1984), sec. 100.

95. I am indebted to correspondence from Michael Lockwood on this point.

96. For discussion of multiple personality disorder, see Hacking (1995) and Wilkes (1988), ch. 4.

97. Miller (1996), p. 56.

98. I am indebted to Michael Lockwood for calling this possibility to my attention.

99. Shoemaker (1984), p. 113.

100. Carter (1982), p. 94. Also see pp. 81–82.

101. Compare McMahan (1995b), p. 119.

102. For a challenge to the idea that two putatively different substances that share all their constituent matter could have different persistence conditions, see Olson (1997), pp. 94–102.

103. Parfit (1994), p. 37.

104. I espoused this view in McMahan (1995b).

105. Quinn (1984), pp. 28–29.

106. Carter (1982), p. 94.

107. This suggestion has been independently developed by Ingmar Persson in his account of "derivative predication." See Persson (1999), sec. 3.

2. Death

1. Plato, *Apology,* p. 374 and *Phaedo,* p. 436, both in Plato (1875), vol. 1.

2. McMahan (1988), pp. 32–40.

3. Arthur Schopenhauer, "Death and Its Relation to the Indestructibility of Our Inner Nature," in Schopenhauer (1966), vol. 2, p. 473.

4. Ibid.

5. Ibid., p. 472.

6. Ibid., p. 477.

7. Ibid., p. 472. And compare p. 473.

8. Ibid., p. 473.

9. Ibid., p. 474.

10. Ibid., p. 479.

11. Tolstoy (1981), pp. 133 and 134.

12. Wilson (1988), p. 366.

13. This is a crude interpretation of the more precise proposal set forth in Lewis (1973).

14. Swift (1941), p. 195.

15. Ibid., p. 197.

16. Ibid., p. 198.

17. Wollheim (1984), pp. 265–66.

18. Snow (1978), p. 148.

19. Williams (1973c), p. 90

20. Ibid., p. 91.

21. Williams (1973b).

22. Alfred, Lord Tennyson, "Tithonus," in Abrams et al. (1968), p. 844.

23. Feldman (1992), pp. 150–51. He defends the same view in a slightly more technical fashion in Feldman (1991). By "extrinsically bad" he means much the same as "comparatively bad"; both contrast with "intrinsically bad."

24. Feldman (1992), pp. 182–90.

25. Marquis (1989), p. 192.

26. One view of this sort is suggested in Williams (1973c).

27. McMahan (1998c), sec. 2.

28. Broome (1993), p. 81.

29. Lewis (1973).

30. Nagel (1979b), p. 9.

31. McMahan (1998d), sec. 1.

32. Nagel (1979b), p. 10.

33. This case is taken from McMahan (1988), p. 45.

34. Feldman (1991), p. 216. I insert the word "nearest" in order to bring the account of the badness of a death into conformity with Feldman's account of "the overall value . . . of states

of affairs for persons," which draws explicitly on Lewis's notion of the nearest possible world. The account is stated on pp. 215–16.

35. Ibid., pp. 225–26.

36. Ibid., p. 226.

37. Ibid.

38. Hanser (1995), p. 185.

39. This example is taken from McMahan and McKim (1993), p. 509. Compare Hanser (1995), p. 199.

40. Schopenhauer (1974), vol. 1, p. 495.

41. Weiss (1997), p. 18.

42. Nagel (1979b), p. 8.

43. Ibid., p. 10.

44. Wollheim (1984), p. 267.

45. Compare the discussion of the case of the Benefactor in sec. 6.1 of this chapter.

46. Nagel (1979b), pp. 8 and 10.

47. Ibid., p. 9.

48. Kaufmann (1961), p. 389.

49. Quoted ibid., p. 381.

50. Ibid., p. 382.

51. Carver (1983), p. 25.

52. Quoted in Halpert (1995), p. 194.

53. Snow (1966), p. 121.

54. Thackeray (1937), p. 257.

55. Brodkey (1996), p. 176.

56. Ibid., p. 13.

57. The Species Norm Account as presented here differs somewhat from the version developed and discussed in McMahan (1996a). However, some of the material in the following paragraphs in the text follows the critique of the Species Norm Account given on pp. 12–14 of this earlier article.

58. The idea that it might take the form of a sufficient condition only was suggested to me by Seana Shiffrin.

59. For other objections to the Species Norm Account, see McMahan (1996a), pp. 16–17 and 20–21.

60. This objection, though somewhat differently formulated, is urged in Arneson (1999), pp. 114–17.

61. The main lines of argument in the following section follow the ideas developed in McMahan (1988) and (1998c), though my views, especially about personal identity, have undergone some significant changes over the years since these essays were written. (The latter article, though published in 1998, was written in 1992.)

62. Morowitz and Trefil (1992), p. 51.

63. Wright (1994), pp. 174–75. Emphases in the original.

64. I owe this objection to Kai Draper and, through him, to some of his colleagues in the philosophy department at Kansas State University.

65. Versions of this objection were put to me, on different occasions, by Fred Feldman and Martin Curd.

66. Compare the earlier discussion in sec. 4.2 of this chapter.

67. MacIntyre (1981), ch. 15. My remarks on narrative unity are also inspired by the insightful discussion in Velleman (1991). Further instructive discussion of the importance of unity within a life may be found in ch. 9 of Hurka (1993).

68. The discussion here draws on that in McMahan (1993b), pp. 336–37.

69. See, for example, the illuminating discussion of experiential and critical interests in chs. 7 and 8 of Dworkin (1993).

70. Velleman (1991), p. 58.

71. MacIntyre (1981), p. 203.

72. Having accepted Epicurus's claim that death cannot be bad for one who does not exist, Dorothy Grover argues that death may still be bad by virtue of its retroactive effects on the value of one's life, for reasons that are related to but somewhat different from those I cite in the text. I believe that this position underestimates the badness of death, perhaps particularly in the case of young children. See Grover (1987).

73. Lockwood (1979), p. 167.

74. The role of investment in the future is noted in McMahan (1988), pp. 57–58. Other works that have given even greater emphasis to the notion of investment are Feldman (1992), pp. 201–4, and Dworkin (1993), pp. 79–101.

75. Feldman (1992), p. 203.

76. Dworkin (1993), p. 79.

77. Ibid., p. 89.

78. Ibid., p. 90.

79. Ibid., p. 71

80. Ibid., p. 87.

81. Velleman (1991), pp. 56–57.

82. Ibid., p. 57.

83. Ibid.

84. Ibid., p. 66.

85. Ibid., pp. 59–60.

86. Williams (1973c), p. 85.

87. McMahan (1998c), pp. 473–80.

88. There is an earlier but unsatisfactory discussion of this problem in McMahan (1988), sec. 3.

3. Killing

1. Rachels (1986), p. 6.

2. Marquis (1989), p. 189.

3. This is denied in Hanser (1999).

4. For example, Marquis (1989).

5. For an argument along these lines, see Singer (1993a), chs. 4 and 5.

6. Mencken (1946), p. 12.

7. Huxley (1959), p. 245.

8. Coetzee (1999), p. 64.

9. Thomson (1990), pp. 292–93.

10. Sacks (1995), p. 281.

11. Ibid., pp. 279–80.

12. Ibid., p. 268.

13. Ibid., pp. 280–81.

14. I offer a limited defense of this claim in McMahan (2002).

15. Compare Singer (1993b), pp. 305–6.

16. See, for example, Regan (1983).

17. Ibid., ch. 7.

18. Dworkin (1993), pp. 69 and 73 and ch. 3 generally. Emphases added.

19. In this and the following paragraph I follow Clark (1993) and Graft (1997), pp. 110–14.

20. Ring species are discussed in Dawkins (1993).

21. This view is discussed in Singer (1993a), pp. 75–76, where it is subject to a rather different critique from that offered here.

22. Finnis (1995b), p. 48.

23. Scanlon (1998), p. 179.

24. Ibid., p. 186.

25. Ibid., p. 185.

26. Ibid.

27. Nozick (1983).

28. The following discussion of the morality of special relations draws on the more extensive discussion in McMahan (1997).

29. Scheffler (1982).

30. Tajfel (1970).

31. In this and the following nine paragraphs, the argument has benefited from comments by and discussion with Jorah Dannenberg.

32. Thomson (1986), p. 108.

33. I discuss this distinction in McMahan (1994b).

34. See McMahan (1994a).

35. I have addressed the issue of the status of moral intuition, though without advancing any decisive arguments, in McMahan (2000).

36. Ramsey (1978), p. 191.

37. I draw here on McMahan (1995a), pp. 10–11. A similar distinction is drawn in Regan (1983), pp. 235–36. Also compare the distinction in Donagan (1977), pp. 64–65, between "respect for human beings" and "respect for fundamental human goods."

38. For discussion, see Dworkin (1993), p. 12.

39. Quinn (1984), p. 49.

40. Ibid., p. 48.

41. This view has obvious affinities with the view sketchily advanced by Robert Nozick under the label "utilitarianism for animals, Kantianism for people," according to which we should "(1) maximize the total happiness of all living beings; (2) place stringent side constraints on what one may do to human beings." See Nozick (1974), p. 39.

42. See Frankena (1986), pp. 160–64, and Donagan (1977), pp. 66–74.

43. Thomson (1990), p. 292.

44. These are variants of examples suggested to me by Kasper Lippert-Rasmussen.

45. For a careful study of some of the pertinent questions that I fail to discuss, see Kamm (1996).

46. Rawls (1972), p. 508.

47. Wikler (1979), p. 384. Compare Buchanan and Brock (1990), pp. 26–29.

48. James (1910), pp. 277–78.

49. Kant (1948), p. 96.

50. Ibid., pp. 111–13. For discussion, see Williams (1973d), pp. 234–36, and Seidler (1986), ch. 2.

51. Rawls (1972), p. 505.

52. Ibid., p. 507.

53. Ibid., p. 512.

54. Ibid., p. 505.

55. Ibid., pp. 510 and 511.

56. Ibid., p. 512. It is unclear what the implied distinction between justice and strict justice amounts to.

57. Ibid., p. 505.

58. Ibid., p. 509.

59. Ibid.

60. Ibid., p. 510.

61. Margalit (1996), p. 70.

62. Ibid., p. 71.

63. Ibid., p. 57. Emphasis added.

64. Ibid., p.81.

65. Ibid., pp. 76 and 77.

66. For a novel and subtle discussion of the implications of rejecting libertarian free will, see Smilansky (2000).

67. Quinn (1984), p. 49.

68. Nozick (1974), p. 50.

69. Ibid., p. 48.

70. Quinn (1989), p. 310.

71. For objections to this sort of counterfactual analysis of the distinction between doing and allowing, see Kagan (1989), pp. 95–99.

72. One recent work that has done much to illuminate the morality of respect, particularly with regard to issues of killing and letting die, is Kamm (1996). Kamm develops at length a subtle understanding of what she refers to as our status as inviolable. She does not, however, attempt to identify the basis of our inviolability, apart from observing that "it is certain properties (here not enumerated) that we have as individuals that would account for our status" as inviolable (p. 273). Hence she has no account of why we are inviolable while animals are not. Nor is there any indication of the scope of her account of inviolability. There is no criterion for determining whether fetuses, infants, young children, or demented individuals share our inviolability.

73. Nietzsche (1973), p. 173.

4. Beginnings

1. Korein (1997), pp. 25–26. For a similar view, see Glover and Fisk (1999).

2. Lockwood (1985), p. 212, note 18.

3. Steinbock (1992), p. 87.

4. Marquis (1989), p. 192.

5. Among those who have defended the Capacity Condition are Singer (1993a), chs. 4 and 5, Harris (1995), p. 9, Cigman (1981), and Velleman (1991).

6. Quinn (1984), p. 34.

7. Ibid., p. 39.

8. Ibid.

9. Ibid., p. 54.

10. The idea that the victim of prenatal harm is not so much the fetus but the later person is advanced by, among others, Steinbock (1992), pp. 89–91.

11. In suggesting that morality may forbid certain acts that have been traditionally condemned as imprudent, I again follow Parfit (1984), sec. 106.

12. Talbot (1999), p. 41.

13. The claim that it is never a reason to prevent someone from existing that the person will have to suffer the evil of death is defended in sec. 9.2 of this chapter.

14. For an extensive discussion of the implications of this kind of case, see Adams (1979).

15. Sacks (1995), pp. 108–52.

16. See note 5.

17. McMahan (1981).

18. Parfit (1984), Pt. III.

19. I say more about the nature of that role in McMahan (1998d), especially secs. IV and V.

20. McMahan (1981), p. 100.

21. A view of this sort is defended in Reichlin (1997).

22. Similar distinctions are drawn in Stone (1987) and Buckle (1988).

23. Parfit (1994), p. 38.

24. Singer (1993a), p. 153.

25. Wade (1999).

26. Reiman (1999), p. 65. (Emphasis added.)

27. Ibid., pp. 65 and 66.

28. There is an echo here of Michael Tooley's example in which kittens, if injected with a certain chemical, will eventually develop into persons. The difference is that the source of the kittens' potential is extrinsic. See Tooley (1973), p. 86.

29. Compare Draper (1999).

30. Dworkin (1993), pp. 73–74.

31. Ibid., p. 73.

32. Ibid., p. 69.

33. Ibid., pp. 12, 194–95, and 198.

34. Ibid., p. 82.

35. Ibid., p. 84.

36. Ibid., p. 93.

37. The argument in the following paragraphs is drawn from McMahan (1995c).

38. Dworkin (1993), p. 80.

39. Frances Kamm makes the same point in Kamm (1995), p. 170.

40. Dworkin (1993), p. 85.

41. Ibid.

42. Dostoyevsky (1992), pp. 238–39.

43. For example, Kuhse and Singer (1985), ch. 5.

44. Ibid.

45. Thomson (1971).

46. Nasar (1999), Sharlet (2000), and Specter (1999).

47. Schaefer (1998).

48. Kuhse and Singer (1985), pp. 156–58; Singer and Kuhse (1993), pp. 160–62; and Singer (1993a), pp. 186–88. As these references indicate, Singer has developed some parts of his view in collaboration with his frequent coauthor, Helga Kuhse. For convenience and simplicity of exposition, I will continue to write as if Singer's arguments were his alone, as they mostly seem to be. Most elements of the replaceability argument were advanced in the first edition of his *Practical Ethics,* published in 1979 (though I will not quote from that edition here, since it represents his thinking at an earlier stage). Because the collaborations with Kuhse came later, I will acknowledge her contributions only in these notes.

49. Kuhse and Singer (1985), pp. 131–33; Singer (1993a), pp. 96–99 and 126. The references are to Tooley (1973) and Tooley (1983).

50. Singer (1993a), p. 97.

51. Ibid., p. 125.

52. Ibid.

53. Ibid., p. 126.

54. Ibid., p. 151.

55. Ibid., p. 169.

56. Kuhse and Singer (1985), p. 134.

57. Ibid., p. 133.

58. Singer (1993a), p. 97.

59. Singer (1994), chs. 2 and 3.

60. Ibid., p. 125.

61. Kuhse and Singer (1985), p. 132; Singer (1993a), p. 171.

62. Singer (1993a), p. 132.

63. Ibid., p. 186. Compare the even more emphatic statements in Kuhse and Singer (1985), pp. 155–61.

64. Singer (1993a), p. 131.

65. Ibid.

66. Kuhse and Singer (1985), p. 134.

67. Jonathan Glover (1977), p. 69. (This paragraph and the four that follow it are revised versions of some passages in McMahan (1998d), pp. 237–39.)

68. Parfit is discussing his own revised version of a principle suggested but ultimately rejected in Kavka (1982). This revised principle is not actually impersonal in character, though it is closely related to an impersonal maximizing principle in that it requires that, other things being equal, one do what would benefit people most on the assumption that people can be benefited by being caused to exist. Thus Parfit does not himself employ his analogy the way that I do here, and my critique of the analogy is not directed against his discussion. See Parfit (1982), pp. 127–32.

69. Ibid., p. 131.

70. I am grateful to Eric Wampler for pressing me to recognize that my view has this sort of implication.

71. Thomson (1971), p. 64.

72. Ibid., pp. 61–62.

73. Ibid., p. 56.

74. Ibid., p. 61.

75. Ibid., p. 49.

76. I believe the objection is decisively refuted in Boonin-Vail (1997a), pp. 290–300.

77. Silverstein (1987) and Boonin-Vail (1997a).

78. Thomson (1971), pp. 57–59.

79. This is a slightly modified version of a case originally presented in Silverstein (1987), pp. 106–7. I take the label from Boonin-Vail (1997a), p. 303, where the case is discussed in detail.

80. Silverstein (1987), pp. 105–9. Silverstein's explanation is endorsed and elaborated in Boonin-Vail (1997a), pp. 301–6.

81. Silverstein (1987), p. 108.

82. This case is presented in Silverstein (1987), p. 107 and is discussed in Boonin-Vail (1997a), p. 304, from which I take the name. Again, their understanding of the significance of the case is rather different from mine.

83. Frances Kamm seems to be giving an answer to this question when she notes that the fetus is "no worse off being dead because it was killed than if it had never existed." See Kamm (1992), p. 80.

84. See McMahan (1981), pp. 104–7 and McMahan (1988), pp. 35–38.

85. The material in this and the following paragraph is taken from McMahan (1991). I presented a compressed version of the argument in McMahan (1993b), p. 335.

86. Lockwood (1985), p. 31.

87. Michael Davis (1983), p. 277.

88. Nagel (1979b), p. 3.

89. This and the following three paragraphs draw on material in McMahan (1993b), pp. 337–38.

90. Kamm (1992), p. 126.

91. This asymmetry is the main focus of McMahan (1991).

92. I have discussed this question briefly and inadequately in sects. 5 and 8.2 of this chapter. See also Parfit (1984), App. G, McMahan (1981), sec. IV, and Heyd (1992).

93. Thomson (1971), p. 64.

94. Ibid., p. 65.

95. Ibid.

96. See Pavlischek (1998).

97. See Blustein (1982) for a survey of some of the historical literature.

98. See, for example, Beckwith (1998), p. 140. I urged this objection in McMahan (1993b), p. 347, though, as the reader will recall from my treatment of the case of the Sperm Donor in sec. 2.3 of ch. 3, I have subsequently changed my mind about the intuitive force of the examples.

99. On the prospects for the development of an artificial uterus, see Powledge (1999).

100. Thomson (1971), pp. 52 and 57.

101. See, for example, Kamm (1992), pp. 74–76.

102. Some of the material in the following discussion is drawn from McMahan (1993a).

103. For a sophisticated elaboration of this view, see Foot (1967), p. 26. Foot sees herself as setting forth a precise distinction that has the moral significance that is ordinarily attributed to the distinction between killing and letting die. But she thinks that our use of the terms "killing" and "letting die" corresponds only imperfectly to the genuinely relevant distinction. Thus she thinks it appropriate to describe the woman's disconnecting the violinist as an act of killing, but she thinks that this is unimportant. What is important is that the act falls on the side of the distinction that includes most or all instances of letting die. Foot's view is discussed in more detail in McMahan (1993a), pp. 251–55.

104. That an unauthorized person's turning off a life-support system seems to involve the same form of agency as an authorized person's doing so is cited by Shelly Kagan as a reason for thinking that the intuitive moral difference between the two acts cannot be explained by claiming that the former is killing whereas the latter is only letting die. See Kagan (1989), p. 101. Compare Boorse and Sorensen (1988), p. 126.

105. I owe this case to Heidi Malm. I used it earlier in McMahan (1993a), p. 256.

106. Some implications of this point are explored in McMahan (1993a), pp. 258–261.

107. McMahan (1998b), pp. 411–16.

108. In this and the following eleven paragraphs, I draw on the argument in McMahan (1993a), pp. 268–71.

109. Foot (1967), p. 26. Also see Foot (1984), pp. 178–80; and Foot (1985), p. 24.

110. Foot (1967), p. 26.

111. Foot (1984), p. 185.

112. Ibid.

113. Foot (1967), p. 26.

114. Levin (1987), pp. 288–89; quoted in Beckwith (1998), p. 144.

115. Cited in Connery (1977), p. 248. I owe this reference to David Boonin.

116. Among the more plausible responses are those presented in Quinn (1989), sec. IV, and Thomson (1999), pp. 504–5.

117. This claim is advanced in Harman (1977), p. 111. For a discussion of this and other reductive explanations of the intuition that killing is worse than letting die, see McMahan (1998b), pp. 398–400.

118. See Walen (1997), sec. IV, esp. pp. 1111–12; and Boonin-Vail (1997b), pp. 338–48.

119. This case was originally presented in McMahan (1993b), sec. III.

120. Kamm (1992), especially ch. 5.

121. See, for example, English (1975) and McDonagh (1996).

122. The seminal article in which this account is developed is Montague (1981). I discuss the account at length in McMahan (1994a).

123. That moral responsibility for a threat, even in the absence of culpability or fault, can be a basis for liability to self-defensive action as a matter of justice is recognized in Draper (1993), Otsuka (1994), and Montague (2000). I overlooked this important point in McMahan (1994a).

124. I borrow the notion of a forced choice among lives from Montague (1981), p. 211.

125. In McMahan (1994a), I sought to cast doubt on the permissibility of killing Innocent Attackers in self-defense by demonstrating how difficult it is to find a relevant difference between an Innocent Attacker and an Innocent Bystander. The argument that follows in the text, in which I compare the Nonresponsible Threat to what I call a Nonresponsible Cause, is a slightly modified version of an argument developed on pp. 266–68 of that article. In an essay published shortly after mine, but written entirely independently, Michael Otsuka argues explicitly that there is no relevant difference between a Nonresponsible Attacker or Threat and an Innocent Bystander. See Otsuka (1994), pp. 84–87. I will discuss this argument later in this section.

126. Walen (1997), p. 1088.

127. Otsuka (1994), p. 87.

128. Ibid., p. 77.

129. For a closely argued defense of the claim that this difference is crucially relevant, see Kamm (1996), ch. 7. The phrases borrowed from Bennett are in his (1981), pp. 101–2.

130. Bennett (1981), p. 111. This discussion of the narrow and broad notions of an intended means draws on McMahan (1994b).

131. See McMahan (1994a), pp. 265–66.

132. This account of the right of self-defense is most ably defended in Thomson (1991) and Uniacke (1994). An early suggestion of the account is in Kadish (1976), p. 885. The account is criticized in McMahan (1994a) and McMahan (1996b).

133. For an earlier elaboration of this objection, see McMahan (1994a), pp. 275–78. A similar objection is advanced in Otsuka (1994), pp. 79–82.

134. See secs. VI–VIII of McMahan (1994a). Other attempts to defend the permissibility of self-defense against a Nonresponsible Threat are found in Kamm (1992), pp. 45–54, Kamm (1987), and Walen (1997), pp. 1100–1107.

135. I am indebted to Alec Walen for this point. My conclusions here coincide with his in Walen (1997), pp. 1104–7.

136. I follow Nancy (Ann) Davis (1984), pp. 190–91.

137. Ibid., p. 190.

138. Ibid., pp. 192–93.

139. I have developed this objection to Davis's view in McMahan (1994a), pp. 268–71.

140. These suggestions are proposed, respectively, in Kamm (1992), pp. 47–50, McMahan (1994a), sec. VI, and Walen (1997), pp. 1100–1104.

141. On the issue of the scope of principles of justice and equality, see McMahan (1996a).

5. Endings

1. Cited in Singer (1994), p. 62. Similar claims by relatives of other people who lapsed into PVS are quoted in Rachels (1986), p. 55.

2. Shewmon (1997), p. 81. Emphasis in the original.

3. Ad Hoc Committee of the Harvard Medical School (1968).

4. For discussion, see Bartlett and Youngner (1988), pp. 201–3.

5. Quoted in Gervais (1986), p. 11.

6. Ibid.

7. Higher-brain criteria are defended by Green and Wikler (1980), Gervais (1986), Bartlett and Youngner (1988), Veatch (1988), and by others whose essays are included in Zaner (1988).

8. For some challenges to certain standard analyses of the death of an organism, see Feldman, 1992), ch. 7.

9. Culver and Gert (1982), p. 183.

10. Lamb (1985), p. 93. Also compare Bernat (1998), pp. 15–16.

11. Rachels (1986), p. 55.

12. Rachels (1986), pp. 5–6 and 24–27.

13. The argument in this section draws extensively on arguments developed earlier in McMahan (1995b) and McMahan (1998a).

14. Lamb (1985), p. 7.

15. President's Commission (1981), p. 32.

16. Lamb (1985), p. 37.

17. Bernat (1998), pp. 19 and 17.

18. Ibid., p. 19.

19. McCullagh (1993), pp. 35–39.

20. Shewmon (1998), p. 136. Shewmon describes another remarkable case with which he had experience in Shewmon (1997), pp. 67–68.

21. Shewmon (1992), p. 38. Compare Truog and Fletcher (1990), p. 206.

22. Shewmon (1997), p. 40.

23. Bernat (1998), p. 19.

24. Ibid.

25. Green and Wikler (1980), p. 113.

26. Shewmon (1997), pp. 65–66, and the references cited there. His discussion includes considerably more detailed discussion of the physiology of the condition than I have presented.

27. See Korein (1997), p. 26 and the references cited there. Korein puts brain life later, at around 20–28 weeks.

28. Shewmon (2001).

29. Shewmon (1997), pp. 79–80.

30. Korein (1997), p. 47.

31. Shewmon (1992), pp. 41–42 and Shewmon (1997), pp. 57–58.

32. Ramachandran and Blakeslee (1998), chs. 2 and 3.

33. Shewmon (1992), p. 36.

34. Singer (1994), p. 32.

35. Ibid., p. 105.

36. Singer (1994), p. 207.

37. Ibid., p. 192.

38. Rachels (1986), p. 43.

39. Ibid., p. 42.

40. Ibid., pp. 24–25.

41. Ibid., p. 26.

42. Ibid., p. 42.

43. Ibid., p. 43.

44. See, for example, Dworkin (1993), pp. 15–16.

45. Homer (1996), Book 11, lines 79–82, p. 251.

46. Herodotus, *Histories* 3.38, cited in Rachels(1993b), pp. 15–17.

47. Dworkin (1993), pp. 180 and 192.

48. Powledge (1999).

49. Shawlot and Behringer, (1995), pp. 425–30.

50. The claim that coerced self-killing is not suicide is defended in Beauchamp (1993), p. 74.

51. McMahan (1994b).

52. Rachels (1986), p. 80; and Jonathan Glover (1977), p. 185.

53. See Davis (1984) and McMahan (1994a), pp. 268–71 and 282–85.

54. Koestler (1980), p. 583.

55. See Rachels (1986), chs. 7 and 8.

56. I originally stated the argument for this claim in McMahan (1978).

57. For a brief discussion of several theological objections, see Rachels (1993a), pp. 51–54.

58. Dworkin (1993), p. 198.

59. Finnis (1995a), pp. 33–34.

60. Dworkin (1993), p. 69.

61. On the different concepts of innocence, and the ways in which noninnocence may compromise a person's moral immunity to being harmed, see McMahan (1994a) and (1994c).

62. See, for example, Finnis (1995a), p. 27.

63. Finnis (1995a), p. 31.

64. Finnis (1995c), p. 69.

65. Ibid.

66. Dworkin (1993), p. 85.

67. His view is developed in Velleman (1999a) and, with specific application to the issues of suicide and euthanasia, in Velleman (1999b).

68. Velleman (1999b), p. 611. Emphases in the original.

69. Ibid., p. 613.

70. Hill (1991), p. 94.

71. Velleman (1999b), p. 616.

72. Ibid., p. 617.

73. Ibid., p. 616.

74. Dworkin (1993), pp. 68–69. Emphasis in the original.

75. Ibid., pp. 215–16.

76. Velleman (1999b), p. 615.

77. Ibid., p. 617.

78. Velleman (1999a), p. 358, n. 72.

79. Ibid., pp. 359–60. The quotation from Kant is from Kant (1948), p. 99. Emphasis is in the original text.

80. Velleman (1999b), p. 614.

81. Ibid., p. 624.

82. Velleman (1999a), p. 344.

83. Velleman (1999b), pp. 616–18.

84. Frances Kamm urges the related objection that Velleman's Kantian view implies the impermissibility of providing modes of pain relief that permanently eliminate a patient's capacity for rational agency—for example, analgesics that foreseeably cause death as a side effect and "terminal sedation." See Kamm (1999), sects. V–VIII.

85. Ibid., p. 615.

86. Kamm (1999), p. 605.

87. Velleman (1999b), p. 624, and also p. 612.

88. Velleman (1999a), p. 360.

89. Kant (1948), p. 99.

90. Velleman (1999b), p. 612.

91. Butler (1933), p. 170.

92. For an extended defense of a view of this sort, see Mayerfeld (1999).

93. For a defense of an analogous claim about preferences, see Fehige (1998).
94. This section draws on McMahan (1994d).
95. Gregg (1994), p. 29.
96. Parfit (1984), p. 317.
97. Dworkin (1993), p. 201.
98. Ibid., p. 202.
99. Ibid., p. 201.
100. Ibid., pp. 201–2.
101. Ibid., p. 230.
102. Ibid., p. 232.
103. Jaworska (1999), p. 130.

REFERENCES

Where reprinted versions are cited, page references in the notes are to the reprint rather than the original.

Abrams, M. H., et al., eds. 1968. *The Norton Anthology of English Literature,* vol. 2, revised edition. New York: W.W. Norton.

Ad Hoc Committee of the Harvard Medical School. 1968. "A Definition of Irreversible Coma." *Journal of the American Medical Association* 205: 337–40.

Adams, Robert M. 1979. "Existence, Self-Interest, and the Problem of Evil." *Nous* 13: 317–32.

Arneson, Richard J. 1999. "What, if Anything, Renders All Humans Morally Equal?" Pp. 103–28 in Dale Jamieson, ed., *Singer and His Critics.* Oxford: Blackwell.

Baillie, James. 1993. *Problems in Personal Identity.* New York: Paragon House.

Bartlett, Edward T., and Youngner, Stuart J. 1988. "Human Death and the Destruction of the Neocortex." Pp. 199–215 in Zaner (1988).

Bate, W. Jackson. 1975. *Samuel Johnson.* New York: Harcourt Brace Jovanovich.

Bayley, John. 1999. *Elegy for Iris.* New York: St. Martin's Press.

Beauchamp, Tom L. 1993. "Suicide." Pp. 69–120 in Regan (1993).

Beckwith, Francis J. 1998. "Arguments from Bodily Rights: A Critical Analysis." Pp. 132–50 in Louis P. Pojman and Francis J. Beckwith, eds., *The Abortion Controversy,* 2d edition. Belmont, Calif: Wadsworth.

Bennett, Jonathan. 1981. "Morality and Consequences." Pp. 46–116 in Stirling McMurrin, ed., *The Tanner Lectures on Human Values,* vol. 2. Salt Lake City: University of Utah Press.

Bermúdez, José Luis. 1996. "The Moral Significance of Birth." *Ethics* 106: 378–403.

Bernat, James L. 1998. "A Defense of the Whole-Brain Concept of Death." *Hastings Center Report* 28: 14–23.

Bluestein, Jeffrey. 1982. *Parents and Children: The Ethics of the Family.* New York: Oxford University Press.

Boonin-Vail, David. 1997a. "A Defense of 'A Defense of Abortion': On the Responsibility Objection to Thomson's Argument." *Ethics* 107: 286–313.

———. 1997b. "Death Comes for the Violinist: On Two Objections to Thomson's 'Defense of Abortion.'" *Social Theory and Practice* 23: 329–64.

Boorse, Christopher, and Sorensen, Roy A. 1988. "Ducking Harm." *Journal of Philosophy* 85: 115–34.

Brodkey, Harold. 1996. *This Wild Darkness.* New York: Henry Holt.

Broome, John. 1993. "Goodness Is Reducible to Betterness: The Evil of Death Is the Value of Life." Pp. 70–86 in Peter Koslowski and Yuichi Shionoya, eds., *The Good and the Economical.* Berlin: Springer.

Buchanan, Allen, and Brock, Dan. 1990. *Deciding for Others: The Ethics of Surrogate Decision Making.* Cambridge: Cambridge University Press.

Buckle, Stephen. 1988. "Arguing From Potential." *Bioethics* 2: 227–53.

Butler, Samuel. 1933. *The Way of All Flesh.* New York: Everyman.

Carter, W. R. 1980. "Once and Future Persons." *American Philosophical Quarterly* 17: 61–66.

———. 1982. "Do Zygotes Become People?" *Mind* 91: 77–95.

———. 1984. "Death and Bodily Transfiguration." *Mind* 93: 412–18.

Carver, Raymond. 1983. "On Writing." Pp. 22–27 in *Fires.* New York: Random House.

Cavalieri, Paolo, and Singer, Peter, eds. 1993. *The Great Ape Project.* New York: St. Martin's Press.

Cigman, Ruth. 1981. "Death, Misfortune, and Species Inequality." *Philosophy and Public Affairs* 10: 47–64.

Clark, Stephen. 1993. "Apes and the Idea of Kindred." Pp. 133–25 in Cavalieri and Singer (1993).

Coetzee, J. M. 1999. *The Lives of Animals.* Princeton: Princeton University Press.

Connery, John, S.J. 1977. *Abortion: The Development of the Roman Catholic Perspective.* Chicago: Loyola University Press.

Culver, Charles M., and Gert, Bernard. 1982. *Philosophy in Medicine.* New York: Oxford University Press.

Davis, Michael. 1983. "Foetuses, Famous Violinists, and the Right to Continued Aid." *Philosophical Quarterly* 33: 259–78.

Davis, Nancy (Ann). 1984. "Abortion and Self-Defense." *Philosophy and Public Affairs* 13: 175–207.

Dawkins, Richard. 1993. "Gaps in the Mind." Pp. 80–87 in Cavalieri and Singer (1993).

Descartes, Rene. 1985. *The Philosophical Writings of Descartes,* vol. 2, trans. J. Cottingham, R. Stoothoff, and D. Murdoch. Cambridge: Cambridge University Press.

———. 1991. *The Philosophical Writings of Descartes,* vol. 3, trans. J. Cottingham, R. Stoothoff, D. Murdoch, and A. Kenny. Cambridge: Cambridge University Press.

Dombrowski, Daniel A., and Deltete, Robert. 2000. *A Brief, Liberal, Catholic Defense of Abortion.* Urbana: University of Illinois Press.

Donagan, Alan. 1977. *The Theory of Morality.* Chicago: University of Chicago Press.

Donceel, Joseph F., S.J. 1984. "A Liberal Catholic's View." Pp. 15–20 in Joel Feinberg, ed., *The Problem of Abortion,* 2d edition. Belmont, Calif: Wadsworth.

Dostoyevsky, Fyodor. 1992. *The Brothers Karamazov.* New York: Everyman's Library.

Draper, Kai. 1993. "Fairness and Self-Defense." *Social Theory and Practice* 19: 73–92.

———. 1999. "Disappointment, Sadness, and Death." *Philosophical Review* 108: 387–414.

Dworkin, Ronald. 1993. *Life's Dominion.* New York: Alfred A. Knopf.

English, Jane. 1975. "Abortion and the Concept of a Person." *Canadian Journal of Philosophy* 5: 233–43.

Fehige, Christoph. 1998. "A Pareto Principle for Possible People." Pp. 508–43 in Fehige and Wessels.

Fehige, Christoph, and Wessels, Ulla, eds. 1998. *Preferences.* Berlin: Walter de Gruyter.

Feldman, Fred. 1991. "Some Puzzles About the Evil of Death." *Philosophical Review* 100: 205–27. Reprinted in Fischer (1993), pp. 307–26.

———. 1992. *Confrontations with the Reaper.* New York: Oxford University Press.

Finnis, John. 1995a. "A Philosophical Case Against Euthanasia." Pp. 23–35 in Keown (1995).

———. 1995b. "The Fragile Case for Euthanasia: A Reply to John Harris." Pp. 46–55 in Keown (1995).

———. 1995c. "Misunderstanding the Case Against Euthanasia: Response to John Harris's First Reply." Pp. 62–71 in Keown (1995).

Fischer, John Martin, ed. 1993. *The Metaphysics of Death.* Stanford: Stanford University Press.

Foot, Philippa. 1967. "The Problem of Abortion and the Doctrine of Double Effect." *Oxford Review* 5: 5–15. Reprinted in Foot (1978), pp. 19–32.

———. 1978. *Virtues and Vices.* Oxford: Basil Blackwell.

———. 1985. "Morality, Action, and Outcome." Pp. 23–38 in Ted Honderich, ed., *Morality and Objectivity.* London: Routledge and Kegan Paul.

———. 1984. "Killing and Letting Die." Pp. 177–85 in Jay L. Garfield and Patricia Hennessey, eds., *Abortion: Moral and Legal Perspectives.* Amherst: University of Massachusetts Press.

Ford, Norman M. 1988. *When Did I Begin? Conception of the Human Individual in History, Philosophy and Science.* Cambridge: Cambridge University Press.

Frankena, William K. 1986. "The Ethics of Respect for Persons." *Philosophical Topics* 14: 149–67.

Gervais, Karen Grandstand. 1986. *Redefining Death.* New Haven: Yale University Press.

Glover, Jonathan. 1977. *Causing Death and Saving Lives.* Harmondsworth: Penguin Books.

———. 1988. *I: The Philosophy and Psychology of Personal Identity.* London: Penguin Books.

Glover, Vivette, and Fisk, Nicholas M. 1999. "Fetal Pain: Implications for Research and Practice." *British Journal of Obstetrics and Gynaecology* 106: 881–86.

Graft, Donald. 1997. "Against Strong Speciesism." *Journal of Applied Philosophy* 14: 107–18.

Gregg, Daphna. 1994. *Alzheimer's Disease.* Boston: Harvard Medical School Health Publications Group.

Green, Michael B., and Wikler, Daniel. 1980. "Brain Death and Personal Identity." *Philosophy and Public Affairs* 9: 105–33.

Grover, Dorothy. 1987. "Death and Life." *Canadian Journal of Philosophy* 17: 711–32.

Hacking, Ian. 1995. *Rewriting the Soul: Multiple Personality and the Sciences of Memory.* Princeton: Princeton University Press.

Halpert, Sam. 1995. *Raymond Carver: An Oral Biography.* Iowa City: University of Iowa Press.

Hanser, Matthew. 1995. "Why Are Killing and Letting Die Wrong?" *Philosophy and Public Affairs* 24: 175–201.

———. 1999. "Killing, Letting Die, and Preventing People from Being Saved." *Utilitas* 11: 277–95.

Harman, Gilbert. 1977. *The Nature of Morality.* New York: Oxford University Press.

Harris, John. 1995. "Euthanasia and the Value of Life." Pp. 6–22 in Keown (1995).

Heyd, David. 1992. *Genethics: Moral Issues in the Creation of People.* Berkeley: University of California Press.

Hill, Thomas E. 1991. "Self-Regarding Suicide: A Modified Kantian View." Pp. 85–103 in his *Autonomy and Self-Respect.* Cambridge: Cambridge University Press.

Holland, Alan. 1990. "A Fortnight of My Life is Missing: A Discussion of the Status of the Human 'Pre-embryo'." *Journal of Applied Philosophy* 7: 25–37.

Homer. 1996. *The Odyssey,* trans. Robert Fagles. New York: Penguin.

Hurka, Thomas. 1993. *Perfectionism.* New York: Oxford University Press.

Huxley, Aldous. 1939. *After Many a Summer Dies the Swan.* New York: Harper.

———. 1952. *The Devils of Loudun.* New York: Harper and Brothers.

———. 1959. *Collected Essays.* New York: Harper.

James, William. 1910. "What Makes a Life Significant?" Pp. 265–301 in his *Talks to Teachers on Psychology: And to Students on Some of Life's Ideals.* London: Longman.

Jaworska, Agnieszka. 1999. "Respecting the Margins of Agency: Alzheimer's Patients and the Capacity to Value." *Philosophy and Public Affairs* 28: 105–38.

Johnston, Mark. 1987. "Human Beings." *Journal of Philosophy* 84: 59–83.

Kadish, Sanford. 1976. "Respect for Life and Regard for Rights in the Criminal Law." *California Law Review* 64: 871–901.

Kagan, Shelly. 1989. *The Limits of Morality.* Oxford: Oxford University Press.

Kamm, Frances Myrna. 1987. "The Insanity Defense, Innocent Threats, and Limited Alternatives." *Criminal Justice Ethics* 6: 61–76.

———. 1992. *Creation and Abortion.* New York: Oxford University Press.

———. 1993. *Morality, Mortality.* Vol. 1: *Death and Whom to Save from It.* New York: Oxford University Press.

———. 1995. "Abortion and the Value of Life: A Discussion of *Life's Dominion.*" *Columbia Law Review* 95: 160–221.

———. 1996. *Morality, Mortality.* Vol. 2: *Rights, Duties, and Status.* New York: Oxford University Press.

———. 1999. "Physician-Assisted Suicide, the Doctrine of Double Effect, and the Ground of Value." *Ethics* 109: 586–605.

Kant, Immanuel. 1948. *Groundwork of the Metaphysic of Morals,* trans. H. J. Paton. London: Hutchinson.

———. 1964. *Critique of Pure Reason,* trans. N. Kemp Smith. London: Macmillan.

Kaufmann, Walter. 1961. *The Faith of a Heretic.* Garden City, N.J.: Doubleday and Co.

Kavka, Gregory S. 1982. "The Paradox of Future Individuals." *Philosophy and Public Affairs* 11: 93–112.

Keown, John, ed. 1995. *Euthanasia Examined: Ethical, Clinical, and Legal Perspectives.* Cambridge: Cambridge University Press.

Koestler, Arthur. 1980. "The Right to Die." Pp. 581–83 in his *Bricks to Babel.* London: Hutchinson.

Korein, Julius. 1997. "Ontogenesis of the Brain in the Human Organism: Definitions of Life and Death of the Human Being and Person." *Advances in Bioethics* 2: 1–74.

Kuhse, Helga and Singer, Peter. 1985. *Should the Baby Live?* Oxford: Oxford University Press.

———. 1990. "Individuals, Humans, and Persons: The Issue of Moral Status." Pp. 65–75 in Singer et al. (1990).

———. 1994. "Abortion and Contraception: The Moral Significance of Fertilization." Pp. 145–61 in F. K. Beller and R. F. Weir, eds., *The Beginning of Human Life.* Dordrecht: Kluwer.

Lamb, David. 1985. *Death, Brain Death, and Ethics.* Albany: State University of New York Press.

Levin, Michael. 1987. *Feminism and Freedom.* New Brunswick, N. J.: Transaction Books.

Lewis, David. 1973. *Counterfactuals.* Oxford: Basil Blackwell.

Locke, John. 1894. *An Essay Concerning Human Understanding,* vol. 1, ed. Alexander Campbell Fraser. Oxford: Clarendon Press.

Lockwood, Michael. 1979. "Singer on Killing and the Preference for Life." *Inquiry* 22: 157–70.

———. 1985. "When Does a Life Begin?" Pp. 9–31 in Michael Lockwood, ed., *Moral Dilemmas in Modern Medicine.* Oxford: Oxford University Press.

———. 1988. "Warnock versus Powell (and Harradine): When Does Potentiality Count?" *Bioethics* 2: 187–213.

———. 1994. "Identity Matters." Pp. 60–74 in K. W. M. Fulford et al., eds., *Medicine and Moral Reasoning.* Cambridge: Cambridge University Press.

MacIntyre, Alasdair. 1981. *After Virtue.* London: Duckworth.

Mackie, John. 1976. *Problems From Locke.* Oxford: Clarendon Press.

Margalit, Avishai. 1996. *The Decent Society.* Cambridge, Mass.: Harvard University Press.

Marquis, Don. 1989. "Why Abortion is Immoral." *Journal of Philosophy* 86: 183–203.

Matthews, Gareth B. 1979. "Life and Death as the Arrival and Departure of the Psyche." *American Philosophical Quarterly* 16: 151–57.

Mayerfeld, Jamie. 1999. *Suffering and Moral Responsibility*. New York: Oxford University Press.

McCullagh, Peter. 1993. *Brain Dead, Brain Absent, Brain Donors: Human Subjects of Human Objects?* Chichester: John Wiley and Sons.

McDonagh, Eileen L. 1996. *Breaking the Abortion Deadlock: From Choice to Consent*. New York: Oxford University Press.

McMahan, Jeff. 1978. "Acts, Omissions, and Supererogation." Unpublished.

———. 1981. "Problems of Population Theory." *Ethics* 92: 96–127.

———. 1988. "Death and the Value of Life," *Ethics* 99: 32–61.

———. 1991. "Nonconception and Early Death." Unpublished.

———. 1993a. "Killing, Letting Die, and Withdrawing Aid." *Ethics* 103: 250–79.

———. 1993b. "The Right to Choose an Abortion." *Philosophy and Public Affairs* 22: 331–48.

———. 1994a. "Self-Defense and the Problem of the Innocent Attacker." *Ethics* 104: 252–90.

———. 1994b. "Revising the Doctrine of Double Effect." *Journal of Applied Philosophy* 11, no. 2: 197–208.

———. 1994c. "Innocence, Self-Defense, and Killing in War." *Journal of Political Philosophy* 2: 193–221.

———. 1994d. "Alzheimer's Disease and Personal Survival." Paper presented at the conference "Alzheimer 1994," May, in Bergamo, Italy.

———. 1995a. "Killing and Equality." *Utilitas* 7: 1–29.

———. 1995b. "The Metaphysics of Brain Death." *Bioethics* 9: 91–126.

———. 1995c. "Kavka on Euthanasia." Paper presented at the American Philosophical Association Pacific Division meetings, April, in San Francisco.

———. 1996a. "Cognitive Disability, Misfortune, and Justice." *Philosophy and Public Affairs* 25: 3–34.

———. 1996b. Review of Suzanne Uniacke, *Permissible Killing: The Self-Defense Justification of Homicide. Ethics* 106: 641–44.

———. 1997. "The Limits of National Partiality." Pp. 107–38 in Robert McKim and Jeff McMahan, eds., *The Morality of Nationalism*. New York: Oxford University Press.

———. 1998a. "Brain Death, Cortical Death, and Persistent Vegetative State." Pp. 250–60 in Helga Kuhse and Peter Singer, eds., *A Companion to Bioethics*. Oxford: Blackwell.

———. 1998b. "A Challenge to Common Sense Morality." *Ethics* 108: 394–418.

———. 1998c. "Preferences, Death, and the Ethics of Killing." Pp. 471–502 in Fehige and Wessels (1998).

———. 1998d. "Wrongful Life: Paradoxes in the Morality of Causing People to Exist." Pp. 208–47 in Jules Coleman and Christopher Morris, eds., *Rational Commitment and Social Justice: Essays for Gregory Kavka*. Cambridge: Cambridge University Press. A revised and abridged version of this article is forthcoming in John Harris, ed., *Oxford Readings in Bioethics*. Oxford: Oxford University Press. The argument of the concluding section is clearer in this revised version.

———. 1999. "Cloning, Killing, and Identity," *Journal of Medical Ethics* 25: 77–86.

———. 2000. "Moral Intuition," Pp. 92–110 in Hugh LaFollette, ed., *The Blackwell Guide to Ethical Theory*. Malden, Mass.: Blackwell.

———. 2002. "Animal Ethics." In R. G. Frey and Christopher Wellman, eds., *Companion to Applied Ethics*. Oxford: Blackwell.

McMahan, Jeff, and McKim, Robert. 1993. "The Just War and the Gulf War," *Canadian Journal of Philosophy* 23: 501–541.

Mencken, H. L. 1946. *Treatise on the Gods,* 2d edition. New York: Alfred A. Knopf.

———. 1982. *A Mencken Chrestomathy.* New York: Vintage Books.

Miller, Kenneth. 1996. "Together Forever." *Life,* April: 44–56.

Monestier, Martin. 1987. *Human Oddities.* New York: Citadel Press.

Montague, Phillip. 1981. "Self-Defense and Choosing among Lives." *Philosophical Studies* 40: 207–19.

———. 2000. "Self-Defense and Innocence: Aggressors and Active Threats." *Utilitas* 12: 62–78.

Morowitz, Harold J. and Trefil, James S. 1992. *The Facts of Life: Science and the Abortion Controversy.* New York: Oxford University Press.

Nagel, Thomas. 1979a. *Mortal Questions.* Cambridge: Cambridge University Press.

———. 1979b. "Death." Pp. 1–10 in Nagel (1979a).

———. 1979c. "Brain Bisection and the Unity of Consciousness." Pp. 147–64 in Nagel (1979a).

———. 1986. *The View From Nowhere.* Oxford: Oxford University Press.

Nasar, Sylvia. 1999. "Princeton's New Philosopher Draws a Stir." *New York Times,* April 10: A1 and A18.

Nietzsche, Friedrich. 1973. *Beyond Good and Evil,* trans. R. J. Hollingsdale. Harmondsworth: Penguin.

Nozick, Robert. 1974. *Anarchy, State, and Utopia.* Oxford: Basil Blackwell.

———. 1983. "About Mammals and People." *New York Times Book Review,* November 27: 11, 29–30.

Oderberg, David S. 1997. "Modal Properties, Moral Status, and Identity." *Philosophy and Public Affairs* 26: 259–98.

Olson, Eric T. 1997. *The Human Animal: Personal Identity Without Psychology.* New York: Oxford University Press.

Otsuka, Michael. 1994. "Killing the Innocent in Self-Defense." *Philosophy and Public Affairs* 23: 74–94.

Parfit, Derek. 1971. "Personal Identity." *Philosophical Review* 80: 3–27.

———. 1982. "Future Generations: Further Problems." *Philosophy and Public Affairs* 11: 113–72.

———. 1984. *Reasons and Persons.* Oxford: Oxford University Press. (All references to this book are to the 1987 reprint, which contains various corrections.)

———. 1994. "Persons, Bodies, and Human Beings." Unpublished.

———. 1995. "The Unimportance of Identity." Pp. 13–45 in Henry Harris, ed., *Identity.* Oxford: Clarendon Press.

———. 1999. "Experiences, Subjects, and Conceptual Schemes." *Philosophical Topics* 26: 217–70.

Pavlischek, Keith. 1998. "Abortion Logic and Paternal Responsibilities." Pp. 176–98 in Pojman and Beckwith (1998).

Percy, Walker. 1991. *Signposts in a Strange Land.* New York: Noonday Press.

Persson, Ingmar. 1999. "Our Identity and the Separability of Persons and Organisms." *Dialogue* 38: 519–33.

Plato. 1875. *The Dialogues of Plato,* 5 vols., 2d edition, ed. and trans. Benjamin Jowett. Oxford: Clarendon Press.

Powledge, Tabitha M. 1999. "The Ultimate Baby Bottle." *Scientific American* 10: 96–99.

President's Commission for the Study of Ethical Problems in Medicine and Biomedical and Behavioral Research. 1981. *Defining Death.* Washington, D.C.: United States Government Printing Office.

Quinn, Warren. 1984. "Abortion: Identity and Loss." *Philosophy and Public Affairs* 13: 24–54.

————. 1989. "Actions, Intentions, and Consequences: The Doctrine of Doing and Allowing." *Philosophical Review* 98: 287–312.

Rachels, James. 1986. *The End of Life: Euthanasia and Morality.* Oxford: Oxford University Press.

————. 1990. *Created From Animals: The Moral Implications of Darwinism.* Oxford: Oxford University Press.

————. 1993a. "Euthanasia." Pp. 30–68 in Regan (1993).

————. 1993b. *The Elements of Moral Philosophy,* 2d edition. New York: McGraw-Hill.

Ramachandran, V. S., and Blakeslee, Sandra. 1998. *Phantoms in the Brain.* New York: William Morrow and Co.

Ramsey, Paul. 1978. *Ethics at the Edges of Life.* New Haven, Conn.: Yale University Press.

Rawls, John. 1972. *A Theory of Justice.* Oxford: Clarendon Press.

Regan, Tom. 1983. *The Case for Animal Rights.* London: Routledge and Kegan Paul.

————., ed. 1993. *Matters of Life and Death,* 3d edition. New York: McGraw-Hill.

Reichlin, Massimo. 1997. "The Argument From Potential: A Reappraisal." *Bioethics* 11: 1–23.

Reiman, Jeffrey. 1999. *Abortion and the Ways We Value Human Life.* Lanham, Md.: Rowman and Littlefield.

Robinson, John. 1988. "Personal Identity and Survival." *Journal of Philosophy* 85: 319–28.

Rovane, Carol. 1994. Critical Notice of Peter Unger, *Identity, Consciousness, and Value. Canadian Journal of Philosophy* 24: 119–34.

Sacks, Oliver. 1987. *The Man Who Mistook his Wife for a Hat.* New York: Perennial Library.

———— 1995. *An Anthropologist on Mars.* New York: Vintage Books.

Scanlon, T. M. 1993. "Partisan for Life." *New York Review of Books,* July 15: 45–50.

————. 1998. *What We Owe to Each Other.* Cambridge, Mass.: Harvard University Press.

Schaefer, Naomi. 1998. "Professor Pleasure - or Professor Death?" *Wall Street Journal,* September 25.

Schechtman, Marya. 1996. *The Constitution of Selves.* Ithaca, N.Y.: Cornell University Press.

Scheffler, Samuel. 1982. *The Rejection of Consequentialism.* Oxford: Oxford University Press.

Schopenhauer, Arthur. 1966. *The World as Will and Representation,* 2 vols., trans. E. F. J. Payne. New York: Dover Publications.

———— 1974. *Parerga and Paralipomena,* 2 vols., trans. E. F. J. Payne. Oxford: Clarendon Press.

Searle, John R. 1992. *The Rediscovery of the Mind.* Cambridge, Mass.: MIT Press.

Seidler, Victor J. 1986. *Kant, Respect and Injustice: The Limits of Liberal Moral Theory.* London: Routledge & Kegan Paul.

Sharlet, Jeff. 2000. "Why Are We Afraid of Peter Singer?" *Chronicle of Higher Education,* March 10: A21–23.

Shawlot, William, and Behringer, Richard R. 1995. "Requirement for Lim 1 in Head-Organization Function." *Nature* 374: 425–30.

Shewmon, D. Alan. 1992. "'Brain Death': A Valid Theme with Invalid Variations, Blurred by Semantic Ambiguity." Pp. 23–51 in R. J. White et al., eds., *The Determination of Brain Death and Its Relationship to Human Death.* Vatican City: Pontifical Academy of Sciences.

————. 1997. "Recovery from 'Brain Death': A Neurologist's Apologia." *Linacre Quarterly* 64: 30–96.

————. 1998. "'Brain-Stem Death', 'Brain Death' and Death: A Critical Re-Evaluation of the Purported Equivalence." *Issues in Law and Medicine* 14: 125–45.

————. 2001, forthcoming. "The Brain and Somatic Integration: Insights Into the Standard Biological Rationale for Equating 'Brain Death' with Death." *Journal of Medicine and Philosophy* 26.

Shoemaker, Sydney. 1984. "A Materialist's Account." Pp. 67–1332 in Shoemaker and Swinburne (1984).

Shoemaker, Sydney, and Swinburne, Richard. 1984. *Personal Identity.* Oxford: Basil Blackwell.

Silverstein, Harry S. 1987. "On a Woman's 'Responsibility' for the Fetus." *Social Theory and Practice* 13: 103–19

Singer, Peter. 1993a. *Practical Ethics,* 2d edition. Cambridge: Cambridge University Press.

———. 1993b. "Animals and the Value of Life." Pp. 280–321 in Regan (1993).

———. 1994. *Rethinking Life and Death: The Collapse of Our Traditional Ethics.* New York: St. Martin's Press.

Singer, Peter, and Dawson, Karen. 1988. "IVF Technology and the Argument From Potential." *Philosophy and Public Affairs* 17: 87–104.

Singer, Peter and Kuhse, Helga. 1993. "More on Euthanasia: A Response to Pauer-Studer." *The Monist* 76: 158–174.

Singer, Peter et. al., eds. 1990. *Embryo Experimentation: Ethical, Legal and Social Issues.* Cambridge: Cambridge University Press.

Smilansky, Saul. 2000. *Free Will and Illusion.* Oxford: Oxford University Press.

Snow, C. P. 1966. *Variety of Men.* New York: Scribners.

———. 1978. *The Realists.* London: Readers Union.

Snowdon, P. F. 1991. "Personal Identity and Brain Transplants." Pp. 109–26 in David Cockburn, ed., *Human Beings.* Cambridge: Cambridge University Press.

Specter, Michael. 1999. "The Dangerous Philosopher." *New Yorker,* September 6: 46–55.

Steinbock, Bonnie. 1992. *Life Before Birth: The Moral and Legal Status of Embryos and Fetuses.* New York: Oxford University Press.

Stone, Jim. 1987. "Why Potentiality Matters." *Canadian Journal of Philosophy* 17: 815–30.

Swift, Jonathan. 1941. *Gulliver's Travels,* in *The Prose Works of Jonathan Swift,* vol. 11. Oxford: Basil Blackwell.

Swinburne, Richard. 1984. "Personal Identity: The Dualist Theory." Pp. 1–66 in Shoemaker and Swinburne (1984).

Tajfel, Henri. 1970. "Experiments in Intergroup Discrimination." *Scientific American* 223: 96–102.

Talbot, Margaret. 1999. "The Little White Bombshell." *New York Times Magazine,* July 11: 39–43, 48, and 61–63.

Thackeray, William Makepeace. 1937. *Vanity Fair.* Garden City, N.J.: Garden City Publishing Co.

Thomson, Judith Jarvis. 1971. "A Defense of Abortion." *Philosophy and Public Affairs* 1: 47–66.

———. 1986. "The Trolley Problem." Pp. 94–116 in her *Rights, Restitution, and Risk: Essays in Moral Theory.* Cambridge, Mass.: Harvard University Press.

———. 1987. "Ruminations on an Account of Personal Identity." Pp. 215–40 in Judith Jarvis Thomson, ed., *On Being and Saying: Essays for Richard Cartwright.* Cambridge, Mass.: MIT Press.

———. 1990. *The Realm of Rights.* Cambridge, Mass.: Harvard University Press.

———. 1991. "Self-Defense." *Philosophy and Public Affairs* 20: 283–310.

———. 1999. "Physician-Assisted Suicide: Two Moral Arguments." *Ethics* 109: 497–518.

Tolstoy, Leo. 1981. *The Death of Ivan Ilych,* trans. Lynn Solotaroff. New York: Bantam Books.

Tooley, Michael. 1973. "A Defense of Abortion and Infanticide." Pp. 51–91 in Joel Feinberg, ed., *The Problem of Abortion,* 2d edition. Belmont, Calif.: Wadsworth.

———. 1983. *Abortion and Infanticide.* Oxford: Oxford University Press.

Truog, Robert D., and Fletcher, John C. 1990. "Brain Death and the Anencephalic Newborn." *Bioethics* 4: 199–215.

Twain, Mark. 1996. *The Tragedy of Pudd'nhead Wilson and the Comedy Those Extraordinary Twins.* New York: Oxford University Press.

Unger, Peter. 1990. *Identity, Consciousness and Value.* New York: Oxford University Press.

Uniacke, Suzanne. 1994. *Permissible Killing: The Self-Defense Justification of Homicide.* Cambridge: Cambridge University Press.

———. 1997. "Replaceability and Infanticide." *Journal of Value Inquiry* 31: 153–66.

Uniacke, Suzanne, and McCloskey, H. J. 1992. "Peter Singer and Non-Voluntary 'Euthanasia': Tripping Down the Slippery Slope." *Journal of Applied Philosophy* 9: 203–19.

van Inwagen, Peter. 1990. *Material Beings.* Ithaca, N.Y.: Cornell University Press.

Veatch, Robert M. 1988. "Whole-brain, Neocortical, and Higher Brain Related Concepts." Pp. 171–186 in Zaner (1988).

Velleman, J. David. 1991. "Well-Being and Time." *Pacific Philosophical Quarterly* 72: 48–77.

———. 1999a. "Love as a Moral Emotion." *Ethics* 109: 338–74.

———. 1999b. "A Right of Self-Termination?" *Ethics* 109: 606–28.

Nicholas Wade. 1999. "Embryo Cell Research: A Clash of Values." *New York Times,* July 2: A11.

Walen, Alec. 1997. "Consensual Sex Without Assuming the Risk of Carrying an Unwanted Fetus: Another Foundation for the Right to an Abortion." *Brooklyn Law Review* 63: 1051–1140.

Weiss, Rick. 1997. "Aging." *National Geographic* 192, no. 5: 2–31.

White, Stephen L. 1989. "Metapsychological Relativism and the Self." *Journal of Philosophy* 86: 298–323.

Wiggins, David. 1967. *Identity and Spatio-Temporal Continuity.* Oxford: Basil Blackwell.

———. 1980. *Sameness and Substance.* Oxford: Basil Blackwell.

Wikler, Daniel. 1979. "Paternalism and the Mildly Retarded," *Philosophy and Public Affairs* 8: 377–92.

Wilkes, Kathleen V. 1988. *Real People: Personal Identity Without Thought Experiments.* Oxford: Clarendon Press.

Williams, Bernard. 1973a. *Problems of the Self.* Cambridge: Cambridge University Press.

———. 1973b. "The Self and the Future." Pp. 46–63 in Williams (1973a).

———. 1973c. "The Makropulos Case: Reflections on the Tedium of Immortality." Pp. 82–100 in Williams (1973a).

———. 1973d. "The Idea of Equality." Pp. 230–49 in Williams (1973a).

———. 1986. "Hylomorphism." Pp. 189–99 in Michael Woods, ed., *Oxford Studies in Ancient Philosophy,* vol. 4. Oxford; Oxford University Press.

Wilson, A. N. 1988. *Tolstoy.* New York: W.W. Norton.

Wilson, Barbara A., and Wearing, Deborah. 1995. "Prisoner of Consciousness: a State of Just Awakening Following Herpes Simplex Encephalitis." Pp. 14–30 in Ruth Campbell and Martin A. Conway, eds., *Broken Memories.* Cambridge, Mass.: Blackwell.

Wollheim, Richard. 1984. *The Thread of Life.* Cambridge: Cambridge University Press.

Wright, Robert. 1994. *The Moral Animal.* New York: Vintage Books.

Zaner, Richard M., ed. 1988. *Death: Beyond Whole-Brain Criteria.* Dordrecht: Kluwer.

INDEX OF CASES

Aborted Rescue, the, 379–80, 384

Accidental Nudge, the, 367–68, 372, 376, 387

Accident Victim, the, 128–32, 141, 173

Advance Directive, the, 497–503

Alzheimer's Patient, the, 283–87

Benefactor, the, 173–74

Brain-Damaged Individual, the, 151, 153, 164, 325–28

Brainstem Transplant, the, 20

Bright, 234–35, 249

Cavalry Officer, the, 118–20, 123

Case 1 (Otsuka), 407–10

Case 2 (Otsuka), 407–10

Case 3 (Otsuka), 407–9

Case 4, 409

Case One (Parfit), 70–72

Case Two (Parfit), 70–72

Cerebrum Transplant, the, 21, 34

Cheerful, 234

Choice between Deaths, the, 185–87, 290–94, 299

Choice between Lives, the, 185–87, 290, 299

Cure, the, 77–78, 174

Deluded Pessimist, the, 257–58

Dependent Child, the, 392–98

Deprogramming, 66, 79

Division, 23–24, 40–43, 48, 51, 52, 56–59, 64, 83, 88

Double Replication, 58–59, 64

Dull, 234–35, 249

Enemy, the, 379–80, 388

Fetus with a Chemical Deficit, the, 309–10, 312, 314

Fetus with Cerebral Deficits, the, 294, 309–12, 314–15, 317–18, 319–29

Fortunate, 234

Fusion, 83

Geriatric Patient, the, 117–20, 133–37, 141

Imperfect Drug, 365–68, 372

Inadvertent Attacker, the, 403, 405

Incurable Patient, the, 115–116

Involuntary Benefactor, the, 363–64, 373, 378–82, 391–92, 393–94, 398

Involuntary Sterilization, 281–82

Loss Followed by Transplantation, 22

Loss of One Hemisphere, 22

Malpractice, 367

Melancholy, 234

Mistaken Attacker, the, 402, 403

Multiple Replication, 57–58

Normal Fetus, the, 309, 310, 312–13, 314, 315, 318

Nuclear Attack, the, 58

Old, 234–35, 237, 238, 239, 244, 245, 247, 249

Pedestrian, the, 111–12, 114

Physical Spectrum, the, 71–72

Pipe Sealer, the, 381

Prenatal Blinding, 294–96, 301–2

Prenatal Injury, 280, 281–82

Prenatal Retardation, 294, 323–28

Prenatal Therapy, 282

Progeria Patient, the, 134–36, 141

Sperm Donor, the, 226, 376, 396

Spontaneous Division, 193, 297, 301

Suicide Mission, the, 57–58

Superchimp, the, 147–49, 152–53, 211,
    216, 324–27

Teletransportation, 56, 61, 68–69, 297
Three-Option Trolley Case, 237
Trapped Miners, the, 405–6

Unfortunate, 234
Unintended Replication, 61, 65

Whole-Body Transplant, the, 20, 31–34

Young, 234–35, 237, 238, 239, 244, 247,
    249
Young Cancer Patient, the, 106–7, 108–11,
    114, 128
Young Pedestrian, the, 117–23, 128–31,
    132, 133, 141

GENERAL INDEX

abortion, 17, 199, 205, 210, 267–421, 436, 451, 489
  early, 267–69, 270–71, 272
  late, 269–80, 288, 489
  merely extractive, 384–92, 394
  "partial birth," 288
abortion pill. *See* RU-486
achievement, importance of, 137–40, 173, 242
adaptation, 294–302, 322, 323–24
additive two-tier view, 471–72
adoption, 341, 344, 347, 359–60, 373–74, 376, 392–93, 396
advance directives, 449, 477, 497–503
afterlife, 9, 10–11, 15, 29, 98, 99, 463
Alzheimer's disease, 15, 43–44, 45, 47–48, 50–51, 54–55, 64–68, 73, 83, 279, 493–503
American Medical Association (AMA), 208
amnesia, 9, 76, 77, 493
Anatomy of Melancholy, The (Burton), 16
anencephalic infants, 147, 208, 210, 214, 225–26, 230–31, 251, 336, 361, 450–55, 468
animals
  badness of death for, 182, 195–98
  causing suffering of, 199–203, 229–30
  consciousness in, 18, 268
  and euthanasia, 199–203, 390–91, 474–75, 487–93
  experimentation on, 18, 200, 203, 207, 222, 224
  Kantian view of, 246, 252
  killing of, 189–232, 234, 243–46, 270–71, 276, 348–49, 360–62, 390–91, 420
  moral status of, 203–32, 234, 251, 272–73, 275, 332, 346, 468–69, 474–75

and overall lifelong fortune, 145–61, 162–63
as pets, 207, 220, 224, 226, 231–32, 390–91
as potential persons, 312, 316, 319–22, 324, 326, 327–28
Rawls's view of, 253–54
and the soul, 13, 17–18
transgenic, 212–13, 452–54
Anthropocentrism, 206, 209–28
Aquinas, Thomas, 10, 12, 13, 16
Aristotle, 10, 12, 13, 14, 175
assisted suicide. *See* suicide, assisted
assumption of correlative variation, 190, 194, 270–71
assumption of proportional significance, 223–25
assumption of proportional variation, 190, 194
Asymmetry, the, 300, 353–54, 492
autonomy, 202, 204, 211, 235, 245, 250, 263, 272–73, 298, 331–32, 464
  as the basis of the worth of persons, 252, 254, 256–59, 260–64, 309, 473
  and paternalism, 287–88

Bayley, John, 82
Bennett, Jonathan, 408, 410
Bernat, James L., 428–29, 432
birth, significance of, 8
brain death, 208, 350, 423–24, 426–43, 446, 448, 450
brain grafting, 84–85
brain life, 436–37
brainstem, 20–21, 424, 427, 431–34, 440–42, 450
brain transplantation, 20–24, 31–35, 429
Brodkey, Harold, 139
Broome, John, 111

533

Buddhism, 82
Burns, Robert, 75
Burton, Robert, 16
Butler, Samuel, 484

Capacity Condition, 274–75, 348, 488–89
capital punishment, 236, 466–67, 470, 471
Carter, W. R., 89, 91–92
Carver, Raymond, 138
Catholic theology, 4, 10, 12
chimeras, 212–13, 454
Christian theology, 4, 10, 16, 463
cloning, 26, 454–55
Coetzee, J. M., 200
coma
    deep, 443, 449–50, 498
    irreversible, 423, 440–43
    see also persistent vegetative state
commissurotomy, 19–20, 23, 24, 36, 38, 86,
    87–88
commonsense intuitions
    about abortion, 274, 288, 289, 344, 389
    about anencephalic infants, 208
    about animals, 204, 206, 210, 219
        227–28, 229, 231, 233, 475
    about causing people to exist, 353–54,
        356
    about death, 104, 167, 179, 426–28
    about duties to strangers, 223–25
    about egoistic concern, 66, 74, 78, 496
    about equality, 249, 254
    about euthanasia, 474
    about infants and infanticide, 163,
        340–42, 362, 374
    about killing and letting die, 360
    about killing an Innocent Bystander, 411
    about killing in self-defense, 413
    about mentally retarded human beings,
        206, 219, 222, 227–28, 229, 231,
        233
    about parental responsibility, 374–75
    about personal survival, 21, 42, 54,
    about potential, 319
    about suicide, 458
    about the wrongness of killing people,
        235, 236, 238–40
commonsense morality, 208, 219, 220,
    223–25, 233, 235, 236, 288, 353–54,
    356, 360, 362, 411, 490–91
competence, as a range property, 250–51

conception
    as the beginning of the existence of a
        human organism, 4, 25–29
    as the beginning of the existence of the
        soul, 16
    as the beginning of our existence, 4, 7–9
consciousness, capacity for
    development of, 267–68
    and egoistic concern, 69
    as necessary for a capacity for well-being,
        147
    as necessary for our existence, 67, 68,
        73–74, 85, 423–24, 439–43
    as necessary for the possession of inter-
        ests, 330, 445, 447, 451
    and the presence of the cartesian soul, 15,
        16, 24
consent, 236, 364, 373–74, 444, 457, 470,
    486
Consistent Elitism, 206–7, 209, 228
constitution, 89–91, 93
contraception, 267, 269, 306, 339, 392, 397
Convergent Assimilation, 206, 209, 228–32,
    260
counterfactuals, 99–100, 113–14, 119
Criterion, the, 298–302, 324, 327
critical interests, 498, 501
Cruzan, Nancy, 423, 464
cryogenics, 438
culpability, 236, 401–4, 412, 415, 418–19
Culpable Attacker, 401–4, 412–13, 414–15
Culpable Cause, 406
Culver, Charles M., 425

Darwinism, 166–68
Davis, Michael, 370
Davis, N. Ann, 415–16
dead donor rule, 431
death
    badness of, 95–188, 241–42, 369–70
    cardio-pulmonary criterion of, 426
    cerebral, 424, 439–40, 443, 444
    concept of, 98, 424–26
    cortical, 439–40, 444
    of fetus, 78, 106, 165–85, 192, 199, 274,
        279–80
    higher-brain criterion of, 424, 427, 444,
        451
    of infant, 78, 162–65, 165–85, 192, 199
    neocortical, 424

Death of Ivan Ilych, The (Tolstoy), 97–98

defeaters, 236, 248

dementia, 3, 43, 45, 47, 66, 73, 74, 79, 82, 104, 172, 175, 204, 227, 260, 279, 298, 479, 480, 493–503

deprogramming, 66, 68, 69, 79, 171–74

Descartes, René, 10, 15–16, 18

desert, 168–69, 181, 183–84

desire
  and the badness of death, 181–84, 197–98, 274–75, 352–53
  categorical, 182–83
  as a prudential unity relation, 182
  and the wrongness of killing, 274–75, 347–48, 352

determinism, 255–56

dicephalus, 35–39, 53, 61–62, 87–88

disability, 280–88, 294–302, 318, 322, 347, 460

discounting misfortunes for previous gains, 140–45

division, 19, 27, 58–59, 192–93, 297, 298

division of the burden, 404, 411–12

doing and allowing, 236, 259, 323, 391, 461, 482

Donceel, Joseph, S. J., 12

Dorff, Rabbi Elliot N., 313

Dostoyevsky, Fyodor, 340

Double Effect, Doctrine of, 408, 456

Down's syndrome, 340–41

dualism
  cartesian, 88
  radical, 91, 426

Dworkin, Ronald, 178–79, 210–11, 212, 330–38, 449, 464–66, 470, 471, 477, 498, 500–502

egoistic concern, 41–43, 48–59, 69–86, 102–3, 170–72, 192, 284, 352–53, 446, 449, 494–95

Einstein, Albert, 138, 155–57, 161, 263

Embodied Mind Account of Egoistic Concern, 68–86, 174, 284, 297, 301

Embodied Mind Account of Identity, 66–94, 98, 101, 267, 268, 271, 279, 303, 426, 427, 441, 446, 447, 449, 453, 494

embryo experimentation, 436

Epicurus, 96

Epistemological Problem, 106–7

equality, 155–56, 160–61, 203–9, 231, 233–65, 469–72

Equal Wrongness Thesis, 235, 237–40, 247–48, 336–38, 470–72, 474

euthanasia, 125, 199–200, 236, 332, 334, 338, 448, 455–93
  active, 457, 460, 462
  concept of, 456–57
  "convenience," 452, 457
  involuntary, 457, 464
  nonvoluntary, 345, 457, 464, 485–93
  passive, 457, 459–60
  side effects of, 485–86
  voluntary, 331–32, 449–50, 457, 462, 464, 483, 485–86

excuses, 401, 402, 417, 419

experiential interests, 498, 501

Extreme Case, 400, 405, 409, 411, 414, 416, 418, 419

Feldman, Fred, 105–6, 119–20, 123, 168–70, 178, 181

Finnis, John, 215, 216, 465, 468

Foot, Philippa, 408

Ford, Norman, 11

forfeiture, 404, 417, 418, 470

fortune
  accounts of, 145–65, 325–28
  defined, 145
  diachronic, 145
  synchronic, 145

free will, 254–56, 468

friendship, 285

functional continuity of the brain, 68–69, 73–74, 75, 79, 86, 172, 193, 198, 298, 321, 446, 449, 495

functionalism, 88

fusion, 26, 83–85, 297, 298–99

genetic therapy, 81, 150, 152–54, 211, 315, 317–24

Gert, Bernard, 425

God, 12, 18, 19, 210, 256, 272, 332, 333, 335, 463

Goya, Francisco, 149

gradualism, 278–80, 308, 494–95

Grandin, Temple, 200–201, 203

Great Chain of Being, 160

Green, Michael B., 69, 432–33

Guillain-Barré Syndrome, 433–34
guilt, 236
Gulliver's Travels (Swift), 99

Hanser, Matthew, 122–23
Harm-Based Account of the wrongness of
    killing, 191–95, 232–33, 243, 270,
    272, 273, 274, 445–46, 464
Hensel, Abigail and Brittany, 35–38,
    87–88
Herodotus, 447
Hill, Jr., Thomas E., 474, 475
Hölderlin, Friedrich, 137–38
Homer, 447
hominization, 12, 14, 17
    delayed, 12, 13, 16
    immediate, 13
Huxley, Aldous, 82, 197, 500
hydranencephalic infants, 440–41
hylomorphism, 10–14
hysterectomy, 383–84
hysterotomy, 384

Iliad, The (Homer), 447
immortality, 98–104, 126–27
impartiality and partiality, 218–28
impersonal value, 246, 299, 301, 329, 330,
    332–38, 348–62, 371, 464, 473, 477
incest, 271, 330
incremental value, 330, 332–33
indeterminacy, 28, 41, 44–46, 48, 72,
    264–65, 268, 272, 494
infanticide, 199, 205, 279, 338–62
Inheritance Strategy, 120–27, 128, 129, 136
innocence, 242, 399, 402, 466–68, 470
Innocent Attacker, 401–4, 412–13
Innocent Bystander, 402, 405–10, 416, 418
Innocent Cause, 406, 419
Innocent Threat, 401, 412, 413–14
instrumental value, 251, 330–31, 332, 334,
    335, 464
intention, moral significance of, 236, 407–8,
    410–11, 455–56, 467–68, 470
Intrinsic Potential Account of fortune,
    153–59, 160–61, 164–65, 326–28
intrinsic value, 330, 332–38
Intrinsic Worth Account of the wrongness of
    killing, 243–65
intuitions, status of, 104, 238, 246–47, 251.
    See also commonsense intuitions

investment as a basis of value, 168, 176–79,
    181, 183, 283, 333–35, 465–66, 467
the isolated subject, 55, 65–66
IUD (intra-uterine device), 384

James, William, 252
Johnson, Samuel, 82
justice, 242, 245, 253–54, 402–5, 412, 413,
    414–15, 418–21, 467, 472
Justice-Based Account of self-defense,
    401–5, 412–14, 418–21

Kamm, Frances, 370–71, 397, 481
Kant, Immanuel, 9, 245–46, 252–53,
    254–55, 259, 473–84
Kaufmann, Walter, 137–39
Keats, John, 104
Kevorkian, Dr. Jack, 460–61
killing
    and letting die, 191–92, 234, 235–37,
        370, 378–92, 394, 459–62
    wrongness of, 95–96, 189–265, 270,
        336–38, 347–62, 444–45, 461,
        46–63, 471–72, 477
Koestler, Arthur, 459
Korein, Julius, 267, 424
Korsakov's syndrome, 76–77
Kuhse, Helga, 26–27

Lamb, David, 425, 428, 429
letting die. *See* killing and letting die
Levin, Michael, 387
Lewis, David, 113–14, 119
liberal egalitarianism, 240, 243
Life Comparative Account of the badness of
    death, 105–6, 119, 165, 168–70, 176,
        186–87, 192, 274, 290–91
life span
    average, 124
    maximum, 124–26
    normal, 124
locked-in state, 9, 16, 431–35, 437
Locke, John, 6, 9–10
Lockwood, Michael, 69, 177, 268, 369
Longevity Pill, 143–44
Lovejoy, A. O., 160

MacIntyre, Alasdair, 174, 176
Margalit, Avishai, 254–56
Marquis, Don, 190–91, 270–71, 272

Martians, 217, 222, 227, 232
meat eating, 203, 222, 224
memory, 16, 21, 22, 39, 44, 45, 46, 59–62,
    67, 69, 75, 76–77, 82, 84, 86, 173, 493
Mencken, H. L., 10–11, 195, 197
mentally retarded human beings, 146, 153,
    155, 161, 164, 203–32, 252, 254,
    309–29, 340–41, 371, 468
Metaphysical Problem, 107–17, 195
mixed two-tier view, 471
moral character, 162, 236, 238–39
moral personality, 253
morality of interests, 245, 253, 254, 302,
    328
morality of respect, 245–65, 272–73,
    275–76, 302, 303, 309, 316, 324, 339,
    346, 360, 398, 470
motivation, moral significance of, 236
Mozart, Wolfgang Amadeus, 138–41
multiple personality disorder, 87, 88
Murdoch, Iris, 82

Nagel, Thomas, 115, 117, 129, 132, 133,
    370
narrative unity, 174–80, 182, 183–84,
    197–98, 283, 499
nationalism, 221
Nietzsche, Friedrich, 263
nonconception, 170–71, 199, 278, 279
nonlethal harms, 247, 271, 280
Nonresponsible Attacker, 401, 404–5, 413,
    416
Nonresponsible Cause, 406, 409
Nonresponsible Projectile, 401, 407–9
Nonresponsible Threat, 401, 404–5,
    413–21
Nonresponsible Victim, 419
Nozick, Robert, 218, 256–57
numbers, moral significance of, 236, 244,
    247, 412–13

Oderberg, David, 26, 27
Odyssey, The (Homer), 447
Olson, Eric, 30
organism, human
    beginning of the existence of, 12, 24–29,
        436–38
    death of, 424–26, 428–39
    killing of, 268–69, 443–50
    relation of person to, 89–94

as what we essentially are, 4, 11, 24–39,
    46, 53, 56, 90, 350, 428, 443, 450
organizational continuity of the brain,
    68–69, 74–82, 172, 193, 198, 449, 495
organ transplantation, 20, 208, 212–13,
    359–61, 427, 431, 443–48, 450–55
other-defense, 400, 404, 414–18, 419–20
Otsuka, Michael, 407–9
overall lifelong fortune, 145–65
overall losses in death, 127–35, 136,
    173–74
overdetermination. *See* Problem of
    Overdetermination

pain, 229–30, 389, 458, 495, 502
Paradox, the, 185–88, 290–93
parental responsibility, 373–78, 393, 396
Parerga and Paralipomena (Schopenhauer),
    125
Parfit, Derek, 7, 20, 39, 40, 41–43, 44–45,
    47, 51, 54, 56–59, 61, 63, 64, 70–72,
    76, 83, 91, 171, 299, 305, 355, 495–96,
    501
parthenogenesis, 26
paternalism, 287–88
paternal responsibility, 368, 397–98
Peak Capacity Account of fortune, 150–53,
    164, 325–26, 327
Percy, Walker, 3–5, 7, 25
persistent vegetative state (PVS), 423–24,
    425, 427–28, 434, 435, 440–41,
    443–50, 464
Personal Priority View, 219–20
personal value, 330–32, 334, 335, 464, 466,
    477
person, concept of, 6, 190
    as phase sortal, 46, 303, 425
    as substance sortal, 45, 46, 55
personhood, moral significance of, 275, 303,
    347–48, 350–62
physical continuity of the brain, 68–73, 172,
    193, 198, 298, 321, 449, 495
pluralism about value, 138–39, 182–83
polytypic species, 212
population theory, 299–300, 491–92
post-persons, 47–51, 54–55, 297, 493
potential, 205, 269, 273, 302–29, 465
    in the evaluation of fortune, 151–59,
        164–65
    extrinsic, 152, 311–16, 327, 328

potential, *(continued)*
  identity-preserving, 304–8, 309–16
  impersonal value of, 306, 335–36
  instrumental value of, 306, 308
  interest in the realization of, 305, 306, 307
  intrinsic, 152–53, 308, 311–16, 326, 327
  nonidentity, 304–308
  as a source of moral status, 254, 260, 306, 308–16
potential persons, 302–16, 370
preformationism, 14
pregnancy, as bodily invasion, 399
prenatal injury, 280–88, 294–302, 318, 323–28, 487
prenatal screening, 347, 358, 451
pre-persons, 46–48, 55, 270, 297
Previous Gain Account of the badness of death, 136–40
Princeton University, 346
Problem of Comparison, 98, 195
Problem of Overdetermination, 117–27, 136, 173–74
Problem of the Terminus, 123–27, 132–33, 136
proportionality, 399, 404, 411, 412–13, 414
prudence, 283–88, 458
prudential unity relations, 42–43, 74, 78, 79–82, 101, 105–6, 170, 172–74, 176, 183–85, 193–95, 198–99, 202, 204, 233, 274–77, 283–84, 298, 353, 487, 488, 492, 495–96, 499, 500–503
Psychological Account of Egoistic Concern, 42–43, 48–66, 69–71, 79, 297
Psychological Account of Identity, 39–66, 69, 79, 269–70, 493
  defined, 40
  narrow version, 56, 63, 69
  wide version, 56, 62, 63
psychological connectedness, 43–45, 49–51, 54–56, 73–82, 102, 171–72
  defined, 39
  as prudential unity relation, 42–43
  "real," 63, 66
psychological connection, concept of, 39, 59–65, 74
psychological continuity, 9, 15, 43–66, 69, 73–82, 102, 171–72, 269–70, 493
  broad, 50, 54, 56, 66, 68

defined, 39–40
  as prudential unity relation, 42, 277, 298, 321, 446, 495
  "real," 63, 66
  strong, 50, 55
  weak, 50
psychological unity, 74–82, 98, 172–74, 179, 193, 198, 475
pure two-tier view, 470–71

quasi-memory, 48, 59–62
quickening, 8, 17, 272
Quinn, Warren, 91, 245–46, 256–59, 260, 278–80

Rachels, James, 190–91, 425–26, 445–46
Radical Egalitarianism, 206, 228
Ramsey, Paul, 240
range property, 249–51, 261–62
rape, 271, 330, 345, 362, 364, 365, 395, 399, 420
rationality, capacity for, 256, 261, 272–73
  as the basis of human worth, 252, 309
  as what distinguishes human beings from animals, 13, 14, 204, 211, 235
rational nature, 473–74, 476–81
Rawls, John, 249–50, 253–54
Realism Condition, 133–35, 136
Reasons and Persons (Parfit), 56
reductionism, 5, 28, 47–48, 51
Rehnquist, William, 332, 465, 466
Reiman, Jeffrey, 313
Rembrandt van Rijn, 335, 337
replaceability argument (Singer), 347–59
replication, 55–59, 66, 68, 69–70
respect for persons, requirement of, 227, 242–65, 276, 389, 464, 470, 473–85, 486
responsibility, moral, 236, 242, 401–11, 413, 415, 418–21
Responsibility Objection (to the Thomson argument), 364–72, 394–96
reticular formation, 21, 85–86, 427, 432, 441–43
retreat, 403–404, 411
retroactive effects on well-being, 176–80, 183, 197–98, 502
right to die, 332

right to life, 207–209, 256, 258, 303,
  331–32, 344, 347, 349, 362, 398, 417,
  418, 464, 470–72
ring species, 214
RU-486, 416

Sacks, Oliver, 76–77, 200–201
sanctity of life, 17, 207–8, 210–11, 243,
  268, 270, 444, 447, 450, 477, 483
  as the basis of an objection to abortion,
    329–38
  as the basis of an objection to euthanasia,
    338, 464–72
Scalia, Antonin, 243, 332, 465, 466
Scanlon, Thomas, 215–16, 217, 218, 246
Schechtman, Marya, 41
Schopenhauer, Arthur, 96–97, 125
self-consciousness, 45, 204, 235, 256, 261,
  272–73, 309
  as a necessary condition of our existence,
    349–50
  as necessary for egoistic concern about
    the future, 352–53
  capacity for, 6, 211, 473
self-defense
  against a Nonresponsible Threat, 405–11
  as a justification for abortion, 273,
    398–421
  killing in, 236, 399–421, 466–67, 486
  national, 399
self-regarding duties, 286–88
sentient creature, 75–77, 475–76
Shakespeare, William, 285
Shaw, George Bernard, 104
Shewmon, Alan, 423, 430, 433, 439
Shoemaker, Sidney, 89
sibling species, 212
Silverstein, Harry, 366
Singer, Peter, 26–27, 76, 346–62, 444–45,
  446, 450, 451, 475
slavery, 480–81
slippery slope, 486
Smith, Reverend Sydney, 82
Smith, Susan, 237, 377
Snow, C. P., 100, 138
Socrates, 96
sortal concepts, 6–7, 278, 425
  phase sortal, 6–7, 24, 30, 46, 303, 304
  substance sortal, 6–7, 24, 45, 46, 55, 279

soul, the, 5, 8, 30, 209–10, 213, 216–17,
  256, 272, 332, 334, 428, 443, 450
  cartesian, 10, 14–20, 23–24, 56
  featureless, 9–10, 16
  hylomorphic, 10–14
special relations, 207, 217–28, 229, 230,
  231–32, 236–37, 248, 285–86, 329,
  343–44, 345, 373–78, 386, 391, 415,
  416
  instrumental significance of, 220–22
  intrinsic significance of, 220–21, 225–27
speciesism, 214, 268, 360, 390
species membership
  criteria of, 211–14
  moral significance of, 209–28, 273, 325,
    454
  relevance to fortune, 144–45, 146–49,
    157–58, 160–61
  as a special relation, 217–28
Species Norm Account of fortune, 146–49,
  157–58, 160–61, 215–16, 323–24, 327
spontaneous abortion, 165–66, 489–90
stem cells, 454–55
strong divergence (between interests and
  time-relative interests), 297
suffering, 98, 134–35, 159, 188, 199–203,
  207, 218, 222, 325, 369–70, 475–76,
  481, 482, 484, 486, 487–93, 495
suicide, 236, 332, 458–64, 465, 466–85, 497
  assisted, 236, 458–60
  concept of, 455–56
  passive, 458, 482
supererogation, 224, 231
Supreme Court, 243, 332, 423, 464
Swift, Jonathan, 99, 104, 127
Swinburne, Richard, 15–16
syngamy, 25, 436

Tennyson, Alfred, 99, 101
terminus. *See* Problem of the Terminus
Thackeray, William Makepeace, 139
Theory of Justice, A (Rawls), 253
third-party intervention, 404, 411, 414–18,
  419–20, 458–59
Thomson argument, the, 344–45, 362–98,
  420
Thomson, Judith Jarvis, 200, 201, 230, 246,
  344, 362–65, 378, 391, 392, 399
Those Extraordinary Twins (Twain), 35–36

threshold of equal worth, 249–50
threshold of respect ("the threshold"), 246,
        248, 249–51, 260–65, 276, 278, 316,
        328, 330, 344, 345–46, 358, 359–61,
        389–91, 398, 473, 486
Time-Relative Interest Account of the
        badness of death, 105–6, 170–74, 176,
        186–87, 274–75
Time-Relative Interest Account of the
        wrongness of killing, 194–95, 201,
        203–6, 209, 233–41, 243, 244, 249,
        274–302, 309, 317, 339, 342–44, 464
time-relative interests, 80, 105, 170–74,
        176, 181, 183–84, 187–88, 192–94,
        198–99, 201–2, 204, 234, 245,
        275–302, 317–19, 323, 352, 487–93
Tithonus, 99, 101
Token Comparison, 103–6, 117–27, 136
Tolstoy, Leo, 97–98
Tooley, Michael, 347, 349
Twain, Mark, 35–36
twinning, monozygotic, 18–19, 25–27
Two-Tiered Account of the wrongness of
        killing, 245–65, 276, 288, 337–38,
        473, 474

Unger, Peter, 52

value of life, 241–42
van Inwagen, Peter, 32–35, 36, 37
Velleman, David, 176, 179–80, 473–85
viability, 8, 272
Viscosi, Daniel, 387
vivisection. *See* animals, experimentation on

Walen, Alec, 407
war, killing in, 236, 466–67
Way of All Flesh, The (Butler), 484
weak divergence (between interests and
        time-relative interests), 297–98
Wearing, Clive, 76–77, 82
well-being, 140, 145–61, 175, 180, 195–96,
        203, 244, 487
    diachronic, 180
    synchronic, 180
Wikler, Daniel, 69, 250, 432–33
Williams, Bernard, 11, 13, 52, 66, 100–103,
        181
Wollheim, Richard, 100, 129, 466
worth of persons, 241–65, 331, 473–85
Wright, Robert, 166–68
Wyeth, Andrew, 337

xenotransplantation, 452–53